# Leviathan

OR THE MATTER, FORME AND

POWER OF A COMMONWEALTH

ECCLESIASTICALL AND CIVIL

THOMAS HOBBES

EDITED BY MICHAEL OAKESHOTT

WITH AN INTRODUCTION BY RICHARD S. PETERS

A TOUCHSTONE BOOK
Published by Simon & Schuster

TOUCHSTONE
Rockefeller Center
1230 Avenue of the Americas
New York, NY 10020

First Touchstone Edition 1997

TOUCHSTONE and colophon are registered
trademarks of Simon & Schuster Inc.

10   9   8   7

Manufactured in the United States of America

Library of Congress Catalog Card Number: A62-8701

ISBN 0-684-84295-5

TO MY MOST HONOR'D FRIEND
## MR. FRANCIS GODOLPHIN
OF *Godolphin*

HONOR'D SIR,

YOUR MOST WORTHY BROTHER, Mr. *Sidney Godophin*, when he lived, was pleased to think my studies something, and otherwise to oblige me, as you know, with real testimonies of his good opinion, great in themselves, and the greater for the worthiness of his person. For there is not any virtue that disposeth a man, either to the service of God, or to the service of his country, to civil society, or private friendship, that did not manifestly appear in his conversation, not as acquired by necessity, or affected upon occasion, but inherent, and shining in a generous constitution of his nature. Therefore, in honour and gratitude to him, and with devotion to yourself, I humbly dedicate unto you this my discourse of Commonwealth. I know not how the world will receive it, nor how it may reflect on those that shall seem to favour it. For in a way beset with those that contend, on one side for too great liberty, and on the other side for too much authority, 'tis hard to pass between the points of both unwounded. But yet, methinks, the endeavour to advance the civil power, should not be by the civil power condemned; nor private men, by reprehending it, declare they think that power too great. Besides, I speak not of the men, but, in the abstract, of the seat of power, (like to those simple and unpartial creatures in the Roman Capitol, that with their noise defended those within it, not because they were they, but there), offending none, I think, but those without, or such within, if there be any such, as favour them. That which perhaps may most offend, are certain texts of Holy Scripture, alleged by me to other purpose than ordinarily they use to be by others. But I have done it with due submission, and also, in order to my subject, necessarily; for they are the outworks of the enemy, from whence they impugn the civil power. If notwithstanding this, you find my labour generally decried, you may be pleased to excuse yourself, and say, I am a man that love my own opinions, and think all true I say, that I honoured your brother, and honour you, and have presumed on that, to assume the title, without your knowledge, of being, as I am.

SIR,

Your most humble,

and most obedient Servant

THOMAS HOBBES

*Paris, April* 15/25, 1651.

# Introduction

MOST OF THE IMPORTANT BOOKS in philosophy have been written by men who were either worried or excited or both. Plato was worried by the profound social changes of his time and excited by mathematics; Kant was both worried and excited by the French Revolution and by Newtonian physics. These thinkers were perplexed by problems arising from new discoveries and social change just as many modern thinkers are perplexed by the implications of Freud, Marx, and Einstein or appalled by the social problems created by rapid industrialization and the development of mass media of communication. Hobbes' *Leviathan* ranks as one of the great books in philosophy because it attempted a systematic answer to the problems posed by the far-reaching social changes of the sixteenth and seventeenth centuries and by the rise of the mathematical sciences. The marriage of his worry with his excitement may have produced a monster—*Leviathan*—which shocked his contemporaries and successors. But it had at least the rare philosophical distinction of being so lucid that on many issues it was obviously wrong, and so readable and stimulating in its conception that even minor clergymen occupied themselves with trying to refute it.

Hobbes loved to make jesting references to his premature birth when his mother heard of the approach of the Spanish Armada in 1588. "Fear and I were born twins," he said, and the fear of death was to dominate his life and thought. But he had good cause to be uneasy. He asked little of life—only the peace and security necessary to pursue his scholarly interests and his occupation as tutor to the Cavendish family, which he embarked on in 1608 after his education at Magdalen Hall, Oxford. Yet he found himself in a country where peace and security were constantly in jeopardy because of the demands for liberty and a greater share in government by the growing class of traders, professional men, and yeomen farmers, who rated the authority of the Bible and of their own consciences above that of the magistrates, bishops, and counsellors of the king. He had encountered such men at Magdalen Hall, which had a strong Puritan tradition, though his later reflections on Oxford indicate that it was the prevalence of drunkenness, wantonness, gaming, and other such

7

vices which impressed him as much as the prevalence of seditious opinions.

Hobbes had little sympathy for the religion of the Puritans and less for their politics. Also, like many others at this time, he lived in daily dread of the Church of Rome which he regarded as an organized conspiracy against the temporal power supported by superstition and sharp practice. The overriding need of every sensible man, he thought, was for peace and security. Yet the ravings of the individual conscience and the sinister authority of Rome were constantly blinding men to what their real interests were. Civil war, the worst calamity that can befall a society, whence proceed "slaughter, solitude, and the want of all things," was upon them. How could this disastrous drift be halted? This was Hobbes' worry.

Hobbes' first attempt to deal with this worry was significant but unexciting. He produced a translation of Thucydides, the Greek historian who had recorded the course of the Peloponnesian War, in order to teach his countrymen the dangers of democracy, which gave too much scope for the ingrained aggressiveness and self-seeking of human nature. Hobbes made a point of remarking in his preface that Thucydides was in favour of kingly power, and, as is well known, one of the main features of his political thought was to be his advocacy of absolute monarchy as the only device for curbing the restless striving of human nature. But it was not the mere advocacy of absolutism that made *Leviathan* a great book; that was a commonplace at the time. It was the reasoning which led up to it. It was this mode of reasoning, quite foreign to the pages of Thucydides, which conveys to us Hobbes' great intellectual excitement. It is important, for the understanding of *Leviathan*, to trace what turned a rather dogmatic classical scholar into a brilliant and ruthless philosopher.

Hobbes had never been merely a classical scholar. For during his first journey to the Continent, which started in 1610, he discovered the disrepute into which Aristotelianism, the system in which he had been nurtured at Oxford, had fallen. Kepler had published his *Astronomia Nova* in 1607 and Galileo had just revealed the satellites of Jupiter by means of his telescope. The new "natural philosophy" was in the ascendant amongst intellectuals. Also, on his return to England, he came under the influence of Francis Bacon, with whom he used to converse, most likely during the period of retirement (1621–26) when Bacon was engaged in writing and scientific research. Bacon probably not only strengthened

Hobbes' growing dissatisfaction with Aristotelianism, but also inspired him with his conviction that knowledge meant power, and that verbal ambiguities, metaphysical vapourings and lack of method were the main obstacles to obtaining such knowledge. Hobbes, however, did not follow Bacon in his belief that the so-called method of induction, which advocated making generalizations on the basis of carefully collected data, would provide such knowledge. For he became enamoured of a very different sort of method which was to have a decisive influence on his life and thought.

At the age of 40, on the second of his journeys to the Continent, he happened to pick up a copy of Euclid's *Elements* in a gentleman's study in Paris. "By God," he said, "this is impossible." He went on tracing the demonstrations back until he was convinced of their truth. "This made him in love with geometry," as his biographer, John Aubrey, put it. But why did geometry consume him with a kind of middle-aged passion? Because it seemed to provide a method of reasoning which would give men certain knowledge. He could use this method to demonstrate to his countrymen that his warnings culled from Thucydides were not simply a piece of shrewd insight; they could be presented as necessary truths like theorems in geometry. Also scientists believed at that time that God had constructed the universe on geometric principles. Geometry thus enabled men to see through the veil of appearances to the underlying real structure of the natural world. Hobbes was excited by the possibility of extending this assumption to man as well as to Nature. Geometry could reveal the ground-plan of human nature and could help Hobbes to set out the bedrock foundations of a secure commonwealth. A science of natural justice could be erected on axioms stemming from such an analysis of human nature. Geometry was the key to peace. It was this kind of fundamental knowledge that would give men power.

It was, however, to Galileo that Hobbes owed his culminating intellectual inspiration. For in 1635, during his third journey to the Continent, Hobbes had made a pilgrimage to Italy to visit the leading exponent of the new natural philosophy. Hobbes relates graphically how, during his return on horseback, the whole world seemed to be full of moving things. He was beginning to conceive the world as Galileo had suggested. In his crude formulation of the law of inertia Galileo had maintained that motion, not rest, was the natural state of bodies. Bodies continued to move unless they were

impeded. Everything was moving. Hobbes extended this idea
to man and society. And so his imaginative idea was born:
"For seeing life is but a motion of limbs . . . For what is the
*heart*, but a *spring;* and the *nerves*, but so many *strings;* and
the *joints*, but so many *wheels*, giving motion to the whole
. . ." Even thinking itself was but the movement of some
internal substance in the head.

Hobbes claimed originality for two main parts of his philosophy—his optics and his civil philosophy, and his first two
contributions to philosophy were in these fields. His *Little
Treatise* (1630?-1637) was an attack on the Aristotelian
theory of sense and a sketch for a new mechanical theory. On
returning to England his thoughts turned again to politics,
owing to the civil dissension. In 1640, he published his
*Elements of Law* during the assembly of Parliament. This
demonstrated the need for undivided sovereignty. (It was
published later in two parts—*Human Nature* and *De Corpore
Politico*.) When Parliament impeached Strafford, Hobbes
feared for his life and fled to the Continent, priding himself
in later times on being "the first of all that fled." His *De Cive*
followed soon after in 1642 (published later in English under
the title of *Philosophical Rudiments Concerning Government
and Society*). In this he tried to demonstrate conclusively the
proper purpose and extent of the civil power, and the relationship between church and state.

Hobbes' originality consisted not simply in his detailed
views about optics and civil philosophy but also in the links
which he tried to forge between them. For he thought that
an all-inclusive theory could be constructed starting with
simple movements studied in geometry and culminating in the
massive movements of men towards and away from each
other in political life. He envisaged a trilogy of Body, Man,
and Citizen, but the march of events constantly interrupted
his project. He started on the *De Corpore* soon after the
publication of *De Cive*, but it was not completed till after his
final return to England.

After the advent of Charles II to Paris (Hobbes was his
tutor for a period) Hobbes turned aside from his physical
speculations and started work on his masterpiece, *Leviathan*.
This really comprised Hobbes' views on Man and Citizen. It
was published in 1651 and soon afterward Cromwell permitted Hobbes to return to England. Indeed, his enemies
later suggested that Hobbes worked his passage home by
means of it. For while he conceded popular representation,

which he conceptualized by means of the social contract
theory, he also used the social contract theory to demonstrate
the necessity of an absolute sovereign—by consent, not Divine
Right. So the major thesis of his book was one which could
be used to justify any *de facto* government, provided that it
governed. It was used to justify the rule both of Cromwell
and of Charles II.

Hobbes' demonstration of the necessity for an absolute
sovereign depended upon a crude kind of psychology culled
from Thucydides. This in turn was underpinned by a mechanical theory which was only loosely connected with it.
Men, Hobbes argued, are really machines moved to and fro
by two basic motions—the desire for power and the fear of
death. The desire for power leads to the state of nature where
the life of man is "solitary, poor, nasty, brutish, and short."
Civilization is based on the fear of death. For men are led
by this overwhelming fear to construct a commonwealth,
*Leviathan*, which is an artificial machine for the enforcement
of social rules and for the provision of security against
sudden death. "For covenants without the sword are but
words and of no strength to secure a man at all." The threat
of civil war and a possible relapse into the state of nature is
ever present unless men, in constructing Leviathan, follow
the logic of the geometer and institute an absolute monarch
to keep the peace with a rule of iron.

Hobbes did not mind much whether Charles or Cromwell was sovereign. What mattered was that the sovereign
should be absolute, so that there could be no other authority
(e.g. a religious one) to which men might appeal to justify
their rebellion. The sovereign must be the final arbiter in all
matters of law, morals and religion. All chains of command
must ascend to him like a pyramid. The liberty of the subject consisted only in those things which were not forbidden
by law, law being simply the command of the sovereign. To
say that a law was unjust could mean nothing except that it
had been abrogated by another law. Hobbes quoted with
delight the old principle that the safety of the people is the
supreme law. He was merely showing men the logical implications of this principle. This was geometry applied to politics
with a vengeance.

Had Hobbes been living in the twentieth century he would
have looked round the world and seen nations in what ap-
proximated to a state of nature in relation to each other. He
would have held that international treaties were of little use

in maintaining peace unless they were backed by overwhelming centralized force. For they would always be broken by any power in whose interest it was to break them and who thought that it could do so with impunity. The only logical solution would be to invest one nation with overwhelming forces—e.g. nuclear weapons—and let this nation keep the peace as it saw fit.

This typified Hobbes' approach to human problems—his contempt for tradition, experience, and laborious trial and error methods. "The skill of making, and maintaining commonwealths," he said, "consisteth in certain rules, as doth arithmetic and geometry; not as tennis-play, on practice only. . ." Englishmen, however, have always valued liberty as highly as they have valued security and have not been prepared to sacrifice liberty for the sake of a geometer's peace. Indeed they have also tended to distrust logical and abstract approaches to political problems altogether and have set much more store by tradition, precedent, and trial and error experimentation.

It was not, therefore, surprising that *Leviathan*, for all its brilliance, ingenuity, and logical clarity, was met with an indignant reception. Hobbes offended Parliament men because, although he held that government was by the consent of the people, he demonstrated that the people must consent to absolute undivided sovereignty. Yet, he offended Royalists, too, because, although he advocated absolute monarchy, he poured scorn on the notion of Divine Right. There could be no legitimacy, he argued, without power. He offended the Common Lawyers because of his forthright attacks on the stupidity of custom and precedent in comparison with geometrical insight. He offended all types of Christians because he maintained that all actions could be mechanically explained and that free-will was therefore an illusion. He gave particular offence to Puritans and Catholics, for he considered that the appeal either to the individual conscience or to the authority of Rome was the most potent of all threats to peace. He even offended the leaders of the Royal Society by his attacks on the Universities as hotbeds of sedition, by his contempt for their experiments and neglect of the science of motion as pioneered by Galileo, Harvey, and Hobbes himself.

The fact, however, that the implications of *Leviathan* for the contemporary scene were either ambiguous or downright distasteful is not really of great permanent significance. For *Leviathan* is a great work in political philosophy, and its argument, like that of all good philosophy, was couched at a level of generality which transcended contemporary concerns, although such concerns generated the impulse to its conception. Hobbes passion for definitions, which he got from geometry, and his espousal of the resoluto-compositive method, which he got from Galileo, combined to produce a ruthless, though somewhat homespun analysis of the presuppositions of civil society and of the concepts which were necessary for its description. The old mediaeval conception of the relationship between the individual and civil society no longer had much application with the rise of individualism and the growth of statute law. *Leviathan* was a brilliant attempt to conceptualize the new form of association that was developing—that of the nation state. Hobbes' greatest contribution to philosophy was in his discussion of what he called the generation of commonwealth; for in this he attempted a kind of Galilean experiment in his imagination to reduce civil society to its simplest elements and to explain political behaviour in terms of its underlying mechanical ground-plan. What emerged was a brilliant analysis within an individualist framework of concepts such as 'right,' 'law,' 'sovereignty,' 'liberty,' 'contract,' and 'commonwealth,' together with a thesis about the justification of government based on a rather crude naturalistic ethical theory which Hobbes tried to deduce from man's desire for peace and self-preservation.

This tendency towards self-preservation, together with desire for power, which led to anarchy, Hobbes tried to exhibit as a particular case of the movement of bodies within the natural world. Man, he held, was a natural machine as distinct from Leviathan, which was an artificial one. Much of the inconsistency in his *Leviathan* was the product of the clash between his analytical acumen and his metaphysical imagination. He saw clearly that the state is an artificial construction which does not develop naturally like a beehive. It depends on agreement, contract, institution and other manifestations of human decision. Laws do not develop naturally; for it is authority, backed by force, that makes a law. In such an account the role of human decision is maximized.

Yet at the same time, Hobbes persistently suggested that man is a machine, like every other part of nature. He was a pioneer in the scientific understanding of man in that he attempted the same *sort* of explanation of the behaviour of men as Galileo had given of the movement of bodies. But this mechanical type of explanation of human actions, together with his belief in determinism and his attempt to develop a naturalistic ethical theory, is a strange theoretical basis on which to erect an account of politics which stresses the role of artifice and convention and the arbitrariness of definitions and institutions. Hobbes has been described as the father of both modern analytic philosophy and modern mechanical psychology. Neither of these are absurd suggestions. But the fact that seeds of both can be found in Hobbes explains very well the deep-seated flaws in *Leviathan*. For careful analysis of the family of concepts necessary for the description and explanation of human actions (especially those connected with social institutions), such as has been conducted by philosophers in recent times, renders a purely mechanical description and explanation of man's behaviour increasingly difficult to defend.

Hobbes' *Leviathan* was an important philosophical work because of its contribution to the philosophy of language and religion as well as because of its contribution to political philosophy, naturalistic ethics, and mechanistic psychology. Indeed, many modern philosophers maintain, somewhat myopically perhaps, that Hobbes' theory of speech was his outstanding contribution to philosophy. In this he tried to combine a mechanical view about the causes of speech with a nominalist account of the meaning of general terms. In his *De Corpore*[1] he provided many more details of his theory, especially about the use of abstract names in science. In his *Leviathan* he was concerned primarily to fashion a tool which enabled him to ridicule the doctrine of essences current in the Schools. He tried to demonstrate that their belief in essences derived from their refusal to distinguish the work done by different types of names. Names could be either of bodies or of properties or of names. If one of these classes of names were interpreted as if it belonged to another class an absurdity would be generated. 'Universal' for instance, was a name of a class of names, not of essences designated by names. Such names are universal because of their use, not because they refer to a special type of entity. Similarly redness (which is a property) is not in blood in the same way as blood (which is a body) is in a bloody cloth (which is another body). Hobbes used crude distinctions; but he anticipated modern techniques of logical analysis by showing how absurdities can be generated if insufficient attention is paid

[1] See Part II.

to the logical behaviour of different classes of terms. Of great importance, too, was his insistence, which he shared with Bacon, on clarity and concreteness of speech, together with his thesis that speech was essential to reasoning and that it was reasoning, in the sense of laying down definitions and drawing out their implications, which distinguishes men from animals.

It is seldom realized that over half of *Leviathan* deals with religious matters. One of Hobbes' main preoccupations was to establish that there are general grounds as well as scriptural authority for his conviction that the sovereign is the best interpreter of God's will. Religion, on his view, was a system of law, not a system of truth. To establish this Hobbes made some illuminating remarks about the distinction between knowledge and faith. He maintained vehemently that we could *know* nothing of the attributes of God; for demonstration was impossible in such matters. The adjectives which we used to describe God were expressions of our adoration, not products of reason. Hobbes waxed particularly eloquent in his defence of what he called the 'true religion' (that of the established Church) against the twin threats of Catholicism, with its extra-mundane authority, and against the Puritans, whose belief in the priesthood of all believers led them to consult their consciences too readily in preference to the dictates of the sovereign. Hobbes' section on the Kingdom of Darkness in which the Pope is compared to the King of the Fairies is one of the wittiest passages in the history of philosophy. In the course of his onslaught Hobbes dealt mercilessly, from the point of view of his mechanical metaphysics, with the concepts of Scripture, such as 'spirits,' 'inspiration,' 'miracles,' and 'the kingdom of God.' On the problem of evil he pointed out, very acutely, that the only solution was to stress God's power. For did not God reply to Job, "Where wast thou when I laid the foundations of the earth?" In brief, Hobbes' *Leviathan* was a great work in rather the same way as Plato's *Republic*. Acute things were said about many facets of human life and these were linked together by an all-inclusive conceptual scheme.

After his return to England Hobbes soon became involved in a dispute with Bishop Bramhall on the subject of free-will. His *Questions Concerning Liberty, Necessity, and Chance* (1656) was the result. Hobbes was then led into a most humiliating controversy; for in Chapter 20 of his *De Corpore*, which he at last published in 1655, he had inserted an attempt to square the circle. This was seized on by John Wallis, professor of geometry at Oxford, and Seth Ward, the professor of astronomy, both of them Puritans and foundation members of the Royal Society. They were irritated by Hobbes' criticisms of the universities and ruthlessly exposed his mathematical ineptitude. The wrangle lasted for about twenty years.

Hobbes' energy, however, which was remarkable for one so advanced in years (he played tennis up to the age of 70), was not completely absorbed in this abortive controversy. In 1657 he published the second part of his trilogy, the *De Homine*. After the Restoration Hobbes was received at Court, where his wit was appreciated. But at the time of the Plague and Great Fire some reason was sought for God's displeasure, and a Bill being brought before Parliament for the suppression of atheism, a committee was set up to look into *Leviathan*. The matter, however, was dropped, probably through the intervention of the king; but Hobbes was forbidden to publish his opinions. He turned to history and in 1668 completed his *Behemoth*, a history of the Civil War, interpreted in the light of his opinions about man and society. It was published posthumously in 1682. He was also sent Bacon's *Elements of Common Law* by his friend John Aubrey and, at the age of 76, produced his *Dialogue between a Philosopher and a Student of the Common Laws of England* (published posthumously in 1681).

At 84 he wrote his own autobiography in Latin verse and at 86 published a translation of the Iliad and Odyssey for want of something better to do. He died in 1679. It is said that before his death he amused himself by allowing his friends to prepare epitaphs for him. He liked best "This is the true philosopher's stone." It was recorded on his tombstone that he was a just man, well-known for his learning at home and abroad. This was accurate; for although Hobbes was one of the most controversial figures of his time, who was constantly engaged in academic debate, no aspersions were ever cast on his integrity as a man. He was also renowned as a wit. Indeed, like Bernard Shaw, by the time of his death he had become almost an English institution.

RICHARD S. PETERS

*Birkbeck College, London University*

# Contents

## The Third Part / **Of a Christian Commonwealth**

## The Fourth Part / **Of the Kingdom of Darkness**

# Author's Introduction

NATURE, the art whereby God hath made and governs the world, is by the *art* of man, as in many other things, so in this also imitated, that it can make an artificial animal. For seeing life is but a motion of limbs, the beginning whereof is in some principal part within; why may we not say, that all *automata* (engines that move themselves by springs and wheels as doth a watch) have an artificial life? For what is the *heart*, but a *spring;* and the *nerves*, but so many *strings;* and the *joints*, but so many *wheels*, giving motion to the whole body, such as was intended by the artificer? *Art* goes yet further, imitating that rational and most excellent work of nature, *man*. For by art is created that great LEVIATHAN called a COMMONWEALTH, or STATE, in Latin CIVITAS, which is but an artificial man; though of greater stature and strength than the natural, for whose protection and defence it was intended; and in which the *sovereignty* is an artificial *soul*, as giving life and motion to the whole body; the *magistrates*, and other *officers* of judicature and execution, artificial *joints;* *reward* and *punishment*, by which fastened to the seat of the sovereignty every joint and member is moved to perform his duty, are the *nerves*, that do the same in the body natural; the *strength; salus populi*, the *people's safety*, its *business; counsellors*, by whom all things needful for it to know are suggested unto it, are the *memory; equity*, and *laws*, an artificial *reason* and *will; concord, health; sedition, sickness;* and *civil war, death*. Lastly, the *pacts* and *covenants*, by which the parts of this body politic were at first made, set together, and united, resemble that *fiat*, or the *let us make man*, pronounced by God in the creation.

To describe the nature of this artificial man, I will consider First, the *matter* thereof, and the *artificer;* both which is *man*.

Secondly, *how*, and by what *covenants* it is made; what are the *rights* and just *power* or *authority* of a *sovereign;* and what it is that *preserveth* and *dissolveth* it.

Thirdly, what is a *Christian commonwealth*.

Lastly, what is the *kingdom of darkness*.

Concerning the first, there is a saying much usurped of late, that *wisdom* is acquired, not by reading of *books*, but of *men*. Consequently whereunto, those persons, that for the most part give no other proof of being wise, take great delight to show what they think they have read in men, by uncharitable censures of one another behind their backs. But there is another saying not of late understood, by which they might learn truly to read one another, if they would take the pains; that is, *nosce teipsum, read thyself:* which was not meant, as it is now used, to countenance, either the barbarous state of men in power, towards their inferiors; or to encourage men of low degree, to a saucy behaviour towards their betters; but to teach us, that for the similitude of the thoughts and passions of one man, to the thoughts and passions of another, whosoever looketh into himself, and considereth what he doth, when he does *think, opine, reason, hope, fear,* &c. and upon what grounds; he shall thereby read and know, what are the thoughts and passions of all other men upon the like occasions. I say the similitude of *passions,* which are the same in all men, *desire, fear, hope,* &c.; not the similitude of the *objects* of the passions, which are the things *desired, feared, hoped,* &c.: for these the constitution individual, and particular education, do so vary, and they are so easy to be kept from our knowledge, that the characters of man's heart, blotted and confounded as they are with dissembling, lying, counterfeiting, and erroneous doctrines, are legible only to him that searcheth hearts. And though by men's actions we do discover their design sometimes; yet to do it without comparing them with our own, and distinguishing all circumstances, by which the case may come to be altered, is to decipher without a key, and be for the most part deceived, by too much trust, or by too much diffidence; as he that reads, is himself a good or evil man.

But let one man read another by his actions never so perfectly, it serves him only with his acquaintance, which are but few. He that is to govern a whole nation, must read in himself, not this or that particular man; but mankind: which though it be hard to do, harder than to learn any language or science; yet when I shall have set down my own reading orderly, and perspicuously, the pains left another, will be only to consider, if he also find not the same in himself. For this kind of doctrine admitteth no other demonstration.

# THE FIRST PART
# OF MAN

## Chapter 1

### Of Sense

*Sense.* Concerning the thoughts of man, I will consider them
first singly, and afterwards in train, or dependence upon one
another. Singly, they are every one a *representation* or *appearance*, of some quality, or other accident of a body without us,
which is commonly called an *object*. Which object worketh
on the eyes, ears, and other parts of a man's body; and by
diversity of working, produceth diversity of appearances.

The original of them all, is that which we call SENSE, for
there is no conception in a man's mind, which hath not at
first, totally, or by parts, been begotten upon the organs of
sense. The rest are derived from that original.

To know the natural cause of sense, is not very necessary
to the business now in hand; and I have elsewhere written of
the same at large. Nevertheless, to fill each part of my present
method, I will briefly deliver the same in this place.

The cause of sense, is the external body, or object, which
presseth the organ proper to each sense, either immediately,
as in the taste and touch; or mediately, as in seeing, hearing,
and smelling; which pressure, by the mediation of the nerves,
and other strings and membranes of the body, continued
inwards to the brain and heart, causeth there a resistance, or
counter-pressure, or endeavour of the heart to deliver itself,
which endeavour, because *outward*, seemeth to be some
matter without. And this *seeming*, or *fancy*, is that which
men call *sense;* and consisteth, as to the eye, in a *light*, or
*colour figured;* to the ear, in a *sound;* to the nostril, in an
*odour;* to the tongue and palate, in a *savour;* and to the rest
of the body, in *heat, cold, hardness, softness,* and such other
qualities as we discern by *feeling.* All which qualities, called
*sensible*, are in the object, that causeth them, but so many
several motions of the matter, by which it presseth our organs
diversely. Neither in us that are pressed, are they any thing
else, but divers motions; for motion produceth nothing but

motion. But their appearance to us is fancy, the same waking, that dreaming. And as pressing, rubbing, or striking the eye, makes us fancy a light; and pressing the ear, produceth a din; so do the bodies also we see, or hear, produce the same by their strong, though unobserved action. For if these colours and sounds were in the bodies, or objects that cause them, they could not be severed from them, as by glasses, and in echoes by reflection, we see they are; where we know the thing we see is in one place, the appearance in another. And though at some certain distance, the real and very object seem invested with the fancy it begets in us; yet the object is one thing, the image or fancy is another. So that sense, in all cases, is nothing else but original fancy, caused, as I have said, by the pressure, that is, by the motion, of external things upon our eyes, ears, and other organs thereunto ordained.

But the philosophy-schools, through all the universities of Christendom, grounded upon certain texts of Aristotle, teach another doctrine, and say, for the cause of *vision*, that the thing seen, sendeth forth on every side a *visible species*, in English, a *visible show, apparition*, or *aspect*, or *a being seen;* the receiving whereof into the eye, is *seeing*. And for the cause of *hearing*, that the thing heard, sendeth forth an *audible species*, that is an *audible aspect*, or *audible being seen;* which entering at the ear, maketh *hearing*. Nay, for the cause of *understanding* also, they say the thing understood, sendeth forth an *intelligible species*, that is, an *intelligible being seen;* which, coming into the understanding, makes us understand. I say not this, as disproving the use of universities; but because I am to speak hereafter of their office in a commonwealth, I must let you see on all occasions by the way, what things would be amended in them; amongst which the frequency of insignificant speech is one.

# Chapter 2

## Of Imagination

*Imagination.* That when a thing lies still, unless somewhat else stir it, it will lie still for ever, is a truth that no man doubts of. But that when a thing is in motion, it will eternally be in motion, unless somewhat else stay it, though the reason be the same, namely, that nothing can change itself, is not so easily assented to. For men measure, not only other men, but all other things, by themselves; and because they find themselves subject after motion to pain, and lassitude, think every thing else grows weary of motion, and seeks repose of its own accord; little considering, whether it be not some other motion, wherein that desire of rest they find in themselves, consisteth. From hence it is, that the schools say, heavy bodies fall downwards, out of an appetite to rest, and to conserve their nature in that place which is most proper for them; ascribing appetite, and knowledge of what is good for their conservation, which is more than man has, to things inanimate, absurdly.

When a body is once in motion, it moveth, unless something else hinder it, eternally; and whatsoever hindreth it, cannot in an instant, but in time, and by degrees, quite extinguish it; and as we see in the water, though the wind cease, the waves give not over rolling for a long time after: so also it happeneth in that motion, which is made in the internal parts of a man, then, when he sees, dreams, &c. For after the object is removed, or the eye shut, we still retain an image of the thing seen, though more obscure than when we see it. And this is it, the Latins call *imagination,* from the image made in seeing; and apply the same, though improperly, to all the other senses. But the Greeks call it *fancy;* which signifies *appearance,* and is as proper to one sense, as to another. IMAGINATION therefore is nothing but *decaying sense;* and is found in men, and many other living creatures, as well sleeping, as waking.

The decay of sense in men waking, is not the decay of the motion made in sense; but an obscuring of it, in such manner as the light of the sun obscureth the light of the stars; which stars do no less exercise their virtue, by which they are visible, in the day than in the night. But because amongst many strokes, which our eyes, ears, and other organs receive from external bodies, the predominant only is sensible; therefore, the light of the sun being predominant, we are not affected with the action of the stars. And any object being removed from our eyes, though the impression it made in us remain, yet other objects more present succeeding, and working on us, the imagination of the past is obscured, and made weak, as the voice of a man is in the noise of the day. From whence if followeth, that the longer the time is, after the sight or sense of any object, the weaker is the imagination. For the continual change of man's body destroys in time the parts which in sense were moved: so that distance of time, and of place, hath one and the same effect in us. For as at a great distance of place, that which we look at appears dim, and without distinction of the smaller parts; and as voices grow weak, and inarticulate; so also, after great distance of time, our imagination of the past is weak; and we lose, for example, of cities we have seen, many particular streets, and of actions, many particular circumstances. This *decaying sense*, when we would express the thing itself, I mean *fancy* itself, we call *imagination*, as I said before: but when we would express the decay, and signify that the sense is fading, old, and past, it is called *memory*. So that imagination and memory are but one thing, which for divers considerations hath divers names.

*Memory.* Much memory, or memory of many things, is called *experience.* Again, imagination being only of those things which have been formerly perceived by sense, either all at once, or by parts at several times; the former, which is the imagining the whole object as it was presented to the sense, is *simple* imagination, as when one imagineth a man, or horse, which he hath seen before. The other is *compounded;* as when, from the sight of a man at one time, and of a horse at another, we conceive in our mind a Centaur. So when a man compoundeth the image of his own person with the image of the actions of another man, as when a man imagines himself a Hercules or an Alexander, which happeneth often to them that are much taken with reading of romances, it is a compound imagination, and properly but a fiction of the mind. There be also other imaginations that rise in men, though waking, from the great impression made in sense: as from gazing upon the sun, the impression leaves an image of the sun before our eyes a long time after; and from being long and vehemently attent upon geometrical figures, a man shall in the dark, though awake, have the images of lines and angles before his eyes; which kind of fancy hath no particular name, as being a thing that doth not commonly fall into men's discourse.

*Dreams*. The imaginations of them that sleep are those we call *dreams*. And these also, as all other imaginations, have been before, either totally or by parcels, in the sense. And because in sense, the brain and nerves, which are the necessary organs of sense, are so benumbed in sleep, as not easily to be moved by the action of external objects, there can happen in sleep no imagination, and therefore no dream, but what proceeds from the agitation of the inward parts of man's body; which inward parts, for the connexion they have with the brain, and other organs, when they be distempered, do keep the same in motion; whereby the imaginations there formerly made, appear as if a man were waking; saving that the organs of sense being now benumbed, so as there is no new object, which can master and obscure them with a more vigorous impression, a dream must needs be more clear, in this silence of sense, than our waking thoughts. And hence it cometh to pass, that it is a hard matter, and by many thought impossible, to distinguish exactly between sense and dreaming. For my part, when I consider that in dreams I do not often nor constantly think of the same persons, places, objects, and actions, that I do waking; nor remember so long a train of coherent thoughts, dreaming, as at other times; and because waking I often observe the absurdity of dreams, but never dream of the absurdities of my waking thoughts; I am well satisfied, that being awake, I know I dream not, though when I dream I think myself awake.

And seeing dreams are caused by the distemper of some of the inward parts of the body, divers distempers must needs cause different dreams. And hence it is that lying cold breedeth dreams of fear, and raiseth the thought and image of some fearful object, the motion from the brain to the inner parts and from the inner parts to the brain being reciprocal; and that as anger causeth heat in some parts of the body when we are awake, so when we sleep the overheating of the same parts causeth anger, and raiseth up in the brain the imagination of an enemy. In the same manner, as natural kindness, when we are awake, causeth desire, and desire makes heat in certain other parts of the body; so also too much heat in those parts, while we sleep, raiseth in the brain an imagination of some kindness shown. In sum, our dreams are the reverse of our waking imaginations; the motion when we are awake beginning at one end, and when we dream at another.

*Apparitions or visions.* The most difficult discerning of a man's dream, from his waking thoughts, is then, when by some accident we observe not that we have slept: which is easy to happen to a man full of fearful thoughts, and whose conscience is much troubled; and that sleepeth, without the circumstances of going to bed or putting off his clothes, as one that noddeth in a chair. For he that taketh pains, and industriously lays himself to sleep, in case any uncouth and exorbitant fancy come unto him, cannot easily think it other than a dream. We read of Marcus Brutus (one that had his life given him by Julius Cæsar, and was also his favourite, and notwithstanding murdered him), how at Philippi, the night before he gave battle to Augustus Cæsar, he saw a fearful apparition, which is commonly related by historians as a vision; but considering the circumstances, one may easily judge to have been but a short dream. For sitting in his tent, pensive and troubled with the horror of his rash act, it was not hard for him, slumbering in the cold, to dream of that which most affrighted him; which fear, as by degrees it made him wake, so also it must needs make the apparition by degrees to vanish; and having no assurance that he slept, he could have no cause to think it a dream, or any thing but a vision. And this is no very rare accident; for even they that be perfectly awake, if they be timorous and superstitious, possessed with fearful tales, and alone in the dark, are subject to the like fancies, and believe they see spirits and dead men's ghosts walking in churchyards; whereas it is either their fancy only, or else the knavery of such persons as make use of such superstitious fear, to pass disguised in the night, to places they would not be known to haunt.

From this ignorance of how to distinguish dreams, and other strong fancies, from vision and sense, did arise the greatest part of the religion of the Gentiles in time past, that worshipped satyrs, fawns, nymphs, and the like; and now-a-days the opinion that rude people have of fairies, ghosts, and goblins, and of the power of witches. For as for witches, I think not that their witchcraft is any real power; but yet that they are justly punished, for the false belief they have that they can do such mischief, joined with their purpose to do it if they can; their trade being nearer to a new religion than to a craft or science. And for fairies, and walking ghosts, the opinion of them has, I think, been on purpose either taught or not confuted, to keep in credit the use of exorcism, of crosses, of holy water, and other such inventions of ghostly men. Nevertheless, there is no doubt, but God can make unnatural apparitions; but that he does it so often, as men need to fear such things, more than they fear the stay or change of the course of nature, which he also can stay, and change, is no point of Christian faith. But evil men under pretext that God can do any thing, are so bold as to say any thing when it serves their turn, though they think it untrue; it is the part of a wise man, to believe them no farther, than right reason makes that which they say, appear credible. If this superstitious fear of spirits were taken away, and with it, prognostics from dreams, false prophecies, and many other things depending thereon, by which crafty ambitious persons abuse the simple people, men would be much more fitted than they are for civil obedience.

And this ought to be the work of the schools: but they rather nourish such doctrine. For, not knowing what imagination or the senses are, what they receive, they teach: some saying, that imaginations rise of themselves, and have no cause; others, that they rise most commonly from the will; and that good thoughts are blown (inspired) into a man by God, and evil thoughts by the Devil; or that good thoughts are poured (infused) into a man by God, and evil ones by the Devil. Some say the senses receive the species of things, and deliver them to the common sense; and the common sense delivers them over to the fancy, and the fancy to the memory, and the memory to the judgment, like handing of things from one to another, with many words making nothing understood.

*Understanding.* The imagination that is raised in man, or any other creature endued with the faculty of imagining, by words, or other voluntary signs, is that we generally call *understanding;* and is common to man and beast. For a dog by custom will understand the call, or the rating of his master; and so will many other beasts. That understanding which is peculiar to man, is the understanding not only his will, but his conceptions and thoughts, by the sequel and contexture of the names of things into affirmations, negations, and other forms of speech; and of this kind of understanding I shall speak hereafter.

# Chapter 3

## Of the Consequence or Train of Imaginations

By *Consequence*, or TRAIN of thoughts, I understand that succession of one thought to another, which is called, to distinguish it from discourse in words, *mental discourse*.

When a man thinketh on any thing whatsoever, his next thought after, is not altogether so casual as it seems to be. Not every thought to every thought succeeds indifferently. But as we have no imagination, whereof we have not formerly had sense, in whole, or in parts; so we have no transition from one imagination to another, whereof we never had the like before in our senses. The reason whereof is this. All fancies are motions within us, relics of those made in the sense: and those motions that immediately succeeded one another in the sense, continue also together after sense: insomuch as the former coming again to take place, and be predominant, the latter followeth, by coherence of the matter moved, in such manner, as water upon a plane table is drawn which way any one part of it is guided by the finger. But because in sense, to one and the same thing perceived, sometimes one thing, sometimes another succeedeth, it comes to pass in time, that in the imagining of any thing, there is no certainty what we shall imagine next; only this is certain, it shall be something that succeeded the same before, at one time or another.

*Train of thoughts unguided.* This train of thoughts, or mental discourse, is of two sorts. The first is *unguided, without design,* and inconstant; wherein there is no passionate thought, to govern and direct those that follow, to itself, as the end and scope of some desire, or other passion: in which case the thoughts are said to wander, and seem impertinent one to another, as in a dream. Such are commonly the thoughts of men, that are not only without company, but also without care of any thing; though even then their thoughts are as busy as at other times, but without harmony; as the sound which a lute out of tune would yield to any man; or in tune, to one that could not play. And yet in this wild ranging of the mind, a man may oft-times perceive the way of it, and the dependence of one thought upon another. For in a discourse of our present civil war, what could seem more impertinent, than to ask, as one did, what was the value of a Roman penny? Yet the coherence to me was manifest enough. For the thought of the war, introduced the thought of the delivering up the king to his enemies; the thought of that, brought in the thought of the delivering up of Christ; and that again the thought of the thirty pence, which was the price of that treason; and thence easily followed that malicious question, and all this in a moment of time; for thought is quick.

*Train of thoughts regulated.* The second is more constant; as being *regulated* by some desire, and design. For the impression made by such things as we desire, or fear, is strong, and permanent, or, if it cease for a time, of quick return: so strong it is sometimes, as to hinder and break our sleep. From desire, ariseth the thought of some means we have seen produce the like of that which we aim at; and from the thought of that, the thought of means to that mean; and so continually, till we come to some beginning within our own power. And because the end, by the greatness of the impression, comes often to mind, in case our thoughts begin to wander, they are quickly again reduced into the way: which observed by one of the seven wise men, made him give men this precept, which is now worn out, *Respice finem;* that is to say, in all your actions, look often upon what you would have, as the thing that directs all your thoughts in the way to attain it.

*Remembrance.* The train of regulated thoughts is of two kinds; one, when of an effect imagined we seek the causes, or means that produce it: and this is common to man and beast. The other is, when imagining any thing whatsoever, we seek all the possible effects, that can by it be produced; that is to say, we imagine what we can do with it, when we have it. Of which I have not at any time seen any sign, but in man only; for this is a curiosity hardly incident to the nature of any living creature that has no other passion but sensual, such as are hunger, thirst, lust, and anger. In sum, the discourse of the mind, when it is governed by design, is nothing but *seeking*, or the faculty of invention, which the Latins called *sagacitas*, and *solertia;* a hunting out of the causes, of some effect, present or past; or of the effects, of some present or past cause. Sometimes a man seeks what he hath lost; and from that place, and time, wherein he misses it, his mind runs back, from place to place, and time to time, to find where, and when he had it; that is to say, to find some certain, and limited time and place, in which to begin a method of seeking. Again, from thence, his thoughts run over the same places and times, to find what action, or other occasion might make him lose it. This we call *remembrance*, or calling to mind: the Latins call it *reminiscentia*, as it were a *re-conning* of our former actions.

Sometimes a man knows a place determinate, within the compass whereof he is to seek; and then his thoughts run over all the parts thereof, in the same manner as one would sweep a room, to find a jewel; or as a spaniel ranges the field, till he find a scent; or as a man should run over the alphabet, to start a rhyme.

*Prudence.* Sometimes a man desires to know the event of an action; and then he thinketh of some like action past, and the events thereof one after another; supposing like events will follow like actions. As he that foresees what will become of a criminal, re-cons what he has seen follow on the like crime before; having this order of thoughts, the crime, the officer, the prison, the judge, and the gallows. Which kind of thoughts, is called *foresight*, and *prudence*, or *providence;* and sometimes *wisdom;* though such conjecture, through the difficulty of observing all circumstances, be very fallacious. But this is certain; by how much one man has more experience of things past, than another, by so much also he is more prudent, and his expectations the seldomer fail him. The *present* only has a being in nature; things *past* have a being in the memory only, but things *to come* have no being at all; the *future* being but a fiction of the mind, applying the sequels of actions past, to the actions that are present; which with most certainty is done by him that has most experience, but not with certainty enough. And though it be called prudence, when the event answereth our expectation; yet in its own nature, it is but presumption. For the foresight of things to come, which is providence, belongs only to him by whose will they are to come. From him only, and supernaturally, proceeds prophecy. The best prophet naturally is the best guesser; and the best guesser, he that is most versed and studied in the matters he guesses at: for he hath most *signs* to guess by.

*Signs.* A *sign* is the evident antecedent of the consequent; and contrarily, the consequent of the antecedent, when the like consequences have been observed, before: and the oftener they have been observed, the less uncertain is the sign. And therefore he that has most experience in any kind of business, has most signs, whereby to guess at the future time; and consequently is the most prudent: and so much more prudent than he that is new in that kind of business, as not to be equalled by any advantage of natural and extemporary wit: though perhaps many young men think the contrary.

Nevertheless it is not prudence that distinguisheth man from beast. There be beasts, that at a year old observe more, and pursue that which is for their good, more prudently, than a child can do at ten.

*Conjecture of the time past.* As prudence is a *presumption* of the *future*, contracted from the *experience* of time *past:* so there is a presumption of things past taken from other things, not future, but past also. For he that hath seen by what courses and degrees a flourishing state hath first come into civil war, and then to ruin; upon the sight of the ruins of any other state, will guess, the like war, and the like courses have been there also. But this conjecture, has the same uncertainty almost with the conjecture of the future; both being grounded only upon experience.

There is no other act of man's mind, that I can remember, naturally planted in him, so as to need no other thing, to the exercise of it, but to be born a man, and live with the use of his five senses. Those other faculties, of which I shall speak by and by, and which seem proper to man only, are acquired and increased by study and industry; and of most men learned by instruction, and discipline; and proceed all from the invention of words, and speech. For besides sense, and thoughts, and the train of thoughts, the mind of man has no other motion; though by the help of speech, and method, the same faculties may be improved to such a height, as to distinguish men from all other living creatures.

*Infinite.* Whatsoever we imagine is *finite*. Therefore there is no idea, or conception of any thing we call *infinite*. No man can have in his mind an image of infinite magnitude; nor conceive infinite swiftness, infinite time, or infinite force, or infinite power. When we say any thing is infinite, we signify only, that we are not able to conceive the ends, and bounds of the things named; having no conception of the thing, but of our own inability. And therefore the name of God is used, not to make us conceive him, for he is incomprehensible; and his greatness, and power are unconceivable; but that we may honour him. Also because, whatsoever, as I said before, we conceive, has been perceived first by sense, either all at once, or by parts; a man can have no thought, representing any thing, not subject to sense. No man therefore can conceive any thing, but he must conceive it in some place; and endued with some determinate magnitude; and which may be divided into parts; nor that any thing is all in this place, and all in another place at the same time; nor that two, or more things can be in one, and the same place at once: for none of these things ever have, nor can be incident to sense; but are absurd speeches, taken upon credit, without any signification at all, from deceived philosophers, and deceived, or deceiving Schoolmen.

# Chapter 4

## Of Speech

*Original of speech.* The invention of *printing*, though ingenious, compared with the invention of *letters*, is no great matter. But who was the first that found the use of letters, is not known. He that first brought them into Greece, men say was Cadmus, the son of Agenor, king of Phœnicia. A profitable invention for continuing the memory of time past, and the conjunction of mankind, dispersed into so many, and distant regions of the earth; and withal difficult, as proceeding from a watchful observation of the divers motions of the tongue, palate, lips, and other organs of speech; whereby to make as many differences of characters, to remember them. But the most noble and profitable invention of all other, was that of SPEECH, consisting of *names* or *appellations*, and their connexion; whereby men register their thoughts; recall them when they are past; and also declare them one to another for mutual utility and conversation; without which, there had been amongst men, neither commonwealth, nor society, nor contract, nor peace, no more than amongst lions, bears, and wolves. The first author of *speech* was God himself, that instructed Adam how to name such creatures as he presented to his sight; for the Scripture goeth no further in this matter. But this was sufficient to direct him to add more names, as the experience and use of the creatures should give him occasion; and to join them in such manner by degrees, as to make himself understood; and so by succession of time, so much language might be gotten, as he had found use for; though not so copious, as an orator or philosopher has need of: for I do not find any thing in the Scripture, out of which, directly or by consequence, can be gathered, that Adam was taught the names of all figures, numbers, measures, colours, sounds, fancies, relations; much less the names of words and speech, as *general, special, affirmative, negative, interrogative, optative, infinitive,* all which are useful; and least of all, of *entity, intentionality, quiddity,* and other insignificant words of the school.

But all this language gotten, and augmented by Adam and his posterity, was again lost at the Tower of Babel, when, by the hand of God, every man was stricken, for his rebellion, with an oblivion of his former language. And being hereby forced to disperse themselves into several parts of the world, it must needs be, that the diversity of tongues that now is, proceeded by degrees from them, in such manner, as need, the mother of all inventions, taught them; and in tract of time grew everywhere more copious.

*The use of speech.* The general use of speech, is to transfer our mental discourse, into verbal; or the train of our thoughts, into a train of words; and that for two commodities, whereof one is the registering of the consequences of our thoughts; which being apt to slip out of our memory, and put us to a new labour, may again be recalled, by such words as they were marked by. So that the first use of names is to serve for *marks,* or *notes* of remembrance. Another is, when many use the same words, to signify, by their connexion and order, one to another, what they conceive, or think of each matter; and also what they desire, fear, or have any other passion for. And for this use they are called *signs.* Special uses of speech are these; first, to register, what by cogitation, we find to be the cause of any thing, present or past; and what we find things present or past may produce, or effect; which in sum, is acquiring of arts. Secondly, to show to others that knowledge which we have attained, which is, to counsel and teach one another. Thirdly, to make known to others our wills and purposes, that we may have the mutual help of one another. Fourthly, to please and delight ourselves and others, by playing with our words, for pleasure or ornament, innocently.

*Abuses of speech.* To these uses, there are also four correspondent abuses. First, when men register their thoughts wrong, by the inconstancy of the signification of their words; by which they register for their conception, that which they never conceived, and so deceive themselves. Secondly, when they use words metaphorically; that is, in other sense than that they are ordained for; and thereby deceive others. Thirdly, by words, when they declare that to be their will, which is not. Fourthly, when they use them to grieve one another; for seeing nature hath armed living creatures, some with teeth, some with horns, and some with hands, to grieve an enemy, it is but an abuse of speech, to grieve him with the tongue, unless it be one whom we are obliged to govern; and then it is not to grieve, but to correct and amend.

The manner how speech serveth to the remembrance of

the consequence of causes and effects, consisteth in the imposing of *names*, and the *connexion* of them.

*Names, proper and common. Universal.* Of names, some are *proper*, and singular to one only thing, as *Peter, John, this man, this tree;* and some are *common* to many things, *man, horse, tree;* every of which, though but one name, is nevertheless the name of divers particular things; in respect of all which together, it is called an *universal;* there being nothing in the world universal but names; for the things named are every one of them individual and singular.

One universal name is imposed on many things, for their similitude in some quality, or other accident; and whereas a proper name bringeth to mind one thing only, universals recall any one of those many.

And of names universal, some are of more, and some of less extent; the larger comprehending the less large; and some again of equal extent, comprehending each other reciprocally. As for example: the name *body* is of larger signification than the word *man*, and comprehendeth it; and the names *man* and *rational*, are of equal extent, comprehending mutually one another. But here we must take notice, that by a name is not always understood, as in grammar, one only word; but sometimes, by circumlocution, many words together. For all these words, *he that in his actions observeth the laws of his country*, make but one name, equivalent to this one word, *just*.

By this imposition of names, some of larger, some of stricter signification, we turn the reckoning of the consequences of things imagined in the mind, into a reckoning of the consequences of appellations. For example: a man that hath no use of speech at all, such as is born and remains perfectly deaf and dumb, if he set before his eyes a triangle, and by it two right angles, such as are the corners of a square figure, he may, by meditation, compare and find, that the three angles of that triangle, are equal to those two right angles that stand by it. But if another triangle be shown him, different in shape from the former, he cannot know, without a new labour, whether the three angles of that also be equal to the same. But he that hath the use of words, when he observes, that such equality was consequent, not to the length of the sides, nor to any other particular thing in his triangle; but only to this, that the sides were straight, and the angles three; and that that was all, for which he named it a triangle; will boldly conclude universally, that such equality of angles is in all triangles whatsoever; and register his invention in these general terms, *every triangle hath its three angles equal to two right angles*. And thus the consequence found in one particular, comes to be registered and remembered, as a universal rule, and discharges our mental reckoning, of time and place, and delivers us from all labour of the mind, saving the first, and makes that which was found true *here*, and *now*, to be true in *all times* and *places*.

But the use of words in registering our thoughts is in nothing so evident as in numbering. A natural fool that could never learn by heart the order of numeral words, as *one, two,* and *three*, may observe every stroke of the clock, and nod to it, or say *one, one, one*, but can never know what hour it strikes. And it seems, there was a time when those names of number were not in use; and men were fain to apply their fingers of one or both hands, to those things they desired to keep account of; and that thence it proceeded, that now our numeral words are but ten, in any nation, and in some but five; and then they begin again. And he that can tell ten, if he recite them out of order, will lose himself, and not know when he has done. Much less will he be able to add, and subtract, and perform all other operations of arithmetic. So that without words there is no possibility of reckoning of numbers; much less of magnitudes, of swiftness, of force, and other things, the reckonings whereof are necessary to the being, or well-being of mankind.

When two names are joined together into a consequence, or affirmation, as thus, *a man is a living creature;* or thus, *if he be a man, he is a living creature;* if the latter name, *living creature*, signify all that the former name *man* signifieth, then the affirmation, or consequence, is *true;* otherwise *false*. For *true* and *false* are attributes of speech, not of things. And where speech is not, there is neither *truth* nor *falsehood; error* there may be, as when we expect that which shall not be, or suspect what has not been; but in neither case can a man be charged with untruth.

*Necessity of definitions.* Seeing then that truth consisteth in the right ordering of names in our affirmations, a man that seeketh precise truth had need to remember what every name he uses stands for, and to place it accordingly, or else he will find himself entangled in words, as a bird in lime twigs, the more he struggles the more belimed. And therefore in geometry, which is the only science that it hath pleased God hitherto to bestow on mankind, men begin at settling the significations of their words; which settling of significations they call *definitions*, and place them in the beginning of their reckoning.

By this it appears how necessary it is for any man that aspires to true knowledge, to examine the definitions of former authors; and either to correct them, where they are negligently set down, or to make them himself. For the errors of definitions multiply themselves according as the reckoning proceeds, and lead men into absurdities, which at last they see, but cannot avoid, without reckoning anew from the beginning, in which lies the foundation of their errors. From whence it happens, that they which trust to books do as they that cast up many little sums into a greater, without considering whether those little sums were rightly cast up or not; and at last finding the error visible, and not mistrusting their first grounds, know not which way to clear themselves, but spend time in fluttering over their books; as birds that entering by the chimney, and finding themselves enclosed in a chamber, flutter at the false light of a glass window, for want of wit to consider which way they came in. So that in the right definition of names lies the first use of speech; which is the acquisition of science: and in wrong, or no definitions, lies the first abuse; from which proceed all false and senseless tenets; which make those men that take their instruction from the authority of books, and not from their own meditation, to be as much below the condition of ignorant men, as men endued with true science are above it. For between true science and erroneous doctrines, ignorance is in the middle. Natural sense and imagination are not subject to absurdity. Nature itself cannot err; and as men abound in copiousness of language, so they become more wise, or more mad than ordinary. Nor is it possible without letters for any man to become either excellently wise, or, unless his memory be hurt by disease or ill constitution of organs, excellently foolish. For words are wise men's counters, they do but reckon by them; but they are the money of fools, that value them by the authority of an Aristotle, a Cicero, or a Thomas, or any other doctor whatsoever, if but a man.

*Subject to names. Subject to names,* is whatsoever can enter into or be considered in an account, and be added one to another to make a sum, or subtracted one from another and leave a remainder. The Latins called accounts of money *rationes,* and accounting *ratiocinatio;* and that which we in bills or books of account call *items,* they call *nomina,* that is, *names;* and thence it seems to proceed, that they extended the word *ratio* to the faculty of reckoning in all other things. The Greeks have but one word, λόγος, for both *speech* and *reason*; not that they thought there was no speech without reason, but no reasoning without speech: and the act of reasoning they called *syllogism*, which signifieth summing up of the consequences of one saying to another. And because the same thing may enter into account for divers accidents, their names are, to show that diversity, diversely wrested and diversified. This diversity of names may be reduced to four general heads.

*Names.* First, a thing may enter into account for *matter* or *body*; as *living, sensible, rational, hot, cold, moved, quiet*; with all which names the word *matter*, or *body*, is understood; all such being names of matter.

Secondly, it may enter into account, or be considered, for some accident or quality which we conceive to be in it; as for *being moved*, for *being so long*, for *being hot*, &c.; and then, of the name of the thing itself, by a little change or wresting, we make a name for that accident, which we consider; and for *living* put into the account *life*; for *moved*, *motion*; for *hot*, *heat*; for *long*, *length*, and the like; and all such names are the names of the accidents and properties by which one matter and body is distinguished from another. These are called *names abstract*, because severed, not from matter, but from the account of matter.

Thirdly, we bring into account the properties of our own bodies, whereby we make such distinction; as when anything is seen by us, we reckon not the thing itself, but the sight, the colour, the idea of it in the fancy: and when anything is heard, we reckon it not, but the hearing or sound only, which is our fancy or conception of it by the ear; and such are names of fancies.

*Use of names positive.* Fourthly, we bring into account, consider, and gives names to, *names* themselves, and to *speeches*: for *general, universal, special, equivocal*, are names of names. And *affirmation, interrogation, commandment, narration, syllogism, sermon, oration*, and many other such, are names of speeches. And this is all the variety of names *positive*; which are put to mark somewhat which is in nature, or may be feigned by the mind of man, as bodies that are, or may be conceived to be; or of bodies, the properties that are, or may be feigned to be; or words and speech.

*Negative names, with their uses.* There be also other names, called *negative*, which are notes to signify that a word is not the name of the thing in question; as these words, *nothing, no man, infinite, indocible, three want four,* and the like; which are nevertheless of use in reckoning, or in correcting of reckoning, and call to mind our past cogitations, though they be not names of any thing, because they make us refuse to admit of names not rightly used.

*Words insignificant.* All other names are but insignificant sounds; and those of two sorts. One when they are new, and yet their meaning not explained by definition; whereof there have been abundance coined by Schoolmen, and puzzled philosophers.

Another, when men make a name of two names, whose significations are contradictory and inconsistent; as this name, an *incorporeal body,* or, which is all one, an *incorporeal substance,* and a great number more. For whensoever any affirmation is false, the two names of which it is composed, put together and made one, signify nothing at all. For example, if it be a false affirmation to say *a quadrangle is round,* the word *round quadrangle* signifies nothing, but is a mere sound. So likewise, if it be false to say that virtue can be poured, or blown up and down, the words *inpoured virtue, inblown virtue,* are as absurd and insignificant as a *round quadrangle.* And therefore you shall hardly meet with a senseless and insignificant word, that is not made up of some Latin or Greek names. A Frenchman seldom hears our Saviour called by the name of *parole,* but by the name of *verbe* often; yet *verbe* and *parole* differ no more, but that one is Latin, the other French.

*Understanding.* When a man, upon the hearing of any speech, hath those thoughts which the words of that speech and their connexion were ordained and constituted to signify, then he is said to understand it; *understanding* being nothing else but conception caused by speech. And therefore if speech be peculiar to man, as for aught I know it is, then is understanding peculiar to him also. And therefore of absurd and false affirmations, in case they be universal, there can be no understanding; though many think they understand then, when they do but repeat the words softly, or con them in their mind.

What kinds of speeches signify the appetites, aversions, and passions of man's mind; and of their use and abuse, I shall speak when I have spoken of the passions.

*Inconstant names.* The names of such things as affect us, that is, which please and displease us, because all men be not alike affected with the same thing, nor the same man at all times, are in the common discourses of men of *inconstant* signification. For seeing all names are imposed to signify our conceptions, and all our affections are but conceptions, when we conceive the same things differently, we can hardly avoid different naming of them. For though the nature of that we conceive, be the same; yet the diversity of our reception of it, in respect of different constitutions of body, and prejudices of opinion, gives every thing a tincture of our different passions. And therefore in reasoning a man must take heed of words; which besides the signification of what we imagine of their nature, have a signification also of the nature, disposition, and interest of the speaker; such as are the names of virtues and vices; for one man calleth *wisdom*, what another calleth *fear*; and one *cruelty*, what another *justice*; one *prodigality*, what another *magnanimity*; and one *gravity*, what another *stupidity*, &c. And therefore such names can never be true grounds of any ratiocination. No more can metaphors, and tropes of speech: but these are less dangerous, because they profess their inconstancy; which the other do not.

Chapter 5

## Of Reason and Science

*Reason, what it is.* When a man *reasoneth*, he does nothing else but conceive a sum total, from *addition* of parcels; or conceive a remainder, from *subtraction* of one sum from another; which, if it be done by words, is conceiving of the consequence of the names of all the parts, to the name of the whole; or from the names of the whole and one part, to the name of the other part. And though in some things, as in numbers, besides adding and subtracting, men name other operations, as *multiplying* and *dividing*, yet they are the same; for multiplication, is but adding together of things equal; and division, but subtracting of one thing, as often as we can. These operations are not incident to numbers only, but to all manner of things that can be added together, and taken one out of another. For as arithmeticians teach to add and subtract in *numbers*; so the geometricians teach the same in *lines, figures*, solid and superficial, *angles, proportions, times*, degrees of *swiftness, force, power*, and the like; the logicians teach the same in *consequences of words*; adding together two *names* to make an *affirmation*, and two *affirmations* to make a *syllogism;* and *many syllogisms* to make a *demonstration*; and from the *sum*, or *conclusion* of a *syllogism*, they subtract one *proposition* to find the other. Writers of politics add together *pactions* to find men's *duties*; and lawyers, *laws* and *facts*, to find what is *right* and *wrong* in the actions of private men. In sum, in what matter soever there is place for *addition* and *subtraction*, there also is place for *reason;* and where these have no place, there *reason* has nothing at all to do.

*Reason defined.* Out of all which we may define, that is to say determine, what that is, which is meant by this word *reason*, when we reckon it amongst the faculties of the mind. For REASON, in this sense, is nothing but *reckoning*, that is adding and subtracting, of the consequences of general names agreed upon for the *marking* and *signifying* of our thoughts; I say *marking* them when we reckon by ourselves, and *signifying*, when we demonstrate or approve our reckonings to other men.

*Right reason, where.* And, as in arithmetic, unpractised men must, and professors themselves may often, err and cast up false; so also in any other subject of reasoning, the ablest, most attentive, and most practised men may deceive themselves, and infer false conclusions; not but that reason itself is always right reason, as well as arithmetic is a certain and infallible art: but no one man's reason, nor the reason of any one number of men, makes the certainty; no more than an account is therefore well cast up, because a great many men have unanimously approved it. And therefore, as when there is a controversy in an account, the parties must by their own accord, set up, for right reason, the reason of some arbitrator, or judge, to whose sentence they will both stand or their controversy must either come to blows or be undecided, for want of a right reason constituted by nature; so is it also in all debates of what kind soever. And when men that think themselves wiser than all others, clamour and demand right reason for judge, yet seek no more, but that things should be determined, by no other men's reason but their own, it is as intolerable in the society of men, as it is in play after trump is turned, to use for trump on every occasion, that suite whereof they have most in their hand. For they do nothing else, that will have every of their passions, as it comes to bear sway in them, to be taken for right reason, and that in their own controversies: bewraying their want of right reason, by the claim they lay to it.

*The use of reason.* The use and end of reason, is not the finding of the sum and truth of one, or a few consequences, remote from the first definitions, and settled significations of names, but to begin at these, and proceed from one consequence to another. For there can be no certainty of the last conclusion, without a certainty of all those affirmations and negations, on which it was grounded and inferred. As when a master of a family, in taking an account, casteth up the sums of all the bills of expense into one sum, and not regarding how each bill is summed up, by those that give them in account; nor what it is he pays for; he advantages himself no more, than if he allowed the account in gross, trusting to every of the accountants' skill and honesty: so also in reasoning of all other things, he that takes up conclusions on the trust of authors, and doth not fetch them from the first items in every reckoning, which are the significations of names settled by definitions, loses his labour; and does not know any thing, but only believeth.

*Of error and absurdity.* When a man reckons without the use of words, which may be done in particular things, as when upon the sight of any one thing, we conjecture what was likely to have preceded, or is likely to follow upon it; if that which he thought likely to follow, follows not, or that which he thought likely to have preceded it, hath not preceded it, this is called *error*; to which even the most prudent men are subject. But when we reason in words of general signification, and fall upon a general inference which is false, though it be commonly called *error*, it is indeed an *absurdity*, or senseless speech. For error is but a deception, in presuming that somewhat is past, or to come; of which, though it were not past, or not to come, yet there was no impossibility discoverable. But when we make a general assertion, unless it be a true one, the possibility of it is inconceivable. And words whereby we conceive nothing but the sound, are those we call *absurd, insignificant,* and *nonsense.* And therefore if a man should talk to me of a *round quadrangle;* or, *accidents of bread in cheese;* or, *immaterial substances;* or of a *free subject*; a *free will*; or any *free*, but free from being hindered by opposition, I should not say he were in an error, but that his words were without meaning, that is to say, absurd.

I have said before in the second chapter, that a man did excel all other animals in this faculty, that when he conceived any thing whatsoever, he was apt to inquire the consequences of it, and what effects he could do with it. And now I add this other degree of the same excellence, that he can by words reduce the consequences he finds to general rules, called *theorems,* or *aphorisms*; that is, he can reason, or reckon, not only in number, but in all other things, whereof one may be added unto, or subtracted from another.

But this privilege is allayed by another; and that is, by the privilege of absurdity; to which no living creature is subject, but man only. And of men, those are of all most subject to it, that profess philosophy. For it is most true that Cicero saith of them somewhere; that there can be nothing so absurd, but may be found in the books of philosophers. And the reason is manifest. For there is not one of them that begins his ratiocination from the definitions, or explications of the names they are to use; which is a method that hath been used only in geometry; whose conclusions have thereby been made indisputable.

*Causes of absurdity.* 1. The first cause of absurd conclusions I ascribe to the want of method; in that they begin not their ratiocination from definitions; that is, from settled significations of their words: as if they could cast account, without knowing the value of the numeral words, *one, two,* and *three*.

And whereas all bodies enter into account upon divers considerations, which I have mentioned in the precedent chapter; these considerations being diversely named, divers absurdities proceed from the confusion, and unfit connexion of their names into assertions. And therefore,

2. The second cause of absurd assertions, I ascribe to the giving of names of *bodies* to *accidents*; or of *accidents* to *bodies*; as they do, that say, *faith is infused,* or *inspired*; when nothing can be *poured,* or *breathed* into anything, but body; and that, *extension* is *body;* that *phantasms* are *spirits,* &c.

3. The third I ascribe to the giving of the names of the *accidents* of *bodies without us,* to the *accidents* of our *own bodies*; as they do that say the *colour is in the body; the sound is in the air,* &c.

4. The fourth, to the giving of the names of *bodies* to *names,* or *speeches*; as they do that say, that *there be things universal*; that *a living creature is genus,* or *a general thing,* &c.

5. The fifth, to the giving of the names of *accidents* to *names* and *speeches*; as they do that say, *the nature of a thing is its definition; a man's command is his will*; and the like.

6. The sixth, to the use of metaphors, tropes, and other rhetorical figures, instead of words proper. For though it be lawful to say, for example, in common speech, *the way goeth, or leadeth hither, or thither; the proverb says this or that,* whereas ways cannot go, nor proverbs speak; yet in reckoning, and seeking of truth, such speeches are not to be admitted.

7. The seventh, to names that signify nothing; but are taken up, and learned by rote from the schools, as *hypostatical, transubstantiate, consubstantiate, eternal-now,* and the like canting of Schoolmen.

To him that can avoid these things it is not easy to fall into any absurdity, unless it be by the length of an account; wherein he may perhaps forget what went before. For all men by nature reason alike, and well, when they have good principles. For who is so stupid, as both to mistake in geometry, and also to persist in it, when another detects his error to him?

*Science.* By this it appears that reason is not, as sense and memory, born with us; nor gotten by experience only, as prudence is; but attained by industry; first in apt imposing of names; and secondly by getting a good and orderly method in proceeding from the elements, which are names, to assertions made by connexion of one of them to another; and so to syllogisms, which are the connexions of one assertion to another, till we come to a knowledge of all the consequences of names appertaining to the subject in hand; and that is it, men call. SCIENCE. And whereas sense and memory are but knowledge of fact, which is a thing past and irrevocable; *Science* is the knowledge of consequences, and dependence of one fact upon another: by which, out of that we can presently do, we know how to do something else when we will, or the like another time; because when we see how any thing comes about, upon what causes, and by what manner; when the like causes come into our power, we see how to make it produce the like effects.

Children therefore are not endued with reason at all, till they have attained the use of speech; but are called reasonable creatures, for the possibility apparent of having the use of reason in time to come. And the most part of men, though they have the use of reasoning a little way, as in numbering to some degree; yet it serves them to little use in common life; in which they govern themselves, some better, some worse, according to their differences of experience, quickness of memory, and inclinations to several ends; but specially according to good or evil fortune, and the errors of one another. For as for *science*, or certain rules of their actions, they are so far from it, that they know not what it is. Geometry they have thought conjuring: but for other sciences, they who have not been taught the beginnings and some progress in them, that they may see how they be acquired and generated, are in this point like children, that having no thought of generation, are made believe by the women that their brothers and sisters are not born, but found in the garden.

But yet they that have no *science*, are in better, and nobler condition, with their natural prudence; than men, that by misreasoning, or by trusting them that reason wrong, fall upon false and absurd general rules. For ignorance of causes, and of rules, does not set men so far out of their way, as relying on false rules, and taking for causes of what they aspire to, those that are not so, but rather causes of the contrary.

To conclude, the light of human minds is perspicuous

words, but by exact definitions first snuffed, and purged from ambiguity; *reason* is the *pace;* increase of *science,* the *way;* and the benefit of mankind, the *end.* And, on the contrary, metaphors, and senseless and ambiguous words, are like *ignes fatui*; and reasoning upon them is wandering amongst innumerable absurdities; and their end, contention and sedition, or contempt.

*Prudence and sapience, with their difference.* As much experience, is *prudence*; so, is much science *sapience.* For though we usually have one name of wisdom for them both, yet the Latins did always distinguish between *prudentia* and *sapientia*; ascribing the former to experience, the latter to science. But to make their difference appear more clearly, let us suppose one man endued with an excellent natural use and dexterity in handling his arms; and another to have added to that dexterity, an acquired science, of where he can offend, or be offended by his adversary, in every possible posture or guard: the ability of the former, would be to the ability of the latter, as prudence to sapience; both useful; but the latter infallible. But they that trusting only to the authority of books, follow the blind blindly, are like him that, trusting to the false rules of a master of fence, ventures presumptuously upon an adversary, that either kills or disgraces him.

*Signs of science.* The signs of science are some, certain and infallible; some, uncertain. Certain, when he that pretendeth the science of any thing, can teach the same; that is to say, demonstrate the truth thereof perspicuously to another; uncertain, when only some particular events answer to his pretence, and upon many occasions prove so as he says they must. Signs of prudence are all uncertain; because to observe by experience, and remember all circumstances that may alter the success, is impossible. But in any business, whereof a man has not infallible science to proceed by; to forsake his own natural judgment, and be guided by general sentences read in authors, and subject to many exceptions, is a sign of folly, and generally scorned by the name of pedantry. And even of those men themselves, that in councils of the commonwealth love to show their reading of politics and history, very few do it in their domestic affairs, where their particular interest is concerned; having prudence enough for their private affairs: but in public they study more the reputation of their own wit, than the success of another's business.

## Chapter 6

### Of the Interior Beginnings of Voluntary Motions, commonly called the Passions; and the Speeches by which they are expressed

*Motion, vital and animal. Endeavour.* There be in animals, two sorts of *motions* peculiar to them: one called *vital*; begun in generation, and continued without interruption through their whole life; such as are the *course* of the *blood,* the *pulse,* the *breathing,* the *concoction, nutrition, excretion,* &c., to which motions there needs no help of imagination: the other is *animal motion,* otherwise called *voluntary motion*; as to *go,* to *speak,* to *move* any of our limbs, in such manner as is first fancied in our minds. That sense is motion in the organs and interior parts of man's body, caused by the action of the things we see, hear, &c.; and that fancy is but the relics of the same motion, remaining after sense, has been already said in the first and second chapters. And because *going, speaking,* and the like voluntary motions, depend always upon a precedent thought of *whither, which way,* and *what*; it is evident, that the imagination is the first internal beginning of all voluntary motion. And although unstudied men do not conceive any motion at all to be there, where the thing moved is invisible; or the space it is moved in is, for the shortness of it, insensible; yet that doth not hinder, but that such motions are. For let a space be never so little, that which is moved over a greater space, whereof that little one is part, must first be moved over that. These small beginnings of motion, within the body of man, before they appear in walking, speaking, striking, and other visible actions, are commonly called ENDEAVOUR.

*Appetite. Desire. Hunger. Thirst. Aversion.* This endeavour, when it is toward something which causes it, is called APPETITE, or DESIRE; the latter, being the general name; and the other oftentimes restrained to signify the desire of food, namely *hunger* and *thirst.* And when the endeavour is fromward something, it is generally called AVERSION. These words, *appetite* and *aversion,* we have from the Latins; and they both of them signify the motions, one of approaching, the other of retiring. So also do the Greek words for the same, which are ὁρμὴ and ἀφορμὴ. For nature itself does often press upon men those truths, which afterwards, when they look for somewhat beyond nature, they stumble at. For the Schools find in mere appetite to go, or move, no actual motion at all: but because some motion they must acknowledge, they call it metaphorical motion; which is but an absurd speech: for though words may be called metaphorical; bodies and motions can not.

*Love. Hate.* That which men desire, they are also said to LOVE: and to HATE those things for which they have aversion. So that desire and love are the same thing; save that by desire, we always signify the absence of the object; by love, most commonly the presence of the same. So also by aversion, we signify the absence; and by hate, the presence of the object.

*Contempt.* Of appetites and aversions, some are born with men; as appetite of food, appetite of excretion, and exoneration, which may also and more properly be called aversions, from somewhat they feel in their bodies; and some other appetites, not many. The rest, which are appetites of particular things, proceed from experience, and trial of their effects upon themselves or other men. For of things we know not at all, or believe not to be, we can have no further desire, than to taste and try. But aversion we have for things, not only which we know have hurt us, but also that we do not know whether they will hurt us, or not.

Those things which we neither desire, nor hate, we are said to *contemn*; CONTEMPT being nothing else but an immobility, or contumacy of the heart, in resisting the action of certain things; and proceeding from that the heart is already moved otherwise, by other more potent objects; or from want of experience of them.

And because the constitution of a man's body is in continual mutation, it is impossible that all the same things should always cause in him the same appetites, and aversions: much less can all men consent, in the desire of almost any one and the same object.

*Good. Evil.* But whatsoever is the object of any man's appetite or desire, that is it which he for his part calleth *good*: and the object of his hate and aversion, *evil*; and of his contempt, *vile* and *inconsiderable*. For these words of good, evil, and contemptible, are ever used with relation to the person that useth them: there being nothing simply and absolutely so; nor any common rule of good and evil, to be taken from the nature of the objects themselves; but from the person of the man, where there is no commonwealth; or, in a commonwealth, from the person that representeth it; or from an arbitrator or judge, whom men disagreeing shall by consent set up, and make his sentence the rule thereof.

*Pulchrum. Turpe. Delightful. Profitable. Unpleasant. Unprofitable.* The Latin tongue has two words, whose significations approach to those of good and evil; but are not precisely the same; and those are *pulchrum* and *turpe.* Whereof the former signifies that, which by some apparent signs promiseth good; and the latter, that which promiseth evil. But in our tongue we have not so general names to express them by. But for *pulchrum* we say in some things, *fair;* in others, *beautiful,* or *handsome,* or *gallant,* or *honourable,* or *comely,* or *amiable;* and for *turpe, foul, deformed, ugly, base, nauseous,* and the like, as the subject shall require; all which words, in their proper places, signify nothing else but the *mien,* or countenance, that promiseth good and evil. So that of good there be three kinds; good in the promise, that is *pulchrum;* good in effect, as the end desired, which is called *jucundum, delightful,* and good as the means, which is called *utile, profitable;* and as many of evil: for *evil* in promise, is that they call *turpe;* evil in effect, and end, is *molestum, unpleasant, troublesome;* and evil in the means, *inutile, unprofitable, hurtful.*

*Delight. Displeasure.* As, in sense, that which is really within us, is, as I have said before, only motion, caused by the action of external objects, but in appearance; to the sight, light and colour; to the ear, sound; to the nostril, odour, &c.: so, when the action of the same object is continued from the eyes, ears, and other organs to the heart, the real effect there is nothing but motion, or endeavour; which consisteth in appetite, or aversion, to or from the object moving. But the appearance, or sense of that motion, is that we either call *delight,* or *trouble of mind.*

*Pleasure. Offence.* This motion, which is called appetite, and for the appearance of it *delight,* and *pleasure,* seemeth to be a corroboration of vital motion, and a help thereunto; and therefore such things as caused delight, were not improperly called *jucunda, à juvando,* from helping or fortifying; and the contrary, *molesta, offensive,* from hindering, and troubling the motion vital.

*Pleasure* therefore, or *delight,* is the appearance or sense of good; and *molestation,* or *displeasure,* the appearance, or sense of evil. And consequently all appetite, desire, and love, is accompanied with some delight more or less; and all hatred and aversion, with more or less displeasure and offence.

*Pleasures of sense. Pleasures of the mind. Joy. Pain. Grief.* Of pleasures or delights, some arise from the sense of an object present; and those may be called *pleasures of sense*; the word *sensual,* as it is used by those only that condemn them, having no place till there be laws. Of this kind are all onerations and exonerations of the body; as also all that is pleasant, in the *sight, hearing, smell, taste,* or *touch.* Others arise from the expectation, that proceeds from foresight of the end, or consequence of things; whether those things in the sense please or displease. And these are *pleasures of the mind* of him that draweth those consequences, and are generally called JOY. In the like manner, displeasures are some in the sense, and called PAIN; others in the expectation of consequences, and are called GRIEF.

These simple passions called *appetite, desire, love, aversion, hate, joy,* and *grief,* have their names for divers considerations diversified. As first, when they one succeed another, they are diversely called from the opinion men have of the likelihood of attaining what they desire. Secondly, from the object loved or hated. Thirdly, from the consideration of many of them together. Fourthly, from the alteration or succession itself.

*Hope.* For *appetite,* with an opinion of attaining, is called HOPE.

*Despair.* The same, without such opinion, DESPAIR.

*Fear. Aversion,* with opinion of HURT from the object, FEAR.

*Courage.* The same, with hope of avoiding that hurt by resistance, COURAGE.

*Anger.* Sudden *courage,* ANGER.

*Confidence.* Constant *hope,* CONFIDENCE of ourselves.

*Diffidence.* Constant *despair,* DIFFIDENCE of ourselves.

*Indignation. Anger* for great hurt done to another, when we conceive the same to be done by injury, INDIGNATION.

*Benevolence. Good nature. Desire* of good to another, BENEVOLENCE, GOOD WILL, CHARITY. If to man generally, GOOD NATURE.

*Covetousness. Desire* of riches, COVETOUSNESS; a name used always in signification of blame; because men contending for them, are displeased with one another attaining them;

though the desire in itself, be to be blamed, or allowed, according to the means by which these riches are sought.

*Ambition. Pusillanimity. Desire* of office, or precedence, AMBITION: a name used also in the worse sense, for the reason before mentioned. *Desire* of things that conduce but a little to our ends, and fear of things that are but of little hindrance, PUSILLANIMITY.

*Magnanimity. Contempt* of little helps and hindrances, MAGNANIMITY.

*Valour. Magnanimity,* in danger of death or wounds, VALOUR, FORTITUDE.

*Liberality. Magnanimity* in the use of riches, LIBERALITY.

*Miserableness. Pusillanimity* in the same, WRETCHEDNESS, MISERABLENESS, or PARSIMONY; as it is liked or disliked.

*Kindness. Love* of persons for society, KINDNESS.

*Natural lust. Love* of persons for pleasing the sense only, NATURAL LUST.

*Luxury. Love* of the same, acquired from rumination, that is, imagination of pleasure past, LUXURY.

*The passion of love. Jealousy. Love* of one singularly, with desire to be singularly beloved, THE PASSION OF LOVE. The same, with fear that the love is not mutual, JEALOUSY.

*Revengefulness. Desire,* by doing hurt to another, to make him condemn some fact of his own, REVENGEFULNESS.

*Curiosity. Desire* to know why, and how, CURIOSITY; such as is in no living creature but *man*: so that man is distinguished, not only by his reason, but also by this singular passion from other *animals;* in whom the appetite of food, and other pleasures of sense, by predominance, take away the care of knowing causes; which is a lust of the mind, that by a perseverance of delight in the continual and indefatigable generation of knowledge, exceedeth the short vehemence of any carnal pleasure.

*Religion. Superstition. True religion. Fear* of power invisible, feigned by the mind, or imagined from tales publicly allowed, RELIGION; not allowed, SUPERSTITION. And when the power imagined, is truly such as we imagine, TRUE RELIGION.

*Panic terror. Fear,* without the apprehension of why, or what, PANIC TERROR, called so from the fables, that make Pan the author of them; whereas, in truth, there is always in him that so feareth, first, some apprehension of the cause, though the rest run away by example, every one supposing his fellow to know why. And therefore this passion happens to none but in a throng, or multitude of people.

*Admiration. Glory. Vain-glory. Joy,* from apprehension of novelty, ADMIRATION; proper to man, because it excites the appetite of knowing the cause.

*Joy,* arising from imagination of a man's own power and ability, is that exultation of the mind which is called GLORY-ING: which if grounded upon the experience of his own former actions, is the same with *confidence*: but if grounded on the flattery of others; or only supposed by himself, for delight in the consequences of it, is called VAIN-GLORY: which name is properly given; because a well grounded *confidence* begetteth attempt; whereas the supposing of power does not, and is therefore rightly called *vain*.

*Dejection. Grief,* from opinion of want of power, is called DEJECTION of mind.

The *vain-glory* which consisteth in the feigning or supposing of abilities in ourselves, which we know are not, is most incident to young men, and nourished by the histories, or fictions of gallant persons; and is corrected oftentimes by age, and employment.

*Sudden glory. Laughter. Sudden glory,* is the passion which maketh those *grimaces* called LAUGHTER; and is caused either by some sudden act of their own, that pleaseth them; or by the apprehension of some deformed thing in another, by comparison whereof they suddenly applaud themselves. And it is incident most to them, that are conscious of the fewest abilities in themselves; who are forced to keep themselves in their own favour, by observing the imperfections of other men. And therefore much laughter at the defects of others, is a sign of pusillanimity. For of great minds, one of the proper works is, to help and free others from scorn; and compare themselves only with the most able.

*Sudden dejection. Weeping.* On the contrary, *sudden dejection,* is the passion that causeth WEEPING; and is caused by such accidents, as suddenly take away some vehement hope, or some prop of their power: and they are most subject to it, that rely principally on helps external, such as are women, and children. Therefore some weep for the loss of friends; others for their unkindness; others for the sudden stop made to their thoughts of revenge, by reconciliation. But in all cases, both laughter, and weeping, are sudden motions; custom taking them both away. For no man laughs at old jests; or weeps for an old calamity.

*Shame. Blushing. Grief,* for the discovery of some defect of ability, is SHAME, or the passion that discovereth itself in

BLUSHING; and consisteth in the apprehension of some thing dishonourable; and in young men, is a sign of the love of good reputation, and commendable: in old men it is a sign of the same; but because it comes too late, not commendable.

*Impudence. Pity.* The *contempt* of good reputation is called IMPUDENCE. *Grief,* for the calamity of another, is PITY; and ariseth from the imagination that the like calamity may befall himself; and therefore is called also COMPASSION, and in the phrase of this present time a FELLOW-FEELING: and therefore for calamity arriving from great wickedness, the best men have the least pity; and for the same calamity, those hate pity, that think themselves least obnoxious to the same.

*Cruelty. Contempt,* or little sense of the calamity of others, is that which men call CRUELTY; proceeding from security of their own fortune. For, that any man should take pleasure in other men's great harms, without other end of his own, I do not conceive it possible.

*Emulation. Envy. Grief,* for the success of a competitor in wealth, honour, or other good, if it be joined with endeavour to enforce our own abilities to equal or exceed him, is called EMULATION: but joined with endeavour to supplant, or hinder a competitor, ENVY.

*Deliberation.* When in the mind of man, appetites, and aversions, hopes, and fears, concerning one and the same thing, arise alternately; and divers good and evil consequences of the doing, or omitting the thing propounded, come successively into our thoughts; so that sometimes we have an appetite to it; sometimes an aversion from it; sometimes hope to be able to do it; sometimes despair, or fear to attempt it; the whole sum of desires, aversions, hopes and fears continued till the thing be either done, or thought impossible, is that we call DELIBERATION.

Therefore of things past, there is no *deliberation*; because manifestly impossible to be changed: nor of things known to be impossible, or thought so; because men know, or think such deliberation vain. But of things impossible, which we think possible, we may deliberate; not knowing it is in vain. And it is called *deliberation*; because it is a putting an end to the *liberty* we had of doing, or omitting, according to our own appetite, or aversion.

This alternate succession of appetites, aversions, hopes and fears, is no less in other living creatures than in man: and therefore beasts also deliberate.

Every *deliberation* is then said to *end,* when that whereof they deliberate, is either done, or thought impossible; because till then we retain the liberty of doing, or omitting; according to our appetite, or aversion.

*The will.* In *deliberation,* the last appetite, or aversion, immediately adhering to the action, or to the omission thereof, is that we call the WILL; the act, not the faculty, of *willing.* And beasts that have *deliberation,* must necessarily also have *will.* The definition of the *will,* given commonly by the Schools, that it is a *rational appetite,* is not good. For if it were, then could there be no voluntary act against reason. For a *voluntary act* is that, which proceedeth from the *will,* and no other. But if instead of a rational appetite, we shall say an appetite resulting from a precedent deliberation, then the definition is the same that I have given here. *Will* therefore *is the last appetite in deliberating.* And though we say in common discourse, a man had a will once to do a thing, that nevertheless he forbore to do; yet that is properly but an inclination, which makes no action voluntary; because the action depends not of it, but of the last inclination, or appetite. For if the intervenient appetites, make any action voluntary; then by the same reason all intervenient aversions, should make the same action involuntary; and so one and the same action, should be both voluntary and involuntary.

By this it is manifest, that not only actions that have their beginning from covetousness, ambition, lust, or other appetites to the thing propounded; but also those that have their beginning from aversion, or fear of those consequences that follow the omission, are *voluntary actions.*

*Forms of speech, in passion.* The forms of speech by which the passions are expressed, are partly the same, and partly different from those, by which we express our thoughts. And first, generally all passions may be expressed *indicatively*; as *I love, I fear, I joy, I deliberate, I will, I command*: but some of them have particular expressions by themselves, which nevertheless are not affirmations, unless it be when they serve to make other inferences, besides that of the passion they proceed from. Deliberation is expressed *subjunctively*; which is a speech proper to signify suppositions, with their consequences; as, *if this be done, then this will follow*; and differs not from the language of reasoning, save that reasoning is in general words; but deliberation for the most part is of particulars. The language of desire, and aversion, is *imperative*; as *do this, forbear that*; which when the party is obliged to do, or forbear, is *command*; otherwise *prayer*; or else *counsel.*

The language of vain-glory, of indignation, pity and revenge-fulness, *optative*: but of the desire to know, there is a peculiar expression, called *interrogative*; as, *what is it, when shall it, how is it done,* and *why so?* other language of the passions I find none: for cursing, swearing, reviling, and the like, do not signify as speech; but as the actions of a tongue accustomed.

These forms of speech, I say, are expressions, or voluntary significations of our passions: but certain signs they be not; because they may be used arbitrarily, whether they that use them, have such passions or not. The best signs of passions present, are either in the countenance, motions of the body, actions, and ends, or aims, which we otherwise know the man to have.

*Good and evil apparent.* And because in deliberation, the appetites, and aversions, are raised by foresight of the good and evil consequences, and sequels of the action whereof we deliberate; the good or evil effect thereof dependeth on the foresight of a long chain of consequences, of which very seldom any man is able to see to the end. But for so far as a man seeth, if the good in those consequences be greater than the evil, the whole chain is that which writers call *apparent,* or *seeming good.* And contrarily, when the evil exceedeth the good, the whole is *apparent,* or *seeming evil*: so that he who hath by experience, or reason, the greatest and surest prospect of consequences, deliberates best himself; and is able when he will, to give the best counsel unto others.

*Felicity. Continual success* in obtaining those things which a man from time to time desireth, that is to say, continual prospering, is that men call FELICITY; I mean the felicity of this life. For there is no such thing as perpetual tranquillity of mind, while we live here; because life itself is but motion, and can never be without desire, nor without fear, no more than without sense. What kind of felicity God hath ordained to them that devoutly honour Him, a man shall no sooner know, than enjoy; being joys, that now are as incomprehensible, as the word of Schoolmen *beatifical vision* is unintelligible.

*Praise. Magnification.* Μακαρισμός. The form of speech whereby men signify their opinion of the goodness of any thing, is PRAISE. That whereby they signify the power and greatness of any thing, is MAGNIFYING. And that whereby they signify the opinion they have of a man's felicity, is by the Greeks called μακαρισμός, for which we have no name in our tongue. And thus much is sufficient for the present pur-pose, to have been said of the PASSIONS.

# Chapter 7

## Of the Ends or Resolutions of Discourse

OF ALL *discourse*, governed by desire of knowledge, there is at last an *end*, either by attaining, or by giving over. And in the chain of discourse, wheresoever it be interrupted, there is an end for that time.

*Judgment, or sentence final. Doubt.* If the discourse be merely mental, it consisteth of thoughts that the thing will be, and will not be; or that it has been, and has not been, alternately. So that wheresoever you break off the chain of a man's discourse, you leave him in a presumption of *it will be,* or, *it will not be;* or, *it has been,* or, *has not been.* All which is *opinion.* And that which is alternate appetite, in deliberating concerning good and evil; the same is alternate opinion, in the enquiry of the truth of *past,* and *future.* And as the last appetite in deliberation, is called the *will;* so the last opinion in search of the truth of past, and future, is called the JUDGMENT, or *resolute* and *final sentence* of him that *discourseth.* And as the whole chain of appetites alternate, in the question of good, or bad, is called *deliberation;* so the whole chain of opinions alternate, in the question of true, or false, is called DOUBT.

No discourse whatsoever, can end in absolute knowledge of fact, past, or to come. For, as for the knowledge of fact, it is originally, sense; and ever after, memory. And for the knowledge of consequence, which I have said before is called science, it is not absolute, but conditional. No man can know by discourse, that this, or that, is, has been, or will be; which is to know absolutely: but only, that if this be, that is; if this has been, that has been; if this shall be, that shall be: which is to know conditionally; and that not the consequence of one thing to another; but of one name of a thing, to another name of the same thing.

*Science. Opinion. Conscious.* And therefore, when the discourse is put into speech, and begins with the definitions of words, and proceeds by connexion of the same into general affirmations, and of these again into syllogisms; the end or last sum is called the conclusion; and the thought of the mind by it signified, is that conditional knowledge, or knowledge of the consequence of words, which is commonly called SCIENCE.

But if the first ground of such discourse, be not definitions; or if the definitions be not rightly joined together into syllogisms, then the end or conclusion, is again OPINION, namely of the truth of somewhat said, though sometimes in absurd and senseless words, without possibility of being understood. When two, or more men, know of one and the same fact, they are said to be CONSCIOUS of it one to another; which is as much as to know it together. And because such are fittest witnesses of the facts of one another, or of a third; it was, and ever will be reputed a very evil act, for any man to speak against his *conscience:* or to corrupt or force another so to do: insomuch that the plea of conscience, has been always hearkened unto very diligently in all times. Afterwards, men made use of the same word metaphorically, for the knowledge of their own secret facts, and secret thoughts, and therefore it is rhetorically said, that the conscience is a thousand witnesses. And last of all, men, vehemently in love with their own new opinions, though never so absurd, and obstinately bent to maintain them, gave those their opinions also that reverenced name of conscience, as if they would have it seem unlawful, to change or speak against them; and so pretend to know they are true, when they know at most, but that they think so.

*Belief. Faith.* When a man's discourse beginneth not at definitions, it beginneth either at some other contemplation of his own, and then it is still called opinion; or it beginneth at some saying of another, of whose ability to know the truth, and of whose honesty in not deceiving, he doubteth not; and then the discourse is not so much concerning the thing, as the person; and the resolution is called BELIEF, and FAITH. *faith, in* the man; *belief,* both *of* the man, and *of* the truth of what he says. So that in belief are two opinions; one of the saying of the man; the other of his virtue. To *have faith in,* or *trust to,* or *believe a man,* signify the same thing; namely, an opinion of the veracity of the man: but to *believe what is said,* signifieth only an opinion of the truth of the saying. But we are to observe that this phrase, *I believe in;* as also the Latin, *credo in;* and the Greek, πιστεύω εἰς, are never used but in the writings of divines. Instead of them, in other writings are put, *I believe him; I trust him; I have faith in him; I rely on him:* and in Latin, *credo illi: fido illi:* and in Greek, πιστεύω αὐτῷ: and that this singularity of the ecclesiastic use of the word hath raised many disputes about the right object of the Christian faith.

But by *believing in*, as it is in the creed, is meant, not trust in the person; but confession and acknowledgment of the doctrine. For not only Christians, but all manner of men do so believe in God, as to hold all for truth they hear him say, whether they understand it, or not; which is all the faith and trust can possibly be had in any person whatsoever: but they do not all believe the doctrine of the creed.

From whence we may infer, that when we believe any saying whatsoever it be, to be true, from arguments taken, not from the thing itself, or from the principles of natural reason, but from the authority, and good opinion we have, of him that hath said it; then is the speaker, or person we believe in, or trust in, and whose word we take, the object of our faith; and the honour done in believing, is done to him only. And consequently, when we believe that the Scriptures are the word of God, having no immediate revelation from God himself, our belief, faith, and trust is in the church; whose word we take, and acquiesce therein. And they that believe that which a prophet relates unto them in the name of God, take the word of the prophet, do honour to him, and in him trust, and believe, touching the truth of what he relateth, whether he be a true, or a false prophet. And so it is also with all other history. For if I should not believe all that is written by historians, of the glorious acts of *Alexander*, or *Cæsar;* I do not think the ghost of *Alexander*, or *Cæsar*, had any just cause to be offended; or any body else, but the historian. If *Livy* say the Gods made once a cow speak, and we believe it not; we distrust not God therein, but *Livy*. So that it is evident, that whatsoever we believe, upon no other reason, than what is drawn from authority of men only, and their writings; whether they be sent from God or not, is faith in men only.

## Chapter 8

### Of the Virtues, commonly called Intellectual; and their contrary Defects

*Intellectual virtue defined.* VIRTUE generally, in all sorts of subjects, is somewhat that is valued for eminence; and consisteth in comparison. For if all things were equal in all men, nothing would be prized. And by *virtues intellectual,* are always understood such abilities of the mind, as men praise, value, and desire should be in themselves; and go commonly under the name of a *good wit;* though the same word *wit,* be used also, to distinguish one certain ability from the rest.

*Wit, natural, or acquired. Natural wit.* These *virtues* are of two sorts; *natural,* and *acquired.* By natural, I mean not, that which a man hath from his birth: for that is nothing else but sense; wherein men differ so little one from another, and from brute beasts, as it is not to be reckoned amongst virtues. But I mean, that *wit,* which is gotten by use only, and experience; without method, culture, or instruction. This NATURAL WIT, consisteth principally in two things; *celerity of imagining,* that is, swift succession of one thought to another; and *steady direction* to some approved end. On the contrary a slow imagination, maketh that defect, or fault of the mind, which is commonly called DULLNESS, *stupidity,* and sometimes by other names that signify slowness of motion, or difficulty to be moved.

*Good wit, or fancy. Good judgment, Discretion.* And this difference of quickness, is caused by the difference of men's passions; that love and dislike, some one thing, some another: and therefore some men's thoughts run one way, some another; and are held to, and observe differently the things that pass through their imagination. And whereas in this succession of men's thoughts, there is nothing to observe in the things they think on, but either in what they be *like one another,* or in what they be *unlike,* or *what they serve for,* or *how they serve to such a purpose;* those that observe their similitudes, in any case they be such as are but rarely observed by others, are said to have a *good wit;* by which, in this occasion, is meant a *good fancy.* But they that observe their differences, and dissimilitudes; which is called *distinguishing,* and *discerning,* and *judging* between thing and thing;

in case, such discerning be not easy, are said to have a *good judgment:* and particularly in matter of conversation and business; wherein, times, places, and persons are to be discerned, this virtue is called DISCRETION. The former, that is, fancy, without the help of judgment, is not commended as a virtue: but the latter which is judgment, and discretion, is commended for itself, without the help of fancy. Besides the discretion of times, places, and persons, necessary to a good fancy, there is required also an often application of his thoughts to their end; that is to say, to some use to be made of them. This done; he that hath this virtue, will be easily fitted with similitudes, that will please, not only by illustrations of his discourse, and adorning it with new and apt metaphors; but also, by the rarity of their invention. But without steadiness, and direction to some end, a great fancy is one kind of madness; such as they have, that entering into any discourse, are snatched from their purpose, by every thing that comes in their thought, into so many, and so long digressions, and parentheses, that they utterly lose themselves: which kind of folly, I know no particular name for: but the cause of it is, sometimes want of experience; whereby that seemeth to a man new and rare, which doth not so to others: sometimes pusillanimity; by which that seems great to him, which other men think a trifle: and whatsoever is new, or great, and therefore thought fit to be told, withdraws a man by degrees from the intended way of his discourse.

In a good poem, whether it be *epic,* or *dramatic;* as also in *sonnets, epigrams,* and other pieces, both judgment and fancy are required: but the fancy must be more eminent; because they please for the extravagancy; but ought not to displease by indiscretion.

In a good history, the judgment must be eminent; because the goodness consisteth, in the method, in the truth, and in the choice of the actions that are most profitable to be known. Fancy has no place, but only in adorning the style.

In orations of praise, and in invectives, the fancy is predominant; because the design is not truth, but to honour or dishonour; which is done by noble, or by vile comparisons. The judgment does but suggest what circumstances make an action laudable, or culpable.

In hortatives, and pleadings, as truth, or disguise serveth best to the design in hand; so is the judgment, or the fancy most required.

In demonstration, in counsel, and all rigorous search of

truth, judgment does all, except sometimes the understanding
have need to be opened by some apt similitude; and then
there is so much use of fancy. But for metaphors, they are
in this case utterly excluded. For seeing they openly profess
deceit; to admit them into counsel, or reasoning, were manifest folly.

And in any discourse whatsoever, if the defect of discretion
be apparent, how extravagant soever the fancy be, the whole
discourse will be taken for a sign of want of wit; and so will
it never when the discretion is manifest, though the fancy be
never so ordinary.

The secret thoughts of a man run over all things, holy,
profane, clean, obscene, grave, and light, without shame, or
blame; which verbal discourse cannot do, farther than the
judgment shall approve of the time, place, and persons. An
anatomist, or a physician may speak, or write his judgment
of unclean things; because it is not to please, but profit: but
for another man to write his extravagant, and pleasant fancies
of the same, is as if a man, from being tumbled into the dirt,
should come and present himself before good company. And
it is the want of discretion that makes the difference. Again,
in professed remissness of mind, and familiar company, a man
may play with the sounds and equivocal significations of
words; and that many times with encounters of extraordinary
fancy: but in a sermon, or in public, or before persons unknown, or whom we ought to reverence; there is no jingling
of words that will not be accounted folly: and the difference
is only in the want of discretion. So that where wit is wanting,
it is not fancy that is wanting, but discretion. Judgment therefore without fancy is wit, but fancy without judgment, not.

*Prudence.* When the thoughts of a man, that has a design
in hand, running over a multitude of things, observes how
they conduce to that design; or what design they may conduce unto; if his observations be such as are not easy, or
usual, this wit of his is called PRUDENCE; and depends on
much experience, and memory of the like things, and their
consequences heretofore. In which there is not so much difference of men; as there is in their fancies and judgment;
because the experience of men equal in age, is not much
unequal, as to the quantity; but lies in different occasions;
every one having his private designs. To govern well a family,
and a kingdom, are not different degrees of prudence; but
different sorts of business; no more than to draw a picture
in little, or as great, or greater than the life, are different

degrees of art. A plain husbandman is more prudent in affairs of his own house, than a privy-councillor in the affairs of another man.

*Craft.* To prudence, if you add the use of unjust, or dishonest means, such as usually are prompted to men by fear, or want; you have that crooked wisdom, which is called CRAFT; which is a sign of pusillanimity. For magnanimity is contempt of unjust, or dishonest helps. And that which the Latins call *versutia,* translated into English, *shifting,* and is a putting off of a present danger or incommodity, by engaging into a greater, as when a man robs one to pay another, is but a shorter-sighted craft, called *versutia,* from *versura,* which signifies taking money at usury for the present payment of interest.

*Acquired wit.* As for *acquired wit,* I mean acquired by method and instruction, there is none but reason; which is grounded on the right use of speech, and produceth the sciences. But of reason and science I have already spoken, in the fifth and sixth chapters.

The causes of this difference of wits, are in the passions; and the difference of passions proceedeth, partly from the different constitution of the body, and partly from different education. For if the difference proceedeth from the temper of the brain, and the organs of sense, either exterior or interior, there would be no less difference of men in their sight, hearing, or other senses, than in their fancies and discretions. It proceeds therefore from the passions; which are different, not only from the difference of men's complexions; but also from their difference of customs, and education.

The passions that most of all cause the difference of wit, are principally, the more or less desire of power, of riches, of knowledge, and of honour. All which may be reduced to the first, that is, desire of power. For riches, knowledge, and honour, are but several sorts of power.

*Giddiness. Madness.* And therefore, a man who has no great passion for any of these things; but is, as men term it, indifferent; though he may be so far a good man, as to be free from giving offence; yet he cannot possibly have either a great fancy, or much judgment. For the thoughts are to the desires, as scouts, and spies, to range abroad, and find the way to the things desired: all steadiness of the mind's motion, and all quickness of the same, proceeding from thence: for as to have no desire, is to be dead: so to have weak passions, is dullness; and to have passions indifferently for every thing,

GIDDINESS, and *distraction;* and to have stronger and more vehement passions for any thing, than is ordinarily seen in others, is that which men call MADNESS.

Whereof there be almost as many kinds, as of the passions themselves. Sometimes the extraordinary and extravagant passion, proceedeth from the evil constitution of the organs of the body, or harm done them; and sometimes the hurt, and indisposition of the organs, is caused by the vehemence, or long continuance of the passion. But in both cases the madness is of one and the same nature.

The passion, whose violence, or continuance, maketh madness, is either great *vain-glory;* which is commonly called *pride,* and *self-conceit;* or great *dejection* of mind.

*Rage.* Pride subjecteth a man to anger, the excess whereof, is the madness called RAGE and FURY. And thus it comes to pass that excessive desire of revenge, when it becomes habitual, hurteth the organs, and becomes rage: that excessive love, with jealousy, becomes also rage: excessive opinion of a man's own self, for divine inspiration, for wisdom, learning, form and the like, becomes distraction and giddiness: the same, joined with envy, rage: vehement opinion of the truth of any thing, contradicted by others, rage.

*Melancholy. Madness.* Dejection subjects a man to causeless fears; which is a madness, commonly called MELANCHOLY; apparent also in divers manners; as in haunting of solitudes and graves; in superstitious behaviour; and in fearing, some one, some another particular thing. In sum, all passions that produce strange and unusual behaviour, are called by the general name of madness. But of the several kinds of madness, he that would take the pains, might enrol a legion. And if the excesses be madness, there is no doubt but the passions themselves, when they tend to evil, are degrees of the same.

For example, though the effect of folly, in them that are possessed of an opinion of being inspired, be not visible always in one man, by any very extravagant action, that proceedeth from such passion; yet, when many of them conspire together, the rage of the whole multitude is visible enough. For what argument of madness can there be greater, than to clamour, strike, and throw stones at our best friends? Yet this is somewhat less than such a multitude will do. For they will clamour, fight against, and destroy those, by whom all their lifetime before, they have been protected, and secured from injury. And if this be madness in the multitude, it is the same in every particular man. For as in the midst of the sea, though a man perceive no sound of that part of the water next him, yet is well assured, that part contributes as much to the roaring of the sea, as any other part of the same quantity; so also, though we perceive no great unquietness in one or two men, yet we may be well assured, that their singular passions, are parts of the seditious roaring of a troubled nation. And if there were nothing else that bewrayed their madness; yet that very arrogating such inspiration to themselves, is argument enough. If some man in Bedlam should entertain you with sober discourse; and you desire in taking leave, to know what he were, that you might another time requite his civility; and he should tell you, he were God the Father; I think you need expect no extravagant action for argument of his madness.

This opinion of inspiration, called commonly, private spirit, begins very often, from some lucky finding of an error generally held by others; and not knowing, or not remembering, by what conduct of reason, they came to so singular a truth, (as they think it, though it be many times an untruth they light on) they presently admire themselves, as being in the special grace of God Almighty, who hath revealed the same to them supernaturally, by his Spirit.

Again, that madness is nothing else, but too much appearing passion, may be gathered out of the effects of wine, which are the same with those of the evil disposition of the organs. For the variety of behaviour in men that have drunk too much, is the same with that of madmen: some of them raging, others loving, others laughing, all extravagantly, but according to their several domineering passions: for the effect of the wine, does but remove dissimulation, and take from them the sight of the deformity of their passions. For, I believe, the most sober men, when they walk alone without care and employment of the mind, would be unwilling the vanity and extravagance of their thoughts at that time should be publicly seen; which is a confession, that passions unguided, are for the most part mere madness.

The opinions of the world, both in ancient and later ages, concerning the cause of madness, have been two. Some deriving them from the passions; some demons, or spirits, either good or bad, which they thought might enter a man, possess him, and move his organs in such strange and uncouth manner, as madmen use to do. The former sort therefore, called such men, madmen: but the latter, called them sometimes *demoniacs*, that is, possessed with spirits; sometimes *energumeni*, that is, agitated or moved with spirits; and now in Italy they are called, not only *pazzi*, madmen; but also *spiritati*, men possessed.

There was once a great conflux of people in Abdera, a city of the Greeks, at the acting of the tragedy of *Andromeda*, upon an extreme hot day; whereupon, a great many of the spectators falling into fevers, had this accident from the heat, and from the tragedy together, that they did nothing but pronounce iambics, with the names of Perseus and Andromeda; which, together with the fever, was cured by the coming on of winter; and this madness was thought to proceed from the passion imprinted by the tragedy. Likewise there reigned a fit of madness in another Grecian city, which seized only the young maidens; and caused many of them to hang themselves. This was by most then thought an act of the Devil. But one that suspected, that contempt of life in them, might proceed from some passion of the mind, and supposing that they did not contemn also their honour, gave counsel to the magistrates, to strip such as so hanged themselves, and let them hang out naked. This, the story says, cured that madness. But on the other side, the same Grecians, did often ascribe madness to the operation of Eumenides, or Furies; and sometimes of Ceres, Phœbus, and other gods; so much did men attribute to phantasms, as to think them aërial living bodies; and generally to call them spirits. And as the Romans in this, held the same opinion with the Greeks, so also did the Jews; for they called madmen prophets, or, according as they thought the spirits good or bad, demoniacs: and some of them called both prophets and demoniacs, madmen; and some called the same man both demoniac, and madman. But for the Gentiles it is no wonder, because diseases and health, vices and virtues, and many natural accidents, were with them termed, and worshipped as demons. So that a man was to understand by demon, as well, sometimes an ague, as a devil. But for the Jews to have such opinion, is somewhat strange. For neither Moses nor Abraham pretended to prophecy by possession of a spirit; but from the voice of God; or by a vision or dream: nor is there anything in his law, moral or ceremonial, by which they were taught, there was any such enthusiasm, or any possession. When God is said, (*Numb*. xi. 25) to take from the spirit that was in Moses, and give to the seventy elders, the Spirit of God (taking it for the substance of God) is not divided. The Scriptures, by the Spirit of God in man, mean a man's spirit, inclined to godliness. And where it is said, (*Exod.* xxviii. 3) *"whom I have filled with the spirit of wisdom to make garments for Aaron,"* is not meant a spirit put into them, that can make garments, but the wisdom of their own spirits in that kind of work. In the like sense, the spirit of man, when it produceth unclean actions, is ordinarily called an unclean spirit, and so other spirits, though not always, yet as often as the virtue or vice so styled, is extraordinary, and eminent. Neither did the other prophets of the old Testament pretend enthusiasm; or, that God spake in them; but to them, by voice, vision, or dream; and the *burthen of the Lord* was not possession, but command. How then could the Jews fall into this opinion of possession? I can imagine no reason, but that which is common to all men. Namely, the want of curiosity to search natural causes: and their placing felicity in the acquisition of the gross pleasures of the senses, and the things that most immediately conduce thereto. For they that see any strange, and unusual ability, or defect, in a man's mind; unless they see withal, from what cause it may probably proceed, can hardly think it natural; and if not natural, they must needs think it supernatural; and then what can it be, but that either God or the Devil is in him? And hence it came to pass, when our Saviour (*Mark* iii. 21) was compassed about with the multitude, those of the house doubted he was mad, and went out to hold him: but the Scribes said he had Beelzebub, and that was it, by which he cast out devils; as if the greater madman had awed the lesser: and that (*John* x. 20) some said, *he hath a devil, and is mad*; whereas others holding him for a prophet, said, *these are not the words of one that hath a devil.* So in the old Testament he that came to anoint Jehu, (2 *Kings* ix. 11) was a prophet; but some of the company asked Jehu, *what came that madman for?* So that in sum, it is manifest, that whosoever behaved himself in extraordinary manner, was thought by the Jews to be possessed either with a good, or evil spirit; except by the Sadducees, who erred so far on the other hand, as not to believe there were at all any spirits, which is very near to indirect atheism; and thereby perhaps the more provoked others, to term such men demoniacs, rather than madmen.

But why then does our Saviour proceed in the curing of

them, as if they were possessed; and not as if they were mad? To which I can give no other kind of answer, but that which is given to those that urge the Scripture in like manner against the opinion of the motion of the earth. The Scripture was written to shew unto men the kingdom of God, and to prepare their minds to become his obedient subjects; leaving the world, and the philosophy thereof, to the disputation of men, for the exercising of their natural reason. Whether the earth's, or sun's motion make the day and night; or whether the exorbitant actions of men, proceed from passion, or from the devil, so we worship him not, it is all one, as to our obedience, and subjection to God Almighty; which is the thing for which the Scripture was written. As for that our Saviour speaketh to the disease, as to a person; it is the usual phrase of all that cure by words only, as Christ did, and enchanters pretend to do, whether they speak to a devil or not. For is not Christ also said (*Matt.* viii. 26) to have rebuked the winds? Is not he said also (*Luke* iv. 39) to rebuke a fever? Yet this does not argue that a fever is a devil. And whereas many of the devils are said to confess Christ; it is not necessary to interpret those places otherwise, than that those madmen confessed him. And whereas our Saviour (*Matt.* xii. 43) speaketh of an unclean spirit, that having gone out of a man, wandereth through dry places, seeking rest, and finding none, and returning into the same man, with seven other spirits worse than himself; it is manifestly a parable, alluding to a man, that after a little endeavour to quit his lusts, is vanquished by the strength of them; and becomes seven times worse than he was. So that I see nothing at all in the Scripture, that requireth a belief, that demoniacs were any other thing but madmen.

*Insignificant speech.* There is yet another fault in the discourses of some men; which may also be numbered amongst the sorts of madness; namely, that abuse of words, whereof I have spoken before in the fifth chapter, by the name of absurdity. And that is, when men speak such words, as put together, have in them no signification at all; but are fallen upon by some, through misunderstanding of the words they have received, and repeat by rote; by others from intention to deceive by obscurity. And this is incident to none but those, that converse in questions of matters incomprehensible, as the Schoolmen; or in questions of abstruse philosophy. The common sort of men seldom speak insignificantly, and are therefore, by those other egregious persons counted idiots. But to be assured their words are without any thing correspondent to them in the mind, there would need some examples; which if any man require, let him take a Schoolman in his hands and see if he can translate any one chapter concerning any difficult point, as the Trinity; the Deity; the nature of Christ; transubstantiation; free-will, &c. into any of the modern tongues, so as to make the same intelligible; or into any tolerable Latin, such as they were acquainted withal, that lived when the Latin tongue was vulgar. What is the meaning of these words, *The first cause does not necessarily inflow any thing into the second, by force of the essential subordination of the second causes, by which it may help it to work?* They are the translation of the title of the sixth chapter of *Suarez'* first book, *Of the concourse, motion, and help of God.* When men write whole volumes of such stuff, are they not mad, or intend to make others so? And particularly, in the question of transubstantiation; where after certain words spoken; they that say, the white*ness*, round*ness*, magni*tude*, quality, corruptibili*ty*, all which are incorporeal, &c. go out of the wafer, into the body of our blessed Saviour, do they not make those *nesses*, *tudes*, and *ties*, to be so many spirits possessing his body? For by spirits, they mean always things, that being incorporeal, are nevertheless moveable from one place to another. So that this kind of absurdity, may rightly be numbered amongst the many sorts of madness; and all the time that guided by clear thoughts of their worldly lust, they forbear disputing, or writing thus, but lucid intervals. And thus much of the virtues and defects intellectual.

# Chapter 9

## Of the Several Subjects of Knowledge

*Knowledge.* There are of KNOWLEDGE two kinds; whereof one is *knowledge of fact:* the other *knowledge of the consequence of one affirmation to another.* The former is nothing else, but sense and memory, and is *absolute knowledge;* as when we see a fact doing, or remember it done: and this is the knowledge required in a witness. The latter is called *science;* and is *conditional;* as when we know, that, *if the figure shown be a circle, then any straight line through the centre shall divide it into two equal parts.* And this is the knowledge required in a philosopher; that is to say, of him that pretends to reasoning.

The register of *knowledge of fact* is called *history.* Whereof there be two sorts: one called *natural history;* which is the history of such facts, or effects of nature, as have no dependence on man's *will;* such as are the histories of *metals, plants, animals, regions,* and the like. The other, is *civil history;* which is the history of the voluntary actions of men in commonwealths.

The registers of science, are such *books* as contain the *demonstrations* of consequences of one affirmation, to another; and are commonly called *books of philosophy;* whereof the sorts are many, according to the diversity of the matter; and may be divided in such manner as I have divided them in the following table.

SCIENCE, that is knowledge of consequences; which is called also PHILOSOPHY.

- Consequences from the accidents of bodies natural; which is called NATURAL PHILOSOPHY

  - Consequences from the accidents common to all bodies natural; which are *quantity*, and *motion*. . . . .

  - PHYSICS or consequences from *qualities*.

    - Consequences from the qualities of bodies *transient*, such as sometimes appear, sometimes vanish, *Meteorology*. . . . . . .

    - Consequences from the qualities of bodies *permanent*.

      - Consequences from the qualities of *the stars* .

      - Consequences of the qualities from *liquid* bodies, that fill the space between the stars; such as are the *air*, or substances ethereal.

      - Consequences from the qualities of *bodies terrestrial*.

- Consequences from the accidents of *politic* bodies; which is called POLITICS, and CIVIL PHILOSOPHY.

  1. Of consequences from the *institution of* COMMONWEALTH, to the *rights*, and *duties* of the *body politic* or *sovereign*.
  2. Of consequences from the same, to the *duty* and *right* of the *subjects*.

Consequences from quantity, and motion *indeterminate;* which being the principles or first foundation of philosophy, is called *Philosophia Prima.* — PHILOSOPHIA PRIMA.

Consequences from motion and quantity *determined.*
- Consequences from quantity, and motion determined.
  - By Figure — GEOMETRY.
  - By Number — ARITHMETIC.
  - *Mathematics.*
- Consequences from the motion, and quantity of bodies in *special.*
  - Consequences from the motion and quantity of the greater parts of the world, as the *earth* and *stars.* — *Cosmography.*
    - ASTRONOMY.
    - GEOGRAPHY.
  - Consequences from the motions of special kinds, and *figures of body.* — *Mechanics.* Doctrine of *weight.*
    - *Science of* ENGINEERS.
    - ARCHITECTURE.
    - NAVIGATION.
  - METEOROLOGY.

Consequences from the *light* of the stars. Out of this, and the motion of the sun, is made the science of — SCIOGRAPHY.

Consequences from the *influences* of the stars — ASTROLOGY.

Consequences from the parts of the earth, that are *without sense.*
- Consequences from the qualities of *minerals,* as *stones, metals,* &c.
- Consequences from the qualities of *vegetables.*

Consequences from the qualities of *animals.*
- Consequences from the qualities of *animals in general.*
  - Consequences from *vision.* — OPTICS.
  - Consequences from *sounds* — MUSIC.
  - Consequences from the rest of the *senses.*
- Consequences from the qualities of *men in special.*
  - Consequences from the *passions* of men — ETHICS.
  - Consequences from *speech.*
    - In *magnifying, vilifying,* &c. — POETRY.
    - In *persuading,* — RHETORIC.
    - In *reasoning,* — LOGIC.
    - In *contracting,* — The *Science* of Just and Unjust.

**Chapter 10**

## Of Power, Worth, Dignity, Honour, and Worthiness

*Power.* The power *of a man,* to take it universally, is his present means, to obtain some future apparent good; and is either *original* or *instrumental.*

*Natural power,* is the eminence of the faculties of body, or mind: as extraordinary strength, form, prudence, arts, eloquence, liberality, nobility. *Instrumental* are those powers, which acquired by these, or by fortune, are means and instruments to acquire more: as riches, reputation, friends, and the secret working of God, which men call good luck. For the nature of power, is in this point, like to fame, increasing as it proceeds; or like the motion of heavy bodies, which the further they go, make still the more haste.

The greatest of human powers, is that which is compounded of the powers of most men, united by consent, in one person, natural, or civil, that has the use of all their powers depending on his will; such as is the power of a commonwealth: or depending on the wills of each particular; such as is the power of a faction or of divers factions leagued. Therefore to have servants, is power; to have friends, is power: for they are strengths united.

Also riches joined with liberality, is power; because it procureth friends, and servants: without liberality, not so; because in this case they defend not; but expose men to envy, as a prey.

Reputation of power, is power; because it draweth with it the adherence of those that need protection.

So is reputation of love of a man's country, called popularity, for the same reason.

Also, what quality soever maketh a man beloved, or feared of many; or the reputation of such quality, is power; because it is a means to have the assistance, and service of many.

Good success is power; because it maketh reputation of wisdom, or good fortune; which makes men either fear him, or rely on him.

Affability of men already in power, is increase of power; because is gaineth love.

Reputation of prudence in the conduct of peace or war, is

power; because to prudent men, we commit the government of ourselves, more willingly than to others.

Nobility is power, not in all places, but only in those commonwealths, where it has privileges: for in such privileges, consisteth their power.

Eloquence is power, because it is seeming prudence.

Form is power; because being a promise of good, it recommendeth men to the favour of women and strangers.

The sciences, are small power; because not eminent; and therefore, not acknowledged in any man; nor are at all, but in a few, and in them, but of a few things. For science is of that nature, as none can understand it to be, but such as in a good measure have attained it.

Arts of public use, as fortification, making of engines, and other instruments of war; because they confer to defence, and victory, are power: and though the true mother of them, be science, namely the mathematics; yet, because they are brought into the light, by the hand of the artificer, they be esteemed, the midwife passing with the vulgar for the mother, as his issue.

*Worth.* The *value,* or WORTH of a man, is as of all other things, his price; that is to say, so much as would be given for the use of his power: and therefore is not absolute; but a thing dependant on the need and judgment of another. An able conductor of soldiers, is of great price in time of war present, or imminent; but in peace not so. A learned and uncorrupt judge, is much worth in time of peace; but not so much in war. And as in other things, so in men, not the seller, but the buyer determines the price. For let a man, as most men do, rate themselves at the highest value they can; yet their true value is no more than it is esteemed by others.

The manifestation of the value we set on one another, is that which is commonly called honouring, and dishonouring. To value a man at a high rate, is to *honour* him; at a low rate, is to *dishonour* him. But high, and low, in this case, is to be understood by comparison to the rate that each man setteth on himself.

*Dignity.* The public worth of a man, which is the value set on him by the commonwealth, is that which men commonly call DIGNITY. And this value of him by the commonwealth, is understood, by offices of command, judicature, public employment; or by names and titles, introduced for distinction of such value.

To pray to another, for aid of any kind, is *to* HONOUR;

because a sign we have an opinion he has power to help; and the more difficult the aid is, the more is the honour.

*To honour and dishonour.* To obey, is to honour, because no man obeys them, whom they think have no power to help, or hurt them. And consequently to disobey, is to *dishonour*.

To give great gifts to a man, is to honour him; because it is buying of protection, and acknowledging of power. To give little gifts, is to dishonour; because it is but alms, and signifies an opinion of the need of small helps.

To be sedulous in promoting another's good; also to flatter, is to honour; as a sign we seek his protection or aid. To neglect, is to dishonour.

To give way, or place to another, in any commodity, is to honour; being a confession of greater power. To arrogate, is to dishonour.

To show any sign of love, or fear of another, is to honour; for both to love, and to fear, is to value. To contemn, or less to love or fear, than he expects, is to dishonour; for it is undervaluing.

To praise, magnify, or call happy, is to honour; because nothing but goodness, power, and felicity is valued. To revile, mock, or pity, is to dishonour.

To speak to another with consideration, to appear before him with decency, and humility, is to honour him; as signs of fear to offend. To speak to him rashly, to do any thing before him obscenely, slovenly, impudently, is to dishonour.

To believe, to trust, to rely on another, is to honour him; sign of opinion of his virtue and power. To distrust, or not believe, is to dishonour.

To hearken to a man's counsel, or discourse of what kind soever is to honour; as a sign we think him wise, or eloquent, or witty. To sleep, or go forth, or talk the while, is to dishonour.

To do those things to another, which he takes for signs of honour, or which the law or custom makes so, is to honour; because in approving the honour done by others, he acknowledgeth the power which others acknowledge. To refuse to do them, is to dishonour.

To agree with in opinion, is to honour; as being a sign of approving his judgment, and wisdom. To dissent, is dishonour, and an upbraiding of error; and, if the dissent be in many things, of folly.

To imitate, is to honour; for it is vehemently to approve. To imitate one's enemy, is to dishonour.

To honour those another honours, is to honour him; as a sign of approbation of his judgment. To honour his enemies, is to dishonour him.

To employ in counsel, or in actions of difficulty, is to honour; as a sign of opinion of his wisdom, or other power. To deny employment in the same cases, to those that seek it, is to dishonour.

All these ways of honouring, are natural; and as well within, as without commonwealths. But in commonwealths, where he, or they that have the supreme authority, can make whatsoever they please, to stand for signs of honour, there be other honours.

A sovereign doth honour a subject, with whatsoever title, or office, or employment, or action, that he himself will have taken for a sign of his will to honour him.

The king of Persia, honoured Mordecai, when he appointed he should be conducted through the streets in the king's garment, upon one of the king's horses, with a crown on his head, and a prince before him, proclaiming, *thus shall it be done to him that the king will honour.* And yet another king of Persia, or the same another time, to one that demanded for some great service, to wear one of the king's robes, gave him leave so to do; but with this addition, that he should wear it as the king's fool; and then it was dishonour. So that of civil honour, the fountain is in the person of the commonwealth, and dependeth on the will of the sovereign; and is therefore temporary, and called *civil honour;* such as magistracy, offices, titles; and in some places coats and scutcheons painted: and men honour such as have them, as having so many signs of favour in the commonwealth; which favour is power.

*Honourable.* Honourable is whatsoever possession, action, or quality, is an argument and sign of power.

*Dishonourable.* And therefore to be honoured, loved, or feared of many, is honourable; as arguments of power. To be honoured of few or none, *dishonourable.*

Dominion, and victory is honourable; because acquired by power; and servitude, for need, or fear, is dishonourable.

Good fortune, if lasting, honourable; as a sign of the favour of God. Ill fortune, and losses, dishonourable. Riches, are honourable; for they are power. Poverty, dishonourable. Magnanimity, liberality, hope, courage, confidence, are honourable; for they proceed from the conscience of power. Pusillanimity, parsimony, fear, diffidence, are dishonourable.

Timely resolution, or determination of what a man is to do, is honourable; as being the contempt of small difficulties, and dangers. And irresolution, dishonourable; as a sign of too much valuing of little impediments, and little advantages: for when a man has weighed things as long as the time permits, and resolves not, the difference of weight is but little; and therefore if he resolve not, he overvalues little things, which is pusillanimity.

All actions, and speeches, that proceed, or seem to proceed, from much experience, science, discretion, or wit, are honourable; for all these are powers. Actions, or words that proceed from error, ignorance, or folly dishonourable.

Gravity, as far forth as it seems to proceed from a mind employed on something else, is honourable; because employment is a sign of power. But if it seem to proceed from a purpose to appear grave, it is dishonourable. For the gravity of the former, is like the steadiness of a ship laden with merchandise; but of the latter, like the steadiness of a ship ballasted with sand, and other trash.

To be conspicuous, that is to say, to be known, for wealth, office, great actions, or any eminent good, is honourable; as a sign of the power for which he is conspicuous. On the contrary, obscurity, is dishonourable.

To be descended from conspicuous parents, is honourable; because they the more easily attain the aids, and friends of their ancestors. On the contrary, to be descended from obscure parentage, is dishonourable.

Actions proceeding from equity, joined with loss, are honourable as signs of magnanimity: for magnanimity is a sign of power. On the contrary, craft, shifting, neglect of equity, is dishonourable.

Covetousness of great riches, and ambition of great honours, are honourable; as signs of power to obtain them. Covetousness, and ambition, of little gains, or preferments, is dishonourable.

Nor does it alter the case of honour, whether an action, so it be great and difficult, and consequently a sign of much power, be just or unjust: for honour consisteth only in the opinion of power. Therefore the ancient heathen did not think they dishonoured, but greatly honoured the Gods, when they introduced them in their poems, committing rapes, thefts, and other great, but unjust, or unclean acts: insomuch as nothing is so much celebrated in Jupiter, as his adulteries; nor in Mercury, as his frauds, and thefts: of whose praises, in a hymn of Homer, the greatest is this, that being born in the morning, he had invented music at noon, and before night, stolen away the cattle of Apollo, from his herdsmen.

Also amongst men, till there were constituted great commonwealths, it was thought no dishonour to be a pirate, or a highway thief; but rather a lawful trade, not only amongst the Greeks, but also amongst all other nations; as is manifest by the histories of ancient time. And at this day, in this part of the world, private duels are, and always will be honourable, though unlawful, till such time as there shall be honour ordained for them that refuse, and ignominy for them that make the challenge. For duels also are many times effects of courage; and the ground of courage is always strength or skill, which are power; though for the most part they be effects of rash speaking, and of the fear of dishonour, in one, or both the combatants; who engaged by rashness, are driven into the lists to avoid disgrace.

*Coats of arms.* Scutcheons, and coats of arms hereditary, where they have any eminent privileges, are honourable; otherwise not: for their power consisteth either in such privileges, or in riches, or some such thing as is equally honoured in other men. This kind of honour, commonly called gentry, hath been derived from the ancient Germans. For there never was any such thing known, where the German customs were unknown. Nor is it now anywhere in use, where the Germans have not inhabited. The ancient Greek commanders, when they went to war, had their shields painted with such devices as they pleased; insomuch as an unpainted buckler was a sign of poverty, and of a common soldier; but they transmitted not the inheritance of them. The Romans transmitted the marks of their families: but they were the images, not the devices of their ancestors. Amongst the people of Asia, Africa, and America, there is not, nor was ever, any such thing. The Germans only had that custom; from whom it has been derived into England, France, Spain, and Italy, when in great numbers they either aided the Romans, or made their own conquests in these western parts of the world.

For Germany, being anciently, as all other countries, in their beginnings, divided amongst an infinite number of little lords, or masters of families, that continually had wars one with another; those masters, or lords, principally to the end they might, when they were covered with arms, be known by their followers; and partly for ornament, both painted their armour, or their scutcheon, or coat, with the picture of some beast, or other thing; and also put some eminent and visible mark upon the crest of their helmets. And this ornament both of the arms, and crest, descended by inheritance to their children; to the eldest pure, and to the rest with some note of diversity, such as the old master, that is to say in Dutch, the *Here-alt* thought fit. But when many such families, joined together, made a greater monarchy, this duty of the Herealt, to distinguish scutcheons, was made a private office apart. And the issue of these lords, is the great and ancient gentry; which for the most part bear living creatures, noted for courage, and rapine; or castles, battlements, belts, weapons, bars, palisadoes, and other notes of war; nothing being then in honour, but virtue military. Afterwards, not only kings, but popular commonwealths, gave divers manners of scutcheons, to such as went forth to the war, or returned from it, for encouragement, or recompense to their service. All which, by an observing reader, may be found in such ancient histories, Greek and Latin, as make mention of the German nation and manners, in their times.

*Titles of honour.* Titles of *honour*, such as are duke, count, marquis, and baron, are honourable; as signifying the value set upon them by the sovereign power of the commonwealth: which titles, were in old time titles of office, and command, derived some from the Romans, some from the Germans and French: dukes, in Latin *duces*, being generals in war: counts, *comites*, such as bear the general company out of friendship, and were left to govern and defend places conquered, and pacified: marquises, *marchiones*, were counts that governed the marches, or bounds of the empire. Which titles of duke, count, and marquis, came into the empire, about the time of Constantine the Great, from the customs of the German *militia*. But baron, seems to have been a title of the Gauls, and signifies a great man; such as were the king's, or prince's men, whom they employed in war about their persons; and seems to be derived from *vir*, to *ber*, and *bar*, that signified the same in the language of the Gauls, that *vir* in Latin; and thence to *bero*, and *baro*: so that such men were called *berones*, and after *barones*; and, in Spanish, *varones*. But he that would know more particularly the original of titles of honour, may find it, as I have done this, in Mr. Selden's most excellent treatise of that subject. In process of time these offices of honour, by occasion of trouble, and for reasons of good and peaceable government, were turned into mere titles; serving for the most part, to distinguish the precedence, place, and order of subjects in the commonwealth: and men were made dukes, counts, marquises, and barons of places, wherein they had neither possession, nor command: and other titles also, were devised to the same end.

*Worthiness. Fitness.* WORTHINESS, is a thing different from the worth, or value of a man; and also from his merit, or desert, and consisteth in a particular power, or ability for that, whereof he is said to be worthy: which particular ability, is usually named FITNESS, or *aptitude.*

For he is worthiest to be a commander, to be a judge, or to have any other charge, that is best fitted, with the qualities required to the well discharging of it; and worthiest of riches, that has the qualities most requisite for the well using of them: any of which qualities being absent, one may nevertheless be a worthy man, and valuable for something else. Again, a man may be worthy of riches, office, and employment, that nevertheless, can plead no right to have it before another; and therefore cannot be said to merit or deserve it. For merit presupposeth a right, and that the thing deserved is due by promise: of which I shall say more hereafter, when I shall speak of contracts.

# Chapter 11

## Of the Difference of Manners

*What is here meant by manners.* By manners, I mean not here, decency of behaviour; as how one should salute another, or how a man should wash his mouth, or pick his teeth before company, and such other points of the *small morals;* but those qualities of mankind, that concern their living together in peace, and unity. To which end we are to consider, that the felicity of this life, consisteth not in the repose of a mind satisfied. For there is no such *finis ultimus,* utmost arm, nor *summum bonum,* greatest good, as is spoken of in the books of the old moral philosophers. Nor can a man any more live, whose desires are at an end, than he, whose senses and imaginations are at a stand. Felicity is a continual progress of the desire, from one object to another; the attaining of the former, being still but the way to the latter. The cause whereof is, that the object of man's desire, is not to enjoy once only, and for one instant of time; but to assure for ever, the way of his future desire. And therefore the voluntary actions, and inclinations of all men, tend, not only to the procuring, but also to the assuring of a contented life; and differ only in the way: which ariseth partly from the diversity of passions, in divers men; and partly from the difference of the knowledge, or opinion each one has of the causes, which produce the effect desired.

*A restless desire of power in all men.* So that in the first place, I put for a general inclination of all mankind, a perpetual and restless desire of power after power, that ceaseth only in death. And the cause of this, is not always that a man hopes for a more intensive delight, than he has already attained to; or that he cannot be content with a moderate power: but because he cannot assure the power and means to live well, which he hath present, without the acquisition of more. And from hence it is, that kings, whose power is greatest, turn their endeavors to the assuring it at home by laws, or abroad by wars: and when that is done, there succeedeth a new desire; in some, of fame from new conquest; in others, of ease and sensual pleasure; in others, of admiration, or being flattered for excellence in some art, or other ability of the mind.

*Love of contention from competition.* Competition of riches, honour, command, or other power, inclineth to contention, enmity, and war: because the way of one competitor, to the attaining of his desire, is to kill, subdue, supplant, or repel the other. Particularly, competition of praise, inclineth to a reverence of antiquity. For men contend with the living, not with the dead; to these ascribing more than due, that they may obscure the glory of the other.

*Civil obedience from love of ease. From fear of death, or wounds.* Desire of ease, and sensual delight, disposeth men to obey a common power: because by such desires, a man doth abandon the protection that might be hoped for from his own industry, and labour. Fear of death, and wounds, disposeth to the same; and for the same reason. On the contrary, needy men, and hardy, not contented with their present condition; as also, all men that are ambitious of military command, are inclined to continue the causes of war; and to stir up trouble and sedition: for there is no honour military but by war; nor any such hope to mend an ill game, as by causing a new shuffle.

*And from love of arts.* Desire of knowledge, and arts of peace, inclineth men to obey a common power: for such desire, containeth a desire of leisure; and consequently protection from some other power than their own.

*Love of virtue from love of praise.* Desire of praise, disposeth to laudable actions, such as please them whose judgment they value; for of those men whom we contemn, we contemn also the praises. Desire of fame after death does the same. And though after death, there be no sense of the praise given us on earth, as being joys, that are either swallowed up in the unspeakable joys of Heaven, or extinguished in the extreme torments of hell: yet is not such fame vain; because men have a present delight therein, from the foresight of it, and of the benefit that may redound thereby to their posterity; which though they now see not, yet they imagine; and any thing that is pleasure to the sense, the same also is pleasure in the imagination.

*Hate, from difficulty of requiting great benefits.* To have received from one, to whom we think ourselves equal, greater benefits than there is hope to requite, disposeth to counterfeit love; but really secret hatred; and puts a man into the estate of a desperate debtor, in that in declining the sight of his creditor, tacitly wishes him there, where he might never see him more. For benefits oblige, and obligation is thraldom; and unrequitable obligation perpetual thraldom; which is to one's equal, hateful. But to have received benefits from one, whom we acknowledge for superior, inclines to love; because the obligation is no new depression: and cheerful acceptation, which men call *gratitude*, is such an honour done to the obliger, as is taken generally for retribution. Also to receive benefits, though from an equal, or inferior, as long as there is hope of requital, disposeth to love: for in the intention of the receiver, the obligation is of aid and service mutual; from whence proceedeth an emulation of who shall exceed in benefiting; the most noble and profitable contention possible; wherein the victor is pleased with his victory, and the other revenged by confessing it.

*And from conscience of deserving to be hated.* To have done more hurt to a man, than he can, or is willing to expiate, inclineth the doer to hate the sufferer. For he must expect revenge, or forgiveness; both which are hateful.

*Promptness to hurt, from fear.* Fear of oppression, disposeth a man to anticipate, or to seek aid by society: for there is no other way by which a man can secure his life and liberty.

*And from distrust of their own wit.* Men that distrust their own subtlety, are, in tumult and sedition, better disposed for victory, than they that suppose themselves wise, or crafty. For these love to consult, the other, fearing to be circumvented, to strike first. And in sedition, men being always in the precincts of battle, to hold together, and use all advantages of force, is a better strategem, than any that can proceed from subtlety of wit.

*Vain undertaking from vain-glory.* Vain-glorious men, such as without being conscious to themselves of great sufficiency, delight in supposing themselves gallant men, are inclined only to ostentation; but not to attempt: because when danger or difficulty appears, they look for nothing but to have their insufficiency discovered.

Vain-glorious men, such as estimate their sufficiency by the flattery of other men, or the fortune of some precedent action, without assured ground of hope from the true knowledge of themselves, are inclined to rash engaging; and in the approach of danger, or difficulty, to retire if they can: because not seeing the way of safety, they will rather hazard their honour, which may be salved with an excuse; than their lives, for which no salve is sufficient.

*Ambition, from opinion of sufficiency.* Men that have a

strong opinion of their own wisdom in matter of government, are disposed to ambition. Because without public employment in council or magistracy, the honour of their wisdom is lost. And therefore eloquent speakers are inclined to ambition; for eloquence seemeth wisdom, both to themselves and others.

*Irresolution, from too great valuing of small matters.* Pusillanimity disposeth men to irresolution, and consequently to lose the occasions, and fittest opportunities of action. For after men have been in deliberation till the time of action approach, if it be not then manifest what is best to be done, it is a sign, the difference of motives, the one way and the other, are not great: therefore not to resolve then, is to lose the occasion by weighing of trifles; which is pusillanimity.

Frugality, though in poor men a virtue, maketh a man unapt to achieve such actions, as require the strength of many men at once: for it weakeneth their endeavour, which is to be nourished and kept in vigour by reward.

*Confidence in others, from ignorance of the marks of wisdom and kindness.* Eloquence, with flattery, disposeth men to confide in them that have it; because the former is seeming wisdom, the latter seeming kindness. Add to them military reputation, and it disposeth men to adhere, and subject themselves to those men that have them. The two former having given them caution against danger from him; the latter gives them caution against danger from others.

*And from ignorance of natural causes.* Want of science, that is, ignorance of causes, disposeth, or rather constraineth a man to rely on the advice, and authority of others. For all men whom the truth concerns, if they rely not on their own, must rely on the opinion of some other, whom they think wiser than themselves, and see not why he should deceive them.

*And from want of understanding.* Ignorance of the signification of words, which is want of understanding, disposeth men to take on trust, not only the truth they know not; but also the errors; and which is more, the nonsense of them they trust: for neither error nor nonsense, can without a perfect understanding of words, be detected.

From the same it proceedeth, that men give different names, to one and the same thing, from the difference of their own passions: as they that approve a private opinion, call it opinion; but they that mislike it, heresy: and yet heresy signifies no more than private opinion; but has only a greater tincture of choler.

From the same also it proceedeth, that men cannot distinguish, without study and great understanding, between one action of many men, and many actions of one multitude; as for example, between one action of all the senators of Rome in killing Cataline, and the many actions of a number of senators in killing Cæsar; and therefore are disposed to take for the action of the people, that which is a multitude of actions done by a multitude of men, led perhaps by the persuasion of one.

*Adherence to custom, from ignorance of the nature of right and wrong.* Ignorance of the causes, and original constitution of right, equity, law, and justice, disposeth a man to make custom and example the rule of his actions; in such manner, as to think that unjust which it hath been the custom to punish; and that just, of the impunity and approbation whereof they can produce an example, or, as the lawyers which only use this false measure of justice barbarously call it, a precedent; like little children, that have no other rule of good and evil manners, but the correction they receive from their parents and masters; save that children are constant to their rule, whereas, men are not so; because grown old, and stubborn, they appeal from custom to reason, and from reason to custom, as it serves their turn; receding from custom when their interest requires it, and setting themselves against reason, as oft as reason is against them: which is the cause, that the doctrine of right and wrong, is perpetually disputed, both by the pen and the sword: whereas the doctrine of lines, and figures, is not so; because men care not, in that subject, what be truth, as a thing that crosses no man's ambition, profit or lust. For I doubt not, but if it had been a thing contrary to any man's right of dominion, or to the interest of men that have dominion, *that the three angles of a triangle, should be equal to two angles of a square;* that doctrine should have been, if not disputed, yet by the burning of all books of geometry, suppressed, as far as he whom it concerned was able.

*Adherence to private men, from ignorance of the causes of peace.* Ignorance of remote causes, disposeth men to attribute all events, to the causes immediate, and instrumental: for these are all the causes they perceive. And hence it comes

to pass, that in all places, men that are grieved with payments
to the public, discharge their anger upon the publicans, that
is to say, farmers, collectors, and other officers of the public
revenue; and adhere to such as find fault with the public
government; and thereby, when they have engaged themselves beyond hope of justification, fall also upon the supreme
authority, for fear of punishment, or shame of receiving
pardon.

*Credulity, from ignorance of nature.* Ignorance of natural
causes, disposeth a man to credulity, so as to believe many
times impossibilities: for such know nothing to the contrary,
but that they may be true; being unable to detect the impossibility. And credulity, because men like to be hearkened
unto in company, disposeth them to lying: so that ignorance
itself without malice, is able to make a man both to believe
lies, and tell them; and sometimes also to invent them.

*Curiosity to know, from care of future time.* Anxiety for
the future time, disposeth men to inquire into the causes of
things: because the knowledge of them, maketh men the
better able to order the present to their best advantage.

*Natural religion from the same.* Curiosity, or love of the
knowledge of causes, draws a man from the consideration of
the effect, to seek the cause; and again, the cause of that
cause; till of necessity he must come to this thought at last,
that there is some cause, whereof there is no former cause,
but is eternal; which is it men call God. So that it is impossible to make any profound inquiry into natural causes, without being inclined thereby to believe there is one God eternal;
though they cannot have any idea of him in their mind,
answerable to his nature. For as a man that is born blind,
hearing men talk of warming themselves by the fire, and being
brought to warm himself by the same, may easily conceive,
and assure himself, there is somewhat there, which men call
*fire,* and is the cause of the heat he feels; but cannot imagine
what it is like; nor have an idea of it in his mind, such as
they have that see it; so also by the visible things in this
world, and their admirable order, a man may conceive there
is a cause of them, which men call God; and yet not have an
idea, or image of him in his mind.

And they that make little, or no inquiry into the natural
causes of things, yet from the fear that proceeds from the
ignorance itself, of what it is that hath the power to do them
much good or harm, are inclined to suppose, and feign themselves, several kinds of powers invisible; and to stand in awe

of their own imaginations; and in time of distress to invoke them; as also in the time of an expected good success, to give them thanks; making the creatures of their own fancy, their gods. By which means it hath come to pass, that from the innumerable variety of fancy, men have created in the world innumerable sorts of gods. And this fear of things invisible, is the natural seed of that, which every one in himself calleth religion; and in them that worship, or fear that power otherwise than they do, superstition.

And this seed of religion, having been observed by many; some of those that have observed it, have been inclined thereby to nourish, dress, and form it into laws; and to add to it of their own invention, any opinion of the causes of future events, by which they thought they should be best able to govern others, and make unto themselves the greatest use of their powers.

# Chapter 12

## Of Religion

*Religion in man only.* Seeing there are no signs, nor fruit of *religion*, but in man only; there is no cause to doubt, but that the seed of *religion*, is also only in man; and consisteth in some peculiar quality, or at least in some eminent degree thereof, not to be found in any other living creatures.

*First, from his desire of knowing causes.* And first, it is peculiar to the nature of man, to be inquisitive into the causes of the events they see, some more, some less; but all men so much, as to be curious in the search of the causes of their own good and evil fortune.

*From the consideration of the beginning of things.* Secondly, upon the sight of any thing that hath a beginning, to think also it had a cause, which determined the same to begin, then when it did, rather than sooner or later.

*From his observation of the sequel of things.* Thirdly, whereas there is no other felicity of beasts, but the enjoying of their quotidian food, ease, and lusts; as having little or no foresight of the time to come, for want of observation, and memory of the order, consequence, and dependence of the things they see; man observeth how one event hath been produced by another; and remembereth in them antecedence and consequence; and when he cannot assure himself of the true causes of things, (for the causes of good and evil fortune for the most part are invisible,) he supposes causes of them, either such as his own fancy suggesteth; or trusteth the authority of other men, such as he thinks to be his friends, and wiser than himself.

*The natural cause of religion, the anxiety of the time to come.* The two first, make anxiety. For being assured that there be causes of all things that have arrived hitherto, or shall arrive hereafter; it is impossible for a man, who continually endeavoureth to secure himself against the evil he fears, and procure the good he desireth, not to be in a perpetual solicitude of the time to come; so that every man, especially those that are over provident, are in a state like to that of Prometheus. For as Prometheus, which interpreted, is, *the prudent man,* was bound to the hill Caucasus, a place of large prospect, where, an eagle feeding on his liver, devoured in the day, as much as was repaired in the night: so that man, which looks too far before him, in the care of future time, hath his heart all the day long, gnawed on by fear of death, poverty, or other calamity; and has no repose, nor pause of his anxiety, but in sleep.

*Which makes them fear the power of invisible things.* This perpetual fear, always accompanying mankind in the ignorance of causes, as it were in the dark, must needs have for object something. And therefore when there is nothing to be seen, there is nothing to accuse, either of their good, or evil fortune, but some *power*, or agent *invisible:* in which sense perhaps it was, that some of the old poets said, that the gods were at first created by human fear: which spoken of the gods, that is to say, of the many gods of the Gentiles, is very true. But the acknowledging of one God, eternal, infinite, and omnipotent, may more easily be derived, from the desire men have to know the causes of natural bodies, and their several virtues, and operations; than from the fear of what was to befall them in time to come. For he that from any effect he seeth come to pass, should reason to the next and immediate cause thereof, and from thence to the cause of that cause, and plunge himself profoundly in the pursuit of causes; shall at last come to this, that there must be, as even the heathen philosophers confessed, one first mover; that is, a first, and an eternal cause of all things; which is that which men mean by the name of God: and all this without thought of their fortune; the solicitude whereof, both inclines to fear, and hinders them from the search of the causes of other things; and thereby gives occasion of feigning of as many gods, as there be men that feign them.

*And suppose them incorporeal.* And for the matter, or substance of the invisible agents, so fancied; they could not by natural cogitation, fall upon any other conceit, but that it was the same with that of the soul of man; and that the soul of man, was of the same substance, with that which appeareth in a dream, to one that sleepeth; or in a looking-glass, to one that is awake; which, men not knowing that such apparitions are nothing else but creatures of the fancy, think to be real, and external substances; and therefore call them ghosts; as the Latins called them *imagines,* and *umbrœ;* and thought them spirits, that is, thin aërial bodies; and those invisible agents, which they feared, to be like them; save that they appear, and vanish when they please. But the opinion that

such spirits were incorporeal, or immaterial, could never
enter into the mind of any man by nature; because, though
men may put together words of contradictory signification,
as *spirit*, and *incorporeal;* yet they can never have the imagination of any thing answering to them: and therefore, men
that by their own meditation, arrive to the acknowledgment
of one infinite, omnipotent, and eternal God, chose rather to
confess he is incomprehensible, and above their understanding, than to define his nature by *spirit incorporeal*, and then
confess their definition to be unintelligible: or if they give
him such a title, it is not *dogmatically,* with intention to make
the divine nature understood; but *piously,* to honour him
with attributes, of significations, as remote as they can from
the grossness of bodies visible.

*But know not the way how they effect any thing.* Then, for
the way by which they think these invisible agents wrought
their effects; that is to say, what immediate causes they used,
in bringing things to pass, men that know not what it is that
we call *causing,* that is, almost all men, have no other rule to
guess by, but by observing, and remembering what they have
seen to precede the like effect at some other time, or times
before, without seeing between the antecedent and subsequent
event, any dependence or connexion at all: and therefore
from the like things past, they expect the like things to come;
and hope for good or evil luck, superstitiously, from things
that have no part at all in the causing of it: as the Athenians
did for their war at Lepanto, demand another Phormio; the
Pompeian faction for their war in Africa, another Scipio; and
others have done in divers other occasions since. In like
manner they attribute their fortune to a stander by, to a
lucky or unlucky place, to words spoken, especially if the
name of God be amongst them; as charming and conjuring,
the liturgy of witches; insomuch as to believe, they have power
to turn a stone into bread, bread into a man, or any thing
into any thing.

*But honour them as they honour men.* Thirdly, for the
worship which naturally men exhibit to powers invisible, it
can be no other, but such expressions of their reverence, as
they would use towards men; gifts, petitions, thanks, submission of body, considerate addresses, sober behaviour, premeditated words, swearing, that is, assuring one another of
their promises, by invoking them. Beyond that reason suggesteth nothing; but leaves them either to rest there; or for

further ceremonies, to rely on those they believe wiser than themselves.

*And attribute to them all extraordinary events.* Lastly, concerning how these invisible powers declare to men the things which shall hereafter come to pass, especially concerning their good or evil fortune in general, or good or ill success in any particular undertaking, men are naturally at a stand; save that using to conjecture of the time to come, by the time past, they are very apt, not only to take casual things, after one or two encounters, for prognostics of the like encounter ever after, but also to believe the like prognostics from other men, of whom they have once conceived a good opinion.

*Four things, natural seeds of religion.* And in these four things, opinion of ghosts, ignorance of second causes, devotion towards what men fear, and taking of things casual for prognostics, consisteth the natural seed of *religion;* which by reason of the different fancies, judgments, and passions of several men, hath grown up into ceremonies so different, that those which are used by one man, are for the most part ridiculous to another.

*Made different by culture.* For these seeds have received culture from two sorts of men. One sort have been they, that have nourished, and ordered them, according to their own invention. The other have done it, by God's commandment, and direction: but both sorts have done it, with a purpose to make those men that relied on them, the more apt to obedience, laws, peace, charity, and civil society. So that the religion of the former sort, is a part of human politics; and teacheth part of the duty which earthly kings require of their subjects. And the religion of the latter sort is divine politics; and containeth precepts to those that have yielded themselves subjects in the kingdom of God. Of the former sort, were all the founders of commonwealths, and the law-givers of the Gentiles: of the latter sort, were Abraham, Moses, and our blessed Saviour; by whom have been derived unto us the laws of the kingdom of God.

*The absurd opinion of Gentilism.* And for that part of religion, which consisteth in opinions concerning the nature of powers invisible, there is almost nothing that has a name, that has not been esteemed amongst the Gentiles, in one place or another, a god, or devil; or by their poets feigned to be inanimated, inhabited, or possessed by some spirit or other.

The unformed matter of the world, was a god, by the name of Chaos.

The heaven, the ocean, the planets, the fire, the earth, the winds, were so many gods.

Men, women, a bird, a crocodile, a calf, a dog, a snake, an onion, a leek, were deified. Besides that, they filled almost all places, with spirits called *demons:* the plains, with Pan, and Panises, or Satyrs; the woods, with Fawns, and Nymphs; the sea, with Tritons, and other Nymphs; every river, and fountain, with a ghost of his name, and with Nymphs; every house with its *Lares,* or familiars; every man with his *Genius;* hell with ghosts, and spiritual officers, as Charon, Cerberus, and the Furies; and in the night time, all places with *larvæ, lemures,* ghosts of men deceased, and a whole kingdom of fairies and bugbears. They have also ascribed divinity, and built temples to mere accidents, and qualities; such as are time, night, day, peace, concord, love, contention, virtue, honour, health, rust, fever, and the like; which when they prayed for, or against, they prayed to, as if there were ghosts of those names hanging over their heads, and letting fall, or withholding that good, or evil, for, or against which they prayed. They invoked also their own wit, by the name of Muses; their own ignorance, by the name of Fortune; their own lusts by the name of Cupid; their own rage, by the name of Furies; their own privy members, by the name of Priapus; and attributed their pollutions, to Incubi, and Succubæ: insomuch as there was nothing, which a poet could introduce as a person in his poem, which they did not make either a *god,* or a *devil.*

The same authors of the religion of the Gentiles, observing the second ground for religion, which is men's ignorance of causes; and thereby their aptness to attribute their fortune to causes, on which there was no dependence at all apparent, took occasion to obtrude on their ignorance, instead of second causes, a kind of second and ministerial gods; ascribing the cause of fecundity, to Venus; the cause of arts, to Apollo; of subtlety and craft, to Mercury; of tempests and storms, to Æolus; and of other effects, to other gods; insomuch as there was amongst the heathen almost as great variety of gods, as of business.

And to the worship, which naturally men conceived fit to be used towards their gods, namely, oblations, prayers, thanks, and the rest formerly named; the same legislators of the Gentiles have added their images, both in picture, and sculpture; that the more ignorant sort, that is to say, the most part or generality of the people, thinking the gods for whose representation they were made, were really included, and as it were housed within them, might so much the more stand in fear of them: and endowed them with lands, and houses, and officers, and revenues, set apart from all other human uses; that is, consecrated, and made holy to those their idols; as caverns, groves, woods, mountains, and whole islands; and have attributed to them, not only the shapes, some of men, some of beasts, some of monsters; but also the faculties, and passions of men and beasts: as sense, speech, sex, lust, generation, and this not only by mixing one with another, to propagate the kind of gods; but also by mixing with men, and women, to beget mongrel gods, and but inmates of heaven, as Bacchus, Hercules, and others; besides anger, revenge, and other passions of living creatures, and the actions proceeding from them, as fraud, theft, adultery, sodomy, and any vice that may be taken for an effect of power, or a cause of pleasure; and all such vices, as amongst men are taken to be against law, rather than against honour.

Lastly, to the prognostics of time to come; which are naturally, but conjectures upon experience of time past; and supernaturally, divine revelation; the same authors of the religion of the Gentiles, partly upon pretended experience, partly upon pretended revelation, have added innumerable other superstitious ways of divination; and made men believe they should find their fortunes, sometimes in the ambiguous or senseless answers of the priests at Delphi, Delos, Ammon, and other famous oracles; which answers, were made ambiguous by design, to own the event both ways; or absurd, by the intoxicating vapour of the place, which is very frequent in sulphurous caverns: sometimes in the leaves of the Sybils; of whose prophecies, like those perhaps of Nostradamus (for the fragments now extant seem to be the invention of later times), there were some books in reputation in the time of the Roman republic: sometimes in the insignificant speeches of madmen, supposed to be possessed with a divine spirit, which possession they called enthusiasm; and these kinds of foretelling events, were accounted theomancy, or prophecy: sometimes in the aspect of the stars at their nativity; which was called horoscopy, and esteemed a part of judiciary astrology: sometimes in their own hopes and fears, called thumomancy, or presage: sometimes in the prediction of witches, that pretended conference with the dead; which is called necromancy, conjuring, and witchcraft; and is but juggling and confederate knavery: sometimes in the casual flight, or feeding of birds; called augury: sometimes in the entrails of a sacrificed beast; which was *aruspicina:* sometimes in dreams: sometimes in croaking of ravens, or chattering of birds: sometimes in the lineaments of the face; which was called metoposcopy; or by palmistry in the lines of the hand; in casual words, called *omina:* sometimes in monsters, or unusual accidents; as eclipses, comets, rare meteors, earthquakes, inundations, uncouth births, and the like, which they called *portenta,* and *ostenta,* because they thought them to portend, or foreshow some great calamity to come; sometimes, in mere lottery, as cross and pile; counting holes in a sieve; dipping of verses in Homer, and Virgil; and innumerable other such vain conceits. So easy are men to be drawn to believe any thing, from such men as have gotten credit with them; and can with gentleness, and dexterity, take hold of their fear, and ignorance.

*The designs of the authors of the religion of the heathen.*
And therefore the first founders, and legislators of commonwealths among the Gentiles, whose ends were only to keep the people in obedience, and peace, have in all places taken care; first, to imprint in their minds a belief, that those precepts which they gave concerning religion, might not be thought to proceed from their own device, but from the dictates of some god, or other spirit; or else that they themselves were of a higher nature than mere mortals, that their laws might the more easily be received: so Numa Pompilius pretended to receive the ceremonies he instituted amongst the Romans, from the nymph Egeria: and the first king and founder of the kingdom of Peru, pretended himself and his wife to be the children of the Sun; and Mahomet, to set up his new religion, pretended to have conferences with the Holy Ghost, in form of a dove. Secondly, they have had a care, to make it believed, that the same things were displeasing to the gods, which were forbidden by the laws. Thirdly, to prescribe ceremonies, supplications, sacrifices, and festivals, by which they were to believe, the anger of the gods might be appeased; and that ill success in war, great contagions of sickness, earthquakes, and each man's private misery, came from the anger of the gods, and their anger from the neglect of their worship, or the forgetting, or mistaking some point of the ceremonies required. And though amongst the ancient Romans, men were not forbidden to deny, that which in the poets is written of the pains, and pleasures after this life: which divers of great authority, and gravity in that state have

in their harangues openly derided; yet that belief was always more cherished, than the contrary.

And by these, and such other institutions, they obtained in order to their end, which was the peace of the commonwealth, that the common people in their misfortunes, laying the fault on neglect, or error in their ceremonies, or on their own disobedience to the laws, were the less apt to mutiny against their governors; and being entertained with the pomp, and pastime of festivals, and public games, made in honour of the gods, needed nothing else but bread to keep them from discontent, murmuring, and commotion against the state. And therefore the Romans, that had conquered the greatest part of the then known world, made no scruple of tolerating any religion whatsoever in the city of Rome itself; unless it had something in it, that could not consist with their civil government; nor do we read, that any religion was there forbidden, but that of the Jews; who, being the peculiar kingdom of God, thought it unlawful to acknowledge subjection to any mortal king or state whatsoever. And thus you see how the religion of the Gentiles was a part of their policy.

*The true religion and the laws of God's kingdom the same.* But where God himself, by supernatural revelation, planted religion; there he also made to himself a peculiar kingdom: and gave laws, not only of behaviour towards himself, but also towards one another; and thereby in the kingdom of God, the policy, and laws civil, are a part of religion; and therefore the distinction of temporal, and spiritual domination, hath there no place. It is true, that God is king of all the earth: yet may he be king of a peculiar, and chosen nation. For there is no more incongruity therein, than that he that hath the general command of the whole army, should have withal a peculiar regiment, or company of his own. God is king of all the earth by his power: but of his chosen people, he is king by covenant. But to speak more largely of the kingdom of God, both by nature, and covenant, I have in the following discourse assigned another place (chapter 35).

*The causes of change in religion.* From the propagation of religion, it is not hard to understand the causes of the resolution of the same into its first seeds, or principles; which are only an opinion of a deity, and powers invisible, and supernatural; that can never be so abolished out of human nature, but that new religions may again be made to spring out of them, by the culture of such men, as for such purpose are in reputation.

For seeing all formed religion, is founded at first, upon the faith which a multitude hath in some one person, whom they believe not only to be a wise man, and to labour to procure their happiness, but also to be a holy man, to whom God himself vouchsafeth to declare his will supernaturally; it followeth necessarily, when they that have the government of religion, shall come to have either the wisdom of those men, their sincerity, or their love suspected; or when they shall be unable to show any probable token of divine revelation; that the religion which they desire to uphold, must be suspected likewise; and, without the fear of the civil sword, contradicted and rejected.

*Enjoining belief of impossibilities.* That which taketh away the reputation of wisdom, in him that formeth a religion, or addeth to it when it is already formed, is the enjoining of a belief of contradictories: for both parts of a contradiction cannot possibly be true: and therefore to enjoin the belief of them, is an argument of ignorance; which detects the author in that; and discredits him in all things else he shall propound as from revelation supernatural: which revelation a man may indeed have of many things above, but of nothing against natural reason.

*Doing contrary to the religion they establish.* That which taketh away the reputation of sincerity, is the doing or saying of such things, as appear to be signs, that what they require other men to believe, is not believed by themselves; all which doings, or sayings are therefore called scandalous, because they be stumbling blocks, that make men to fall in the way of religion; as injustice, cruelty, profaneness, avarice, and luxury. For who can believe, that he that doth ordinarily such actions as proceed from any of these roots, believeth there is any such invisible power to be feared, as he affrighteth other men withal, for lesser faults?

That which taketh away the reputation of love, is the being detected of private ends: as when the belief they require of others, conduceth or seemeth to conduce to the acquiring of dominion, riches, dignity, or secure pleasure, to themselves only, or specially. For that which men reap benefit by to themselves, they are thought to do for their own sakes, and not for love of others.

*Want of the testimony of miracles.* Lastly, the testimony

that men can render of divine calling, can be no other, than
the operation of miracles; or true prophecy, which also is a
miracle; or extraordinary felicity. And therefore, to those
points of religion, which have been received from them that
did such miracles; those that are added by such, as approve
not their calling by some miracle, obtain no greater belief,
than what the custom and laws of the places, in which they
be educated, have wrought into them. For as in natural
things, men of judgment require natural signs, and arguments; so in supernatural things, they require signs supernatural, which are miracles, before they consent inwardly,
and from their hearts.

All which causes of the weakening of men's faith, do
manifestly appear in the examples following. First, we have
the example of the children of Israel; who when Moses, that
had approved his calling to them by miracles, and by the
happy conduct of them out of Egypt, was absent but forty
days, revolted from the worship of the true God, recommended to them by him; and setting up (*Exod*. xxxii. 1, 2)
a golden calf for their god, relapsed into the idolatry of the
Egyptians; from whom they had been so lately delivered.
And again, after Moses, Aaron, Joshua, and that generation
which had seen the great works of God in Israel, (*Judges* ii.
11) were dead; another generation arose, and served Baal.
So that miracles failing, faith also failed.

Again, when the sons of Samuel, (1 *Sam*. viii. 3) being
constituted by their father judges in Bersabee, received bribes,
and judged unjustly, the people of Israel refused any more to
have God to be their king, in other manner than he was king
of other people; and therefore cried out to Samuel, to choose
them a king after the manner of the nations. So that justice
failing, faith also failed; insomuch, as they deposed their God,
from reigning over them.

And whereas in the planting of Christian religion, the
oracles ceased in all parts of the Roman empire, and the
number of Christians increased wonderfully every day, and
in every place, by the preaching of the Apostles, and Evangelists; a great part of that success, may reasonably be attributed, to the contempt, into which the priests of the Gentiles
of that time, had brought themselves, by their uncleanness,
avarice, and juggling between princes. Also the religion of the
church of Rome, was partly, for the same cause abolished in
England, and many other parts of Christendom; insomuch,
as the failing of virtue in the pastors, maketh faith fail in

the people: and partly from bringing of the philosophy, and doctrine of Aristotle into religion, by the Schoolmen; from whence there arose so many contradictions, and absurdities, as brought the clergy into a reputation both of ignorance, and of fraudulent intention; and inclined people to revolt from them, either against the will of their own princes, as in France and Holland; or with their will, as in England.

Lastly, amongst the points by the church of Rome declared necessary for salvation, there be so many, manifestly to the advantage of the Pope, and of his spiritual subjects, residing in the territories of other Christian princes, that were it not for the mutual emulation of those princes, they might without war, or trouble, exclude all foreign authority, as easily as it has been excluded in England. For who is there that does not see, to whose benefit it conduceth, to have it believed, that a king hath not his authority from Christ, unless a bishop crown him? That a king, if he be a priest, cannot marry? That whether a prince be born in lawful marriage, or not, must be judged by authority from Rome? That subjects may be freed from their allegiance, if by the court of Rome, the king be judged an heretic? That a king, as Childeric of France, may be deposed by a pope, as Pope Zachary, for no cause; and his kingdom given to one of his subjects? That the clergy and regulars, in what country soever, shall be exempt from the jurisdiction of their king in cases criminal? Or who does not see, to whose profit redound the fees of private masses, and vales of purgatory; with other signs of private interest, enough to mortify the most lively faith, if, as I said, the civil magistrate, and custom did not more sustain it, than any opinion they have of the sanctity, wisdom, or probity of their teachers? So that I may attribute all the changes of religion in the world, to one and the same cause; and that is, unpleasing priests; and those not only amongst Catholics, but even in that church that hath presumed most of reformation.

# Chapter 13

## Of the Natural Condition of Mankind as concerning their Felicity and Misery

*Men by nature equal.* Nature hath made men so equal, in the faculties of the body, and mind; as that though there be found one man sometimes manifestly stronger in body, or of quicker mind than another; yet when all is reckoned together, the difference between man, and man, is not so considerable, as that one man can thereupon claim to himself any benefit, to which another may not pretend, as well as he. For as to the strength of body, the weakest has strength enough to kill the strongest, either by secret machination, or by confederacy with others, that are in the same danger with himself.

And as to the faculties of the mind, setting aside the arts grounded upon words, and especially that skill of proceeding upon general, and infallible rules, called science; which very few have, and but in few things; as being not a native faculty, born with us; nor attained, as prudence, while we look after somewhat else, I find yet a greater equality amongst men, than that of strength. For prudence, is but experience; which equal time, equally bestows on all men, in those things they equally apply themselves unto. That which may perhaps make such equality incredible, is but a vain conceit of one's own wisdom, which almost all men think they have in a greater degree, than the vulgar; that is, than all men but themselves, and a few others, whom by fame, or for concurring with themselves, they approve. For such is the nature of men, that howsoever they may acknowledge many others to be more witty, or more eloquent, or more learned; yet they will hardly believe there be many so wise as themselves; for they see their own wit at hand, and other men's at a distance. But this proveth rather that men are in that point equal, than unequal. For there is not ordinarily a greater sign of the equal distribution of any thing, than that every man is contented with his share.

*From equality proceeds diffidence.* From this equality of ability, ariseth equality of hope in the attaining of our ends. And therefore if any two men desire the same thing, which nevertheless they cannot both enjoy, they become enemies;

and in the way to their end, which is principally their own conservation, and sometimes their delectation only, endeavour to destroy, or subdue one another. And from hence it comes to pass, that where an invader hath no more to fear, than another man's single power; if one plant, sow, build, or possess a convenient seat, others may probably be expected to come prepared with forces united, to dispossess, and deprive him, not only of the fruit of his labour, but also of his life, or liberty. And the invader again is in the like danger of another.

*From diffidence war.* And from this diffidence of one another, there is no way for any man to secure himself, so reasonable, as anticipation; that is, by force, or wiles, to master the persons of all men he can, so long, till he see no other power great enough to endanger him: and this is no more than his own conservation requireth, and is generally allowed. Also because there be some, that taking pleasure in contemplating their own power in the acts of conquest, which they pursue farther than their security requires; if others, that otherwise would be glad to be at ease within modest bounds, should not by invasion increase their power, they would not be able, long time, by standing only on their defence, to subsist. And by consequence, such augmentation of dominion over men being necessary to a man's conservation, it ought to be allowed him.

Again, men have no pleasure, but on the contrary a great deal of grief, in keeping company, where there is no power able to over-awe them all. For every man looketh that his companion should value him, at the same rate he sets upon himself: and upon all signs of contempt, or undervaluing, naturally endeavours, as far as he dares, (which amongst them that have no common power to keep them in quiet, is far enough to make them destroy each other), to extort a greater value from his contemners, by damage; and from others, by the example.

So that in the nature of man, we find three principal causes of quarrel. First, competition; secondly, diffidence; thirdly, glory.

The first, maketh men invade for gain; the second, for safety; and the third, for reputation. The first use violence, to make themselves masters of other men's persons, wives, children, and cattle; the second, to defend them; the third, for trifles, as a word, a smile, a different opinion, and any other sign of undervalue, either direct in their persons, or by reflection in their kindred, their friends, their nation, their profession, or their name.

*Out of civil states, there is always war of every one against every one.* Hereby it is manifest, that during the time men live without a common power to keep them all in awe, they are in that condition which is called war; and such a war, as is of every man, against every man. For WAR, consisteth not in battle only, or the act of fighting; but in a tract of time, wherein the will to contend by battle is sufficiently known: and therefore the notion of *time,* is to be considered in the nature of war; as it is in the nature of weather. For as the nature of foul weather, lieth not in a shower or two of rain; but in an inclination thereto of many days together: so the nature of war, consisteth not in actual fighting; but in the known disposition thereto, during all the time there is no assurance to the contrary. All other time is PEACE.

*The incommodities of such a war.* Whatsoever therefore is consequent to a time of war, where every man is enemy to every man; the same is consequent to the time, wherein men live without other security, than what their own strength, and their own invention shall furnish them withal. In such condition, there is no place for industry; because the fruit thereof is uncertain: and consequently no culture of the earth; no navigation, nor use of the commodities that may be imported by sea; no commodious building; no instruments of moving, and removing, such things as require much force; no knowledge of the face of the earth; no account of time; no arts; no letters; no society; and which is worst of all, continual fear, and danger of violent death; and the life of man, solitary, poor, nasty, brutish, and short.

It may seem strange to some man, that has not well weighed these things; that nature should thus dissociate, and render men apt to invade, and destroy one another: and he may therefore, not trusting to this inference, made from the passions, desire perhaps to have the same confirmed by experience. Let him therefore consider with himself, when taking a journey, he arms himself, and seeks to go well accompanied; when going to sleep, he locks his doors; when even in his house he locks his chests; and this when he knows there be laws, and public officers, armed, to revenge all injuries shall be done him; what opinion he has of his fellow-subjects, when he rides armed; of his fellow citizens, when he locks his doors; and of his children, and servants, when he locks his chests. Does he not there as much accuse mankind by his actions, as I do by my words? But neither of us accuse man's nature in it. The desires, and other passions of man, are in themselves no sin. No more are the actions, that proceed from those passions, till they know a law that forbids them: which till laws be made they cannot know: nor can any law be made, till they have agreed upon the person that shall make it.

It may peradventure be thought, there was never such a time, nor condition of war as this; and I believe it was never generally so, over all the world: but there are many places, where they live so now. For the savage people in many places of America, except the government of small families, the concord whereof dependeth on natural lust, have no government at all; and live at this day in that brutish manner, as I said before. Howsoever, it may be perceived what manner of life there would be, where there were no common power to fear, by the manner of life, which men that have formerly lived under a peaceful government, use to degenerate into, in a civil war.

But though there had never been any time, wherein particular men were in a condition of war one against another; yet in all times, kings, and persons of sovereign authority, because of their independency, are in continual jealousies, and in the state and posture of gladiators; having their weapons pointing, and their eyes fixed on one another; that is, their forts, garrisons, and guns upon the frontiers of their kingdoms; and continual spies upon their neighbours; which is a posture of war. But because they uphold thereby, the industry of their subjects; there does not follow from it, that misery, which accompanies the liberty of particular men.

*In such a war nothing is unjust.* To this war of every man, against every man, this also is consequent; that nothing can be unjust. The notions of right and wrong, justice and injustice have there no place. Where there is no common power, there is no law: where no law, no injustice. Force, and fraud, are in war the two cardinal virtues. Justice, and injustice are none of the faculties neither of the body, nor mind. If they were, they might be in a man that were alone in the world, as well as his senses, and passions. They are qualities, that relate to men in society, not in solitude. It is consequent also to the same condition, that there be no propriety, no dominion, no *mine* and *thine* distinct; but only that to be every man's, that he can get: and for so long, as he can keep it. And thus much for the ill condition, which man by mere nature is actually placed in; though with a possibility to come out of it, consisting partly in the passions, partly in his reason.

*The passions that incline men to peace.* The passions that incline men to peace, are fear of death; desire of such things as are necessary to commodious living; and a hope by their industry to obtain them. And reason suggesteth convenient articles of peace, upon which men may be drawn to agreement. These articles, are they, which otherwise are called the Laws of Nature: whereof I shall speak more particularly, in the two following chapters.

## Chapter 14

## Of the First and Second Natural Laws, and of Contracts

*Right of nature what.* THE RIGHT OF NATURE, which writers commonly call *jus naturale*, is the liberty each man hath, to use his own power, as he will himself, for the preservation of his own nature; that is to say, of his own life; and consequently, of doing any thing, which in his own judgment, and reason, he shall conceive to be the aptest means thereunto.

*Liberty what.* By LIBERTY, is understood, according to the proper signification of the word, the absence of external impediments: which impediments, may oft take away part of a man's power to do what he would; but cannot hinder him from using the power left him, according as his judgment, and reason shall dictate to him.

*A law of nature what. Difference of right and law.* A LAW OF NATURE, *lex naturalis,* is a precept or general rule, found out by reason, by which a man is forbidden to do that, which is destructive of his life, or taketh away the means of preserving the same; and to omit that, by which he thinketh it may be best preserved. For though they that speak of this subject, use to confound *jus,* and *lex, right* and *law:* yet they ought to be distinguished; because RIGHT, consisteth in liberty to do, or to forbear: whereas LAW, determineth, and bindeth to one of them: so that law, and right, differ as much, as obligation, and liberty; which in one and the same matter are inconsistent.

*Naturally every man has right to every thing. The fundamental law of nature.* And because the condition of man, as hath been declared in the precedent chapter, is a condition of war of every one against every one; in which case every one is governed by his own reason; and there is nothing he can make use of, that may not be a help unto him, in preserving his life against his enemies; it followeth, that in such a condition, every man has a right to every thing; even to one another's body. And therefore, as long as this natural right of every man to every thing endureth, there can be no security to any man, how strong or wise soever he be, of living out the time, which nature ordinarily alloweth men to live. And consequently it is a precept, or general rule of reason, *that every man, ought to endeavour peace, as far as he has hope of obtaining it; and when he cannot obtain it, that he may seek, and use, all helps, and advantages of war.* The first branch of which rule, containeth the first, and fundamental law of nature; which is, *to seek peace, and follow it.* The second, the sum of the right of nature; which is, *by all means we can, to defend ourselves.*

*The second law of nature.* From this fundamental law of nature, by which men are commanded to endeavour peace, is derived this second law; *that a man be willing, when others are so too, as far-forth, as for peace, and defence of himself he shall think it necessary, to lay down this right to all things; and be contented with so much liberty against other men, as he would allow other men against himself.* For as long as every man holdeth this right, of doing any thing he liketh; so long are all men in the condition of war. But if other men will not lay down their right, as well as he; then there is no reason for any one, to divest himself of his: for that were to expose himself to prey, which no man is bound to, rather than to dispose himself to peace. This is that law of the Gospel; *whatsoever you require that others should do to you, that do ye to them.* And that law of all men, *quod tibi fieri non vis, alteri ne feceris.*

*What it is to lay down a right.* To *lay down* a man's *right* to any thing, is to *divest* himself of the *liberty,* of hindering another of the benefit of his own right to the same. For he that renounceth, or passeth away his right, giveth not to any other man a right which he had not before; because there is nothing to which every man had not right by nature: but only standeth out of his way, that he may enjoy his own original right, without hindrance from him; not without hindrance from another. So that the effect which redoundeth to one man, by another man's defect of right, is but so much diminution of impediments to the use of his own right original.

*Renouncing a right, what it is. Transferring right what. Obligation. Duty. Injustice.* Right is laid aside, either by simply renouncing it; or by transferring it to another. By *simply* RENOUNCING; when he cares not to whom the benefit thereof redoundeth. By TRANSFERRING; when he intendeth the benefit thereof to some certain person, or persons. And when a man hath in either manner abandoned, or granted away his right; then he is said to be OBLIGED, or BOUND, not to hinder those, to whom such right is granted, or abandoned, from the benefit of it: and that he *ought,* and it is his DUTY, not to make void that voluntary act of his own: and that such hindrance is INJUSTICE, and INJURY, as being *sine jure;* the right being before renounced, or transferred. So that *injury,* or *injustice,* in the controversies of the world, is somewhat like to that, which in the disputations of scholars is called *absurdity.* For as it is there called an absurdity, to contradict what one maintained in the beginning: so in the world, it is called injustice, and injury, voluntarily to undo that, which from the beginning he had voluntarily done. The way by which a man either simply renounceth, or transferreth his right, is a declaration, or signification, by some voluntary and sufficient sign, or signs, that he doth so renounce, or transfer; or hath so renounced, or transferred the same, to him that accepteth it. And these signs are either words only, or actions only; or, as it happeneth most often, both words, and actions. And the same are the BONDS, by which men are bound, and obliged: bonds, that have their strength, not from their own nature, for nothing is more easily broken than a man's word, but from fear of some evil consequence upon the rupture.

*Not all rights are alienable.* Whensoever a man transferreth his right, or renounceth it; it is either in consideration of some right reciprocally transferred to himself; or for some other good he hopeth for thereby. For it is a voluntary act: and of the voluntary acts of every man, the object is some *good to himself.* And therefore there be some rights, which no man can be understood by any words, or other signs, to have abandoned, or transferred. As first a man cannot lay down the right of resisting them, that assault him by force, to take away his life; because he cannot be understood to aim thereby, at any good to himself. The same may be said of wounds, and chains, and imprisonment; both because there is no benefit consequent to such patience; as there is to the patience of suffering another to be wounded, or imprisoned: as also because a man cannot tell, when he seeth men proceed against him by violence, whether they intend his death or not. And lastly the motive, and end for which this renouncing, and transferring of right is introduced, is nothing else but the security of a man's person, in his life, and in the means of so preserving life, as not to be weary of it. And therefore if a man by words, or other signs, seem to despoil himself of the end, for which those signs were intended; he is not to be understood as if he meant it, or that it was his will; but that he was ignorant of how such words and actions were to be interpreted.

*Contract what*. The mutual transferring of right, is that which men call CONTRACT.

There is difference between transferring of right to the thing; and transferring, or tradition, that is delivery of the thing itself. For the thing may be delivered together with the translation of the right; as in buying and selling with ready-money; or exchange of goods, or lands: and it may be delivered some time after.

*Covenant what*. Again, one of the contractors, may deliver the thing contracted for on his part, and leave the other to perform his part at some determinate time after, and in the mean time be trusted; and then the contract on his part, is called PACT, or COVENANT: or both parts may contract now, to perform hereafter: in which cases, he that is to perform in time to come, being trusted, his performance is called *keeping of promise*, or faith; and the failing of performance, if it be voluntary, *violation of faith*.

*Free-gift*. When the transferring of right, is not mutual; but one of the parties transferreth, in hope to gain thereby friendship, or service from another, or from his friends; or in hope to gain the reputation of charity, or magnanimity; or to deliver his mind from the pain of compassion; or in hope of reward in heaven; this is not contract, but GIFT, FREE-GIFT, GRACE: which words signify one and the same thing.

*Signs of contract express. Promise*. Signs of contract, are either *express*, or *by inference*. Express, are words spoken with understanding of what they signify: and such words are either of the time *present*, or *past*; as, *I give, I grant, I have given, I have granted, I will that this be yours*: or of the future; as, *I will give, I will grant*: which words of the future are called PROMISE.

*Signs of contract by inference*. Signs by inference, are sometimes the consequence of words; sometimes the consequence of silence; sometimes the consequence of actions; sometimes the consequence of forbearing an action: and generally a sign by inference, of any contract, is whatsoever sufficiently argues the will of the contractor.

*Free gift passeth by words of the present or past*. Words alone, if they be of the time to come, and contain a bare promise, are an insufficient sign of a free-gift, and therefore not obligatory. For if they be of the time to come, as *to-morrow I will give*, they are a sign I have not given yet, and consequently that my right is not transferred, but remaineth till I transfer it by some other act. But if the words be of the time present, or past, as, *I have given,* or, *do give to be delivered to-morrow,* then is my to-morrow's right given away to-day; and that by the virtue of the words, though there were no other argument of my will. And there is a great difference in the signification of these words, *volo hoc tuum esse cras,* and *cras dabo;* that is, between *I will that this be thine to-morrow,* and, *I will give it thee to-morrow:* for the word *I will,* in the former manner of speech, signifies an act of the will present; but in the latter, it signifies a promise of an act of the will to come: and therefore the former words, being of the present, transfer a future right; the latter, that be of the future, transfer nothing. But if there be other signs of the will to transfer a right, besides words; then, though the gift be free, yet may the right be understood to pass by words of the future: as if a man propound a prize to him that comes first to the end of a race, the gift is free; and though the words be of the future, yet the right passeth: for if he would not have his words so be understood, he should not have let them run.

*Signs of contract are words both of the past, present, and future.* In contracts, the right passeth, not only where the words are of the time present, or past, but also where they are of the future: because all contract is mutual translation, or change of right; and therefore he that promiseth only, because he hath already received the benefit for which he promiseth, is to be understood as if he intended the right should pass: for unless he had been content to have his words so understood, the other would not have performed his part first. And for that cause, in buying, and selling, and other acts of contract, a promise is equivalent to a covenant; and therefore obligatory.

*Merit what.* He that performeth first in the case of a contract, is said to MERIT that which he is to receive by the performance of the other; and he hath it as *due.* Also when a prize is propounded to many, which is to be given to him only that winneth; or money is thrown amongst many, to be enjoyed by them that catch it; though this be a free gift; yet so to win, or so to catch, is to *merit,* and to have it as DUE. For the right is transferred in the propounding of the prize, and in throwing down the money; though it be not determined to whom, but by the event of the contention. But there is between these two sorts of merit, this difference, that in contract, I merit by virtue of my own power, and the contractor's need; but in this case of free gift, I am enabled to merit only by the benignity of the giver: in contract, I merit at the contractor's hand that he should depart with his right; in this case of gift, I merit not that the giver should part with his right; but that when he has parted with it, it should be mine, rather than another's. And this I think to be the meaning of that distinction of the Schools, between *meritum congrui*, and *meritum condigni*. For God Almighty, having promised Paradise to those men, hoodwinked with carnal desires, that can walk through this world according to the precepts, and limits prescribed by him; they say, he that shall so walk, shall merit Paradise *ex congruo*. But because no man can demand a right to it, by his own righteousness, or any other power in himself, but by the free grace of God only; they say, no man can merit Paradise *ex condigno*. This I say, I think is the meaning of that distinction; but because disputers do not agree upon the signification of their own terms of art, longer than it serves their turn; I will not affirm any thing of their meaning: only this I say; when a gift is given indefinitely, as a prize to be contended for, he that winneth meriteth, and may claim the prize as due.

*Covenants of mutual trust, when invalid.* If a covenant be made, wherein neither of the parties perform presently, but trust one another; in the condition of mere nature, which is a condition of war of every man against every man, upon any reasonable suspicion, it is void: but if there be a common power set over them both, with right and force sufficient to compel performance, it is not void. For he that performeth first, has no assurance the other will perform after; because the bonds of words are too weak to bridle men's ambition, avarice, anger, and other passions, without the fear of some coercive power; which in the condition of mere nature, where all men are equal, and judges of the justness of their own fears, cannot possibly be supposed. And therefore he which performeth first, does but betray himself to his enemy; contrary to the right, he can never abandon, of defending his life, and means of living.

But in a civil estate, where there is a power set up to constrain those that would otherwise violate their faith, that fear is no more reasonable; and for that cause, he which by the covenant is to perform first, is obliged so to do.

The cause of fear, which maketh such a covenant invalid, must be always something arising after the covenant made; as some new fact, or other sign of the will not to perform: else it cannot make the covenant void. For that which could not hinder a man from promising, ought not to be admitted as a hindrance of performing.

*Right to the end, containeth right to the means.* He that transferreth any right, transferreth the means of enjoying it, as far as lieth in his power. As he that selleth land, is understood to transfer the herbage, and whatsoever grows upon it: nor can he that sells a mill turn away the stream that drives it. And they that give to a man the right of government in sovereignty, are understood to give him the right of levying money to maintain soldiers; and of appointing magistrates for the administration of justice.

*No covenant with beasts.* To make covenants with brute beasts, is impossible; because not understanding our speech, they understand not, nor accept of any translation of right; nor can translate any right to another: and without mutual acceptation, there is no covenant.

*Nor with God without special revelation.* To make covenant with God, is impossible, but by mediation of such as God speaketh to, either by revelation supernatural, or by his lieutenants that govern under him, and in his name: for otherwise we know not whether our covenants be accepted, or not. And therefore they that vow any thing contrary to any law of nature, vow in vain; as being a thing unjust to pay such vow. And if it be a thing commanded by the law of nature, it is not the vow, but the law that binds them.

*No covenant, but of possible and future.* The matter, or subject of a covenant, is always something that falleth under deliberation; for to covenant, is an act of the will; that is to say, an act, and the last act of deliberation; and is therefore always understood to be something to come; and which is judged possible for him that covenanteth, to perform.

And therefore, to promise that which is known to be impossible, is no covenant. But if that prove impossible afterwards, which before was thought possible, the covenant is valid, and bindeth, though not to the thing itself, yet to the value; or, if that also be impossible, to the unfeigned endeavour of performing as much as is possible: for to more no man can be obliged.

*Covenants how made void.* Men are freed of their covenants two ways; by performing; or by being forgiven. For performance, is the natural end of obligation; and forgiveness, the restitution of liberty; as being a retransferring of that right, in which the obligation consisted.

*Covenants extorted by fear are valid*. Covenants entered into by fear, in the condition of mere nature, are obligatory. For example, if I covenant to pay a ransom, or service for my life, to an enemy; I am bound by it: for it is a contract, wherein one receiveth the benefit of life; the other is to receive money, or service for it; and consequently, where no other law, as in the condition of mere nature, forbiddeth the performance, the covenant is valid. Therefore prisoners of war, if trusted with the payment of their ransom, are obliged to pay it: and if a weaker prince, make a disadvantageous peace with a stronger, for fear; he is bound to keep it; unless, as hath been said before, there ariseth some new, and just cause of fear, to renew the war. And even in commonwealths, if I be forced to redeem myself from a thief by promising him money, I am bound to pay it, till the civil law discharge me. For whatsoever I may lawfully do without obligation, the same I may lawfully covenant to do through fear: and what I lawfully covenant, I cannot lawfully break.

*The former covenant to one, makes void the later to another*. A former covenant, makes void a later. For a man that hath passed away his right to one man to-day, hath it not to pass to-morrow to another: and therefore the later promise passeth no right, but is null.

*A man's covenant not to defend himself is void*. A covenant not to defend myself from force, by force, is always void. For, as I have showed before, no man can transfer, or lay down his right to save himself from death, wounds, and imprisonment, the avoiding whereof is the only end of laying down any right; and therefore the promise of not resisting force, in no covenant transferreth any right; nor is obliging. For though a man may covenant thus, *unless I do so, or so, kill me;* he cannot covenant thus, *unless I do so, or so, I will not resist you, when you come to kill me*. For man by nature chooseth the lesser evil, which is danger of death in resisting; rather than the greater, which is certain and present death in not resisting. And this is granted to be true by all men, in that they lead criminals to execution, and prison, with armed men, notwithstanding that such criminals have consented to the law, by which they are condemned.

*No man obliged to accuse himself*. A covenant to accuse oneself, without assurance of pardon, is likewise invalid. For in the condition of nature, where every man is judge, there is no place for accusation: and in the civil state, the accusation is followed with punishment; which being force, a man is not obliged not to resist. The same is also true, of the accusation of those, by whose condemnation a man falls into misery; as of a father, wife, or benefactor. For the testimony of such an accuser, if it be not willingly given, is presumed to be corrupted by nature; and therefore not to be received: and where a man's testimony is not to be credited, he is not bound to give it. Also accusations upon torture, are not to be reputed as testimonies. For torture is to be used as means of conjecture, and light, in the further examination, and search of truth: and what is in that case confessed, tendeth to the ease of him that is tortured; not to the informing of the torturers: and therefore ought not to have the credit of a sufficient testimony: for whether he deliver himself by true, or false accusation, he does it by the right of preserving his own life.

*The end of an oath. The form of an oath.* The force of words, being, as I have formerly noted, too weak to hold men to the performance of their covenants; there are in man's nature, but two imaginable helps to strengthen it. And those are either a fear of the consequence of breaking their word; or a glory, or pride in appearing not to need to break it. This latter is a generosity too rarely found to be presumed on, especially in the pursuers of wealth, command, or sensual pleasure; which are the greatest part of mankind. The passion to be reckoned upon, is fear; whereof there be two very general objects: one, the power of spirits invisible; the other, the power of those men they shall therein offend. Of these two, though the former be the greater power, yet the fear of the latter is commonly the greater fear. The fear of the former is in every man, his own religion: which hath place in the nature of man before civil society. The latter hath not so; at least not place enough, to keep men to their promises; because in the condition of mere nature, the inequality of power is not discerned, but by the event of battle. So that before the time of civil society, or in the interruption thereof by war, there is nothing can strengthen a covenant of peace agreed on, against the temptations of avarice, ambition, lust, or other strong desire, but the fear of that invisible power, which they every one worship as God; and fear as a revenger of their perfidy. All therefore that can be done between two men not subject to civil power, is to put one another to swear by the God he feareth: which *swearing*, or OATH, is a *form of speech, added to a promise; by which he that promiseth, signifieth, that unless he perform, he renounceth the*

*mercy of his God, or calleth to him for vengeance on himself.*
Such was the heathen form, *Let* Jupiter *kill me else, as I kill
this beast.* So is our form, *I shall do thus, and thus, so help
me God.* And this, with the rites and ceremonies, which every
one useth in his own religion, that the fear of breaking faith
might be the greater.

*No oath but by God.* By this it appears, that an oath taken
according to any other form, or rite, than his, that sweareth,
is in vain; and no oath: and that there is no swearing by any
thing which the swearer thinks not God. For though men
have sometimes used to swear by their kings, for fear, or
flattery; yet they would have it thereby understood, they
attributed to them divine honour. And that swearing unneces-
sarily by God, is but profaning of his name: and swearing
by other things, as men do in common discourse, is not
swearing, but an impious custom, gotten by too much vehemence of talking.

*An oath adds nothing to the obligation.* It appears also,
that the oath adds nothing to the obligation. For a covenant,
if lawful, binds in the sight of God, without the oath, as much
as with it: if unlawful, bindeth not at all; though it be confirmed with an oath.

# Chapter 15

## Of other Laws of Nature

*The third law of nature, justice.* From that law of nature, by which we are obliged to transfer to another, such rights, as being retained, hinder the peace of mankind, there followeth a third; which is this, *that men perform their covenants made:* without which, covenants are in vain, and but empty words; and the right of all men to all things remaining, we are still in the condition of war.

*Justice and injustice what.* And in this law of nature, consisteth the fountain and original of JUSTICE. For where no covenant hath preceded, there hath no right been transferred, and every man has right to every thing; and consequently, no action can be unjust. But when a covenant is made, then to break it is *unjust:* and the definition of INJUSTICE, is no other than *the not performance of covenant.* And whatsoever is not unjust, is *just.*

*Justice and propriety begin with the constitution of commonwealth.* But because covenants of mutual trust, where there is a fear of not performance on either part, as hath been said in the former chapter, are invalid; though the original of justice be the making of covenants; yet injustice actually there can be none, till the cause of such fear be taken away; which while men are in the natural condition of war, cannot be done. Therefore before the names of just, and unjust can have place, there must be some coercive power, to compel men equally to the performance of their covenants, by the terror of some punishment, greater than the benefit they expect by the breach of their covenant; and to make good that propriety, which by mutual contract men acquire, in recompense of the universal right they abandon: and such power there is none before the erection of a commonwealth. And this is also to be gathered out of the ordinary definition of justice in the Schools: for they say, that *justice is the constant will of giving to every man his own.* And therefore where there is no *own,* that is no propriety, there is no injustice; and where there is no coercive power erected, that is, where there is no commonwealth, there is no propriety; all men having right to all things: therefore where there is no commonwealth, there nothing is unjust. So that the nature of justice, consisteth in keeping of valid covenants: but the validity of covenants begins not but with the constitution of a civil power, sufficient to compel men to keep them: and then it is also that propriety begins.

*Justice not contrary to reason.* The fool hath said in his heart, there is no such thing as justice; and sometimes also with his tongue; seriously alleging, that every man's conservation, and contentment, being committed to his own care, there could be no reason, why every man might not do what he thought conduced thereunto: and therefore also to make, or not make; keep, or not keep covenants, was not against reason, when it conduced to one's benefit. He does not therein deny, that there be covenants; and that they are sometimes broken, sometimes kept; and that such breach of them may be called injustice, and the observance of them justice: but he questioneth, whether injustice, taking away the fear of God, for the same fool hath said in his heart there is no God, may not sometimes stand with that reason, which dictateth to every man his own good; and particularly then, when it conduceth to such a benefit, as shall put a man in a condition, to neglect not only the dispraise, and revilings, but also the power of other men. The kingdom of God is gotten by violence: but what if it could be gotten by unjust violence? were it against reason so to get it, when it is impossible to receive hurt by it? and if it be not against reason, it is not against justice; or else justice is not to be approved for good. From such reasoning as this, successful wickedness hath obtained the name of virtue: and some that in all other things have disallowed the violation of faith; yet have allowed it, when it is for the getting of a kingdom. And the heathen that believed, that Saturn was deposed by his son Jupiter, believed nevertheless the same Jupiter to be the avenger of injustice: somewhat like to a piece of law in Coke's *Commentaries on Littleton;* where he says, if the right heir of the crown be attainted of treason; yet the crown shall descend to him, and *eo instante* the attainder be void: from which instances a man will be very prone to infer; that when the heir apparent of a kingdom, shall kill him that is in possession, though his father; you may call it injustice, or by what other name you will; yet it can never be against reason, seeing all the voluntary actions of men tend to the benefit of themselves; and those actions are most reasonable, that conduce most to their ends. This specious reasoning is nevertheless false.

For the question is not of promises mutual, where there is no security of performance on either side; as when there is no civil power erected over the parties promising; for such promises are no covenants: but either where one of the parties has performed already; or where there is a power to make him perform; there is the question whether it be against reason, that is, against the benefit of the other to perform, or not. And I say it is not against reason. For the manifestation whereof, we are to consider; first, that when a man doth a thing, which notwithstanding any thing can be foreseen, and reckoned on, tendeth to his own destruction, howsoever some accident which he could not expect, arriving may turn it to his benefit; yet such events do not make it reasonably or wisely done. Secondly, that in a condition of war, wherein every man to every man, for want of a common power to keep them all in awe, is an enemy, there is no man who can hope by his own strength, or wit, to defend himself from destruction, without the help of confederates; where every one expects the same defence by the confederation, that any one else does: and therefore he which declares he thinks it reason to deceive those that help him, can in reason expect no other means of safety, than what can be had from his own single power. He therefore that breaketh his covenant, and consequently declareth that he thinks he may with reason do so, cannot be received into any society, that unite themselves for peace and defence, but by the error of them that receive him; nor when he is received, be retained in it, without seeing the danger of their error; which errors a man cannot reasonably reckon upon as the means of his security: and therefore if he be left, or cast out of society, he perisheth; and if he live in society, it is by the errors of other men, which he could not foresee, nor reckon upon; and consequently against the reason of his preservation; and so, as all men that contribute not to his destruction, forbear him only out of ignorance of what is good for themselves.

As for the instance of gaining the secure and perpetual felicity of heaven, by any way; it is frivolous: there being but one way imaginable; and that is not breaking, but keeping of covenant.

And for the other instance of attaining sovereignty by rebellion; it is manifest, that though the event follow, yet because it cannot reasonably be expected, but rather the contrary; and because by gaining it so, others are taught to gain the same in like manner, the attempt thereof is against reason. Justice therefore, that is to say, keeping of covenant, is a rule of reason, by which we are forbidden to do any thing destructive to our life; and consequently a law of nature.

There be some that proceed further; and will not have the law of nature, to be those rules which conduce to the preservation of man's life on earth; but to the attaining of an eternal felicity after death; to which they think the breach of covenant may conduce; and consequently be just and reasonable; such are they that think it a work of merit to kill, or depose, or rebel against, the sovereign power constituted over them by their own consent. But because there is no natural knowledge of man's estate after death; much less of the reward that is then to be given to breach of faith; but only a belief grounded upon other men's saying, that they know it supernaturally, or that they know those, that knew them, that knew others, that knew it supernaturally; breach of faith cannot be called a precept of reason, or nature.

*Covenants not discharged by the vice of the person to whom they are made.* Others, that allow for a law of nature, the keeping of faith, do nevertheless make exception of certain persons; as heretics, and such as use not to perform their covenant to others: and this also is against reason. For if any fault of a man, be sufficient to discharge our covenant made; the same ought in reason to have been sufficient to have hindered the making of it.

*Justice of men and justice of actions what.* The names of just, and unjust, when they are attributed to men, signify one thing; and when they are attributed to actions, another. When they are attributed to men, they signify conformity, or inconformity of manners, to reason. But when they are attributed to actions, they signify the conformity, or inconformity to reason, not of manners, or manner of life, but of particular actions. A just man therefore, is he that taketh all the care he can, that his actions may be all just: and an unjust man, is he that neglecteth it. And such men are more often in our language styled by the names of righteous, and unrighteous; than just, and unjust; though the meaning be the same. Therefore a righteous man, does not lose that title, by one, or a few unjust actions, that proceed from sudden passion, or mistake of things, or persons: nor does an unrighteous man, lose his character, for such actions, as he does, or forbears to do, for fear: because his will is not framed by the justice, but by the apparent benefit of what he is to do. That which gives to human actions the relish of justice, is a certain nobleness or gallantness of courage, rarely found, by which a man scorns to be beholden for the contentment of his life, to fraud, or breach of promise. This justice of the manners, is that which is meant, where justice is called a virtue; and injustice a vice.

But the justice of actions denominates men, not just, but *guiltless:* and the injustice of the same, which is also called injury, gives them but the name of *guilty.*

*Justice of manners, and justice of actions.* Again, the injustice of manners, is the disposition, or aptitude to do injury; and is injustice before it proceed to act; and without supposing any individual person injured. But the injustice of an action, that is to say injury, supposeth an individual person injured; namely him, to whom the covenant was made: and therefore many times the injury is received by one man, when the damage redoundeth to another. As when the master commandeth his servant to give money to a stranger; if it be not done, the injury is done to the master, whom he had before covenanted to obey; but the damage redoundeth to the stranger, to whom he had no obligation; and therefore could not injure him. And so also in commonwealths, private men may remit to one another their debts; but not robberies or other violences, whereby they are endamaged; because the detaining of debt, is an injury to themselves; but robbery and violence, are injuries to the person of the commonwealth.

*Nothing done to a man by his own consent can be injury.* Whatsoever is done to a man, conformable to his own will signified to the doer, is no injury to him. For if he that doeth it, hath not passed away his original right to do what he please, by some antecedent covenant, there is no breach of covenant; and therefore no injury done him. And if he have; then his will to have it done being signified, is a release of that covenant: and so again there is no injury done him.

*Justice commutative and distributive.* Justice of actions, is by writers divided into *commutative,* and *distributive:* and the former they say consisteth in proportion arithmetical; the latter in proportion geometrical. Commutative therefore, they place in the equality of value of the things contracted for; and distributive, in the distribution of equal benefit, to men of equal merit. As if it were injustice to sell dearer than we buy; or to give more to a man than he merits. The value of all things contracted for, is measured by the appetite of the contractors: and therefore the just value, is that which they be contented to give. And merit (besides that which is by covenant, where the performance on one part, meriteth the performance on the other part, and falls under justice commutative, not distributive) is not due to justice; but is rewarded of grace only. And therefore this distinction, in the sense wherein it useth to be expounded, is not right. To speak properly, commutative justice, is the justice, of a contractor; that is, a performance of covenant, in buying, and selling; hiring, and letting to hire; lending, and borrowing; exchanging, bartering, and other acts of contract.

And distributive justice, the justice of an arbitrator; that is to say, the act of defining what is just. Wherein, being trusted by them that make him arbitrator, if he perform his trust, he is said to distribute to every man his own: and this is indeed just distribution, and may be called, though improperly, distributive justice; but more properly equity; which also is a law of nature, as shall be shown in due place.

*The fourth law of nature, gratitude.* As justice dependeth on antecedent covenant; so does GRATITUDE depend on antecedent grace; that is to say, antecedent free gift: and is the fourth law of nature; which may be conceived in this form, *that a man which receiveth benefit from another of mere grace, endeavour that he which giveth it, have no reasonable cause to repent him of his good will.* For no man giveth, but with intention of good to himself; because gift is voluntary; and of all voluntary acts, the object is to every man his own good; of which if men see they shall be frustrated, there will be no beginning of benevolence, or trust; nor consequently of mutual help; nor of reconciliation of one man to another; of *war;* which is contrary to the first and fundamental law of nature, which commandeth men to *seek peace.* The breach of this law, is called *ingratitude;* and hath the same relation to grace, that injustice hath to obligation by covenant.

*The fifth mutual accommodation, or complaisance.* A fifth law of nature, is COMPLAISANCE; that is to say, *that every man strive to accommodate himself to the rest.* For the understanding whereof, we may consider, that there is in men's aptness to society, a diversity of nature, rising from their diversity of affections; not unlike to that we see in stones brought together for building of an edifice. For as that stone which by the asperity, and irregularity of figure, takes more room from others, than itself fills; and for the hardness, cannot be easily made plain, and thereby hindereth the building, is by the builders cast away as unprofitable, and troublesome: so also, a man that by asperity of nature, will strive to retain those things which to himself are superfluous, and to others necessary; and for the stubbornness of his passions, cannot be corrected, is to be left, or cast out of society, as cumbersome thereunto. For seeing every man, not only by right, but also by necessity of nature, is supposed to endeavour all he can, to obtain that which is necessary for his conservation; he that shall oppose himself against it, for things superfluous, is guilty of the war that thereupon is to follow; and therefore doth that, which is contrary to the fundamental law of nature, which commandeth *to seek peace*. The observers of this law, may be called SOCIABLE, the Latins call them *commodi*; the contrary, *stubborn, insociable, forward, intractable*.

*The sixth, facility to pardon*. A sixth law of nature, is this, *that upon caution of the future time, a man ought to pardon the offences past of them that repenting, desire it*. For PARDON, is nothing but granting of peace; which though granted to them that persevere in their hostility, be not peace, but fear; yet not granted to them that give caution of the future time, is sign of an aversion to peace; and therefore contrary to the law of nature.

*The seventh, that in revenges, men respect only the future good*. A seventh is, *that in revenges*, that is, retribution of evil for evil, *men look not at the greatness of the evil past, but the greatness of the good to follow*. Whereby we are forbidden to inflict punishment with any other design, than for correction of the offender, or direction of others. For this law is consequent to the next before it, that commandeth pardon, upon security of the future time. Besides, revenge without respect to the example, and profit to come, is a triumph, or glorying in the hurt of another, tending to no end; for the end is always somewhat to come; and glorying to no end, is vain-glory, and contrary to reason, and to hurt without reason, tendeth to the introduction of war; which is against the law of nature; and is commonly styled by the name of *cruelty*.

*The eight, against contumely*. And because all signs of hatred, or contempt, provoke to fight; insomuch as most men choose rather to hazard their life, than not to be revenged; we may in the eighth place, for a law of nature, set down this precept, *that no man by deed, word, countenance, or gesture, declare hatred, or contempt of another*. The breach of which law, is commonly called *contumely*.

*The ninth, against pride*. The question who is the better man, has no place in the condition of mere nature; where, as has been shewn before, all men are equal. The inequality that now is, has been introduced by the laws civil. I know that

Aristotle in the first book of his *Politics*, for a foundation of his doctrine, maketh men by nature, some more worthy to command, meaning the wiser sort, such as he thought himself to be for his philosophy; others to serve, meaning those that had strong bodies, but were not philosophers as he; as if master and servant were not introduced by consent of men, but by difference of wit: which is not only against reason; but also against experience. For there are very few so foolish, that had not rather govern themselves, than be governed by others: nor when the wise in their own conceit, contend by force, with them who distrust their own wisdom, do they always, or often, or almost at any time, get the victory. If nature therefore have made men equal, that equality is to be acknowledged: or if nature have made men unequal; yet because men that think themselves equal, will not enter into conditions of peace, but upon equal terms, such equality must be admitted. And therefore for the ninth law of nature, I put this, *that every man acknowledge another for his equal by nature.* The breach of this precept is *pride.*

*The tenth, against arrogance.* On this law, dependeth another, *that at the entrance into conditions of peace, no man require to reserve to himself any right, which he is not content should be reserved to every one of the rest.* As it is necessary for all men that seek peace, to lay down certain rights of nature; that is to say, not to have liberty to do all they list: so is it necessary for man's life, to retain some; as right to govern their own bodies; enjoy air, water, motion, ways to go from place to place; and all things else, without which a man cannot live, or not live well. If in this case, at the making of peace, men require for themselves, that which they would not have to be granted to others, they do contrary to the precedent law, that commandeth the acknowledgment of natural equality, and therefore also against the law of nature. The observers of this law, are those we call *modest,* and the breakers *arrogant* men. The Greeks call the violation of this law πλεονεξία; that is, a desire of more than their share.

*The eleventh, equity.* Also if *a man be trusted to judge between man and man,* it is a precept of the law of nature, *that he deal equally between them.* For without that, the controversies of men cannot be determined but by war. He therefore that is partial in judgment, doth what in him lies, to deter men from the use of judges, and arbitrators; and consequently, against the fundamental law of nature, is the cause of war.

The observance of this law, from the equal distribution to each man, of that which in reason belongeth to him, is called EQUITY, and, as I have said before, distributive justice: the violation, *acception of persons*, προσωποληψία.

*The twelfth, equal use of things common*. And from this followeth another law, *that such things as cannot be divided, be enjoyed in common, if it can be; and if the equality of the thing permit, without stint; otherwise proportionably to the number of them that have right*. For otherwise the distribution is unequal, and contrary to equity.

*The thirteenth, of lot*. But some things there be, that can neither be divided, nor enjoyed in common. Then, the law of nature, which prescribeth equity, requireth, *that the entire right; or else, making the use alternate, the first possession, be determined by lot*. For equal distribution, is of the law of nature; and other means of equal distribution cannot be imagined.

*The fourteenth, of primogeniture, and first seizing*. Of *lots* there be two sorts, *arbitrary*, and *natural*. Arbitrary, is that which is agreed on by the competitors: natural, is either *primogeniture*, which the Greek calls κληρονομία, which signifies, *given by lot;* or *first seizure*.

And therefore those things which cannot be enjoyed in common, nor divided, ought to be adjudged to the first possessor; and in some cases in the first born, as acquired by lot.

*The fifteenth, of mediators*. It is also a law of nature, *that all men that mediate peace, be allowed safe conduct*. For the law that commandeth peace, as the *end*, commandeth intercession, as the *means;* and to intercession the means is safe conduct.

*The sixteenth, of submission to arbitrement*. And because, though men be never so willing to observe these laws, there may nevertheless arise questions concerning a man's action; first, whether it were done, or not done; secondly, if done, whether against the law, or not against the law; the former whereof, is called a question *of fact;* the latter a question *of right*, therefore unless the parties to the question, covenant mutually to stand to the sentence of another, they are as far from peace as ever. This other to whose sentence they submit is called an ARBITRATOR. And therefore it is of the law of nature, *that they that are at controversy, submit their right to the judgment of an arbitrator*.

*The seventeenth, no man is his own judge*. And seeing

every man is presumed to do all things in order to his own benefit, no man is a fit arbitrator in his own cause; and if he were never so fit; yet equity allowing to each party equal benefit, if one be admitted to be judge, the other is to be admitted also; and so the controversy, that is, the cause of war, remains, against the law of nature.

*The eighteenth, no man to be judge, that has in him a natural cause of partiality.* For the same reason no man in any cause ought to be received for arbitrator, to whom greater profit, or honour, or pleasure apparently ariseth out of the victory of one party, than of the other: for he hath taken, though an unavoidable bribe, yet a bribe; and no man can be obliged to trust him. And thus also the controversy, and the condition of war remaineth, contrary to the law of nature.

*The nineteenth, of witnesses.* And in a controversy of *fact*, the judge being to give no more credit to one, than to the other, if there be no other arguments, must give credit to a third; or to a third and fourth; or more: for else the question is undecided, and left to force, contrary to the law of nature.

These are the laws of nature, dictating peace, for a means of the conservation of men in multitudes; and which only concern the doctrine of civil society. There be other things tending to the destruction of particular men; as drunkenness, and all other parts of intemperance; which may therefore also be reckoned amongst those things which the law of nature hath forbidden; but are not necessary to be mentioned, nor are pertinent enough to this place.

*A rule, by which the laws of nature may easily be examined.* And though this may seem too subtle a deduction of the laws of nature, to be taken notice of by all men; whereof the most part are too busy in getting food, and the rest too negligent to understand; yet to leave all men inexcusable, they have been contracted into one easy sum, intelligible even to the meanest capacity; and that is, *Do not that to another, which thou wouldest not have done to thyself;* which sheweth him, that he had no more to do in learning the laws of nature, but, when weighing the actions of other men with his own, they seem too heavy, to put them into the other part of the balance, and his own into their place, that his own passions, and self-love, may add nothing to the weight; and then there is none of these laws of nature that will not appear unto him very reasonable.

*The laws of nature oblige in conscience always, but in*

*effect then only when there is security.* The laws of nature oblige *in foro interno;* that is to say, they bind to a desire they should take place: but *in foro externo;* this is, to the putting them in act, not always. For he that should be modest, and tractable, and perform all he promises, in such time, and place, where no man else should do so, should but make himself a prey to others, and procure his own certain ruin, contrary to the ground of all laws of nature, which tend to nature's preservation. And again, he that having sufficient security, that others shall observe the same laws towards him, observes them not himself, seeketh not peace, but war; and consequently the destruction of his nature by violence.

And whatsoever laws bind *in foro interno,* may be broken, not only by a fact contrary to the law, but also by a fact according to it, in case a man think it contrary. For though his action in this case, be according to the law; yet his purpose was against the law; which, where the obligation is *in foro interno,* is a breach.

*The laws of nature are eternal.* The laws of nature are immutable and eternal; for injustice, ingratitude, arrogance, pride, iniquity, acception of persons, and the rest, can never be made lawful. For it can never be that war shall preserve life, and peace destroy it.

*And yet easy.* The same laws, because they oblige only to a desire, and endeavour, I mean an unfeigned and constant endeavour, are easy to be observed. For in that they require nothing but endeavor, he that endeavoureth their performance, fufilleth them; and he that fulfilleth the law, is just.

*The science of these laws, is the true moral philosophy.* And the science of them, is the true and only moral philosophy. For moral philosophy is nothing else but the science of what is *good,* and *evil,* in the conversation, and society of mankind. *Good,* and *evil,* are names that signify our appetites, and aversions; which in different tempers, customs, and doctrines of men, are different: and divers men, differ not only in their judgment, on the senses of what is pleasant, and unpleasant to the taste, smell, hearing, touch, and sight; but also of what is conformable, or disagreeable to reason, in the actions of common life. Nay, the same man, in divers times, differs from himself; and one time praiseth, that is, calleth good, what another time he dispraiseth, and calleth evil: from whence arise disputes, controversies, and at last war. And therefore so long as a man is in the condition of mere nature, which is a condition of war, as private appetite is the measure of good, and evil: and consequently all men agree on this, that peace is good, and therefore also the way, or means of peace, which, as I have shewed before, are *justice, gratitude, modesty, equity, mercy,* and the rest of the laws of nature, are good; that is to say; *moral virtues;* and their contrary *vices,* evil. Now the science of virtue and vice, is moral philosophy; and therefore the true doctrine of the laws of nature, is the true moral philosophy. But the writers of moral philosophy, though they acknowledge the same virtues and vices; yet not seeing wherein consisted their goodness; nor that they come to be praised, as the means of peaceable, sociable, and comfortable living, place them in a mediocrity of passions: as if not the cause, but the degree of daring, made fortitude; or not the cause, but the quantity of a gift, made liberality.

These dictates of reason, men used to call by the names of laws, but improperly: for they are but conclusions, or theorems concerning what conduceth to the conservation and defence of themselves; whereas law, properly, is the word of him, that by right hath command over others. But yet if we consider the same theorems, as delivered in the word of God, that by right commandeth all things; then are they properly called laws.

# Chapter 16

## Of Persons, Authors, and Things Personated

*A person what.* A person, is he, *whose words or actions are considered, either as his own, or as representing the words or actions of another man, or of any other thing, to whom they are attributed, whether truly or by fiction.*

*Person natural, and artificial.* When they are considered as his own, then is he called a *natural person:* and when they are considered as representing the words and actions of another, then is he a *feigned* or *artificial person.*

*The word person, whence.* The word person is Latin: instead whereof the Greeks have πρόσωπον, which signifies the *face*, as *persona* in Latin signifies the *disguise*, or *outward appearance* of a man, counterfeited on the stage; and sometimes more particularly that part of it, which disguiseth the face, as a mask or vizard: and from the stage, hath been translated to any representer of speech and action, as well in tribunals, as theatres. So that a *person*, is the same that an *actor* is, both on the stage and in common conversation; and to *personate*, is to *act*, or *represent* himself, or another; and he that acteth another, is said to bear his person, or act in his name; in which sense Cicero useth it where he says, *Unus sustineo tres personas; mei, adversarii, et judicis:* I bear three persons; my own, my adversary's, and the judge's; and is called in divers occasions, diversely; as a *representer*, or *representative*, a *lieutenant*, a *vicar*, an *attorney*, a *deputy*, a *procurator*, an *actor*, and the like.

*Actor. Author. Authority.* Of persons artificial, some have their words and actions *owned* by those whom they represent. And then the person is the *actor;* and he that owneth his words and actions, is the AUTHOR: in which case the actor acteth by authority. For that which in speaking of goods and possessions, is called an *owner*, and in Latin *dominus*, in Greek κύριος speaking of actions, is called author. And as the right of possession, is called dominion; so the right of doing any action, is called AUTHORITY. So that by authority, is always understood a right of doing any act; and *done by authority*, done by commission, or licence from him whose right it is.

*Covenants by authority, bind the author.* From hence it followeth, that when the actor maketh a covenant by authority, he bindeth thereby the author, no less than if he had made it himself; and no less subjecteth him to all the consequences of the same. And therefore all that hath been said formerly, (chap. 14) of the nature of covenants between man and man in their natural capacity, is true also when they are made by their actors, representers, or procurators, that have authority from them, so far forth as is in their commission, but no further.

And therefore he that maketh a covenant with the actor, or representer, not knowing the authority he hath, doth it at his own peril. For no man is obliged by a covenant, whereof he is not author; nor consequently by a covenant made against, or beside the authority he gave.

*But not the actor.* When the actor doth any thing against the law of nature by command of the author, if he be obliged by former covenant to obey him, not he, but the author breaketh the law of nature; for though the action be against the law of nature; yet it is not his: but contrarily, to refuse to do it, is against the law of nature, that forbiddeth breach of covenant.

*The authority is to be shown.* And he that maketh a covenant with the author, by mediation of the actor, not knowing what authority he hath, but only takes his word; in case such authority be not made manifest unto him upon demand, is no longer obliged: for the covenant made with the author, is not valid, without his counter-assurance. But if he that so covenanteth, knew beforehand he was to expect no other assurance, than the actor's word; then is the covenant valid; because the actor in this case maketh himself the author. And therefore, as when the authority is evident, the covenant obligeth the author, not the actor; so when the authority is feigned, it obligeth the actor only; there being no author but himself.

*Things personated, inanimate.* There are few things, that are incapable of being represented by fiction. Inanimate things, as a church, an hospital, a bridge, may be personated by a rector, master, or overseer. But things inanimate, cannot be authors, nor therefore give authority to their actors: yet the actors may have authority to procure their maintenance, given them by those that are owners, or governors of those things. And therefore, such things cannot be personated, before there be some state of civil government.

*Irrational.* Likewise children, fools, and madmen that have no use of reason, may be personated by guardians, or curators; but can be no authors, during that time, of any action done by them, longer than, when they shall recover the use of reason, they shall judge the same reasonable. Yet during the folly, he that hath right of governing them, may give authority to the guardian. But this again has no place but in a state civil, because before such estate, there is no dominion of persons.

*False gods.* An idol, or mere figment of the brain, may be personated; as were the gods of the heathen: which by such officers as the state appointed, were personated, and held possessions, and other goods, and rights, which men from time to time dedicated, and consecrated unto them. But idols cannot be authors: for an idol is nothing. The authority proceeded from the state: and therefore before introduction of civil government, the gods of the heathen could not be personated.

*The true God.* The true God may be personated. As he was; first, by Moses; who governed the Israelites, that were not his, but God's people, not in his own name, with *hoc dicit Moses;* but in God's name, with *hoc dicit Dominus.* Secondly, by the Son of man, his own Son, our blessed Saviour Jesus Christ, that came to reduce the Jews, and induce all nations into the kingdom of his father; not as of himself, but as sent from his father. And thirdly, by the Holy Ghost, or Comforter, speaking, and working in the Apostles: which Holy Ghost, was a Comforter that came not of himself; but was sent, and proceeded from them both.

*A multitude of men, how one person.* A multitude of men, are made *one* person, when they are by one man, or one person, represented; so that it be done with the consent of every one of that multitude in particular. For it is the *unity* of the representer, not the *unity* of the represented, that maketh the person *one.* And it is the representer that beareth the person, and but one person: and *unity,* cannot otherwise be understood in multitude.

*Every one is author.* And because the multitude naturally is not *one,* but *many;* they cannot be understood for one; but many authors, of every thing their representative saith, or doth in their name; every man giving their common representer, authority from himself in particular; and owning all the actions the representer doth, in case they give him authority without stint: otherwise, when they limit him in what, and how far he shall represent them, none of them owneth more that they gave him commission to act.

*An actor may be many men made one by plurality of voices.* And if the representative consist of many men, the voice of the greater number, must be considered as the voice of them all. For if the lesser number pronounce, for example, in the affirmative, and the greater in the negative, there will be negatives more than enough to destroy the affirmatives; and thereby the excess of negatives, standing uncontradicted, are the only voice the representative hath.

*Representatives, when the number is even, unprofitable.* And a representative of even number, especially when the number is not great, whereby the contradictory voices are oftentimes equal, is therefore oftentimes mute, and incapable of action. Yet in some cases contradictory voices equal in number, may determine a question; as in condemning, or absolving, equality of votes, even in that they condemn not, do absolve; but not on the contrary condemn, in that they absolve not. For when a cause is heard; not to condemn, is to absolve: but on the contrary, to say that not absolving, is condemning, is not true. The like it is in a deliberation of executing presently, or deferring till another time: for when the voices are equal, the not decreeing execution, is a decree of dilation.

*Negative voice.* Or if the number be odd, as three, or more, men or assemblies; whereof every one has by a negative voice, authority to take away the effect of all the affirmative voices of the rest, this number is no representative; because by the diversity of opinions, and interests of men, it becomes oftentimes, and in cases of the greatest consequence, a mute person, and unapt, as for many things else, so for the government of a multitude, especially in time of war.

Of authors there be two sorts. The first simply so called; which I have before defined to be him, that owneth the action of another simply. The second is he, that owneth an action, or covenant of another conditionally; that is to say, he undertaketh to do it, if the other doth it not, at, or before a certain time. And these authors conditional, are generally called SURETIES, in Latin, *fidejussores*, and *sponsores*; and particularly for debt, *prædes;* and for appearance before a judge, or magistrate, *vades.*

# THE SECOND PART
# OF COMMONWEALTH

Chapter 17

## Of the Causes, Generation, and Definition of a Commonwealth

*The end of commonwealth, particular security.* The final cause, end, or design of men, who naturally love liberty, and dominion over others, in the introduction of that restraint upon themselves, in which we see them live in commonwealths, is the foresight of their own preservation, and of a more contented life thereby; that is to say, of getting themselves out from that miserable condition of war, which is necessarily consequent, as hath been shown (chapter 13), to the natural passions of men, when there is no visible power to keep them in awe, and tie them by fear of punishment to the performance of their covenants, and observation of those laws of nature set down in the fourteenth and fifteenth chapters.

*Which is not to be had from the law of nature.* For the laws of nature, as *justice, equity, modesty, mercy,* and, in sum, *doing to others, as we would be done to,* of themselves, without the terror of some power, to cause them to be observed, are contrary to our natural passions, that carry us to partiality, pride, revenge, and the like. And covenants, without the sword, are but words, and of no strength to secure a man at all. Therefore notwithstanding the laws of nature (which every one hath then kept, when he has the will to keep them, when he can do it safely) if there be no power erected, or not great enough for our security; every man will, and may lawfully rely on his own strength and art, for caution against all other men. And in all places, where men have lived by small families, to rob and spoil one another, has been a trade, and so far from being reputed against the law of nature, that the greater spoils they gained, the greater was their honour; and men observed no other laws therein, but the laws of honour; that is, to abstain from cruelty, leaving to men their lives, and instruments of husbandry. And as small families did then; so now do cities and kingdoms which are but greater families, for their own security, enlarge their dominions, upon all pretences of danger, and fear of invasion, or assistance that may be given to invaders, and endeavour as much as they can, to subdue, or weaken their neighbours, by open force, and secret arts, for want of other caution, justly; and are remembered for it in after ages with honour.

*Nor from the conjunction of a few men or families.* Nor is it the joining together of a small number of men, that gives them this security; because in small numbers, small additions on the one side or the other, make the advantage of strength so great, as is sufficient to carry the victory; and therefore gives encouragement to an invasion. The multitude sufficient to confide in for our security, is not determined by any certain number, but by comparison with the enemy we fear; and is then sufficient, when the odds of the enemy is not of so visible and conspicuous moment, to determine the event of war, as to move him to attempt.

*Nor from a great multitude, unless directed by one judgment.* And be there never so great a multitude; yet if their actions be directed according to their particular judgments, and particular appetites, they can expect thereby no defence, nor protection, neither against a common enemy, nor against the injuries of one another. For being distracted in opinions concerning the best use and application of their strength, they do not help but hinder one another; and reduce their strength by mutual opposition to nothing: whereby they are easily, not only subdued by a very few that agree together; but also when there is no common enemy, they make war upon each other, for their particular interests. For if we could suppose a great multitude of men to consent in the observation of justice, and other laws of nature, without a common power to keep them all in awe; we might as well suppose all mankind to do the same; and then there neither would be, nor need to be any civil government, or commonwealth at all; because there would be peace without subjection.

*And that continually.* Nor is it enough for the security, which men desire should last all the time of their life, that they be governed, and directed by one judgment, for a limited time; as in one battle, or one war. For though they obtain a victory by their unanimous endeavour against a foreign enemy; yet afterwards, when either they have no common enemy, or he that by one part is held for an enemy, is by another part held for a friend, they must needs by the differ-

ence of their interests dissolve, and fall again into a war
amongst themselves.

*Why certain creatures without reason, or speech, do never-
theless live in society, without any coercive power.* It is true,
that certain living creatures, as bees, and ants, live sociably
one with another, which are therefore by Aristotle numbered
amongst political creatures; and yet have no other direction,
than their particular judgments and appetites; nor speech,
whereby one of them can signify to another, what he thinks
expedient for the common benefit: and therefore some man
may perhaps desire to know, why mankind cannot do the
same. To which I answer,

First, that men are continually in competition for honour
and dignity, which these creatures are not; and consequently
amongst men there ariseth on that ground, envy and hatred,
and finally war; but amongst these not so.

Secondly, that amongst these creatures, the common good
differeth not from the private; and being by nature inclined
to their private, they procure thereby the common benefit.
But man, whose joy consisteth in comparing himself with
other men, can relish nothing but what is eminent.

Thirdly, that these creatures, having not, as man, the use of
reason, do not see, nor think they see any fault, in the administration of their common business; whereas amongst men,
there are very many, that think themselves wiser, and abler
to govern the public, better than the rest; and these strive to
reform and innovate, one this way, another that way; and
thereby bring it into distraction and civil war.

Fourthly, that these creatures, though they have some use
of voice, in making known to one another their desires, and
other affections; yet they want that art of words, by which
some men can represent to others, that which is good, in the
likeness of evil; and evil, in the likeness of good; and aug-
ment, or diminish the apparent greatness of good and evil;
discontenting men, and troubling their peace at their pleasure.

Fifthly, irrational creatures cannot distinguish between *injury,* and *damage;* and therefore as long as they be at ease,
they are not offended with their fellows: whereas man is then
most troublesome, when he is most at ease: for then it is that
he loves to shew his wisdom, and control the actions of them
that govern the commonwealth.

Lastly, the agreement of these creatures is natural; that of
men, is by covenant only, which is artificial: and therefore it

is no wonder if there be somewhat else required, besides covenant, to make their agreement constant and lasting; which is a common power, to keep them in awe, and to direct their actions to the common benefit.

*The generation of a commonwealth. The definition of a commonwealth.* The only way to erect such a common power, as may be able to defend them from the invasion of foreigners, and the injuries of one another, and thereby to secure them in such sort, as that by their own industry, and by the fruits of the earth, they may nourish themselves and live contentedly; is, to confer all their power and strength upon one man, or upon one assembly of men, that may reduce all their wills, by plurality of voices, unto one will: which is as much as to say, to appoint one man, or assembly of men, to bear their person; and every one to own, and acknowledge himself to be author of whatsoever he that so beareth their person, shall act, or cause to be acted, in those things which concern the common peace and safety; and therein to submit their wills, every one to his will, and their judgments, to his judgment. This is more than consent, or concord; it is a real unity of them all, in one and the same person, made by covenant of every man with every man, in such manner, as if every man should say to every man, *I authorize and give up my right of governing myself, to this man, or to this assembly of men, on this condition, that thou give up thy right to him, and authorize all his actions in like manner.* This done, the multitude so united in one person, is called a COMMONWEALTH, in Latin CIVITAS. This is the generation of that great LEVIATHAN, or rather, to speak more reverently, of that *mortal god,* to which we owe under the *immortal God,* our peace and defence. For by this authority, given him by every particular man in the commonwealth, he hath the use of so much power and strength conferred on him, that by terror thereof, he is enabled to form the wills of them all, to peace at home, and mutual aid against their enemies abroad. And in him consisteth the essence of the commonwealth; which, to define it, is *one person, of whose acts a great multitude, by mutual covenants one with another, have made themselves every one the author, to the end he may use the strength and means of them all, as he shall think expedient, for their peace and common defence.*

*Sovereign, and subject, what.* And he that carrieth this person is called SOVEREIGN, and said to have *sovereign power;* and every one besides, his SUBJECT.

The attaining to this sovereign power, is by two ways. One by natural force; as when a man maketh his children, to submit themselves, and their childen to his government, as being able to destroy them if they refuse; or by war subdueth his enemies to his will, giving them their lives on that condition. The other, is when men agree amongst themselves, to submit to some man, or assembly of men, voluntarily, on confidence to be protected by him against all others. This latter, may be called a political commonwealth, or commonwealth by *institution;* and the former, a commonwealth by *acquisition.* And first, I shall speak of a commonwealth by institution.

## Chapter 18

## Of the Rights of Sovereigns by Institution

*The act of instituting a commonwealth, what.* A *commonwealth* is said to be *instituted,* when a *multitude* of men do agree, and *covenant, every one, with every one,* that to whatsoever *man,* or *assembly of men,* shall be given by the major part, the *right* to *present* the person of them all, that is to say, to be their *representative;* every one, as well he that *voted for it,* as he that *voted against it,* shall *authorize* all the actions and judgments, of that man, or assembly of men, in the same manner, as if they were his own, to the end, to live peaceably amongst themselves, and be protected against other men.

*The consequences to such institutions, are:* From this institution of a commonwealth are derived all the *rights,* and *faculties* of him, or them, on whom the sovereign power is conferred by the consent of the people assembled.

1. *The subjects cannot change the form of government.* First, because they covenant, it is to be understood, they are not obliged by former covenant to any thing repugnant hereunto. And consequently they that have already instituted a commonwealth, being thereby bound by covenant, to own the actions, and judgments of one, cannot lawfully make a new covenant, amongst themselves, to be obedient to any other, in any thing whatsoever, without his permission. And therefore, they that are subjects to a monarch, cannot without his leave cast off monarchy, and return to the confusion of a disunited multitude; nor transfer their person from him that beareth it, to another man, or other assembly of men: for they are bound, every man to every man, to own, and be reputed author of all, that he that already is their sovereign, shall do, and judge fit to be done: so that any one man dissenting, all the rest should break their covenant made to that man, which is injustice: and they have also every man given the sovereignty to him that beareth their person; and therefore if they depose him, they take from him that which is his own, and so again it is injustice. Besides, if he that attempteth to depose his sovereign, be killed, or punished by him for such attempt, he is author of his own punishment, as being by the institu-

tion, author of all his sovereign shall do: and because it is injustice for a man to do any thing, for which he may be punished by his own authority, he is also upon that title, unjust. And whereas some men have pretended for their disobedience to their sovereign, a new covenant, made, not with men, but with God; this also is unjust: for there is no covenant with God, but by mediation of somebody that representeth God's person; which none doth but God's lieutenant, who hath the sovereignty under God. But this pretence of covenant with God, is so evident a lie, even in the pretenders' own consciences, that it is not only an act of an unjust, but also of a vile, and unmanly disposition.

2. *Sovereign power cannot be forfeited.* Secondly, because the right of bearing the person of them all, is given to him they make sovereign, by covenant only of one to another, and not of him to any of them; there can happen no breach of covenant on the part of the sovereign; and consequently none of his subjects, by any pretence of forfeiture, can be freed from his subjection. That he which is made sovereign maketh no covenant with his subjects beforehand, is manifest; because either he must make it with the whole multitude, as one party to the covenant; or he must make a several covenant with every man. With the whole, as one party, it is impossible; because as yet they are not one person: and if he make so many several covenants as there be men, those covenants after he hath the sovereignty are void; because what act soever can be pretended by any one of them for breach thereof, is the act both of himself, and of all the rest, because done in the person, and by the right of every one of them in particular. Besides, if any one, or more of them, pretend a breach of the covenant made by the sovereign at his institution; and others, or one other of his subjects, or himself alone, pretend there was no such breach, there is in this case, no judge to decide the controversy; it returns therefore to the sword again; and every man recovereth the right of protecting himself by his own strength, contrary to the design they had in the institution. It is therefore in vain to grant sovereignty by way of precedent covenant. The opinion that any monarch receiveth his power by covenant, this is to say, on condition, proceedeth from want of understanding this easy truth, that covenants being but words and breath, have no force to oblige, contain, constrain, or protect any man, but what it has from the public sword; that is, from the untied hands of that man, or assembly of men that hath the sovereignty, and

whose actions are avouched by them all, and performed by the strength of them all, in him united. But when an assembly of men is made sovereign; then no man imagineth any such covenant to have passed in the institution; for no man is so dull as to say, for example, the people of Rome made a covenant with the Romans, to hold the sovereignty on such or such conditions; which not performed, the Romans might lawfully depose the Roman people. That men see not the reason to be alike in a monarchy, and in a popular government, proceedeth from the ambition of some, that are kinder to the government of an assembly, whereof they may hope to participate, than of monarchy, which they despair to enjoy.

3. *No man can without injustice protest against the institution of the sovereign declared by the major part.* Thirdly, because the major part hath by consenting voices declared a sovereign; he that dissented must now consent with the rest; that is, be contented to avow all the actions he shall do, or else justly be destroyed by the rest. For if he voluntarily entered into the congregation of them that were assembled, he sufficiently declared thereby his will, and therefore tacitly covenanted, to stand to what the major part should ordain: and therefore if he refuse to stand thereto, or make protestation against any of their decrees, he does contrary to his covenant, and therefore unjustly. And whether he be of the congregation, or not; and whether his consent be asked, or not, he must either submit to their decrees, or be left in the condition of war he was in before; wherein he might without injustice be destroyed by any man whatsoever.

4. *The sovereign's actions cannot be justly accused by the subject.* Fourthly, because every subject is by this institution author of all the actions, and judgments of the sovereign instituted; it follows, that whatsoever he doth, it can be no injury to any of his subjects; nor ought he to be by any of them accused of injustice. For he that doth anything by authority from another, doth therein no injury to him by whose authority he acteth: but by this institution of a commonwealth, every particular man is author of all the sovereign doth: and consequently he that complaineth of injury from his sovereign, complaineth of that whereof he himself is author; and therefore ought not to accuse any man but himself; no nor himself of injury; because to do injury to one's self, is impossible. It is true that they that have sovereign power may commit iniquity; but not injustice, or injury in the proper signification.

5. *Whatsoever the sovereign doth is unpunishable by the subject.* Fifthly, and consequently to that which was said last, no man that hath sovereign power can justly be put to death, or otherwise in any manner by his subjects punished. For seeing every subject is author of the actions of his sovereign; he punisheth another for the actions committed by himself.

6. *The sovereign is judge of what is necessary for the peace and defence of his subjects.* And because the end of this institution, is the peace and defence of them all; and whosoever has right to the end, has right to the means; it belongeth of right, to whatsoever man, or assembly that hath the sovereignty, to be judge both of the means of peace and defence, and also of the hindrances, and disturbances of the same; and to do whatsoever he shall think necessary to be done, both beforehand, for the preserving of peace and security, by prevention of discord at home, and hostility from abroad; and, when peace and security are lost, for the recovery of the same. And therefore,

*And judge of what doctrines are fit to be taught them.* Sixthly, it is annexed to the sovereignty, to be judge of what opinions and doctrines are averse, and what conducing to peace; and consequently, on what occasions, how far, and what men are to be trusted withal, in speaking to multitudes of people; and who shall examine the doctrines of all books before they be published. For the actions of men proceed from their opinions; and in the well-governing of opinions, consisteth the well-governing of men's actions, in order to their peace, and concord. And though in matter of doctrine, nothing ought to be regarded but the truth; yet this is not repugnant to regulating the same by peace. For doctrine repugnant to peace, can no more be true, than peace and concord can be against the law of nature. It is true, that in a commonwealth, where by the negligence, or unskilfulness of governors, and teachers, false doctrines are by time generally received; the contrary truths may be generally offensive. Yet the most sudden, and rough busling in of a new truth, that can be, does never break the peace, but only sometimes awake the war. For those men that are so remissly governed, that they dare take up arms to defend, or introduce an opinion, are still in war; and their condition not peace, but only a cessation of arms for fear of one another; and they live, as it were, in the precincts of battle continually. It belongeth therefore to him that hath the sovereign power, to be judge, or constitute all judges of opinions and doctrines, as a thing necessary to peace; thereby to prevent discord and civil war.

7. *The right of making rules; whereby the subjects may every man know what is so his own, as no other subject can without injustice take it from him.* Seventhly, is annexed to the sovereignty, the whole power of prescribing the rules, whereby every man may know, what goods he may enjoy, and what actions he may do, without being molested by any of his fellow-subjects; and this is it men call *propriety*. For before constitution of sovereign power, as hath already been shown, all men had right to all things; which necessarily causeth war: and therefore this propriety, being necessary to peace, and depending on sovereign power, is the act of that power, in order to the public peace. These rules of propriety, or *meum* and *tuum*, and of *good, evil, lawful,* and *unlawful* in the actions of subjects, are the civil laws; that is to say, the laws of each commonwealth in particular; though the name of civil law be now restrained to the ancient civil laws of the city of Rome; which being the head of a great part of the world, her laws at that time were in these parts the civil law.

8. *To him also belongeth the right of judicature and decision of controversy.* Eighthly, is annexed to the sovereignty, the right of judicature; that is to say, of hearing and deciding all controversies, which may arise concerning law, either civil, or natural; or concerning fact. For without the decision of controversies, there is no protection of one subject, against the injuries of another; the laws concerning *meum* and *tuum* are in vain; and to every man remaineth, from the natural and necessary appetite of his own conservation, the right of protecting himself by his private strength, which is the condition of war, and contrary to the end for which every commonwealth is instituted.

9. *And of making war, and peace, as he shall think best.* Ninthly, is annexed to the sovereignty, the right of making war and peace with other nations, and commonwealths; that is to say, of judging when it is for the public good, and how great forces are to be assembled, armed, and paid for that end; and to levy money upon the subjects, to defray the expenses thereof. For the power by which the people are to be defended, consisteth in their armies; and the strength of an army, in the union of their strength under one command; which command the sovereign instituted, therefore hath; because the command of the *militia*, without other institution, maketh him that hath it sovereign. And therefore whosoever

is made general of an army, he that hath the sovereign power is always generalissimo.

10. *And of choosing all counsellors and ministers, both of peace and war.* Tenthly, is annexed to the sovereignty, the choosing of all counsellors, ministers, magistrates, and officers, both in peace, and war. For seeing the sovereign is charged with the end, which is the common peace and defence, he is understood to have power to use such means, as he shall think most fit for his discharge.

11. *And of rewarding and punishing, and that (where no former law hath determined the measure of it) arbitrarily.* Eleventhly, to the sovereign is committed the power of rewarding with riches, or honour, and of punishing with corporal or pecuniary punishment, or with ignominy, every subject according to the law he hath formerly made; or if there be no law made, according as he shall judge most to conduce to the encouraging of men to serve the commonwealth, or deterring of them from doing disservice to the same.

12. *And of honour and order.* Lastly, considering what value men are naturally apt to set upon themselves; what respect they look for from others; and how little they value other men; from whence continually arise amongst them, emulation, quarrels, factions, and at last war, to the destroying of one another, and diminution of their strength against a common enemy; it is necessary that there be laws of honour, and a public rate of the worth of such men as have deserved, or are able to deserve well of the commonwealth; and that there be force in the hands of some or other, to put those laws in execution. But it hath already been shown, that not only the whole *militia*, or forces of the commonwealth; but also the judicature of all controversies, is annexed to the sovereignty. To the sovereign therefore it belongeth also to give titles of honour; and to appoint what order of place, and dignity, each man shall hold; and what signs of respect, in public or private meetings, they shall give to one another.

*These rights are indivisible.* These are the rights, which make the essence of sovereignty; and which are the marks, whereby a man may discern in what man, or assembly of men, the sovereign power is placed, and resideth. For these are incommunicable, and inseparable. The power to coin money; to dispose of the estate and persons of infant heirs; to have præemption in markets; and all other statute prerogatives, may be transferred by the sovereign; and yet the power to protect his subjects be retained. But if he transfer the *militia,* he retains the judicature in vain, for want of execution of the laws: or if he grant away the power of raising money; the *militia* is in vain; or if he give away the government of doctrines, men will be frighted into rebellion with the fear of spirits. And so if we consider any one of the said rights, we shall presently see, that the holding of all the rest will produce no effect, in the conservation of peace and justice, the end for which all commonwealths are instituted. And this division is it, whereof it is said, *a kingdom divided in itself cannot stand:* for unless this division precede, division into opposite armies can never happen. If there had not first been an opinion received of the greatest part of England, that these powers were divided between the King, and the Lords, and the House of Commons, the people had never been divided and fallen into this civil war; first between those that disagreed in politics; and after between the dissenters about the liberty of religion; which have so instructed men in this point of sovereign right, that there be few now in England that do not see, that these rights are inseparable, and will be so generally acknowledged at the next return of peace; and so continue, till their miseries are forgotten; and no longer, except the vulgar be better taught than they have hitherto been.

*And can by no grant pass away without direct renouncing of the sovereign power.* And because they are essential and inseparable rights, it follows necessarily, that in whatsoever words any of them seem to be granted away, yet if the sovereign power itself be not in direct terms renounced, and the name of sovereign no more given by the grantees to him that grants them, the grant is void: for when he has granted all he can, if we grant back the sovereignty, all is restored, as inseparably annexed thereunto.

*The power and honour of subjects vanisheth in the presence of the power sovereign.* This great authority being indivisible, and inseparably annexed to the sovereignty, there is little ground for the opinion of them, that say of sovereign kings, though they be *singulis majores,* of greater power than every one of their subjects, yet they be *universis minores,* of less power than them all together. For if by *all together,* they mean not the collective body as one person, then *all together,* and *every one,* signify the same; and the speech is absurd. But if by *all together,* they understand them as one person, which person the sovereign bears, then the power of all together, is the same with the sovereign's power; and so again the speech is absurd: which absurdity they see well enough, when the sovereignty is in an assembly of the people; but in a monarch they see it not; and yet the power of sovereignty is the same in whomsoever it be placed.

And as the power, so also the honour of the sovereign, ought to be greater, than that of any, or all the subjects. For in the sovereignty is the fountain of honor. The dignities of lord, earl, duke, and prince are his creatures. As in the presence of the master, the servants are equal, and without any honour at all; so are the subjects, in the presence of the sovereign. And though they shine some more, some less, when they are out of his sight; yet in his presence, they shine no more than the stars in the presence of the sun.

*Sovereign power not so hurtful as the want of it, and the hurt proceeds for the greatest part from not submitting readily to a less.* But a man may here object, that the condition of subjects is very miserable; as being obnoxious to the lusts, and other irregular passions of him, or them that have so unlimited a power in their hands. And commonly they that live under a monarch, think it the fault of monarchy; and they that live under the government of democracy, or other sovereign assembly, attribute all the, inconvenience to that form of commonwealth; whereas the power in all forms, if they be perfect enough to protect them, is the same: not considering that the state of man can never be without some incommodity or other; and that the greatest, that in any form of government can possibly happen to the people in general, is scarce sensible in respect of the miseries, and horrible calamities, that accompany a civil war, or that dissolute condition of masterless men, without subjection to laws, and a coercive power to tie their hands from rapine and revenge: nor considering that the greatest pressure of sovereign governors, proceedeth not from any delight, or profit they can expect in the damage or weakening of their subjects, in whose vigour, consisteth their own strength and glory; but in the restiveness of themselves, that unwillingly contributing to their own defence, make it necessary for their governors to draw from them what they can in time of peace, that they may have means on any emergent occasion, or sudden need, to resist, or take advantage on their enemies. For all men are by nature provided of notable multiplying glasses, that is their passions and self-love, through which, every little payment appeareth a great grievance; but are destitute of those prospective glasses, namely moral and civil science, to see afar off the miseries that hang over them, and cannot without such payments be avoided.

## Chapter 19

### Of the several kinds of Commonwealth by Institution; and of Succession to the Sovereign Power

*The different forms of commonwealths but three.* The difference of commonwealths, consisteth in the difference of the sovereign, or the person representative of all and every one of the multitude. And because the sovereignty is either in one man, or in an assembly of more than one; and into that assembly either every man hath right to enter, or not every one, but certain men distinguished from the rest; it is manifest, there can be but three kinds of commonwealth. For the representative must needs be one man, or more: and if more, then it is the assembly of all, or but of a part. When the representative is one man, then is the commonwealth a MONARCHY: when an assembly of all that will come together, then it is a DEMOCRACY, or popular commonwealth: when an assembly of a part only, then it is called an ARISTOCRACY. Other kind of commonwealth there can be none: for either one, or more, or all, must have the sovereign power, which I have shown to be indivisible, entire.

*Tyranny and oligarchy, but different names of monarchy, and aristocracy.* There be other names of government, in the histories, and books of policy; as *tyranny*, and *oligarchy*: but they are not the names of other forms of government, but of the same forms misliked For they that are discontented under *monarchy*, call it *tyranny*; and they that are displeased with *aristocracy*, call it *oligarchy*: so also, they which find themselves grieved under a *democracy*, call it *anarchy*, which signifies want of government; and yet I think no man believes, that want of government, is any new kind of government: nor by the same reason ought they to believe, that the government is of one kind, when they like it, and another, when they mislike it, or are oppressed by the governors.

*Subordinate representatives dangerous.* It is manifest, that men who are in absolute liberty, may, if they please, give authority to one man, to represent them every one; as well as give such authority to any assembly of men whatsoever; and consequently may subject themselves, if they think good, to a monarch, as absolutely, as to any other representative. Therefore, where there is already erected a sovereign power, there can be no other representative of the same people, but only to certain particular ends, by the sovereign limited. For that were to erect two sovereigns; and every man to have his person represented by two actors, that by opposing one another, must needs divide that power, which, if men will live in peace, is indivisible; and thereby reduce the multitude into the condition of war, contrary to the end for which all sovereignty is instituted. And therefore as it is absurd, to think that a sovereign assembly, inviting the people of their dominion, to send up their deputies, with power to make known their advice, or desires, should therefore hold such deputies, rather than themselves, for the absolute representatives of the people: so it is absurd also, to think the same in a monarchy. And I know not how this so manifest a truth, should of late be so little observed; that in a monarchy, he that had the sovereignty from a descent of six hundred years, was alone called sovereign, had the title of Majesty from every one of his subjects, and was unquestionably taken by them for their king, was notwithstanding never considered as their representative; the name without contradiction passing for the title of those men, which at his command were sent up by the people to carry their petitions, and give him, if he permitted it, their advice. Which may serve as an admonition, for those that are the true, and absolute representative of a people, to instruct men in the nature of that office, and to take heed how they admit of any other general representation upon any occasion whatsoever, if they mean to discharge the trust committed to them.

*Comparison of monarchy, with sovereign assemblies.* The difference between these three kinds of commonwealth, consisteth not in the difference of power; but in the difference of convenience, or aptitude to produce the peace, and security of the people; for which end they were instituted. And to compare monarchy with the other two, we may observe; first, that whosoever beareth the person of the people, or is one of that assembly that bears it, beareth also his own natural person. And though he be careful in his politic person to procure the common interest; yet he is more, or no less careful to procure the private good of himself, his family, kindred, and friends; and for the most part, if the public interest chance to cross the private, he prefers the private: for the passions of men, are commonly more potent than their reason. From whence it follows, that where the public and private interest are most closely united, there is the public most advanced. Now in monarchy, the private interest is the same with the public. The riches, power, and honour of a monarch arise only from the riches, strength, and reputation of his subjects. For no king can be rich, nor glorious, nor secure, whose subjects are either poor, or contemptible, or too weak through want or dissention, to maintain a war against their enemies: whereas in a democracy, or aristocracy, the public prosperity confers not so much to the private fortune of one that is corrupt, or ambitious, as doth many times a perfidious advice, a treacherous action, or a civil war.

Secondly, that a monarch receiveth counsel of whom, when, and where he pleaseth; and consequently may hear the opinion of men versed in the matter about which he deliberates, of what rank or quality soever, and as long before the time of action, and with as much secrecy, as he will. But when a sovereign assembly has need of counsel, none are admitted but such as have a right thereto from the beginning; which for the most part are of those who have been versed more in the acquisition of wealth than of knowledge; and are to give their advice in long discourses, which may, and do commonly excite men to action, but not govern them in it. For the *understanding* is by the flame of the passions, never enlightened, but dazzled. Nor is there any place, or time, wherein an assembly can receive counsel with secrecy, because of their own multitude.

Thirdly, that the resolutions of a monarch, are subject to no other inconstancy, than that of human nature; but in assemblies, besides that of nature, there ariseth an inconstancy from the number. For the absence of a few, that would have the resolution once taken, continue firm, which may happen by security, negligence, or private impediments, or the diligent appearance of a few of the contrary opinion, undoes to-day, all that was concluded yesterday.

Fourthly, that a monarch cannot disagree with himself, out of envy, or interest; but an assembly may; and that to such a height, as may produce a civil war.

Fifthly, that in monarchy there is this inconvenience; that any subject, by the power of one man, for the enriching of a favourite or flatterer, may be deprived of all he possesseth; which I confess is a great and inevitable inconvenience. But the same may as well happen, where the sovereign power is in an assembly: for their power is the same; and they are as subject to evil counsel, and to be seduced by orators, as a monarch by flatterers; and becoming one another's flatterers, serve one another's covetousness and ambition by turns. And whereas the favourites of monarchs, are few, and they have none else to advance but their own kindred; the favourites of an assembly, are many; and the kindred much more numerous, than of any monarch. Besides, there is no favourite of a monarch, which cannot as well succour his friends, as hurt his enemies: but orators, that is to say, favourites of sovereign assemblies, though they have great power to hurt, have little to save. For to accuse, requires less eloquence, such is man's nature, than to excuse; and condemnation, than absolution more resembles justice.

Sixthly, that it is an inconvenience in monarchy, that the sovereignty may descend upon an infant, or one that cannot discern between good and evil: and consisteth in this, that the use of his power, must be in the hand of another man, or of some assembly of men, which are to govern by his right, and in his name; as curators, and protectors of his person, and authority. But to say there is inconvenience, in putting the use of the sovereign power, into the hand of a man, or an assembly of men; is to say that all government is more inconvenient, than confusion, and civil war. And therefore all the danger that can be pretended, must arise from the contention of those, that for an office of so great honour, and profit, may become competitors. To make it appear, that this inconvenience, proceedeth not from that form of government we call monarchy, we are to consider, that the precedent monarch hath appointed who shall have the tuition of his infant successor, either expressly by testament, or tacitly, by not controlling the custom in that case received: and then such inconvenience, if it happen, is to be attributed, not to the monarchy, but to the ambition, and injustice of the subjects; which in all kinds of government, where the people are not well instructed in their duty, and the rights of sovereignty, is the same. Or else the precedent monarch hath not at all taken order for such tuition; and then the law of nature hath provided this sufficient rule, that the tuition shall be in him, that hath by nature most interest in the preservation of the authority of the infant, and to whom least benefit can accrue by his death, or diminution. For seeing every man by nature seeketh his own benefit, and promotion; to put an infant into the power of those, that can promote themselves by his destruction, or damage, is not tuition, but treachery. So that sufficient provision being taken, against all just quarrel, about the government under a child, if any contention arise to the disturbance of the public peace, it is not to be attributed to the form of monarchy, but to the ambition of subjects, and ignorance of their duty. On the other side, there is no great commonwealth, the sovereignty whereof is in a great assembly, which is not, as to consultations of peace, and war, and making of laws, in the same condition, as if the government were in a child. For as a child wants the judgment to dissent from counsel given him, and is thereby necessitated to take the advice of them, or him, to whom he is committed: so an assembly wanteth the liberty, to dissent from the counsel of the major part, be it good, or bad. And as a child has need of a tutor, or protector, to preserve his person and authority: so also, in great commonwealths, the sovereign assembly, in all great dangers and troubles, have need of *custodes libertatis;* that is of dictators, or protectors of their authority; which are as much as temporary monarchs, to whom for a time, they may commit the entire exercise of power; and have, at the end of that time, been oftener deprived thereof, than infant kings, by their protectors, regents, or any other tutors.

*Definition of monarchy, and other forms.* Though the kinds of sovereignty be, as I have now shown, but three; that is to say, monarchy, where one man has it; or democracy, where the general assembly of subjects hath it; or aristocracy, where it is in an assembly of certain persons nominated, or otherwise distinguished from the rest: yet he that shall consider the particular commonwealths that have been, and are in the world, will not perhaps easily reduce them to three, and may thereby be inclined to think there be other forms, arising from these mingled together. As for example, elective kingdoms; where kings have the sovereign power put into their hands for a time; or kingdoms, wherein the king hath a power limited: which governments, are nevertheless by most writers called monarchy. Likewise if a popular, or aristocratical commonwealth, subdue an enemy's country, and govern the same, by a president, procurator, or other magistrate; this may seem perhaps at first sight, to be a democratical, or aristocratical government. But it is not so. For elective kings, are not sovereigns, but ministers of the sovereign; nor limited kings, sovereigns, but ministers of them that have the sovereign power: nor are those provinces which are in subjection to a democracy, or aristocracy of another commonwealth, democratically or aristocratically governed, but monarchically.

And first, concerning an elective king, whose power is limited to his life, as it is in many places of Christendom at this day; or to certain years or months, as the dictator's power amongst the Romans; if he have right to appoint his successor, he is no more elective but hereditary. But if he have no power to elect his successor, then there is some other man, or assembly known, after his decease may elect anew, or else the commonwealth dieth, and dissolveth with him, and returneth to the condition of war. If it be known who have the power to give the sovereignty after his death, it is known also that the sovereignty was in them before: for none have right to give that which they have not right to possess, and keep to themselves, if they think good. But if there be none that can give the sovereignty, after the decease of him that was first elected; then has he power, nay he is obliged by the law of nature, to provide, by establishing his successor, to keep those that had trusted him with the government, from relapsing into the miserable condition of civil war. And consequently he was, when elected, a sovereign absolute.

Secondly, that king whose power is limited, is not superior to him, or them that have the power to limit it; and he that is not superior, is not supreme; that is to say, not sovereign. The sovereignty therefore was always in that assembly which had the right to limit him; and by consequence the government not monarchy, but either democracy, or aristocracy; as of old time in Sparta; where the kings had a privilege to lead their armies; but the sovereignty was in the Ephori.

Thirdly, whereas heretofore the Roman people governed the land of Judea, for example, by a president; yet was not Judea therefore a democracy; because they were not governed by any assembly, into the which, any of them, had right to enter; nor an aristocracy; because they were not governed by any assembly, into which, any man could enter by their election: but they were governed by one person, which, though as to the people of Rome, was an assembly of the people, or democracy; yet as to the people of Judea, which had no right at all of participating in the government, was a monarch. For though where the people are governed by an assembly, chosen by themselves out of their own number, the government is called a democracy, or aristocracy; yet when they are governed by an assembly, not of their own choosing, it is a monarchy; not of *one* man, over another man; but of one people, over another people.

*Of the right of succession.* Of all these forms of government, the matter being mortal, so that not only monarchs, but also whole assemblies die, it is necessary for the conservation of the peace of men, that as there was order taken for an artificial man, so there be order also taken, for an artificial eternity of life; without which, men that are governed by an assembly, should return into the condition of war in every age; and they that are governed by one man, as soon as their governor dieth. This artificial eternity, is that which men call the right of *succession*.

There is no perfect form of government, where the disposing of the succession is not in the present sovereign. For if it be in any other particular man, or private assembly, it is in a person subject, and may be assumed by the sovereign at his pleasure; and consequently the right is in himself. And if it be in no particular man, but left to a new choice; then is the commonwealth dissolved; and the right is in him that can get it; contrary to the intention of them that did institute the commonwealth, for their perpetual, and not temporary security.

In a democracy, the whole assembly cannot fail, unless the multitude that are to be governed fail. And therefore questions of the right of succession, have in that form of government no place at all.

In an aristocracy, when any of the assembly dieth, the election of another into his room belongeth to the assembly, as the sovereign, to whom belongeth the choosing of all counsellors and officers. For that which the representative doth, as actor, every one of the subjects doth, as author. And though the sovereign assembly may give power to others, to elect new men, for supply of their court; yet it is still by their authority, that the election is made; and by the same it may, when the public shall require it, be recalled.

*The present monarch hath right to dispose of the succession.* The greatest difficulty about the right of succession, is in monarchy: and the difficulty ariseth from this, that at first sight, it is not manifest who is to appoint the successor; nor many times, who it is whom he hath appointed. For in both these cases, there is required a more exact ratiocination, than every man is accustomed to use. As to the question, who shall appoint the successor, of a monarch that hath the sovereign authority; that is to say, who shall determine of the right of inheritance, (for elective kings and princes have not the sovereign power in propriety, but in use only), we are to consider, that either he that is in possession, has right to dispose of the succession, or else that right is again in the dissolved multitude. For the death of him that hath the sovereign power in propriety, leaves the multitude without any sovereign at all; that is, without any representative in whom they should be united, and be capable of doing any one action at all: and therefore they are incapable of election of any new monarch; every man having equal right to submit himself to such as he thinks best able to protect him; or if he can, protect himself by his own sword; which is a return to confusion, and to the condition of a war of every man against every man, contrary to the end for which monarchy had its first institution. Therefore it is manifest, that by the institution of monarchy, the disposing of the successor, is always left to the judgment and will of the present possessor.

And for the question, which may arise sometimes, who it is that the monarch in possession, hath designed to the succession and inheritance of his power; it is determined by his express words, and testament; or by other tacit signs sufficient.

*Succession passeth by express words.* By express words, or testament, when it is declared by him in his lifetime, *viva voce*, or by writing; as the first emperors of Rome declared who should be their heirs. For the word heir does not of itself imply the children, or nearest kindred of a man; but whomsoever a man shall any way declare, he would have to succeed him in his estate. If therefore a monarch declare expressly, that such a man shall be his heir, either by word or writing, then is that man immediately after the decease of his predecessor, invested in the right of being monarch.

*Or, by not controlling a custom.* But where testament, and express words are wanting, other natural signs of the will are to be followed: whereof the one is custom. And therefore where the custom is, that the next of kindred absolutely succeedeth, there also the next of kindred hath right to the succession; for that, if the will of him that was in possession had been otherwise, he might easily have declared the same in his life-time. And likewise where the custom is, that the next of the male kindred succeedeth, there also the right of succession is in the next of the kindred male, for the same reason. And so it is if the custom were to advance the female. For whatsoever custom a man by a word control, and does not, it is a natural sign he would have that custom stand.

*Or, by presumption of natural affection.* But where neither custom, nor testament hath preceded, there it is to be understood, first, that a monarch's will is, that the government remain monarchical; because he hath approved that government in himself. Secondly, that a child of his own, male, or female, be preferred before any other; because men are presumed to be more inclined by nature, to advance their own children, than the children of other men; and of their own, rather a male than a female; because men, are naturally fitter than women, for actions of labour and danger. Thirdly, where his own issue faileth, rather a brother than a stranger; and so still the nearer in blood, rather than the more remote; because it is always presumed that the nearer of kin, is the nearer in affection; and it is evident that a man receives always, by reflection, the most honour from the greatness of his nearest kindred.

*To dispose of the succession, though to a king of another nation, not unlawful.* But if it be lawful for a monarch to dispose of the succession by words of contract, or testament, men may perhaps object a great inconvenience: for he may sell, or give his right of governing to a stranger; which, because strangers, that is, men not used to live under the same government, nor speaking the same language, do commonly undervalue one another, may turn to the oppression of his subjects; which is indeed a great inconvenience: but it proceedeth not necessarily from the subjection to a stranger's government, but from the unskilfulness of the governors, ignorant of the true rules of politics. And therefore the Romans when they had subdued many nations, to make their government digestible, were wont to take away that grievance, as much as they thought necessary, by giving sometimes to whole nations, and sometimes to principal men of every nation they conquered, not only the privileges, but also the name of Romans; and took many of them into the senate, and offices of charge, even in the Roman city. And this was it our most wise king, king James, aimed at, in endeavouring the union of his two realms of England and Scotland. Which if he could have obtained, had in all likelihood prevented the civil wars, which make both those kingdoms, at this present, miserable. It is not therefore any injury to the people, for a monarch to dispose of the succession by will; though by the fault of many princes, it hath been sometimes found inconvenient. Of the lawfulness of it, this also is an argument, that whatsoever inconvenience can arrive by giving a kingdom to a stranger, may arrive also by so marrying with strangers, as the right of succession may descend upon them: yet this by all men is accounted lawful.

## Chapter 20

## Of Dominion Paternal, and Despotical

*A Commonwealth by acquisition.* A commonwealth *by acquisition*, is that, where the sovereign power is acquired by force; and it is acquired by force, when men singly, or many together by plurality of voices, for fear of death, or bonds, do authorize all the actions of that man, or assembly, that hath their lives and liberty in his power.

*Wherein different from a commonwealth by institution.* And this kind of dominion, or sovereignty, differeth from sovereignty by institution, only in this, that men who choose their sovereign, do it for fear of one another, and not of him whom they institute: but in this case, they subject themselves, to him they are afraid of. In both cases they do it for fear: which is to be noted by them, that hold all such covenants, as proceed from fear of death or violence, void: which if it were true, no man, in any kind of commonwealth, could be obliged to obedience. It is true, that in a commonwealth once instituted, or acquired, promises proceeding from fear of death or violence, are no covenants, nor obliging, when the thing promised is contrary to the laws; but the reason is not, because it was made upon fear, but because he that promiseth, hath no right in the thing promised. Also, when he may lawfully perform, and doth not, it is not the invalidity of the covenant, that absolveth him, but the sentence of the sovereign. Otherwise, whensoever a man lawfully promiseth, he unlawfully breaketh: but when the sovereign, who is the actor, acquitteth him, then he is acquitted by him that extorted the promise, as by the author of such absolution.

*The rights of sovereignty the same in both.* But the rights, and consequences of sovereignty, are the same in both. His power cannot, without his consent, be transferred to another: he cannot forfeit it: he cannot be accused by any of his subjects, of injury: he cannot be punished by them: he is judge of what is necessary for peace; and judge of doctrines: he is sole legislator; and supreme judge of controversies; and of the times, and occasions of war, and peace: to him it belongeth to choose magistrates, counsellors, commanders, and all other officers, and ministers; and to determine of rewards, and punishments, honour, and order. The reasons whereof, are the same which are alleged in the precedent chapter, for the same rights, and consequences of sovereignty by institution.

*Dominion paternal how attained. Not by generation, but by contract.* Dominion is acquired two ways; by generation, and by conquest. The right of dominion by generation, is that, which the parent hath over his children; and is called PATERNAL. And is not so derived from the generation, as if therefore the parent had dominion over his child because he begat him; but from the child's consent, either express, or by other sufficient arguments declared. For as to the generation, God hath ordained to man a helper; and there be always two that are equally parents: the dominion therefore over the child, should belong equally to both; and he be equally subject to both, which is impossible; for no man can obey two masters. And whereas some have attributed the dominion to the man only, as being of the more excellent sex; they misreckon in it. For there is not always that difference of strength, or prudence between the man and the woman, as that the right can be determined without war. In commonwealths, this controversy is decided by the civil law; and for the most part, but not always, the sentence is in favour of the father; because for the most part commonwealths have been erected by the fathers, not by the mothers of families. But the question lieth now in the state of mere nature; where there are supposed no laws of matrimony; no laws for the education of children; but the law of nature, and the natural inclination of the sexes, one to another, and to their children. In this condition of mere nature, either the parents between themselves dispose of the dominion over the child by contract; or do not dispose thereof at all. If they dispose thereof, the right passeth according to the contract. We find in history that the Amazons contracted with the men of the neighbouring countries, to whom they had recourse for issue, that the issue male should be sent back, but the female remain with themselves: so that the dominion of the females was in the mother.

*Or education.* If there be no contract, the dominion is in the mother. For in the condition of mere nature, where there are no matrimonial laws, it cannot be known who is the father, unless it be declared by the mother: and therefore the right of dominion over the child dependeth on her will, and is consequently hers. Again, seeing the infant is first in the power of the mother, so as she may either nourish, or expose it; if she nourish it, it oweth its life to the mother; and is therefore obliged to obey her, rather than any other; and by consequence the dominion over it is hers. But if she expose it, and another find and nourish it, the dominion is in him that nourisheth it. For it ought to obey him by whom it is preserved; because preservation of life being the end, for which one man becomes subject to another, every man is supposed to promise obedience, to him, in whose power it is to save, or destroy him.

*Or precedent subjection of one of the parents to the other.* If the mother be the father's subject, the child is in the father's power: and if the father be the mother's subject, as when a sovereign queen marrieth one of her subjects, the child is subject to the mother; because the father also is her subject.

If a man and woman, monarchs of two several kingdoms, have a child, and contract concerning who shall have the dominion of him, the right of the dominion passeth by the contract. If they contract not, the dominion followeth the dominion of the place of his residence. For the sovereign of each country hath dominion over all that reside therein.

He that hath the dominion over the child, hath dominion also over the children of the child; and over their children's children. For he that hath dominion over the person of a man, hath dominion over all that is his; without which, dominion were but a title, without the effect.

*The right of succession followeth the rules of the right of possession.* The right of succession to paternal dominion, proceedeth in the same manner, as doth the right of succession of monarchy; of which I have already sufficiently spoken in the precedent chapter.

*Despotical dominion how attained.* Dominion acquired by conquest, or victory in war, is that which some writers call DESPOTICAL, from Δεσπότης, which signifieth a *lord,* or *master;* and is the dominion of the master over his servant. And this dominion is then acquired to the victor, when the vanquished, to avoid the present stroke of death, covenanteth either in express words, or by other sufficient signs of the will, that so long as his life, and the liberty of his body is allowed him, the victor shall have the use thereof, at his pleasure. And after such covenant made, the vanquished is a SERVANT, and not before: for by the word *servant,* whether it be derived from *servire,* to serve, or from *servare,* to save, which I leave to grammarians to dispute, is not meant a captive, which is kept in prison, or bonds, till the owner of him that took him, or brought him of one that did, shall consider what to do with him: for such men, commonly called slaves, have no obligation at all; but may break their bonds, or the prison; and kill, or carry away captive their master, justly: but one, that being taken, hath corporal liberty allowed him; and upon promise not to run away, nor to do violence to his master, is trusted by him.

*Not by the victory, but by the consent of the vanquished.* It is not therefore the victory, that giveth the right of dominion over the vanquished, but his own covenant. Nor is he obliged because he is conquered; that is to say, beaten, and taken, or put to flight; but because he cometh in, and submitteth to the victor; nor is the victor obliged by an enemy's rendering himself, without promise of life, to spare him for this his yielding to discretion; which obliges not the victor longer, than in his own discretion he shall think fit.

And that which men do, when they demand, as it is now called, *quarter,* which the Greeks called Ζωγρία, *taking alive,* is to evade the present fury of the victor, by submission, and to compound for their life, with ransom, or service: and therefore he that hath quarter, hath not his life given, but deferred till farther deliberation; for it is not a yielding on condition of life, but to discretion. And then only is his life in security, and his service due, when the victor hath trusted him with his corporal liberty. For slaves that work in prisons; or fetters, do it not of duty, but to avoid the cruelty of their task-masters.

The master of the servant, is master also of all he hath: and may exact the use thereof; that is to say, of his goods, of his labour, of his servants, and of his children, as often as he shall think fit. For he holdeth his life of his master, by the covenant of obedience; that is, of owning, and authorizing whatsoever the master shall do. And in case the master, if he refuse, kill him, or cast him into bonds, or otherwise punish him for his disobedience, he is himself the author of the same; and cannot accuse him of injury.

In sum, the rights and consequences of both *paternal* and *despotical* dominion, are the very same with those of a sovereign by institution; and for the same reasons: which reasons are set down in the precedent chapter. So that for a man that is monarch of divers nations, whereof he hath, in one the sovereignty by institution of the people assembled, and in another by conquest, that is by the submission of each particular, to avoid death or bonds; to demand of one nation more than of the other, from the title of conquest, as being a conquered nation, is an act of ignorance of the rights of sovereignty; for the sovereign is absolute over both alike; or else there is no sovereignty at all; and so every man may lawfully protect himself, if he can, with his own sword, which is the condition of war.

*Difference between a family and a kingdom.* By this it appears; that a great family, if it be not part of some commonwealth, is of itself, as to the rights of sovereignty, a little monarchy: whether that family consist of a man and his children; or of a man and his servants; or of a man, and his children, and servants together: wherein the father or master is the sovereign. But yet a family is not properly a commonwealth; unless it be that power by its own number, or by other opportunities, as not to be subdued without the hazard of war. For where a number of men are manifestly too weak to defend themselves united, every one may use his own reason in time of danger, to save his own life, either by flight, or by submission to the enemy, as he shall think best; in the same manner as a very small company of soldiers, surprised by an army, may cast down their arms, and demand quarter, or run away, rather than be put to the sword. And thus much shall suffice, concerning what I find by speculation, and deduction, of sovereign rights, from the nature, need, and designs of men, in erecting of commonwealths, and putting themselves under monarchs, or assemblies, entrusted with power enough for their protection.

*The rights of monarchy from Scripture.* Let us now consider what the Scripture teacheth in the same point. To Moses, the children of Israel say thus: *Speak thou to us, and we will hear thee; but let not God speak to us, lest we die.* (*Exod.* xx. 19.) This is absolute obedience to Moses. Concerning the right of kings, God himself by the mouth of Samuel, saith, (1 *Sam.* viii. 11, 12, &c.) *This shall be the right of the king you will have to reign over you. He shall take your sons, and set them to drive his chariots, and to be his horsemen, and to run before his chariots; and gather in his harvest; and to make his engines of war, and instruments of his chariots; and shall take your daughters to make perfumes, to be his cooks, and bakers. He shall take your fields, your vineyards, and your olive-yards, and give them to his servants. He shall take the tithe of your corn and wine, and give it to the men of his chamber, and to his other servants. He shall take your man-servants, and your maid-servants, and the choice of your youth, and employ them in his business. He shall take the tithe of your flocks; and you shall be his servants.* This is absolute power, and summed up in the last words, *you shall be his servants.* Again, when the people heard what power their king was to have, yet then consented thereto, and say thus, (*verse 19*) *we will be as all other nations, and our king shall judge our causes, and go before us, to conduct our wars.* Here is confirmed the right that sovereigns have, both to the *militia,* and to all *judicature;* in which is contained as absolute power, as one man can possibly transfer to another. Again, the prayer of king Solomon to God, was this (1*Kings* iii. 9): *Give to thy servant understanding, to judge thy people, and to discern between good and evil.* It belongeth therefore to the sovereign to be *judge,* and to prescribe the rules of *discerning good* and *evil:* which rules are laws; and therefore in him is the legislative power. Saul sought the life of David; yet when it was in his power to slay Saul, and his servants would have done it. David forbad them, saying, (1 *Sam.* xxiv. 6) *God forbid I should do such an act against my Lord, the anointed of God.* For obedience of servants St. Paul saith: (*Col.* iii. 22) *Servants obey your masters in all things;* and, (*Col.* iii. 20) *children obey your parents in all things.* There is simple obedience in those that are subject to paternal, or despotical dominion. Again, (*Matt.* xxiii. 2, 3) *The Scribes and Pharisees sit in Moses' chair, and therefore all that they shall bid you observe, that observe and do.* There again is simple obedience. And St. Paul, (*Titus* iii. 2) *Warn them that they subject themselves to princes, and to those that are in authority, and obey them.* This obedience is also simple. Lastly, our Saviour himself acknowledges, that men ought to pay such taxes as are by kings imposed, where he says, *give to Cæsar that which is Cæsar's;* and paid such taxes himself. And that the king's word, is sufficient to take any thing from any subject, when there is need; and that the king is judge of that need: for he himself, as king of the Jews, commanded his disciples to take the ass, and ass's colt to carry him into Jerusalem, saying, (*Matt.* xxi. 2, 3) *Go into the village over against you, and you shall find a she ass tied, and her colt with her, untie them, and bring them to me. And if any man ask you, what you mean by it, say the Lord hath need of them: and they will let them go.* They will not ask whether his necessity be a sufficient title; nor whether he be judge of that necessity; but acquiesce in the will of the Lord.

To these places may be added also that of *Genesis,* (iii. 5)

*Ye shall be as gods, knowing good and evil.* And (*verse* 11)
*Who told thee that thou wast naked? hast thou eaten of the
tree, of which I commanded thee thou shouldest not eat?* For
the cognizance or judicature of *good* and *evil*, being forbidden
by the name of the fruit of the tree of knowledge, as a trial
of Adam's obedience; the devil to inflame the ambition of the
woman, to whom that fruit already seemed beautiful, told her
that by tasting it, they should be as gods, knowing *good* and
*evil*. Whereupon having both eaten, they did indeed take upon
them God's office, which is judicature of good and evil; but
acquired no new ability to distinguish between them aright.
And whereas it is said, that having eaten, they saw they were
naked; no man hath so interpreted that place, as if they had
been formerly blind, and saw not their own skins: the meaning is plain, that it was then they first judged their nakedness,
wherein it was God's will to create them, to be uncomely; and
by being ashamed, did tacitly censure God himself. And
thereupon God saith, *Hast thou eaten, &c.* as if he should say,
doest thou that owest me obedience, take upon thee to judge
of my commandments? Whereby it is clearly, though allegorically, signified, that the commands of them that have the
right to command, are not by their subjects to be censured,
nor disputed.

*Sovereign power ought in all commonwealths to be absolute.*
So that it appeareth plainly, to my understanding, both from
reason, and Scripture, that the sovereign power, whether
placed in one man, as in monarchy, or in one assembly of
men, as in popular, and aristocratical commonwealths, is as
great, as possibly men can be imagined to make it. And
though of so unlimited a power, men may fancy many evil
consequences, yet the consequences of the want of it, which
is perpetual war of every man against his neighbour, are
much worse. The condition of man in this life shall never be
without inconveniences; but there happeneth in no commonwealth any great inconvenience, but what proceeds from the
subject's disobedience, and breach of those covenants, from
which the commonwealth hath its being. And whosoever
thinking sovereign power too great, will seek to make it less,
must subject himself, to the power, that can limit it; that is to
say, to a greater.

The greatest objection is, that of the practice; when men
ask, where, and when, such power has by subjects been acknowledged. But one may ask them again, when, or where
has there been a kingdom long free from sedition and civil

war. In those nations, whose commonwealths have been long-lived, and not been destroyed but by foreign war, the subjects never did dispute of the sovereign power. But howsoever, an argument from the practice of men, that have not sifted to the bottom, and with exact reason weighed the causes, and nature of commonwealths, and suffer daily those miseries, that proceed from the ignorance thereof, is invalid. For though in all places of the world, men should lay the foundation of their houses on the sand, it could not thence be inferred, that so it ought to be. The skill of making, and maintaining commonwealths, consisteth in certain rules, as doth arithmetic and geometry; not, as tennis-play, on practice only: which rules, neither poor men have the leisure, nor men that have had the leisure, have hitherto had the curiosity, or the method to find out.

## Chapter 21

## Of the Liberty of Subjects

*Liberty, what.* LIBERTY, or FREEDOM, signifieth, properly, the absence of opposition; by opposition, I mean external impediments of motion; and may be applied no less to irrational, and inanimate creatures, than to rational. For whatsoever is so tied, or environed, as it cannot move but within a certain space, which space is determined by the opposition of some external body, we say it hath not liberty to go further. And so of all living creatures, whilst they are imprisoned, or restrained, with walls, or chains; and of the water whilst it is kept in by banks, or vessels, that otherwise would spread itself into a larger space, we use to say, they are not at liberty, to move in such manner, as without those external impediments they would. But when the impediment of motion, is in the constitution of the thing itself, we use not to say; it wants the liberty; but the power to move; as when a stone lieth still, or a man is fastened to his bed by sickness.

*What it is to be free.* And according to this proper, and generally received meaning of the word, a FREEMAN, *is he, that in those things, which by his strength and wit he is able to do, is not hindered to do what he has a will to.* But when the words *free*, and *liberty*, are applied to any thing but *bodies*, they are abused; for that which is not subject to motion, is not subject to impediment: and therefore, when it is said, for example, the way is free, no liberty of the way is signified, but of those that walk in it without stop. And when we say a gift is free, there is not meant any liberty of the gift, but of the giver, that was not bound by any law or covenant to give it. So when we *speak freely*, it is not the liberty of voice, or pronunciation, but of the man, whom no law hath obliged to speak otherwise than he did. Lastly, from the use of the word *free-will*, no liberty can be inferred of the will, desire, or inclination, but the liberty of the man; which consisteth in this, that he finds no stop, in doing what he has the will, desire, or inclination to do.

*Fear and liberty consistent.* Fear and liberty are consistent; as when a man throweth his goods into the sea for *fear* the ship should sink, he doth it nevertheless very willingly, and may refuse to do it if he will: it is therefore the action of one that was *free:* so a man sometimes pays his debt, only for *fear* of imprisonment, which because nobody hindered him from detaining, was the action of a man at *liberty*. And generally all actions which men do in commonwealths, for *fear* of the law, are actions, which the doers had *liberty* to omit.

*Liberty and necessity consistent. Liberty,* and *necessity* are consistent: as in the water, that hath not only *liberty,* but a *necessity* of descending by the channel; so likewise in the actions which men voluntarily do: which, because they proceed from their will, proceed from *liberty;* and yet, because every act of man's will, and every desire, and inclination proceedeth from some cause, and that from another cause, in a continual chain, whose first link is in the hand of God the first of all causes, proceed from *necessity*. So that to him that could see the connexion of those causes, the *necessity* of all men's voluntary actions, would appear manifest. And therefore God, that seeth, and disposeth all things, seeth also that the *liberty* of man in doing what he will, is accompanied with the *necessity* of doing that which God will, and no more, nor less. For though men may do many things, which God does not command, nor is therefore author of them; yet they can have no passion, nor appetite to any thing, of which appetite God's will is not the cause. And did not his will assure the *necessity* of man's will, and consequently of all that on man's will dependeth, the *liberty* of men would be a contradiction, and impediment to the omnipotence and *liberty* of God. And this shall suffice, as to the matter in hand, of that natural *liberty,* which only is properly called *liberty*.

*Artificial bonds, or covenants.* But as men, for the attaining of peace, and conservation of themselves thereby, have made an artificial man, which we call a commonwealth; so also have they made artificial chains, called *civil laws,* which they themselves, by mutual covenants, have fastened at one end, to the lips of that man, or assembly, to whom they have given the sovereign power; and at the other end to their own ears. These bonds, in their own nature but weak, may nevertheless be made to hold, by the danger, though not by the difficulty of breaking them.

*Liberty of subjects consisteth in liberty from covenants.* In relation to these bonds only it is, that I am to speak now, of the *liberty* of *subjects*. For seeing there is no commonwealth in the world, wherein there be rules enough set down, for the regulating of all the actions, and words of men;

as being a thing impossible: it followeth necessarily, that in all kinds of actions by the laws prætermitted, men have the liberty, of doing what their own reasons shall suggest, for the most profitable to themselves. For if we take liberty in the proper sense, for corporal liberty; that is to say, freedom from chains and prison; it were very absurd for men to clamour as they do, for the liberty they so manifestly enjoy. Again, if we take liberty, for an exemption from laws, it is no less absurd, for men to demand as they do, that liberty, by which all other men may be masters of their lives. And yet, as absurd as it is, this is it they demand; not knowing that the laws are of no power to protect them, without a sword in the hands of a man, or men, to cause those laws to be put in execution. The liberty of a subject, lieth therefore only in those things, which in regulating their actions, the sovereign hath prætermitted: such as is the liberty to buy, and sell, and otherwise contract with one another; to choose their own abode, their own diet, their own trade of life, and institute their children as they themselves think fit; and the like.

*Liberty of the subject consistent with the unlimited power of the sovereign.* Nevertheless we are not to understand, that by such liberty, the sovereign power of life and death, is either abolished, or limited. For it has been already shown, that nothing the sovereign representative can do to a subject, on what pretence soever, can properly be called injustice, or injury; because every subject is author of every act the sovereign doth; so that he never wanteth right to any thing, otherwise, than as he himself is the subject of God, and bound thereby to observe the laws of nature. And therefore it may, and doth often happen in commonwealths, that a subject may be put to death, by the command of the sovereign power; and yet neither do the other wrong: as when Jephtha caused his daughter to be sacrificed: in which, and the like cases, he that so dieth, had liberty to do the action, for which he is nevertheless, without injury put to death. And the same holdeth also in a sovereign prince, that putteth to death an innocent subject. For though the action be against the law of nature, as being contrary to equity, as was the killing of Uriah, by David; yet it was not an injury to Uriah, but to God. Not to Uriah, because the right to do what he pleased was given him by Uriah himself: and yet to God, because David was God's subject, and prohibited all iniquity by the law of nature: which distinction, David himself, when he repented the fact, evidently confirmed, saying, *To thee only have I sinned.* In the same manner, the people of Athens, when they banished the most potent of their commonwealth for ten years, thought they committed no injustice; and yet they never questioned what crime he had done; but what hurt he would do: nay they commanded the banishment of they knew not whom; and every citizen bringing his oystershell into the market place, written with the name of him he desired should be banished, without actually accusing him, sometimes banished an Aristides, for his reputation of justice; and sometimes a scurrilous jester, as Hyperbolus, to make a jest of it. And yet a man cannot say, the sovereign people of Athens wanted right to banish them; or an Athenian the liberty to jest, or to be just.

*The liberty which writers praise, is the liberty of sovereigns; not of private men.* The liberty, whereof there is so frequent and honourable mention, in the histories, and philosophy of the ancient Greeks, and Romans, and in the writings, and discourse of those that from them have received all their learning in the politics, is not the liberty of particular men; but the liberty of the commonwealth: which is the same with that which every man then should have, if there were no civil laws, nor commonwealth at all. And the effects of it also be the same. For as amongst masterless men, there is perpetual war, of every man against his neighbour; no inheritance, to transmit to the son, nor to expect from the father; no propriety of goods, or lands; no security; but a full and absolute liberty in every particular man: so in states, and commonwealths not dependent on one another, every commonwealth, not every man, has an absolute liberty, to do what it shall judge, that is to say, what that man, or assembly that representeth it, shall judge most conducing to their benefit. But withal, they live in the condition of a perpetual war, and upon the confines of battle, with their frontiers armed, and cannons planted against their neighbours round about. The Athenians, and Romans were free; that is, free commonwealths: not that any particular men had the liberty to resist their own representative; but that their representative had the liberty to resist, or invade other people. There is written on the turrets of the city of Lucca in great characters at this day, the word LIBERTAS; yet no man can thence infer, that a particular man has more liberty, or immunity from the service of the commonwealth there, than in Constantinople. Whether a commonwealth be monarchical, or popular, the freedom is still the same.

But it is an easy thing, for men to be deceived, by the specious name of liberty; and for want of judgment to distinguish, mistake that for their private inheritance, and birthright, which is the right of the public only. And when the same error is confirmed by the authority of men in reputation for their writings on this subject, it is no wonder if it produce sedition, and change of government. In these western parts of the world, we are made to receive our opinions concerning the institution, and rights of commonwealths, from Aristotle, Cicero, and other men, Greeks and Romans, that living under popular states, derived those rights, not from the principles of nature, but transcribed them into their books, out of the practice of their own commonwealths, which were popular; as the grammarians describe the rules of language, out of the practice of the time; or the rules of poetry, out of the poems of Homer and Virgil. And because the Athenians were taught, to keep them from desire of changing their government, that they were freemen, and all that lived under monarchy were slaves; therefore Aristotle puts it down in his *Politics*, (*lib.* 6. *cap.* ii.) *In democracy,* LIBERTY *is to be supposed: for it is commonly held, that no man is* FREE *in any other government.* And as Aristotle; so Cicero, and other writers have grounded their civil doctrine, on the opinions of the Romans, who were taught to hate monarchy, at first, by them that having deposed their sovereign, shared amongst them the sovereignty of Rome; and afterwards by their successors. And by reading of these Greek, and Latin authors, men from their childhood have gotten a habit, under a false show of liberty, of favouring tumults, and of licentious controlling the actions of their sovereigns, and again of controlling those controllers; with the effusion of so much blood, as I think I may truly say, there was never any thing so dearly bought, as these western parts have bought the learning of the Greek and Latin tongues.

*Liberty of subjects how to be measured.* To come now to the particulars of the true liberty of a subject; that is to say, what are the things, which though commanded by the sovereign, he may nevertheless, without injustice, refuse to do; we are to consider, what rights we pass away, when we make a commonwealth; or, which is all one, what liberty we deny ourselves, by owning all the actions, without exception, of the man, or assembly we make our sovereign. For in the act of our *submission,* consisteth both our *obligation,* and our *liberty;* which must therefore be inferred by arguments taken from thence; there being no obligation on any man, which ariseth not from some act of his own; for all men equally, are by nature free. And because such arguments, must either be drawn from the express words, *I authorize all his actions*, or from the intention of him that submitteth himself to his power, which intention is to be understood by the end for which he so submitteth; the obligation, and liberty of the subject, is to be derived, either from those words, or others equivalent; or else from the end of the institution of sovereignty, namely, the peace of the subjects within themselves, and their defence against a common enemy.

*Subjects have liberty to defend their own bodies, even against them that lawfully invade them.* First therefore, seeing sovereignty by institution, is by covenant of every one to every one; and sovereignty by acquisition, by covenants of the vanquished to the victor, or child to the parent; it is manifest, that every subject has liberty in all those things, the right whereof cannot by covenant be transferred. I have shewn before in the 14th chapter, that covenants, not to defend a man's own body, are void. Therefore,

*Are not bound to hurt themselves.* If the sovereign command a man, though justly condemned, to kill, wound, or maim himself; or not to resist those that assault him; or to abstain from the use of food, air, medicine, or any other thing, without which he cannot live; yet hath that man the liberty to disobey.

If a man be interrogated by the sovereign, or his authority, concerning a crime done by himself, he is not bound, without assurance of pardon, to confess it; because no man, as I have shown in the same chapter, can be obliged by covenant to accuse himself.

Again, the consent of a subject to sovereign power, is contained in these words, *I authorize, or take upon me, all his actions;* in which there is no restriction at all, of his own former natural liberty: for by allowing him to *kill me*, I am not bound to kill myself when he commands me. It is one thing to say, *kill me, or my fellow, if you please;* another thing to say, *I will kill myself, or my fellow.* It followeth therefore, that

No man is bound by these words themselves, either to kill himself, or any other man; and consequently, that the obligation a man may sometimes have, upon the command of the sovereign to execute any dangerous, or dishonourable office, dependeth not on the words of our submission; but on the

intention, which is to be understood by the end thereof. When
therefore our refusal to obey, frustrates the end for which the
sovereignty was ordained; then there is no liberty to refuse:
otherwise there is.

*Nor to warfare, unless they voluntarily undertake it.* Upon
this ground, a man that is commanded as a soldier to fight
against the enemy, though his sovereign have right enough to
punish his refusal with death, may nevertheless in many cases
refuse, without injustice; as when he substituteth a sufficient
soldier in his place: for in this case he deserteth not the
service of the commonwealth. And there is allowance to be
made for natural timorousness; not only to women, of whom
no such dangerous duty is expected, but also to men of
feminine courage. When armies fight, there is on one side, or
both, a running away; yet when they do it not out of treachery, but fear, they are not esteemed to do it unjustly, but
dishonourably. For the same reason, to avoid battle, is not
injustice, but cowardice. But he that enrolleth himself a soldier or taketh imprest money, taketh away the excuse of a
timorous nature; and is obliged, not only to go to the battle,
but also not to run from it, without his captain's leave. And
when the defence of the commonwealth, requireth at once
the help of all that are able to bear arms, every one is obliged;
because otherwise the institution of the commonwealth, which
they have not the purpose, or courage to preserve, was in vain.

To resist the sword of the commonwealth, in defence of another man, guilty, or innocent, no man hath liberty; because
such liberty, takes away from the sovereign, the means of
protecting us; and is therefore destructive of the very essence
of government. But in case a great many men together, have
already resisted the sovereign power unjustly, or committed
some capital crime, for which every one of them expecteth
death, whether have they not the liberty then to join together,
and assist, and defend one another? Certainly they have: for
they but defend their lives, which the guilty man may as well
do, as the innocent. There was indeed injustice in the first
breach of their duty; their bearing of arms subsequent to it,
though it be to maintain what they have done, is no new unjust act. And if it be only to defend their persons, it is not
unjust at all. But the offer of pardon taketh from them, to
whom it is offered, the plea of self-defence, and maketh their
perseverance in assisting, or defending the rest, unlawful.

*The greatest liberty of subjects, dependeth on the silence of
the law.* As for other liberties, they depend on the silence of

the law. In cases where the sovereign has prescribed no rule, there the subject hath the liberty to do, or forbear, according to his own discretion. And therefore such liberty is in some places more, and in some less; and in some times more, in other times less, according as they that have the sovereignty shall think most convenient. As for example, there was a time, when in England a man might enter into his own land, and dispossess such as wrongfully possessed it, by force. But in aftertimes, that liberty of forcible entry, was taken away by a statute made, by the king, in parliament. And in some places of the world, men have the liberty of many wives: in other places, such liberty is not allowed.

If a subject have a controversy with his sovereign, of debt, or of right of possession of lands or goods, or concerning any service required at his hands, or concerning any penalty, corporal, or pecuniary, grounded on a precedent law; he hath the same liberty to sue for his right, as if it were against a subject; and before such judges, as are appointed by the sovereign. For seeing the sovereign demandeth by force of a former law, and not by virtue of his power; he declareth thereby, that he requireth no more, than shall appear to be due by that law. The suit therefore is not contrary to the will of the sovereign; and consequently the subject hath the liberty to demand the hearing of his cause; and sentence, according to that law. But if he demand, or take any thing by pretence of his power; there lieth, in that case, no action of law; for all that is done by him in virtue of his power, is done by the authority of every subject, and consequently he that brings an action against the sovereign, brings it against himself.

If a monarch, or sovereign assembly, grant a liberty to all, or any of his subjects, which grant standing, he is disabled to provide for their safety, the grant is void; unless he directly renounce, or transfer the sovereignty to another. For in that he might openly, if it had been his will, and in plain terms, have renounced, or transferred it, and did not; it is to be understood it was not his will, but that the grant proceeded from ignorance of the repugnancy between such a liberty and the sovereign power; and therefore the sovereignty is still retained; and consequently all those powers, which are necessary to the exercising thereof; such as are the power of war, and peace, of judicature, of appointing officers, and councillors, of levying money, and the rest named in the eighteenth chapter.

*In what cases subjects are absolved of their obedience to*

*their sovereign*. The obligation of subjects to the sovereign, is understood to last as long, and no longer, than the power lasteth, by which he is able to protect them. For the right men have by nature to protect themselves, when none else can protect them, can by no covenant be relinquished. The sovereignty is the soul of the commonwealth; which once departed from the body, the members do no more receive their motion from it. The end of obedience is protection; which, wheresoever a man seeth it, either in his own, or in another's sword, nature applieth his obedience to it, and his endeavour to maintain it. And though sovereignty, in the intention of them that make it, be immortal; yet is it in its own nature, not only subject to violent death, by foreign war; but also through the ignorance, and passions of men, it hath in it, from the very institution, many seeds of a natural mortality, by intestine discord.

*In case of captivity.* If a subject be taken prisoner in war; or his person, or his means of life be within the guards of the enemy, and hath his life and corporal liberty given him, on condition to be subject to the victor, he hath liberty to accept the condition; and having accepted it, is the subject of him that took him; because he had no other way to preserve himself. The case is the same, if he be detained on the same terms, in a foreign country. But if a man be held in prison, or bonds, or is not trusted with the liberty of his body; he cannot be understood to be bound by covenant to subjection; and therefore may, if he can, make his escape by any means whatsoever.

*In case the sovereign cast off the government from himself and his heirs.* If a monarch shall relinquish the sovereignty, both for himself, and his heirs; his subjects return to the absolute liberty of nature; because, though nature may declare who are his sons, and who are the nearest of his kin; yet it dependeth on his own will, as hath been said in the precedent chapter, who shall be his heir. If therefore he will have no heir, there is no sovereignty, nor subjection. The case is the same, if he die without known kindred, and without declaration of his heir. For then there can no heir be known, and consequently no subjection be due.

*In case of banishment.* If the sovereign banish his subject; during the banishment, he is not subject. But he that is sent on a message, or hath leave to travel, is still subject; but it is, by contract between sovereigns, not by virtue of the covenant of subjection. For whosoever entereth into another's dominion, is subject to all the laws thereof; unless he have a privilege by the amity of the sovereigns, or by special license.

*In case the sovereign render himself subject to another*. If a monarch subdued by war, render himself subject to the victor; his subjects are delivered from their former obligation, and become obliged to the victor. But if he be held prisoner, or have not the liberty of his own body; he is not understood to have given away the right of sovereignty; and therefore his subjects are obliged to yield obedience to the magistrates formerly placed, governing not in their own name, but in his. For, his right remaining, the question is only of the administration; that is to say, of the magistrates and officers; which, if he have not means to name, he is supposed to approve those, which he himself had formerly appointed.

# Chapter 22

## Of Systems Subject, Political, and Private

*The divers sorts of systems of people.* Having spoken of the generation, form, and power of commonwealth, I am in order to speak next of the parts thereof. And first of systems, which resemble the similar parts, or muscles of a body natural. By SYSTEMS, I understand any numbers of men joined in one interest, or one business. Of which, some are *regular*, and some *irregular*. *Regular* are those, where one man, or assembly of men, is constituted representative of the whole number. All other are *irregular*.

Of regular, some are *absolute*, and *independent*, subject to none but their own representative: such are only commonwealths; of which I have spoken already in the five last precedent chapters. Others are dependent; that is to say, subordinate to some sovereign power, to which every one, as also their representative is *subject*.

Of systems subordinate, some are *political*, and some *private*. Political, otherwise called *bodies politic*, and *persons in law*, are those, which are made by authority from the sovereign power of the commonwealth. *Private*, are those, which are constituted by subjects amongst themselves, or by authority from a stranger. For no authority derived from foreign power, within the dominion of another, is public there, but private.

And of private systems, some are *lawful;* some *unlawful. Lawful,* are those which are allowed by the commonwealth: all other are *unlawful. Irregular* systems, are those which having no representative, consist only in concourse of people; which if not forbidden by the commonwealth, nor made on evil design, such as are conflux of people to markets, or shows, or any other harmless end, are lawful. But when the intention is evil, or (if the number be considerable), unknown, they are unlawful.

*In all bodies politic the power of the representative is limited.* In bodies politic, the power of the representative is always limited: and that which prescribeth the limits thereof, is the power sovereign. For power unlimited, is absolute sovereignty. And the sovereign in every commonwealth, is the absolute representative of all the subjects; and therefore no other can be representative of any part of them, but so far forth, as he shall give leave. And to give leave to a body politic of subjects, to have an absolute representative to all intents and purposes, were to abandon the government of so much of the commonwealth, and to divide the dominion, contrary to their peace and defence; which the sovereign cannot be understood to do, by any grant, that does not plainly, and directly discharge them of their subjection. For consequences of words, are not the signs of his will, when other consequences are signs of the contrary; but rather signs of error, and misreckoning; to which all mankind is too prone.

The bounds of that power, which is given to the representative of a body politic, are to be taken notice of, from two things. One is their writ, or letters from the sovereign: the other is the law of the commonwealth.

*By letters patent:* For though in the institution or acquisition of a commonwealth, which is independent, there needs no writing, because the power of the representative has there no other bounds, but such as are set out by the unwritten law of nature; yet in subordinate bodies, there are such diversities of limitation necessary, concerning their business, times, and places, as can neither be remembered without letters, nor taken notice of, unless such letters be patent, that they may be read to them, and withal sealed, or testified, with the seals, or other permanent signs of the authority sovereign.

*And the laws.* And because such limitation is not always easy, or perhaps possible to be described in writing; the ordinary laws, common to all subjects, must determine what the representative may lawfully do, in all cases, where the letters themselves are silent. And therefore,

*When the representative is one man, his unwarranted acts are his own only.* In a body politic, if the representative be one man, whatsoever he does in the person of the body, which is not warranted in his letters, nor by the laws, is his own act, and not the act of the body, nor of any other member thereof besides himself: because further than his letters, or the laws limit, he representeth no man's person, but his own. But what he does according to these, is the act of every one: for of the act of the sovereign every one is author, because he is their representative unlimited; and the act of him that recedes not from the letters of the sovereign, is the act of the sovereign, and therefore every member of the body is author of it.

*When it is an assembly, it is the act of them that assented*

*only*. But if the representative be an assembly; whatsoever that assembly shall decree, not warranted by their letters, or the laws, is the act of the assembly, or body politic, and the act of every one by whose vote the decree was made; but not the act of any man that being present voted to the contrary; nor of any man absent, unless he voted it by procuration. It is the act of the assembly, because voted by the major part; and if it be a crime, the assembly may be punished, as far forth as it is capable, as by dissolution, or forfeiture of their letters (which is to such artificial, and fictitious bodies, capital) or, if the assembly have a common stock, wherein none of the innocent members have propriety, by pecuniary mulct. For from corporal penalties nature hath exempted all bodies politic. But they that gave not their vote, are therefore innocent, because the assembly cannot represent any man in things unwarranted by their letters, and consequently are not involved in their votes.

*When the representative is one man, if he borrow money, or owe it, by contract, he is liable only, the members not*. If the person of the body politic being in one man, borrow money of a stranger, that is, of one that is not of the same body, (for no letters need limit borrowing, seeing it is left to men's own inclinations to limit lending), the debt is the representative's. For if he should have authority from his letters, to make the members pay what he borroweth, he should have by consequence the sovereignty of them; and therefore that grant were either void, as proceeding from error, commonly incident to human nature, and an insufficient sign of the will of the granter; or if it be avowed by him, then is the representer sovereign, and falleth not under the present question, which is only of bodies subordinate. No member therefore is obliged to pay the debt so borrowed, but the representative himself: because he that lendeth it, being a stranger to the letters, and to the qualification of the body, understandeth those only for his debtors, that are engaged: and seeing the representer can engage himself, and none else, has him only for debtor; who must therefore pay him, out of the common stock, if there be any, or, if there be none, out of his own estate.

If he come into debt by contract, or mulct, the case is the same.

*When it is an assembly, they only are liable that have assented*. But when the representative is an assembly, and the debt to a stranger; all they, and only they are responsible for the debt, that gave their votes to the borrowing of it, or to the contract that made it due, or to the fact for which the mulct was imposed; because every one of those in voting did engage himself for the payment: for he that is author of the borrowing, is obliged to the payment, even of the whole debt; though when paid by any one, he be discharged.

*If the debt be to one of the assembly, the body only is obliged.* But if the debt be to one of the assembly, the assembly only is obliged to the payment, out of their common stock, if they have any: for having liberty of vote, if he vote the money shall be borrowed, he votes it shall be paid; if he vote it shall not be borrowed, or be absent, yet because in lending, he voteth the borrowing, he contradicteth his former vote, and is obliged by the latter, and becomes both borrower and lender, and consequently cannot demand payment from any particular man, but from the common treasure only; which failing he hath no remedy, nor complaint, but against himself, that being privy to the acts of the assembly, and to their means to pay, and not being enforced, did nevertheless through his own folly lend his money.

*Protestation against the decrees of bodies politic sometimes lawful, but against sovereign power never.* It is manifest by this, that in bodies politic subordinate, and subject to a sovereign power, it is sometimes not only lawful, but expedient, for a particular man to make open protestation against the decrees of the representative assembly, and cause their dissent to be registered, or to take witness of it; because otherwise they may be obliged to pay debts contracted, and be responsible for crimes committed by other men. But in a sovereign assembly, that liberty is taken away, both because he that protesteth there, denies their sovereignty; and also because whatsoever is commanded by the sovereign power, is as to the subject, though not so always in the sight of God, justified by the command: for of such command every subject is the author.

*Bodies politic for government of a province, colony, or town.* The variety of bodies politic, is almost infinite: for they are not only distinguished by the several affairs, for which they are constituted, wherein there is an unspeakable diversity; but also by the times, places, and numbers, subject to many limitations. And as to their affairs, some are ordained for government; as first, the government of a province may be committed to an assembly of men, wherein all resolutions shall depend on the votes of the major part; and then this assembly is a body politic, and their power limited by commission. This word province signifies a charge, or care of business, which he whose business it is, committeth to another man, to be administered for, and under him; and therefore when in one commonwealth there be divers countries, that have their laws distinct one from another, or are far distant in place, the administration of the government being committed to divers persons, those countries where the sovereign is not resident, but governs by commission, are called provinces. But of the government of a province, by an assembly residing in the province itself, there be few examples. The Romans who had the sovereignty of many provinces; yet governed them always by presidents, and prætors; and not by assemblies, as they governed the city of Rome, and territories adjacent. In like manner, when there were colonies sent from England, to plant Virginia, and Sommer-islands; though the governments of them here, were committed to assemblies in London, yet did those assemblies never commit the government under them to any assembly there, but did to each plantation send one governor. For though every man, where he can be present by nature, desires to participate of government; yet where they cannot be present, they are by nature also inclined, to commit the government of their common interest rather to a monarchical, than a popular form of government: which is also evident in those men that have great private estates; who when they are unwilling to take the pains of administering the business that belongs to them, choose rather to trust one servant, than an assembly either of their friends or servants. But howsoever it be in fact, yet we may suppose the government of a province, or colony committed to an assembly: and when it is, that which in this place I have to say, is this; that whatsoever debt is by that assembly contracted; or whatsoever unlawful act is decreed, is the act only of those that assented, and not of any that dissented, or were absent, for the reasons before alleged. Also that an assembly residing out of the bounds of that colony whereof they have the government, cannot execute any power over the persons, or goods of any of the colony, to seize on them for debt, or other duty, in any place without the colony itself, as having no jurisdiction, nor authority elsewhere, but are left to the remedy, which the law of the place alloweth them. And though the assembly have right, to impose a mulct upon any of their members, that shall break the laws they make; yet out of the colony itself, they have no right to execute the same. And that which is said here, of the rights of an assembly, for the government of a province, or a colony, is applicable also to an assembly for the government of a town, an university, or a college, or a church, or for any other government over the persons of men.

And generally, in all bodies politic, if any particular member conceive himself injured by the body itself, the cognizance of his cause belongeth to the sovereign, and those the sovereign hath ordained for judges in such causes, or shall ordain for that particular cause; and not to the body itself. For the whole body is in this case his fellow-subject, which in a sovereign assembly, is otherwise: for there, if the sovereign be not judge, though in his own cause, there can be no judge at all.

*Bodies politic for ordering of trade.* In a body politic, for the well ordering of foreign traffic, the most commodious representative is an assembly of all the members; that is to say, such a one, as every one that adventureth his money, may be present at all the deliberations, and resolutions of the body, if they will themselves. For proof whereof, we are to consider the end, for which men that are merchants, and may buy and sell, export, and import their merchandise, according to their own discretions, do nevertheless bind themselves up in one corporation. It is true, there be few merchants, that with the merchandise they buy at home, can freight a ship, to export it; or with that they buy abroad, to bring it home; and have therefore need to join together in one society; where every man may either participate of the gain, according to the proportion of his adventure; or take his own, and sell what he transports, or imports, at such prices as he thinks fit. But this is no body politic, there being no common representative to oblige them to any other law, than that which is common to all other subjects. The end of their incorporating, is to make their gain the greater; which is done two ways; by sole buying, and sole selling, both at home, and abroad. So that to grant a company of merchants to be a corporation, or body politic, is to grant them a double monopoly, whereof one is to be sole buyers; another to be sole sellers. For when there is a company incorporate for any particular foreign country, they only export the commodities vendible in that country; which is sole buying at home, and sole selling abroad. For at home there is but one buyer, and abroad but one that selleth: both which is gainful to the merchant, because thereby they buy at home at lower, and sell abroad at higher rates: and abroad there is but one buyer of foreign merchandize, and but one that sells them at home; both which again are gainful to the adventurers.

Of this double monopoly one part is disadvantageous to the people at home, the other to foreigners. For at home by their sole exportation they set what price they please on the husbandry, and handyworks of the people; and by the sole importation, what price they please on all foreign commodities the people have need of; both which are ill for the people. On the contrary, by the sole selling of the native commodities abroad, and sole buying the foreign commodities upon the place, they raise the price of those, and abate the price of these, to the disadvantage of the foreigner: for where but one selleth, the merchandize is the dearer; and where but one buyeth, the cheaper. Such corporations therefore are no other than monopolies; though they would be very profitable for a commonwealth, if being bound up into one body in foreign markets they were at liberty at home, every man to buy, and sell at what price he could.

The end then of these bodies of merchants, being not a common benefit to the whole body, which have in this case no common stock, but what is deducted out of the particular adventures, for building, buying, victualling and manning of ships, but the particular gain of every adventurer, it is reason that every one be acquainted with the employment of his own; that is, that every one be of the assembly, that shall have the power to order the same; and be acquainted with their accounts. And therefore the representative of such a body must be an assembly, where every member of the body may be present at the consultations, if he will.

If a body politic of merchants, contract a debt to a stranger by the act of their representative assembly, every member is liable by himself for the whole. For a stranger can take no notice of their private laws, but considereth them as so many particular men, obliged every one to the whole payment, till payment made by one dischargeth all the rest: but if the debt be to one of the company, the creditor is debtor for the whole to himself, and cannot therefore demand his debt, but only from the common stock, if there be any.

If the commonwealth impose a tax upon the body, it is understood to be laid upon every member proportionably to his particular adventure in the company. For there is in this case no other common stock, but what is made of their particular adventures.

If a mulct be laid upon the body for some unlawful act, they only are liable by whose votes the act was decreed, or by whose assistance it was executed; for in none of the rest is there any other crime but being of the body; which if a crime, because the body was ordained by the authority of the commonwealth, is not his.

If one of the members be indebted to the body, he may be sued by the body; but his goods cannot be taken, nor his person imprisoned by the authority of the body; but only by authority of the commonwealth: for if they can do it by their own authority, they can by their own authority give judgment that the debt is due; which is as much as to be judge in their own cause.

*A body politic for counsel to be given to the sovereign.* These bodies made for the government of men, or of traffic, be either perpetual, or for a time prescribed by writing. But there be bodies also whose times are limited, and that only by the nature of their business. For example, if a sovereign monarch, or a sovereign assembly, shall think fit to give command to the towns, and other several parts of their territory, to send to him their deputies, to inform him of the condition, and necessities of the subjects, or to advise with him for the making of good laws, or for any other cause, as with one person representing the whole country, such deputies, having a place and time of meeting assigned them, are there, and at that time, a body politic, representing every subject of that dominion; but it is only for such matters as shall be propounded unto them by that man, or assembly, that by the sovereign authority sent for them; and when it shall be declared that nothing more shall be propounded, nor debated by them, the body is dissolved. For if they were the absolute representatives of the people, then were it the sovereign assembly; and so there would be two sovereign assemblies, or two sovereigns, over the same people; which cannot consist with their peace. And therefore where there is once a sovereignty, there can be no absolute representation of the people, but by it. And for the limits of how far such a body shall represent the whole people, they are set forth in the writing by which they were sent for. For the people cannot choose their deputies to other intent, than is in the writing directed to them from their sovereign expressed.

*A regular private body, lawful, as a family.* Private bodies regular, and lawful, are those that are constituted without letters, or other written authority, saving the laws common to all other subjects. And because they be united in one person representative, they are held for regular; such as are all families, in which the father, or master ordereth the whole family. For he obligeth his children, and servants, as far as the law permitteth, though not further, because none of them are bound to obedience in those actions, which the law hath forbidden to be done. In all other actions, during the time they are under domestic government, they are subject to their fathers, and masters, as to their immediate sovereigns. For the father and master, being before the institution of commonwealth, absolute sovereigns in their own families, they lose afterward no more of their authority, than the law of the commonwealth taketh from them.

*Private bodies regular, but unlawful.* Private bodies regular, but unlawful, are those that unite themselves into one person representative, without any public authority at all; such as are the corporations of beggars, thieves, and gipsies, the better to order their trade of begging and stealing; and the corporations of men, that by authority from any foreign person, unite themselves in another's dominion, for the easier propagation of doctrines, and for making a party, against the power of the commonwealth.

*Systems irregular, such as are private leagues.* Irregular systems, in their nature but leagues, or sometimes mere concourse of people, without union to any particular design, not by obligation of one to another, but proceeding only from a similitude of wills and inclinations, become lawful, or unlawful, according to the lawfulness, or unlawfulness of every particular man's design therein: and his design is to be understood by the occasion.

The leagues of subjects, because leagues are commonly made for mutual defence, are in a commonwealth, which is no more than a league of all the subjects together, for the most part unnecessary, and savour of unlawful design; and are for that cause unlawful, and go commonly by the name of factions, or conspiracies. For a league being a connexion of men by covenants, if there be no power given to any one man or assembly, as in the condition of mere nature, to compel them to performance, is so long only valid, as there ariseth no just cause of distrust: and therefore leagues between commonwealths, over whom there is no human power established, to keep them all in awe, are not only lawful, but also profitable for the time they last. But leagues of the subjects of one and the same commonwealth, where every one may obtain his right by means of the sovereign power, are unnecessary to the maintaining of peace and justice, and, in case the design of them be evil or unknown to the commonwealth, unlawful. For all uniting of strength by private men, is, if for evil intent, unjust; if for intent unknown, dangerous to the public, and unjustly concealed.

*Secret cabals.* If the sovereign power be in a great assembly, and a number of men, part of the assembly, without authority, consult apart, to contrive the guidance of the rest; this is a faction, or conspiracy unlawful, as being fraudulent seducing of the assembly for their particular interest. But if he, whose private interest is to be debated and judged in the assembly, make as many friends as he can; in him it is no injustice; because in this case he is no part of the assembly. And though he hire such friends with money, unless there be an express law against it, yet it is not injustice. For sometimes, as men's manners are, justice cannot be had without money; and every man may think his own cause just, till it be heard, and judged.

*Feuds of private families.* In all commonwealths, if private men entertain more servants, than the government of his estate, and lawful employment he has for them requires, it is faction, and unlawful. For having the protection of the commonwealth, he needeth not the defence of private force. And whereas in nations not thoroughly civilized, several numerous families have lived in continual hostility, and invaded one another with private force; yet it is evident enough, that they have done unjustly; or else they had no commonwealth.

*Factions for government.* And as factions for kindred, so also factions for government of religion, as of Papists, Protestants, &c. or of state, as patricians, and plebeians of old time in Rome, and of aristocraticals and democraticals of old time in Greece, are unjust, as being contrary to the peace and safety of the people, and a taking of the sword out of the hand of the sovereign.

*Concourse of people.* Concourse of people is an irregular system, the lawfulness, or unlawfulness, whereof dependeth on the occasion, and on the number of them that are assembled. If the occasion be lawful, and manifest, the concourse is lawful; as the usual meeting of men at church, or at a public show, in usual numbers: for if the numbers be extraordinarily great, the occasion is not evident; and consequently he that cannot render a particular and good account of his being amongst them, is to be judged conscious of an unlawful, and tumultuous design. It may be lawful for a thousand men, to join to a petition to be delivered to a judge, or magistrate;

yet if a thousand men come to present it, it is a tumultuous assembly; because there needs but one or two for that purpose. But in such cases as these, it is not a set number that makes the assembly unlawful, but such a number, as the present officers are not able to suppress, and bring to justice.

When an unusual number of men, assemble against a man whom they accuse; the assembly is an unlawful tumult; because they may deliver their accusation to the magistrate by a few, or by one man. Such was the case of St. Paul at Ephesus; where Demetrius and a great number of other men, brought two of Paul's companions before the magistrate, saying with one voice, *Great is Diana of the Ephesians;* which was their way of demanding justice against them for teaching the people such doctrine, as was against their religion, and trade. The occasion here, consisting the laws of that people, was just; yet was their assembly judged unlawful, and the magistrate reprehended them for it in these words (*Acts* xix. 38-40), *If Demetrius and the other workmen can accuse any man, of any thing, there be pleas, and deputies, let them accuse one another. And if you have any other thing to demand, your case may be judged in an assembly lawfully called. For we are in danger to be accused for this day's sedition; because there is no cause by which any man can render any reason of this concourse of people.* Where he calleth an assembly, whereof men can give no just account, a sedition, and such as they could not answer for. And this is all I shall say concerning *systems*, and assemblies of people, which may be compared, as I said, to the similar parts of man's body; such as be lawful, to the muscles; such as are unlawful, to wens, biles, and apostems, engendered by the unnatural conflux of evil humours.

## Chapter 23

### Of the Public Ministers of Sovereign Power

In the last chapter I have spoken of the similar parts of a commonwealth: in this I shall speak of the parts organical, which are public ministers.

*Public minister, who.* A public minister, is he, that by the sovereign, whether a monarch or an assembly, is employed in any affairs, with authority to represent in that employment, the person of the commonwealth. And whereas every man, or assembly that hath sovereignty, representeth two persons, or, as the more common phrase is, has two capacities, one natural, and another politic: as a monarch, hath the person not only of the commonwealth, but also of a man; and a sovereign assembly hath the person not only of the commonwealth, but also of the assembly: they that be servants to them in their natural capacity, are not public ministers; but those only that serve them in the administration of the public business. And therefore neither ushers, nor sergeants, nor other officers that wait on the assembly, for no other purpose, but for the commodity of the men assembled, in an aristocracy, or democracy; nor stewards, chamberlains, cofferers, or any other officers of the household of a monarch, are public ministers in a monarchy.

*Ministers for the general administration.* Of public ministers, some have charge committed to them for a general administration, either of the whole dominion, or of a part thereof. Of the whole, as to a protector, or regent, may be committed by the predecessor of an infant king, during his minority, the whole administration of his kingdom. In which case, every subject is so far obliged to obedience, as the ordinances he shall make, and the commands he shall give be in the king's name, and not inconsistent with his sovereign power. Of a part, or province; as when either a monarch, or a sovereign assembly, shall give the general charge thereof to a governor, lieutenant, præfect, or viceroy: and in this case also, every one of that province is obliged to all he shall do in the name of the sovereign, and that not incompatible with the sovereign's right. For such protectors, viceroys, and governors, have no other right, but what depends on the sovereign's will;

and no commission that can be given them, can be interpreted for a declaration of the will to transfer the sovereignty, without express and perspicuous words to that purpose. And this kind of public ministers resembleth the nerves, and tendons that move the several limbs of a body natural.

*For special administration, as for economy*. Others have special administration, that is to say, charges of some special business, either at home, or abroad: as at home, first, for the economy of a commonwealth, they that have authority concerning the *treasure*, as tributes, impositions, rents, fines or whatsoever public revenue, to collect, receive, issue, or take the accounts thereof, are public ministers: ministers, because they serve the person representative, and can do nothing against his command, nor without his authority: public, because they serve him in his political capacity.

Secondly, they that have authority concerning the *militia;* to have the custody of arms, forts, ports; to levy, pay, or conduct soldiers; or to provide for any necessary thing for the use of war, either by land or sea, are public ministers. But a soldier without command, though he fight for the commonwealth, does not therefore represent the person of it; because there is none to represent it to. For every one that hath command, represents it to them only whom he commandeth.

*For instruction of the people*. They also that have authority to teach, or to enable others to teach the people their duty to the sovereign power, and instruct them in the knowledge of what is just, and unjust, thereby to render them more apt to live in godliness, and in peace amongst themselves, and resist the public enemy, are public ministers: ministers, in that they do it not by their own authority, but by another's; and public, because they do it, or should do it, by no authority but that of the sovereign. The monarch, or the sovereign assembly only hath immediate authority from God, to teach and instruct the people; and no man but the sovereign, receiveth his power *Dei gratiâ* simply; that is to say, from the favour of none but God: all other, receive theirs from the favour and providence of God, and their sovereigns; as in a monarchy *Dei gratiâ et regis;* or *Dei providentiâ et voluntate regis*.

*For judicature*. They also to whom jurisdiction is given, are public ministers. For in their seats of justice they represent the person of the sovereign; and their sentence, is his sentence: for, as hath been before declared, all judicature is essentially annexed to the sovereignty; and therefore all other judges are but ministers of him or them that have the sovereign power.

And as controversies are of two sorts, namely of *fact*, and of *law;* so are judgments, some of fact, some of law: and consequently in the same controversy, there may be two judges, one of fact, another of law.

And in both these controversies, there may arise a controversy between the party judged, and the judge; which because they be both subjects to the sovereign, ought in equity to be judged by men agreed on by consent of both; for no man can be judge in his own cause. But the sovereign is already agreed on for judge by them both, and is therefore either to hear the cause, and determine it himself, or appoint for judge such as they shall both agree on. And this agreement is then understood to be made between them divers ways; as first, if the defendant be allowed to except against such of his judges, whose interest maketh him suspect them, (for as to the complainant, he hath already chosen his own judge), those which he excepteth not against, are judges he himself agrees on. Secondly, if he appeal to any other judge, he can appeal no further; for his appeal is his choice. Thirdly, if he appeal to the sovereign himself, and he by himself, or by delegates which the parties shall agree on, give sentence; that sentence is final: for the defendant is judged by his own judges, that is to say, by himself.

These properties of just and rational judicature considered, I cannot forbear to observe the excellent constitution of the courts of justice, established both for Common, and also for Public Pleas in England. By Common Pleas, I mean those, where both the complainant and defendant are subjects: and by public, which are also called Pleas of the Crown, those where the complainant is the sovereign. For whereas there were two orders of men, whereof one was Lords, the other Commons; the Lords had this privilege, to have for judges in all capital crimes, none but Lords; and of them, as many as would be present; which being ever acknowledged as a privilege of favour, their judges were none but such as they had themselves desired. And in all controversies, every subject, (as also in civil controversies the Lords), had for judges, men of the country where the matter in controversy lay; against which he might make his exceptions, till at last twelve men without exception being agreed on, they were judged by those twelve. So that having his own judges, there could be nothing alleged by the party, why the sentence should not be final. These public persons, with authority from the sovereign power, either to instruct, or judge the people, are such members of the commonwealth, as may fitly be compared to the organs of voice in a body natural.

*For execution.* Public ministers are also all those, that have authority from the sovereign, to procure the execution of judgments given; to publish the sovereign's commands; to suppress tumults; to apprehend, and imprison malefactors; and other acts tending to the conservation of the peace. For every act they do by such authority, is the act of the commonwealth; and their service, answerable to that of the hands, in a body natural.

Public ministers abroad, are those that represent the person of their own sovereign, to foreign states. Such are ambassadors, messengers, agents, and heralds, sent by public authority, and on public business.

But such as are sent by authority only of some private party of a troubled state, though they be received, are neither public, nor private ministers of the commonwealth; because none of their actions have the commonwealth for author. Likewise, an ambassador sent from a prince, to congratulate, condole, or to assist at a solemnity; though the authority be public; yet because the business is private, and belonging to him in his natural capacity; is a private person. Also if a man be sent into another country, secretly to explore their counsels, and strength; though both the authority, and the business be public; yet because there is none to take notice of any person in him, but his own; he is but a private minister; but yet a minister of the commonwealth; and may be compared to an eye in the body natural. And those that are appointed to receive the petitions or other informations of the people, and are as it were the public ear, are public ministers, and represent their sovereign in that office.

*Councillors without other employment than to advise are not public ministers.* Neither a councillor, nor a council of state, if we consider it with no authority of judicature or command, but only of giving advice to the sovereign when it is required, or of offering it when it is not required, is a public person. For the advice is addressed to the sovereign only, whose person cannot in his own presence, be represented to him, by another. But a body of councillors, are never without some other authority, either of judicature, or of immediate administration: as in a monarchy, they represent the monarch, in delivering his commands to the public ministers: in a democracy, the council, or senate propounds the result of their deliberations to the people, as a council; but when they appoint judges, or hear causes, or give audience to ambassadors, it is in the quality of a minister of the people: and in an aristocracy, the council of state is the sovereign assembly itself; and gives counsel to none but themselves.

# Chapter 24

## Of the Nutrition, and Procreation
## of a Commonwealth

*The nourishment of a commonwealth consisteth in the commodities of sea and land:* THE NUTRITION of a commonwealth consisteth, in the *plenty,* and *distribution* of *materials* conducing to life: in *concoction,* or *preparation;* and, when concocted, in the *conveyance* of it, by convenient conduits, to the public use.

As for the plenty of matter, it is a thing limited by nature, to those commodities, which from the two breasts of our common mother, land and sea, God usually either freely giveth, or for labour selleth to mankind.

For the matter of this nutriment, consisting in animals, vegetals, and minerals, God hath freely laid them before us, in or near to the face of the earth; so as there needeth no more but the labour, and industry of receiving them. Insomuch as plenty dependeth, next to God's favour, merely on the labour and industry of men.

This matter, commonly called commodities, is partly *native,* and partly *foreign: native,* that which is to be had within the territory of the commonwealth: *foreign,* that which is imported from without. And because there is no territory under the dominion of one commonwealth, except it be of very vast extent, that produceth all things needful for the maintenance, and motion of the whole body; and few that produce not some thing more than necessary; the superfluous commodities to be had within, become no more superfluous, but supply these wants at home, by importation of that which may be had abroad, either by exchange, or by just war, or by labour. For a man's labour also, is a commodity exchangeable for benefit, as well as any other thing: and there have been commonwealths that having no more territory, than hath served them for habitation, have nevertheless, not only maintained, but also increased their power, partly by the labour of trading from one place to another, and partly by selling the manufactures whereof the materials were brought in from other places.

*And the right distribution of them.* The distribution of the materials of this nourishment, is the constitution of *mine,* and *thine,* and *his;* that is to say, in one word *propriety;* and belongeth in all kinds of commonwealth to the sovereign power. For where there is no commonwealth, there is, as hath been already shown, a perpetual war of every man against his neighbour; and therefore every thing is his that getteth it, and keepeth it by force; which is neither *propriety,* nor *community;* but *uncertainty.* Which is so evident, that even Cicero, a passionate defender of liberty, in a public pleading, attributeth all propriety to the law civil. *Let the civil law,* saith he, *be once abandoned, or but negligently guarded, not to say oppressed, and there is nothing, that any man can be sure to receive from his ancestor, or leave to his children.* And again; *Take away the civil law, and no man knows what is his own, and what another man's.* Seeing therefore the introduction of *propriety* is an effect of commonwealth, which can do nothing but by the person that represents it, it is the act only of the sovereign; and consisteth in the laws, which none can make that have not the sovereign power. And this they well knew of old, who called that Νόμος, that is to say, *distribution,* which we call law; and defined justice, by *distributing* to every man *his own.*

*All private estates of land proceed originally from the arbitrary distribution of the sovereign.* In this distribution, the first law, is for division of the land itself: wherein the sovereign assigneth to every man a portion, according as he, and not according as any subject, or any number of them, shall judge agreeable to equity, and the common good. The children of Israel, were a commonwealth in the wilderness; but wanted the commodities of the earth, till they were masters of the Land of Promise; which afterward was divided amongst them, not by their own discretion, but by the discretion of Eleazar the Priest, and Joshua their General, who, when there were twelve tribes, making them thirteen by subdivision of the tribe of Joseph, made nevertheless but twelve portions of the land; and ordained for the tribe of Levi no land; but assigned them the tenth part of the whole fruits; which division was therefore arbitrary. And though a people coming into possession of a land by war, do not always exterminate the ancient inhabitants, as did the Jews, but leave to many, or most or all of them their estates; yet it is manifest they hold them afterwards, as of the victors' distribution; as the people of England held all theirs of William the Conqueror.

*Propriety of a subject excludes not the dominion of the sovereign, but only of another subject.* From whence we may collect, that the propriety which a subject hath in his lands, consisteth in a right to exclude all other subjects from the use of them; and not to exclude their sovereign, be it an assembly, or a monarch. For seeing the sovereign, that is to say, the commonwealth, whose person he representeth, is understood to do nothing but in order to the common peace and security, this distribution of lands, is to be understood as done in order to the same: and consequently, whatsoever distribution he shall make in prejudice thereof, is contrary to the will of every subject, that committed his peace, and safety to his discretion, and conscience; and therefore by the will of every one of them, is to be reputed void. It is true, that a sovereign monarch, or the greater part of a sovereign assembly, may ordain the doing of many things in pursuit of their passions, contrary to their own consciences, which is a breach of trust, and of the law of nature; but this is not enough to authorize any subject, either to make war upon, or so much as to accuse of injustice, or any way to speak evil of their sovereign; because they have authorized all his actions, and in bestowing the sovereign power, made them their own. But in what cases the commands of sovereigns are contrary to equity, and the law of nature, is to be considered hereafter in another place.

*The public is not to be dieted.* In the distribution of land, the commonwealth itself, may be conceived to have a portion, and possess, and improve the same by their representative; and that such portion may be made sufficient, to sustain the whole expense to the common peace, and defence necessarily required. Which were very true, if there could be any representative conceived free from human passions, and infirmities. But the nature of men being as it is, the setting forth of public land, or of any certain revenue for the commonwealth, is in vain; and tendeth to the dissolution of government, and to the condition of mere nature, and war, as soon as ever the sovereign power falleth into the hands of a monarch, or of an assembly, that are either too negligent of money, or too hazardous in engaging the public stock into a long or costly war. Commonwealths can endure no diet: for seeing their expense is not limited by their own appetite, but by external accidents, and the appetites of their neighbours, the public riches cannot be limited by other limits, than those which the emergent occasions shall require. And whereas in England, there were by the Conqueror, divers lands reserved to his own use, besides forests and chases, either for his recreation, or preservation of woods, and divers services reserved on the land he gave his subjects; yet it seems they were not reserved for his maintenance in his public, but in his natural capacity. For he, and his successors did for all that, lay arbitrary taxes on all subjects' land, when they judged it necessary. Or if those public lands, and services, were ordained as a sufficient maintenance of the commonwealth, it was contrary to the scope of the institution; being, as it appeared by those ensuing taxes, insufficient, and, as it appears by the late small revenue of the crown, subject to alienation and diminution. It is therefore in vain, to assign a portion to the commonwealth; which may sell, or give it away; and does sell and give it away, when it is done by their representative.

*The places and matter of traffic depend, as their distribution, on the sovereign.* As the distribution of lands at home; so also to assign in what places, and for what commodities, the subject shall traffic abroad, belongeth to the sovereign. For if it did belong to private persons to use their own discretion therein, some of them would be drawn for gain, both to furnish the enemy with means to hurt the commonwealth, and hurt it themselves, by importing such things, as pleasing men's appetites, be nevertheless noxious, or at least unprofitable to them. And therefore it belongeth to the commonwealth, that is, to the sovereign only, to approve, or disapprove both of the places, and matter of foreign traffic.

*The laws of transferring propriety belong also to the sovereign.* Further, seeing it is not enough to the sustentation of a commonwealth, that every man have a propriety in a portion of land, or in some few commodities, or a natural property in some useful art, and there is no art in the world, but is necessary either for the being, or well-being almost of every particular man; it is necessary, that men distribute that which they can spare, and transfer their propriety therein, mutually one to another, by exchange, and mutual contract. And therefore it belongeth to the commonwealth, that is to say, to the sovereign, to appoint in what manner all kinds of contract between subjects, as buying, selling, exchanging, borrowing, lending, letting, and taking to hire, are to be made; and by what words and signs they shall be understood for valid. And for the matter, and distribution of the nourishment, to the several members of the commonwealth, thus much, considering the model of the whole work, is sufficient.

*Money the blood of a commonwealth.* By concoction, I understand the reducing of all commodities, which are not presently consumed, but reserved for nourishment in time to

come, to something of equal value, and withal so portable, as
not to hinder the motion of men from place to place; to the
end a man may have in what place soever, such nourishment
as the place affordeth. And this is nothing else but gold, and
silver, and money. For gold and silver, being, as it happens,
almost in all countries of the world highly valued, is a commodious measure of the value of all things else between
nations; and money, of what matter soever coined by the sovereign of a commonwealth, is a sufficient measure of the value
of all things else, between the subjects of that commonwealth.
By the means of which measure, all commodities, movable
and immovable, are made to accompany a man to all places
of his resort, within and without the place of his ordinary
residence; and the same passeth from man to man, within the
commonwealth; and goes round about, nourishing, as it
passeth, every part thereof; in so much as this concoction, is
as it were the sanguification of the commonwealth: for natural
blood is in like manner made of the fruits of the earth; and
circulating, nourisheth by the way every member of the body
of man.

And because silver and gold have their value from the
matter itself; they have first this privilege, that the value of
them cannot be altered by the power of one, nor of a few
commonwealths; as being a common measure of the commodities of all places. But base money, may easily be en-
hanced, or abased. Secondly, they have the privilege to make
commonwealths move, and stretch out their arms, when need
is, into foreign countries: and supply, not only private subjects that travel, but also whole armies with provision. But
that coin, which is not considerable for the matter, but for the
stamp of the place, being unable to endure change of air, hath
its effect at home only; where also it is subject to the change
of laws, and thereby to have the value diminished, to the
prejudice many times of those that have it.

*The conduits and way of money to the public use.* The conduits, and ways by which it is conveyed to the public use, are
of two sorts: one, that conveyeth it to the public coffers; the
other, that issueth the same out again for public payments. Of
the first sort, are collectors, receivers, and treasurers; of the
second, are the treasurers again, and the officers appointed for
payment of several public or private ministers. And in this
also, the artificial man maintains his resemblance with the
natural; whose veins receiving the blood from the several parts
of the body, carry it to the heart; where being made vital, the

heart by the arteries sends it out again, to enliven, and enable for motion all the members of the same.

*The children of a commonwealth colonies.* The procreation or children of a commonwealth, are those we call *plantations,* or *colonies;* which are numbers of men sent out from the commonwealth, under a conductor, or governor, to inhabit a foreign country, either formerly void of inhabitants, or made void then by war. And when a colony is settled, they are either a commonwealth of themselves, discharged of their subjection to their sovereign that sent them, as hath been done by many commonwealths, of ancient time, in which case the commonwealth from which they went, was called their metropolis or mother, and requires no more of them, than fathers require of the children, whom they emancipate and make free from their domestic government, which is honour, and friendship; or else they remain united to their metropolis, as were the colonies of the people of Rome; and then they are no commonwealths themselves, but provinces, and parts of the commonwealth that sent them. So that the right of colonies, saving honour and league with their metropolis, dependeth wholly on their licence or letters, by which their sovereign authorised them to plant.

# Chapter 25

## Of Counsel

*Counsel, what.* How fallacious it is to judge of the nature of things by the ordinary and inconstant use of words, appeareth in nothing more, than in the confusion of counsels, and commands, arising from the imperative manner of speaking in them both, and in many other occasions besides. For the words *do this*, are the words not only of him that commandeth; but also of him that giveth counsel; and of him that exhorteth; and yet there are but few, that see not that these are very different things, or that cannot distinguish between them, when they perceive who it is that speaketh, and to whom the speech is directed, and upon what occasion. But finding those phrases in men's writings, and being not able, or not willing to enter into a consideration of the circumstances, they mistake sometimes the precepts of counsellors, for the precepts of them that command; and sometimes the contrary; according as it best agreeth with the conclusions they would infer, or the actions they approve. To avoid which mistakes, and render to those terms of commanding, counselling, and exhorting, their proper and distinct significations, I define them thus.

*Differences between command and counsel.* COMMAND is, where a man saith, *do this*, or *do not this*, without expecting other reason than the will of him that says it. From this it followeth manifestly, that he that commandeth, pretendeth thereby his own benefit: for the reason of his command is his own will only, and the proper object of every man's will, is some good to himself.

COUNSEL, is where a man saith, *do*, or *do not this*, and deduceth his reasons from the benefit that arriveth by it to him to whom he saith it. And from this it is evident, that he that giveth counsel, pretendeth only, whatsoever he intendeth, the good of him, to whom he giveth it.

Therefore between counsel and command, one great difference is, that command is directed to a man's own benefit; and counsel to the benefit of another man. And from this ariseth another difference, that a man may be obliged to do what he is commanded; as when he hath covenanted to obey; but he cannot be obliged to do as he is counselled, because the hurt of not following it, is his own; or if he should covenant to follow it, then is the counsel turned into the nature of a command. A third difference between them is, that no man can pretend a right to be of another man's counsel; because he is not to pretend benefit by it to himself: but to demand right to counsel another, argues a will to know his designs, or to gain some other good to himself: which, as I said before, is of every man's will the proper object.

This also is incident to the nature of counsel; that whatsoever it be, he that asketh it, cannot in equity accuse, or punish it: for to ask counsel of another, is to permit him to give such counsel as he shall think best; and consequently, he that giveth counsel to his sovereign, whether a monarch, or an assembly, when he asketh it, cannot in equity be punished for it, whether the same be conformable to the opinion of the most, or not, so it be to the proposition in debate. For if the sense of the assembly can be taken notice of, before the debate be ended, they should neither ask, nor take any further counsel; for the sense of the assembly, is the resolution of the debate, and end of all deliberation. And generally he that demandeth counsel, is author of it; and therefore cannot punish it; and what the sovereign cannot, no man else can. But if one subject giveth counsel to another, to do anything contrary to the laws, whether that counsel proceed from evil intention, or from ignorance only, it is punishable by the commonwealth; because ignorance of the law is no good excuse, where every man is bound to take notice of the laws to which he is subject.

*Exhortation and dehortation, what.* EXHORTATION and DE-HORTATION is counsel, accompanied with signs in him that giveth it, of vehement desire to have it followed: or to say it more briefly, *counsel vehemently pressed.* For he that exhorteth, doth not deduce the consequences of what he adviseth to be done, and tie himself therein to the rigour of true reasoning; but encourages him he counselleth to action: as he that dehorteth, deterreth him from it. And, therefore, they have in their speeches, a regard to the common passions and opinions of men, in deducing their reasons; and make use of similitudes, metaphors, examples, and other tools of oratory, to persuade their hearers of the utility, honour, or justice of following their advice.

From whence may be inferred, first, that exhortation and dehortation is directed to the good of him that giveth the counsel, not of him that asketh it, which is contrary to the duty of a counsellor; who, by the definition of counsel, ought to regard not his own benefit, but his whom he adviseth. And that he directeth his counsel to his own benefit, is manifest enough, by the long and vehement urging, or by the artificial giving thereof; which being not required of him, and consequently proceeding from his own occasions, is directed principally to his own benefit, and but accidentally to the good of him that is counselled, or not at all.

Secondly, that the use of exhortation and dehortation lieth only where a man is to speak to a multitude; because when the speech is addressed to one, he may interrupt him, and examine his reasons more rigorously than can be done in a multitude; which are too many to enter into dispute, and dialogue with him that speaketh indifferently to them all at once.

Thirdly, that they that exhort and dehort, where they are required to give counsel, are corrupt counsellors, and as it were bribed by their own interest. For though the counsel they give be never so good; yet he that gives it, is no more a good counsellor, than he that giveth a just sentence for a reward, is a just judge. But where a man may lawfully command, as a father in his family, or a leader in an army, his exhortations and dehortations, are not only lawful, but also necessary, and laudable. But then they are no more counsels, but commands; which when they are for execution of sour labour, sometimes necessity, and always humanity requireth to be sweetened in the delivery, by encouragement, and in the tune and phrase of counsel, rather than in harsher language of command.

Examples of the difference between command and counsel, we may take from the forms of speech that express them in Holy Scripture. *Have no other Gods but me; make to thyself no graven image; take not God's name in vain; sanctify the sabbath; honour thy parents; kill not; steal not, &c.* are commands; because the reason for which we are to obey them, is drawn from the will of God our king, whom we are obliged to obey. But these words, *Sell all thou hast; give it to the poor; and follow me,* are counsel; because the reason for which we are to do so, is drawn from our own benefit; which is this, that we shall have *treasure in Heaven.* These words, *Go into the village over against you, and you shall find an ass tied, and her colt; loose her, and bring her to me,* are a command: for the reason of their fact is drawn from the will of their Master: but these words, *Repent and be baptized in the name of Jesus,* are counsel; because the reason why we should so do, tendeth not to any benefit of God Almighty, who shall still be king in what manner soever we rebel; but of ourselves, who have no other means of avoiding the punishment hanging over us for our sins.

*Differences of fit and unfit counsellors.* As the difference of counsel from command, hath been now deduced from the nature of counsel, consisting in a deducing of the benefit, or hurt that may arise to him that is to be counselled, by the necessary or probable consequences of the action he propoundeth; so may also the differences between *apt* and *inept* counsellors be derived from the same. For experience, being but memory of the consequences of like actions formerly observed, and counsel but the speech whereby that experience is made known to another; the virtues, and defects of counsel, are the same with the virtues, and defects intellectual: and to the person of a commonwealth, his counsellors serve him in the place of memory, and mental discourse. But with this resemblance of the commonwealth, to a natural man, there is one dissimilitude joined, of great importance; which is, that a natural man receiveth his experience, from the natural objects of sense, which work upon him without passion, or interest of their own; whereas they that give counsel to the representative person of a commonwealth, may have, and have often their particular ends and passions, that render their counsels always suspected, and many times unfaithful. And therefore we may set down for the first condition of a good counsellor, *that his ends, and interests, be not inconsistent with the ends and interests of him he counselleth.*

Secondly, because the office of a counsellor, when an action comes into deliberation, is to make manifest the consequences of it, in such manner, as he that is counselled may be truly and evidently informed; he ought to propound his advice, in such form of speech, as may make the truth most evidently appear; that is to say, with as firm ratiocination, as significant and proper language, and as briefly, as the evidence will permit. And therefore *rash unevident inferences,* such as are fetched only from examples, or authority of books, and are not arguments of what is good, or evil, but witnesses of fact, or of opinion; *obscure, confused, and ambiguous expressions, also all metaphorical speeches, tending to the stirring up of passion,* (because such reasoning, and such expressions, are useful only to deceive, or to lead him we counsel towards other ends than his own) *are repugnant to the office of a counsellor.*

Thirdly, because the ability of counselling proceedeth from

experience, and long study; and no man is presumed to have experience in all those things that to the administration of a great commonwealth are necessary to be known, *no man is presumed to be a good counsellor, but in such business, as he hath not only been much versed in, but hath also much meditated on, and considered.* For seeing the business of a commonwealth is this, to preserve the people in peace at home, and defend them against foreign invasion, we shall find, it requires great knowledge of the disposition of mankind, of the rights of government, and of the nature of equity, law, justice, and honour, not to be attained without study; and of the strength, commodities, places, both of their own country, and their neighbours; as also of the inclinations, and designs of all nations that may any way annoy them. And this is not attained to, without much experience. Of which things, not only the whole sum, but every one of the particulars requires the age, and observation of a man in years, and of more than ordinary study. The wit required for counsel, as I have said before (chap. 8) is judgment. And the differences of men in that point come from different education, of some to one kind of study or business, and of others to another. When for the doing of any thing, there be infallible rules, as in engines and edifices, the rules of geometry, all the experience of the world cannot equal his counsel, that has learnt, or found out the rule. And when there is no such rule, he that hath most experience in that particular kind of business, has therein the best judgment, and is the best counsellor.

Fourthly, to be able to give counsel to a commonwealth, in a business that hath reference to another commonwealth, *it is necessary to be acquainted with the intelligences, and letters* that come from thence, *and with all the records of treaties, and other transactions of state* between them; which none can do, but such as the representative shall think fit. By which we may see, that they who are not called to counsel, can have no good counsel in such cases to obtrude.

Fifthly, supposing the number of counsellors equal, a man is better counselled by hearing them apart, than in an assembly; and that for many causes. First, in hearing them apart, you have the advice of every man; but in an assembly many of them deliver their advice with *aye,* or *no,* or with their hands, or feet, not moved by their own sense, but by the eloquence of another, or for fear of displeasing some that have spoken, or the whole assembly, by contradiction; or for fear of appearing duller in apprehension, than those that have applauded the contrary opinion. Secondly, in an assembly of many, there cannot choose but be some whose interests are contrary to that of the public; and these their interests make passionate, and passion eloquent, and eloquence draws others into the same advice. For the passions of men, which asunder are moderate, as the heat of one brand; in an assembly are like many brands, that inflame one another, especially when they blow one another with orations, to the setting of the commonwealth on fire, under pretence of counselling it. Thirdly, in hearing every man apart, one may examine, when there is need, the truth, or probability of his reasons, and of the grounds of the advice he gives, by frequent interruptions, and objections; which cannot be done in an assembly, where, in every difficult question, a man is rather astonied, and dazzled with the variety of discourse upon it, than informed of the course he ought to take. Besides, there cannot be an assembly of many, called together for advice, wherein there be not some, that have the ambition to be thought eloquent, and also learned in the politics; and give not their advice with care of the business propounded, but of the applause of their motley orations, made of the divers coloured threads, or shreds of authors; which is an impertinence at least, that takes away the time of serious consultation, and in the secret way of counselling apart, is easily avoided. Fourthly, in deliberations that ought to be kept secret, whereof there be many occasions in public business, the counsels of many, and especially in assemblies, are dangerous; and therefore great assemblies are necessitated to commit such affairs to lesser numbers, and of such persons as are most versed, and in whose fidelity they have most confidence.

To conclude, who is there that so far approves the taking of counsel from a great assembly of counsellors, that wisheth for, or would accept of their pains, when there is a question of marrying his children, disposing of his lands, governing his household, or managing his private estate, especially if there be amongst them such as wish not his prosperity? A man that doth his business by the help of many and prudent counsellors, with every one consulting apart in his proper element, does it best, as he that useth able seconds at tennis play, placed in their proper stations. He does next best, that useth his own judgment only; as he that has no second at all. But he that is carried up and down to his business in a framed counsel, which cannot move but by the plurality of consenting opinions, the execution whereof is commonly, out of envy or interest, retarded by the part dissenting, does it worst of all, and like one that is carried to the ball, though by good players, yet in a wheel-barrow, or other frame, heavy of itself, and retarded also by the inconcurrent judgments, and endeavours of them that drive it; and so much the more, as they be more that set their hands to it; and most of all, when there is one, or more amongst them, that desire to have him lose. And though it be true, that many eyes see more than one; yet it is not to be understood of many counsellors; but then only, when the final resolution is in one man. Otherwise, because many eyes see the same thing in divers lines, and are apt to look asquint towards their private benefit; they that desire not to miss their mark, though they look about with two eyes, yet they never aim but with one; and therefore no great popular commonwealth was ever kept up, but either by a foreign enemy that united them; or by the reputation of some eminent man amongst them; or by the secret counsel of a few; or by the mutual fear of equal factions; and not by the open consultations of the assembly. And as for very little commonwealths, be they popular, or monarchical, there is no human wisdom can uphold them, longer than the jealousy lasteth of their potent neighbours.

# Chapter 26

## Of Civil Laws

*Civil law, what.* By civil laws, I understand the laws, that men are therefore bound to observe, because they are members, not of this, or that commonwealth in particular, but of a commonwealth. For the knowledge of particular laws belongeth to them, that profess the study of the laws of their several countries; but the knowledge of civil law in general, to any man. The ancient law of Rome was called their *civil law,* from the word *civitas,* which signifies a commonwealth: and those countries, which having been under the Roman empire, and governed by that law, retain still such part thereof as they think fit, call that part the civil law, to distinguish it from the rest of their own civil laws. But that is not it I intend to speak of here; my design being not to show what is law here, and there; but what is law; as Plato, Aristotle, Cicero, and divers others have done, without taking upon them the profession of the study of the law.

And first it is manifest, that law in general, is not counsel, but command; nor a command of any man to any man; but only of him, whose command is addressed to one formerly obliged to obey him. And as for civil law, it addeth only the name of the person commanding, which is *persona civitatis,* the person of the commonwealth.

Which considered, I define civil law in this manner. CIVIL LAW, *is to every subject, those rules, which the commonwealth hath commanded him, by word, writing, or other sufficient sign of the will, to make use of, for the distinction of right, and wrong; that is to say, of what is contrary, and what is not contrary to the rule.*

In which definition, there is nothing that is not at first sight evident. For every man seeth, that some laws are addressed to all the subjects in general; some to particular provinces; some to particular vocations; and some to particular men; and are therefore laws, to every of those to whom the command is directed, and to none else. As also, that laws are the rules of just, and unjust; nothing being reputed unjust, that is not contrary to some law. Likewise, that none can make laws but the commonwealth; because our subjection is to the commonwealth only: and that commands, are to be signified by sufficient signs; because a man knows not otherwise how to obey them. And therefore, whatsoever can from this definition by necessary consequence be deduced, ought to be acknowledged for truth. Now I deduce from it this that followeth.

*The sovereign is legislator.* 1. The legislator in all commonwealths, is only the sovereign, be he one man, as in a monarchy, or one assembly of men, as in a democracy, or aristocracy. For the legislator is he that maketh the law. And the commonwealth only prescribes, and commandeth the observation of those rules, which we call law: therefore the commonwealth is the legislator. But the commonwealth is no person, nor has capacity to do any thing, but by the representative, that is, the sovereign; and therefore the sovereign is the sole legislator. For the same reason, none can abrogate a law made, but the sovereign; because a law is not abrogated, but by another law, that forbiddeth it to be put in execution.

*And not subject to civil law.* 2. The sovereign of a commonwealth, be it an assembly, or one man, is not subject to the civil laws. For having power to make, and repeal laws, he may when he pleaseth, free himself from that subjection, by repealing those laws that trouble him, and making of new; and consequently he was free before. For he is free, that can be free when he will: nor is it possible for any person to be bound to himself; because he that can bind, can release; and therefore he that is bound to himself only, is not bound.

*Use, a law not by virtue of time, but of the sovereign's consent.* 3. When long use obtaineth the authority of a law, it is not the length of time that maketh the authority, but the will of the sovereign signified by his silence, for silence is sometimes an argument of consent; and it is no longer law, than the sovereign shall be silent therein. And therefore if the sovereign shall have a question of right grounded, not upon his present will, but upon the laws formerly made; the length of time shall bring no prejudice to his right; but the question shall be judged by equity. For many unjust actions, and unjust sentences, go uncontrolled a longer time than any man can remember. And our lawyers account no customs law, but such as are reasonable, and that evil customs are to be abolished. But the judgment of what is reasonable, and of what is to be abolished, belongeth to him that maketh the law, which is the sovereign assembly, or monarch.

*The law of nature, and the civil law contain each other.* 4. The law of nature, and the civil law, contain each other, and are of equal extent. For the laws of nature, which consist in equity, justice, gratitude, and other moral virtues on these depending, in the condition of mere nature, as I have said before in the end of the fifteenth chapter, are not properly laws, but qualities that dispose men to peace and obedience. When a commonwealth is once settled, then are they actually laws, and not before; as being then the commands of the commonwealth; and therefore also civil laws: for it is the sovereign power that obliges men to obey them. For in the differences of private men, to declare, what is equity, what is justice, and what is moral virtue, and to make them binding, there is need of the ordinances of sovereign power, and punishments to be ordained for such as shall break them; which ordinances are therefore part of the civil law. The law of nature therefore is a part of the civil law in all commonwealths of the world. Reciprocally also, the civil law is a part of the dictates of nature. For justice, that is to say, performance of covenant, and giving to every man his own, is a dictate of the law of nature. But every subject in a commonwealth, hath covenanted to obey the civil law; either one with another, as when they assemble to make a common representative, or with the representative itself one by one, when subdued by the sword they promise obedience, that they may receive life; and therefore obedience to the civil law is part also of the law of nature. Civil, and natural law are not different kinds, but different parts of law; whereof one part being written, is called civil, the other unwritten, natural. But the right of nature, that is, the natural liberty of man, may by the civil law be abridged, and restrained: nay, the end of making laws, is no other, but such restraint; without the which there cannot possibly be any peace. And law was brought into the world for nothing else, but to limit the natural liberty of particular men, in such manner, as they might not hurt, but assist one another, and join together against a common enemy.

*Provincial laws are not made by custom, but by the sovereign power.* 5. If the sovereign of one commonwealth, subdue a people that have lived under other written laws, and afterwards govern them by the same laws, by which they were governed before; yet those laws are the civil laws of the victor, and not of the vanquished commonwealth. For the legislator is he, not by whose authority the laws were first made, but by whose authority they now continue to be laws. And therefore where there be divers provinces, within the dominion of a commonwealth, and in those provinces diversity of laws, which commonly are called the customs of each several province, we are not to understand that such customs have their force, only from length of time; but that they were anciently laws written, or otherwise made known for the constitutions, and statutes of their sovereigns; and are now laws, not by virtue of the prescription of time, but by the constitutions of their present sovereigns. But if an unwritten law, in all the provinces of a dominion, shall be generally observed, and no iniquity appear in the use thereof; that law can be no other but a law of nature, equally obliging all mankind.

*Some foolish opinions of lawyers concerning the making of laws.* 6. Seeing then all laws, written and unwritten, have their authority and force, from the will of the commonwealth: that is to say, from the will of the representative; which in a monarchy is the monarch, and in other commonwealths the sovereign assembly; a man may wonder from whence proceed such opinions, as are found in the books of lawyers of eminence in several commonwealths, directly, or by consequence making the legislative power depend on private men, or subordinate judges. As for example, *that the common law, hath no controller but the parliament;* which is true only where a parliament has the sovereign power, and cannot be assembled, nor dissolved, but by their own discretion. For if there be a right in any else to dissolve them, there is a right also to control them, and consequently to control their controllings. And if there be no such right, then the controller of laws is not *parliamentum,* but *rex in parliamento.* And where a parliament is sovereign, if it should assemble never so many, or so wise men, from the countries subject to them, for whatsoever cause; yet there is no man will believe, that such an assembly hath thereby acquired to themselves a legislative power. *Item,* that the two arms of a commonwealth, are *force and justice; the first whereof is in the king; the other deposited in the hands of the parliament.* As if a commonwealth could consist, where the force were in any hand, which justice had not the authority to command and govern.

*Sir Edw. Coke upon Littleton, lib.* 2, *ch.* 6, *fol.* 97, *b.* 7. That law can never be against reason, our lawyers are agreed; and that not the letter, that is every construction of it, but that which is according to the intention of the legislator, is the law. And it is true: but the doubt is of whose reason it is, that shall be received for law. It is not meant of any private reason; for then there would be as much contradiction in the laws, as there is in the Schools; nor yet, as Sir Edward Coke makes it, an *artificial perfection of reason, gotten by long study, ob-*

*servation, and experience,* as his was. For it is possible long study may increase, and confirm erroneous sentences: and where men build on false grounds, the more they build, the greater is the ruin: and of those that study, and observe with equal time and diligence, the reasons and resolutions are, and must remain discordant: and therefore it is not that *juris prudentia,* or wisdom of subordinate judges; but the reason of this our artificial man the commonwealth, and his command, that maketh law: and the commonwealth being in their representative but one person, there cannot easily arise any contradiction in the laws; and when there doth, the same reason is able, by interpretation, or alteration, to take it away. In all courts of justice, the sovereign, which is the person of the commonwealth, is he that judgeth: the subordinate judge, ought to have regard to the reason, which moved his sovereign to make such law, that his sentence may be according thereunto; which then is his sovereign's sentence; otherwise it is his own, and an unjust one.

*Law made, if not also made known, is no law.* 8. From this, that the law is a command, and a command consisteth in declaration, or manifestation of the will of him that commandeth, by voice, writing, or some other sufficient argument of the same, we may understand, that the command of the commonwealth is law only to those, that have means to take notice of it. Over natural fools, children, or madmen, there is no law, no more than over brute beasts; nor are they capable of the title of just, or unjust; because they had never power to make any covenant, or to understand the consequences thereof; and consequently never took upon them to authorize the actions of any sovereign, as they must do that make to themselves a commonwealth. And as those from whom nature or accident hath taken away the notice of all laws in general; so also every man, from whom any accident, not proceeding from his own default, hath taken away the means to take notice of any particular law, is excused, if he observe it not: and to speak properly, that law is no law to him. It is therefore necessary, to consider in this place, what arguments, and signs be sufficient for the knowledge of what is the law; that is to say, what is the will of the sovereign, as well in monarchies, as in other forms of government.

*Unwritten laws are all of them laws of nature.* And first, if it be a law that obliges all the subjects without exception, and is not written, nor otherwise published in such places as they may take notice thereof, it is a law of nature. For whatsoever men are to take knowledge of for law, not upon other men's words, but every one from his own reason, must be such as is agreeable to the reason of all men; which no law can be, but the law of nature. The laws of nature therefore need not any publishing, nor proclamation; as being contained in this one sentence, approved by all the world. *Do not that to another, which thou thinkest unreasonable to be done by another to thyself.*

Secondly, if it be a law that obliges only some condition of men, or one particular man, and be not written, nor published by word, then also it is a law of nature; and known by the same arguments, and signs, that distinguish those in such a condition, from other subjects. For whatsoever law is not written, or some way published by him that makes it law, can be known no way, but by the reason of him that is to obey it; and is therefore also a law not only civil, but natural. For example, if the sovereign employ a public minister, without written instructions what to do; he is obliged to take for instructions the dictates of reason; as if he make a judge, the judge is to take notice, that his sentence ought to be according to the reason of his sovereign, which being always understood to be equity, he is bound to it by the law of nature: or if an ambassador, he is, in all things not contained in his written instructions, to take for instruction that which reason dictates to be most conducing to his sovereign's interests; and so of all other ministers of the sovereignty, public and private. All which instructions of natural reason may be comprehended under one name of *fidelity;* which is a branch of natural justice.

The law of nature excepted, it belongeth to the essence of all other laws, to be made known, to every man that shall be obliged to obey them, either by word, or writing, or some other act, known to proceed from the sovereign authority. For the will of another cannot be understood, but by his own word, or act, or by conjecture taken from his scope and purpose; which in the person of the commonwealth, is to be supposed always consonant to equity and reason. And in ancient time, before letters were in common use, the laws were many times put into verse; that the rude people taking pleasure in singing, or reciting them, might the more easily retain them in memory. And for the same reason Solomon (*Prov.* vii. 3) adviseth a man, to bind the ten commandments upon his ten fingers. And for the law which Moses gave to the people of Israel at the renewing of the covenant (*Deut.* xi.

19), he biddeth them to teach it their children, by discoursing of it both at home, and upon the way; at going to bed, and at rising from bed; and to write it upon the posts, and doors of their houses; and (*Deut.* xxxi. 12) to assemble the people, man, woman, and child, to hear it read.

*Nothing is law where the legislator cannot be known. Difference between verifying and authorizing.* Nor is it enough the law be written, and published; but also that there be manifest signs, that it proceedeth from the will of the sovereign. For private men, when they have, or think they have force enough to secure their unjust designs, and convoy them safely to their ambitious ends, may publish for laws what they please, without, or against the legislative authority. There is therefore requisite, not only a declaration of the law, but also sufficient signs of the author and authority. The author, or legislator is supposed in every commonwealth to be evident, because he is the sovereign, who having been constituted by the consent of every one, is supposed by every one to be sufficiently known. And though the ignorance and security of men be such, for the most part, as that when the memory of the first constitution of their commonwealth is worn out, they do not consider, by whose power they used to be defended against their enemies, and to have their industry protected, and to be righted when injury is done them; yet because no man that considers, can make question of it, no excuse can be derived from the ignorance of where the sovereignty is placed. And it is a dictate of natural reason, and consequently an evident law of nature, that no man ought to weaken that power, the protection whereof he hath himself demanded, or wittingly received against others. Therefore of who is sovereign, no man, but by his own fault, (whatsoever evil men suggest), can make any doubt. The difficulty consisteth in the evidence of the authority derived from him; the removing whereof, dependeth on the knowledge of the public registers, public counsels, public ministers, and public seals; by which all laws are sufficiently verified; verified, I say, not authorized: for the verification, is but the testimony and record, not the authority of the law; which consisteth in the command of the sovereign only.

*The law verified by the subordinate judge.* If therefore a man have a question of injury, depending on the law of nature; that is to say, on common equity; the sentence of the judge, that by commission hath authority to take cognizance of such causes, is a sufficient verification of the law of nature in that individual case. For though the advice of one that professeth the study of the law, be useful for the avoiding of contention; yet it is but advice: it is the judge must tell men what is law, upon the hearing of the controversy.

*By the public registers.* But when the question is of injury, or crime, upon a written law; every man by recourse to the registers, by himself or others, may, if he will, be sufficiently informed, before he do such injury, or commit the crime, whether it be an injury, or not: nay he ought to do so: for when a man doubts whether the act he goeth about, be just, or unjust; and may inform himself, if he will; the doing is unlawful. In like manner, he that supposeth himself injured, in a case determined by the written law, which he may, by himself or others, see and consider; if he complain before he consults with the law, he does unjustly, and bewrayeth a disposition rather to vex other men, than to demand his own right.

*By letters patent and public seal.* If the question be of obedience to a public officer; to have seen his commission, with the public seal, and heard it read; or to have had the means to be informed of it, if a man would, is a sufficient verification of his authority. For every man is obliged to do his best endeavour, to inform himself of all written laws, that may concern his own future actions.

*The interpretation of the law dependeth on the sovereign power.* The legislator known; and the laws, either by writing, or by the light of nature, sufficiently published; there wanteth yet another very material circumstance to make them obligatory. For it is not the letter, but the intendment, or meaning, that is to say, the authentic interpretation of the law (which is the sense of the legislator), in which the nature of the law consisteth; and therefore the interpretation of all laws dependeth on the authority sovereign; and the interpreters can be none but those, which the sovereign, to whom only the subject oweth obedience, shall appoint. For else, by the craft of an interpreter, the law may be made to bear a sense, contrary to that of the sovereign: by which means the interpreter becomes the legislator.

*All laws need interpretation.* All laws, written, and unwritten, have need of interpretation. The unwritten law of nature, though it be easy to such, as without partiality and passion, make use of their natural reason, and therefore leaves the violators thereof without excuse; yet considering there be very few, perhaps none, that in some cases are not blinded by self-love, or some other passion; it is now become of all laws the most obscure, and has consequently the greatest need of able interpreters. The written laws, if they be short, are easily misinterpreted, from the divers significations of a word, or two: if long, they be more obscure by the divers significations of many words: insomuch as no written law, delivered in few, or many words, can be well understood, without a perfect understanding of the final causes, for which the law was made; the knowledge of which final causes is in the legislator. To him therefore there cannot be any knot in the law, insoluble; either by finding out the ends, to undo it by; or else by making what ends he will, as Alexander did with his sword in the Gordian knot, by the legislative power; which no other interpreter can do.

*The authentical interpretation of law is not that of writers.* The interpretation of the laws of nature, in a commonwealth, dependeth not on the books of moral philosophy. The authority of writers, without the authority of the commonwealth, maketh not their opinions law, be they never so true. That which I have written in this treatise, concerning the moral virtues, and of their necessity for the procuring, and maintaining peace, though it be evident truth, is not therefore presently law; but because in all commonwealths in the world, it is part of the civil law. For though it be naturally reasonable; yet it is by the sovereign power that it is law: otherwise, it were a great error, to call the laws of nature unwritten law; whereof we see so many volumes published, and in them so many contradictions of one another, and of themselves.

*The interpreter of the law is the judge giving sentence* viva voce *in every particular case.* The interpretation of the law of nature, is the sentence of the judge constituted by the sovereign authority, to hear and determine such controversies, as depend thereon; and consisteth in the application of the law to the present case. For in the act of judicature, the judge doth no more but to consider, whether the demand of the party, be consonant to natural reason, and equity; and the sentence he giveth, is therefore the interpretation of the law of nature; which interpretation is authentic; not because it is his private sentence; but because he giveth it by authority of the sovereign, whereby it becomes the sovereign's sentence; which is law for that time, to the parties pleading.

*The sentence of a judge does not bind him, or another judge to give like sentence in like cases ever after. The sentence of a judge does not bind him, &c.* But because there is no judge

subordinate, nor sovereign, but may err in a judgment of
equity; if afterward in another like case he find it more consonant to equity to give a contrary sentence, he is obliged to
do it. No man's error becomes his own law; nor obliges him
to persist in it. Neither, for the same reason, becomes it a law
to other judges, though sworn to follow it. For though a wrong
sentence given by authority of the sovereign, if he know and
allow it, in such laws as are mutable, be a constitution of a
new law, in cases, in which every little circumstance is the
same; yet in laws immutable, such as are the laws of nature,
they are no laws to the same or other judges, in the like cases
for ever after. Princes succeed one another; and one judge
passeth, another cometh; nay, heaven and earth shall pass; but
not one tittle of the law of nature shall pass; for it is the
eternal law of God. Therefore all the sentences of precedent
judges that have ever been, cannot altogether make a law
contrary to natural equity: nor any examples of former
judges, can warrant an unreasonable sentence, or discharge
the present judge of the trouble of studying what is equity, in
the case he is to judge, from the principles of his own
natural reason. For example sake, it is against the law of
nature, *to punish the innocent;* and innocent is he that acquitteth himself judicially, and is acknowledged for innocent by
the judge. Put the case now, that a man is accused of a capital
crime, and seeing the power and malice of some enemy, and
the frequent corruption and partiality of judges, runneth away
for fear of the event, and afterwards is taken, and brought to
a legal trial, and maketh it sufficiently appear, he was not
guilty of the crime, and being thereof acquitted, is nevertheless
condemned to lose his goods; this is a manifest condemnation
of the innocent. I say therefore, that there is no place in the
world, where this can be an interpretation of a law of nature,
or be made a law by the sentences of precedent judges, that
had done the same. For he that judged it first, judged unjustly;
and no injustice can be a pattern of judgment to succeeding
judges. A written law may forbid innocent men to fly, and
they may be punished for flying: but that flying for fear of
injury, should be taken for presumption of guilt, after a man
is already absolved of the crime judicially, is contrary to the
nature of a presumption, which hath no place after judgment
given. Yet this is set down by a great lawyer for the common
law of England. *If a man,* saith he, *that is innocent, be accused
of felony, and for fear flyeth for the same; albeit he judicially
acquitteth himself of the felony; yet if it be found that he fled*

*for the felony, he shall notwithstanding his innocency, forfeit all his goods, chattels, debts, and duties. For as to the forfeiture of them, the law will admit no proof against the presumption in law, grounded upon his flight.* Here you see, *an innocent man judicially acquitted, notwithstanding his innocency,* when no written law forbad him to fly, after his acquittal, *upon a presumption in law,* condemned to lose all the goods he hath. If the law ground upon his flight a presumption of the fact, which was capital, the sentence ought to have been capital: if the presumption were not of the fact, for what then ought he to lose his goods? This therefore is no law of England; nor is the condemnation grounded upon a presumption of law, but upon the presumption of the judges. It is also against law, to say that no proof shall be admitted against a presumption of law. For all judges, sovereign and subordinate, if they refuse to hear proof, refuse to do justice: for though the sentence be just, yet the judges that condemn without hearing the proofs offered, are unjust judges; and their presumption is but prejudice; which no man ought to bring with him to the seat of justice, whatsoever precedent judgments, or examples he shall pretend to follow. There be other things of this nature, wherein men's judgments have been perverted, by trusting to precedents: but this is enough to show, that though the sentence of the judge, be a law to the party pleading, yet it is no law to any judge, that shall succeed him in that office.

In like manner, when question is of the meaning of written laws, he is not the interpreter of them, that writeth a commentary upon them. For commentaries are commonly more subject to cavil, than the text; and therefore need other commentaries; and so there will be no end of such interpretation. And therefore unless there be an interpreter authorized by the sovereign, from which the subordinate judges are not to recede, the interpreter can be no other than the ordinary judges, in the same manner, as they are in cases of the unwritten law; and their sentences are to be taken by them that plead, for laws in that particular case; but not to bind other judges, in like cases to give like judgments. For a judge may err in the interpretation even of written laws; but no error of a subordinate judge, can change the law, which is the general sentence of the sovereign.

*The difference between the letter and sentence of the law.* In written laws, men use to make a difference between the letter, and the sentence of the law: and when by the letter, is meant whatsoever can be gathered from the bare words, it is well distinguished. For the significations of almost all words, are either in themselves, or in the metaphorical use of them, ambiguous; and may be drawn in argument, to make many senses; but there is only one sense of the law. But if by the letter, be meant the literal sense, then the letter, and the sentence or intention of the law, is all one. For the literal sense is that, which the legislator intended, should by the letter of the law be signified. Now the intention of the legislator is always supposed to be equity: for it were a great contumely for a judge to think otherwise of the sovereign. He ought therefore, if the word of the law do not fully authorize a reasonable sentence, to supply it with the law of nature; or if the case be difficult, to respite judgment till he have received more ample authority. For example, a written law ordaineth, that he which is thrust out of his house by force, shall be restored by force: it happens that a man by negligence leaves his house empty, and returning is kept out by force, in which case there is no special law ordained. It is evident that this case is contained in the same law: for else there is no remedy for him at all; which is to be supposed against the intention of the legislator. Again, the word of the law commandeth to judge according to the evidence: a man is accused falsely of a fact, which the judge himself saw done by another, and not by him that is accused. In this case neither shall the letter of the law be followed to the condemnation of the innocent, nor shall the judge give sentence against the evidence of the witnesses; because the letter of the law is to the contrary: but procure of the sovereign that another be made judge, and himself witness. So that the incommodity that follows the bare words of a written law, may lead him to the intention of the law, whereby to interpret the same the better; though no incommodity can warrant a sentence against the law. For every judge of right, and wrong, is not judge of what is commodious, or incommodious to the commonwealth.

*The abilities required in a judge.* The abilities required in a good interpreter of the law, that is to say, in a good judge, are not the same with those of an advocate; namely the study of the laws. For a judge, as he ought to take notice of the fact, from none but the witnesses; so also he ought to take notice of the law from nothing but the statutes, and constitutions of the sovereign, alleged in the pleading, or declared to him by some that have authority from the sovereign power to declare them; and need not take care beforehand, what he shall judge;

for it shall be given him what he shall say concerning the fact, by witnesses; and what he shall say in point of law, from those that shall in their pleadings show it, and by authority interpret it upon the place. The Lords of Parliament in England were judges, and most difficult causes have been heard and determined by them; yet few of them were much versed in the study of the laws, and fewer had made profession of them: and though they consulted with lawyers, that were appointed to be present there for that purpose; yet they alone had the authority of giving sentence. In like manner, in the ordinary trials of right, twelve men of the common people, are the judges, and give sentence, not only of the fact, but of the right; and pronounce simply for the complainant, or for the defendant; that is to say, are judges, not only of the fact, but also of the right: and in a question of crime, not only determine whether done, or not done; but also whether it be *murder, homicide, felony, assault,* and the like, which are determinations of law: but because they are not supposed to know the law of themselves, there is one that hath authority to inform them of it, in the particular case they are to judge of. But yet if they judge not according to that he tells them, they are not subject thereby to any penalty; unless it be made appear, that they did it against their consciences, or had been corrupted by reward.

The things that make a good judge, or good interpreter of the laws, are, first, *a right understanding* of that principal law of nature called *equity;* which depending not on the reading of other men's writings, but on the goodness of a man's own natural reason, and meditation, is presumed to be in those most, that have had most leisure, and had the most inclination to meditate thereon. Secondly, *contempt of unnecessary riches, and preferments.* Thirdly, *to be able in judgment to divest himself of all fear, anger, hatred, love, and compassion.* Fourthly, and lastly, *patience to hear; diligent attention in hearing; and memory to retain, digest, and apply what he hath heard.*

*Divisions of law.* The difference and division of the laws, has been made in divers manners, according to the different methods, of those men that have written of them. For it is a thing that dependeth not on nature, but on the scope of the writer; and is subservient to every man's proper method. In the Institutions of Justinian, we find seven sorts of civil laws:

1. The *edicts, constitutions,* and *epistles of the prince,* that is, of the emperor; because the whole power of the people was

in him. Like these, are the proclamations of the kings of England.

2. *The decrees of the whole people of Rome,* comprehending the senate, when they were put to the question by the *senate.* These were laws, at first, by the virtue of the sovereign power residing in the people; and such of them as by the emperors were not abrogated, remained laws, by the authority imperial. For all laws that bind, are understood to be laws by his authority that has power to repeal them. Somewhat like to these laws, are the Acts of Parliament in England.

3. *The decrees of the common people,* excluding the senate, when they were put to the question by the *tribune* of the people. For such of them as were not abrogated by the emperors, remained laws by the authority imperial. Like to these, were the orders of the House of Commons in England.

4. *Senatus consulta,* the *orders of the senate;* because when the people of Rome grew so numerous, as it was inconvenient to assemble them; it was thought fit by the emperor, that men should consult the senate, instead of the people; and these have some resemblance with the acts of council.

5. *The edicts of prætors,* and in some cases, of *ædiles:* such as are the chief justices in the courts of England.

6. *Responsa prudentum;* which were the sentences, and opinion of those lawyers, to whom the emperor gave authority to interpret the law, and to give answer to such as in matter of law demanded their advice; which answers, the judges in giving judgment were obliged by the constitutions of the emperor to observe: and should be like the reports of cases judged, if other judges be by the law of England bound to observe them. For the judges of the common law of England, are not properly judges, but *juris consulti;* of whom the judges, who are either the lords, or twelve men of the country, are in point of law to ask advice.

7. Also, *unwritten customs,* which in their own nature are an imitation of law, by the tacit consent of the emperor, in case they be not contrary to the law of nature, are very laws.

*Another division of law.* Another division of laws, is into *natural* and *positive. Natural* are those which have been laws from all eternity; and are called not only *natural,* but also *moral* laws; consisting in the moral virtues, as justice, equity, and all habits of the mind that conduce to peace, and charity; of which I have already spoken in the fourteenth and fifteenth chapters.

*Positive,* are those which have not been from eternity; but have been made laws by the will of those that have had the sovereign power over others; and are either written, or made known to men, by some other argument of the will of their legislator.

Again, of positive laws some are *human,* some *divine;* and of human positive laws, some are *distributive,* some *penal. Distributive* are those that determine the rights of the subjects, declaring to every man what it is, by which he acquireth and holdeth a propriety in lands, or goods, and a right or liberty of action: and these speak to all the subjects. *Penal* are those, which declare, what penalty shall be inflicted on those that violate the law; and speak to the ministers and officers ordained for execution. For though every one ought to be informed of the punishments ordained beforehand for their transgression; nevertheless the command is not addressed to the delinquent, who cannot be supposed will faithfully punish himself, but to public ministers appointed to see the penalty executed. And these penal laws are for the most part written together with the laws distributive; and are sometimes called judgments. For all laws are general judgments, or sentences of the legislator; as also every particular judgment, is a law to him, whose case is judged.

*Divine positive law how made known to be law. Divine positive laws* (for natural laws being eternal, and universal, are all divine), are those, which being the commandments of God, not from all eternity, nor universally addressed to all men, but only to a certain people, or to certain persons, are declared for such, by those whom God hath authorized to declare them. But this authority of man to declare what be these positive laws of God, how can it be known? God may command a man by a supernatural way, to deliver laws to other men. But because it is of the essence of law, that he who is to be obliged, be assured of the authority of him that declareth it, which we cannot naturally take notice to be from God, *how can a man without supernatural revelation be assured of the revelation received by the declarer?* and *how can he be bound to obey them?* For the first question, how a man can be assured of the revelation of another, without a revelation particularly to himself, it is evidently impossible. For though a man may be induced to believe such revelation, from the miracles they see him do, or from seeing the extraordinary sanctity of his life, or from seeing the extraordinary wisdom, or extraordinary felicity of his actions, all which are marks of God's extraordinary favour; yet they are not assured evidences of special revelation. Miracles are marvellous works: but that which is marvellous to one, may not be so to another. Sanctity may be feigned; and the visible felicities of this world, are most often the work of God by natural, and ordinary causes. And therefore no man can infallibly know by natural reason, that another has had a supernatural revelation of God's will; but only a belief; every one, as the signs thereof shall appear greater or lesser, a firmer or a weaker belief.

But for the second, how can he be bound to obey them; it is not so hard. For if the law declared, be not against the law of nature, which is undoubtedly God's law, and he undertake to obey it, he is bound by his own act; bound I say to obey it, but not bound to believe it: for men's belief, and interior cogitations, are not subject to the commands, but only to the operation of God, ordinary, or extraordinary. Faith of supernatural law, is not a fulfilling, but only an assenting to the same; and not a duty that we exhibit to God, but a gift which God freely giveth to whom he pleaseth; as also unbelief is not a breach of any of his laws; but a rejection of them all, except the laws natural. But this that I say, will be made yet clearer, by the examples and testimonies concerning this point in holy Scripture. The covenant God made with Abraham, in a supernatural manner, was thus, (*Gen.* xvii. 10) *This is the covenant which thou shalt observe between me and thee and thy seed after thee.* Abraham's seed had not this revelation, nor were yet in being; yet they are a party to the covenant, and bound to obey what Abraham should declare to them for God's law; which they could not be, but in virtue of the obedience they owed to their parents; who, if they be subject to no other earthly power, as here in the case of Abraham, have sovereign power over their children and servants. Again, where God saith to Abraham, *In thee shall all nations of the earth be blessed; for I know thou wilt command thy children, and thy house after thee to keep the way of the Lord, and to observe righteousness and judgment,* it is manifest, the obedience of his family, who had no revelation, depended on their former obligation to obey their sovereign. At Mount Sinai Moses only went up to God; the people were forbidden to approach on pain of death; yet they were bound to obey all that Moses declared to them for God's law. Upon what ground, but on this submission of their own, *Speak thou to us, and we will hear thee; but let not God speak to us, lest we die?* By which two places it sufficiently appeareth, that in a commonwealth, a subject that has no certain and assured revelation particularly to himself concerning the will of God, is to obey for such, the command of the commonwealth: for if men were at liberty, to take for God's commandments, their own dreams and fancies, or the dreams and fancies of private men; scarce two men would agree upon what is God's commandment; and yet in respect of them, every man would despise the commandments of the commonwealth. I conclude therefore, that in all things not contrary to the moral law, that is to say, to the law of nature, all subjects are bound to obey that for divine law, which is declared to be so, by the laws of the commonwealth. Which also is evident to any man's reason; for whatsoever is not against the law of nature, may be made law in the name of them that have the sovereign power; and there is no reason men should be the less obliged by it, when it is propounded in the name of God. Besides, there is no place in the world where men are permitted to pretend other commandments of God, than are declared for such by the commonwealth. Christian states punish those that revolt from the Christian religion, and all other states, those that set up any religion by them forbidden. For in whatsoever is not regulated by the commonwealth, it is equity, which is the law of nature, and therefore an eternal law of God, that every man equally enjoy his liberty.

*Another division of laws.* There is also another distinction of laws, into *fundamental* and *not fundamental;* but I could never see in any author, what a fundamental law signifieth. Nevertheless one may very reasonably distinguish laws in that manner.

*A fundamental law, what.* For a fundamental law in every commonwealth is that, which being taken away, the commonwealth faileth, and is utterly dissolved; as a building whose foundation is destroyed. And therefore a fundamental law is that, by which subjects are bound to uphold whatsoever power is given to the sovereign, whether a monarch, or a sovereign assembly, without which the commonwealth cannot stand; such as is the power of war and peace, of judicature, of election of officers, and of doing whatsoever he shall think necessary for the public good. Not fundamental is that, the abrogating whereof, draweth not with it the dissolution of the commonwealth; such as are the laws concerning controversies between subject and subject. Thus much of the division of laws.

*Difference between law and right.* I find the words *lex civilis,* and *jus civile,* that is to say *law* and *right civil,* promiscuously used for the same thing, even in the most learned authors; which nevertheless ought not to be so. For *right* is *liberty*, namely that liberty which the civil law leaves us: but *civil law* is an *obligation*, and takes from us the liberty which the law of nature gave us. Nature gave a right to every man to secure himself by his own strength, and to invade a suspected neighbour, by way of prevention: but the civil law takes away that liberty, in all cases where the protection of the law may be safely stayed for. Insomuch as *lex* and *jus*, are as different as *obligation* and *liberty*.

*And between a law and a charter.* Likewise *laws* and *charters* are taken promiscuously for the same thing. Yet charters are donations of the sovereign; and not laws, but exemptions from law. The phrase of a law is, *jubeo, injungo, I command* and *enjoin:* the phrase of a charter is, *dedi, concessi, I have given, I have granted:* but what is given or granted, to a man, is not forced upon him, by a law. A law may be made to bind all the subjects of a commonwealth: a liberty, or charter is only to one man, or some one part of the people. For to say all the people of a commonwealth, have liberty in any case whatsoever, is to say, that in such case, there hath been no law made; or else having been made, is now abrogated.

# Chapter 27

## Of Crimes, Excuses, and Extenuations

*Sin, what.* A SIN, is not only a transgression of a law, but also any contempt of the legislator. For such contempt, is a breach of all his laws at once. And therefore may consist, not only in the *commission* of a fact, or in speaking of words by the laws forbidden, or in the *omission* of what the law commandeth, but also in the *intention,* or purpose to transgress. For the purpose to break the law, is some degree of contempt of him, to whom it belongeth to see it executed. To be delighted in the imagination only, of being possessed of another man's goods, servants, or wife, without any intention to take them from him by force or fraud, is no breach of the law, that saith, *Thou shalt not covet:* nor is the pleasure a man may have in imagining or dreaming of the death of him, from whose life he expecteth nothing but damage, and displeasure, a sin; but the resolving to put some act in execution, that tendeth thereto. For to be pleased in the fiction of that, which would please a man if it were real, is a passion so adherent to the nature both of man, and every other living creature, as to make it a sin, were to make sin of being a man. The consideration of this, has made me think them too severe, both to themselves, and others, that maintain, that the first motions of the mind, though checked with the fear of God, be sins. But I confess it is safer to err on that hand, than on the other.

*A crime, what.* A CRIME, is a sin, consisting in the committing, by deed or word, of that which the law forbiddeth, or the omission of what it hath commanded. So that every crime is a sin; but not every sin a crime. To intend to steal, or kill, is a sin, though it never appear in word, or fact: for God that seeth the thoughts of man, can lay it to his charge: but till it appear by something done, or said, by which the intention may be argued by a human judge, it hath not the name of crime: which distinction the Greeks observed, in the word ἁμάρτημα, and ἔγκλημα or αἰτία; whereof the former, which is translated *sin,* signifieth any swerving from the law whatsoever; but the two latter, which are translated *crime,* signify that sin only, whereof one man may accuse another. But of intentions, which never appear by any outward act, there is no place for human accusation. In like manner the Latins by *peccatum*, which is *sin*, signify all manner of deviation from the law; but by *crimen*, which word they derive from *cerno*, which signifies *to perceive*, they mean only such sins, as may be made appear before a judge; and therefore are not mere intentions.

*Where no civil law is, there is no crime.* From this relation of sin to the law, and of crime to the civil law, may be inferred, first, that where law ceaseth, sin ceaseth. But because the law of nature is eternal, violation of covenants, ingratitude, arrogance, and all facts contrary to any moral virtue, can never cease to be sin. Secondly, that the civil law ceasing, crimes cease: for there being no other law remaining, but that of nature, there is no place for accusation; every man being his own judge, and accused only by his own conscience, and cleared by the uprightness of his own intention. When therefore his intention is right, his fact is no sin: if otherwise, his fact is sin; but not crime. Thirdly, that when the sovereign power ceaseth, crime also ceaseth; for where there is no such power, there is no protection to be had from the law; and therefore every one may protect himself by his own power: for no man in the institution of sovereign power can be supposed to give away the right of preserving his own body; for the safety whereof all sovereignty was ordained. But this is to be understood only of those, that have not themselves contributed to the taking away of the power that protected them; for that was a crime from the beginning.

*Ignorance of the law of nature excuseth no man.* The source of every crime, is some defect of the understanding; or some error in reasoning; or some sudden force of the passions. Defect in the understanding, is *ignorance;* in reasoning, *erroneous opinion.* Again, ignorance is of three sorts; of the *law,* and of the *sovereign,* and of the *penalty.* Ignorance of the law of nature excuseth no man; because every man that hath attained to the use of reason, is supposed to know, he ought not to do to another, what he would not have done to himself. Therefore into what place soever a man shall come, if he do any thing contrary to that law, it is a crime. If a man come from the Indies hither, and persuade men here to receive a new religion, or teach them any thing that tendeth to disobedience of the laws of this country, though he be never so well persuaded of the truth of what he teacheth, he commits a crime, and may be justly punished for the same, not only because his doctrine is false, but also because he does that which he would not approve in another, namely, that coming from hence, he should endeavour to alter the religion there. But ignorance of the civil law, shall excuse a man in a strange country, till it be declared to him; because, till then no civil law is binding.

*Ignorance of the civil law excuseth sometimes.* In the like manner, if the civil law of a man's own country, be not so sufficiently declared, as he may know it if he will; nor the action against the law of nature; the ignorance is a good excuse: in other cases ignorance of the civil law, excuseth not.

*Ignorance of the sovereign excuseth not.* Ignorance of the sovereign power, in the place of a man's ordinary residence, excuseth him not; because he ought to take notice of the power, by which he hath been protected there.

*Ignorance of the penalty excuseth not.* Ignorance of the penalty, where the law is declared, excuseth no man: for in breaking the law, which without a fear of penalty to follow, were not a law, but vain words, he undergoeth the penalty, though he know not what it is; because, whosoever voluntarily doth any action, accepteth all the known consequences of it; but punishment is a known consequence of the violation of the laws, in every commonwealth; which punishment, if it be determined already by the law, he is subject to that; if not, then he is subject to arbitrary punishment. For it is reason, that he which does injury, without other limitation than that of his own will, should suffer punishment without other limitation, than that of his will whose law is thereby violated.

*Punishments declared before the fact, excuse from greater punishments after it.* But when a penalty, is either annexed to the crime in the law itself, or hath been usually inflicted in the like cases; there the delinquent is excused from a greater penalty. For the punishment foreknown, if not great enough to deter men from the action, is an invitement to it: because when men compare the benefit of their injustice, with the harm of their punishment, by necessity of nature they choose that which appeareth best for themselves: and therefore when they are punished more than the law had formerly determined, or more than others were punished for the same crime; it is the law that tempted, and deceiveth them.

*Nothing can be made a crime by a law made after the fact.* No law, made after a fact done, can make it a crime: because if the fact be against the law of nature, the law was before the fact; and a positive law cannot be taken notice of, before it be made; and therefore cannot be obligatory. But when the law that forbiddeth a fact, is made before the fact be done; yet he that doth the fact, is liable to the penalty ordained after, in case no lesser penalty were made known before, neither by writing, nor by example, for the reason immediately before alleged.

*False principles of right and wrong causes of crime.* From defect in reasoning, that is to say, from error, men are prone to violate the laws, three ways. First, by presumption of false principles: as when men, from having observed how in all places, and in all ages, unjust actions have been authorized, by the force, and victories of those who have committed them; and that potent men, breaking through the cobweb laws of their country, the weaker sort, and those that have failed in their enterprises, have been esteemed the only criminals; have thereupon taken for principles, and grounds of their reasoning, *that justice is but a vain word: that whatsoever a man can get by his own industry, and hazard, is his own: that the practice of all nations cannot be unjust: that examples of former times are good arguments of doing the like again;* and many more of that kind: which being granted, no act in itself can be a crime, but must be made so, not by the law, but by the success of them that commit it; and the same fact be virtuous, or vicious, as fortune pleaseth; so that what Marius makes a crime, Sylla shall make meritorious, and Cæsar, the same laws standing, turn again into a crime, to the perpetual disturbance of the peace of the commonwealth.

*False teachers misinterpreting the law of nature.* Secondly, by false teachers, that either misinterpret the law of nature, making it thereby repugnant to the law civil; or by teaching for laws, such doctrines of their own, or traditions of former times, as are inconsistent with the duty of a subject.

*And false inferences from true principles, by teachers.* Thirdly, by erroneous inferences from true principles; which happens commonly to men that are hasty, and precipitate in concluding, and resolving what to do; such as are they, that have both a great opinion of their own understanding, and believe that things of this nature require not time and study, but only common experience, and a good natural wit; whereof no man thinks himself unprovided: whereas the knowledge, of right and wrong, which is no less difficult, there is no man will pretend to, without great and long study. And of those defects in reasoning, there is none that can excuse, though some of them may extenuate, a crime in any man, that pretendeth to the administration of his own private business;

much less in them that undertake a public charge; because they pretend to the reason, upon the want whereof they would ground their excuse.

*By their passions.* Of the passions that most frequently are the causes of crime, one, is vain-glory, or a foolish overrating of their own worth; as if difference of worth, were an effect of their wit, or riches, or blood, or some other natural quality, not depending on the will of those that have the sovereign authority. From whence proceedeth a presumption that the punishments ordained by the laws, and extended generally to all subjects, ought not to be inflicted on them, with the same rigour they are inflicted on poor, obscure, and simple men, comprehended under the name of the *vulgar*.

*Presumption of riches.* Therefore it happeneth commonly, that such as value themselves by the greatness of their wealth, adventure on crimes, upon hope of escaping punishment, by corrupting public justice, or obtaining pardon by money, or other rewards.

*And friends.* And that such as have multitude of potent kindred; and popular men, that have gained reputation amongst the multitude, take courage to violate the laws, from a hope of oppressing the power, to whom it belongeth to put them in execution.

*Wisdom.* And that such as have a great, and false opinion of their own wisdom, take upon them to reprehend the actions, and call in question the authority of them that govern, and so to unsettle the laws with their public discourse, as that nothing shall be a crime, but what their own designs require should be so. It happeneth also to the same men, to be prone to all such crimes, as consist in craft, and in deceiving of their neighbours; because they think their designs are too subtle to be perceived. These I say are effects of a false presumption of their own wisdom. For of them that are the first movers in the disturbance of commonwealth, which can never happen without a civil war, very few are left alive long enough, to see their new designs established: so that the benefit of their crimes redoundeth to posterity, and such as would least have wished it: which argues they were not so wise, as they thought they were. And those that deceive upon hope of not being observed, do commonly deceive themselves, the darkness in which they believe they lie hidden, being nothing else but their own blindness; and are no wiser than children, that think all hid, by hiding their own eyes.

And generally all vain-glorious men, unless they be withal

timorous, are subject to anger; as being more prone than others to interpret for contempt, the ordinary liberty of conversation: and there are few crimes that may not be produced by anger.

*Hatred, lust, ambition, covetousness, causes of crime.* As for the passions, of hate, lust, ambition, and covetousness, what crimes they are apt to produce, is so obvious to every man's experience and understanding, as there needeth nothing to be said of them, saving that they are infirmities, so annexed to the nature, both of man, and all other living creatures, as that their effects cannot be hindered, but by extraordinary use of reason, or a constant severity in punishing them. For in those things men hate, they find a continual, and unavoidable molestation; whereby either a man's patience must be everlasting, or he must be eased by removing the power of that which molesteth him. The former is difficult; the latter is many times impossible, without some violation of the law. Ambition, and covetousness are passions also that are perpetually incumbent, and pressing; whereas reason is not perpetually present, to resist them: and therefore whensoever the hope of impunity appears, their effects proceed. And for lust, what it wants in the lasting, it hath in the vehemence, which sufficeth to weigh down the apprehension of all easy, or uncertain punishments.

*Fear sometimes cause of crime, as when the danger is neither present nor corporeal.* Of all passions, that which inclineth men least to break the laws, is fear. Nay, excepting some generous natures, it is the only thing, when there is appearance of profit or pleasure by breaking the laws, that makes men keep them. And yet in many cases a crime may be committed through fear.

For not every fear justifies the action it produceth, but the fear only of corporeal hurt, which we call *bodily fear,* and from which a man cannot see how to be delivered, but by the action. A man is assaulted, fears present death, from which he sees not how to escape, but by wounding him that assaulteth him: if he wound him to death, this is no crime; because no man is supposed at the making of a commonwealth, to have abandoned the defence of his life, or limbs, where the law cannot arrive time enough to his assistance. But to kill a man, because from his actions, or his threatenings, I may argue he will kill me when he can, seeing I have time, and means to demand protection, from the sovereign power, is a crime. Again, a man receives words of disgrace or some little injuries, for which they that made the laws, had assigned no punishment, nor thought it worthy of a man that hath the use of reason, to take notice of, and is afraid, unless he revenge it, he shall fall into contempt, and consequently be obnoxious to the like injuries from others; and to avoid this, breaks the law, and protects himself for the future, by the terror of his private revenge. This is a crime: for the hurt is not corporeal, but phantastical, and, though in this corner of the world, made sensible by a custom not many years since begun, amongst young and vain men, so light, as a gallant man, and one that is assured of his own courage, cannot take notice of. Also a man may stand in fear of spirits, either through his own superstition, or through too much credit given to other men, that tell him of strange dreams and visions; and thereby be made believe they will hurt him, for doing, or omitting divers things, which nevertheless, to do, or omit, is contrary to the laws; and that which is so done, or omitted, is not to be excused by this fear; but is a crime. For, as I have shown before in the second chapter, dreams be naturally but the fancies remaining in sleep, after the impressions our senses had formerly received waking; and when men are by any accident unassured they have slept, seem to be real visions; and therefore he that presumes to break the law upon his own, or another's dream, or pretended vision, or upon other fancy of the power of invisible spirits, than is permitted by the commonwealth, leaveth the law of nature, which is a certain offence, and followeth the imagery of his own, or another private man's brain, which he can never know whether it signifieth any thing or nothing, nor whether he that tells his dream, say true, or lie; which if every private man should have leave to do, as they must by the law of nature, if any one have it, there could no law be made to hold, and so all commonwealth would be dissolved.

*Crimes not equal.* From these different sources of crimes, it appears already, that all crimes are not, as the Stoics of old time maintained, of the same alloy. There is place, not only for EXCUSE, by which that which seemed a crime, is proved to be none at all; but also for EXTENUATION, by which the crime, that seemed great, is made less. For though all crimes do equally deserve the name of injustice, as all deviation from a straight line is equally crookedness, which the Stoics rightly observed: yet it does not follow that all crimes are equally unjust, no more than that all crooked lines are equally crooked; which the Stoics not observing, held it as great a crime, to kill a hen, against the law, as to kill one's father.

*Total excuses.* That which totally excuseth a fact, and takes away from it the nature of a crime, can be none but that, which at the same time, taketh away the obligation of the law. For the fact committed once against the law, if he that committed it be obliged to the law, can be no other than a crime.

The want of means to know the law, totally excuseth. For the law whereof a man has no means to inform himself, is not obligatory. But the want of diligence to inquire, shall not be considered as a want of means; nor shall any man, that pretendeth to reason enough for the government of his own affairs, be supposed to want means to know the laws of nature; because they are known by the reason he pretends to: only children, and madmen are excused from offences against the law natural.

Where a man is captive, or in the power of the enemy (and he is then in the power of the enemy, when his person, or his means of living, is so), if it be without his own fault, the obligation of the law ceaseth; because he must obey the enemy, or die; and consequently such obedience is no crime: for no man is obliged, when the protection of the law faileth, not to protect himself, by the best means he can.

If a man, by the terror of present death, be compelled to do a fact against the law, he is totally excused; because no law can oblige a man to abandon his own preservation. And supposing such a law were obligatory; yet a man would reason thus, *If I do not, I die presently; if I do it, I die afterwards; therefore by doing it, there is time of life gained;* nature therefore compels him to the fact.

When a man is destitute of food, or other thing necessary for his life, and cannot preserve himself any other way, but by some fact against the law; as if in a great famine he take food by force, or stealth, which he cannot obtain for money nor charity; or in defence of his life, snatch away another man's sword; he is totally excused, for the reason next before alleged.

*Excuses against the author.* Again, facts done against the law by the authority of another, are by that authority excused against the author; because no man ought to accuse his own fact in another, that is but his instrument: but it is not excused against a third person thereby injured; because in the violation of the law, both the author and actor are criminals.

From hence it followeth that when that man, or assembly, that hath the sovereign power, commandeth a man to do that which is contrary to a former law, the doing of it is totally excused: for he ought not to condemn it himself, because he is the author; and what cannot justly be condemned by the sovereign, cannot justly be punished by any other. Besides, when the sovereign commandeth any thing to be done against his own former law, the command, as to that particular fact, is an abrogation of the law.

If that man, or assembly, that hath the sovereign power, disclaim any right essential to the sovereignty, whereby there accrueth to the subject, any liberty inconsistent with the sovereign power, that is to say, with the very being of a commonwealth, if the subject shall refuse to obey the command in any thing contrary to the liberty granted, this is nevertheless a sin, and contrary to the duty of the subject: for he ought to take notice of what is inconsistent with the sovereignty, because it was erected by his own consent and for his own defence; and that such liberty as is inconsistent with it, was granted through ignorance of the evil consequence thereof. But if he not only disobey, but also resist a public minister in the execution of it, then it is a crime; because he might have been righted, without any breach of the peace, upon complaint.

The degrees of crime are taken on divers scales, and measured, first by the malignity of the source, or cause; secondly, by the contagion of the example; thirdly, by the mischief of the effect; and fourthly, by the concurrence of times, places, and persons.

*Presumption of power aggravateth.* The same fact done against the law, if it proceed from presumption of strength, riches, or friends to resist those that are to execute the law, is a greater crime than if it proceed from hope of not being discovered, or of escape by flight: for presumption of impunity by force, is a root, from whence springeth, at all times, and upon all temptations, a contempt of all laws; whereas in the latter case, the apprehension of danger, that makes a man fly, renders him more obedient for the future. A crime which we know to be so, is greater than the same crime proceeding from a false persuasion that it is lawful; for he that committeth it against his own conscience, presumeth on his force, or other power, which encourages him to commit the same again: but he that doth it by error, after the error is shewn him, is conformable to the law.

*Evil teachers extenuate.* He, whose error proceeds from the authority of a teacher, or an interpreter of the law publicly authorized, is not so faulty as he whose error proceedeth from a peremptory pursuit of his own principles and reasoning: for what is taught by one that teacheth by public authority, the commonwealth teacheth, and hath a resemblance of law, till the same authority controlleth it; and in all crimes that contain not in them a denial of the sovereign power, nor are against an evident law, excuseth totally: whereas he that groundeth his actions on his private judgment, ought, according to the rectitude, or error thereof, to stand or fall.

*Examples of impunity extenuate.* The same fact, if it have been constantly punished in other men, is a greater crime, than if there have been many precedent examples of impunity. For those examples are so many hopes of impunity, given by the sovereign himself: and because he which furnishes a man with such a hope and presumption of mercy, as encourageth him to offend, hath his part in the offence; he cannot reasonably charge the offender with the whole.

*Premeditation aggravateth.* A crime from a sudden passion, is not so great, as when the same ariseth from long meditation: for in the former case there is a place for extenuation, in the common infirmity of human nature: but he that doth it with premeditation, has used circumspection, and cast his eye on the law, on the punishment, and on the consequence thereof to human society; all which, in committing the crime, he hath contemned and postponed to his own appetite. But there is no suddenness of passion sufficient for a total excuse: for all the time between the first knowing of the law, and the commission of the fact, shall be taken for a time of deliberation; because he ought by meditation of the law, to rectify the irregularity of his passions.

Where the law is publicly, and with assiduity, before all the people read and interpreted, a fact done against it, is a greater crime, than where men are left without such instruction, to enquire of it with difficulty, uncertainty, and interruption of their callings, and be informed by private men: for in this case, part of the fault is discharged upon common infirmity; but, in the former, there is apparent negligence, which is not without some contempt of the sovereign power.

*Tacit approbation of the sovereign extenuates.* Those facts which the law expressly condemneth, but the law-maker by other manifest signs of his will tacitly approveth, are less crimes, than the same facts, condemned both by the law and law-maker. For seeing the will of the law-maker is a law, there appear in this case two contradictory laws; which would totally excuse, if men were bound to take notice of the sovereign's approbation, by other arguments than are expressed by his command. But because there are punishments consequent, not only to the transgression of his law, but also to the observing of it, he is in part a cause of the transgression, and therefore cannot reasonably impute the whole crime to the delinquent. For example, the law condemneth duels; the punishment is made capital: on the contrary part, he that refuseth duel, is subject to contempt and scorn, without remedy; and sometimes by the sovereign himself thought unworthy to have any charge, or preferment in war. If thereupon he accept duel, considering all men lawfully endeavour to obtain the good opinion of them that have the sovereign power, he ought not in reason to be rigorously punished; seeing part of the fault may be discharged on the punisher: which I say, not as wishing liberty of private revenges, or any other kind of disobedience; but a care in governors, not to countenance any thing obliquely, which directly they forbid. The examples of princes, to those that see them, are, and ever have been, more potent to govern their actions, than the laws themselves. And though it be our duty to do, not what they do, but what they say; yet will that duty never be performed, till it please God to give man an extraordinary, and supernatural grace to follow that precept.

*Comparison of crimes from their effects.* Again, if we compare crimes by the mischief of their effects; first, the same fact, when it redounds to the damage of many, is greater, than when it redounds to the hurt of few. And therefore, when a fact hurteth, not only in the present, but also, by example, in the future, it is a greater crime, than if it hurt only in the present: for the former, is a fertile crime, and multiplies to the hurt of many; the latter is barren. To maintain doctrines contrary to the religion established in the commonwealth, is a greater fault, in an authorized preacher, than in a private person: so also is it, to live profanely, incontinently, or do any irreligious act whatsoever. Likewise in a professor of the law, to maintain any point, or do any act, that tendeth to the weakening of the sovereign power, is a greater crime, than in another man: also in a man that hath such reputation for wisdom, as that his counsels are followed, or his actions imitated by many, his fact against the law, is a greater crime, than the same fact in another: for such men not only commit crime, but teach it for law to all other men. And generally all crimes are the greater, by the scandal they give; that is to say, by becoming stumbling-blocks to the weak, that look not so much upon the way they go in, as upon the light that other man carry before them.

*Læsa Majestas.* Also facts of hostility against the present state of the commonwealth, are greater crimes, than the same acts done to private men: for the damage extends itself to all: such are the betraying of the strengths, or revealing of the secrets of the commonwealth to an enemy; also all attempts upon the representative of the commonwealth, be it a monarch, or an assembly; and all endeavours by word, or deed, to diminish the authority of the same, either in the present time, or in succession: which crimes the Latins understand by *crimina læsæ majestatis,* and consist in design, or act, contrary to a fundamental law.

*Bribery and false testimony.* Likewise those crimes, which render judgments of no effect, are greater crimes, than injuries done to one, or a few persons; as to receive money to give false judgment, or testimony, is a greater crime, than otherwise to deceive a man of the like, or a greater sum; because not only he has wrong, that falls by such judgments; but all judgments are rendered useless, and occasion ministered to force, and private revenges.

*Depeculation.* Also robbery, and depeculation of the public treasure, or revenues, is a greater crime, than the robbing, or defrauding of a private man; because to rob the public, is to rob many at once.

*Counterfeiting authority.* Also the counterfeit usurpation of public ministry, the counterfeiting of public seals or public coin, than counterfeiting of a private man's person, or his seal; because the fraud thereof, extendeth to the damage of many.

*Crimes against private men compared.* Of facts against the law, done to private men, the greater crime, is that, where the damage in the common opinion of men, is most sensible. And therefore

To kill against the law, is a greater crime, than any other injury, life preserved.

And to kill with torment, greater, than simply to kill.

And mutilation of a limb, greater, than the spoiling a man of his goods.

And the spoiling a man of his goods, by terror of death, or wounds, than by clandestine surreption.

And by clandestine surreption, than by consent fraudulently obtained.

And the violation of chastity by force, greater, than by flattery.

And of a woman married, than of a woman not married.

For all these things are commonly so valued: though some men are more, and some less sensible of the same offence. But the law regardeth not the particular, but the general inclination of mankind.

And therefore the offence men take, from contumely, in words, or gesture, when they produce no other harm, than the present grief of him that is reproached, hath been neglected in the laws of the Greeks, Romans, and other both ancient and modern commonwealths; supposing the true cause of such grief to consist, not in the contumely, which takes no hold upon men conscious of their own virtue, but in the pusillanimity of him that is offended by it.

Also a crime against a private man, is much aggravated by the person, time, and place. For to kill one's parent, is a greater crime, than to kill another: for the parent ought to have the honour of a sovereign, though he surrendered his power to the civil law; because he had it originally by nature. And to rob a poor man, is a greater crime, than to rob a rich man; because it is to the poor a more sensible damage.

And a crime committed in the time or place appointed for devotion, is greater, than if committed at another time or place: for it proceeds from a greater contempt of the law.

Many other cases of aggravation, and extenuation might be added: but by these I have set down, it is obvious to every man, to take the altitude of any other crime proposed.

*Public crimes, what.* Lastly, because in almost all crimes there is an injury done, not only to some private men, but also to the commonwealth; the same crime, when the accusation is in the name of the commonwealth, is called public crime: and when in the name of a private man, a private crime; and the pleas according thereunto called public, *judicia publica*, Pleas of the Crown; or Private Pleas. As in an accusation of murder, if the accuser be a private man, the plea is a Private Plea; if the accuser be the sovereign, the plea is a Public Plea.

## Chapter 28

## Of Punishments and Rewards

*The definition of punishment.* A PUNISHMENT, *is an evil inflicted by public authority, on him that hath done, or omitted that which is judged by the same authority to be a transgression of the law; to the end that the will of men may thereby the better be disposed to obedience.*

*Right to punish whence derived.* Before I infer any thing from this definition, there is a question to be answered, of much importance; which is, by what door the right or authority of punishing in any case, came in. For by that which has been said before, no man is supposed bound by covenant, not to resist violence; and consequently it cannot be intended, that he gave any right to another to lay violent hands upon his person. In the making of a commonwealth, every man giveth away the right of defending another; but not of defending himself. Also he obligeth himself, to assist him that hath the sovereignty, in the punishing of another; but of himself not. But to covenant to assist the sovereign, in doing hurt to another, unless he that so covenanteth have a right to do it himself, is not to give him a right to punish. It is manifest therefore that the right which the commonwealth, that is, he, or they that represent it, hath to punish, is not grounded on any concession, or gift of the subjects. But I have also showed formerly, that before the institution of commonwealth, every man had a right to every thing, and to do whatsoever he thought necessary to his own preservation; subduing, hurting, or killing any man in order thereunto. And this is the foundation of that right of punishing, which is exercised in every commonwealth. For the subjects did not give the sovereign that right; but only in laying down theirs, strengthened him to use his own, as he should think fit, for the preservation of them all: so that it was not given, but left to him, and to him only; and (excepting the limits set him by natural law) as entire, as in the condition of mere nature, and of war of every one against his neighbour.

*Private injuries and revenges no punishments.* From the definition of punishment, I infer, first, that neither private revenges, nor injuries of private men, can properly be styled punishment; because they proceed not from public authority.

*Nor denial of preferment.* Secondly, that to be neglected, and unpreferred by the public favour, is not a punishment; because no new evil is thereby on any man inflicted; he is only left in the estate he was in before.

*Nor pain inflicted without public hearing.* Thirdly, that the evil inflicted by public authority, without precedent public condemnation, is not to be styled by the name of punishment; but of an hostile act; because the fact for which a man is punished, ought first to be judged by public authority, to be a transgression of the law.

*Nor pain inflicted by usurped power.* Fourthly, that the evil inflicted by usurped power, and judges without authority from the sovereign, is not punishment; but an act of hostility; because the acts of power usurped, have not for author, the person condemned; and therefore are not acts of public authority.

*Nor pain inflicted without respect to the future good.* Fifthly, that all evil which is inflicted without intention, or possibility of disposing the delinquent, or, by his example, other men, to obey the laws, is not punishment; but an act of hostility: because without such an end, no hurt done is contained under that name.

*Natural evil consequences no punishments.* Sixthly, whereas to certain actions, there be annexed by nature, divers hurtful consequences; as when a man in assaulting another, is himself slain, or wounded; or when he falleth into sickness by the doing of some unlawful act; such hurt, though in respect of God, who is the author of nature, it may be said to be inflicted, and therefore a punishment divine; yet it is not contained in the name of punishment in respect of men, because it is not inflicted by the authority of man.

*Hurt inflicted, if less than the benefit of transgressing, is not punishment.* Seventhly, if the harm inflicted be less than the benefit, or contentment that naturally followeth the crime committed, that harm is not within the definition; and is rather the price, or redemption, than the punishment of a crime: because it is of the nature of punishment, to have for end, the disposing of men to obey the law; which end, if it be less than the benefit of the transgression, it attaineth not, but worketh a contrary effect.

*Where the punishment is annexed to the law, a greater hurt is not punishment, but hostility.* Eighthly, if a punishment be determined and prescribed in the law itself, and after the crime committed, there be a greater punishment inflicted, the excess is not punishment, but an act of hostility. For seeing the aim of punishment is not a revenge, but terror; and the terror of a great punishment unknown, is taken away by the declaration of a less, the unexpected addition is no part of the punishment. But where there is no punishment at all determined by the law, there whatsoever is inflicted, hath the nature of punishment. For he that goes about the violation of a law, wherein no penalty is determined, expecteth an indeterminate, that is to say, an arbitrary punishment.

*Hurt inflicted for a fact done before the law, no punishment.* Ninthly, harm inflicted for a fact done before there was a law that forbade it, is not punishment, but an act of hostility: for before the law, there is no transgression of the law: but punishment supposeth a fact judged, to have been a transgression of the law; therefore harm inflicted before the law made, is not punishment, but an act of hostility.

*The representative of the commonwealth unpunishable.* Tenthly, hurt inflicted on the representative of the commonwealth, is not punishment, but an act of hostility: because it is of the nature of punishment, to be inflicted by public authority, which is the authority only of the representative itself.

*Hurt to revolted subjects is done by right of war, not by way of punishment.* Lastly, harm inflicted upon one that is a declared enemy, falls not under the name of punishment: because seeing they were either never subject to the law, and therefore cannot transgress it; or having been subject to it, and professing to be no longer so, by consequence deny they can transgress it, all the harms that can be done them, must be taken as acts of hostility. But in declared hostility, all infliction of evil is lawful. From whence it followeth, that if a subject shall by fact, or word, wittingly, and deliberately deny the authority of the representative of the commonwealth (whatsoever penalty hath been formerly ordained for treason) he may lawfully be made to suffer whatsoever the representative will. For in denying subjection, he denies such punishment as by the law hath been ordained; and therefore suffers as an enemy of the commonwealth; that is, according to the will of the representative. For the punishments set down in the law, are to subjects, not to enemies; such as are they, that having been by their own acts subjects, deliberately revolting, deny the sovereign power.

The first, and most general distribution of punishments, is

into *divine,* and *human.* Of the former I shall have occasion to speak, in a more convenient place hereafter.

*Human,* are those punishments that be inflicted by the commandment of man; and are either *corporal,* or *pecuniary,* or *ignominy,* or *imprisonment,* or *exile,* or mixed of these.

*Punishments corporal. Corporal punishment* is that, which is inflicted on the body directly, and according to the intention of him that inflicteth it: such as are stripes, or wounds, or deprivation of such pleasures of the body, as were before lawfully enjoyed.

*Capital.* And of these, some be *capital,* some *less* than *capital.* Capital, is the infliction of death; and that either simply, or with torment. Less than capital, are stripes, wounds, chains, and any other corporal pain, not in its own nature mortal. For if upon the infliction of a punishment death follow not in the intention of the inflictor, the punishment is not to be esteemed capital, though the harm prove mortal by an accident not to be foreseen; in which case death is not inflicted, but hastened.

*Pecuniary punishment,* is that which consisteth not only in the deprivation of a sum of money, but also of lands, or any other goods which are usually bought and sold for money. And in case the law, that ordaineth such a punishment, be made with design to gather money, from such as shall transgress the same, it is not properly a punishment, but the price of privilege and exemption from the law, which doth not absolutely forbid the fact, but only to those that are not able to pay the money: except where the law is natural, or part of religion; for in that case it is not an exemption from the law, but a transgression of it. As where a law exacteth a pecuniary mulct, of them that take the name of God in vain, the payment of the mulct, is not the price of a dispensation to swear, but the punishment of the transgression of a law indispensable. In like manner if the law impose a sum of money to be paid, to him that has been injured; this is but a satisfaction for the hurt done him; and extinguisheth the accusation of the party injured, not the crime of the offender.

*Ignominy. Ignominy,* is the infliction of such evil, as is made dishonourable; or the deprivation of such good, as is made honourable by the commonwealth. For there be some things honourable by nature; as the effects of courage, magnanimity, strength, wisdom, and other abilities of body and mind: others made honourable by the commonwealth; as badges, titles, offices, or any other singular mark of the sovereign's favour. The former, though they may fail by nature, or accident, cannot be taken away by a law; and therefore the loss of them is not punishment. But the latter, may be taken away by the public authority that made them honourable, and are properly punishments: such are degrading men condemned, of their badges, titles, and offices; or declaring them incapable of the like in time to come.

*Imprisonment.* Imprisonment, is when a man is by public authority deprived of liberty; and may happen from two divers ends; whereof one is the safe custody of a man accused; the other is the inflicting of pain on a man condemned. The former is not punishment; because no man is supposed to be punished, before he be judicially heard, and declared guilty. And therefore whatsoever hurt a man is made to suffer by bonds, or restraint, before his cause be heard, over and above that which is necessary to assure his custody, is against the law of nature. But the latter is punishment, because evil, and inflicted by public authority, for somewhat that has by the same authority been judged a transgression of the law. Under this word imprisonment, I comprehend all restraint of motion, caused by an external obstacle, be it a house, which is called by the general name of a prison; or an island, as when men are said to be confined to it; or a place where men are set to work, as in old time men have been condemned to quarries, and in these times to galleys; or be it a chain, or any other such impediment.

*Exile.* Exile (banishment) is when a man is for a crime, condemned to depart out of the dominion of the commonwealth, or out of a certain part thereof: and during a prefixed time, or for ever, not to return into it: and seemeth not in its own nature, without other circumstances, to be a punishment; but rather an escape, or a public commandment to avoid punishment by flight. And Cicero says, there was never any such punishment ordained in the city of Rome; but calls it a refuge of men in danger. For if a man banished, be nevertheless permitted to enjoy his goods, and the revenue of his lands, the mere change of air is no punishment, nor does it tend to that benefit of the commonwealth, for which all punishments are ordained, that is to say, to the forming of men's wills to the observation of the law; but many times to the damage of the commonwealth. For a banished man, is a lawful enemy of the commonwealth that banished him; as being no more a member of the same. But if he be withal deprived of his lands, or goods, then the punishment lieth not in the exile, but is to be reckoned amongst punishments pecuniary.

*The punishment of innocent subjects is contrary to the law of nature.* All punishments of innocent subjects, be they great or little, are against the law of nature; for punishment is only for transgression of the law, and therefore there can be no punishment of the innocent. It is therefore a violation, first, of that law of nature, which forbiddeth all men, in their revenges, to look at any thing but some future good: for there can arrive no good to the commonwealth, by punishing the innocent. Secondly, of that, which forbiddeth ingratitude: for seeing all sovereign power, is originally given by the consent of every one of the subjects, to the end they should as long as they are obedient, be protected thereby; the punishment of the innocent, is a rendering of evil for good. And thirdly, of the law that commandeth equity; that is to say, an equal distribution of justice; which in punishing the innocent is not observed.

*But the harm done to innocents in war not so. Nor that which is done to declared rebels.* But the infliction of what evil soever, on an innocent man, that is not a subject, if it be for the benefit of the commonwealth, and without violation of any former covenant, is no breach of the law of nature. For all men that are not subjects, are either enemies, or else they have ceased from being so by some precedent covenants. But against enemies, whom the commonwealth judgeth capable to do them hurt, it is lawful by the original right of nature to make war; wherein the sword judgeth not, nor doth the victor make distinction of nocent, and innocent, as to the time past nor has other respect of mercy, than as it conduceth to the good of his own people. And upon this ground it is, that also in subjects, who deliberately deny the authority of the commonwealth established, the vengeance is lawfully extended, not only to the fathers, but also to the third and fourth generation not yet in being, and consequently innocent of the fact, for which they are afflicted: because the nature of this offence, consisteth in the renouncing of subjection; which is a relapse into the condition of war, commonly called rebellion; and they that so offend, suffer not as subjects, but as enemies. For *rebellion,* is but war renewed.

*Reward is either salary or grace.* REWARD, is either of *gift,* or by *contract.* When by contract, it is called *salary,* and *wages;* which is benefit due for service performed, or promised. When of gift, it is benefit proceeding from the *grace* of them that bestow it, to encourage, or enable men to do them service. And therefore when the sovereign of a commonwealth appointeth a salary to any public office, he that receiveth it, is bound in justice to perform his office; otherwise, he is bound only in honour, to acknowledgment, and an endeavour of requital. For though men have no lawful remedy, when they be commanded to quit their private business, to serve the public, without reward or salary; yet they are not bound thereto, by the law of nature, nor by the institution of the commonwealth, unless the service cannot otherwise be done; because it is supposed the sovereign may make use of all their means, insomuch as the most common soldier, may demand the wages of his warfare, as a debt.

*Benefits bestowed for fear are not rewards.* The benefits which a sovereign bestoweth on a subject, for fear of some power and ability he hath to do hurt to the commonwealth, are not properly rewards; for they are not salaries; because there is in this case no contract supposed, every man being obliged already not to do the commonwealth disservice: nor are they graces; because they be extorted by fear, which ought not to be incident to the sovereign power: but are rather sacrifices, which the sovereign, considered in his natural person, and not in the person of the commonwealth, makes, for the appeasing the discontent of him he thinks more potent than himself; and encourage not to obedience, but on the contrary, to the continuance, and increasing of further extortion.

*Salaries certain and casual.* And whereas some salaries are certain, and proceed from the public treasure; and others uncertain, and casual, proceeding from the execution of the office for which the salary is ordained; the latter is in some cases hurtful to the commonwealth; as in the case of judicature. For where the benefit of the judges, and ministers of a court of justice ariseth from the multitude of causes that are brought to their cognizance, there must needs follow two inconveniences: one, is the nourishing of suits; for the more suits, the greater benefit: and another that depends on that, which is contention about jurisdiction; each court drawing to itself, as many causes as it can. But in offices of execution there are not those inconveniences; because their employment cannot be increased by any endeavour of their own. And thus much shall suffice for the nature of punishment and reward; which are, as it were, the nerves and tendons, that move the limbs and joints of a commonwealth.

Hitherto I have set forth the nature of man, whose pride

and other passions have compelled him to submit himself to government: together with the great power of his governor, whom I compared to *Leviathan*, taking that comparison out of the two last verses of the one-and-fortieth of *Job;* where God having set forth the great power of *Leviathan*, calleth him King of the Proud. *There is nothing*, saith he, *on earth, to be compared with him. He is made so as not to be afraid. He seeth every high thing below him; and is king of all the children of pride.* But because he is mortal, and subject to decay, as all other earthly creatures are; and because there is that in heaven, though not on earth, that he should stand in fear of, and whose laws he ought to obey; I shall in the next following chapters speak of his diseases, and the causes of his mortality; and of what laws of nature he is bound to obey.

# Chapter 29

## Of those things that weaken, or tend to the Dissolution of a Commonwealth

*Dissolution of commonwealths proceedeth from their imperfect institution.* Though nothing can be immortal, which mortals make; yet, if men had the use of reason they pretend to, their commonwealths might be secured, at least from perishing by internal diseases. For by the nature of their institution, they are designed to live, as long as mankind, or as the laws of nature, or as justice itself, which gives them life. Therefore when they come to be dissolved, not by external violence, but intestine disorder, the fault is not in men, as they are the *matter;* but as they are the *makers,* and orderers of them. For men, as they become at last weary of irregular jostling, and hewing one another, and desire with all their hearts, to conform themselves into one firm and lasting edifice: so for want, both of the art of making fit laws, to square their actions by, and also of humility, and patience, to suffer the rude and cumbersome points of their present greatness to be taken off, they cannot without the help of a very able architect, be compiled into any other than a crazy building, such as hardly lasting out their own time, must assuredly fall upon the heads of their posterity.

Amongst the *infirmities* therefore of a commonwealth, I will reckon in the first place, those that arise from an imperfect institution, and resemble the diseases of a natural body, which proceed from a defectuous procreation.

*Want of absolute power.* Of which, this is one, *that a man to obtain a kingdom, is sometimes content with less power, than to the peace, and defence of the commonwealth is necessarily required.* From whence it cometh to pass, that when the exercise of the power laid by, is for the public safety to be resumed, it hath the resemblance of an unjust act; which disposeth great numbers of men, when occasion is presented, to rebel; in the same manner as the bodies of children, gotten by diseased parents, are subject either to untimely death, or to purge the ill quality, derived from their vicious conception, by breaking out into biles and scabs. And when kings deny themselves some such necessary power, it is not always, though sometimes, out of ignorance of what is necessary to the office they undertake; but many times out of a hope to recover the same again at their pleasure. Wherein they reason not well; because such as will hold them to their promises, shall be maintained against them by foreign commonwealths; who in order to the good of their own subjects let slip few occasions to *weaken* the estate of their neighbours. So was Thomas Beckett, archbishop of Canterbury, supported against Henry the Second, by the Pope; the subjection of ecclesiastics to the commonwealth, having been dispensed with by William the Conqueror at his reception, when he took an oath, not to infringe the liberty of the church. And so were the barons, whose power was by William Rufus, to have their help in transferring the succession from his elder brother to himself, increased to a degree inconsistent with the sovereign power, maintained in their rebellion against king John, by the French.

Nor does this happen in monarchy only. For whereas the style of the ancient Roman commonwealth, was, *The Senate and People of Rome;* neither senate, nor people pretended to the whole power; which first caused the seditions, of Tiberius Gracchus, Caius Gracchus, Lucius Saturninus, and others; and afterwards the wars between the senate and the people, under Marius and Sylla; and again under Pompey and Cæsar, to the extinction of their democracy, and the setting up of monarchy.

The people of Athens bound themselves but from one only action; which was, that no man on pain of death should propound the renewing of the war for the island of Salamis; and yet thereby, if Solon had not caused to be given out he was mad, and afterwards in gesture and habit of a madman, and in verse, propounded it to the people that flocked about him, they had had an enemy perpetually in readiness, even at the gates of their city; such damage, or shifts, are all commonwealths forced to, that have their power never so little limited.

*Private judgment of good and evil.* In the second place, I observe the *diseases* of a commonwealth, that proceed from the poison of seditious doctrines, whereof one is, *That every private man is judge of good and evil actions.* This is true in the condition of mere nature, where there are no civil laws; and also under civil government, in such cases as are not determined by the law. But otherwise, it is manifest, that the measure of good and evil actions, is the civil law; and the judge the legislator, who is always representative of the commonwealth. From this false doctrine, men are disposed to debate with themselves, and dispute the commands of the commonwealth; and afterwards to obey, or disobey them, as in their private judgments they shall think fit; whereby the commonwealth is distracted and *weakened*.

*Erroneous conscience*. Another doctrine repugnant to civil society, is, that *whatsoever a man does against his conscience, is sin;* and it dependeth on the presumption of making himself judge of good and evil. For a man's conscience, and his judgment is the same thing, and as the judgment, so also the conscience may be erroneous. Therefore, though he that is subject to no civil law, sinneth in all he does against his conscience, because he has no other rule to follow but his own reason; yet it is not so with him that lives in a commonwealth; because the law is the public conscience, by which he hath already undertaken to be guided. Otherwise in such diversity, as there is of private consciences, which are but private opinions, the commonwealth must needs be distracted, and no man dare to obey the sovereign power, further than it shall seem good in his own eyes.

*Pretence of inspiration*. It hath been also commonly taught, *that faith and sanctity, are not to be attained by study and reason, but by supernatural inspiration, or infusion*. Which granted, I see not why any man should render a reason of his faith; or why every Christian should not be also a prophet; or why any man should take the law of his country, rather than his own inspiration, for the rule of his action. And thus we fall again in the fault of taking upon us to judge of good and evil; or to make judges of it, such private men as pretend to be supernaturally inspired, to the dissolution of all civil government. Faith comes by hearing, and hearing by those accidents, which guide us into the presence of them that speak to us; which accidents are all contrived by God Almighty; and yet are not supernatural, but only, for the great number of them that concur to every effect, unobservable. Faith and sanctity, are indeed not very frequent; but yet they are not miracles, but brought to pass by education, discipline, correction, and other natural ways, by which God worketh them in his elect, at such times as he thinketh fit. And these three opinions, pernicious to peace and government, have in this part of the world, proceeded chiefly from the tongues, and pens of unlearned divines, who joining the words of Holy Scripture together, otherwise than is agreeable to reason, do what they can, to make men think, that sanctity and natural reason, cannot stand together.

*Subjecting the sovereign power to civil laws.* A fourth opinion, repugnant to the nature of a commonwealth, is this, *that he that hath the sovereign power is subject to the civil laws.* It is true, that sovereigns are all subject to the laws of nature; because such laws be divine, and cannot by any man, or commonwealth be abrogated. But to those laws which the sovereign himself, that is, which the commonwealth maketh, he is not subject. For to be subject to laws, is to be subject to the commonwealth, that is to the sovereign representative, that is to himself; which is not subjection, but freedom from the laws. Which error, because it setteth the laws above the sovereign, setteth also a judge above him, and a power to punish him; which is to make a new sovereign; and again for the same reason a third, to punish the second; and so continually without end, to the confusion, and dissolution of the commonwealth.

*Attributing of absolute propriety to subjects.* A fifth doctrine, that tendeth to the dissolution of a commonwealth, is, *that every private man has an absolute propriety in his goods; such, as excludeth the right of the sovereign.* Every man has indeed a propriety that excludes the right of every other subject: and he has it only from the sovereign power; without the protection whereof, every other man should have equal right to the same. But if the right of the sovereign also be excluded, he cannot perform the office they have put him into; which is, to defend them both from foreign enemies, and from the injuries of one another; and consequently there is no longer a commonwealth.

And if the propriety of subjects, exclude not the right of the sovereign representative to their goods; much less to their offices of judicature, or execution, in which they represent the sovereign himself.

*Dividing of the sovereign power.* There is a sixth doctrine, plainly, and directly against the essence of a commonwealth; and it is this, *that the sovereign power may be divided.* For what is it to divide the power of a commonwealth, but to dissolve it; for powers divided mutually destroy each other. And for these doctrines, men are chiefly beholding to some of those, that making profession of the laws, endeavour to make them depend upon their own learning, and not upon the legislative power.

*Imitation of neighbour nations.* And as false doctrine, so also oftentimes the example of different government in a neighbouring nation, disposeth men to alteration of the form already settled. So the people of the Jews were stirred up to reject God, and to call upon the prophet Samuel, for a king after the manner of the nations: so also the lesser cities of Greece, were continually disturbed, with seditions of the aristocratical, and democratical factions; one part of almost every commonwealth, desiring to imitate the Lacedemonians; the other, the Athenians. And I doubt not, but many men have been contented to see the late troubles in England, out of an imitation of the Low Countries; supposing there needed no more to grow rich, than to change, as they had done, the form of their government. For the constitution of man's nature, is of itself subject to desire novelty. When therefore they are provoked to the same, by the neighbourhood also of those that have been enriched by it, it is almost impossible for them, not to be content with those that solicit them to change; and love the first beginnings, though they be grieved with the continuance of disorder; like hot bloods, that having gotten the itch, tear themselves with their own nails, till they can endure the smart no longer.

*Imitation of the Greeks and Romans*. And as to rebellion in particular against monarchy; one of the most frequent causes of it, is the reading of the books of policy, and histories of the ancient Greeks, and Romans; from which, young men, and all others that are unprovided of the antidote of solid reason, receiving a strong, and delightful impression, of the great exploits of war, achieved by the conductors of their armies, receive withal a pleasing idea, of all they have done besides; and imagine their great prosperity, not to have proceeded from the emulation of particular men, but from the virtue of their popular form of government: not considering the frequent seditions, and civil wars, produced by the imperfection of their policy. From the reading, I say, of such books, men have undertaken to kill their kings, because the Greek and Latin writers, in their books, and discourses of policy, make it lawful, and laudable, for any man so to do; provided, before he do it, he call him tyrant. For they say not *regicide*, that is, killing a king, but *tyrannicide*, that is killing of a tyrant is lawful. From the same books, they that live under a monarch conceive an opinion, that the subjects in a popular commonwealth enjoy liberty; but that in a monarchy they are all slaves. I say, they that live under a monarchy conceive such an opinion; not they that live under a popular government: for they find no such matter. In sum, I cannot imagine, how any thing can be more prejudicial to a monarchy, than the allowing of such books to be publicly read, without present applying such correctives of discreet masters, as are fit to take away their venom: which venom I will not doubt to compare to the biting of a mad dog, which is a disease the physicians call *hydrophobia*, or *fear of water*. For as he that is so bitten, has a continual torment of thirst, and yet abhorreth water; and is in such an estate, as if the poison endeavoured to convert him into a dog: so when a monarchy is once bitten to the quick, by those democratical writers, that continually snarl at that estate; it wanteth nothing more than a strong monarch, which nevertheless out of a certain *tyrannophobia,* or fear of being strongly governed, when they have him, they abhor.

*The opinion that there be more sovereigns than one in the commonwealth.* As there have been doctors, that hold there be three souls in a man; so there be also that think there may be more souls, that is, more sovereigns, than one, in a commonwealth; and set up a *supremacy* against the *sovereignty; canons* against *laws;* and a *ghostly authority* against the *civil;* working on men's minds, with words and distinctions, that of themselves signify nothing, but bewray by their obscurity; that there walketh, as some think, invisibly another kingdom, as it were a kingdom of fairies, in the dark. Now seeing it is manifest, that the civil power, and the power of the commonwealth is the same thing; and that supremacy, and the power of making canons, and granting faculties, implieth a commonwealth; it followeth, that where one is sovereign, another supreme; where one can make laws, and another make canons; there must needs be two commonwealths, of one and the same subjects; which is a kingdom divided in itself, and cannot stand. For notwithstanding the insignificant distinction of *temporal,* and *ghostly,* they are still two kingdoms, and every subject is subject to two masters. For seeing the *ghostly* power challengeth the right to declare what is sin, it challengeth by consequence to declare what is law, sin being nothing but the transgression of the law; and again, the civil power challenging to declare what is law, every subject must obey two masters, who both will have their commands be observed as law; which is impossible. Or, if it be but one kingdom, either the *civil,* which is the power of the commonwealth, must be subordinate to the *ghostly,* and then there is no sovereignty but the *ghostly;* or the *ghostly* must be subordinate to the *temporal,* and then there is no *supremacy* but the *temporal.* When therefore these two powers oppose one another, the commonwealth cannot but be in great danger of civil war and dissolution. For the *civil* authority being more visible, and standing in the clearer light of natural reason, cannot choose but draw to it in all times a very considerable part of the people: and the *spiritual,* though it stand in the darkness of School distinctions, and hard words, yet because the fear of darkness and ghosts, is greater than other fears, cannot want a party sufficient to trouble, and sometimes to destroy a commonwealth. And this is a disease which not un-fitly may be compared to the epilepsy, or falling sickness, which the Jews took to be one kind of possession by spirits, in the body natural. For as in this disease, there is an un-natural spirit, or wind in the head that obstructeth the roots of the nerves, and moving them violently, taketh away the motion which naturally they should have from the power of the soul in the brain, and thereby causeth violent, and ir-regular motions, which men call convulsions, in the parts; insomuch as he that is seized therewith, falleth down some-times into the water, and sometimes into the fire, as a man deprived of his senses; so also in the body politic, when the spiritual power, moveth the members of a commonwealth, by the terror of punishments, and hope of rewards, which are the nerves of it, otherwise than by the civil power, which is the soul of the commonwealth, they ought to be moved; and by strange, and hard words suffocates their understanding, it must needs thereby distract the people, and either overwhelm the commonwealth with oppression, or cast it into the fire of a civil war.

*Mixed government.* Sometimes also in the merely civil gov-ernment, there be more than one soul; as when the power of levying money, which is the nutritive faculty, has depended on a general assembly; the power of conduct and command, which is the motive faculty, on one man; and the power of making laws, which is the rational faculty, on the accidental consent, not only of those two, but also of a third; this en-dangereth the commonwealth, sometimes for want of consent to good laws: but most often for want of such nourishment, as is necessary to life, and motion. For although few perceive, that such government, is not government, but division of the commonwealth into three factions, and call it mixed mon-archy; yet the truth is, that it is not one independent com-monwealth, but three independent factions; nor one representative person, but three. In the kingdom of God, there may be three persons independent, without breach of unity in God that reigneth; but where men reign, that be subject to diversity of opinions, it cannot be so. And therefore if the king bear the person of the people, and the general assembly bear also the person of the people, and another assembly bear the person of a part of the people, they are not one person, nor one sovereign, but three persons, and three sovereigns.

To what disease in the natural body of man, I may exactly compare this irregularity of a commonwealth, I know not. But I have seen a man, that had another man growing out of his side, with a head, arms, breast, and stomach, of his own; if he had had another man growing out of his other side, the comparison might then have been exact.

*Want of money*. Hitherto I have named such diseases of a commonwealth, as are of the greatest, and most present danger. There be other not so great; which nevertheless are not unfit to be observed. At first, the difficulty of raising money, for the necessary uses of the commonwealth; especially in the approach of war. This difficulty ariseth from the opinion, that every subject hath a propriety in his lands and goods, exclusive of the sovereign's right to the use of the same. From whence it cometh to pass, that the sovereign power, which foreseeth the necessities and dangers of the commonwealth, finding the passage of money to the public treasury obstructed, by the tenacity of the people, whereas it ought to extend itself, to encounter, and prevent such dangers in their beginnings, contracteth itself as long as it can, and when it cannot longer, struggles with the people by stratagems of law, to obtain little sums, which not sufficing, he is fain at last violently to open the way for present supply, or perish; and being put often to these extremities, at last reduceth the people to their due temper; or else the commonwealth must perish. Insomuch as we may compare this distemper very aptly to an ague; wherein, the fleshly parts being congealed, or by venomous matter obstructed, the veins which by their natural course empty themselves into the heart, are not, as they ought to be, supplied from the arteries, whereby there succeedeth at first a cold contraction, and trembling of the limbs; and afterward a hot, and strong endeavour of the heart, to force a passage for the blood; and before it can do that, contenteth itself with the small refreshments of such things as cool for a time, till, if nature be strong enough, it break at last the contumacy of the parts obstructed, and dissipateth the venom into sweat; or, if nature be too weak, the patient dieth.

*Monopolies, and abuses of publicans*. Again, there is sometimes in a commonwealth, a disease, which resembleth the pleurisy; and that is, when the treasure of the commonwealth, flowing out of its due course, is gathered together in too much abundance, in one, or a few private men, by monopolies, or by farms of the public revenues; in the same manner as the blood in a pleurisy, getting into the membrane of the breast, breedeth there an inflammation, accompanied with a fever, and painful stitches.

*Popular men.* Also, the popularity of a potent subject, unless the commonwealth have very good caution of his fidelity, is a dangerous disease; because the people, which should receive their motion from the authority of the sovereign, by the flattery and by the reputation of an ambitious man are drawn away from their obedience to the laws, to follow a man, of whose virtues, and designs they have no knowledge. And this is commonly of more danger in a popular government, than in a monarchy; because an army is of so great force, and multitude, as it may easily be made believe, they are the people. By this means it was, that Julius Cæsar, who was set up by the people against the senate, having won to himself the affections of his army, made himself master both of senate and people. And this proceeding of popular, and ambitious men, is plain rebellion; and may be resembled to the effects of witchcraft.

*Excessive greatness of a town, multitude of corporations. Liberty of disputing against sovereign power.* Another infirmity of a commonwealth, is the immoderate greatness of a town, when it is able to furnish out of its own circuit, the number, and expense of a great army: as also the great number of corporations; which are as it were many lesser commonwealths in the bowels of a greater, like worms in the entrails of a natural man. To which may be added, the liberty of disputing against absolute power, by pretenders to political prudence; which though bred for the most part in the lees of the people, yet animated by false doctrines, are perpetually meddling with the fundamental laws, to the molestation of the commonwealth; like the little worms, which physicians call *ascarides*.

We may further add, the insatiable appetite, or βουλιμία, of enlarging dominion; with the incurable *wounds* thereby many times received from the enemy; and the *wens,* of ununited conquests, which are many times a burthen, and with less danger lost, than kept; as also the *lethargy* of ease, and *consumption* of riot and vain expense.

*Dissolution of the commonwealth.* Lastly, when in a war, foreign or intestine, the enemies get a final victory; so as, the forces of the commonwealth keeping the field no longer, there is no further protection of subjects in their loyalty; then is the commonwealth DISSOLVED, and every man at liberty to protect himself by such courses as his own discretion shall suggest unto him. For the sovereign is the public soul, giving life and motion to the commonwealth; which expiring, the members are governed by it no more, than the carcase of a man, by his departed, though immortal, soul. For though the right of a sovereign monarch cannot be extinguished by the act of another; yet the obligation of the members may. For he that wants protection, may seek it anywhere; and when he hath it, is obliged, without fraudulent pretence of having submitted himself out of fear, to protect his protection as long as he is able. But when the power of an assembly is once suppressed, the right of the same perisheth utterly; because the assembly itself is extinct; and consequently, there is no possibility for the sovereignty to re-enter.

# Chapter 30

## Of the Office of the Sovereign Representative

*The procuration of the good of the people.* The office of the sovereign, be it a monarch or an assembly, consisteth in the end, for which he was trusted with the sovereign power, namely the procuration of *the safety of the people;* to which he is obliged by the law of nature, and to render an account thereof to God, the author of that law, and to none but him. But by safety here, is not meant a bare preservation, but also all other contentments of life, which every man by lawful industry, without danger, or hurt to the commonwealth, shall acquire to himself.

*By instruction and laws.* And this is intended should be done, not by care applied to individuals, further than their protection from injuries, when they shall complain; but by a general providence, contained in public instruction, both of doctrine, and example; and in the making and executing of good laws, to which individual persons may apply their own cases.

*Against the duty of a sovereign to relinquish any essential right of sovereignty. Or not to see the people taught the grounds of them.* And because, if the essential rights of sovereignty, specified before in the eighteenth chapter, be taken away, the commonwealth is thereby dissolved, and every man returneth into the condition, and calamity of a war with every other man, which is the greatest evil that can happen in this life; it is the office of the sovereign, to maintain those rights entire; and consequently against his duty, first, to transfer to another, or to lay from himself any of them. For he that deserteth the means, deserteth the ends; and he deserteth the means, that being the sovereign, acknowledgeth himself subject to the civil laws; and renounceth the power of supreme judicature; or of making war, or peace by his own authority; or of judging of the necessities of the commonwealth; or of levying money and soldiers, when, and as much as in his own conscience he shall judge necessary; or of making officers, and ministers both of war and peace; or of appointing teachers, and examining what doctrines are conformable, or contrary to the defence, peace, and good of the people. Secondly, it is against his duty, to let the people be ignorant, or misinformed of the grounds, and reasons of those his essential rights; because thereby men are easy to be seduced, and drawn to resist him, when the commonwealth shall require their use and exercise.

And the grounds of these rights, have the rather need to be diligently, and truly taught; because they cannot be maintained by any civil law, or terror of legal punishment. For a civil law, that shall forbid rebellion, (and such is all resistance to the essential rights of the sovereignty), is not, as a civil law, any obligation, but by virtue only of the law of nature, that forbiddeth the violation of faith; which natural obligation, if men know not, they cannot know the right of any law the sovereign maketh. And for the punishment, they take it but for an act of hostility; which when they think they have strength enough, they will endeavour by acts of hostility, to avoid.

*Objection of those that say there are no principles of reason for absolute sovereignty.* As I have heard some say, that justice is but a word, without substance; and that whatsoever a man can by force, or art, acquire to himself, not only in the condition of war, but also in a commonwealth, is his own, which I have already showed to be false: so there be also that maintain, that there are no grounds, nor principles of reason, to sustain those essential rights, which make sovereignty absolute. For if there were, they would have been found out in some place, or other; whereas we see, there has not hitherto been any commonwealth, where those rights have been acknowledged, or challenged. Wherein they argue as ill, as if the savage people of America, should deny there were any grounds, or principles of reason, so to build a house, as to last as long as the materials, because they never yet saw any so well built. Time, and industry, produce every day new knowledge. And as the art of well building is derived from principles of reason, observed by industrious men, that had long studied the nature of materials, and the divers effects of figure, and proportion, long after mankind began, though poorly, to build: so, long time after men have begun to constitute commonwealths, imperfect, and apt to relapse into disorder, there may principles of reason be found out, by industrious meditation, to make their constitution, excepting by external violence, everlasting. And such are those which I have in this discourse set forth: which whether they come not into the sight of those that have power to make use of them, or be neglected by them, or not, concerneth my particular interests, at this day, very little. But supposing that these of mine are not such principles of reason; yet I am sure they are principles from authority of Scripture; as I shall make it appear, when I shall come to speak of the kingdom of God, administered by Moses, over the Jews, his peculiar people by covenant.

*Objection from the incapacity of the vulgar.* But they say again, that though the principles be right, yet common people are not of capacity enough to be made to understand them. I should be glad, that the rich and potent subjects of a kingdom, or those that are accounted the most learned, were no less incapable than they. But all men know, that the obstructions to this kind of doctrine, proceed not so much from the difficulty of the matter, as from the interest of them that are to learn. Potent men, digest hardly any thing that setteth up a power to bridle their affections; and learned men, any thing that discovereth their errors, and thereby lesseneth their authority: whereas the common people's minds, unless they be tainted with dependence on the potent, or scribbled over with the opinions of their doctors, are like clean paper, fit to receive whatsoever by public authority shall be imprinted in them. Shall whole nations be brought to *acquiesce* in the great mysteries of the Christian religion, which are above reason, and millions of men be made believe, that the same body may be in innumerable places at one and the same time, which is against reason; and shall not men be able, by their teaching, and preaching, protected by the law, to make that received, which is so consonant to reason, that any unprejudicated man, needs no more to learn it, than to hear it? I conclude therefore, that in the instruction of the people in the essential rights which are the natural and fundamental laws of sovereignty, there is no difficulty, whilst a sovereign has his power entire, but what proceeds from his own fault, or the fault of those whom he trusteth in the administration of the commonwealth; and consequently, it is his duty, to cause them so to be instructed; and not only his duty, but his benefit also, and security against the danger that may arrive to himself in his natural person from rebellion.

*Subjects are to be taught not to affect change of government:* And, to descend to particulars, the people are to be taught, first, that they ought not to be in love with any form of government they see in their neighbour nations, more than with their own, nor, whatsoever present prosperity they behold in nations that are otherwise governed than they, to desire change. For the prosperity of a people ruled by an aristocratical, or democratical assembly, cometh not from aristocracy, nor from democracy, but from the obedience, and concord of the subjects: nor do the people flourish in a monarchy, because one man has the right to rule them, but because they obey him. Take away in any kind of state, the obedience, and consequently the concord of the people, and they shall not only not flourish, but in short time be dissolved. And they that go about by disobedience, to do no more than reform the commonwealth, shall find they do thereby destroy it; like the foolish daughters of Peleus, in the fable; which desiring to renew the youth of their decrepit father, did by the counsel of Medea, cut him in pieces, and boil him, together with strange herbs, but made not of him a new man. This desire of change, is like the breach of the first of God's commandments: for there God says, *Non habebis Deos alienos;* Thou shalt not have the Gods of other nations; and in another place concerning *kings,* that they are *Gods.*

*Nor adhere, against the sovereign, to popular men.* Secondly, they are to be taught, that they ought not to be led with admiration of the virtue of any of their fellow-subjects, how high soever he stand, or how conspicuously soever he shine in the commonwealth; nor of any assembly, except the sovereign assembly, so as to defer to them any obedience, or honour, appropriate to the sovereign only, whom, in their particular stations, they represent; nor to receive any influence from them, but such as is conveyed by them from the sovereign authority. For that sovereign cannot be imagined to love his people as he ought, that is not jealous of them, but suffers them by the flattery of popular men, to be seduced from their loyalty, as they have often been, not only secretly, but openly, so as to proclaim marriage with them *in facie ecclesiæ* by preachers, and by publishing the same in the open streets: which may fitly be compared to the violation of the second of the ten commandments.

*Nor to dispute the sovereign power.* Thirdly, in consequence to this, they ought to be informed, how great a fault it is, to speak evil of the sovereign representative, whether one man, or an assembly of men; or to argue and dispute his power; or any way to use his name irreverently, whereby he may be brought into contempt with his people, and their obedience, in which the safety of the commonwealth consisteth, slackened. Which doctrine the third commandment by resemblance pointeth to.

*And to have days set apart to learn their duty.* Fourthly, seeing people cannot be taught this, nor when it is taught, remember it, nor after one generation past, so much as know in whom the sovereign power is placed, without setting apart from their ordinary labour, some certain times, in which they may attend those that are appointed to instruct them; it is necessary that some such times be determined, wherein they may assemble together, and, after prayers and praises given to God, the sovereign of sovereigns, hear those their duties told them, and the positive laws, such as generally concern them all, read and expounded, and be put in mind of the authority that maketh them laws. To this end had the Jews every seventh day, a sabbath, in which the law was read and expounded; and in the solemnity whereof they were put in mind, that their king was God; that having created the world in six days, he rested the seventh day; and by their resting on it from their labour, that that God was their king, which redeemed them from their servile, and painful labour in Egypt, and gave them a time, after they had rejoiced in God, to take joy also in themselves, by lawful recreation. So that the first table of the commandments, is spent all in setting down the sum of God's absolute power; not only as God, but as king by pact, in peculiar, of the Jews; and may therefore give light, to those that have sovereign power conferred on them by the consent of men, to see what doctrine they ought to teach their subjects.

*And to honour their parents.* And because the first instruction of children, dependeth on the care of their parents, it is necessary that they should be obedient to them, whilst they are under their tuition; and not only so, but that also afterwards, as gratitude requireth, they acknowledge the benefit of their education, by external signs of honour. To which end they are to be taught, that originally the father of every man was also his sovereign lord, with power over him of life and death; and that the fathers of families, when by instituting a commonwealth, they resigned that absolute power, yet it was never intended, they should lose the honour due unto them for their education. For to relinquish such right, was not necessary to the institution of sovereign power; nor would there be any reason, why any man should desire to have children, or take the care to nourish and instruct them, if they were afterwards to have no other benefit from them, than from other men. And this accordeth with the fifth commandment.

*And to avoid doing of injury.* Again, every sovereign ought to cause justice to be taught, which, consisting in taking from no man what is his, is as much as to say, to cause men to be taught not to deprive their neighbours, by violence or fraud, of any thing which by the sovereign authority is theirs. Of things held in propriety, those that are dearest to a man are his own life, and limbs; and in the next degree, in most men, those that concern conjugal affection; and after them, riches and means of living. Therefore the people are to be taught, to abstain from violence to one another's person, by private revenges; from violation of conjugal honour; and from forcible rapine, and fraudulent surreption of one another's goods. For which purpose also it is necessary they be showed the evil consequences of false judgment, by corruption either of judges or witnesses, whereby the distinction of propriety is taken away, and justice becomes of no effect: all which things are intimated in the sixth, seventh, eighth, and ninth commandments.

*And to do all this sincerely from the heart.* Lastly, they are to be taught, that not only the unjust facts, but the designs and intentions to do them, though by accident hindered, are injustice; which consisteth in the pravity of the will, as well as in the irregularity of the act. And this is the intention of the tenth commandment, and the sum of the second table; which is reduced all to this one commandment of mutual charity, *thou shalt love thy neighbour as thyself:* as the sum of the first table is reduced to *the love of God;* whom they had then newly received as their king.

*The use of universities.* As for the means, and conduits, by which the people may receive this instruction, we are to search, by what means so many opinions, contrary to the peace of mankind, upon weak and false principles, have nevertheless been so deeply rooted in them. I mean those, which I have in the precedent chapter specified: as that men shall judge of what is lawful and unlawful, not by the law itself, but by their own consciences; that is to say, by their own private judgments: that subjects sin in obeying the commands of the commonwealth, unless they themselves have first judged them to be lawful: that their propriety in their riches is such, as to exclude the dominion, which the commonwealth hath over the same: that it is lawful for subjects to kill such, as they call tyrants: that the sovereign power may be divided, and the like; which come to be instilled into the people by this means. They whom necessity, or covetousness keepeth attent on their trades, and labour; and they, on the other side, whom superfluity, or sloth carrieth after their sensual pleasures; which two sorts of men take up the greatest part of mankind; being diverted from the deep meditation, which the learning of truth, not only in the matter of natural justice, but also of all other sciences necessarily requireth, receive the notions of their duty, chiefly from divines in the pulpit, and partly from such of their neighbours or familiar acquaintance, as having the faculty of discoursing readily, and plausibly, seem wiser and better learned in cases of law and conscience, than themselves. And the divines, and such others as make show of learning, derive their knowledge from the universities, and from the schools of law, or from the books, which by men, eminent in those schools and universities, have been published. It is therefore manifest, that the instruction of the people, dependeth wholly, on the right teaching of youth in the universities. But are not, may some man say, the universities of England learned enough already to do that? or is it you, will undertake to teach the universities? Hard questions. Yet to the first, I doubt not to answer; that till towards the latter end of Henry the Eighth, the power of the Pope, was always upheld against the power of the commonwealth, principally by the universities; and that the doctrines maintained by so many preachers, against the sovereign power of the king, and by so many lawyers, and others, that had their education there, is a sufficient argument, that though the universities were not authors of those false doctrines, yet they knew not how to plant the true. For in such a contradiction of opinions, it is most certain, that they have not been sufficiently instructed; and it is no wonder, if they yet retain a relish of that subtle liquor, wherewith they were first seasoned, against the civil authority. But to the latter question, it is not fit, nor needful for me to say either aye, or no: for any man that sees what I am doing, may easily perceive what I think.

The safety of the people, requireth further, from him, or them that have the sovereign power, that justice be equally administered to all degrees of people; that is, that as well the rich and mighty, as poor and obscure persons, may be righted of the injuries done them; so as the great may have no greater hope of impunity, when they do violence, dishonour, or any injury to the meaner sort, than when one of these, does the like to one of them: for in this consisteth equity; to which, as being precept of the law of nature, a sovereign is as much subject, as any of the meanest of his people. All breaches of the law, are offences against the commonwealth: but there be some, that are also against private persons. Those that concern the commonwealth only, may without breach of equity be pardoned; for every man may pardon what is done against himself, according to his own discretion. But an offence against a private man, cannot in equity be pardoned, without the consent of him that is injured; or reasonable satisfaction.

The inequality of subjects, proceedeth from the acts of sovereign power; and therefore has no more place in the presence of the sovereign, that is to say, in a court of justice, than the inequality between kings and their subjects, in the presence of the King of kings. The honour of great persons, is to be valued for their beneficence and the aids they give to men of inferior rank, or not at all. And the violences, oppressions, and injuries they do, are not extenuated, but aggravated by the greatness of their persons; because they have least need to commit them. The consequences of this partiality towards the great, proceed in this manner. Impunity maketh insolence; insolence, hatred; and hatred, an endeavour to pull down all oppressing and contumelious greatness, though with the ruin of the commonwealth.

*Equal taxes.* To equal justice, appertaineth also the equal imposition of taxes; the equality whereof dependeth not on the equality of riches, but on the equality of the debt that every man oweth to the commonwealth for his defence. It is not enough, for a man to labour for the maintenance of his life; but also to fight, if need be, for the securing of his labour. They must either do as the Jews did after their return from captivity, in re-edifying the temple, build with one hand, and hold the sword in the other; or else they must hire others to fight for them. For the impositions, that are laid on the people by the sovereign power, are nothing else but the wages, due to them that hold the public sword, to defend private men in the exercise of their several trades, and callings. Seeing then the benefit that every one receiveth thereby, is the enjoyment of life, which is equally dear to poor and rich; the debt which a poor man oweth them that defend his life, is the same which a rich man oweth for the defence of his; saving that the rich, who have the service of the poor, may be debtors not only for their own persons but for many more. Which considered, the equality of imposition, consisteth rather in the equality of that which is consumed, than of the riches of the persons that consume the same. For what reason is there, that he which laboureth much, and sparing the fruits of his labour, consumeth little, should be more charged, than he that living idly, getteth little, and spendeth all he gets; seeing the one hath no more protection from the commonwealth, than the other? But when the impositions, are laid upon those things which men consume, every man payeth equally for what he useth: nor is the commonwealth defrauded by the luxurious waste of private men.

*Public charity.* And whereas many men, by accident inevitable, become unable to maintain themselves by their labour; they ought not to be left to the charity of private persons; but to be provided for, as far forth as the necessities of nature require, by the laws of the commonwealth. For as it is uncharitableness in any man, to neglect the impotent; so it is in the sovereign of a commonwealth, to expose them to the hazard of such uncertain charity.

*Prevention of idleness.* But for such as have strong bodies, the case is otherwise: they are to be forced to work; and to avoid the excuse of not finding employment, there ought to be such laws, as may encourage all manner of arts; as navigation, agriculture, fishing, and all manner of manufacture that requires labour. The multitude of poor, and yet strong people still increasing, they are to be transplanted into countries not sufficiently inhabited: where nevertheless, they are not to exterminate those they find there; but constrain them to inhabit closer together, and not to range a great deal of ground, to snatch what they find; but to court each little plot with art and labour, to give them their sustenance in due season. And when all the world is overcharged with inhabitants, then the last remedy of all is war; which provideth for every man, by victory, or death.

*Good laws, what.* To the care of the sovereign, belongeth the making of good laws. But what is a good law? By a good law, I mean not a just law: for no law can be unjust. The law is made by the sovereign power, and all that is done by such power, is warranted, and owned by every one of the people; and that which every man will have so, no man can say is unjust. It is in the laws of a commonwealth, as in the laws of gaming: whatsoever the gamesters all agree on, is injustice to none of them. A good law is that, which is *needful,* for the *good of the people,* and withal *perspicuous.*

*Such as are necessary.* For the use of laws, which are but

rules authorized, is not to bind the people from all voluntary actions; but to direct and keep them in such a motion, as not to hurt themselves by their own impetuous desires, rashness or indiscretion; as hedges are set, not to stop travellers, but to keep them in their way. And therefore a law that is not needful, having not the true end of a law, is not good. A law may be conceived to be good, when it is for the benefit of the sovereign; though it be not necessary for the people; but it is not so. For the good of the sovereign and people, cannot be separated. It is a weak sovereign, that has weak subjects; and a weak people, whose sovereign wanteth power to rule them at his will. Unnecessary laws are not good laws; but traps for money: which where the right of sovereign power is acknowledged, are superfluous; and where it is not acknowledged, insufficient to defend the people.

*Such as are perspicuous.* The perspicuity, consisteth not so much in the words of the law itself, as in a declaration of the causes, and motives for which it was made. That is it, that shows us the meaning of the legislator; and the meaning of the legislator known, the law is more easily understood by few, than many words. For all words, are subject to ambiguity; and therefore multiplication of words in the body of the law, is multiplication of ambiguity: besides it seems to imply, by too much diligence, that whosoever can evade the words, is without the compass of the law. And this is a cause of many unnecessary processes. For when I consider how short were the laws of ancient times; and how they grew by degrees still longer; methinks I see a contention between the penners, and pleaders of the law; the former seeking to circumscribe the latter; and the latter to evade their circumscriptions; and that the pleaders have got the victory. It belongeth therefore to the office of a legislator, (such as is in all commonwealths the supreme representative, be it one man, or an assembly), to make the reason perspicuous, why the law was made; and the body of the law itself, as short, but in as proper, and significant terms, as may be.

*Punishments.* It belongeth also to the office of the sovereign, to make a right application of punishments, and rewards. And seeing the end of punishing is not revenge, and discharge of choler; but correction, either of the offender, or of others by his example; the severest punishments are to be inflicted for those crimes, that are of most danger to the public; such as are those which proceed from malice to the government established; those that spring from contempt of justice; those that provoke indignation in the multitude; and those, which unpunished, seem authorized, as when they are committed by sons, servants, or favourites of men in authority. For indignation carrieth men, not only against the actors, and authors of injustice; but against all power that is likely to protect them; as in the case of Tarquin; when for the insolent act of one of his sons, he was driven out of Rome, and the monarchy itself dissolved. But crimes of infirmity; such as are those which proceed from great provocation, from great fear, great need, or from ignorance whether the fact be a great crime, or not, there is place many times for lenity, without prejudice to the commonwealth; and lenity, when there is such place for it, is required by the law of nature. The punishment of the leaders and teachers in a commotion, not the poor seduced people, when they are punished, can profit the commonwealth by their example. To be severe to the people, is to punish that ignorance, which may in great part be imputed to the sovereign, whose fault it was, that they were no better instructed.

*Rewards.* In like manner it belongeth to the office, and duty of the sovereign, to apply his rewards always so, as there may arise from them benefit to the commonwealth; wherein consisteth their use, and end; and is then done, when they that have well served the commonwealth, are with as little expense of the common treasure, as is possible, so well recompensed, as others thereby may be encouraged, both to serve the same as faithfully as they can, and to study the arts by which they may be enabled to do it better. To buy with money, or preferment, from a popular ambitious subject, to be quiet, and desist from making ill impressions in the minds of the people, has nothing of the nature of reward; (which is ordained not for disservice, but for service past;) nor a sign of gratitude, but of fear; nor does it tend to the benefit, but to the damage of the public. It is a contention with ambition, like that of Hercules with the monster Hydra, which having many heads, for every one that was vanquished, there grew up three. For in like manner, when the stubbornness of one popular man, is overcome with reward, there arise many more, by the example, that do the same mischief, in hope of like benefit: and as all sorts of manufacture, so also malice increaseth by being vendible. And though sometimes a civil war, may be deferred by such ways as that, yet the danger grows still the greater, and the public ruin more assured. It is therefore against the duty of the sovereign, to whom the public safety is committed, to reward those that aspire to greatness by disturbing the peace of their country, and not rather to oppose the beginnings of such men, with a little danger, than after a longer time with greater.

*Counsellors*. Another business of the sovereign, is to choose good counsellors; I mean such, whose advice he is to take in the government of the commonwealth. For this word counsel, *consilium*, corrupted from *considium*, is of a large signification, and comprehendeth all assemblies of men that sit together, not only to deliberate what is to be done hereafter, but also to judge of facts past, and of law for the present. I take it here in the first sense only: and in this sense, there is no choice of counsel, neither in a democracy, nor aristocracy; because the persons counselling are members of the person counselled. The choice of counsellors therefore is proper to monarchy; in which, the sovereign that endeavoureth not to make choice of those, that in every kind are the most able, dischargeth not his office as he ought to do. The most able counsellors, are they that have least hope of benefit by giving evil counsel, and most knowledge of those things that conduce to the peace, and defence of the commonwealth. It is a hard matter to know who expecteth benefit from public troubles; but the signs that guide to a just suspicion, is the soothing of the people in their unreasonable, or irremediable grievances, by men whose estates are not sufficient to discharge their accustomed expenses, and may easily be observed by any one whom it concerns to know it. But to know, who has most knowledge of the public affairs, is yet harder; and they that know them, need them a great deal the less. For to know, who knows the rules almost of any art, is a great degree of the knowledge of the same art; because no man can be assured of the truth of another's rules, but he that is first taught to understand them. But the best signs of knowledge of any art, are, much conversing in it, and constant good effects of it. Good counsel comes not by lot, nor by inheritance; and therefore there is no more reason to expect good advice from the rich or noble, in matter of state, than in delineating the dimensions of a fortress; unless we shall think there needs no method in the study of the politics, as there does in the study of geometry, but only to be lookers on; which is not so. For the politics is the harder study of the two. Whereas in these parts of Europe, it hath been taken for a right of certain persons, to have place in the highest council of state by inheritance; it is derived from the conquests of the ancient Germans;

wherein many absolute lords joining together to conquer other nations, would not enter into the confederacy, without such privileges, as might be marks of difference in time following, between their posterity, and the posterity of their subjects; which privileges being inconsistent with the sovereign power, by the favour of the sovereign, they may seem to keep; but contending for them as their right, they must needs by degrees let them go, and have at last no further honour, than adhereth naturally to their abilities.

And how able soever be the counsellors in any affair, the benefit of their counsel is greater, when they give every one his advice, and the reasons of it apart, than when they do it in an assembly, by way of orations; and when they have premeditated, than when they speak on the sudden; both because they have more time, to survey the consequences of action; and are less subject to be carried away to contradiction, through envy, emulation, or other passions arising from the difference of opinion.

The best counsel, in those things that concern not other nations, but only the ease and benefit the subjects may enjoy, by laws that look only inward, is to be taken from the general informations, and complaints of the people of each province, who are best acquainted with their own wants, and ought therefore, when they demand nothing in derogation of the essential rights of sovereignty, to be diligently taken notice of. For without those essential rights, as I have often before said, the commonwealth cannot at all subsist.

*Commanders.* A commander of an army in chief, if he be not popular, shall not be beloved nor feared as he ought to be by his army; and consequently, cannot perform that office with good success. He must therefore be industrious, valiant, affable, liberal and fortunate, that he may gain an opinion both of sufficiency, and of loving his soldiers. This is popularity, and breeds in the soldiers both desire, and courage, to recommend themselves to his favour; and protects the severity of the general in punishing, when need is, the mutinous, or negligent soldiers. But this love of soldiers, if caution be not given of the commander's fidelity, is a dangerous thing to sovereign power; especially when it is in the hands of an assembly not popular. It belongeth therefore to the safety of the people, both that they be good conductors, and faithful subjects, to whom the sovereign commits his armies.

But when the sovereign himself is popular; that is, reverenced and beloved of his people, there is no danger at all from the popularity of a subject. For soldiers are never so generally unjust, as to side with their captain though they love him, against their sovereign, when they love not only his person, but also his cause. And therefore those, who by violence have at any time suppressed the power of their lawful sovereign, before they could settle themselves in his place, have been always put to the trouble of contriving their titles, to save the people from the shame of receiving them. To have a known right to sovereign power, is so popular a quality, as he that has it needs no more, for his own part, to turn the hearts of his subjects to him, but that they see him able absolutely to govern his own family: nor, on the part of his enemies, but a disbanding of their armies. For the greatest and most active part of mankind, has never hitherto been well contented with the present.

Concerning the offices of one sovereign to another, which are comprehended in that law, which is commonly called the *law of nations*, I need not say any thing in this place; because the law of nations, and the law of nature, is the same thing. And every sovereign hath the same right, in procuring the safety of his people, that any particular man can have, in procuring the safety of his own body. And the same law, that dictateth to men that have no civil government, what they ought to do, and what to avoid in regard of one another, dictateth the same to commonwealths, that is, to the consciences of sovereign princes and sovereign assemblies; there being no court of natural justice, but in the conscience only; where not man, but God reigneth; whose laws, such of them as oblige all mankind, in respect of God, as he is the author of nature, are *natural;* and in respect of the same God, as he is King of kings, are *laws*. But of the kingdom of God, as King of kings, and as King also of a peculiar people, I shall speak in the rest of this discourse.

# Chapter 31

## Of the Kingdom of God by Nature

*The scope of the following chapters.* That the condition of mere nature, that is to say, of absolute liberty, such as is theirs, that neither are sovereigns, nor subjects, is anarchy, and the condition of war: that the precepts, by which men are guided to avoid that condition, are the laws of nature: that a commonwealth, without sovereign power, is but a word without substance, and cannot stand: that subjects owe to sovereign simple obedience, in all things wherein their obedience is not repugnant to the laws of God, I have sufficiently proved, in that which I have already written. There wants only, for the entire knowledge of civil duty, to know what are those laws of God. For without that, a man knows not, when he is commanded any thing by the civil power, whether it be contrary to the law of God, or not: and so, either by too much civil obedience, offends the Divine Majesty; or through fear of offending God, transgresses the commandments of the commonwealth. To avoid both these rocks, it is necessary to know what are the laws divine. And seeing the knowledge of all law, dependeth on the knowledge of the sovereign power, I shall say something in that which followeth, of the KINGDOM OF GOD.

*Who are subjects in the kingdom of God.* God is king, let the earth rejoice, saith the psalmist (xcvii. 1). And again, (*Psalm* xcix. 1) *God is king, though the nations be angry; and he that sitteth on the cherubims, though the earth be moved.* Whether men will or not, they must be subject always to the divine power. By denying the existence, or providence of God, men may shake off their ease, but not their yoke. But to call this power of God, which extendeth itself not only to man, but also to beasts, and plants, and bodies inanimate, by the name of kingdom, is but a metaphorical use of the word. For he only is properly said to reign, that governs his subjects by his word, and by promise of rewards to those that obey it, and by threatening them with punishment that obey it not. Subjects therefore in the kingdom of God, are not bodies inanimate, nor creatures irrational; because they understand no precepts as his: nor atheists, nor they that be-

lieve not that God has any care of the actions of mankind;
because they acknowledge no word for his, nor have hope of
his rewards or fear of his threatenings. They therefore that
believe there is a God that governeth the world, and hath
given precepts, and propounded rewards, and punishments to
mankind, are God's subjects; all the rest, are to be understood
as enemies.

*A threefold word of God, reason, revelation, prophecy.* To
rule by words, requires that such words be manifestly made
known; for else they are no laws: for to the nature of laws
belongeth a sufficient, and clear promulgation, such as may
take away the excuse of ignorance; which in the laws of men
is but of one only kind, and that is, proclamation, or
promulgation by the voice of man. But God declareth his laws
three ways; by the dictates of *natural reason,* by *revelation,*
and by the *voice* of some *man* to whom by the operation of
miracles, he procureth credit with the rest. From hence there
ariseth a triple word of God, *rational, sensible,* and *prophetic:*
to which correspondeth a triple hearing; *right reason, sense
supernatural,* and *faith.* As for sense supernatural, which consisteth in revelation or inspiration, there have not been any
universal laws so given, because God speaketh not in that
manner but to particular persons, and divers men divers
things.

*A twofold kingdom of God, natural and prophetic.* From
the difference between the other two kinds of God's word,
*rational,* and *prophetic,* there may be attributed to God, a
twofold kingdom, *natural,* and *prophetic:* natural, wherein he
governeth as many of mankind as acknowledge his providence,
by the natural dictates of right reason; and prophetic, wherein
having chosen out one peculiar nation, the Jews, for his subjects, he governed them, and none but them, not only by
natural reason, but by positive laws, which he gave them by
the mouths of his holy prophets. Of the natural kingdom of
God I intend to speak in this chapter.

*The right of God's sovereignty is derived from his omni-
potence.* The right of nature, whereby God reigneth over
men, and punisheth those that break his laws, is to be derived,
not from his creating them, as if he required obedience as of
gratitude for his benefits; but from his *irresistible power.* I
have formerly shown, how the sovereign right ariseth from
pact: to show how the same right may arise from nature, requires no more, but to show in what case it is never taken
away. Seeing all men by nature had right to all things, they

had right every one to reign over all the rest. But because this right could not be obtained by force, it concerned the safety of every one, laying by that right, to set up men, with sovereign authority, by common consent, to rule and defend them: whereas if there had been any man of power irresistible, there had been no reason, why he should not by that power have ruled and defended both himself, and them, according to his own discretion. To those therefore whose power is irresistible, the dominion of all men adhereth naturally by their excellence or power; and consequently it is from that power, that the kingdom over men, and the right of afflicting men at his pleasure, belongeth naturally to God Almighty; not as Creator, and gracious; but as omnipotent. And though punishment be due for sin only, because by that word is understood affliction for sin; yet the right of afflicting, is not always derived from men's sin, but from God's power.

*Sin not the cause of all affliction.* This question, *why evil men often prosper, and good men suffer adversity,* has been much disputed by the ancient, and is the same with this of ours, *by what right God dispenseth the prosperities and adversities of this life;* and is of that difficulty, as it hath shaken the faith, not only of the vulgar, but of philosophers, and which is more, of the Saints, concerning the Divine Providence. *How good,* saith David, (*Psalm* lxxiii. 1, 2, 3,) *is the God of Israel to those that are upright in heart; and yet my feet were almost gone, my treadings had well-nigh slipt; for I was grieved at the wicked, when I saw the ungodly in such prosperity.* And Job, how earnestly does he expostulate with God, for the many afflictions he suffered, notwithstanding his righteousness? This question in the case of Job, is decided by God himself, not by arguments derived from Job's sin, but his own power. For whereas the friends of Job drew their arguments from his affliction to his sin, and he defended himself by the conscience of his innocence, God himself taketh up the matter, and having justified the affliction by arguments drawn from his power, such as this, (*Job* xxxviii. 4) *Where wast thou, when I laid the foundations of the earth?* and the like, both approved Job's innocence, and reproved the erroneous doctrine of his friends. Conformable to this doctrine is the sentence of our Saviour, concerning the man that was born blind, in these words, *Neither hath this man sinned, nor his fathers; but that the works of God might be made manifest in him.* And though it be said, *that death entered into the world by sin,* (by which is meant, that if Adam had never sinned, he had never died, that is, never suffered any separation of his soul from his body,) it follows not thence, that God could not justly have afflicted him, though he had not sinned, as well as he afflicteth other living creatures, that cannot sin.

*Divine laws.* Having spoken of the right of God's sovereignty, as grounded only on nature; we are to consider next, what are the Divine laws, or dictates of natural reason; which laws concern either the natural duties of one man to another, or the honour naturally due to our Divine Sovereign. The first are the same laws of nature, of which I have spoken already in the fourteenth and fifteenth chapters of this treatise; namely, equity, justice, mercy, humility, and the rest of the moral virtues. It remaineth therefore that we consider, what precepts are dictated to men, by their natural reason only, without other word of God, touching the honour and worship of the Divine Majesty.

*Honour and worship, what.* Honour consisteth in the inward thought, and opinion of the power, and goodness of another; and therefore to honour God, is to think as highly of his power and goodness, as is possible. And of that opinion, the external signs appearing in the words and actions of men, are called *worship;* which is one part of that which the Latins understand by the word *cultus.* For *cultus* signifieth properly, and constantly, that labour which a man bestows on any thing, with a purpose to make benefit by it. Now those things whereof we make benefit, are either subject to us, and the profit they yield, followeth the labour we bestow upon them, as a natural effect; or they are not subject to us, but answer our labour, according to their own wills. In the first sense the labour bestowed on the earth, is called *culture;* and the education of children, a *culture* of their minds. In the second sense, where men's wills are to be wrought to our purpose, not by force, but by complaisance, it signifieth as much as courting, that is, a winning of favour by good offices; as by praises, by acknowledging their power, and by whatsoever is pleasing to them from whom we look for any benefit. And this is properly *worship:* in which sense *Publicola,* is understood for a worshipper of the people; and *cultus Dei,* for the worship of God.

*Several signs of honour.* From internal honour, consisting in the opinion of power and goodness, arise three passions; *love,* which hath reference to goodness; and *hope,* and *fear,* that relate to power: and three parts of external worship; *praise, magnifying,* and *blessing:* the subject of praise, being goodness: the subject of magnifying and blessing, being power, and the effect thereof felicity. Praise, and magnifying are signified both by words, and actions: by words, when we say a man is good, or great: by actions, when we thank him for his bounty, and obey his power. The opinion of the happiness of another, can only be expressed by words.

*Worship natural and arbitrary.* There be some signs of honour, both in attributes and actions, that be naturally so; as amongst attributes, *good, just, liberal,* and the like; and amongst actions, *prayers, thanks,* and *obedience.* Others are so by institution, or custom of men; and in some times and places are honourable; in others, dishonourable; in others, indifferent: such as are the gestures in salutation, prayer, and thanksgiving, in different times and places, differently used. The former is *natural:* the latter *arbitrary* worship.

*Worship commanded and free.* And of arbitrary worship, there be two differences: for sometimes it is a *commanded,* sometimes *voluntary* worship: commanded, when it is such as he requireth, who is worshipped: free, when it is such as the worshipper thinks fit. When it is commanded, not the words, or gesture, but the obedience is the worship. But when free, the worship consists in the opinion of the beholders: for if to them the words, or actions by which we intend honour, seem ridiculous, and tending to contumely, they are no worship, because no signs of honour; and no signs of honour, because a sign is not a sign to him that giveth it, but to him to whom it is made, that is, to the spectator.

*Worship public and private.* Again, there is a *public,* and a *private* worship. Public, is the worship that a commonwealth performeth, as one person. Private, is that which a private person exhibiteth. Public, in respect of the whole commonwealth is free; but in respect of particular men, it is not so. Private, is in secret free; but in the sight of the multitude, it is never without some restraint, either from the laws, or from the opinion of men; which is contrary to the nature of liberty.

*The end of worship.* The end of worship amongst men, is power. For where a man seeth another worshipped, he supposeth him powerful, and is the readier to obey him; which makes his power greater. But God has no ends: the worship we do him, proceeds from our duty, and is directed according to our capacity, by those rules of honour, that reason dictateth to be done by the weak to the more potent men, in hope of benefit, for fear of damage, or in thankfulness for good already received from them.

*Attributes of divine honour.* That we may know what worship of God is taught us by the light of nature, I will begin with his attributes. Where, first, it is manifest, we ought to attribute to him *existence.* For no man can have the will to honour that, which he thinks not to have any being.

Secondly, that those philosophers, who said the world, or the soul of the world was God, spake unworthily of him; and denied his existence. For by God, is understood the cause of the world; and to say the world is God, is to say there is no cause of it, that is, no God.

Thirdly, to say the world was not created, but eternal, seeing that which is eternal has no cause, is to deny there is a God.

Fourthly, that they who attributing, as they think, ease to God, take from him the care of mankind; take from him his honour: for it takes away men's love, and fear of him; which is the root of honour.

Fifthly, in those things that signify greatness, and power; to say he is *finite,* is not to honour him: for it is not a sign of the will to honour God, to attribute to him less than we can; and finite, is less than we can; because to finite, it is easy to add more.

Therefore to attribute *figure* to him, is not honour; for all figure is finite:

Nor to say we conceive, and imagine, or have an *idea* of him, in our mind: for whatsoever we conceive is finite:

Nor to attribute to him *parts,* or *totality;* which are the attributes only of things finite:

Nor to say he is in this, or that *place:* for whatsoever is in place, is bounded, and finite:

Nor that he is *moved,* or *resteth:* for both these attributes ascribe to him place:

Nor that there be more Gods than one; because it implies them all finite: for there cannot be more than one infinite:

Nor to ascribe to him, (unless metaphorically, meaning not the passion but the effect,) passions that partake of grief; as *repentance, anger, mercy:* or of want; as *appetite, hope, desire;* or of any passive faculty: for passion, is power limited by somewhat else.

And therefore when we ascribe to God a *will,* it is not to be understood, as that of man, for a *rational appetite;* but as the power, by which he effecteth every thing.

Likewise when we attribute to him *sight,* and other acts of sense; as also *knowledge,* and *understanding;* which in us is nothing else, but a tumult of the mind, raised by external things that press the organical parts of man's body: for there is no such thing in God; and being things that depend on natural causes, cannot be attributed to him.

He that will attribute to God, nothing but what is warranted by natural reason, must either use such negative attributes, as *infinite, eternal, incomprehensible;* or superlatives, as *most high, most great,* and the like; or indefinite, as *good, just, holy, creator;* and in such sense, as if he meant not to declare what he is, (for that were to circumscribe him within the limits of our fancy,) but how much we admire him, and how ready we would be to obey him; which is a sign of humility, and of a will to honour him as much as we can. For there is but one name to signify our conception of his nature, and that is, I AM: and but one name of his relation to us, and that is, *God;* in which is contained Father, King, and Lord.

*Actions that are signs of divine honour.* Concerning the actions of divine worship, it is a most general precept of reason, that they be signs of the intention to honour God; such as are, first, *prayers.* For not the carvers, when they made images, were thought to make them gods; but the people that *prayed* to them.

Secondly, *thanksgiving;* which differeth from prayer in divine worship, no otherwise, than that prayers precede, and thanks succeed the benefit; the end, both of the one and the other, being to acknowledge God, for author of all benefits, as well past, as future.

Thirdly, *gifts,* that is to say, *sacrifices* and *oblations,* if they be of the best, are signs of honour: for they are thanksgivings.

Fourthly, *not to swear by any but God,* is naturally a sign of honour: for it is a confession that God only knoweth the heart; and that no man's wit or strength can protect a man against God's vengeance on the perjured.

Fifthly, it is a part of rational worship, to speak considerately of God; for it argues a fear of him, and fear is a confession of his power. Hence followeth, that the name of God is not to be used rashly, and to no purpose; for that is as much, as in vain: and it is to no purpose, unless it be by way of oath, and by order of the commonwealth, to make judgments certain; or between commonwealths, to avoid war. And that disputing of God's nature is contrary to his honour: for it is supposed, that in this natural kingdom of God, there is no other way to know any thing, but by natural reason, that is, from the principles of natural science; which are so far from teaching us any thing of God's nature, as they cannot teach us our own nature, nor the nature of the smallest creature living. And therefore, when men out of the principles of natural reason, dispute of the attributes of God, they but dishonour him: for in the attributes which we give to God, we are not to consider the signification of philosophical truth; but the signification of pious intention, to do him the greatest honour we are able. From the want of which consideration, have proceeded the volumes of disputation about the nature of God, that tend not to his honour, but to the honour of our own wits and learning; and are nothing else but inconsiderate and vain abuses of his sacred name.

Sixthly, in *prayers, thanksgiving, offerings,* and *sacrifices,* it is a dictate of natural reason, that they be every one in his kind the best, and most significant of honour. As for example, that prayers and thanksgiving, be made in words and phrases, not sudden, nor light, nor plebeian; but beautiful, and well composed. For else we do not God as much honour as we can. And therefore the heathens did absurdly, to worship images for gods: but their doing it in verse, and with music, both of voice and instruments, was reasonable. Also that the beasts they offered in sacrifice, and the gifts they offered, and in their actions in worshipping, were full of submission, and commemorative of benefits received, was according to reason, as proceeding from an intention to honour him.

Seventhly, reason directeth not only to worship God in secret; but also, and especially, in public, and in the sight of men. For without that, that which in honour is most acceptable, the procuring others to honour him, is lost.

Lastly, obedience to his laws, that is, in this case to the laws of nature, is the greatest worship of all. For as obedience is more acceptable to God than sacrifice; so also to set light by his commandments, is the greatest of all contumelies. And these are the laws of that divine worship, which natural reason dictateth to private men.

*Public worship consisteth in uniformity.* But seeing a commonwealth is but one person, it ought also to exhibit to God but one worship; which then it doth, when it commandeth it to be exhibited by private men, publicly. And this is public worship; the property whereof, is to be *uniform:* for those actions that are done differently, by different men, cannot be said to be a public worship. And therefore, where many sorts of worship be allowed, proceeding from the different religions of private men, it cannot be said there is any public worship, nor that the commonwealth is of any religion at all.

*All attributes depend on the laws civil.* And because words, and consequently the attributes of God, have their signification by agreement and constitution of men, those attributes are to be held significative of honour, that men intend shall so be; and whatsoever may be done by the wills of particular men, where there is no law but reason, may be done by the will of the commonwealth, by laws civil. And because a commonwealth hath no will, nor makes no laws, but those that are made by the will of him, or them that have the sovereign power; it followeth that those attributes which the sovereign ordaineth, in the worship of God, for signs of honour, ought to be taken and used for such, by private men in their public worship.

*Not all actions.* But because not all actions are signs by constitution, but some are naturally signs of honour, others of contumely; these latter, which are those that men are ashamed to do in the sight of them they reverence, cannot be made by human power a part of Divine worship; nor the former, such as are decent, modest, humble behaviour, ever be separated from it. But whereas there be an infinite number of actions and gestures of an indifferent nature; such of them as the commonwealth shall ordain to be publicly and universally in use, as signs of honour, and part of God's worship, are to be taken and used for such by the subjects. And that which is said in the Scripture, *It is better to obey God than man,* hath place in the kingdom of God by pact, and not by nature.

*Natural punishments.* Having thus briefly spoken of the natural kingdom of God, and his natural laws, I will add only to this chapter a short declaration of his natural punishments. There is no action of man in this life, that is not the beginning of so long a chain of consequences, as no human providence is high enough, to give a man a prospect to the end. And in this chain, there are linked together both pleasing and unpleasing events; in such manner, as he that will do any thing for his pleasure, must engage himself to suffer all the pains annexed to it; and these pains, are the natural punishments of those actions, which are the beginning of more harm than good. And hereby it comes to pass, that intemperance is naturally punished with diseases; rashness, with mischances; injustice, with the violence of enemies; pride, with ruin; cowardice, with oppression; negligent government of princes, with rebellion; and rebellion, with slaughter. For seeing punishments are consequent to the breach of laws; natural punishments must be naturally consequent to the breach of the laws of nature; and therefore follow them as their natural, not arbitrary effects.

*The conclusion of the second part.* And thus far concerning the constitution, nature, and right of sovereigns, and concerning the duty of subjects, derived from the principles of natural reason. And now, considering how different this doctrine is, from the practice of the greatest part of the world, especially of these western parts, that have received their moral learning from Rome and Athens; and how much depth of moral philosophy is required, in them that have the administration of the sovereign power; I am at the point of believing this my labour, as useless, as the commonwealth of Plato. For he also is of opinion that it is impossible for the disorders of state, and change of governments by civil war, ever to be taken away, till sovereigns be philosophers. But when I consider again, that the science of natural justice, is the only science necessary for sovereigns and their principal ministers; and that they need not be charged with the sciences mathematical, as by Plato they are, farther than by good laws to encourage men to the study of them; and that neither Plato, nor any other philosopher hitherto, hath put into order, and sufficiently or probably proved all the theorems of moral doctrine, that men may learn thereby, both how to govern, and how to obey; I recover some hope, that one time or other, this writing of mine may fall into the hands of a sovereign, who will consider it himself, (for it is short, and I think clear,) without the help of any interested, or envious interpreter; and by the exercise of entire sovereignty, in protecting the public teaching of it, convert this truth of speculation, into the utility of practice.

# THE THIRD PART

# OF A CHRISTIAN COMMONWEALTH

## Chapter 32

### Of the Principles of Christian Politics

*The word of God delivered by prophets is the main principle of Christian politics.* I have derived the rights of sovereign power, and the duty of subjects, hitherto from the principles of nature only; such as experience has found true, or consent concerning the use of words has made so; that is to say, from the nature of men, known to us by experience, and from definitions of such words as are essential to all political reasoning, universally agreed on. But in that I am next to handle, which is the nature and rights of a CHRISTIAN COMMONWEALTH, whereof there dependeth much upon supernatural revelations of the will of God; the ground of my discourse must be, not only the natural word of God, but also the prophetical.

*Yet is not natural reason to be renounced.* Nevertheless, we are not to renounce our senses, and experience; nor, that which is the undoubted word of God, our natural reason. For they are the talents which he hath put into our hands to negotiate, till the coming again of our blessed Saviour; and therefore not to be folded up in the napkin of an implicit faith, but employed in the purchase of justice, peace, and true religion. For though there be many things in God's word above reason; that is to say, which cannot by natural reason be either demonstrated, or confused; yet there is nothing contrary to it; but when it seemeth so, the fault is either in our unskillful interpretation, or erroneous ratiocination.

Therefore, when any thing therein written is too hard for our examination, we are bidden to captivate our understanding to the words; and not to labour in sifting out a philosophical truth by logic, of such mysteries as are not comprehensible, nor fall under any rule of natural science. For it is with the mysteries of our religion, as with wholesome pills for the sick; which swallowed whole, have the virtue of cure; but chewed, are for the most part cast up again without effect.

*What it is to captivate the understanding.* But by the captivity of our understanding, is not meant a submission of the intellectual faculty to the opinion of any other man; but of the will to obedience, where obedience is due. For sense, memory, understanding, reason, and opinion are not in our power to change; but always, and necessarily such, as the things we see, hear, and consider suggest unto us; and therefore are not effects of our will, but our will of them. We then captivate our understanding and reason, when we forbear contradiction; when we so speak, as by lawful authority we are commanded; and when we live accordingly; which in sum, is trust and faith reposed in him that speaketh, though the mind be incapable of any notion at all from the words spoken.

*How God speaketh to men.* When God speaketh to man, it must be either immediately; or by meditation of another man, to whom he had formerly spoken by himself immediately. How God speaketh to a man immediately, may be understood by those well enough, to whom he hath so spoken; but how the same should be understood by another, is hard, if not impossible to know. For if a man pretend to me, that God hath spoken to him supernaturally and immediately, and I make doubt of it, I cannot easily perceive what argument he can produce, to oblige me to believe it. It is true, that if he be my sovereign, he may oblige me to obedience, so, as not by act or word to declare I believe him not; but not to think any otherwise than my reason persuades me. But if one that hath not such authority over me, should pretend the same, there is nothing that exacteth either belief, or obedience.

For to say that God hath spoken to him in the Holy Scripture, is not to say God hath spoken to him immediately, but by mediation of the prophets, or of the apostles, or of the church, in such manner as he speaks to all other Christian men. To say he hath spoken to him in a dream, is no more than to say he dreamed that God spake to him; which is not of force to win belief from any man, that knows dreams are for the most part natural, and may proceed from former thoughts; and such dreams as that, from self-deceit, and foolish arrogance, and false opinion of a man's own godliness, or other virtue, by which he thinks he hath merited the favour of extraordinary revelation. To say he hath seen a vision, or heard a voice, is to say, that he hath dreamed between sleeping and waking: for in such manner a man doth many times naturally take his dream for a vision, as not having well observed his own slumbering. To say he speaks by supernatural inspiration, is to say he finds an ardent desire to speak, or some strong opinion of himself, for which he can allege no natural and sufficient reason. So that though God Almighty can speak to a man by dreams, visions, voice, and inspiration; yet he obliges no man to believe he hath so done to him that pretends it; who, being a man, may err, and, which is more, may lie.

*By what marks prophets are known.* How then can he, to whom God hath never revealed his will immediately, saving by the way of natural reason, know when he is to obey, or not to obey his word, delivered by him that says he is a prophet? Of four hundred prophets, of whom the king of Israel asked counsel, concerning the war he made against Ramoth Gilead, (1 *Kings* xxii) only Micaiah was a true one. The prophet that was sent to prophesy against the altar set up by Jeroboam, (1 *Kings* xiii) though a true prophet, and that by two miracles done in his presence, appears to be a prophet sent from God, was yet deceived by another old prophet, that persuaded him as from the mouth of God, to eat and drink with him. If one prophet deceive another, what certainty is there of knowing the will of God, by other way than that of reason? To which I answer out of the Holy Scripture, that there be two marks, by which together, not asunder, a true prophet is to be known. One is the doing of miracles; the other is the not teaching any other religion than that which is already established. Asunder, I say, neither of these is sufficient. *If a prophet rise amongst you, or a dreamer of dreams, and shall pretend the doing of a miracle, and the miracle come to pass; if he say, Let us follow strange Gods, which thou hast not known, thou shalt not hearken to him, &c. But that prophet and dreamer of dreams shall be put to death, because he hath spoken to you to revolt from the Lord your God.* (*Deut.* xiii. 1-5.) In which words two things are to be observed; first, that God will not have miracles alone serve for arguments, to approve the prophet's calling; but, as it is in the third verse, for an experiment of the constancy of our adherence to himself. For the works of the Egyptian sorcerers, though not so great as those of Moses, yet were great miracles. Secondly, that how great soever the miracle be, yet if it tend to stir up revolt against the king, or him that governeth by the king's authority, he that doth such miracle, is not to be considered otherwise than as sent to make trial of their alle-

giance. For these words, *revolt from the Lord your God,* are
in this place equivalent to *revolt from your king.* For they
had made God their king by pact at the foot of Mount Sinai;
who ruled them by Moses only; for he only spake with God,
and from time to time declared God's commandments to the
people. In like manner, after our Saviour Christ had made
his disciples acknowledge him for the Messiah, (that is to say,
for God's anointed, whom the nation of the Jews daily
expected for their king, but refused when he came,) he
omitted not to advertise them of the danger of miracles. *There
shall arise,* saith he, *false Christs, and false prophets, and shall
do great wonders and miracles, even to the seducing, if it were
possible, of the very elect.* (*Matt.* xxiv. 24.) By which it
appears, that false prophets may have the power of miracles;
yet are we not to take doctrine for God's word. St. Paul says
further to the Galatians, (*Gal.* i. 8) that *if himself, or an angel
from heaven preach another gospel to them, than he had
preached, let him be accursed.* That gospel was, that Christ
was King; so that all preaching against the power of the king
received, in consequence to these words, is by St. Paul accursed. For his speech is addressed to those, who by his
preaching had already received Jesus for the Christ, that is to
say, for King of the Jews.

*The marks of a prophet in the old law, miracles, and doc-
trine conformable to the law.* And as miracles, without preaching that doctrine which God hath established; so preaching
the true doctrine, without the doing of miracles, is an insufficient argument of immediate revelation. For if a man that
teacheth not false doctrine, should pretend to be a prophet
without showing any miracle, he is never the more to be
regarded for his pretence, as is evident by *Deut.* xviii. 21, 22,
*If thou say in thy heart, How shall we know that the word
(of the prophet) is not that which the Lord hath spoken?
when the prophet shall have spoken in the name of the Lord,
that which shall not come to pass, that is the word which the
Lord hath not spoken, but the prophet has spoken it out of the
pride of his own heart, fear him not.* But a man may here
again ask, when the prophet hath foretold a thing, how shall
we know whether it will come to pass or not? For he may
foretell it as a thing to arrive after a certain long time, longer
than the time of man's life; or indefinitely, that it will come to
pass one time or other: in which case this mark of a prophet
is unuseful; and therefore the miracles that oblige us to believe
a prophet, ought to be confirmed by an immediate, or a not

long deferred event. So that it is manifest, that the teaching of the religion which God hath established, and the showing of a present miracle, joined together, were the only marks whereby the Scripture would have a true prophet, that is to say, immediate revelation, to be acknowledged; neither of them being singly sufficient to oblige any other man to regard what he saith.

*Miracles ceasing, prophets cease, and the Scripture supplies their place.* Seeing therefore miracles now cease, we have no sign left, whereby to acknowledge the pretended revelations or inspirations of any private man; nor obligation to give ear to any doctrine, farther than it is conformable to the Holy Scriptures, which since the time of our Saviour, supply the place, and sufficiently recompense the want of all other prophecy; and from which, by wise and learned interpretation, and careful ratiocination, all rules and precepts necessary to the knowledge of our duty both to God and man, without enthusiasm or supernatural inspiration, may easily be deduced. And this Scripture is it, out of which I am to take the principles of my discourse, concerning the rights of those that are the supreme governors on earth of Christian commonwealths; and of the duty of Christian subjects toward their sovereigns. And to that end, I shall speak in the next chapter, of the books, writers, scope, and authority of the Bible.

## Chapter 33

### Of the Number, Antiquity, Scope, Authority, and Interpreters of the Books of Holy Scripture

*Of the books of Holy Scripture.* By the Books of HOLY SCRIPTURE, are understood those, which ought to be the *canon,* that is to say, the rules of Christian life.

And because all rules of life, which men are in conscience bound to observe, are laws; the question of the Scripture, is the question of what is law throughout all Christendom, both natural and civil. For though it be not determined in Scripture, what laws every Christian king shall constitute in his own dominions; yet it is determined what laws he shall not constitute. Seeing therefore I have already proved, that sovereigns in their own dominions are the sole legislators; those books only are canonical, that is, law, in every nation, which are established for such by the sovereign authority. It is true, that God is the sovereign of all sovereigns; and therefore, when he speaks to any subject, he ought to be obeyed, whatsoever any earthly potentate command to the contrary. But the question is not of obedience to God, but of *when* and *what* God hath said; which to subjects that have no supernatural revelation, cannot be known, but by that natural reason, which guideth them, for the obtaining of peace and justice, to obey the authority of their several commonwealths, that is to say, of their lawful sovereigns. According to this obligation, I can acknowledge no other books of the Old Testament, to be Holy Scripture, but those which have been commanded to be acknowledged for such, by the authority of the Church of England. What books these are, is sufficiently known, without a catalogue of them here; and they are the same that are acknowledged by St. Jerome, who holdeth the rest, namely, the *Wisdom of Solomon, Ecclesiasticus, Judith, Tobias,* the first and the second of *Maccabees,* (though he had seen the first in Hebrew,) and the third and fourth of *Esdras,* for *Apocrypha.* Of the canonical, Josephus, a learned Jew, that wrote in the time of the emperor Domitian, reckoneth *twenty-two,* making the number agree with the Hebrew alphabet. St. Jerome does the same, though they reckon them in different manner. For Josephus numbers *five* Books of *Moses, thirteen* of *Prophets*, that writ the history of their own times, (which how it agrees with the prophets' writings contained in the Bible we shall see hereafter,) and *four* of *hymns* and moral precepts. But St. Jerome reckons *five* books of *Moses*, *eight* of *Prophets*, and *nine* of other Holy Writ, which he calls of ἁγιόγραφα. The Septuagint, who were seventy learned men of the Jews, sent for by Ptolemy, king of Egypt, to translate the Jewish law out of the Hebrew into the Greek, have left us no other for Holy Scripture in the Greek tongue, but the same that are received in the Church of England.

As for the Books of the New Testament, they are equally acknowledged for canon by all Christian churches, and by all sects of Christians, that admit any books at all for canonical.

*Their antiquity.* Who were the original writers of the several Books of Holy Scripture, has not been made evident by any sufficient testimony of other history, which is the only proof of matter of fact; nor can be, by any arguments of natural reason: for reason serves only to convince the truth, not of fact, but, of consequence. The light therefore that must guide us in this question, must be that which is held out unto us from the books themselves: and this light, though it show us not the writer of every book, yet it is not unuseful to give us knowledge of the time, wherein they were written.

*The Pentateuch not written by Moses.* And first, for the *Pentateuch*, it is not argument enough that they were written by Moses, because they are called the five Books of *Moses;* no more than these titles, the book of *Joshua*, the Book of *Judges*, the Book of *Ruth*, and the Books of the *Kings*, are arguments sufficient to prove, that they were written by *Joshua*, by the *Judges*, by *Ruth*, and by the *Kings*. For in titles of books, the subject is marked, as often as the writer. The history of Livy, denotes the writer; but the history of Scanderberg, is denominated from the subject. We read in the last chapter of *Deuteronomy*, verse 6, concerning the sepulchre of Moses, *that no man knoweth of his sepulchre to this day*, that is, to the day wherein those words were written. It is therefore manifest, that those words were written after his interment. For it were a strange interpretation, to say Moses spake of his own sepulchre, though by prophecy, that it was not found to that day, wherein he was yet living. But it may perhaps be alleged, that the last chapter only, not the whole *Pentateuch*, was written by some other man, but the rest not. Let us therefore consider that which we find in the book of *Genesis*, (xii. 6) *And Abraham passed through the land to the place of Sichem, unto the plain of Moreh, and the* Canaanite *was then in the land;* which must needs be the words of one that wrote when the Canaanite was not in the land; and consequently, not of Moses, who died before he came into it. Likewise *Numbers* xxi. 14, the writer citeth another more ancient book, entitled, *The Book of the Wars of the Lord,* wherein were registered the acts of Moses, at the Red Sea, and at the brook of Arnon. It is therefore sufficiently evident, that the five Books of Moses were written after his time, though how long after it be not so manifest.

But though Moses did not compile those books entirely, and in the form we have them; yet he wrote all that which he is there said to have written: as for example, the Volume of the Law, which is contained, as it seemeth, in the xith of *Deuteronomy,* and the following chapters to the xxviith which was also commanded to be written on stones, in their entry into the land of Canaan. And this did Moses himself write, (*Deut.* xxxi. 9, 10) and deliver to the priests and elders of Israel, to be read every seventh year to all Israel, at their assembling in the Feast of Tabernacles. And this is that law which God commanded, that their kings, when they should have established that form of government, should take a copy of from the priests and Levites: and which Moses commanded the priests and Levites to lay in the side of the ark, (*Deut.* xxxi. 26); and the same which having been lost, was long time after found again by Hilkiah, and sent to king Josias (2 *Kings* xxii. 8) who causing it to be read to the people, (2 *Kings* xxiii. 1, 2, 3) renewed the covenant between God and them.

*The book of Joshua written after his time.* That the book of *Joshua* was also written long after the time of Joshua, may be gathered out of many places of the book itself. Joshua had set up twelve stones in the midst of Jordan, for a monument of their passage; of which the writer saith thus, *They are there unto this day* (*Josh.* iv. 9); for *unto this day,* is a phrase that signifieth a time past, beyond the memory of man. In like manner, upon the saying of the Lord, that he had rolled off from the people the reproach of Egypt, the writer saith, *The place is called Gilgal unto this day* (*Josh.* v. 9); which to have said in the time of Joshua had been improper. So also the name of the valley of Achor, from the trouble that Achan raised in the camp, the writer saith, *remaineth unto this day* (*Josh.* vii. 26); which must needs be therefore long after the time of Joshua. Arguments of this kind there be many other; as *Josh.* viii. 29, xiii. 13, xiv. 14, xv. 63.

*The books of Judges and Ruth written long after the captivity.* The same is manifest by like arguments of the book of *Judges*, chap. i. 21, 26, vi. 24, x. 4, xv. 19, xvii. 6, and *Ruth* i. 1; but especially *Judg.* xviii. 30, where it is said, that *Jonathan and his sons were priests to the tribe of Dan, until the day of the captivity of the land.*

*The like of the books of Samuel.* That the books of *Samuel* were also written after his own time, there are the like arguments, 1 *Sam.* v. 5, vii. 13, 15; xxvii. 6, and xxx. 25, where, after David had adjudged equal part of the spoils, to them that guarded the ammunition, with them that fought, the writer saith, *He made it a statute and an ordinance to Israel to this day.* Again, when David, displeased, that the Lord had slain Uzzah, for putting out his hand to sustain the ark, called the place Perez-Uzzah, the writer saith, (2 *Sam.* vi. 8) it is called so *to this day:* the time therefore of writing of that book, must be long after the time of the fact; that is, long after the time of David.

*The books of the Kings, and the Chronicles.* As for the two books of the *Kings*, and the two books of the *Chronicles*, besides the places which mention such monuments, as the writer saith, remained till his own days; such as are 1 *Kings* ix. 13, ix. 21, x. 12, xii. 19. 2 *Kings* ii. 22, viii. 22, x. 27, xiv. 7, xvi. 6, xvii. 23, xvii. 34, xvii. 41, and 1 *Chron.* iv. 41, v. 26: it is argument sufficient they were written after the captivity in Babylon, that the history of them is continued till that time. For the facts registered are always more ancient than the register; and much more ancient than such books as make mention of, and quote the register; as these books do in divers places, referring the reader to the Chronicles of the Kings of Judah, to the Chronicles of the Kings of Israel, to the Books of the prophet Samuel, of the prophet Nathan, of the prophet Ahijah; to the Vision of Jehdo, to the books of the prophet Serveiah, and of the prophet Addo.

*Ezra and Nehemiah.* The books of *Ezra* and *Nehemiah* were written certainly after their return from captivity; because their return, the re-edification of the walls and houses of Jerusalem, the renovation of the covenant, and ordination of their policy, are therein contained.

*Esther.* The history of *Queen Esther* is of the time of the captivity; and therefore the writer must have been of the same time, or after it.

*Job.* The book of *Job* hath no mark in it of the time wherein it was written; and though it appear sufficiently (*Ezekiel* xiv. 14, and *James* v. 11) that he was no feigned person; yet the book itself seemeth not to be a history, but a treatise concerning a question in ancient time much disputed, *why wicked men have often prospered in this world, and good men have been afflicted;* and this is the more probable, because from the beginning, to the third verse of the third chapter, where the complaint of Job beginneth, the Hebrew is, as St. Jerome testifies, in prose; and from thence to the sixth verse of the last chapter, in hexameter verses; and the rest of that chapter again in prose. So that the dispute is all in verse; and the prose is added, but as a preface in the beginning, and an epilogue in the end. But verse is no usual style of such, as either are themselves in great pain, as Job; or of such as come to comfort them, as his friends; but in philosophy, especially moral philosophy, in ancient time frequent.

*The Psalter.* The *Psalms* were written the most part by David, for the use of the choir. To these are added some songs of Moses, and other holy men; and some of them after the return from the captivity, as the 137th and the 126th, whereby it is manifest that the Psalter was compiled, and put into the form it now hath, after the return of the Jews from Babylon.

*The Proverbs.* The *Proverbs,* being a collection of wise and godly sayings, partly of Solomon, partly of Agur, the son of Jaketh, and partly of the mother of king Lemuel, cannot probably be thought to have been collected by Solomon, rather than by Agur, or the mother of Lemuel; and that, though the sentences be theirs, yet the collection or compiling them into this one book, was the work of some other godly man, that lived after them all.

*Ecclesiastes and the Canticles.* The books of *Ecclesiastes* and the *Canticles* have nothing that was not Solomon's except it be the titles, or inscriptions. For *The Words of the Preacher, the son of David, king in Jerusalem;* and, *The Song of Songs,* which is Solomon's, seem to have been made for distinction's sake, then, when the Books of Scripture were gathered into one body of the law; to the end, that not the doctrine only, but the authors also might be extant.

*The Prophets.* Of the prophets, the most ancient, are Zephaniah, Jonah, Amos, Hosea, Isaiah, and Micah, who lived in the time of Amaziah and Azariah, otherwise Ozias, kings of Judah. But the book of Jonah is not properly a register of his prophecy; for that is contained in these few words, *Forty days and Nineveh shall be destroyed;* but a history or narration of his frowardness and disputing God's commandments; so that there is small probability he should be the author, seeing he is the subject of it. But the book of *Amos* is his prophecy.

Jeremiah, Obadiah, Nahum, and Habakkuk prophesied in the time of Josiah.

Ezekiel, Daniel, Haggai, and Zechariah, in the captivity.

When Joel and Malachi prophesied, is not evident by their writings. But considering the inscriptions, or titles of their books, it is manifest enough, that the whole Scripture of the Old Testament, was set forth in the form we have it, after the return of the Jews from their captivity in Babylon, and before the time of Ptolomæus Philadelphus, that caused it to be translated into Greek by seventy men, which were sent him out of Judea for that purpose. And if the books of Apocrypha, which are recommended to us by the church, though not for canonical, yet for profitable books for our instruction, may in this point be credited, the Scripture was set forth in the form we have it in, by Esdras: as may appear by that which he himself saith, in the second book, (chapter xiv. verse 21, 22, &c.) where speaking to God, he saith thus, *Thy law is burnt; therefore no man knoweth the things which thou hast done, or the works that are to begin. But if I have found grace before thee, send down the holy spirit into me, and I shall write all that hath been done in the world, since the beginning, which were written in thy law, that men may find thy path, and that they which will live in the latter day, may live.* And verse 45: *And it came to pass when the forty days were fulfilled, that the highest spake, saying, The first that thou hast written, publish openly, that the worthy and unworthy may read it; but keep the seventy last, that thou mayest deliver them only to such as be wise among the people.* And thus much concerning the time of the writing of the books of the Old Testament.

*The New Testament.* The writers of the New Testament lived all in less than an age after Christ's ascension, and had all of them seen our Saviour, or been his disciples, except St. Paul, and St. Luke; and consequently whatsoever was written by them, is as ancient as the time of the apostles. But the time wherein the books of the New Testament were received, and acknowledged by the church to be of their writing, is not altogether so ancient. For, as the books of the Old Testament are derived to us, from no other time than that of Esdras, who by the direction of God's spirit retrieved them, when they were lost: those of the New Testament, of which the copies were not many, nor could easily be all in any one private man's hand, cannot be derived from a higher time, than that wherein the governors of the church collected, approved, and recommended them to us, as the writings of those apostles and disciples, under whose names they go. The first enumeration of all the books, both of the Old and New Testament, is in the canons of the apostles, supposed to be collected by Clement, the first (after St. Peter) bishop of Rome. But because that is but supposed, and by many questioned, the Council of Laodicea is the first so we know, that recommended the Bible to the then Christian churches, for the writings of the prophets and apostles: and this Council was held in the 364th year after Christ. At which time, though ambition had so far prevailed on the great doctors of the church, as no more to esteem emperors, though Christian, for the shepherds of the people, but for sheep; and emperors not Christian, for wolves; and endeavoured to pass their doctrine, not for counsel and information, as preachers; but for laws, as absolute governors; and thought such frauds as tended to make the people the more obedient to Christian doctrine, to be pious; yet I am persuaded they did not therefore falsify the Scriptures, though the copies of the books of the New Testament, were in the hands of the ecclesiastics; because if they had had an intention so to do, they would surely have made them more favourable to their power over Christian princes, and civil sovereignty, than they are. I see not therefore any reason to doubt but that the Old and New Testament, as we have them now, are the true registers of those things, which were done and said by the prophets and apostles. And so perhaps are some of those books which are called apocrypha, if left out of the canon, not for inconformity of doctrine with the rest, but only because they are not found in the Hebrew. For after the conquest of Asia by Alexander the Great, there were few learned Jews, that were not perfect in the Greek tongue. For the seventy interpreters that converted the Bible into Greek, were all of them Hebrews; and we have extant the works of Philo and Josephus, both Jews, written by them eloquently in Greek. But it is not the writer, but the authority of the church, that maketh the book canonical.

*Their scope.* And although these books were written by divers men, yet it is manifest the writers were all endued with one and the same spirit, in that they conspire to one and the same end, which is setting forth of the rights of the Kingdom of God, the Father, Son, and Holy Ghost. For the book of *Genesis*, deriveth the genealogy of God's people, from the creation of the world, to the going into Egypt: the other four books of Moses contain the election of God for their king, and the laws which he prescribed for their government: the books of *Joshua, Judges, Ruth*, and *Samuel*, to the time of Saul, describe the acts of God's people, till the time they cast off God's yoke, and called for a king, after the manner of their neighbour nations. The rest of the history of the Old Testament derives the succession of the line of David, to the captivity, out of which line was to spring the restorer of the Kingdom of God, even our blessed Saviour God the Son, whose coming was foretold in the books of the prophets, after whom the Evangelists wrote his life, and actions, and his claim to the kingdom, whilst he lived on earth: and lastly, the *Acts*, and *Epistles* of the Apostles, declare the coming of God the Holy Ghost, and the authority he left with them and their successors, for the direction of the Jews, and for the invitation of the Gentiles. In sum, the histories and the prophecies of the Old Testament, and the gospels and epistles of the New Testament, have had one and the same scope, to convert men to the obedience of God; i., in Moses, and the Priests; ii., in the man Christ; and iii., in the Apostles and the successors to apostolical power. For these three at several times did represent the person of God: Moses, and his successors the High Priests, and Kings of Judah, in the Old Testament: Christ himself, in the time he lived on earth: and the Apostles, and their successors, from the day of Pentecost, when the Holy Ghost descended on them, to this day.

*The question of the authority of the Scriptures stated.* It is a question much disputed between the divers sects of Christian religion, *from whence the Scriptures derive their authority;* which question is also propounded sometimes in other terms, as, *how we know them to be the word of God,* or, *why we believe them to be so:* and the difficulty of resolving it, ariseth chiefly from the improperness of the words wherein the question itself is couched. For it is believed on all hands, that the first and original *author* of them is God; and consequently the question disputed, is not that. Again, it is manifest, that none can know they are God's word, (though all true Christians believe it,) but those to whom God himself hath revealed it supernaturally; and therefore the question is not rightly moved, of our *knowledge* of it. Lastly, when the question is propounded of our *belief;* because some are moved to believe for one, and others for other reasons; there can be rendered no one general answer for them all. The question truly stated is, *by what authority they are made law*.

*Their authority and interpretation.* As far as they differ not from laws of nature, there is no doubt, but they are the law of God, and carry their authority with them, legible to all men that have the use of natural reason: but this is no other authority, than that of all other moral doctrine consonant to reason; the dictates whereof are laws, not *made,* but *eternal*.

If they be made law by God himself, they are of the nature of written law, which are laws to them only to whom God hath so sufficiently published them, as no man can excuse himself, by saying, he knew not they were his.

He therefore to whom God hath not supernaturally revealed that they are his, nor that those that published them, were sent by him, is not obliged to obey them, by any authority, but his, whose commands have already the force of laws; that is to say, by any other authority, than that of the commonwealth, residing in the sovereign, who only has the legislative power. Again, if it be not the legislative authority of the commonwealth, that giveth them the force of laws, it must be some other authority derived from God, either private, or public: if private, it obliges only him, to whom in particular God hath been pleased to reveal it. For if every man should be obliged, to take for God's law, what particular men, on pretence of private inspiration, or revelation, should obtrude upon him, in such a number of men, that out of pride and ignorance, take their own dreams, and extravagant fancies, and madness, for testimonies of God's spirit; or out of ambition, pretend to such divine testimonits, falsely, and contrary to their own consciences, it were impossible that any divine law should be acknowledged. If public, it is the authority of the *commonwealth*, or of the *chudch*. But the church, if it be one person, is the same thing with a commonwealth of Christians; called a *commonwealth*, because it consisteth of men united in one person, their sovereign; and a *church*, because it consisteth in Christian men, united in one Christian sovereign. But if the church be not one person, then it hath no authority at all: it can neither command, nor do any action at all; nor is capable of having any power, or right to any thing: nor has any will, reason nor voice; for all the qualities are personal. Now if the whole number of Christians be not contained in one commonwealth, they are not one person; nor is there an universal church that hath any authority over them; and therefore the Scriptures are not made laws, by the universal church: or if it be one commonwealth, then all Christian monarchs and states are private persons, and subject to be judged, deposed, and punished by an universal sovereign of all Christendom. So that the question of the authority of the Scriptures, is reduced to this, *whether Christian kings, and the sovereign assemblies in Christian commonwealths, be absolute in their own territories, immediately under God; or subject to one Vicar of Christ, constituted of the universal church; to be judged, condemned, deposed, and put to death, as he shall think expedient, or necessary for the common good.*

Which question cannot be resolved, without a more particular consideration of the Kingdom of God; from whence also, we are to judge of the authority of interpreting the Scripture. For, whosoever hath a lawful power over any writing, to make it law, hath the power also to approve, or disapprove the interpretation of the same.

# Chapter 34

## Of the Signification of Spirit, Angel, and Inspiration, in the Books of Holy Scripture

*Body and spirit how taken in the Scripture.* Seeing the foundation of all true ratiocination, is the constant signification of words; which in the doctrine following, dependeth not, as in natural science, on the will of the writer, nor, as in common conversation, on vulgar use, but on the sense they carry in the Scripture; it is necessary, before I proceed any further, to determine, out of the Bible, the meaning of such words, as by their ambiguity, may render what I am to infer upon them, obscure, or disputable. I will begin with the words BODY and SPIRIT, which in the language of the Schools are termed, *substances, corporeal,* and *incorporeal.*

The word *body,* in the most general acceptation, signifieth that which filleth, or occupieth some certain room, or imagined place; and dependeth not on the imagination, but is a real part of that we call the *universe.* For the *universe,* being the aggregate of all bodies, there is no real part thereof that is not also *body;* nor any thing properly a *body,* that is not also part of that aggregate of all *bodies,* the *universe.* The same also, because bodies are subject to change, that is to say, to variety of appearance to the sense of living creatures, is called *substance,* that is to say, *subject* to various accidents: as sometimes to be moved; sometimes to stand still; and to seem to our senses sometimes hot, sometimes cold, sometimes of one colour, smell, taste, or sound, sometimes of another. And this diversity of seeming, produced by the diversity of the operation of bodies on the organs of our sense, we attribute to alterations of the bodies that operate, and call them *accidents* of those bodies. And according to this acceptation of the word, *substance* and *body* signify the same thing; and therefore *substance incorporeal* are words, which when they are joined together, destroy one another, as if a man should say, an *incorporeal body.*

But in the sense of common people, not all the universe is called body, but only such parts thereof as they can discern by the sense of feeling, to resist their force, or by the sense of their eyes, to hinder them from a farther prospect. Therefore in the common language of men, *air*, and *aërial substances*, use not to be taken for *bodies*, but, (as often as men are sensible of their effects) are called *wind*, or *breath*, or (because the same are called in the Latin *spiritus*) *spirits;* as when they call that aërial substance, which in the body of any living creature gives it life and motion, *vital* and *animal spirits*. But for those idols of the brain, which represent bodies to us, where they are not, as in a looking-glass in a dream, or to a distempered brain waking, they are, as the apostle saith generally of all idols, nothing; nothing at all, I say, there where they seem to be; and in the brain itself, nothing but tumult, proceeding either from the action of the objects, or from the disorderly agitation of the organs of our sense. And men, that are otherwise employed, than to search into their causes, know not of themselves, what to call them; and may therefore easily be persuaded, by those whose knowledge they much reverence, some to call them *bodies,* and think them made of air compacted by a power supernatural, because the sight judges them corporeal; and some to call them *spirits,* because the sense of touch discerneth nothing in the place where they appear, to resist their fingers: so that the proper signification of *spirit* in common speech, is either a subtle, fluid, and invisible body, or a ghost, or other idol or phantasm of the imagination. But for metaphorical significations, there be many: for sometimes it is taken for disposition or inclination of the mind; as when for the disposition to control the sayings of other men, we say, *a spirit of contradiction;* for *a disposition to uncleanness, an unclean spirit,* for *perverseness, a froward spirit;* for *sullenness, a dumb spirit;* and for *inclination to godliness and God's service, the Spirit of God:* sometimes for any eminent ability or extraordinary passion, or disease of the mind, as when *great wisdom* is called the *spirit of wisdom;* and *madmen* are said to be *possessed with a spirit.*

Other signification of *spirit* I find nowhere any; and where none of these can satisfy the sense of that word in Scripture, the place falleth not under human understanding; and our faith therein consisteth not in our opinion, but in our submission; as in all places where God is said to be a *Spirit;* or where by the *Spirit of God,* is meant God himself. For the nature of God is incomprehensible; that is to say, we understand nothing of *what he is,* but only *that he is;* and therefore the attributes we give him, are not to tell one another, *what he is,* nor to signify our opinion of his nature, but our desire to honour him with such names as we conceive most honourable amongst ourselves.

*The spirit of God taken in the Scripture sometimes for a wind, or breath.* Gen. i. 2. *The Spirit of God moved upon the face of the waters.* Here if by the *Spirit of God* be meant God himself, then is *motion* attributed to God, and consequently *place*, which are intelligible only of bodies, and not of substances incorporeal; and so the place is above our understanding, that can conceive nothing moved that changes not place, or that has not dimension; and whatsoever has dimension, is body. But the meaning of those words is best understood by the like place, (*Gen.* viii. 1) where when earth was covered with waters, as in the beginning, God intending to abate them, and again to discover the dry land, useth the like words, *I will bring my Spirit upon the earth, and the waters shall be diminished:* in which place, by *Spirit* is understood a wind, that is an air or *spirit moved,* which might be called, as in the former place, the *Spirit of God,* because it was God's work.

*Secondly, for extraordinary gifts of the understanding.* Gen. xli. 38, Pharaoh calleth the Wisdom of Joseph, the *spirit of God.* For Joseph having advised him to look out a wise and discreet man, and to set him over the land of Egypt, he saith thus, *Can we find such a man as this is, in whom is the Spirit of God?* And *Exod.* xxviii. 3, *Thou shalt speak,* saith God, *to all the wise hearted, whom I have filled with the spirit of wisdom, to make Aaron garments, to consecrate him:* where extraordinary understanding, though but in making garments, as being the *gift* of God, is called the *Spirit of God.* The same is found again, *Exod.* xxxi. 3, 4, 5, 6, *and* xxxv. 31. And *Isaiah* xi. 2, 3, where the prophet speaking of the Messiah, saith, *the Spirit of the Lord shall abide upon him, the spirit of wisdom and understanding, the spirit of counsel and fortitude, and the spirit of the fear of the Lord.* Where manifestly is meant, not so many ghosts, but so many eminent graces that God would give him.

*Thirdly, for extraordinary affections.* In the book of the *Judges,* an extraordinary zeal and courage in the defence of God's people, is called the *Spirit* of God; as when it excited Othniel, Gideon, Jephtha, and Sampson to deliver them from servitude, *Judges* iii. 10, vi. 34, xi. 29, xiii. 25, xiv. 6, 19. And of Saul, upon the news of the insolence of the Ammonites towards the men of Jabesh Gilead, it is said, (1 *Sam.* xi. 6) that *the Spirit of God came upon Saul, and his anger,* (or, as it is in the Latin, *his fury*), *was kindled greatly.* Where it is not probable was meant a ghost, but an extraordinary *zeal* to punish the cruelty of the Ammonites. In like manner by the *Spirit* of God, that came upon Saul, when he was amongst the prophets that praised God in songs and music, (1 *Sam.* xix. 20), is to be understood, not a ghost, but an unexpected and sudden *zeal* to join with them in their devotion.

*Fourthly, for the gift of prediction by dreams and visions.* The false prophet Zedekiah saith to Micaiah (1 *Kings* xxii. 24), *which way went the Spirit of the Lord from me to speak to thee?* Which cannot be understood of a ghost; for Micaiah declared before the kings of Israel and Judah, the event of the battle, as from a *vision*, and not as from a *spirit* speaking in him.

In the same manner it appeareth in the books of the Prophets, that though they spake by the *spirit* of God, that is to say, by a special grace of prediction; yet their knowledge of the future, was not by a ghost within them, but by some supernatural *dream* or *vision*.

*Fifthly, for life. Gen.* ii. 7, it is said, *God made man of the dust of the earth, and breathed into his nostrils* (spiraculum vitæ) *the breath of life, and man was made a living soul.* There the *breath of life* inspired by God, signifies no more, but that God gave him life; and (*Job* xxvii. 3) *as long as the Spirit of God is in my nostrils,* is no more than to say, *as long as I live.* So in *Ezek.* i. 20, *the spirit of life was in the wheels,* is equivalent to, *the wheels were alive.* And, (*Ezek.* ii. 2) *the Spirit entered into me, and set me on my feet,* that is, *I recovered my vital strength;* not that any ghost or incorporeal substance entered into, and possessed his body.

*Sixthly, for a subordination to authority.* In the xith chap. of *Numbers,* v. 17, *I will take,* saith God, *of the Spirit, which is upon thee, and will put it upon them, and they shall bear the burthen of the people with thee;* that is, upon the seventy elders: whereupon two of the seventy are said to prophesy in the camp; of whom some complained, and Joshua desired Moses to forbid them; which Moses would not do. Whereby it appears, that Joshua knew not that they had received authority so to do, and prophesied according to the mind of Moses, that is to say, by a *spirit*, or *authority* subordinate to his own.

In the like sense we read, (*Deut,* xxxiv. 9) that *Joshua was full of the spirit of wisdom, because Moses had laid his hands upon him:* that is because he was *ordained* by Moses, to prosecute the work he had himself begun, namely the bringing of

God's people into the promised land, but prevented by death, could not finish.

In the like sense it is said, (*Rom.* viii. 9) *If any man have not the Spirit of Christ, he is none of his:* not meaning thereby the *ghost* of Christ, but a *submission* to his doctrine. As also, (1 *John* iv. 2) *Hereby you shall know the Spirit of God: every spirit that confesseth that Jesus Christ is come in the flesh, is of God;* by which is meant the spirit of unfeigned Christianity, or *submission* to that main article of Christian faith, that Jesus is the Christ; which cannot be interpreted of a ghost.

Likewise these words, (*Luke* iv. 1) *And Jesus full of the Holy Ghost,* (that is, as it is expressed, *Matt.* iv. 1, and *Mark* i. 12, *of the Holy Spirit,*) may be understood, for *zeal* to do the work for which he was sent by God the Father: but to interpret it of a ghost, is to say, that God himself, for so our Saviour was, was filled with God; which is very improper and significant. How we came to translate *spirits,* by the word *ghosts,* which signifieth nothing, neither in heaven, nor earth, but the imaginary inhabitants of man's brain, I examine not: but this I say, the word *spirit* in the text signifieth no such thing; but either properly a real *substance,* or metaphorically, some extraordinary *ability* or *affection* of the mind, or of the body.

*Seventhly, for aërial bodies.* The disciples of Chirst, seeing him walking upon the sea, (*Matt.* xiv. 26, and *Mark* vi. 49) supposed him to be a *Spirit,* meaning thereby an aërial *body,* and not a phantasm; for it is said, they all saw him; which cannot be understood of the delusions of the brain, (which are not common to many at once, as visible bodies are; but singular, because of the differences of fancies,) but of bodies only. In like manner, where he was taken for a *spirit,* by the same apostles, (*Luke* xxiv. 37): so also (*Acts* xii. 15) when St. Peter was delivered out of prison, it would not be believed; but when the maid said he was at the door, they said it was his *angel;* by which must be meant a corporeal substance, or we must say, the disciples themselves did follow the common opinion of both Jews and Gentiles, that some such apparitions were not imaginary, but real, and such as needed not the fancy of man for their existence. There the Jews called *spirits,* and *angels,* good or bad; as the Greeks called the same by the name of *demons.* And some such apparitions may be real, and substantial; that is to say, subtle bodies, which God can form by the same power, by which he formed all things, and make use of, as of ministers, and messengers, that is to say, angels, to declare his will, and execute the same when he pleaseth, in extraordinary and supernatural manner. But when he hath so formed them, they are substances, endued with dimensions, and take up room, and can be moved from place to place, which is peculiar to bodies; and therefore are not ghosts *incorporeal*, that is to say, ghosts that are in *no place;* that is to say, that are *nowhere;* that is to say, that seeming to be *somewhat*, are *nothing*. But if corporeal be taken in the most vulgar manner, for such substances as are perceptible by our external senses; then is substance incorporeal, a thing not imaginary, but real; namely, a thin substance invisible, but that hath the same dimensions that are in grosser bodies.

*Angel, what.* By the name of ANGEL, is signified generally, a *messenger;* and most often, a *messenger of God;* and by a messenger of God, is signified, any thing that makes known his extraordinary presence; that is to say, the extraordinary manifestation of his power, especially by a dream or vision.

Concerning the creation of *angels,* there is nothing delivered in the Scriptures. That they are spirits, is often repeated; but by the name of spirit, is signified both in Scripture, and vulgarly, both amongst Jews and Gentiles, sometimes thin bodies: as the air, the wind, the spirits vital and animal of living creatures; and sometimes the images that rise in the fancy in dreams and visions; which are not real substances, nor last any longer than the dream, or vision they appear in; which apparitions, though no real substances, but accidents of the brain; yet when God raiseth them supernaturally, to signify his will, they are not improperly termed God's messengers, that is to say, his *angels*.

And as the Gentiles did vulgarly conceive the imagery of the brain, for things really subsistent without them, and not dependent on the fancy; and out of them framed their opinions of *demons,* good and evil; which because they seemed to subsist really, they called *substances;* and, because they could not feel them with their hands, *incorporeal:* so also the Jews, upon the same ground, without any thing in the Old Testament that constrained them thereunto, had generally an opinion, except the sect of the Sadducees, that those apparitions, which it pleased God sometimes to produce in the fancy of men, for his own service, and therefore called them his *angels,* were substances, not dependent on the fancy, but permanent creatures of God; whereof those which they thought were good to them, they esteemed the *angels of God,* and those they thought would hurt them, they called *evil angels,* or evil spirits; such as was the spirit of Python, and the spirits of madmen, of lunatics and epileptics: for they esteemed such as were troubled with such diseases, *demoniacs*.

But if we consider the places of the Old Testament where angels are mentioned, we shall find, that in most of them, there can nothing else be understood by the word *angel*, but some image raised, supernaturally, in the fancy, to signify the presence of God in the execution of some supernatural work; and therefore in the rest, where their nature is not expressed, it may be understood in the same manner.

For we read, (*Gen.* xvi) that the same apparition is called, not only an *angel*, but *God;* where that which (verse 7) is called the *angel* of the Lord, in the tenth verse, saith to Agar, *I will multiply thy seed exceedingly;* that is, speaketh in the person of God. Neither was this apparition a fancy figured, but a voice. By which it is manifest, that *angel* signifieth there, nothing but *God* himself, that caused Agar supernaturally to apprehend a voice from heaven; or rather, nothing else but a voice supernatural, testifying God's special presence there. Why therefore may not the angels that appeared to Lot, and are called (*Gen.* xix. 12) *men;* and to whom, though they were two, Lot speaketh (verse 18) as but to one, and that one, as God, (for the words are, *Lot said unto them, Oh, not so, my Lord*), be understood of images of men, supernaturally formed in the fancy; as well as before by *angel* was understood a fancied voice? When the angel called to Abraham out of heaven, to stay his hand (*Gen.* xxii. 11) from slaying Isaac, there was no apparition, but a voice; which nevertheless was called properly enough a messenger or *angel* of God, because it declared God's will supernaturally, and saves the labour of supposing any permanent ghosts. The angels which Jacob saw on the ladder of Heaven, (*Gen.* xxviii. 12) were a vision of his sleep; therefore only fancy, and a dream; yet being supernatural, and signs of God's special presence, those apparitions are not improperly called *angels*. The same is to be understood, (*Gen.* xxxi. 11) where Jacob saith thus, *The Angel of the Lord appeared to me in my sleep.* For an apparition made to a man in his sleep, is that which all men call a dream, whether such dream be natural, or supernatural: and that which there Jacob calleth an *angel*, was God himself; for the same angel saith, verse 13, *I am the God of Bethel.*

Also (*Exod.* xiv. 19) the angel that went before the army of Israel to the Red Sea, and then came behind it, is (verse 24) the Lord himself; and he appeared, not in the form of

a beautiful man, but in form, (*Exod*. xiii. 21) by day, of a
*pillar of cloud*, and, by night, in form of a *pillar of fire;* and
yet this pillar was all the apparition and *angel* promised to
Moses, (*Exod*. xxxiii. 2) for the army's guide: for this cloudy
pillar (*Exod*. xxxiii. 9) is said to have descended, and stood
at the door of the Tabernacle, and to have talked with Moses.

There you see motion and speech, which are commonly
attributed to angels, attributed to a cloud, because the cloud
served as a sign of God's presence; and was no less an angel,
than if it had had the form of a man, or child of never so
great beauty; or wings, as usually they are painted, for the
false instruction of common people. For it is not the shape;
but their use that makes them angels. But their use is to be
significations of God's presence in supernatural operations;
as when Moses (*Exod*. xxxiii. 14) had desired God to go
along with the camp, as he had done always before the making
of the golden calf, God did not answer, *I will go*, nor, *I will
send an angel in my stead;* but thus, *My presence shall go
with thee.*

To mention all the places of the Old Testament where the
name of angel is found, would be too long. Therefore to comprehend them all at once, I say, there is no text in that part
of the Old Testament, which the Church of England holdeth
for canonical, from which we can conclude, there is, or hath
been created, any permanent thing, understood by the name of
*spirit* or *angel*, that hath not quantity; and that may not be
by the understanding divided; that is to say, considered by
parts; so as one part may be in one place, and the next part
in the next place to it; and, in sum, which is not (taking body
for that, which is somewhat or somewhere,) corporeal; but in
every place, the sense will bear the interpretation of angel,
for messenger; as John Baptist is called an angel, and Christ
the Angel of the Covenant; and as, according to the same
analogy, the dove and the fiery tongues, in that they were signs
of God's special presence, might also be called angels. Though
we find in *Daniel* two names of angels, Gabriel and Michael;
yet it is clear out of the text itself, (*Dan*. xii 1) that by
Michael is meant Christ, not as an angel, but as a prince: and
that Gabriel, as the like apparitions made to other holy men
in their sleep, was nothing but a supernatural phantasm, by
which it seemed to Daniel, in his dream, that two saints being
in talk, one of them said to the other, *Gabriel, Let us make
this man understand his vision:* for God needeth not to distinguish his celestial servants by names, which are useful only to

the short memories of mortals. Nor in the New Testament is there any place, out of which it can be proved, that angels, except when they are put for such men as God hath made the messengers and ministers of his word or works, are things permanent, and withal incorporeal. That they are permanent, may be gathered from the words of our Saviour himself, (*Matt.* xxv. 41) where he saith, it shall be said to the wicked in the last day, *Go ye cursed into everlasting fire prepared for the Devil and his angels:* which place is manifest for the permanence of evil angels, (unless we might think the name of Devil and his angels may be understood of the Church's adversaries and their ministers); but then it is repugnant to their immateriality; because everlasting fire is no punishment to impatible substances, such as are all things incorporeal. Angels therefore are not thence proved to be incorporeal. In like manner where St. Paul says, (1 *Cor.* vi 3) *Know ye not that we shall judge the angels?* and 2 *Pet.* ii. 4, *For if God spared not the angels that sinned, but cast them down into hell:* and (*Jude* i. 6) *And the angels that kept not their first estate, but left their own habitation, he hath reserved in everlasting chains under darkness unto the judgment of the last day:* though it prove the permanence of angelical nature, it confirmeth also their materiality. And (*Matt.* xxii. 30) *In the resurrection men do neither marry nor give in marriage, but are as the angels of God in heaven:* but in the resurrection men shall be permanent, and not incorporeal: so therefore also are the angels.

There be divers other places out of which may be drawn the like conclusion. To men that understand the signification of these words, *substance,* and *incorporeal; as incorporeal* is taken, not for subtle body, but for *not body;* they imply a contradiction: insomuch as to say, an angel or spirit is in that sense an incorporeal substance, is to say in effect, there is no angel nor spirit at all. Considering therefore the signification of the word *angel* in the Old Testament, and the nature of dreams and visions that happen to men by the ordinary way of nature; I was inclined to this opinion, that angels were nothing but supernatural apparitions of the fancy, raised by the special and extraordinary operation of God, thereby to make his presence and commandments known to mankind, and chiefly to his own people. But the many places of the New Testament, and our Saviour's own words, and in such texts, wherein is no suspicion of corruption of the Scripture, have extorted from my feeble reason, an acknowledgment and belief, that there be also angels substantial, and permanent. But to believe they be in no place, that is to say, nowhere, that is to say, nothing, as they, though indirectly, say, that will have them incorporeal, cannot by Scripture be evinced.

*Inspiration, what.* On the signification of the word *spirit*, dependeth that of the word INSPIRATION; which must either be taken properly; and then it is nothing but the blowing into a man some thin and subtle air or wind, in such manner as a man filleth a bladder with his breath; or if spirits be not corporeal, but have their existence only in the fancy, it is nothing but the blowing in of a phantasm; which is improper to say, and impossible; for phantasms are not, but only seem to be, somewhat. That word therefore is used in the Scripture metaphorically only: as (*Gen.* ii 7) where it is said that God *inspired* into man the breath of life, no more is meant, than that God gave unto him vital motion. For we are not to think that God made first a living breath and then blew it into Adam after he was made, whether that breath were real, or seeming; but only as it is, (*Acts* xvii. 25) *that he gave him life, and breath;* that is, made him a living creature. And where it is said, (2 *Tim.* iii. 16) *all Scripture is given by inspiration from God,* speaking there of the Scripture of the Old Testament, it is an easy metaphor, to signify, that God inclined the spirit or mind of those writers, to write that which should be useful, in teaching, reproving, correcting, and instructing men in the way of righteous living. But where St. Peter, (2 *Pet.* i. 21) saith, that *Prophecy came not in old time by the will of man, but the holy men of God spake as they were moved by the Holy Spirit,* by the Holy Spirit is meant the voice of God, in a dream or vision supernatural, which is not *inspiration.* Nor, when our Saviour breathing on his disciples, said, *Receive the Holy Spirit,* was that breath the Spirit, but a sign of the spiritual graces he gave unto them. And though it be said of many, and of our Saviour himself, that he was full of the Holy Spirit; yet that fulness is not to be understood for *infusion* of the substance of God, but for accumulation of his gifts, such as are the gift of sanctity of life, of tongues, and the like, whether attained supernaturally, or by study and industry; for in all cases they are the gifts of God. So likewise where God says (*Joel* ii. 28) *I will pour out my Spirit upon all flesh, and your sons and your daughters shall prophesy, your old men shall dream dreams, and your young men shall see visions,* we are not to understand it in the proper sense, as if his *Spirit* were like water, subject to effusion or infusion; but as if God had promised to give them prophetical dreams, and visions. For the proper use of the word *infused*, in speaking of the graces of God, is an abuse of it; for those grace are virtues, not bodies to be carried hither and thither, and to be poured into men as into barrels.

In the same manner, to take *inspiration* in the proper sense, or to say that good *spirits* entered into men to make them prophesy, or evil *spirits* into those that became phrenetic, lunatic, or epileptic, is not to take the word in the sense of the Scripture; for the Spirit there is taken for the power of God, working by causes to us unknown. As also (*Acts* ii. 2) the wind, that is there said to fill the house wherein the apostles were assembled on the day of Pentecost, is not to be understood for the *Holy Spirit*, which is the Diety itself; but for an external sign of God's special working on their hearts, to effect in them the internal graces, and holy virtues he thought requisite for the performance of their apostleship.

# Chapter 35

## Of the Signification in Scripture of the Kingdom of God, of Holy, Sacred, and Sacrament

*The kingdom of God taken by divines metaphorically, but in the Scriptures properly.* The *Kingdom of God* in the writings of divines, and specially in sermons and treatises of devotion, is taken most commonly for eternal felicity, after this life, in the highest heaven, which they also call the *kingdom of glory;* and sometimes for the earnest of that felicity, sanctification, which they term the *kingdom of grace;* but never for the monarchy, that is to say, the sovereign power of God over any subjects acquired by their own consent, which is the proper signification of kingdom.

To the contrary, I find the KINGDOM OF GOD to signify, in most places of Scripture, a *kingdom properly so named,* constituted by the votes of the people of Israel in peculiar manner; wherein they chose God for their king by covenant made with him, upon God's promising them the possession of the land of Canaan; and but seldom metaphorically; and then it is taken for *dominion over sin;* (and only in the New Testament;) because such a dominion as that, every subject shall have in the kingdom of God, and without prejudice to the sovereign.

From the very creation, God not only reigned over all men *naturally* by his might; but also had *peculiar* subjects, whom he commanded by a voice, as one man speaketh to another. In which manner he *reigned* over Adam, and gave him commandment to abstain from the tree of cognizance of good and evil; which when he obeyed not, but tasting thereof, took upon him to be as God, judging between good and evil, not by his creator's commandment, but by his own sense, his punishment was a privation of the estate of eternal life, wherein God had at first created him: and afterwards God punished his posterity for their vices, all but eight persons, with an universal deluge; and in these eight did consist the then kingdom of God.

*The original of the kingdom of God.* After this it pleased God to speak to Abraham, and (*Gen.* xvii. 7, 8) to make a covenant with him in these words, *I will establish my cove-*

*nant between me, and thee, and thy seed after thee in their generations, for an everlasting covenant, to be a God to thee, and to thy seed after thee; and I will give unto thee, and to thy seed after thee, the land wherein thou art a stranger, all the land of Canaan for an everlasting possession.* In this covenant *Abraham promiseth for himself and his posterity, to obey as God,* the Lord that spake to him; and God on his part promiseth to Abraham the land of Canaan for an everlasting possession. And for a memorial, and a token of this covenant, he ordaineth (*Gen.* xvii. 11) the *sacrament of circumcision.* This is it which is called the *old covenant* or *testament;* and containeth a contract between God and Abraham; by which Abraham obligeth himself, and his posterity, in a peculiar manner to be subject to God's positive law; for to the law moral he was obliged before, as by an oath of allegiance. And though the name of *King* be not yet given to God, nor of *kingdom* to Abraham and his seed; yet the thing is the same; namely, an institution by pact, of God's peculiar sovereignty over the seed of Abraham; which in the renewing of the same covenant by Moses, at Mount Sinai, is expressly called a peculiar *kingdom of God* over the Jews: and it is of Abraham, not of Moses, St. Paul saith (*Rom.* iv. 11) that he is the *father of the faithful;* that is, of those that are loyal, and do not violate their allegiance sworn to God, then by circumcision, and afterwards in the *new covenant* by baptism.

*That the kingdom of God is properly his civil sovereignty over a peculiar people by pact.* This covenant, at the foot of Mount Sinai, was renewed by Moses, (*Exod.* xix. 5) where the Lord commandeth Moses to speak to the people in this manner, *If you will obey my voice indeed, and keep my covenant, then ye shall be a peculiar people to me, for all the earth is mine; and ye shall be unto me a sacerdotal kingdom, and an holy nation.* For a *peculiar people,* the vulgar Latin hath *peculium de cunctis populis:* the English translation, made in the beginning of the reign of King James, hath a *peculiar treasure unto me above all nations;* and the Geneva French, *the most precious jewel of all nations.* But the truest translation is the first, because it is confirmed by St. Paul himself (*Tit.* ii. 14) where he saith, alluding to that place, that our blessed Saviour *gave himself for us, that he might purify us to himself, a peculiar,* that is, an extraordinary, *people:* for the word is in the Greek περιούσιος, which is opposed commonly to the word ἐπιούσιος: and as this signifieth *ordinary, quotidian,* or, as in the Lord's Prayer, *of daily use;*

so the other signifieth that which is *overplus,* and *stored up,* and *enjoyed in a special manner;* which the Latins call *peculium:* and this meaning of the place is confirmed by the reason God rendereth of it, which followeth immediately, in that he addeth, *For all earth is mine,* as if he should say, *All the nations of world are mine;* but it is not so that you are mine, but in a *special manner:* for they are all mine, by reason of my power; but you shall be mine, by your own consent, and covenant; which is an addition to his ordinary title, to all nations.

The same is again confirmed in express words in the same text, *Ye shall be to me a sacerdotal kingdom, and an holy nation.* The vulgar Latin hath it, *regnum sacerdotale,* to which agreeth the translation of that place (1 *Pet.* ii. 9) *Sacerdotium regale, a regal priesthood;* as also the institution itself, by which no man might enter into the *Sanctum Sanctorum,* that is to say, no man might enquire God's will immediately of God himself, but only the high-priest. The English translation before mentioned, following that of Geneva, has, *a kingdom of priests;* which is either meant of the succession of one high-priest after another, or else it accordeth not with St. Peter, nor with the exercise of the high-priesthood: for there was never any but the high-priest only, that was to inform the people of God's will; nor any convocation of priests ever allowed to enter into the *Sanctum Sanctorum.*

Again, the title of a *holy nation* confirms the same: for *holy* signifies, that which is God's by special, not by general right. All the earth, as is said in the text, is God's; but all the earth is not called *holy,* but that only which is set apart for his especial service, as was the nation of the Jews. It is therefore manifest enough by this one place, that by the *kingdom of God,* is properly meant a commonwealth, instituted, by the consent of those which were to be subject thereto, for their civil government, and the regulating of their behaviour, not only towards God their king, but also towards one another in point of justice, and towards other nations both in peace and war; which properly was a kingdom wherein God was king, and the high-priest was to be, after the death of Moses, his sole viceroy or lieutenant.

But there be many other places that clearly prove the same. As first (1 *Samuel* viii. 7) when the Elders of Israel, grieved with the corruption of the sons of Samuel, demanded a king, Samuel displeased therewith, prayed unto the Lord, and the Lord answering said unto him, *Hearken unto the voice of the people, for they have not rejected thee, but they have rejected me, that I should not reign over them,* Out of which it is evident, that God himself was then their king; and Samuel did not command the people, but only delivered to them that which God from time to time appointed him.

Again, (1 *Sam.* xii. 12) where Samuel saith to the people, *When ye saw that Nahash, king of the children of Ammon, came against you, ye said unto me, Nay, but a king shall reign over us; when the Lord your God was your king.* It is manifest that God was their king, and governed the civil state of their commonwealth.

And after the Israelites had rejected God, the prophets did foretell his restitution; as (*Isaiah* xxiv. 23) *Then the moon shall be confounded, and the sun ashamed, when the Lord of hosts shall reign in Mount Zion, and in Jerusalem;* where he speaketh expressly of his reign in Zion and Jerusalem; that is, on earth. And (*Micah* iv. 7) *And the Lord shall reign over them in Mount Zion:* this Mount Zion is in Jerusalem, upon the earth. And (*Ezek.* xx. 33) *As I live, saith the Lord God, surely with a mighty hand, and a stretched out arm, and with fury poured out, I will rule over you;* and (verse 37) *I will cause you to pass under the rod, and I will bring you into the bond of the covenant;* that is, I will reign over you, and make you to stand to that covenant which you made with me by Moses, and brake in your rebellion against me in the days of Samuel, and in your election of another king.

And in the New Testament, the angel Gabriel saith of our Saviour (*Luke* i. 32, 33) *He shall be great, and be called the Son of the most High, and the Lord shall give unto him the throne of his father David; and he shall reign over the house of Jacob for ever; and of his kingdom there shall be no end.* This is also a kingdom upon earth; for the claim whereof, as an enemy to Cæsar, he was put to death; the title of his cross, was, *Jesus of Nazareth, King of the Jews;* he was crowned in scorn with a crown of thorns; and for the proclaiming of him, it is said of the disciples (*Acts* xvii. 7) *That they did all of them contrary to the decrees of Cæsar, saying there was another king, one Jesus.* The kingdom therefore of God is a real, not a metaphorical kingdom; and so taken, not only in the Old Testament, but in the New; when we say, *For thine is the kingdom, the power, and glory,* it is to be understood of God's kingdom, by force of our covenant, not by the right of God's power; for such a kingdom God always hath; so that it were superfluous to say in our prayer, *Thy kingdom come,* unless it be meant of the restoration of that kingdom of God by Christ, which by revolt of the Israelites had been interrupted in the election of Saul. Nor had it been proper to say, *The kingdom of heaven is at hand;* or to pray, *Thy kingdom come*, if it had still continued.

There be so many other places that confirm this interpretation, that it were a wonder there is no greater notice taken of it, but that it gives too much light to Christian kings to see their right of ecclesiastical government. This they have observed, that instead of a *sacerdotal kingdom*, translate, *a kingdom of priests;* for they may as well translate a *royal priesthood*, as it is in St. Peter, into a *priesthood of kings*. And whereas, for a *peculiar people*, they put a *precious jewel*, or *treasure*, a man might as well call the special regiment, or company of a general, the general's precious jewel, or his treasure.

In short, the kingdom of God is a civil kingdom; which consisted, first, in the obligation of the people of Israel to those laws, which Moses should bring unto them from Mount Sinai; and which afterwards the high-priest for the time being, should deliver to them from before the cherubims in the *sanctum sanctorum;* and which kingdom having been cast off in the election of Saul, the prophets foretold, should be restored by Christ; and the restoration whereof we daily pray for, when we say in the Lord's Prayer, *Thy kingdom come;* and the right whereof we acknowledge, when we add, *For thine is the kingdom, the power, and glory, for ever and ever, Amen;* and the proclaiming whereof, was the preaching of the apostles; and to which men are prepared, by the teachers of the Gospel; to embrace which Gospel, that is to say, to promise obedience to God's government, is to be in the *kingdom of grace*, because God hath *gratis* given to such the power to be the subjects, that is children, of God hereafter, when Christ shall come in majesty to judge the world, and actually to govern his own people, which is called *the kingdom of glory*. If the kingdom of God, called also the kingdom of heaven, from the gloriousness and admirable height of that throne, were not a kingdom which God by his lieutenants, or vicars, who deliver his commandments to the people, did exercise on earth; there would not have been so much contention, and war, about who it is, by whom God speaketh to us; neither would many priests have troubled themselves with spiritual jurisdiction, nor any king have denied it them.

*Holy, what.* Out of this literal interpretation of the *kingdom of God*, ariseth also the true interpretation of the word HOLY. For it is a word, which in God's kingdom answereth to that, which men in their kingdoms use to call *public*, or the *king's*.

The king of any country is the *public* person, or representative of all his own subjects. And God the king of Israel was the *Holy One* of Israel. The nation which is subject to one earthly sovereign, is the nation of that sovereign, that is, of the public person. So the Jews, who were God's nation, were called (*Exod.* xix. 6) *a holy nation.* For by *holy*, is always understood either God himself, or that which is God's in propriety; as by public is always meant, either the person of the commonwealth itself, or something that is so the commonwealth's, as no private person can claim any propriety therein.

Therefore the Sabbath, God's day, is a *holy day;* the temple, God's house, *a holy house;* sacrifices, tithes, and offerings, God's tribute, *holy duties;* priests, prophets, and anointed kings, under Christ, God's ministers, *holy men;* the celestial ministering spirits, God's messengers, *holy angels;* and the like: and wheresoever the word *holy* is taken properly, there is still something signified of propriety, gotten by consent. In saying, *Hallowed be thy name,* we do but pray to God for grace to keep the first commandment, of *having no other Gods but him.* Mankind is God's nation in propriety: but the Jews only were a *holy nation.* Why, but because they became his propriety by covenant?

*Sacred, what.* And the word *profane*, is usually taken in the Scripture for the same with *common;* and consequently their contraries, *holy* and *proper*, in the kingdom of God, must be the same also. But figuratively, those men also are called *holy*, that led such godly lives, as if they had forsaken all worldly designs, and wholly devoted and given themselves to God. In the proper sense, that which is made *holy* by God's appropriating or separating it to his own use, is said to be *sanctified* by God, as the seventh day in the fourth commandment; and as the elect in the New Testament were said to be *sanctified*, when they were endued with the spirit of godliness. And that which is made *holy* by the dedication of men, and given to God, so as to be used only in his public service, is called also SACRED, and said to be consecrated, as temples, and other houses of public prayer, and their utensils, priests, and ministers, victims, offerings, and the external matter of sacraments.

*Degrees of sanctity.* Of *holiness* there be degrees: for of those things that are set apart for the service of God, there may be some set apart again, for a nearer and more especial service. The whole nation of Israelites were a people holy to God; yet the tribe of Levi was amongst the Israelites a holy tribe; and amongst the Levites, the priests were yet more holy; and amongst the priests, the high-priest was the most holy. So the land of Judea was the Holy Land; but the holy city wherein God was to be worshipped, was more holy; and again the Temple more holy than the city, and the *sanctum sanctorum* more holy than the rest of the Temple.

*Sacrament.* A SACRAMENT, is a separation of some visible thing from common use; and a consecration of it to God's service, for a sign either of our admission into the kingdom of God, to be of the number of his peculiar people, or for a commemoration of the same. In the Old Testament, the sign of admission was *circumcision;* in the New Testament, *baptism.* The commemoration of it in the Old Testament, was the *eating,* at a certain time which was anniversary, of the *Paschal Lamb;* by which they were put in mind of the night wherein they were delivered out of their bondage in Egypt; and in the New Testament, the celebrating of the *Lord's Supper;* by which, we are put in mind of our deliverance from the bondage of sin, by our blessed Saviour's death upon the cross. The sacraments of *admission,* are but once to be used, because there needs but one *admission;* but because we have need of being often put in mind of our deliverance, and of our allegiance, the sacraments of *commemoration* have need to be reiterated. And these are the principal sacraments, and as it were the solemn oaths we make of our allegiance. There be also other consecrations, that may be called sacraments, as the word implieth only consecration to God's service; but as it implies an oath, or promise of allegiance to God, there were no other in the Old Testament, but *circumcision,* and the *passover;* nor are there any other in the New Testament, but *baptism* and the *Lord's Supper.*

# Chapter 36

## Of the Word of God, and of Prophets

*Word, what.* When there is mention of the *word of God,* or of *man,* it doth not signify a part of speech, such as grammarians call a noun, or a verb, or any simple voice, without a contexture with other words to make it significative; but a perfect speech or discourse, whereby the speaker *affirmeth, denieth, commandeth, promiseth, threateneth, wisheth,* or *interrogateth.* In which sense it is not *vocabulum,* that signifies a *word;* but *sermo,* (in Greek λόγος) that is, some *speech, discourse,* or *saying.*

*The words spoken by God, and concerning God, both are called God's word in Scripture.* Again, if we say the *word of God,* or of *man,* it may be understood sometimes of the speaker: as the words that God hath spoken, or that a man hath spoken; in which sense, when we say, the Gospel of St. Matthew, we understand St. Matthew to be the writer of it: and sometimes of the subject; in which sense, when we read in the Bible, *the words of the days of the kings of Israel, or Judah,* it is meant, that the acts that were done in those days, were the subject of those words; and in the Greek, which, in the Scripture, retaineth many Hebraisms, by the word of God is oftentimes meant, not that which is spoken by God, but concerning God, and his government; that is to say, the doctrine of religion: insomuch, as it is all one, to say λόγος Θεοῦ, and *theologia;* which is, that doctrine which we usually call *divinity,* as is manifest by the places following, (*Acts* xiii. 46) *Then Paul and Barnabas waxed bold, and said, it was necessary that the word of God should first have been spoken to you, but seeing you put it from you, and judge yourselves unworthy of everlasting life, lo, we turn to the Gentiles.* That which is here called the word of God, was the doctrine of Christian religion; as it appears evidently by that which goes before. And (*Acts* v. 20) where it is said to the apostles by an angel, *Go stand and speak in the Temple, all the words of this life;* by the words of this life, is meant, the doctrine of the Gospel; as is evident by what they did in the Temple, and is expressed in the last verse of the same chapter, *Daily in the Temple, and in every house they ceased not to teach and preach Christ Jesus:* in which place it is manifest, that Jesus Christ was the subject of this *word of life;* or, which is all one, the subject of the *words of this life eternal,* that our Saviour offered them. So (*Acts* xv. 7) the word of God, is called *the word of the Gospel,* because it containeth the doctrine of the kingdom of Christ; and the same word (*Rom.* x. 8, 9) is called *the word of faith;* that is, as there expressed, the doctrine of Christ come, and raised from the dead. Also (*Matt.* xiii. 19) *When any one heareth the word of the kingdom;* that is, the doctrine of the kingdom taught by Christ. Again, the same word, is said (*Acts* xii. 24) *to grow and to be multiplied;* which to understand of the evangelical doctrine is easy, but of the voice or speech of God, hard and strange. In the same sense (1 *Tim.* iv. 1) the *doctrine of devils* signifieth not the words of any devil, but the doctrine of heathen men concerning *demons,* and those phantasms which they worshipped as gods.

*The word of God metaphorically used, first, for the decrees and power of God.* Considering these two significations of the WORD OF GOD, as it is taken in Scripture, it is manifest in this latter sense, where it is taken for the doctrine of Christian religion, that the whole Scripture is the word of God: but in the former sense, not so. For example, though these words, *I am the Lord thy God, &c.* to the end of the Ten Commandments, were spoken by God to Moses; yet the preface, *God spake these words and said,* is to be understood for the words of him that wrote the holy history. The *word of God,* as it is taken for that which he hath spoken, is understood sometimes *properly,* sometimes *metaphorically. Properly,* as the words he hath spoken to his prophets: *metaphorically,* for his wisdom, power, and eternal decree, in making the world; in which sense, those fiats, *Let there be light, Let there be a firmament, Let us make man, &c.* (*Gen.* i) are the word of God. And in the same sense it is said (*John* i. 3) *All things were made by it, and without it was nothing made that was made:* and (*Heb.* i. 3) *He upholdeth all things by the word of his power;* that is, by the power of his word; that is, by his power: and (*Heb.* xi. 3) *The worlds were framed by the word of God;* and many other places to the same sense: as also amongst the Latins, the name of *fate,* which signifieth properly *the word spoken,* is taken in the same sense.

*Secondly, for the effect of his word.* Secondly, for the effect of his word; that is to say, for the thing itself, which his word is affirmed, commanded, threatened, or promised; as (*Psalm* cv. 19) where Joseph is said to have been kept in prison, *till his word was come;* that is, till that was come to pass which he had foretold to Pharaoh's butler (*Gen*. xl. 13) concerning his being restored to his office: for there, by *his word was come,* is meant, the thing itself was come to pass. So also (1 *Kings* xviii. 36) Elijah saith to God, *I have done all these thy words,* instead of *I have done all these things at thy word,* or commandment; and (*Jer*. xvii. 15) *Where is the word of the Lord,* is put for, *Where is the evil he threatened.* And (*Ezek.* xii. 28) *There shall none of my words be prolonged any more:* by *words* are understood those *things,* which God promised to his people. And in the New Testament (*Matt*. xxiv. 35) *heaven and earth shall pass away, but my words shall not pass away;* that is, there is nothing that I have promised or foretold, that shall not come to pass. And in this sense it is, that St. John the Evangelist, and, I think, St. John only, calleth our Saviour himself as in the flesh *the word of God,* as (*John* i. 14) *the word was made flesh;* that is to say, the word, or promise that Christ should come into the world; *who in the beginning was with God;* that is to say, it was in the purpose of God the Father, to send God the Son into the world, to enlighten men in the way of eternal life; but it was not till then put in execution, and actually incarnate. So that our Saviour is there called the *word,* not because he was the promise, but the thing promised. They that taking occasion from this place, do commonly call him the verb of God, do but render the text more obscure. They might as well term him the noun of God: for as by *noun,* so also by *verb,* men understand nothing but a part of speech, a voice, a sound, that neither affirms, nor denies, nor commands, nor promiseth, nor is any substance corporeal, or spiritual; and therefore it cannot be said to be either God, or man; whereas our Saviour is both. And this *word,* which St. John in his gospel saith was with God, is (in this *first Epistle,* verse 1) called the *word of life;* and (verse 2) *the eternal life, which was with the Father.* So that he can be in no other sense called the *word,* than in that, wherein he is called eternal life; that is, *he that hath procured us eternal life,* by his coming in the flesh. So also (*Apocalypse* xix. 13) the apostle speaking of Christ, clothed in a garment dipped in blood, saith, his name is *the word of God;* which is to be understood, as if he had said his name had been, *He that was come according to the purpose of God from the beginning, and according to his word and promises delivered by the prophets.* So that there is nothing here of the incarnation of a word, but of the incarnation of God the Son, therefore called *the word*, because his incarnation was the performance of the promise; in like manner as the Holy Ghost is called (*Acts* i. 4; *Luke* xxiv. 49) *the promise*.

*Thirdly, for the words of reason and equity*. There are also places of the Scripture, where, by the *word of God*, is signified such words as are consonant to reason and equity, though spoken sometimes neither by prophet, nor by a holy man. For Pharaoh-Necho was an idolater; yet his words to the good king Josiah, in which he advised him by messengers, not to oppose him in his march against Charchemish, are said to have proceeded from the mouth of God; and that Josiah, not hearkening to them, was slain in the battle; as is to be read (2 *Chron.* xxxv. 21, 22, 23). It is true, that as the same history is related in the first book of Esdras, not Pharaoh, but Jeremiah, spake these words to Josiah, from the mouth of the Lord. But we are to give credit to the canonical Scripture, whatsoever be written in the Apocrypha.

The *word of God*, is then also to be taken for the dictates of reason and equity, when the same is said in the Scriptures to be written in man's heart; as *Psalm* xxxvii. 31; *Jer.* xxxi. 33; *Deut.* xxx. 11, 14, and many other like places.

*Divers acceptions of the word prophet*. The name of PROPHET signifieth in Scripture, sometimes *prolocutor;* that is, he that speaketh from God to man, or from man to God: and sometimes *predictor*, or a foreteller of things to come: and sometimes one that speaketh incoherently, as men that are distracted. It is most frequently used in the sense of speaking from God to the people. So Moses, Samuel, Elijah, Isaiah, Jeremiah, and others were *prophets*. And in this sense the high-priest was a *prophet*, for he only went into the *sanctum sanctorum*, to enquire of God; and was to declare his answer to the people. And therefore when Caiaphas said, it was expedient that one man should die for the people, St. John saith (chapter 11. 51) that *He spake not this of himself, but being high-priest that year, he prophesied that one man should die for the nation*. Also they that in Christian congregations taught the people, (1 *Cor.* xiv. 3) are said to prophesy. In the like sense it is, that God saith to Moses (*Exod.* iv. 16) concerning Aaron, *He shall be thy spokesman to the people; and he shall be to thee a mouth, and thou shalt be to him instead of God:* that which here is *spokesman*, is (*Exod.* vii. 1) interpreted prophet; *See*, saith God, *I have made thee a God to Pharaoh, and Aaron thy brother shall be thy prophet*. In the sense of speaking from man to God, Abraham is called a prophet (*Gen.* xx. 7) where God in a dream speaketh to Abimelech in this manner, *Now therefore restore the man his wife, for he is a prophet, and shall pray for thee;* whereby may be also gathered, that the name of prophet may be given, not unproperly, to them that in Christian churches, have a calling to say public prayers for the congregation. In the same sense, the prophets that came down from the high place, or hill of God, with a psaltery, and a tabret, and a pipe, and a harp (1 *Sam.* x. 5, 6, and 10), Saul amongst them, are said to prophesy, in that they praised God in that manner publicly. In the like sense, is Miriam (*Exod.* xv. 20) called a prophetess. So is it also to be taken (1 *Cor.* xi. 4, 5), where St. Paul saith, *Every man that prayeth or prophesieth with his head covered, &c., and every woman that prayeth or prophesieth with her head uncovered:* for prophecy, in that place, signifieth no more, but praising God in psalms and holy songs; which women might do in the church, though it were not lawful for them to speak to the congregation. And in this signification it is, that the poets of the heathen, that composed hymns and other sorts of poems in the honour of their gods, were called *vates*, prophets; as is well enough known by all that are versed in the books of the Gentiles, and as is evident. (*Tit.* i. 12), where St. Paul saith of the Cretans, that a prophet of their own said, they were liars; not that St. Paul held their poets for prophets, but acknowledgeth that the word prophet was commonly used to signify them that celebrated the honour of God in verse.

*Prediction of future contingents, not always prophecy.* When by prophecy is meant prediction, or foretelling of future contingents; not only they were prophets, who were God's spokesmen, and foretold those things to others, which God had foretold to them; but also all those impostors, that pretend, by help of familiar spirits, or by superstitious divination of events past, from false causes, to foretell the like events in time to come: of which, as I have declared already in the twelfth chapter of this discourse, there be many kinds, who gain in the opinion of the common sort of men, a greater reputation of prophecy, by one casual event that may be but wrested to their purpose, than can be lost again by never so many failings. Prophecy is not an art, nor, when it is taken for prediction, a constant vocation; but an extraordinary, and temporary employment from God, most often of good men, but sometimes also of the wicked. The woman of Endor, who is said to have had a familiar spirit, and thereby to have raised a phantasm of Samuel, and foretold Saul his death, was not therefore a prophetess; for neither had she any science, whereby she could raise such a phantasm; nor does it appear that God commanded the raising of it; but only guided that imposture to be a means of Saul's terror and discouragement, and by consequent, of the discomfiture by which he fell. And for incoherent speech, it was amongst the Gentiles taken for one sort of prophecy, because the prophets of their oracles, intoxicated with a spirit or vapour from the cave of the Pythian oracle at Delphi, were for the time really mad, and spake like madmen; of whose loose words a sense might be made to fit any event, in such sort, as all bodies are said to be made of *materia prima*. In Scripture I find it also so taken (1 *Sam.* xviii. 10) in these words, *And the evil spirit came upon Saul, and he prophesied in the midst of the house.*

*The manner how God hath spoken to the prophets.* And although there be so many significations in Scripture of the word *prophet;* yet is that the most frequent, in which it is taken for him, to whom God speaketh immediately that which the prophet is to say from him, to some other man, or to the people. And hereupon a question may be asked, in what manner God speaketh to such a prophet. Can it, may some say, be properly said, that God hath voice and language, when it cannot be properly said, he hath a tongue, or other organs, as a man? The prophet David argueth thus, (*Psalm* xciv. 9) *Shall he that made the eye, not see? or he that made the ear, not hear?* But this may be spoken, not as usually, to signify God's nature, but to signify our intention to honour him. For to *see,* and *hear,* are honourable attributes, and may be given to God, to declare, as far as our capacity can conceive, his almighty power. But if it were to be taken in the strict and proper sense, one might argue from his making of all other parts of man's body, that he had also the same use of them which we have; which would be many of them so uncomely, as it would be the greatest contumely in the world to ascribe them to him. Therefore we are to interpret God's speaking to men immediately, for that way, whatsoever it be, by which God makes them understand his will. And the ways whereby he doth this, are many, and to be sought only in the Holy Scripture: where though many times it be said, that God spake to this, and that person, without declaring in what manner; yet there be again many places, that deliver also the signs by which they were to acknowledge his presence, and commandment; and by these may be understood, how he spake to many of the rest.

*To the extraordinary prophets of the Old Testament he spake by dreams, or visions.* In what manner God spake to Adam, and Eve, and Cain, and Noah, is not expressed; nor how he spake to Abraham, till such time as he came out of his own country to Sichem in the land of Canaan; and then (*Gen.* xii. 7) God is said to have *appeared* to him. So there is one way, whereby God made his presence manifest; that is, by an *apparition, or vision.* And again, (*Gen.* xv. 1) *the word of the Lord came to Abraham in a vision;* that is to say, somewhat, as a sign of God's presence, appeared as God's messenger, to speak to him. Again, the Lord appeared to Abraham (*Gen.* xviii. 1) by an apparition of three angels; and to Abimelech (*Gen.* xx. 3) in a dream: to Lot (*Gen.* xix. 1) by an apparition of two angels: and to Agar (*Gen.* xxi. 17) by the apparition of one angel: and to Abraham again (*Gen.* xxii. 11) by the apparition of a voice from heaven: and (*Gen.* xxvi. 24) to Isaac in the night, that is, in his sleep, or by dream: and to Jacob (*Gen.* xxviii. 12) in a dream; that is to say, as are the words of the text, *Jacob dreamed that he saw a ladder, &c.:* and (*Gen.* xxxii. 1) in a vision of angels: and to Moses (*Exod.* iii. 2) in the apparition of a flame of fire out of the midst of a bush. And after the time of Moses, where the manner how God spake immediately to man in the Old Testament is expressed, he spake always by a vision, or by a dream; as to Gideon, Samuel, Elijah, Elisha, Isaiah, Ezekiel, and the rest of the prophets; and often in the New Testament, as to Joseph, to St. Peter, to St. Paul, and to St. John the Evangelist in the Apocalypse.

Only to Moses he spake in a more extraordinary manner in Mount Sinai, and in the Tabernacle; and to the high-priest in the Tabernacle, and in the *sanctum sanctorum* of the Temple. But Moses, and after him the high-priests, were prophets of a more eminent place and degree in God's favour; and God himself in express words declareth, that to other prophets he spake in dreams and visions, but to his servant Moses, in such manner as a man speaketh to his friend. The words are these (*Numb.* xii. 6, 7, 8) *If there be a prophet among you, I the Lord will make myself known to him in a vision, and will speak unto him in a dream. My servant Moses is not so, who is faithful in all my house; with him I will speak mouth to mouth, even apparently, not in dark speeches; and the similitude of the Lord shall he behold.* And (*Exod.* xxxiii. 11) *The*

*Lord spake to Moses face to face, as a man speaketh to his friend.* And yet this speaking of God to Moses, was by mediation of an angel, or angels, as appears expressly, *Acts* vii. 35 and 53, and *Gal.* iii. 19; and was therefore a vision, though a more clear vision than was given to other prophets. And conformable hereunto, where God saith (*Deut.* xiii. 1) *If there arise amongst you a prophet, or dreamer of dreams,* the latter word is but the interpretation of the former. And (*Joel* ii. 28) *Your sons and your daughters shall prophesy; your old men shall dream dreams, and your young men shall see visions;* where again, the word *prophesy* is expounded by *dream,* and *vision.* And in the same manner it was, that God spake to Solomon, promising him wisdom, riches, and honour; for the text saith, (1 *Kings* iii. 15) *And Solomon awoke, and behold it was a dream;* so that generally the prophets extraordinary in the Old Testament took notice of the word of God no otherwise than from their dreams, or visions; that is to say, from the imaginations which they had in their sleep, or in an extasy: which imaginations in every true prophet were supernatural; but in false prophets were either natural or feigned.

The same prophets were nevertheless said to speak by the spirit; as (*Zech.* vii. 12); where the prophet speaking of the Jews, saith, *They made their hearts hard as adamant, lest they should hear the law, and the words which the Lord of Hosts hath sent in his Spirit by the former prophets.* By which it is manifest, that speaking by the *spirit,* or *inspiration,* was not a particular manner of God's speaking, different from vision, when they, that were said to speak by the Spirit, were extraordinary prophets, such as for every new message, were to have a peculiar commission, or, which is all one, a new dream, or vision.

*To prophets of perpetual calling, and supreme, God spake in the Old Testament from the mercy-seat, in a manner not expressed in the Scripture.* Of prophets, that were so by a perpetual calling in the Old Testament, some were *supreme,* and some *subordinate:* supreme were first Moses; and after him the high-priests, every one for his time, as long as the priesthood was royal; and after the people of the Jews had rejected God, that he should no more reign over them, those kings which submitted themselves to God's government, were also his chief prophets; and the high-priest's office became ministerial. And when God was to be consulted, they put on the holy vestments, and enquired of the Lord, as the king commanded

them, and were deprived of their office, when the king thought
fit. For king Saul (1 *Sam*. xiii. 9) commanded the burnt offering to be brought, and (1 *Sam*. xiv. 18) he commands the
priests to bring the ark near him; and (verse 19) again to let
it alone, because he saw an advantage upon his enemies. And
in the same chapter (verse 37) Saul asketh counsel of God.
In like manner king David, after his being anointed, though
before he had possession of the kingdom, is said to *enquire of
the Lord* (1 *Sam*. xxiii. 2) whether he should fight against
the Philistines at Keilah; and (verse 9) David commandeth the
priest to bring him the ephod, to enquire whether he should
stay in Keilah, or not. And king Solomon (1 *Kings* ii. 27)
took the priesthood from Abiathar, and gave it (verse 35) to
Zadok. Therefore Moses, and the high-priests, and the pious
kings, who enquired of God on all extraordinary occasions,
how they were to carry themselves, or what event they were
to have, were all sovereign prophets. But in what manner God
spake unto them is not manifest. To say that when Moses
went up to God in Mount Sinai, it was a dream or vision,
such as other prophets had, is contrary to that distinction
which God made between Moses and other prophets (*Numb*.
xii. 6, 7, 8). To say God spake or appeared as he is in his own
nature, is to deny his infiniteness, invisibility, incomprehensibility. To say he spake by inspiration, or infusion of the
Holy Spirit, as the Holy Spirit, signifieth the Deity, is to make
Moses equal with Christ, in whom only the Godhead (as St.
Paul speaketh, *Col*. ii. 9) dwelleth bodily. And lastly, to say
he spake by the Holy Spirit, as it signifieth the graces or gifts
of the Holy Spirit, is to attribute nothing to him supernatural.
For God disposeth men to piety, justice, mercy, truth, faith,
and all manner of virtue, both moral and intellectual, by doctrine, example, and by several occasions, and natural and
ordinary.

And as these ways cannot be applied to God in his speaking
to Moses, at Mount Sinai; so also, they cannot be applied to
him, in his speaking to the high-priests, from the mercy-seat.
Therefore in what manner God spake to those sovereign
prophets of the Old Testament, whose office it was to enquire
of him, is not intelligible. In the time of the New Testament,
there was no sovereign prophet, but our Saviour; who was
both God that spake, and the prophet to whom he spake.

*To prophets of perpetual calling, but subordinate, God
spake by the spirit*. To subordinate prophets of perpetual calling, I find not any place that proveth God spake to them

supernaturally; but only in such manner, as naturally he inclineth men to piety, to belief, to righteousness, and to other virtues all other Christian men. Which way, though it consist in constitution, instruction, education, and the occasions and invitements men have to Christian virtues; yet it is truly attributed to the operation of the Spirit of God, or Holy Spirit, which we in our language call the Holy Ghost: for there is no good inclination, that is not of the operation of God. But these operations are not always supernatural. When therefore a prophet is said to speak in the spirit, or by the spirit of God, we are to understand no more, but that he speaks according to God's will, declared by the supreme prophet. For the most common acceptation of the word spirit, is in the signification of a man's intention, mind, or disposition.

In the time of Moses, there were seventy men besides himself, that *prophesied* in the camp of the Israelites. In what manner God spake to them, is declared in *Numbers,* chap. xi, verse 25. *The Lord came down in a cloud, and spake unto Moses, and took of the spirit that was upon him, and gave it to the seventy elders. And it came to pass, when the spirit rested upon them, they prophesied and did not cease.* By which it is manifest, first, that their prophesying to the people was subservient and subordinate to the prophesying of Moses; for that God took of the spirit of Moses, to put upon them; so that they prophesied as Moses would have them: otherwise they had not been suffered to prophesy at all. For there was (verse 27) a complaint made against them to Moses; and Joshua would have Moses to have forbidden them; which he did not, but said to Joshua, *be not jealous in my behalf.* Secondly, that the spirit of God in that place signifieth nothing but the mind and disposition to obey and assist Moses in the administration of the government. For if it were meant they had the substantial spirit of God; that is, the divine nature, inspired into them, then they had it in no less manner than Christ himself, in whom only the spirit of God dwelt bodily. It is meant therefore of the gift and grace of God, that guided them to co-operate with Moses; from whom their spirit was derived. And it appeareth (*Numb.* xi. 16) that they were such as Moses himself should appoint for elders and officers of the people: for the words are, *Gather unto me seventy men, whom thou knowest to be elders and officers of the people:* where, *thou knowest,* is the same with *thou appointest,* or *hast appointed to be such.* For we are told before (*Exod.* xviii. 24) that Moses following the counsel of Jethro, his father-in-

law, did appoint judges and officers over the people, such as
feared God; and of these were those seventy, whom God, by
putting upon them Moses' spirit, inclined to aid Moses in the
administration of the kingdom: and in this sense the spirit
of God is said (1 *Sam.* xvi. 13, 14) presently upon the anoint-
ing of David, to have come upon David, and left Saul; God
giving his graces to him he chose to govern his people, and
taking them away from him he rejected. So that by the spirit
is meant inclination to God's service; and not any supernatural
revelation.

*God sometimes also spake by lots.* God spake also many
times by the event of lots; which were ordered by such as he
had put in authority over his people. So we read that God
manifested by the lots which Saul caused to be drawn (1 *Sam.*
xiv. 43) the fault that Jonathan had committed, in eating a
honey-comb, contrary to the oath taken by the people. And
(*Josh.* xviii. 10) God divided the land of Canaan amongst
the Israelites, by the *lots that Joshua did cast before the Lord
in Shiloh.* In the same manner it seemeth to be, that God discovered (*Josh.* vii. 16, &c.) the crime of Achan. And these
are the ways whereby God declared his will in the Old Testament.

All which ways he used also in the New Testament. To the
Virgin Mary, by a vision of an angel: to Joseph in a dream:
again, to Paul, in the way to Damascus, in a vision of our
Saviour: and to Peter in the vision of a sheet let down from
heaven, with divers sorts of flesh; of clean, and unclean
beasts; and in prison, by vision of an angel: and to all the
apostles, and writers of the New Testament, by the graces of
his spirit; and to the apostles again, at the choosing of
Matthias in the place of Judas Iscariot, by lot.

*Every man ought to examine the probability of a pretended
prophet's calling.* Seeing then, all prophecy supposeth vision,
or dream, (which two, when they be natural, are the same),
or some especial gift of God so rarely observed in mankind
as to be admired where observed; and seeing as well such
gifts, as the most extraordinary dreams and visions, may proceed from God, not only by his supernatural, and immediate,
but also by his natural operation, and by mediation of second
causes; there is need of reason and judgment to discern between natural, and supernatural gifts, and between natural,
and supernatural visions or dreams. And consequently men
had need to be very circumspect and wary, in obeying the
voice of man, that pretending himself to be a prophet, re-

quires us to obey God in that way, which he in God's name
telleth us to be the way to happiness. For he that pretends to
teach men the way of so great felicity, pretends to govern
them; that is to say, to rule and reign over them; which is a
thing, that all men naturally desire, and is therefore worthy
to be suspected of ambition and imposture; and consequently,
ought to be examined and tried by every man, before he yield
them obedience; unless he have yielded it them already, in the
institution of a commonwealth; as when the prophet is the
civil sovereign, or by the civil sovereign authorized. And if
this examination of prophets and spirits, were not allowed to
every one of the people, it had been to no purpose to set out
the marks, by which every man might be able to distinguish
between those, whom they ought, and those whom they ought
not to follow. Seeing therefore such marks are set out (*Deut.*
xiii. 1, &c.) to know a prophet by; and (1 *John* iv. 1, &c.)
to know a spirit by: and seeing there is so much prophesying
in the Old Testament, and so much preaching in the New
Testament, against prophets; and so much greater a number
ordinarily of false prophets, than of true; every one is to beware of obeying their directions, at their own peril. And first,
that there were many more false than true prophets, appears
by this, that when Ahab (1 *Kings* xxii) consulted four hundred prophets, they were all false impostors, but only one
Micaiah. And a little before the time of the captivity, the
prophets were generally liars. *The prophets*, (saith the Lord,
by *Jeremiah*, chapter xiv. 14) *prophesy lies in my name. I
sent them not, neither have I commanded them, nor spake
unto them; they prophesy to you a false vision, a thing of
nought, and the deceit of their heart.* Insomuch as God commanded the people by the mouth of the prophet Jeremiah
(chapter xxiii. 16) not to obey them: *Thus saith the Lord of
hosts, hearken not unto the words of the prophets, that prophesy to you. They make you vain, they speak a vision of their
own heart, and not out of the mouth of the Lord.*

*All prophecy but of the sovereign prophet, is to be ex-
amined by every subject.* Seeing then there was in the time of
the Old Testament, such quarrels amongst the visionary prophets, one contesting with another, and asking, *when departed
the Spirit from me, to go to thee?* as between Micaiah and the
rest of the four hundred; and such giving of the lie to one
another, (as in *Jer.* xiv. 14) and such controversies in the
New Testament at this day, amongst the spiritual prophets;
every man then was, and now is bound to make use of his

natural reason, to apply to all prophecy those rules which God hath given us, to discern the true from false. Of which rules, in the Old Testament, one was, conformable doctrine to that which Moses the sovereign prophet had taught them; and the other, the miraculous power of foretelling what God would bring to pass, as I have already showed out of *Deut.* xiii. 1, &c. And in the New Testament there was but one only mark; and that was the preaching of this doctrine, *that Jesus is the Christ,* that is, king of the Jews, promised in the Old Testament. Whosoever denied that article, he was a false prophet, whatsoever miracles he might seem to work; and he that taught it was a true prophet. For St. John (1 *John* iv. 2, &c.) speaking expressly of the means to examine spirits, whether they be of God, or not; after he had told them that there would arise false prophets, saith thus, *Hereby know ye the Spirit of God. Every spirit that confesseth that Jesus Christ is come in the flesh, is of God;* that is, is approved and allowed as a prophet of God; not that he is a godly man, or one of the elect, for this, that he confesseth, professeth, or preacheth Jesus to be the Christ; but for that he is a prophet avowed. For God sometimes speaketh by prophets, whose persons he hath not accepted; as he did by Balaam; and as he foretold Saul of his death, by the Witch of Endor. Again in the next verse, *Every spirit that confesseth not that Jesus Christ is come in the flesh, is not of Christ; and this is the spirit of Anti-Christ.* So that the rule is perfect on both sides; that he is a true prophet, which preacheth the Messiah already come, in the person of Jesus; and he a false one that denieth him come, and looketh for him in some future impostor, that shall take upon him that honour falsely, whom the apostle there properly calleth Anti-Christ. Every man therefore ought to consider who is the sovereign prophet; that is to say, who it is, that is God's vicegerent on earth; and hath next under God, the authority of governing Christian men; and to observe for a rule, that doctrine, which in the name of God, he hath commanded to be taught; and thereby to examine and try out the truth of those doctrines, which pretended prophets with miracle, or without, shall at any time advance: and if they find it contrary to that rule, to do as they did, that came to Moses, and complained that there were some that prophesied in the camp, whose authority so to do they doubted of; and leave to the sovereign, as they did to Moses, to uphold, or to forbid them, as he should see cause; and if he disavow them, then no more to obey their voice; or if he approve them, then to obey them, as men to whom God hath given a part of the spirit of their sovereign. For when Christian men, take not their Christian sovereign, for God's prophet; they must either take their own dreams, for the prophecy they mean to be governed by, and the tumour of their own hearts for the Spirit of God; or they must suffer themselves to be led by some strange prince; or by some of their fellow-subjects, that can bewitch them, by slander of the government, into rebellion, without other miracle to confirm their calling, than sometimes an extraordinary success and impunity; and by this means destroying all laws, both divine and human, reduce all order, government, and society, to the first chaos of violence and civil war.

## Chapter 37

### Of Miracles, and their Use

*A miracle is a work that causeth admiration.* By *miracles* are signified the admirable works of God: and therefore they are also called *wonders.* And because they are for the most part, done, for a signification of his commandment, in such occasions, as without them, men are apt to doubt, (following their private natural reasoning,) what he hath commanded, and what not, they are commonly, in holy Scripture, called *signs,* in the same sense, as they are called by the Latins, *ostenta,* and *portenta,* from showing and foresignifying that, which the Almighty is about to bring to pass.

*And must therefore be rare, and whereof there is no natural cause known.* To understand therefore what is a miracle, we must first understand what works they are, which men wonder at, and call admirable. And there be but two things which make men wonder at any event: the one is, if it be strange, that is to say, such as the like of it hath never, or very rarely been produced: the other is, if when it is produced, we cannot imagine it to have been done by natural means, but only by the immediate hand of God. But when we see some possible, natural cause of it, how rarely soever the like has been done, or if the like have been often done, how impossible soever it be to imagine a natural means thereof, we no more wonder, nor esteem it for a miracle.

Therefore, if a horse or cow should speak, it were a miracle; because both the thing is strange, and the natural cause difficult to imagine. So also were it to see a strange deviation of nature, in the production of some new shape of a living creature. But when a man, or other animal, engenders his like, though we know no more how this is done, than the other; yet because it is usual, it is no miracle. In like manner, if a man be metamorphosed into a stone, or into a pillar, it is a miracle; because strange: but if a piece of wood be so changed; because we see it often, it is no miracle: and yet we know no more by what operation of God, the one is brought to pass, than the other.

The first rainbow that was seen in the world, was a miracle, because the first; and consequently strange; and served for a sign from God, placed in heaven, to assure his people, there should be no more any universal destruction of the world by water. But at this day, because they are frequent, they are not miracles, neither to them that know their natural causes, nor to them who know them not. Again, there be many rare works produced by the art of man: yet when we know they are done; because thereby we know also the means how they are done, we count them not for miracles, because not wrought by the immediate hand of God, but by mediation of human industry.

*That which seemeth a miracle to one man, may seem otherwise to another.* Furthermore, seeing admiration and wonder are consequent to the knowledge and experience, wherewith men are endued, some more, some less; it followeth, that the same thing may be a miracle to one, and not to another. And thence it is, that ignorant and superstitious men make great wonders of those works, which other men, knowing to proceed from nature, (which is not the immediate, but the ordinary work of God), admire not at all: as when eclipses of the sun and moon have been taken for supernatural works, by the common people; when nevertheless, there were others, who could from their natural causes have foretold the very hour they should arrive; or, as when a man, by confederacy and secret intelligence, getting knowledge of the private actions of an ignorant, unwary man, thereby tells him what he has done in former time; it seems to him a miraculous thing; but amongst wise, and cautelous men, such miracles as those, cannot easily be done.

*The end of miracles.* Again, it belongeth to the nature of a miracle, that it be wrought for the procuring of credit to God's messengers, ministers, and prophets, that thereby men may know, they are called, sent, and employed by God, and thereby be the better inclined to obey them. And therefore, though the creation of the world, and after that the destruction of all living creatures in the universal deluge, were admirable works; yet because they were not done to procure credit to any prophet, or other minister of God, they use not to be called miracles. For how admirable soever any work be, the admiration consisteth not in that it could be done; because men naturally believe the Almighty can do all things; but because he does it at the prayer or word of a man. But the works of God in Egypt, by the hand of Moses, were properly miracles; because they were done with intention to make the people of Israel believe, that Moses came unto them, not out of any design of his own interest, but as sent from God. Therefore, after God had commanded him to deliver the Israelites from the Egyptian bondage, when he said (*Exod. iv.* 1) *They will not believe me, but will say, the Lord hath not appeared unto me,* God gave him power, to turn the rod he had in his hand into a serpent, and again to return it into a rod; and by putting his hand into his bosom, to make it leprous; and again by pulling it out, to make it whole; to make the children of Israel believe (as it is verse 5) that the God of their fathers had appeared unto him: and if that were not enough, he gave him power to turn their waters into blood. And when he had done these miracles before the people, it is said (verse 31) that *they believed him.* Nevertheless, for fear of Pharaoh, they durst not yet obey him. Therefore the other works which were done to plague Pharaoh and the Egyptians, tended all to make the Israelites believe in Moses, and were properly miracles. In like manner if we consider all the miracles done by the hand of Moses, and all the rest of the prophets, till the captivity; and those of our Saviour, and his apostles afterwards; we shall find, their end was always to beget or confirm belief, that they came not of their own motion, but were sent by God. We may further observe in Scripture, that the end of miracles, was to beget belief, not universally in all men, elect and reprobate; but in the elect only; that is to say, in such as God had determined should become his subjects. For those miraculous plagues of Egypt, had not for their end, the conversion of Pharaoh; for God had told Moses before, that he would harden the heart of Pharaoh, that he should not let the people go: and when he let them go at last, not the miracles persuaded him, but the plagues forced him to it. So also of our Saviour, it is written (*Matt.* xiii. 58), that he wrought not many miracles in his own country, because of their unbelief; and (in *Mark* vi. 5) instead of, *He wrought not many,* it is, *He could work none.* It was not because he wanted power; which to say, were blasphemy against God; nor that the end of miracles was not to convert incredulous men to Christ; for the end of all the miracles of Moses, of the prophets, of our Saviour, and of his apostles was to add men to the church: but it was, because the end of their miracles, was to add to the church, not all men, but such as should be saved; that is to say, such as God had elected. Seeing therefore our Saviour was sent from his Father, he could not use his power in the conversion of those, whom his Father had rejected. They that expounding this place of *St. Mark*, say, that this word, *He could not*, is put for, *He would not*, do it without example in the Greek tongue: where *would not*, is put sometimes for *could not*, in things inanimate, that have no will; but *could not*, for *would not* never: and thereby lay a stumbling block before weak Christians; as if Christ could do no miracles, but amongst the credulous.

*The definition of a miracle.* From that which I have here set down, of the nature and use of a miracle, we may define it thus: A MIRACLE *is a work of God, (besides his operation by the way of nature, ordained in the creation) done, for the making manifest to his elect, the mission of an extraordinary minister for their salvation.*

And from this definition, we may infer; first, that in all miracles, the work done, is not the effect of any virtue in the prophet; because it is the effect of the immediate hand of God; that is to say God hath done it, without using the prophet therein, as a subordinate cause.

Secondly, that no devil, angel, or other created spirit, can do a miracle. For it must either be by virtue of some natural science, or by incantation, that is, by virtue of words. For if the enchanters do it by their own power independent, there is some power that proceedeth not from God; which all men deny: and if they do it by power given them, then is the work not from the immediate hand of God, but natural, and consequently no miracle.

There be some texts of Scripture, that seem to attribute the power of working wonders, equal to some of those immediate miracles wrought by God himself, to certain arts of magic and incantation. As for example, when we read that after the rod of Moses being cast on the ground became a serpent, (*Exod.* vii. 11) *the magicians of Egypt did the like by their enchantments;* and that after Moses had turned the waters of the Egyptian streams, rivers, ponds, and pools of water into blood, (*Exod.* vii. 22) *the magicians did so likewise with their enchantments;* and that after Moses had by the power of God brought frogs upon the land, (*Exod.* viii. 7) *the magicians also did so with their enchantments, and brought up frogs upon the land of Egypt;* will not a man be apt to attribute miracles to enchantments; that is to say, to the efficacy of the sound of words; and think the same very well proved out of this, and other such places? And yet there is no place of Scripture, that telleth us what an enchantment is. If therefore enchantment be not, as many think it, a working of strange effects by spells and words; but imposture and delusion, wrought by ordinary means; and so far from supernatural, as the impostors need not the study so much as of natural causes, but the ordinary ignorance, stupidity, and superstition of mankind, to do them; those texts that seem to countenance the power of magic, witchcraft, and enchantment, must needs have another sense, than at first sight they seem to bear.

For it is evident enough, that words have no effect, but on those that understand them; and then they have no other, but to signify the intentions or passions of them that speak; and thereby produce hope, fear, or other passions or conceptions in the hearer. Therefore when a rod seemeth a serpent, or the waters blood, or any other miracle seemeth done by enchantment; if it be not to the edification of God's people, not the rod, nor the water, nor any other thing in enchanted; that is to say, wrought upon by the words, but the spectator. So that all the miracle consisteth in this, that the enchanter has deceived a man; which is no miracle, but a very easy matter to do.

*That men are apt to be deceived by false miracles.* For such is the ignorance and aptitude to error generally of all men, but especially of them that have not much knowledge of natural causes, and of the nature and interests of men; as by innumerable and easy tricks to be abused. What opinion of miraculous power, before it was known there was a science of the course of the stars, might a man have gained, that should have told the people, this hour or day the sun should be darkened? A juggler by the handling of his goblets and other trinkets, if it were not now ordinarily practised, would be thought to do his wonders by the power at least of the devil. A man that hath practised to speak by drawing in of his breath, (which kind of men in ancient time were called *ventriloqui*), and so make the weakness of his voice seem to proceed, not from the weak impulsion of the organs of speech, but from distance of place, is able to make very many men believe it is a voice from Heaven, whatsoever he please to tell them. And for a crafty man, that hath enquired into the secrets, and familiar confessions that one man ordinarily maketh to another of his actions and adventures past, to tell them him again is no hard matter; and yet there be many, that by such means as that obtain the reputation of being conjurers. But it is too long a business, to reckon up the several sorts of those men, which the Greeks called θαυματουργοι, that is to say, workers of things wonderful: and yet these do all they do, by their own single dexterity. But if we look upon the impostures wrought by confederacy, there is nothing how impossible soever to be done, that is impossible to be believed. For two men conspiring, one to seem lame, the other to cure him with a charm, will deceive many: but many conspiring, one to seem lame, another so to cure him, and all the rest to bear witness, will deceive many more.

*Cautions against the imposture of miracles.* In this aptitude of mankind, to give too hasty belief to pretended miracles, there can be no better, nor I think any other caution, than that which God hath prescribed, first by Moses, as I have said before in the precedent chapter, in the beginning of the xiiith and the end of the xviiith of *Deuteronomy;* that we take not any for prophets, that teach any other religion, than that which God's lieutenant, which at that time was Moses, hath established; nor any, though he teach the same religion, whose prediction we do not see come to pass. Moses therefore in his time, and Aaron and his successors in their times, and the sovereign governor of God's people, next under God himself, that is to say, the head of the Church, in all times, are to be consulted, what doctrine he hath established, before we give credit to a pretended miracle or prophet. And when that is done, the thing they pretend to be a miracle, we must both see it done, and use all means possible to consider, whether it be really done; and not only so, but whether it be such, as no man can do the like by his natural power, but that it requires the immediate hand of God. And in this also we must have recourse to God's lieutenant, to whom in all doubtful cases, we have submitted our private judgments. For example; if a man pretend, after certain words spoken over a piece of bread, that presently God hath made it not bread, but a god, or a man, or both, and nevertheless it looketh still as like bread as ever it did; there is no reason for any man to think it really done, nor consequently to fear him, till he enquire of God, by his vicar or lieutenant, whether it be done, or not. If he say, not, then followeth that which Moses saith (*Deut.* xviii. 22) *he hath spoken it presumptuously, thou shalt not fear him.* If he say, it is done, then he is not to contradict it. So also if we see not, but only hear tell of a miracle, we are to consult the lawful Church; that is to say, the lawful head thereof, how far we are to give credit to the relators of it. And this is chiefly the case of men, that in these days live under Christian sovereigns. For in these times, I do not know one man, that ever saw any such wondrous work, done by the charm, or at the word, or prayer of a man, that a man endued but with a mediocrity of reason would think supernatural: and the question is no more, whether what we see done, be a miracle; whether the miracle we hear, or read of, were a real work, and not the act of a tongue, or pen; but in plain terms, whether the report be true, or a lie. In which question we are not every one, to make our own private reason, or conscience, but the public reason, that is, the reason of God's supreme lieutenant, judge; and indeed we have made him judge already, if we have given him a sovereign power, to do all that is necessary for our peace and defence. A private man has always the liberty, because thought is free, to believe or not believe in his heart those acts that have been given out for miracles, according as he shall see what benefit can accrue by men's belief, to those that pretend or countenance them, and thereby conjecture whether they be miracles or lies. But when it comes to confession of that faith, the private reason must submit to the public; that is to say, to God's lieutenant. But who is this lieutenant of God, and head of the Church, shall be considered in its proper place hereafter.

# Chapter 38

## Of the Signification in Scripture of Eternal Life, Hell, Salvation, the World to Come, and Redemption

THE MAINTENANCE OF civil society depending on justice, and justice on the power of life and death, and other less rewards and punishments, residing in them that have the sovereignty of the commonwealth; it is impossible a commonwealth should stand, where any other than the sovereign hath a power of giving greater rewards than life, and of inflicting greater punishments than death. Now seeing *eternal life* is a greater reward than the *life present;* and *eternal torment* a greater punishment than the *death of nature;* it is a thing worthy to be well considered of all men that desire, by obeying authority, to avoid the calamities of confusion and civil war, what is meant in Holy Scripture, by *life eternal,* and *torment eternal;* and for what offences, and against whom committed, men are to be *eternally tormented;* and for what actions they are to obtain *eternal life.*

*The place of Adam's eternity, if he had not sinned, had been the terrestrial Paradise.* And first we find that Adam was created in such a condition of life, as had he not broken the commandment of God, he had enjoyed it in the paradise of Eden everlastingly. For there was the *tree of life,* whereof he was so long allowed to eat, as he should forbear to eat of the tree of knowledge of good and evil; which was not allowed him. And therefore as soon as he had eaten of it, God thrust him out of Paradise, (*Gen.* iii. 22) *lest he should put forth his hand, and take also of the tree of life and live for ever.* By which it seemeth to me, (with submission nevertheless both in this, and in all questions whereof the determination dependeth on the Scriptures, to the interpretation of the Bible authorized by the commonwealth, whose subject I am), that Adam, if he had not sinned, had had an eternal life on earth, and that mortality entered upon himself and his posterity by his first sin. Not that actual death then entered; for Adam then could never have had children; whereas he lived long after, and saw a numerous posterity ere he died. But where it is said, (*Gen.* ii. 17) *In the day that thou eatest thereof, thou shalt surely die,* it must needs be meant of his mortality, and certitude of death. Seeing then eternal life was lost by Adam's forfeiture in committing sin, he that should cancel that forfeiture, was to recover thereby that life again. Now Jesus Christ hath satisfied for the sins of all that believe in him; and therefore recovered to all believers, that eternal life which was lost by the sin of Adam. And in this sense it is that the comparison of St. Paul holdeth, (*Rom.* v. 18, 19) *As by the offence of one, judgment came upon all men to condemnation, even so by the righteousness of one, the free gift came upon all men to justification of life;* which is again (1 *Cor.* xv. 21, 22) more perspicuously delivered in these words, *For since by man came death, by man came also the resurrection of the dead. For as in Adam all die, even so in Christ shall all be made alive.*

*Texts concerning the place of life eternal, for believers.* Concerning the place wherein men shall enjoy that eternal life which Christ hath obtained for them, the texts next before alleged seem to make it on earth. For if as in Adam all die, that is, have forfeited paradise and eternal life on earth, even so in Christ all shall be made alive; then all men shall be made to live on earth; for else the comparison were not proper. Hereunto seemeth to agree that of the psalmist (*Psalm* cxxxiii. 3) *upon Zion God commanded the blessing, even life for evermore:* for Zion is in Jerusalem upon earth: as also that of St. John (*Rev.* ii. 7) *To him that overcometh I will give to eat of the tree of life, which is in the midst of the paradise of God.* This was the tree of Adam's eternal life; but his life was to have been on earth. The same seemeth to be confirmed again by St. John (*Rev.* xxi. 2), where he saith, *I John saw the holy city, new Jerusalem, coming down from God out of heaven, prepared as a bride adorned for her husband:* and again (verse 10) to the same effect: as if he should say, the new *Jerusalem,* the paradise of God, at the coming again of Christ, should come down to God's people from heaven, and not they go up to it from earth. And this differs nothing from that, which the two men in white clothing, that is the two angels, said to the apostles that were looking upon Christ ascending (*Acts* i. 11) *This same Jesus, who is taken up from you into heaven, shall so come, as you have seen him go up into heaven.* Which soundeth as if they had said he should come down to govern them under his Father eternally here, and not take them up to govern them in heaven; and is conformable to the restoration of the kingdom of God instituted under Moses, which was a political government of the Jews on earth. Again, that saying of our Saviour (*Matt.* xxii. 30), *that in the resurrection they neither marry, nor are given in marriage, but are as the angels of God in heaven,* is a description of an eternal life, resembling that which we lost in Adam in the point of marriage. For seeing Adam and Eve, if they had not sinned, had lived on earth eternally in their individual persons; it is manifest, they should not continually have procreated their kind; for if immortals should have generated as mankind doth now, the earth in a small time would not have been able to afford them place to stand on. The Jews that asked our Saviour the question, whose wife the woman that had married many brothers should be in the resurrection, knew not what were the consequences of life eternal: and therefore our Saviour puts them in mind of this consequence of immortality; that there shall be no generation, and consequently no marriage, no more than there is marriage or generation among the angels. The comparison between that eternal life which Adam lost, and our Saviour by his victory over death hath recovered, holdeth also in this; that as Adam lost eternal life by his sin, and yet lived after it for a time, so the faithful Christian hath recovered eternal life by Christ's passion, though he die a natural death, and remain dead for a time, namely, till the resurrection. For as death is reckoned from the condemnation of Adam, not from the execution; so life is reckoned from the absolution, not from the resurrection of them that are elected in Christ.

*Ascension into heaven.* That the place wherein men are to live eternally, after the resurrection, is the heavens, (meaning by heaven, those parts of the world, which are the most remote from earth, as where the stars are, or above the stars, in another higher heaven, called *cælum empyreum,* whereof there is no mention in Scripture, nor ground in reason), is not easily to be drawn from any text that I can find. By the Kingdom of Heaven, is meant the kingdom of the King that dwelleth in heaven; and his kingdom was the people of Israel, whom he ruled by the prophets, his lieutenants; first Moses, and after him Eleazar, and the sovereign priests, till in the days of Samuel they rebelled, and would have a mortal man for their king, after the manner of other nations. And when our Saviour Christ, by the preaching of his ministers, shall have persuaded the Jews to return, and called the Gentiles to his obedience, then shall there be a new kingdom of heaven;

because our king shall then be God, whose *throne* is heaven: without any necessity evident in the Scripture, that man shall ascend to his happiness any higher than God's *footstool* the earth. On the contrary, we find written (*John* iii. 13) that *no man hath ascended into heaven, but he that came down from heaven, even the son of man, that is in heaven.* Where I observe by the way, that these words are not, as those which go immediately before, the words of our Saviour, but of St. John himself; for Christ was then not in heaven, but upon the earth. The like is said of David (*Acts* ii. 34) where St. Peter, to prove the ascension of Christ, using the words of the Psalmist (*Psalm* xvi. 10), *Thou wilt not leave my soul in hell, nor suffer thine holy one to see corruption,* saith, they were spoken, not of David, but of Christ; and to prove it, addeth this reason, *For David is not ascended into heaven.* But to this a man may easily answer, and say, that though their bodies were not to ascend till the general day of judgment, yet their souls were in heaven as soon as they were departed from their bodies; which also seemeth to be confirmed by the words of our Saviour (*Luke* xx. 37, 38), who proving the resurrection out of the words of Moses, saith thus, *That the dead are raised, even Moses shewed at the bush, when he calleth the Lord, the God of Abraham, and the God of Isaac, and the God of Jacob. For he is not a God of the dead, but of the living; for they all live to him.* But if these words be to be understood only of the immortality of the soul, they prove not at all that which our Saviour intended to prove, which was the resurrection of the body, that is to say, the immortality of the man. Therefore our Saviour meaneth, that those patriarchs were immortal; not by a property consequent to the essence and nature of mankind; but by the will of God, that was pleased of his mere grace, to bestow *eternal life* upon the faithful. And though at that time the patriarchs and many other faithful men were *dead,* yet as it is in the text, they *lived to God;* that is, they were written in the Book of Life with them that were absolved of their sins, and ordained to life eternal at the resurrection. That the soul of man is in its own nature eternal, and a living creature independent on the body, or that any mere man is immortal, otherwise than by the resurrection in the last day, except Enoch and Elias, is a doctrine not apparent in Scripture. The whole of the xivth chapter of *Job,* which is the speech not of his friends, but of himself, is a complaint of this mortality of nature; and yet no contradiction of the immortality at the resurrection. *There is hope of a tree,* saith he, (verse 7) *if it be cast down. Though the root thereof wax old, and the stock thereof die in the ground, yet when it scenteth the water it will bud, and bring forth boughs like a plant. But man dieth and wasteth away, yea, man giveth up the ghost, and where is he?* And (verse 12) *Man lieth down, and riseth not, till the heavens be no more.* But when is it, that the heavens shall be no more? St. Peter tells us, that it is at the general resurrection. For in his 2nd *Epistle,* chap. iii, verse 7, he saith, that *the heavens and the earth that are now, are reserved unto fire against the day of judgment, and perdition of ungodly men,* and (verse 12) *looking for, and hasting to the coming of God, wherein the heavens shall be on fire and shall be dissolved, and the elements shall melt with fervent heat. Nevertheless, we according to the promise look for new heavens, and a new earth, wherein dwelleth righteousness.* Therefore where Job saith, *man riseth not till the heavens be no more;* it is all one, as if he had said, the immortal life, (and soul and life in the Scripture do usually signify the same thing), beginneth not in man, till the resurrection and day of judgment; and hath for cause, not his specifical nature and generation, but the promise. For St. Peter says, not *We look for new heavens and a new earth, from nature,* but *from promise.*

Lastly, seeing it hath been already proved out of divers evident places of Scripture, in chap. 35 of this book, that the kingdom of God is a civil commonwealth, where God himself is sovereign, by virtue first of the *old,* and since of the *new* covenant, wherein he reigneth by his vicar or lieutenant; the same places do therefore also prove, that after the coming again of our Saviour in his majesty and glory, to reign actually and eternally, the kingdom of God is to be on earth. But because this doctrine, though proved out of places of Scripture not few nor obscure, will appear to most men a novelty, I do but propound it; maintaining nothing in this, or any other paradox of religion; but attending the end of that dispute of the sword, concerning the authority, not yet amongst my countrymen decided, by which all sorts of doctrine are to be approved or rejected; and whose commands, both in speech and writing, whatsoever be the opinions of private men, must by all men, that mean to be protected by their laws, be obeyed. For the points of doctrine concerning the kingdom of God, have so great influence on the kingdom of man, as not to be determined, but by them, that under God have the sovereign power.

*The place after judgment of those who were never in the kingdom of God, or having been in, are cast out. Tartarus.* As the kingdom of God, and eternal life, so also God's enemies, and their torments after judgment, appear by the Scripture to have their place on earth. The name of the place, where all men remain till the resurrection, that were either buried, or swallowed up of the earth, is usually called in Scripture by words that signify *under ground;* which the Latins read generally *infernus,* and *inferi,* and the Greek ᾄδης, that is to say, a place where men cannot see; and containeth as well the grave, as any other deeper place. But for the place of the damned after the resurrection, it is not determined, neither in the Old nor New Testament, by any note of situation; but only by the company: as that it shall be, where such wicked men were, as God in former times, in extraordinary and miraculous manner, had destroyed from off the face of the earth: as for example, that they are *in Inferno,* in *Tartarus,* or in the bottomless pit; because Korah, Dathan, and Abiram, were swallowed up alive into the earth. Not that the writers of the Scripture would have us believe, there could be in the globe of the earth, which is not only finite, but also, compared to the height of the stars, of no considerable magnitude, a pit without a bottom, that is, a hole of infinite depth, such as the Greeks in their *demonology,* (that is to say, in their doctrine concerning *demons*), and after them the Romans, called *Tartarus;* of which Virgil (*Æn.* VI. 578, 579) says,

Bis patet in præceps tantum, tenditque sub umbras,
Quantus ad ætherium cœli suspectus Olympum:

for that is a thing the proportion of earth to heaven cannot bear: but that we should believe them there, indefinitely, where those men are, on whom God inflicted that exemplary punishment.

*The congregation of giants. Lake of fire.* Again, because those mighty men of the earth, that lived in the time of Noah, before the flood, (which the Greeks call *heroes,* and the Scripture *giants,* and both say were begotten by copulation of the children of God with the children of men,) were for their wicked life destroyed by the general deluge; the place of the damned, is therefore also sometimes marked out, by the company of those deceased giants; as *Proverbs* xxi. 16, *The man that wandereth out of the way of understanding, shall remain in the congregation of the giants;* and *Job* xxvi. 5, *Behold the giants groan under water, and they that dwell with them.* Here the place of the damned is under the water. And Isaiah xiv. 9, *Hell is troubled how to meet thee* (that is, the King of Babylon) *and will displace the giants for thee:* and here again the place of the damned, if the sense be literal, is to be under water. Thirdly, because the cities of Sodom and Gomorrah, by the extraordinary wrath of God, were consumed for their wickedness with fire and brimstone, and together with them the country about made a stinking bituminous lake: the place of the damned is sometimes expressed by fire, and a fiery lake, as in the *Apocalypse,* xxi. 8, *But the timorous, incredulous, and abominable, and murderers, and whoremongers, and sorcerers, and idolaters, and all liars, shall have their part in the lake that burneth with fire and brimstone; which is the second death.* So that it is manifest, that hell fire, which is here expressed by metaphor from the real fire of Sodom, signifieth not any certain kind or place of torment; but is to be taken indefinitely, for destruction, as it is in *Rev.* xx. 14, where it is said, that *death and hell were cast into the lake of fire;* that is to say, were abolished and destroyed; as if after the day of judgment, there shall be no more dying, nor no more going into hell; that is, no more going to *Hades,* (from which word perhaps our word Hell is derived,) which is the same with no more dying.

*Utter darkness.* Fourthly, from the plague of darkness inflicted on the Egyptians, of which it is written (*Exod.* x. 23) *They saw not one another, neither rose any man from his place for three days; but all the children of Israel had light in their dwellings;* the place of the wicked after judgment, is called *utter darkness,* or, as it is in the original, *darkness without.* And so it is expressed (*Matt.* xxii. 13) where the king commanded his servants, *to bind hand and foot the man that had not on his wedding garment, and to cast him out,* εἰς τὸ σκότος τὸ ἐξώτερον, *into external darkness,* or *darkness without:* which though translated *utter darkness,* does not signify *how great,* but *where* that darkness is to be; namely, *without the habitation* of God's elect.

*Gehenna, and Tophet.* Lastly, whereas there was a place near Jerusalem, called the *Valley of the Children of Hinnon;* in a part whereof, called *Tophet,* the Jews had committed most grievous idolatry, sacrificing their children to the idol Moloch; and wherein also God had afflicted his enemies with most grievous punishments; and wherein Josiah had burned the priests of Moloch upon their own altars, as appeareth at large in the 2nd of *Kings*, chap. xxiii: the place served afterwards to receive the filth and garbage which was carried thither out of the city; and there used to be fires made from time to time, to purify the air, and take away the stench of carrion. From this abominable place, the Jews used ever after to call the place of the damned, by the name of *Gehenna*, or *Valley of Hinnon*. And this *Gehenna*, is that word which is usually now translated HELL; and from the fires from time to time there burning, we have the notion of *everlasting* and *unquenchable fire*.

*Of the literal sense of the Scripture concerning hell*. Seeing now there is none, that so interprets the Scripture, as that after the day of judgment, the wicked are all eternally to be punished in the Valley of Hinnon; or that they shall so rise again, as to be ever after under ground or under water; or that after the resurrection, they shall no more see one another, nor stir from one place to another: it followeth, methinks, very necessarily, that that which is thus said concerning hell fire, is spoken metaphorically; and that therefore there is a proper sense to be enquired after, (for of all metaphors there is some real ground, that may be expressed in proper words,) both of the *place* of *hell*, and the nature of *hellish torments*, and *tormenters*.

*Satan, Devil, not proper names, but appellatives*. And first for the tormenters, we have their nature and properties, exactly and properly delivered by the names of, *the Enemy*, or *Satan; the Accuser*, or *Diabolus; the Destroyer*, or *Abaddon*. Which significant names, *Satan, Devil, Abaddon*, set not forth to us any individual person, as proper names use to do; but only an office, or quality; and are therefore appellatives; which ought not to have been left untranslated, as they are in the Latin and modern Bibles; because thereby they seem to be proper names of *demons;* and men are the more easily seduced to believe the doctrine of devils; which at that time was the religion of the Gentiles, and contrary to that of Moses and of Christ.

And because by the *Enemy*, the *Accuser*, and *Destroyer*, is meant the enemy of them that shall be in the kingdom of God; therefore if the kingdom of God after the resurrection, be upon the earth, as in the former chapter I have shown

by Scripture it seems to be, the Enemy and his kingdom must
be on earth also. For so also was it, in the time before the
Jews had deposed God. For God's kingdom was in Palestine;
and the nations round about, were the kingdoms of the
Enemy; and consequently by *Satan,* is meant any earthly
enemy of the Church.

*Torments of hell.* The torments of hell, are expressed
sometimes, by *weeping,* and *gnashing of teeth,* as *Matt.* viii.
12. Sometimes by *the worm of conscience;* as *Isaiah* lxvi. 24,
and *Mark* ix. 44, 46, 48: sometimes, by fire, as in the place
now quoted, *where the worm dieth not, and the fire is not
quenched,* and many places beside: sometimes by *shame and
contempt,* as *Dan.* xii. 2. *And many of them that sleep in the
dust of the earth, shall awake; some to everlasting life; and
some to shame, and everlasting contempt.* All which places
design metaphorically a grief and discontent of mind, from
the sight of that eternal felicity in others, which they themselves through their own incredulity and disobedience have
lost. And because such felicity in others, is not sensible but
by comparison with their own actual miseries; it followeth that
they are to suffer such bodily pains, and calamities, as are incident to those, who not only live under evil and cruel
governors, but have also for enemy the eternal king of the
saints, God Almighty. And amongst these bodily pains, is to
be reckoned also to every one of the wicked a second death.
For though the Scripture be clear for an universal resurrection; yet we do not read, that to any of the reprobate is
promised an eternal life. For whereas St. Paul (1 *Cor.* xv. 42,
43) to the question concerning what bodies men shall rise
with again, saith, that *The body is sown in corruption, and is
raised in incorruption; it is sown in dishonour, it is raised in
glory; it is sown in weakness, it is raised in power.* Glory and
power cannot be applied to the bodies of the wicked: nor can
the name of *second death* be applied to those that can never
die but once: and although in metaphorical speech, a calami-
tous life everlasting, may be called an everlasting death, yet it
cannot well be understood of a *second death.*

The fire prepared for the wicked, is an everlasting fire: that
is to say, the estate wherein no man can be without torture,
both of body and mind, after the resurrection, shall endure
for ever; and in that sense the fire shall be unquenchable, and
the torments everlasting: but it cannot thence be inferred, that
he who shall cast into that fire, or be tormented with those
torments, shall endure and resist them so as to be eternally

burnt, and tortured, and yet never be destroyed, nor die. And though there be many places that affirm everlasting fire and torments, into which men may be cast successively one after another as long as the world lasts, yet I find none that affirm there shall be an eternal life therein of any individual person; but to the contrary, an everlasting death, which is the second death: (*Rev.* xx. 13, 14) *For after death and the grave shall have delivered up the dead which were in them, and every man be judged according to his works; death and the grave shall also be cast into the lake of fire. This is the second death.* Whereby it is evident that there is to be a second death of every one that shall be condemned at the day of judgment, after which he shall die no more.

*The joys of life eternal, and salvation, the same thing. Salvation from sin, and from misery, all one.* The joys of life eternal, are in Scripture comprehended all under the name of SALVATION, or *being saved.* To be saved, is to be secured, either respectively, against special evils, or absolutely, against all evils, comprehending want, sickness, and death itself. And because man was created in a condition immortal, not subject to corruption, and consequently to nothing that tendeth to the dissolution of his nature; and fell from that happiness by the sin of Adam; it followeth, that to be *saved* from sin, is to be saved from all the evil and calamities that sin hath brought upon us. And therefore in the holy Scripture, remission of sin, and salvation from death and misery, is the same thing, as it appears by the words of our Saviour, who having cured a man sick of the palsy, by saying, (*Matt.* ix. 2) *Son be of good cheer, thy sins be forgiven thee;* and knowing that the Scribes took for blasphemy, that a man should pretend to forgive sins, asked them (verse 5) *whether it were easier to say, Thy sins be forgiven thee, or, Arise and walk;* signifying thereby, that it was all one, as to the saving of the sick, to say, *Thy sins are forgiven,* and *Arise and walk;* and that he used that form of speech, only to shew he had power to forgive sins. And it is besides evident in reason, that since death and misery were the punishments of sin, the discharge of sin must also be a discharge of death and misery; that is to say, salvation absolute, such as the faithful are to enjoy after the day of judgment, by the power and favour of Jesus Christ, who for that cause is called our SAVIOUR.

Concerning particular salvations, such as are understood, (1 *Sam.* xiv. 39) *as the Lord liveth that saveth Israel,* that is, from their temporary enemies, and (2 *Sam.* xxii. 3) *Thou art my Saviour, thou savest me from violence;* and, (2 *Kings* xiii. 5) *God gave the Israelites a Saviour, and so they were delivered from the hand of the Assyrians,* and the like, I need say nothing; there being neither difficulty, nor interest to corrupt the interpretation of texts of that kind.

*The place of eternal salvation.* But concerning the general salvation, because it must be in the kingdom of heaven, there is great difficulty concerning the place. On one side, by *kingdom,* which is an estate ordained by men for their perpetual security against enemies and want, it seemeth that this salvation should be on earth. For by salvation is set forth unto us, a glorious reign of our king, by conquest; not a safety by escape: and therefore there where we look for salvation, we must look also for triumph; and before triumph, for victory; and before victory, for battle; which cannot well be supposed, shall be in heaven. But how good soever this reason may be, I will not trust to it, without very evident places of Scripture. The state of salvation is described at large, *Isaiah* xxxiii. 20, 21, 22, 23, 24:

*Look upon Zion, the city of our solemnities; thine eyes shall see Jerusalem a quiet habitation, a tabernacle that shall not be taken down; not one of the stakes thereof shall ever be removed, neither shall any of the cords thereof be broken.*

*But there the glorious Lord will be unto us a place of broad rivers and streams; wherein shall go no galley with oars, neither shall gallant ship pass thereby.*

*For the Lord is our Judge, the Lord is our law-giver, the Lord is our king, he will save us.*

*Thy tacklings are loosed; they could not well strengthen their mast; they could not spread the sail: then is the prey of a great spoil divided; the lame take the prey:*

*And the inhabitant shall not say, I am sick; the people that shall dwell therein shall be forgiven their iniquity.*

In which words we have the place from whence salvation is to proceed, *Jerusalem, a quiet habitation;* the eternity of it, *a tabernacle that shall not be taken down, &c.;* the Saviour of it, *the Lord, their judge, their law-giver, their king, he will save us;* the salvation, *the Lord shall be to them as a broad moat of swift waters, &c.;* the condition of their enemies, *their tacklings are loose, their masts weak, the lame shall take the spoil of them;* the condition of the saved, *the inhabitant shall not say, I am sick:* and lastly, all this is comprehended in forgiveness of sin, *the people that dwell therein shall be forgiven their iniquity.* By which it is evident, that salvation shall be on earth, then, when God shall reign, at the coming again of Christ, in Jerusalem; and from Jerusalem shall proceed the salvation of the Gentiles that shall be received into God's kingdom: as is also more expressly declared by the same prophet, (*Isaiah* lxvi. 20, 21), *And they* (that is the Gentiles who had any Jew in bondage) *shall bring all your brethren, for an offering to the Lord, out of all nations, upon horses, and in chariots, and in litters, and upon mules, and upon swift beasts, to my holy mountain, Jerusalem, saith the Lord, as the children of Israel bring an offering in a clean vessel into the house of the Lord. And I will also take of them for priests and for Levites, saith the Lord.* Whereby it is manifest, that the chief seat of God's kingdom, which is the place from whence the salvation of us that were Gentiles shall proceed, shall be Jerusalem: and the same is also confirmed by our Saviour in his discourse with the woman of Samaria, concerning the place of God's worship; to whom he saith (*John* iv. 22) that the Samaritans worshipped they knew not what, but the Jews worshipped what they knew, *for salvation is of the Jews* (*ex Judæis,* that is, begins at the Jews): as if he should say, you worship God, but know not by whom he will save you, as we do, that know it shall be by one of the tribe of Judah; a Jew, not a Samaritan. And therefore also the woman not impertinently answered him again, *We know the Messias shall come.* So that which our Saviour saith, *Salvation is from the Jews,* is the same that Paul says (*Rom.* i. 16, 17) *The Gospel is the power of God to salvation to every one that believeth: to the Jew first, and also to the Greek. For therein is the righteousness of God revealed from faith to faith;* from the faith of the Jew to the faith of the Gentile. In the like sense the prophet Joel describing the day of Judgment, (chap. ii. 30, 31) that God would *shew wonders in heaven, and in earth, blood, and fire, and pillars of smoke; the sun shall be turned to darkness, and the moon into blood, before the great and terrible day of the Lord come:* he addeth, (verse 32) *and it shall come to pass, that whatsoever shall call upon the name of the Lord shall be saved. For in Mount Zion and in Jerusalem shall be salvation.* And *Obadiah,* (verse 17) saith the same, *Upon Mount Zion shall be deliverance; and there shall be holiness, and the house of Jacob shall possess their possessions,* that is the possessions of the *heathen,* which *possessions,* he expresseth more particularly in the following verses, by the *mount of Esau,* the *Land of the Philistines,* the *fields of Ephraim,* of *Samaria, Gilead,* and the *cities of the south,* and concludes with these words, *the kingdom shall be the Lord's*. All these places are for salvation, and the kingdom of God, after the day of judgment, upon earth. On the other side, I have not found any text that can probably be drawn, to prove any ascension of the saints into heaven; that is to say, into any *cælum empyreum*, or other ætherial region; saving that it is called the kingdom of Heaven: which name it may have because God, that was king of the Jews, governed them by his commands, sent to Moses by angels from heaven; and after the revolt, sent his Son from heaven to reduce them to their obedience; and shall send him thence again to rule both them, and all other faithful men, from the day of judgment, everlastingly: or from that, that the throne of this our great king is in heaven; whereas the earth is but his footstool. But that the subjects of God should have any place as high as his throne, or higher than his footstool, it seemeth not suitable to the dignity of a king, nor can I find any evident text for it in Holy Scripture.

*The world to come*. From this that hath been said of the kingdom of God, and of salvation, it is not hard to interpret what is meant by the WORLD TO COME. There are three worlds mentioned in Scripture, the *old world*, the *present world*, and the *world to come*. Of the first, St. Peter speaks, (2 *Pet*. ii. 5) *If God spared not the old world, but saved Noah the eighth person, a preacher of righteousness, bringing the flood upon the world of the ungodly, &c*. So the *first world*, was from Adam to the general flood. Of the present world, our Saviour speaks (*John* xviii. 36) *My kingdom is not of this world*. For he came only to teach men the way of salvation, and to renew the kingdom of his Father, by his doctrine. Of the world to come, St. Peter speaks (2 *Pet*. iii. 13) *Nevertheless we according to his promise look for new heavens, and a new earth*. This is that WORLD, wherein Christ coming down from heaven in the clouds, with great power, and glory, shall send his angels, and shall gather together his elect, from the four winds, and from the uttermost parts of the earth, and thenceforth reign over them, under his Father, everlastingly.

*Redemption*. *Salvation* of a sinner, supposeth a precedent REDEMPTION; for he that is once guilty of sin, is obnoxious to the penalty of the same; and must pay, or some other for him, such ransom as he that is offended, and has him in his power, shall require. And seeing the person offended, is Almighty God, in whose power are all things; such ransom is to be paid before salvation can be acquired, as God hath been pleased to require. By this ransom, is not intended a satisfaction for sin, equivalent to the offence; which no sinner for himself, nor righteous man can ever be able to make for another: the damage a man does to another, he may make amends for by restitution or recompense; but sin cannot be taken away by recompense; for that were to make the liberty to sin, a thing vendible. But sins may be pardoned to the repentant, either *gratis,* or upon such penalty as God is pleased to accept. That which God usually accepted in the Old Testament, was some sacrifice or oblation. To forgive sin is not an act of injustice, though the punishment have been threatened. Even amongst men, though the promise of good, bind the promiser; yet threats, that is to say, promises of evil, bind them not; much less shall they bind God, who is infinitely more merciful than men. Our Saviour Christ therefore to *redeem* us, did not in that sense satisfy for the sins of men, as that his death, of its own virtue, could make it unjust in God to punish sinners with eternal death; but did make that sacrifice and oblation of himself, at his first coming, which God was pleased to require for the salvation, at his second coming, of such as in the meantime should repent, and believe in him. And though this act of our *redemption,* be not always in Scripture called a *sacrifice,* and *oblation,* but sometimes a *price;* yet by *price* we are not to understand any thing, by the value whereof, he could claim right to a pardon for us, from his offended Father; but that price which God the Father was pleased in mercy to demand.

## Chapter 39

## Of the Signification in Scripture of the word Church

*Church the Lord's house.* The word Church, (*Ecclesia*) signifieth in the books of Holy Scripture divers things. Sometimes, though not often, it is taken for *God's house,* that is to say, for a temple, wherein Christians assembled to perform holy duties, publicly, as (1 *Cor.* xiv. 34) *Let your women keep silence in the Churches:* but this is metaphorically put for the congregation there assembled; and hath been since used for the edifice itself, to distinguish between the temples of Christians and idolaters. The Temple of Jerusalem was *God's house,* and the house of prayer; and so is any edifice dedicated by Christians to the worship of Christ, *Christ's house:* and therefore the Greek fathers call it Κυριακὴ, *the Lord's house:* and thence in our language it came to be called *kirk,* and *church.*

Ecclesia, *properly what.* Church, when not taken for a house, signifieth the same that *ecclesia* signified in the Grecian commonwealth, that is to say, a congregation, or an assembly of citizens, called forth to hear the magistrate speak unto them; and which in the commonwealth of Rome was called *concio:* as he that spake was called *ecclesiastes,* and *concionator.* And when they were called forth by lawful authority, (*Acts* xix. 39) it was *Ecclesia legitima,* a *lawful Church,* ἔννομος ἐκκλησία. But when they were excited by tumultuous and seditious clamour, then it was a confused Church, ἐκκλησία συγκεχυμένη.

It is taken also sometimes for the men that have right to be of the congregation, though not actually assembled, that is to say, for the whole multitude of Christian men, how far soever they be dispersed: as (*Acts* viii. 3) where it is said, that *Saul made havoc of the Church:* and in this sense is Christ said to be the head of the Church. And sometimes for a certain part of Christians, as (*Col.* iv. 15) *Salute the Church that is in his house.* Sometimes also for the elect only; as (*Eph.* v. 27) *A glorious Church, without spot, or wrinkle, holy, and without blemish;* which is meant of the *Church triumphant,* or *Church to come.* Sometimes, for a congregation assembled of professors of Christianity, whether their profession be true or counterfeit; as it is understood, (*Matt.* xviii. 17) where it is said, *Tell it to the Church; and if he neglect to hear the Church, let him be to thee as a Gentile, or publican.*

*In what sense the church is one person. Church defined.* And in this last sense only it is that the *Church* can be taken for one person; that is to say, that it can be said to have power to will, to pronounce, to command, to be obeyed, to make laws, or to do any other action whatsoever. For without authority from a lawful congregation, whatsoever act be done in a concourse of people, it is the particular act of every one of those that were present, and gave their aid to the performance of it; and not the act of them all in gross, as of one body; much less the act of them that were absent, or that being present, were not willing it should be done. According to this sense, I define a CHURCH to be, *a company of men professing Christian religion, united in the person of one sovereign, at whose command they ought to assemble, and without whose authority they ought not to assemble.* And because in all commonwealths, that assembly, which is without warrant from the civil sovereign, is unlawful; that Church also, which is assembled in any commonwealth that hath forbidden them to assemble, is an unlawful assembly.

*A Christian commonwealth and a church all one.* It followeth also, that there is on earth, no such universal Church, as all Christians are bound to obey; because there is no power on earth, to which all other commonwealths are subject. There are Christians, in the dominions of several princes and states; but every one of them is subject to that commonwealth, whereof he is him self a member; and consequently, cannot be subject to the commands of any other person. And therefore a Church, such a one as is capable to command, to judge, absolve, condemn, or do any other act, is the same thing with a civil commonwealth, consisting of Christian men; and is called a *civil state,* for that the subjects of it are *men:* and a *Church,* for that the subjects thereof are *Christians. Temporal* and *spiritual* government, are but two words brought into the world, to make men see double, and mistake their *lawful sovereign.* It is true, that the bodies of the faithful, after the resurrection, shall be not only spiritual, but eternal; but in this life they are gross, and corruptible. There is therefore no other government in this life, neither of state, nor religion, but temporal; nor teaching of any doctrine, lawful to any subject, which the governor both of the state, and of the religion forbiddeth to be taught. And that governor must be one; or else there must needs follow faction and civil war in the commonwealth, between the *Church* and *State;* between *spiritualists* and *temporalists;* between the *sword of justice,* and the *shield of faith:* and, which is more, in every Christian man's own breast, between the *Christian,* and the *man.* The doctors of the Church, are called pastors; so also are civil sovereigns. But if pastors be not subordinate one to another, so as that there may be one chief pastor, men will be taught contrary doctrines; whereof both may be, and one must be false. Who that one chief pastor is, according to the law of nature, hath been already shown; namely, that it is the civil sovereign: and to whom the Scripture hath assigned that office, we shall see in the chapters following.

Chapter 40

### Of the Rights of the Kingdom of God, in Abraham, Moses, the High-Priests, and the Kings of Judah

*The sovereign right of Abraham.* The father of the faithful, and first in the kingdom of God by covenant, was Abraham. For with him was the covenant first made; wherein he obliged himself, and his seed after him, to acknowledge and obey the commands of God; not only such, as he could take notice of (as moral laws) by the light of nature; but also such, as God should in special manner deliver to him by dreams and visions. For as to the moral law, they were already obliged, and needed not have been contracted withal, by promise of the land of Canaan. Nor was there any contract, that could add to, or strengthen the obligation, by which both they, and all men else were bound naturally to obey God Almighty: and therefore the covenant which Abraham made with God, was to take for the commandment of God, that which in the name of God was commanded him in a dream, or vision; and to deliver it to his family, and cause them to observe the same.

*Abraham had the sole power of ordering the religion of his own people.* In this contract of God with Abraham, we may observe three points of important consequence in the government of God's people. First, that at the making of this covenant, God spake only to Abraham; and therefore contracted not with any of his family, or seed, otherwise than as their wills, which make the essence of all covenants, were before the contract involved in the will of Abraham; who was therefore supposed to have had a lawful power, to make them perform all that he covenanted for them. According whereunto (*Gen.* xviii. 18, 19) God saith, *All the nations of the earth shall be blessed in him; for I know him that he will command his children and his household after him, and they shall keep the way of the Lord.* From whence may be concluded this first point, that they to whom God hath not spoken immediately, are to receive the positive commandments of God, from their sovereign; as the family and seed of Abraham did from Abraham their father, and Lord, and civil sovereign. And consequently in every commonwealth, they

who have no supernatural revelation to the contrary, ought
to obey the laws of their own sovereign, in the external acts
and profession of religion. As for the inward *thought*, and
*belief* of men, which human governors can take no notice of
(for God only knoweth the heart), they are not voluntary,
nor the effect of the laws, but of the unrevealed will and of
the power of God; and consequently fall not under obligation.

*No pretence of private spirit against the religion of Abra-
ham.* From whence proceedeth another point, that it was not
unlawful for Abraham, when any of his subjects should pretend private vision or spirit, or other revelation from God,
for the countenancing of any doctrine which Abraham should
forbid, or when they followed or adhered to any such pretender, to punish them; and consequently that it is lawful
now for the sovereign to punish any man that shall oppose
his private spirit against the laws: for he hath the same place
in the commonwealth, that Abraham had in his own family.

*Abraham sole judge and interpreter of what God spake.*
There ariseth also from the same, a third point; that as none
but Abraham in his family, so none but the sovereign in a
Christian commonwealth, can take notice what is, or what
is not the word of God. For God spake only to Abraham;
and it was he only, that was able to know what God said, and
to interpret the same to his family: and therefore also, they
that have the place of Abraham in a commonwealth, are the
only interpreters of what God hath spoken.

*The authority of Moses, whereon grounded.* The same
covenant was renewed with Isaac; and afterwards with Jacob;
but afterwards no more, till the Israelites were freed from the
Egyptians, and arrived at the foot of Mount Sinai: and then
it was renewed by Moses, (as I have said before, chap. 35)
in such manner, as they became from that time forward the
peculiar kingdom of God; whose lieutenant was Moses, for
his own time; and the succession to that office was settled
upon Aaron, and his heirs after him, to be to God a sacerdotal kingdom for ever.

By this constitution, a kingdom is acquired to God. But
seeing Moses had no authority to govern the Israelites, as a
successor to the right of Abraham, because he could not
claim it by inheritance; it appeareth not as yet, that the
people were obliged to take him for God's lieutenant, longer
than they believed that God spake unto him. And therefore
his authority, notwithstanding the covenant they made with
God, depended yet merely upon the opinion they had of his

sanctity, and of the reality of his conferences with God, and the verity of his miracles; which opinion coming to change, they were no more obliged to take any thing for the law of God, which he propounded to them in God's name. We are therefore to consider, what other ground there was, of their obligation to obey him. For it could not be the commandment of God that could oblige them; because God spake not to them immediately, but by the mediation of Moses himself: and our Saviour saith of himself, (*John* v. 31) *If I bear witness of myself, my witness is not true;* much less if Moses bear witness of himself, especially in a claim of kingly power over God's people, ought his testimony to be received. His authority therefore, as the authority of all other princes, must be grounded on the consent of the people, and their promise to obey him. And so it was: for *the people* (*Exod.* xx. 18, 19) *when they saw the thunderings, and the lightnings, and the noise of the trumpets, and the mountain smoking, removed, and stood afar off. And they said unto Moses, speak thou with us, and we will hear, but let not God speak with us lest we die.* Here was their promise of obedience; and by this it was they obliged themselves to obey whatsoever he should deliver unto them for the commandment of God.

*Moses was, under God, sovereign of the Jews all his own time, though Aaron had the priesthood.* And notwithstanding the covenant constituted a sacerdotal kingdom, that is to say, a kingdom hereditary to Aaron; yet that is to be understood of the succession after Moses should be dead. For whosoever ordereth and establisheth the policy, as first founder of a commonwealth, be it monarchy, aristocracy, or democracy, must needs have sovereign power over the people all the while he is doing of it. And that Moses had that power all his own time, is evidently affirmed in the Scripture. First, in the text last before cited, because the people promised obedience, not to Aaron, but to him. Secondly, (*Exod.* xxiv. 1, 2) *And God said unto Moses, Come up unto the Lord, thou and Aaron, Nadab and Abihu, and seventy of the Elders of Israel. And Moses alone shall come near the Lord, but they shall not come nigh, neither shall the people go up with him.* By which it is plain, that Moses, who was alone called up to God (and not Aaron, nor the other priests, nor the seventy elders, nor the people who were forbidden to come up) was alone he, that represented to the Israelites the person of God, that is to say, was their sole sovereign under God. And though afterwards it be said (verses 9, 10) *Then went up Moses and Aaron, Nadab and Abihu, and seventy of the* *elders of Israel, and they saw the God of Israel, and there* *was under his feet, as it were a paved work of a sapphire* *stone, &c.;* yet this was not till after Moses had been with God before, and had brought to the people the words which God had said to him. He only went for the business of the people; the others, as the nobles of his retinue, were admitted for honour to that special grace, which was not allowed to the people; which was, as in the verse after appeareth, to see God and live, *God laid not his hand upon them, they saw* *God and did eat and drink,* that is, did live: but did not carry any commandment from him to the people. Again, it is everywhere said, *the Lord spake unto Moses,* as in all other occasions of government, so also in the ordering of the ceremonies of religion, contained in chapters xxv, xxvi, xxvii, xxviii, xxix, xxx, and xxxi of *Exodus,* and throughout *Leviticus:* to Aaron seldom. The calf that Aaron made, Moses threw into the fire. Lastly, the question of the authority of Aaron, by occasion of his and Miriam's mutiny against Moses, was (*Numb.* xii) judged by God himself for Moses. So also in the question between Moses and the people, who had the right of governing the people, when Korah, Dathan, and Abiram, and two hundred and fifty princes of the assembly, *gathered themselves together (Numb.* xvi. 3) *against* *Moses, and against Aaron, and said unto them, ye take too* *much upon you, seeing all the congregation are holy, every* *one of them, and the Lord is amongst them, why lift you up* *yourselves above the congregation of the Lord?* God caused the earth to swallow Korah, Dathan, and Abiram, with their wives and children, alive, and consumed those two hundred and fifty princes with fire. Therefore neither Aaron, nor the people, nor any aristocracy of the chief princes of the people, but Moses alone had next under God the sovereignty over the Israelites: and that not only in causes of civil policy, but also of religion: for Moses only spake with God, and therefore only could tell the people what it was that God required at their hands. No man upon pain of death might be so presumptuous as to approach the mountain where God talked with Moses. *Thou shalt set bounds* (saith the Lord, *Exod.* xix. 12) *to the people round about, and say, Take heed to yourselves that you go not up into the Mount, or touch the border of it; whosoever toucheth the Mount shall surely be put to* *death.* And again (verse 21) *Go down, charge the people,* *lest they break through unto the Lord to gaze.* Out of which we may conclude, that whosoever in a Christian commonwealth holdeth the place of Moses, is the sole messenger of God, and interpreter of his commandments. And according hereunto, no man ought in the interpretation of the Scripture to proceed further than the bounds which are set by their several sovereigns. For the Scriptures, since God now speaketh in them, are the Mount Sinai; the bounds whereof are the laws of them that represent God's person on earth. To look upon them, and therein to behold the wondrous works of God, and learn to fear him, is allowed; but to interpret them, that is, to pry into what God saith to him whom he appointeth to govern under him, and make themselves judges whether he govern as God commandeth him, or not, is to transgress the bounds God hath set us, and to gaze upon God irreverently.

*All spirits were subordinate to the spirit of Moses.* There was no prophet in the time of Moses, nor pretender to the spirit of God, but such as Moses had approved and authorized. For there were in his time but seventy men, that are said to prophesy by the spirit of God, and these were all of Moses his election; concerning whom God said to Moses, (*Numb.* xi. 16) *Gather to me seventy of the elders of Israel, whom thou knowest to be the elders of the people.* To these God imparted his spirit; but it was not a different spirit from that of Moses; for it is said (verse 25) *God came down in a cloud, and took of the spirit that was upon Moses, and gave it to the seventy elders.* But as I have shown before (chap. 36) by *spirit,* is understood the *mind;* so that the sense of the place is no other than this, that God endued them with a mind conformable and subordinate to that of Moses, that they might prophesy, that is to say, speak to the people in God's name, in such manner, as to set forward, as ministers of Moses and by his authority, such doctrine as was agreeable to Moses his doctrine. For they were but ministers; and when two of them prophesied in the camp, it was thought a new and unlawful thing; and as it is in verses 27 and 28 of the same chapter, they were accused of it, and Joshua advised Moses to forbid them, as not knowing that it was by Moses his spirit that they prophesied. By which it is manifest, that no subject ought to pretend to prophesy, or to the spirit, in opposition to the doctrine established by him whom God hath set in the place of Moses.

*After Moses the sovereignty was in the high-priest.* Aaron being dead, and after him also Moses, the kingdom, as being a sacerdotal kingdom, descended by virtue of the covenant, to Aaron's son Eleazar the high-priest: and God declared him, next under himself, for sovereign, at the same time that he appointed Joshua for the General of their army. For thus God saith expressly (*Numb.* xxvii. 21) concerning Joshua: *He shall stand before Eleazar the priest, who shall ask counsel for him before the Lord; at his word shall they go out, and at his word they shall come in, both he, and all the children of Israel with him.* Therefore the supreme power of making war and peace, was in the priest. The supreme power of judicature belonged also to the high-priest: for the book of the law was in their keeping; and the priests and Levites only were the subordinate judges in causes civil, as appears in *Deut.* xvii. 8, 9, 10. And for the manner of God's worship, there was never doubt made, but that the high-priest till the time of Saul, had the supreme authority. Therefore the civil and ecclesiastical power were both joined together in one and the same person, the high-priest; and ought to be so, in whosoever governeth by divine right, that is, by authority immediate from God.

*Of the sovereign power between the time of Joshua and of Saul.* After the death of Joshua, till the time of Saul, the time between is noted frequently in the Book of *Judges, That there was in those days no king in Israel;* and sometimes with this addition, that *every man did that which was right in his own eyes.* By which is to be understood, that where it is said, *there was no king,* is meant, *there was no sovereign power* in Israel. And so it was, if we consider the act and exercise of such power. For after the death of Joshua and Eleazar, *there arose another generation* (*Judges* ii. 10, 11) *that knew not the Lord, nor the works which he had done for Israel, but did evil in the sight of the Lord, and served Baalim.* And the Jews had that quality which St. Paul noteth, *to look for a sign,* not only before they would submit themselves to the government of Moses, but also after they had obliged themselves by their submission. Whereas signs and miracles had for end to procure faith, not to keep men from violating it, when they have once given it; for to that men are obliged by the law of nature. But if we consider not the exercise, but the right of governing, the sovereign power was still in the high-priest. Therefore whatsoever obedience was yielded to any of the Judges, who were men chosen by God extraordinarily to save his rebellious subjects out of the hands of the enemy, it cannot be drawn into argument against the right the high-priest had to the sovereign power, in all matters both of policy and religion. And neither the Judges nor Samuel himself had an ordinary, but an extraordinary calling to the government; and were obeyed by the Israelites, not out of duty, but out of reverence to their favour with God, appearing in their wisdom, courage, or felicity. Hitherto therefore the right of regulating both the policy, and the religion, were inseparable.

*Of the rights of the kings of Israel.* To the Judges succeeded kings: and whereas before, all authority, both in religion and policy, was in the high-priest; so now it was all in the king. For the sovereignty over the people, which was before, not only by virtue of the divine power, but also by a particular pact of the Israelites, in God, and next under him, in the high-priest, as his vice-gerent on earth, was cast off by the people, with the consent of God himself. For when they said to Samuel (1 *Sam.* viii. 5) *Make us a king to judge us like all the nations,* they signified that they would no more be governed by the commands that should be laid upon them by the priest, in the name of God; but by one that should command them in the same manner that all other nations were commanded; and consequently in deposing the high-priest of royal authority, they deposed that peculiar government of God. And yet God consented to it, saying to Samuel (1 *Sam.* viii. 7) *Hearken unto the voice of the people, in all that they shall say unto thee; for they have not rejected thee, but they have rejected me, that I should not reign over them.* Having therefore rejected God, in whose right the priests governed, there was no authority left to the priests, but such as the king was pleased to allow them; which was more or less, according as the kings were good or evil. And for the government of civil affairs, it is manifest, it was all in the hands of the king. For in the same chapter, (verse 20), they say *they will be like all the nations; that their king shall be their judge, and go before them, and fight their battles;* that is, he shall have the whole authority, both in peace and war. In which is contained also the ordering of religion: for there was no other word of God in that time, by which to regulate religion, but the law of Moses, which was their civil law. Besides, we read (1 *Kings* ii. 27) that *Solomon thrust out Abiathar from being priest before the Lord:* he had therefore authority over the high-priest, as over any other subject; which is a great mark of supremacy in religion. And we read also, (1 *Kings* viii) that he dedicated the Temple; that he blessed the people; and that he himself in person made that excellent prayer, used in the consecration of all churches and houses of prayer; which is another great mark of supremacy in religion. Again, we read (2 *Kings* xxii) that when there was question concerning the Book of the Law found in the Temple, the same was not decided by the high-priest, but Josiah sent both him and others to enquire concerning it, of Huldah, the prophetess; which is another mark of supremacy in religion. Lastly, we read (1 *Chron.* xxvi. 30) that David made Hashabiah and his brethren, Hebronites, officers of Israel among them westward, *in all the business of the Lord, and in the service of the king.* Likewise (verse 32) that he made other Hebronites, *rulers over the Reubenites, the Gadites, and the half tribe of Manasseh* (these were the rest of Israel that dwelt beyond Jordan) *for every matter pertaining to God, and affairs of the king.* Is not this full power, both *temporal* and *spiritual,* as they call it that would divide it? To conclude; from the first institution of God's kingdom, to the captivity, the supremacy of religion was in the same hand with that of the civil sovereignty; and the priest's office after the election of Saul, was not magisterial, but ministerial.

*The practice of supremacy in religion was not, in the time of the kings, according to the right thereof.* Notwithstanding the government both in policy and religion, were joined, first in the high-priests, and afterwards in the kings, so far forth as concerned the right; yet it appeareth by the same holy history, that the people understood it not: but there being amongst them a great part, and probably the greatest part, that no longer than they saw great miracles, or, what is equivalent to a miracle, great abilities, or great felicity in the enterprises of their governors, gave sufficient credit either to the fame of Moses or to the colloquies between God and the priests; they took occasion, as oft as their governors displeased them, by blaming sometimes the policy, sometimes the religion, to change the government or revolt from their obedience at their pleasure: and from thence proceeded from time to time the civil troubles, divisions, and calamities of the nation. As for example, after the death of Eleazar and Joshua, the next generation which had not seen the wonders of God, but were left to their own weak reason, not knowing themselves obliged by the covenant of a sacerdotal kingdom, regarded no more the commandment of the priest nor any law of Moses, but did every man that which was right in his own eyes, and obeyed in civil affairs such men, as from time to time they thought able to deliver them from the neighbour nations that oppressed them; and consulted not with God, as they ought to do, but with such men or women, as they guessed to be prophets by their predictions of things to come; and though they had an idol in their chapel, yet if they had a Levite for their chaplain, they made account they worshipped the God of Israel.

And afterwards when they demanded a king after the manner of the nations; yet it was not with a design to depart from the worship of God their king; but despairing of the justice of the sons of Samuel, they would have a king to judge them in civil actions; but not that they would allow their king to change the religion which they thought was recommended to them by Moses. So that they always kept in store a pretext, either of justice or religion, to discharge themselves of their obedience, whensoever they had hope to prevail. Samuel was displeased with the people, for that they desired a king; for God was their king already, and Samuel had but an authority under him; yet did Samuel, when Saul observed not his counsel, in destroying Agag as God had commanded, anoint another king, namely David, to take the succession from his heirs. Rehoboam was no idolater; but when the people thought him an oppressor, that civil pretence carried from him ten tribes to Jeroboam an idolater. And generally through the whole history of the kings, as well of Judah as of Israel, there were prophets that always controlled the kings, for transgressing the religion; and sometimes also for errors of state; as Jehosaphat was reproved (2 *Chron.* xix. 2) by the prophet Jehu, for aiding the king of Israel against the Syrians; and Hezekiah, by Isaiah, (xxxix. 3-7) for shewing his treasures to the ambassadors of Babylon. By all which it appeareth, that though the power both of state and religion were in the kings; yet none of them were uncontrolled in the use of it, but such as were gracious for their own natural abilities or felicities. So that from the practice of those times, there can no argument be drawn, that the right of supremacy in religion was not in the kings, unless we place it in the prophets, and conclude, that because Hezekiah praying to the Lord before the cherubims, was not answered from thence, nor then, but afterwards by the prophet Isaiah, therefore Isaiah was supreme head of the church; or because Josiah consulted Huldah the prophetess, concerning the Book of the Law, that therefore neither he nor the high-priest, but Huldah the prophetess, had the supreme authority in matter of religion; which I think is not the opinion of any doctor.

*After the captivity, the Jews had no settled commonwealth.* During the captivity, the Jews had no commonwealth at all: and after their return, though they renewed their covenant with God, yet there was no promise made of obedience, neither to Esdras, nor to any other: and presently after, they became subjects to the Greeks, from whose customs and demonology, and from the doctrine of the Cabalists, their religion became much corrupted: in such sort as nothing can be gathered from their confusion, both in state and religion, concerning the supremacy in either. And therefore so far forth as concerneth the Old Testament, we may conclude, that whosoever had the sovereignty of the commonwealth amongst the Jews, the same had also the supreme authority in matter of God's external worship, and represented God's person; that is, the person of God the Father; though he were not called by the name of Father, till such time as he sent into the world his son Jesus Christ, to redeem mankind from their sins, and bring them into his everlasting kingdom, to be saved for evermore. Of which we are to speak in the chapter following.

# Chapter 41

## Of the Office of Our Blessed Saviour

*Three parts of the office of Christ.* We find in Holy Scripture three parts of the office of the Messiah: the first of a *Redeemer* or *Saviour;* the second of a *pastor, counsellor,* or *teacher,* that is, of a prophet sent from God to convert such as God hath elected to salvation: the third of a *king,* an *eternal king,* but under his Father, as Moses and the high-priests were in their several times. And to these three parts are correspondent three times. For our redemption he wrought at his first coming, by the sacrifice wherein he offered up himself for our sins upon the cross: our conversion he wrought partly then in his own person, and partly worketh now by his ministers, and will continue to work till his coming again. And after his coming again, shall begin that his glorious reign over his elect, which is to last eternally.

*His office as a Redeemer.* To the office of a Redeemer, that is, of one that payeth the ransom of sin, which ransom is death, it appertaineth, that he was sacrificed, and thereby bare upon his own head and carried away from us our iniquities, in such sort as God had required. Not that the death of one man, though without sin, can satisfy for the offences of all men, in the rigour of justice, but in the mercy of God, that ordained such sacrifices for sin, as he was pleased in his mercy to accept. In the old law (as we may read, *Levit.* xvi) the Lord required that there should, every year once, be made an atonement for the sins of all Israel, both priests and others; for the doing whereof, Aaron alone was to sacrifice for himself and the priests a young bullock; and for the rest of the people, he was to receive from them two young goats, of which he was to *sacrifice* one; but as for the other, which was the *scape-goat,* he was to lay his hands on the head thereof, and by a confession of the iniquities of the people, to lay them all on that head, and then by some opportune man, to cause the goat to be led into the wilderness, and there to *escape,* and carry away with him the iniquities of the people. As the sacrifice of the one goat was a sufficient, because an acceptable, price for the ransom of all Israel; so the death of the Messiah, is a sufficient price for the sins of all mankind, because there was no more required. Our Saviour Christ's sufferings seem to be here figured, as clearly as in the oblation of Isaac, or in any other type of him in the Old Testament. He was both the sacrificed goat, and the scapegoat; *he was oppressed, and he was afflicted (Isaiah liii. 7); he opened not his mouth; he is brought as a lamb to the slaughter, and as a sheep is dumb before the shearer, so he opened not his mouth:* here is he the *sacrificed goat. He hath borne our griefs* (verse 4), *and carried our sorrows:* and again, (verse 6), *the Lord hath laid upon him the iniquities of us all:* and so he is the *scape-goat. He was cut off from the land of the living* (verse 8) *for the transgression of my people:* there again he is the *sacrificed goat.* And again, (verse 11) *he shall bear their sins:* he is the *scape-goat.* Thus is the lamb of God equivalent to both those goats; sacrificed, in that he died; and escaping, in his resurrection; being raised opportunely by his Father, and removed from the habitation of men in his ascension.

*Christ's kingdom not of this world.* For as much therefore, as he that *redeemeth* hath no title to the *thing redeemed,* before *the redemption,* and ransom paid; and this ransom was the death of the Redeemer; it is manifest, that our Saviour, as man, was not king of those that he redeemed, before he suffered death; that is, during that time he conversed bodily on the earth. I say, he was not then king in present, by virtue of the pact, which the faithful make with him in baptism. Nevertheless, by the renewing of their pact with God in baptism, they were obliged to obey him for king, under his Father, whensoever he should be pleased to take the kingdom upon him. According whereunto, our Saviour himself expressly saith, *(John* xviii. 36) *My kingdom is not of this world.* Now seeing the Scripture maketh mention but of two worlds; this that is now, and shall remain unto the day of judgment, which is therefore also called the *last day;* and that which shall be after the day of judgment, when there shall be a new heaven, and a new earth: the kingdom of Christ is not to begin till the general resurrection. And that is it which our Saviour saith, *(Matt.* xvi. 27) *The Son of man shall come in the glory of his Father, with his angels; and then he shall reward every man according to his works.* To reward every man according to his works, is to execute the office of a king; and this is not to be till he come in the glory of his Father, with his angels. When our Saviour saith, *(Matt.* xxiii. 2, 3) *The Scribes and Pharisees sit in Moses' seat; all therefore whatso-*

*ever they bid you do, that observe and do;* he declared plainly, that he ascribed kingly power, for that time, not to himself, but to them. And so he doth also, where he saith (*Luke* xii. 14) *Who made me a judge or divider over you?* And (*John* xii. 47) *I came not to judge the world, but to save the world.* And yet our Saviour came into this world that he might be a king and a judge in the world to come: for he was the Messiah, that is, the Christ, that is, the anointed priest, and the sovereign prophet of God; that is to say, he was to have all the power that was in Moses the prophet, in the high-priests that succeeded Moses, and in the kings that succeeded the priests. And St. John says expressly (chap. v. verse 22) *the Father judgeth no man, but hath committed all judgment to the Son.* And this is not repugnant to that other place, *I came not to judge the world:* for this is spoken of the world present, the other of the world to come; as also where it is said, that at the second coming of Christ, (*Matt.* xix. 28) *Ye that have followed me in the regeneration, when the Son of Man shall sit in the throne of his glory, ye shall also sit on twelve thrones, judging the twelve tribes of Israel.*

*The end of Christ's coming was to renew the covenant of the kingdom of God, and to persuade the elect to embrace it, which was the second part of his office.* If then Christ, whilst he was on earth, had no kingdom in this world, to what end was his first coming? It was to restore unto God, by a new covenant, the kingdom, which being his by the old covenant, had been cut off by the rebellion of the Israelites in the election of Saul. Which to do, he was to preach unto them, that he was the *Messiah*, that is, the king promised to them by the prophets; and to offer himself in sacrifice for the sins of them that should by faith submit themselves thereto; and in case the nation generally should refuse him, to call to his obedience such as should believe in him amongst the Gentiles. So that there are two parts of our Saviour's office during his abode upon the earth: one to proclaim himself the Christ; and another by teaching, and by working of miracles, to persuade and prepare men to live so, as to be worthy of the immortality believers were to enjoy, at such time as he should come in majesty to take possession of his Father's kingdom. And therefore it is, that the time of his preaching is often by himself called the *regeneration;* which is not properly a kingdom, and thereby a warrant to deny obedience to the magistrates that then were; for he commanded to obey those that sat then in Moses' chair, and to pay tribute to Cæsar; but only an earnest of the kingdom of God that was to come, to those to whom God had given the grace to be his disciples, and to believe in him; for which cause the godly are said to be already in the *kingdom of grace*, as naturalized in that heavenly kingdom.

*The preaching of Christ not contrary to the then law of the Jews, nor of Cæsar.* Hitherto, therefore, there is nothing done or taught by Christ, that tendeth to the diminution of the civil right of the Jews or of Cæsar. For as touching the commonwealth which then was amongst the Jews, both they that bare rule amongst them, and they that were governed, did all expect the Messiah and kingdom of God; which they could not have done, if their laws had forbidden him, when he came, to manifest and declare himself. Seeing therefore he did nothing, but by preaching and miracles go about to prove himself to be that Messiah, he did therein nothing against their laws. The kingdom he claimed was to be in another world: he taught all men to obey in the meantime them that sat in Moses' seat: he allowed them to give Cæsar his tribute, and refused to take upon himsef to be a judge. How then could his words or actions be seditious, or tend to the overthrow of their then civil government? But God having determined his sacrifice for the reduction of his elect to their former covenanted obedience, for the means, whereby he would bring the same to effect, made use of their malice and ingratitude. Nor was it contrary to the laws of Cæsar. For though Pilate himself, to gratify the Jews, delivered him to be crucified; yet before he did so, he pronounced openly, that he found no fault in him: and put for title of his condemnation, not as the Jews required, *that he pretended to be king;* but simply, *that he was king of the Jews;* and notwithstanding their clamour, refused to alter it; saying, *What I have written, I have written.*

*The third part of his office was to be king, under his Father, of the elect.* As for the third part of his office, which was to be *king,* I have already shewn that his kingdom was not to begin till the resurrection. But then he shall be king, not only as God, in which sense he is king already, and ever shall be, of all the earth, in virtue of his omnipotence; but also peculiarly of his own elect, by virtue of the pact they make with him in their baptism. And therefore it is, that our Saviour saith (*Matt.* xix. 28) that his apostles should sit upon twelve thrones, judging the twelve tribes of Israel, *When the*

*Son of Man shall sit in the throne of his glory:* whereby he signified that he should reign then in his human nature; and (*Matt.* xvi. 27) *The Son of Man shall come in the glory of his Father, with his angels, and then he shall reward every man according to his works.* The same we may read, *Mark* xiii. 26, and xiv. 62; and more expressly for the time, *Luke* xxii. 29, 30, *I appoint unto you a kingdom, as my Father hath appointed to me, that you may eat and drink at my table in my kingdom, and sit on thrones judging the twelve tribes of Israel.* By which it is manifest, that the kingdom of Christ appointed to him by his Father, is not to be before the Son of Man shall come in glory, and make his apostles judges of the twelve tribes of Israel. But a man may here ask, seeing there is no marriage in the kingdom of heaven, whether men shall then eat and drink? What eating therefore is meant in this place? This is expounded by our Saviour (*John* vi. 27), where he saith, *Labour not for the meat which perisheth, but for that meat which endureth unto everlasting life, which the Son of Man shall give you.* So that by eating at Christ's table, is meant the eating of the tree of life; that is to say, the enjoying of immortality, in the kingdom of the Son of Man. By which places and many more, it is evident that our Saviour's kingdom is to be exercised by him in his human nature.

*Christ's authority in the kingdom of God, subordinate to that of his Father.* Again, he is to be king then, no otherwise than as subordinate or vicegerent of God the Father, as Moses was in the wilderness; and as the high-priests were before the reign of Saul; and as the kings were after it. For it is one of the prophecies concerning Christ, that he should be like, in office, to Moses: *I will raise them up a prophet,* saith the Lord (*Deut.* xviii. 18) *from amongst their brethren, like unto thee, and will put my words into his mouth;* and this similitude with Moses, is also apparent in the actions of our Saviour himself, whilst he was conversant on earth. For as Moses chose twelve princes of the tribes, to govern under him; so did our Saviour choose twelve apostles, who shall sit on twelve thrones, and judge the twelve tribes of Israel. And as Moses authorized seventy elders, to receive the Spirit of God, and to prophesy to the people, that is, as I have said before, to speak unto them in the name of God; so our Saviour also ordained seventy disciples, to preach his kingdom and salvation to all nations. And as when a complaint was made to Moses, against those of the seventy that prophesied in the camp of Israel, he justified them in it, as being subservient therein to his government; so also our Saviour, when St. John complained to him of a certain man that cast out devils in his name, justified him therein, saying, (*Luke* ix. 50) *Forbid him not, for he that is not against us, is on our part.*

Again, our Saviour resembled Moses in the institution of *sacraments*, both of *admission* into the kingdom of God, and of *commemoration* of his deliverance of his elect from their miserable condition. As the children of Israel had for sacrament of their reception into the kingdom of God, before the time of Moses, the rite of *circumcision*, which rite having been omitted in the wilderness, was again restored as soon as they came into the Land of Promise; so also the Jews, before the coming of our Saviour, had a rite of *baptizing*, that is, of washing with water, all those that being Gentiles embraced the God of Israel. This rite St. John the Baptist used in the reception of all them that gave their names to the Christ, whom he preached to be already come into the world; and our Saviour instituted the same for a sacrament to be taken by all that believed in him. From what cause the rite of baptism first proceeded, is not expressed formally in the Scripture; but it may be probably thought to be an imitation of the law of Moses, concerning leprosy; wherein the leprous man was commanded to be kept out of the camp of Israel for a certain time; after which time being judged by the priest to be clean, he was admitted into the camp after a solemn washing. And this may therefore be a type of the washing in baptism; wherein such men as are cleansed of the leprosy of sin by faith, are received into the Church with the solemnity of baptism. There is another conjecture, drawn from the ceremonies of the Gentiles, in a certain case that rarely happens: and that is, when a man that was thought dead chanced to recover, other men made scruple to converse with him, as they would do to converse with a ghost, unless he were received again into the number of men by washing, as children new-born were washed from the uncleanness of their nativity; which was a kind of new birth. This ceremony of the Greeks, in the time that Judea was under the dominion of Alexander and the Greeks his successors, may probably enough have crept into the religion of the Jews. But seeing it is not likely our Saviour would countenance a heathen rite, it is most likely it proceeded from the legal ceremony of washing after leprosy. And for the other sacrament of eating the *Paschal lamb,* it is manifestly imitated in the sacrament of the *Lord's Supper;* in which the breaking of the bread, and the pouring out of the wine, do keep in memory our deliverance from the misery of sin, by Christ's passion, as the eating of the Paschal lamb kept in memory the deliverance of the Jews out of the bondage of Egypt. Seeing therefore the authority of Moses was but subordinate, and he but a lieutenant of God; it followeth that Christ, whose authority, as man, was to be like that of Moses, was no more but subordinate to the authority of his Father. The same is more expressly signified, by that that he teacheth us to pray, *Our Father, let thy kingdom come;* and, *For thine is the kingdom, the power and the glory;* and by that it is said, that *He shall come in the glory of his Father;* and by that which St. Paul saith, (1 *Cor.* xv. 24) *then cometh the end, when he shall have delivered up the kingdom to God, even the Father;* and by many other most express places.

*One and the same God is the person represented by Moses and Christ.* Our Saviour, therefore, both in teaching and reigning, representeth, as Moses did, the person of God; which God from that time forward, but not before, is called the Father; and being still one and the same substance, is one person as represented by Moses, and another person as represented by his son the Christ. For *person* being a relative to a *representer,* it is consequent to plurality of representers, that there be a plurality of persons, though of one and the same substance.

# Chapter 42

## Of Power Ecclesiastical

FOR the understanding of POWER ECCLESIASTICAL, what, and in whom it is, we are to distinguish the time from the ascension of our Saviour, into two parts; one before the conversion of kings, and men endued with sovereign civil power; the other after their conversion. For it was long after the ascension, before any king or civil sovereign embraced and publicly allowed the teaching of Christian religion.

*Of the holy spirit that fell on the apostles.* And for the time between, it is manifest, that the *power ecclesiastical* was in the apostles; and after them in such as were by them ordained to preach the gospel, and to convert men to Christianity, and to direct them that were converted in the way of salvation; and after these, the power was delivered again to others by these ordained, and this was done by imposition of hands upon such as were ordained; by which was signified the giving of the Holy Spirit, or Spirit of God, to those whom they ordained ministers of God, to advance his kingdom. So that imposition of hands was nothing else but the seal of their commission to preach Christ, and teach his doctrine; and the giving of the Holy Ghost by that ceremony of imposition of hands, was an imitation of that which Moses did. For Moses used the same ceremony to his minister Joshua, as we read (*Deut.* xxxiv. 9) *And Joshua the son of Nun was full of the spirit of wisdom; for Moses had laid his hands upon him.* Our Saviour therefore, between his resurrection and ascension, gave his spirit to the apostles; first, by *breathing on them, and saying,* (*John* xx. 22) *Receive ye the Holy Spirit;* and after his ascension (*Acts* ii. 2, 3) by sending down upon them *a mighty wind, and cloven tongues of fire;* and not by imposition of hands; as neither did God lay his hands on Moses: and his apostles afterward transmitted the same spirit by imposition of hands, as Moses did to Joshua. So that it is manifest hereby, in whom the power ecclesiastical continually remained, in those first times where there was not any Christian commonwealth; namely, in them that received the same from the apostles, by successive laying on of hands.

*Of the Trinity.* Here we have the person of God born now

the third time. For as Moses, and the high-priests, were God's representative in the Old Testament; and our Saviour himself, as man, during his abode on earth: so the Holy Ghost, that is to say the apostles and their successors, in the office of preaching and teaching, that had received the Holy Spirit, have represented him ever since. But a person, as I have shown before, (chap. 13) is he that is represented, as often as he is represented; and therefore God, who has been represented, that is personated, thrice, may properly enough be said to be three persons; though neither the word *Person,* nor *Trinity,* be ascribed to him in the Bible. *St. John,* indeed (1 *John* v. 7) saith, *There be three that bear witness in heaven, the Father, the Word, and the Holy Spirit; and these three are One.* But· this disagreeth not, but accordeth fitly with three persons in the proper signification of persons; which is, that which is represented by another. For so God the Father, as represented by Moses, is one person; and as represented by his Son, another person; and as represented by the apostles, and by the doctors that taught by authority from them derived, is a third person; and yet every person here, is the person of one and the same God. But a man may here ask, what it was whereof these three bear witness. *St. John* therefore tells us (verse 11) that they bear witness, that *God hath given us eternal life in his Son.* Again, if it should be asked, wherein that testimony appeareth, the answer is easy; for he hath testified the same by the miracles he wrought, first by Moses; secondly, by his Son himself; and lastly by his apostles, that had received the Holy Spirit; all which in their times represented the person of God, and either prophesied or preached Jesus Christ. And as for the apostles, it was the character of the apostleship, in the twelve first and great apostles, to bear witness of his resurrection; as appeareth expressly (*Acts* i. 21, 22), where St. Peter, when a new apostle was to be chosen in the place of Judas Iscariot, useth these words, *Of these men which have companied with us all the time that the Lord Jesus went in and out amongst us, beginning at the baptism of John, unto that same day that he was taken up from us, must one be ordained to be a witness with us of his resurrection:* which words interpret the *bearing of witness,* mentioned by St. John. There is in the same place mentioned another Trinity of witnesses in earth. For (1 *John* v. 8) he saith, *there are three that bear witness in earth, the Spirit, and the water, and the blood, and these three agree in one:* that is to say, the graces of God's spirit, and the two sacraments, baptism, and the Lord's supper, which all agree in one testimony to assure the consciences of believers, of eternal life; of which testimony he saith (verse 10) *He that believeth on the Son of man hath the witness in himself.* In this Trinity on earth, the unity is not of the thing; for the spirit, the water, and the blood, are not the same substance, though they give the same testimony: but in the Trinity of heaven, the persons are the persons of one and the same God, though represented in three different times and occasions. To conclude, the doctrine of the Trinity, as far as can be gathered directly from the Scripture, is in substance this, that God who is always one and the same, was the person represented by Moses; the person represented by his Son incarnate; and the person represented by the apostles. As represented by the apostles, the Holy Spirit, by which they spake, is God; as represented by his Son, that was God and man, the Son is that God; as represented by Moses and the high-priests, the Father, that is to say, the Father of our Lord Jesus Christ, is that God. From whence we may gather the reason why those names *Father, Son,* and *Holy Spirit,* in the signification of the Godhead, are never used in the Old Testament: for they are persons, that is, they have their names from representing; which could not be, till divers men had represented God's person in ruling or in directing under him.

Thus we see how the power ecclesiastical was left by our Saviour to the apostles; and how they were, to the end they might the better exercise that power, endued with the Holy Spirit, which is therefore called sometimes in the New Testament *paracletus,* which signifieth an *assister,* or one called to for help, though it be commonly translated a *comforter.* Let us now consider the power itself, what it was, and over whom.

*The power ecclesiastical is but the power to teach.* Cardinal Bellarmine, in his third general controversy, hath handled a great many questions concerning the ecclesiastical power of the pope of Rome; and begins with this, whether it ought to be monarchical, aristocratical, or democratical: all which sorts of power are sovereign and coercive. If now it should appear, that there is no coercive power left them by our Saviour, but only a power to proclaim the kingdom of Christ, and to persuade men to submit themselves thereunto; and by precepts and good counsel, to teach them that have submitted, what they are to do, that they may be received into the kingdom of God when it comes; and that the apostles, and other ministers of the Gospel, are our schoolmasters, and not our commanders, and their precepts not laws, but wholesome counsels: then were all that dispute in vain.

*An argument thereof, the power of Christ himself.* I have shown already, in the last chapter, that the kingdom of Christ is not of this world: therefore neither can his ministers, unless they be kings, require obedience in his name. For if the supreme king have not his regal power in this world; by what authority can obedience be required to his officers? *As my Father sent me,* so saith our Saviour, *(John* xx. 21) *I send you.* But our Saviour was sent to persuade the Jews to return to, and to invite the Gentiles to receive, the kingdom of his Father, and not to reign in majesty, no not as his Father's lieutenant, till the day of judgment.

*From the name of regeneration.* The time between the ascension and the general resurrection, is called, not a reigning, but a regeneration; that is, a preparation of men for the second and glorious coming of Christ, at the day of judgment; as appeareth by the words of our Saviour, *(Matt.* xix. 28), *You that have followed me in the regeneration, when the Son of man shall sit in the throne of his glory, you shall also sit upon twelve thrones;* and of St. Paul *(Eph.* vi. 15) *Having your feet shod with the preparation of the gospel of peace.*

*From the comparison of it, with fishing, leaven, seed.* And is compared by our Saviour, to fishing, that is, to winning men to obedience, not by coercion and punishing, but by persuasion: and therefore he said not to his apostles, he would make them so many Nimrods, *hunters of men; but fishers of men.* It is compared also to leaven, to sowing of seed, and to the multiplication of a grain of mustard-seed; by all which compulsion is excluded; and consequently there can in that time be no actual reigning. The work of Christ's ministers, is evangelization; that is, a proclamation of Christ, and a preparation for his second coming, as the evangelization of John the Baptist was a preparation to his first coming.

*From the nature of faith.* Again, the office of Christ's ministers in this world, is to make men believe and have faith in Christ; but faith hath no relation to, nor dependence at all upon compulsion or commandment; but only upon certainty or probability of arguments drawn from reason, or from something men believe already. Therefore the ministers of Christ in this world, have no power, by that title, to punish any man for not believing or for contradicting what they say; they have I say no power by that title of Christ's ministers, to punish such; but if they have sovereign civil power, by politic institution, then they may indeed lawfully punish any contradiction to their laws whatsoever: and St. Paul, of himself and other the then preachers of the gospel, saith in express words (2 *Cor.* i. 24), *We have no dominion over your faith, but are helpers of your joy.*

*From the authority Christ hath left to civil princes.* Another argument, that the ministers of Christ in this present world have no right of commanding, may be drawn from the lawful authority which Christ hath left to all princes, as well Christians as infidels. St. Paul saith (*Col.* iii. 20) *Children obey your parents in all things; for this is well pleasing to the Lord:* and (verse 22) *Servants, obey in all things your masters according to the flesh; not with eye-service, as men-pleasers, but in singleness of heart, as fearing the Lord;* this is spoken to them whose masters were infidels; and yet they are bidden to obey them *in all things.* And again, concerning obedience to princes (*Rom.* xiii the first six verses), exhorting *to be subject to the higher powers,* he saith, *that all power is ordained of God;* and *that we ought to be subject to them, not only for fear of incurring their wrath, but also for conscience sake.* And St. Peter (1 *Pet.* ii. 13, 14, 15), *Submit yourselves to every ordinance of man, for the Lord's sake, whether it be to the king, as supreme; or unto governors, as to them that be sent by him for the punishment of evil doers, and for the praise of them that do well; for so is the will of God.* And again St. Paul (*Titus* iii. 1), *Put men in mind to be subject to principalities and powers, and to obey magistrates.* These princes and powers, whereof St. Peter and St. Paul here speak, were all infidels: much more therefore we are to obey those Christians, whom God hath ordained to have sovereign power over us. How then can we be obliged to obey any minister of Christ, if he should command us to do any thing contrary to the command of the king, or other sovereign representant of the commonwealth whereof we are members, and by whom we look to be protected? It is therefore manifest, that Christ hath not left to his ministers in this world, unless they be also endued with civil authority, any authority to command other men.

*What Christians may do to avoid persecution.* But what, may some object, if a king, or a senate, or other sovereign person forbid us to believe in Christ? To this I answer, that such forbidding is of no effect; because belief and unbelief never follow men's commands. Faith is a gift of God, which man can neither give, nor take away by promise of rewards, or menaces of torture. And if it be further asked, what if we be commanded by our lawful prince to say with our tongue, we believe not; must we obey such command? Profession with the tongue is but an external thing, and no more than any other gesture whereby we signify our obedience; and wherein a Christian, holding firmly in his heart the faith of Christ, hath the same liberty which the prophet Elisha allowed to Naaman the Syrian. Naaman was converted in his heart to the God of Israel; for he saith (2 *Kings* v. 17, 18) *Thy servant will henceforth offer neither burnt offering nor sacrifice unto other gods, but unto the Lord. In this thing the Lord pardon thy servant, that when my master goeth into the house of Rimmon to worship there, and he leaneth on my hand, and I bow myself in the house of Rimmon: when I bow down myself in the house of Rimmon, the Lord pardon thy servant in this thing.* This the prophet approved, and bid him *Go in peace.* Here Naaman believed in his heart; but by bowing before the idol Rimmon, he denied the true God in effect, as much as if he had done it with his lips. But then what shall we answer to our Saviour's saying, (*Matt.* x. 33) *Whosoever denieth me before men, I will deny him before my Father which is in heaven.* This we may say, that whatsoever a subject, as Naaman was, is compelled to do in obedience to his sovereign, and doth it not in order to his own mind, but in order to the laws of his country, that action is not his, but his sovereign's; nor is it he that in this case denieth Christ before men, but his governor, and the law of his country. If any man shall accuse this doctrine, as repugnant to true and unfeigned Christianity; I ask him, in case there should be a subject in any Christian commonwealth, that should be inwardly in his heart of the Mahomedan religion, whether if his sovereign command him to be present at the divine service of the Christian church, and that on pain of death, he think that Mahomedan obliged in conscience to suffer death for that cause, rather than obey that command of his lawful prince. If he say, he ought rather to suffer death, then he authorizeth all private men to disobey their princes in maintenance of their religion, true or false: if he say, he ought to be obedient, then he alloweth to himself that which he denieth to another, contrary to the words of our Saviour, (*Luke* vi. 31) *Whatsoever you would that men should do unto you, that do ye unto them;* and contrary to the law of nature, which is the indubitable everlasting law of God, *Do not to another, that which thou wouldest not he should do unto thee.*

*Of martyrs.* But what then shall we say of all those martyrs we read of in the history of the Church, that they have needlessly cast away their lives? For answer hereunto, we are to distinguish the persons that have been for that cause put to death: whereof some have received a calling to preach, and profess the kingdom of Christ openly; others have had no such calling, nor more has been required of them than their own faith. The former sort, if they have been put to death, for bearing witness to this point, that Jesus Christ is risen from the dead, were true martyrs; for a *martyr* is, (to give the true definition of the word) a witness of the resurrection of Jesus the Messiah; which none can be but those that conversed with him on earth, and saw him after he was risen: for a witness must have seen what he testifieth, or else his testimony is not good. And that none but such can properly be called martyrs of Christ, is manifest out of the words of St. Peter, (*Acts* i. 21, 22) *Wherefore of these men which have companied with us all the time that the Lord Jesus went in and out amongst us, beginning from the baptism of John unto that same day he was taken up from us, must one be ordained to be a martyr* (that is a witness) *with us of his resurrection:* where we may observe, that he which is to be a witness of the truth of the resurrection of Christ, that is to say, of the truth of this fundamental article of Christian religion, that Jesus was the Christ, must be some disciple that conversed with him, and saw him before and after his resurrection; and consequently must be one of his original disciples: whereas they which were not so, can witness no more but that their antecessors said it, and are therefore but witnesses of other men's testimony; and are but second martyrs, or martyrs of Christ's witnesses.

He, that to maintain every doctrine which he himself draweth out of the history of our Saviour's life, and of the Acts or Epistles of the apostles, or which he believeth upon the authority of a private man, will oppose the laws and authority of the civil state, is very far from being a martyr of Christ, or a martyr of his martyrs. It is one article only, which to die for, meriteth so honourable a name; and that article is this, that *Jesus is the Christ;* that is to say, He that hath redeemed us, and shall come again to give us salvation, and eternal life in his glorious kingdom. To die for every tenet that serveth the ambition or profit of the clergy, is not required; nor is it the death of the witness, but the testimony itself that makes the martyr: for the word signifieth nothing else, but the man that beareth witness, whether he be put to death for his testimony, or not.

Also he that is not sent to preach this fundamental article, but taketh it upon him of his private authority, though he be a witness, and consequently a martyr, either primary of Christ, or secondary of his apostles, disciples, or their successors: yet is he not obliged to suffer death for that cause; because being not called thereto, it is not required at his hands; nor ought he to complain, if he loseth the reward he expecteth from those that never set him on work. None therefore can be a martyr, neither of the first nor second degree, that have not a warrant to preach Christ come in the flesh; that is to say, none, but such as are sent to the conversion of infidels. For no man is a witness to him that already believeth, and therefore needs no witness; but to them that deny, or doubt, or have not heard it. Christ sent his apostles, and his seventy disciples, with authority to preach; he sent not all that believed. And he sent them to unbelievers; *I send you,* saith he, (*Matt.* x. 16) *as sheep amongst wolves;* not as sheep to other sheep.

*Argument from the points of their commission.* Lastly, the points of their commission, as they are expressly set down in the gospel, contain, none of them, any authority over the congregation.

*To preach.* We have first (*Matt.* x. 6, 7) that the twelve apostles were sent *to the lost sheep of the house of Israel,* and commanded to preach *that the kingdom of God was at hand.* Now preaching, in the original, is that act, which a crier, herald, or other officer useth to do publicly in proclaiming of a king. But a crier hath not right to command any man. And (*Luke* x. 2) the seventy disciples are sent out as *Labourers, not as Lords of the harvest; and are bidden* (verse 9) to say, *The kingdom of God is come nigh unto you;* and by kingdom here is meant, not the kingdom of grace, but the kingdom of glory; for they are bidden (verses 11, 12) to denounce it to those cities which shall not receive them, as a threatening *that it shall be more tolerable in that day for Sodom, than for such a city.* And (*Matt.* xx. 28) our Saviour telleth his disciples, that sought priority of place, their office was to minister, *even as the Son of Man came, not to be ministered unto, but to minister.* Preachers therefore have not magisterial, but ministerial

power: *Be not called masters,* saith our Saviour, (*Matt.*
xxiii. 10) *for one is your master, even Christ.*

*And teach.* Another point of their commission, is, to *Teach
all nations;* as it is in *St. Matt.* xxviii. 19, or as in *St. Mark*
xvi. 15; *Go into all the world, and preach the gospel to every
creature.* Teaching therefore, and preaching, is the same thing.
For they that proclaim the coming of a king, must withal
make known by what right he cometh, if they mean men
shall submit themselves unto him: as St. Paul did to the
Jews of Thessalonica, when (*Acts* xvii. 2, 3) *three Sabbath
days he reasoned with them out of the Scriptures, opening,
and alleging that Christ must needs have suffered, and risen
again from the dead, and that this Jesus is Christ.* But to
teach out of the Old Testament that Jesus was Christ, that is
to say, king, and risen from the dead, is not to say that men
are bound, after they believe it, to obey those that tell them
so, against the laws and commands of their sovereigns; but
that they shall do wisely, to expect the coming of Christ hereafter, in patience and faith, with obedience to their present
magistrates.

*To baptize.* Another point of their commission, is to *baptize, in the name of the Father, and of the Son, and of the
Holy Ghost.* What is baptism? Dipping into water. But what
is it to dip a man into the water in the name of any thing?
The meaning of these words of baptism is this. He that is baptized, is dipped or washed, as a sign of becoming a new man,
and a loyal subject to that God, whose person was represented in old time by Moses, and the high-priests, when he
reigned over the Jews; and to Jesus Christ his Son, God and
Man, that hath redeemed us, and shall in his human nature
represent his Father's person in his eternal kingdom after the
resurrection; and to acknowledge the doctrine of the apostles,
who, assisted by the spirit of the Father and of the Son, were
left for guides to bring us into that kingdom, to be the only and
assured way thereunto. This being our promise in baptism;
and the authority of earthly sovereigns being not to be put
down till the day of judgment; for that is expressly affirmed
by St. Paul (1 *Cor.* xv. 22, 23, 24) where he saith, *As in
Adam all die, so in Christ all shall be made alive. But every
man in his own order, Christ the first fruits, afterward they
that are Christ's at his coming; then cometh the end, when
he shall have delivered up the kingdom to God, even the
Father, when he shall have put down all rule, and all authority and power:* it is manifest, that we do not in baptism

constitute over us another authority, by which our external actions are to be governed in this life; but promise to take the doctrine of the apostles for our direction in the way to life eternal.

*And to forgive, and retain sins.* The power of *remission and retention of sins,* called also the power of *loosing* and *binding,* and sometimes the *keys of the kingdom of heaven,* is a consequence of the authority to baptize, or refuse to baptize. For baptism is the sacrament of allegiance of them that are to be received into the kingdom of God; that is to say, into eternal life; that is to say, to remission of sin; for as eternal life was lost by the committing, so it is recovered by the remitting of men's sins. The end of baptism is remission of sins: and therefore St. Peter, when they that were converted by his sermon on the day of Pentecost, asked what they were to do, advised them (*Acts* ii. 38) to *repent, and be baptized in the name of Jesus, for the remission of sins.* And therefore, seeing to baptize is to declare the reception of men into God's kingdom; and to refuse to baptize is to declare their exclusion; it followeth, that the power to declare them cast out, or retained in it, was given to the same apostles, and their substitutes and successors. And therefore after our Saviour had breathed upon them, saying (*John* xx. 22) *Receive the Holy Ghost,* he added in the next verse, *Whosesoever sins ye remit, they are remitted unto them; and whosesoever sins ye retain, they are retained.* By which words, is not granted an authority to forgive or retain sins, simply and absolutely, as God forgiveth or retaineth them, who knoweth the heart of man, and truth of his penitence and conversion; but conditionally, to the penitent: and this forgiveness, or absolution, in case the absolved have but a feigned repentance, is thereby, without other act, or sentence of the absolved, made void, and hath no effect at all to salvation, but on the contrary to the aggravation of his sin. Therefore the apostles, and their successors, are to follow but the outward marks of repentance; which appearing, they have no authority to deny absolution; and if they appear not, they have no authority to absolve. The same also is to be observed in baptism: for to a converted Jew, or Gentile, the apostles had not the power to deny baptism; nor to grant it to the unpenitent. But seeing no man is able to discern the truth of another man's repentance, further than by external marks, taken from his words and actions, which are subject to hypocrisy; another question will arise, who it is that is constituted judge of those marks? And this question is decided by our Saviour himself; *If thy brother,* saith he, (*Matt.* xviii. 15, 16, 17) *shall trespass against thee, go and tell him his fault, between thee and him alone; if he shall hear thee, thou hast gained thy brother. But if he will not hear thee, then take with thee one or two more. And if he shall neglect to hear them, tell it unto the Church; but if he negect to hear the Church, let him be unto thee as an heathen man and a publican.* By which it is manifest, that the judgment concerning the truth of repentance, belonged not to any one man, but to the Church, that is, to the assembly of the faithful, or to them that have authority to be their representant. But besides the judgment, there is necessary also the pronouncing of sentence. And this belonged always to the apostle, or some pastor of the Church, as prolocutor; and of this our Saviour speaketh in the 18th verse, *Whatsoever ye shall bind on earth, shall be bound in heaven; and whatsoever ye shall loose on earth, shall be loosed in heaven.* And conformable hereunto was the practice of St. Paul, (1 *Cor.* v. 3, 4, 5) where he saith, *For I verily, as absent in body, but present in spirit, have determined already, as though I were present, concerning him that hath so done this deed; in the name of our Lord Jesus Christ, when ye are gathered together, and my spirit, with the power of our Lord Jesus Christ, to deliver such a one to Satan;* that is to say, to cast him out of the Church, as a man whose sins are not forgiven. Paul here pronounceth the sentence; but the assembly was first to hear the cause, for St. Paul was absent, and by consequence to condemn him. But in the same chapter (verses 11, 12) the judgment in such a case is more expressly attributed to the assembly: *But now I have written unto you, not to keep company, if any man that is called a brother be a fornicator, &c. with such a one, no not to eat. For what have I to do to judge them that are without? Do not ye judge them that are within?* The sentence therefore by which a man was put out of the Church, was pronounced by the apostle, or pastor; but the judgment concerning the merit of the cause, was in the Church; that is to say, as the times were before the conversion of kings, and men that had sovereign authority in the commonwealth, the assembly of the Christians dwelling in the same city: as in Corinth, in the assembly of the Christians of Corinth.

*Of excommunication.* This part of the power of the keys, by which men were thrust out from the kingdom of God, is that which is called *excommunication;* and to *excommunicate,* is in the original, ἀποσυνάγωγον ποιεῖν, *to cast out of the synagogue;* that is, out of the place of divine service; a word drawn from the custom of the Jews, to cast out of their synagogues such as they thought, in manners or doctrine, contagious, as lepers were by the law of Moses separated from the congregation of Israel, till such time as they should be by the priest pronounced clean.

*The use of excommunication without civil power.* The use and effect of excommunication, whilst it was not yet strengthened with the civil power, was no more than that they, who were not excommunicate, were to avoid the company of them that were. It was not enough to repute them as heathen, that never had been Christians; for with such they might eat and drink; which with excommunicate persons they might not do; as appeareth by the words of St. Paul, (1 *Cor.* v. 9, 10, &c.) where he telleth them, he had formerly forbidden them to *company with fornicators;* but, because that could not be without going out of the world, he restraineth it to such fornicators, and otherwise vicious persons, as were of the brethren; *with such a one,* he saith, they ought not to keep company, *no not to eat.* And this is no more than our Saviour saith (*Matt.* xviii. 17), *Let him be to thee as a heathen, and as a publican.* For publicans, which signifieth farmers and receivers of the revenue of the commonwealth, were so hated and detested by the Jews that were to pay it, as that *publican* and *sinner* were taken amongst them for the same thing: insomuch, as when our Saviour accepted the invitation of Zacchæus a publican; though it were to convert him, yet it was objected to him as a crime. And therefore, when our Saviour to *heathen* added *publican,* he did forbid them to eat with a man excommunicate.

As for keeping them out of their synagogues, or places of assembly, they had no power to do it, but that of the owner of the place, whether he were Christian, or heathen. And because all places are by right in the dominion of the commonwealth; as well he that was excommunicated, as he that never was baptized, might enter into them by commission from the civil magistrate; as Paul before his conversion entered into their synagogues at Damascus, (*Acts* ix. 2) to apprehend Christians, men and women, and to carry them bound to Jerusalem, by commission from the high-priest.

*Of no effect upon an apostate.* By which it appears, that upon a Christian, that should become an apostate, in a place where the civil power did persecute, or not assist the Church, the effect of excommunication had nothing in it, neither of damage in this world, nor of terror; not of terror, because of their unbelief; nor of damage, because they returned thereby into the favour of the world; and in the world to come were to be in no worse estate, than they which never had believed. The damage redounded rather to the Church, by provocation of them they cast out, to a freer execution of their malice.

*But upon the faithful only.* Excommunication therefore had its effect only upon those, that believed that Jesus Christ was to come again in glory, to reign over and to judge both the quick and the dead, and should therefore refuse entrance into his kingdom to those whose sins were retained, that is, to those that were excommunicated by the Church. And thence it is, that St. Paul calleth excommunication, a delivery of the excommunicate person to Satan. For without the kingdom of Christ, all other kingdoms, after judgment, are comprehended in the kingdom of Satan. This is it that the faithful stood in fear of, as long as they stood excommunicate, that is to say, in an estate wherein their sins were not forgiven. Whereby we may understand, that excommunication, in the time that Christian religion was not authorized by the civil power, was used only for a correction of manners, not of errors in opinion: for it is a punishment, whereof none could be sensible but such as believed, and expected the coming again of our Saviour to judge the world; and they who so believed, needed no other opinion, but uprightness of life, to be saved.

*For what fault lieth excommunication.* There lieth excommunication for injustice; as (*Matt.* xviii), If thy brother offend thee, tell it him privately; then with witnesses; lastly, tell the Church; and then if he obey not, *Let him be to thee as an heathen man and a publican.* And there lieth excommunication for a scandalous life, as (1 *Cor.* v. 11) *If any man that is called a brother, be a fornicator, or covetous, or an idolater, or a drunkard, or an extortioner, with such a one ye are not to eat.* But to excommunicate a man that held this foundation, that *Jesus was the Christ,* for difference of opinion in other points, by which that foundation was not destroyed, there appeareth no authority in the Scripture, nor example in the apostles. There is indeed in St. Paul (*Titus* iii. 10) a text that seemeth to be to the contrary; *A man that is an heretic, after the first and second admonition, reject.* For an *heretic,* is he, that being a member of the Church, teacheth nevertheless some private opinion, which the Church has for-

bidden; and such a one, St. Paul adviseth Titus, after the first
and second admonition, to *reject*. But to *reject*, in this place, is
not to *excommunicate* the man; but to *give over admonishing
him, to let him alone, to set by disputing with him,* as one
that is to be convinced only by himself. The same apostle
saith (2 *Tim*. ii. 23) *Foolish and unlearned questions avoid:*
the word *avoid* in this place, and *reject* in the former, is the
same in the original, παραιτοῦ: but foolish questions may be
set by without excommunication. And again, (*Titus* iii. 9)
*Avoid foolish questions,* where the original περίστασο (*set
them by*) is equivalent to the former word *reject*. There is
no other place that can so much as colourably be drawn, to
countenance the casting out of the Church faithful men, such
as believed the foundation, only for a singular superstructure
of their own, proceeding perhaps from a good and pious
conscience. But on the contrary, all such places as command
avoiding such disputes, are written for a lesson to pastors,
such as Timothy and Titus were, not to make new articles of
faith, by determining every small controversy, which oblige
men to a needless burthen of conscience, or provoke them to
break the union of the Church. Which lesson the apostles
themselves observed well. St. Peter and St. Paul, though their
controversy were great, as we may read in *Gal*. ii. 11, yet
they did not cast one another out of the Church. Nevertheless, during the apostles' times, there were other pastors that
observed it not; as Diotrephes (3 *John*, 9, &c.) who cast out
of the Church such as St. John himself thought fit to be
received into it, out of a pride he took in pre-eminence. So
early it was, that vain-glory and ambition had found entrance
into the Church of Christ.

*Of persons liable to excommunication.* That a man be
liable to excommunication, there be many conditions requisite; as first, that he be a member of some commonalty, that
is to say, of some lawful assembly, that is to say, of some
Christian Church, that hath power to judge of the cause for
which he is to be excommunicated. For where there is no
community, there can be no excommunication; nor where
there is no power to judge, can there be any power to give
sentence.

From hence it followeth, that one Church cannot be excommunicated by another: for either they have equal power
to excommunicate each other, in which case excommunication is not discipline, nor an act of authority, but schism, and
dissolution of charity; or one is so subordinate to the other,

as that they both have but one voice; and then they be but one Church; and the part excommunicated is no more a Church, but a dissolute number of individual persons.

And because the sentence of excommunication, importeth an advice, not to keep company nor so much as to eat with him that is excommunicate, if a sovereign prince or assembly be excommunicate, the sentence is of no effect. For all subjects are bound to be in the company and presence of their own sovereign, when he requireth it, by the law of nature; nor can they lawfully either expel him from any place of his own dominion, whether profane or holy; nor go out of his dominion without his leave; much less, if he call them to that honour, refuse to eat with him. And as to other princes and states, because they are not parts of one and the same congregation, they need not any other sentence to keep from keeping company with the state excommunicate: for the very institution, as it uniteth many men into one community, so it dissociateth one community from another: so that excommunication is not needful for keeping kings and states asunder; nor has any further effect than is in the nature of policy itself, unless it be to instigate princes to war upon one another.

Nor is the excommunication of a Christian subject, that obeyeth the laws of his own sovereign, whether Christian or heathen, of any effect. For if he believe that *Jesus is the Christ, he hath the Spirit of God* (1 *John* v. 1): *and God dwelleth in him, and he in God* (1 *John* iv. 15). But he that hath the spirit of God; he that dwelleth in God; he in whom God dwelleth, can receive no harm by the excommunication of men. Therefore, he that believeth Jesus to be the Christ, is free from all the dangers threatened to persons excommunicate. He that believeth it not, is no Christian. Therefore a true and unfeigned Christian is not liable to excommunication: nor he also that is a professed Christian, till his hypocrisy appear in his manners, that is, till his behaviour be contrary to the law of his sovereign, which is the rule of manners, and which Christ and his apostles have commanded us to be subject to. For the Church cannot judge of manners but by external actions, which actions can never be unlawful, but when they are against the law of the commonwealth.

If a man's father, or mother, or master, be excommunicate, yet are not the children forbidden to keep them company, nor to eat with them: for that were, for the most part, to oblige them not to eat at all, for want of means to get food;

and to authorize them to disobey their parents and masters, contrary to the precept of the apostles.

In sum, the power of excommunication cannot be extended further than to the end for which the apostles and pastors of the Church have their commission from our Saviour; which is not to rule by command and coercion, but by teaching and direction of men in the way of salvation in the world to come. And as a master in any science may abandon his scholar, when he obstinately neglecteth the practice of his rules; but not accuse him of injustice, because he was never bound to obey him: so a teacher of Christian doctrine may abandon his disciples that obstinately continue in an unchristian life; but he cannot say, they do him wrong, because they are not obliged to obey him. For to a teacher that shall so complain, may be applied the answer of God to Samuel in the like place, (1 *Sam*. viii. 7) *They have not rejected thee, but me*. Excommunication therefore, when it wanteth the assistance of the civil power, as it doth, when a Christian state or prince is excommunicate by a foreign authority, is without effect; and consequently ought to be without terror. The name of *Fulmen excommunicationis*, that is, *the thunderbolt of excommunication*, proceedeth from an imagination of the Bishop of Rome, which first used it, that he was king of kings; as the heathen made Jupiter king of the gods, and assigned him, in their poems, and pictures, a thunderbolt, wherewith to subdue and punish the giants, that should dare to deny his power. Which imagination was grounded on two errors; one, that the kingdom of Christ is of this world, contrary to our Saviour's own words, (*John* xviii. 36) *My kingdom is not of this world*; the other, that he is Christ's vicar, not only over his own subjects, but over all the Christians of the world; whereof there is no ground in Scripture, and the contrary shall be proved in its due place.

*Of the interpreter of the Scriptures, before civil sovereigns became Christians.* St. Paul coming to Thessalonica, where was a Synagogue of the Jews, (*Acts* xvii. 2, 3) *as his manner was, went in unto them, and three Sabbath days reasoned with them out of the Scriptures, opening and alleging, that Christ must needs have suffered and risen again from the dead; and that this Jesus whom he preached was the Christ.* The Scriptures here mentioned were the Scriptures of the Jews, that is, the Old Testament. The men, to whom he was to prove that Jesus was the Christ and risen again from the dead, were also Jews, and did believe already, that they were

the word of God. Hereupon (as it is in verse 4) some of
them believed, and (as it is in verse 5) some believed not.
What was the reason, when they all believed the Scripture,
that they did not all believe alike; but that some approved,
others disapproved the interpretation of St. Paul that cited
them; and every one interpreted them to himself? It was this;
St. Paul came to them without any legal commission, and in
the manner of one that would not command, but persuade;
which he must needs do, either by miracles, as Moses did to
the Israelites in Egypt, that they might see his authority in
God's works; or by reasoning from the already received
Scripture, that they might see the truth of his doctrine in
God's word. But whosoever persuadeth by reasoning from
principles written, maketh him to whom he speaketh judge,
both of the meaning of those principles, and also of the force
of his inferences upon them. If these Jews of Thessalonica
were not, who else was the judge of what St. Paul alleged
out of Scripture? If St. Paul, what needed he to quote any
places to prove his doctrine? It had been enough to have said,
I find it so in Scripture, that is to say, in your laws, of which
I am interpreter, as sent by Christ. The interpreter therefore
of the Scripture, to whose interpretation the Jews of Thessalonica were bound to stand, could be none: every one might
believe, or not believe, according as the allegation seemed to
himself to be aggreeable, or not agreeable to the meaning of
the places alleged. And generally in all cases of the world,
he that pretendeth any proof, maketh judge of his proof him
to whom he addresseth his speech. And as to the case of the
Jews in particular, they were bound by express words (*Deut.*
xvii) to receive the determination of all hard questions, from
the priests and judges of Israel for the time being. But this
is to be understood of the Jews that were yet unconverted.

For the conversion of the Gentiles, there was no use of
alleging the Scriptures, which they believed not. The apostles
therefore laboured by reason to confute their idolatry; and
that done, to persuade them to the faith of Christ, by their
testimony of his life and resurrection. So that there could not
yet be any controversy concerning the authority to interpret
Scripture; seeing no man was obliged, during his infidelity,
to follow any man's interpretation of any Scripture, except
his sovereign's interpretation of the laws of his country.

Let us now consider the conversion itself, and see what
there was therein that could be cause of such an obligation.
Men were converted to no other thing than to the belief of

that which the apostles preached: and the apostles preached nothing, but that Jesus was the Christ, that is to say, the king that was to save them, and reign over them eternally in the world to come; and consequently that he was not dead, but risen again from the dead, and gone up into heaven, and should come again one day to judge the world, (which also should rise again to be judged,) and reward every man according to his works. None of them preached that himself, or any other apostle, was such an interpreter of the Scripture, as all that became Christians, ought to take their interpretation for law. For to interpret the laws, is part of the administration of a present kingdom; which the apostles had not. They prayed then, and all other pastors ever since, *let thy kingdom come;* and exhorted their converts to obey their then ethnic princes. The New Testament was not yet published in one body. Every of the evangelists was interpreter of his own gospel; and every apostle of his own epistle; and of the Old Testament our Saviour himself saith to the Jews (*John* v. 39) *Search the Scriptures; for in them ye think to have eternal life, and they are they that testify of me.* If he had not meant they should interpret them, he would not have bidden them take thence the proof of his being the Christ: he would either have interpreted them himself, or referred them to the interpretation of the priests.

When a difficulty arose, the apostles and elders of the Church assembled themselves together, and determined what should be preached and taught, and how they should interpret the Scriptures to the people; but took not from the people the liberty to read and interpret them to themselves. The apostles sent divers letters to the Churches, and other writings for their instruction; which had been in vain, if they had not allowed them to interpret, that is, to consider the meaning of them. And as it was in the apostles' time, it must be till such time as there should be pastors, that could authorize an interpreter, whose interpretation should generally be stood to: but that could not be till kings were pastors, or pastors kings.

*Of the power to make Scripture, law.* There be two senses, wherein a writing may be said to be *canonical;* for *canon,* signifieth a *rule;* and a rule is a precept, by which a man is guided and directed in any action whatsoever. Such precepts, though given by a teacher to his disciple, or a counsellor to his friend, without power to compel him to observe them, are nevertheless canons; because they are rules. But when they are given by one, whom he that receiveth them is bound to obey, then are those canons, not only rules, but laws. The question therefore here, is of the power to make the Scriptures, which are the rules of Christian faith, laws.

*Of the ten commandments.* That part of the Scripture, which was first law, was the Ten Commandments, written in two tables of stone, and delivered by God himself to Moses; and by Moses made known to the people. Before that time there was no written law of God, who as yet having not chosen any people to be his peculiar kingdom, had given no law to men, but the law of nature, that is to say, the precepts of natural reason, written in every man's own heart. Of these two tables, the first containeth the law of sovereignty; 1. That they should not obey, nor honour the gods of other nations, in these words, *Non habebis deos alienos coram me,* that is, *thou shalt not have for gods, the gods that other nations worship, but only me:* whereby they were forbidden to obey, or honour, as their king and governor, any other God, than him that spake unto them then by Moses, and afterwards by the high-priest. 2. That they *should not make any image to represent him;* that is to say, they were not to choose to themselves, neither in heaven, nor in earth, any representative of their own fancying, but obey Moses and Aaron, whom he had appointed to that office. 3. That *they should not take the name of God in vain;* that is, they should not speak rashly of their king, nor dispute his right, nor the commissions of Moses and Aaron, his lieutenants. 4. That *they should every seventh day abstain from their ordinary labour,* and employ that time in doing him public honour. The second table containeth the duty of one man towards another, as to *honour parents; not to kill; not to commit adultery; not to steal; not to corrupt judgment by false witness;* and finally, *not so much as to design in their heart the doing of any injury one to another.* The question now is, who it was that gave to these written tables the obligatory force of laws. There is no doubt but they were made laws by God himself: but because a law obliges not, nor is law to any, but to them that acknowledge it to be the act of the sovereign; how could the people of Israel, that were forbidden to approach the mountain to hear what God said to Moses, he obliged to obedience to all those laws which Moses propounded to them? Some of them were indeed the laws of nature, as all the second table; and therefore to be acknowledged for God's laws; not to the Israelites alone, but to all people: but of those that were peculiar to the Israelites, as those of the first table, the question remains; saving that they had obliged themselves, presently after the propounding of them, to obey Moses, in these words (*Exod.* xx. 19), *Speak thou to us, and we will hear thee; but let not God speak to us, lest we die.* It was therefore only Moses then, and after him the high-priest, whom, by Moses, God declared should administer this his peculiar kingdom, that had on earth the power to make this short Scripture of the Decalogue to be law in the commonwealth of Israel. But Moses, and Aaron, and the succeeding high-priests, were the civil sovereigns. Therefore hitherto, the canonizing or making the Scripture law, belonged to the civil sovereign.

*Of the judicial and Levitical law.* The judicial law, that is to say, the laws that God prescribed to the magistrates of Israel for the rule of their administration of justice, and of the sentences or judgments they should pronounce in pleas between man and man; and the Levitical law, that is to say, the rule that God prescribed touching the rites and cere-monies of the priests and Levites, were all delivered to them by Moses only; and therefore also became laws, by virtue of the same promise of obedience to Moses. Whether these laws were then written, or not written, but dictated to the people by Moses, after his being forty days with God in the Mount, by word of mouth, is not expressed in the text; but they were all positive laws, and equivalent to holy Scripture, and made canonical by Moses the civil sovereign.

*The second law.* After the Israelites were come into the plains of Moab over against Jericho, and ready to enter into the land of promise, Moses to the former laws added divers others; which therefore are called *Deuteronomy;* that is, *second laws.* And are, (as it is written *Deut.* xxix. 1) *the words of a covenant which the Lord commanded Moses to make with the children of Israel, besides the covenant which he made with them in Horeb.* For having explained those former laws, in the beginning of the book of *Deuteronomy,* he added others, that begin at the xiith chapter, and continue to the end of the xxvith of the same book. This law (*Deut.* xxvii. 3) they were commanded to write upon great stones plastered over, at their passing over Jordan: this law also was written by Moses himself in a book, and delivered into the hands of the *priests, and to the elders of Israel* (*Deut.* xxxi. 9), and commanded (verse 26) *to be put in the side of the ark;* for in the ark itself was nothing but the *ten com-mandments.* This was the law, which Moses (*Deut.* xvii. 18) commanded the kings of Israel should keep a copy of: and this is the law, which having been long time lost, was found again in the temple in the time of Josiah, and by his authority received for the law of God. But both Moses at the writing, and Josiah at the recovery thereof, had both of them the civil sovereignty. Hitherto therefore the power of making Scripture canonical, was in the civil sovereign.

Besides this book of the law, there was no other book, from the time of Moses till after the Captivity, received amongst the Jews for the law of God. For the prophets, except a few, lived in the time of the Captivity itself; and the rest lived but a little before it; and were so far from having their prophecies generally received for laws, as that their persons were persecuted, partly by false prophets, and partly by the kings which were seduced by them. And this book itself, which was confirmed by Josiah for the law of God, and with it all the history of the works of God, was lost in the Captivity and sack of the city of Jerusalem, as appears by that of 2 *Esdras* xiv. 21, *thy law is burnt; therefore no man knoweth the things that are done of thee, or the works that shall begin.* And before the Captivity, between the time when the law was lost, (which is not mentioned in the Scripture, but may probably be thought to be the time of Rehoboam, when (1 *Kings* xiv. 26) Shishak, king of Egypt, took the spoil of the temple), and the time of Josiah when it was found again, they had no written word of God, but ruled according to their own discretion, or by the direction of such as each of them esteemed prophets.

*The Old Testament when made canonical.* From hence we may infer, that the Scriptures of the Old Testament, which we have at this day, were not canonical nor a law unto the Jews, till the renovation of their covenant with God at their return from the Captivity, and restoration of their commonwealth under Esdras. But from that time forward they were accounted the law of the Jews, and for such translated into Greek by seventy elders of Judea, and put into the library of Ptolemy at Alexandria, and approved for the word of God. Now seeing Esdras was the high-priest, and the high-priest was their civil sovereign, it is manifest that the Scriptures were never made laws, but by the sovereign civil power.

*The New Testament began to be canonical under Christian sovereigns.* By the writings of the Fathers that lived in the time before that the Christian religion was received, and authorized by Constantine the emperor, we may find, that the books we now have of the New Testament were held by the Christians of that time, except a few, (in respect of whose paucity the rest were called the Catholic Church, and others heretics), for the dictates of the Holy Ghost, and consequently for the canon or rule of faith: such was the reverence and opinion they had of their teachers; as generally the reverence, that the disciples bear to their first masters in all manner of doctrine they receive from them, is not small. Therefore there is no doubt, but when St. Paul wrote to the Churches he had converted; or any other apostle or disciple of Christ, to those which had then embraced Christ; they received those their writings for the true Christian doctrine. But in that time, when not the power and authority of the teacher, but the faith of the hearer, caused them to receive it, it was not the apostles that made their own writings canonical, but every convert made them so to himself.

But the question here, is not what any Christian made a law or canon to himself, which he might again reject by the same right he received it; but what was so made a canon to them, as without injustice they could not do any thing contrary thereunto. That the New Testament should in this sense be canonical, that is to say a law, in any place where the law of the commonwealth had not made it so, is contrary to the nature of a law. For a law, as has been already shown, is the commandment of that man or assembly, to whom we have given sovereign authority to make such rules for the direction of our actions as he shall think fit, and to punish us when we do anything contrary to the same. When therefore any other man shall offer unto us any other rules, which the sovereign ruler hath not prescribed, they are but counsel and advice; which, whether good or bad, he that is counselled, may without injustice refuse to observe; and when contrary to the laws already established, without injustice cannot observe, how good soever he conceiveth it to be. I say, he cannot in this case observe the same in his actions, nor in his discourse with other men; though he may without blame believe his private teachers, and wish he had the liberty to practise their advice, and that it were publicly received for law. For internal faith is in its own nature invisible, and consequently exempted from all human jurisdiction; whereas the words and actions that proceed from it, as breaches of our civil obedience, are injustice both before God and man. Seeing then our Saviour hath denied his kingdom to be in this world, seeing he hath said, he came not to judge, but to save the world, he hath not subjected us to other laws than those of the commonwealth; that is, the Jews to the law of Moses, which he saith (*Matt.* v. 17) he came not to destroy, but to fulfil; and other nations to the laws of their several sovereigns, and all men to the laws of nature; the observing whereof, both he himself, and his apostles, have in their teaching recommended to us, as a necessary condition of being admitted by him in the last day into his eternal kingdom, wherein shall be protection, and life everlasting. Seeing then our Saviour, and his apostles, left not new laws to oblige us in this world, but new doctrine to prepare us for the next; the books of the New Testament, which contain that doctrine, until obedience to them was commanded by them that God had given power to on earth to be legislators, were not obligatory canons, that is, laws, but only good and safe advice, for the direction of sinners in the way to salvation, which every man might take and refuse at his own peril, without injustice.

Again, our Saviour Christ's commission to his apostles and disciples, was to proclaim his kingdom, not present, but to come; and to teach all nations, and to baptize them that should believe; and to enter into the houses of them that should receive them, and where they were not received, to shake off the dust of their feet against them; but not to call for fire from heaven to destroy them, nor to compel them to obedience by the sword. In all which there is nothing of power, but of persuasion. He sent them out as sheep unto wolves, not as kings to their subjects. They had not in commission to make laws; but to obey, and teach obedience to laws made; and consequently they could not make their writings obligatory canons, without the help of the sovereign civil power. And therefore the Scripture of the New Testament is there only law, where the lawful civil power hath made it so. And there also the king, or sovereign, maketh it a law to himself; by which he subjecteth himself, not to the doctor or apostle that converted him, but to God himself and his Son Jesus Christ, as immediately as did the apostles themselves.

*Of the power of councils to make the Scriptures law.* That which may seem to give the New Testament, in respect of those that have embraced Christian doctrine, the force of laws, in the times and places of persecution, is the decrees they made amongst themselves in their synod. For we read (*Acts* xv. 28) the style of the council of the apostles, the elders, and the whole Church, in this manner; *It seemed good to the Holy Ghost, and to us, to lay upon you no greater burthen than these necessary things, &c.;* which is a style that signifieth a power to lay a burthen on them that had received their doctrine. Now *to lay a burthen on another,* seemeth the same as *to oblige;* and therefore the acts of that council were laws to the then Christians. Nevertheless, they were no more laws than are these other precepts, *Repent; be baptized; keep the commandments; believe the gospel; come unto me; sell all that thou hast; give it to the poor; and follow me;* which are not commands, but invitations, and callings of men to Christianity, like that of *Isaiah* lv. 1; *Ho, every man that thirsteth, come ye to the waters, come, and buy wine and milk without money.* For first, the apostles' power was no other than that of our Saviour, to invite men to embrace the kingdom of God; which they themselves acknowledged for a kingdom, not present, but to come; and they that have no kingdom, can make no laws. And secondly, if their acts of council were laws, they could not without sin be disobeyed. But we read not any where, that they who received not the doctrine of Christ, did therein sin; but that they died in their sins; that is, that their sins against the laws to which they owed obedience, were not pardoned. And those laws were the laws of nature, and the civil laws of the state, whereto every Christian man had by pact submitted himself. And therefore by the burthen, which the apostles might lay on such as they had converted, are not to be understood laws, but conditions proposed to those that sought salvation; which they might accept or refuse at their own peril, without a new sin, though not without the hazard of being condemned and excluded out of the kingdom of God for their sins past. And therefore of infidels, St. John saith not, the wrath of God shall *come* upon them, but (*John* iii. 36) *the wrath of God remaineth upon them;* and not that they shall be condemned, but that (*John* iii. 18) *they are condemned already.* Nor can it be conceived, that the benefit of faith *is remission of sins,* unless we conceive withal, that the damage of infidelity *is the retention of the same sins.*

But to what end is it, may some man ask, that the apostles, and other pastors of the Church after their time, should meet together to agree upon what doctrine should be taught, both for faith and manners, if no man were obliged to observe their decrees? To this may be answered, that the apostles and elders of that council were obliged even by their entrance into it, to teach the doctrine therein concluded and decreed to be taught, so far forth, as no precedent law, to which they were obliged to yield obedience, was to the contrary; but not that all other Christians should be obliged to observe what they taught. For though they might deliberate what each of them should teach; yet they could not deliberate what others should do, unless their assembly had had a legislative power; which none could have but civil sovereigns. For though God be the sovereign of all the world, we are not bound to take for his law whatsoever is propounded by every man in his name; nor anything contrary to the civil law, which God hath expressly commanded us to obey.

Seeing then the acts of council of the apostles, were then no laws, but counsels; much less are laws the acts of any other doctors or council since, if assembled without the authority of the civil sovereign. And consequently, the Books of the New Testament, though most perfect rules of Christian doctrine, could not be made laws by any other authority than that of kings or sovereign assemblies.

The first council, that made the Scriptures we now have canon, is not extant: for that collection of the canons of the apostles, attributed to Clement, the first bishop of Rome after St. Peter, is subject to question. For though the canonical books be there reckoned up; yet these words, *sint vobis omnibus clericis et laicis libri venerandi, etc.* contain a distinction of clergy and laity, that was not in use so near St. Peter's time. The first council for settling the canonical Scripture, that is extant, is that of Laodicea, (*Can.* lix) which forbids the reading of other books than those in the churches; which is a mandate that is not addressed to every Christian, but to those only that had authority to read anything publicly in the church; that is, to ecclesiastics only.

*Of the right of constituting ecclesiastical officers in the time of the apostles.* Of ecclesiastical officers in the time of the apostles, some were magisterial, some ministerial. Magisterial were the offices of the preaching of the gospel of the kingdom of God to infidels; of administering the sacraments, and divine service; and of teaching the rules of faith and manners to those that were converted. Ministerial was the office of deacons, that is, of them that were appointed to the administration of the secular necessities of the church, at such time as they lived upon a common stock of money, raised out of the voluntary contributions of the faithful.

Amongst the officers magisterial, the first and principal were the apostles; whereof there were at first but twelve; and these were chosen and constituted by our Saviour himself; and their office was not only to preach, teach, and baptize, but also to be martyrs, witnesses of our Saviour's resurrection. This testimony was the specifical and essential mark, whereby the apostleship was distinguished from other magistracy ecclesiastical; as being necessary for an apostle, either to have seen our Saviour after his resurrection, or to have conversed with him before, and seen his works, and other arguments of his divinity; whereby they might be taken for sufficient witnesses. And therefore at the election of a new apostle in the place of Judas Iscariot, St. Peter saith (*Acts* i. 21, 22) *Of these men that have companied with us, all the time that the Lord Jesus went in and out amongst us, beginning from the baptism of John unto that same day that he was taken up from us, must one be ordained to be a witness with us of his resurrection:* where by this word *must,* is implied a necessary property of an apostle, to have companied with the first and prime apostles, in the time that our Saviour manifested himself in the flesh.

*Matthias made apostle by the congregation.* The first apostle, of those which were not constituted by Christ in the time he was upon the earth, was Matthias, chosen in this manner. There were assembled together in Jerusalem about one hundred and twenty Christians (*Acts* i. 15). These (verse 23) appointed two, Joseph the Just and Matthias, and caused lots to be drawn; *and* (verse 26) *the lot fell on Matthias, and he was numbered with the apostles.* So that here we see the ordination of this apostle was the act of the congregation, and not of St. Peter nor of the eleven, otherwise than as members of the assembly.

*Paul and Barnabas made apostles by the Church of Antioch.* After him there was never any other apostle ordained, but Paul and Barnabas; which was done as we read (*Acts* xiii. 1, 2, 3) in this manner. *There were in the Church that was at Antioch, certain prophets and teachers; as Barnabas, and Simeon that was called Niger, and Lucius of Cyrene, and Manaen; which had been brought up with Herod the Tetrarch, and Saul. As they ministered unto the Lord, and fasted, the Holy Ghost said, Separate me Barnabas and Saul for the work whereunto I have called them. And when they had fasted and prayed, and laid their hands on them, they sent them away.*

By which it is manifest, that though they were called by the Holy Ghost, their calling was declared unto them and

their mission authorized by the particular Church of Antioch.
And that this their calling was to the apostleship, is apparent
by that, that they are both called (*Acts* xiv. 14) apostles: and
that it was by virtue of this act of the Church of Antioch,
that they were apostles, St. Paul declareth plainly (*Rom.* i. 1),
in that he useth the word, which the Holy Ghost used at his
calling: for he styleth himself, *An apostle separated unto the
gospel of God;* alluding to the words of the Holy Ghost,
*Separate me Barnabas and Saul, &c.* But seeing the work of
an apostle, was to be a witness of the resurrection of Christ,
a man may here ask, how St. Paul, that conversed not with
our Saviour before his passion, could know he was risen? To
which is easily answered, that our Saviour himself appeared
to him in the way to Damascus, from heaven, after his ascension; *and chose him for a vessel to bear his name before the
Gentiles, and kings, and children of Israel:* and consequently,
having seen the Lord after his passion, he was a competent
witness of his resurrection. And as for Barnabas, he was a
disciple before the passion. It is therefore evident that Paul
and Barnabas were apostles; and yet chosen and authorized,
not by the first apostles alone, but by the Church of Antioch;
as Matthias was chosen and authorized by the Church of
Jerusalem.

*What offices in the church are magisterial. Bishop,* a word
formed in our language out of the Greek Ἐπίσκοπος, signifieth an overseer or superintendent of any business, and particularly a pastor or shepherd; and thence by metaphor was
taken, not only amongst the Jews that were originally shepherds, but also amongst the heathen, to signify the office of a
king, or any other rule or guide of people, whether he ruled
by laws or doctrine. And so the apostles were the first Christian bishops, instituted by Christ himself: in which sense the
apostleship of Judas is called (*Acts* i. 20) *his bishopric.* And
afterwards, when there were constituted elders in the Christian Churches, with charge to guide Christ's flock by their
doctrine and advice; these elders were also called bishops.
Timothy was an elder, (which word *elder,* in the New Testament, is a name of office, as well as of age); yet he was also
a bishop. And bishops were then content with the title of
elders. Nay St. John himself, the apostle beloved of our Lord,
beginneth his second Epistle with these words, *The elder to
the elect lady.* By which it is evident, that *bishop, pastor,
elder, doctor,* that is to say, *teacher,* were but so many divers
names of the same office in the time of the apostles; for

there was then no government by coercion, but only by doctrine and persuading. The kingdom of God was yet to come, in a new world: so that there could be no authority to compel in any Church, till the commonwealth had embraced the Christian faith: and consequently no diversity of authority, though there were diversity of employment.

Besides these magisterial employments in the Church, namely, apostles, bishops, elders, pastors, and doctors, whose calling was to proclaim Christ to the Jews and infidels, and to direct and to teach those that believed, we read in the New Testament of no other. For by the names of *evangelists* and *prophets*, is not signified any office, but several gifts, by which several men were profitable to the Church: as evangelists, by writing the life and acts of our Saviour; such as were St. Matthew and St. John apostles, and St. Mark and St. Luke disciples, and whosoever else wrote of that subject, (as St. Thomas, and St. Barnabas are said to have done, though the Church have not received the books that have gone under their names): and as prophets, by the gift of interpreting the Old Testament, and sometimes by declaring their special revelations to the Church. For neither these gifts, nor the gifts of languages, nor the gift of casting out devils, nor of curing other diseases, nor any thing else, did make an officer in the Church, save only the due calling and election to the charge of teaching.

*Ordination of teachers.* As the apostles, Matthias, Paul, and Barnabas, were not made by our Saviour himself, but were elected by the Church, that is, by the assembly of Christians; namely, Matthias by the Church of Jerusalem, and Paul and Barnabas by the Church of Antioch; so were also the *presbyters* and *pastors* in other cities, elected by the Churches of those cities. For proof whereof let us consider, first, how St. Paul proceeded in the ordination of presbyters, in the cities where he had converted men to the Christian faith, immediately after he and Barnabas had received their apostleship. We read (*Acts* xiv. 23) that *they ordained elders in every Church;* which at first sight may be taken for an argument, that they themselves chose, and gave them their authority: but if we consider the original text, it will be manifest that they were authorized and chosen by the assembly of the Christians of each city. For the words there are, χειροτονήσαντες αὐτοῖς πρεσβυτέρους κατ' ἐκκλησίαν, that is, *when they had ordained them elders by the holding up of hands in every congregation.* Now it is well enough known, that in all those cities the manner of choosing magistrates and officers, was by plurality of suffrages; and, because the ordinary way of distinguishing the affirmative votes from the negatives, was by holding up of hands, to ordain an officer in any of the cities, was no more but to bring the people together, to elect them by plurality of votes, whether it were by plurality of elevated hands, or by plurality of voices, or plurality of balls, or beans, or small stones, of which every man cast in one, into a vessel marked for the affirmative or negative; for divers cities had divers customs in that point. It was therefore the assembly that elected their own elders: the apostles were only presidents of the assembly, to call them together for such election, and to pronunce them elected, and to give them the benediction which now is called consecration. And for this cause, they that were presidents of the assemblies, as in the absence of the apostles the elders were, were called προεστῶτες, and in Latin *antistites;* which words signify the principal person of the assembly, whose office was to number the votes, and to declare thereby who was chosen; and where the votes were equal, to decide the matter in question, by adding his own; which is the office of a president in council. And, because all the Churches had their presbyters ordained in the same manner, where the word is *constitute,* (as *Titus i.* 5) ἵνα καταστήσῃς κατά πόλιν πρεσβυτέρους, *For this cause left I thee in Crete, that thou shouldest constitute elders in every city,* we are to understand the same thing, namely, that he should call the faithful together, and ordain them presbyters by plurality of suffrages. It had been a strange thing, if in a town, where men perhaps had never seen any magistrate otherwise chosen than by an assembly, those of the town becoming Christians should so much as have thought on any other way of election of their teachers and guides, that is to say, of their presbyters, (otherwise called bishops) than this of plurality of suffrages, intimated by St. Paul (*Acts* xiv. 23) in the word χειροτονήσαντες. Nor was there ever any choosing of bishops, before the emperors found it necessary to regulate them, in order to the keeping of the peace amongst them, but by the assemblies of the Christians in every several town.

The same is also confirmed by the continual practice, even to this day, in the election of the bishops of Rome. For if the bishop of any place had the right of choosing another, to the succession of the pastoral office, in any city, at such times as he went from thence to plant the same in another place;

much more had he the right to appoint his successors in that place, in which he last resided and died: and we find not that ever any bishop of Rome appointed his successor. For they were a long time chosen by the people, as we may see by the sedition raised about the election between *Damascus* and *Ursicinus;* which Ammianus Marcellinus saith was so great, that *Juventius* the præfect, unable to keep the peace between them, was forced to go out of the city; and that there were above an hundred men found dead upon that occasion in the church itself. And though they afterwards were chosen, first, by the whole clergy of Rome, and afterwards by the cardinals; yet never any was appointed to the succession by his predecessor. If therefore they pretended no right to appoint their own successors, I think I may reasonably conclude they had no right to appoint the successors of other bishops, without receiving some new power; which none could take from the Church to bestow on them, but such as had a lawful authority, not only to teach, but to command the Church; which none could do, but the civil sovereign.

*Ministers of the Church, what:* The word *minister,* in the original Διάκονος, signifieth one that voluntarily doth the business of another man; and differeth from a servant only in this, that servants are obliged by their condition, to do what is commanded them; whereas ministers are obliged only by their undertaking, and bound therefore to no more than that they have undertaken: so that both they that teach the word of God, and they that administer the secular affairs of the Church, are both ministers, but they are ministers of different persons. For the pastors of the Church, called (*Acts* vi. 4) *the ministers of the word,* are ministers of Christ, whose word it is: but the ministry of a deacon, which is called (verse 2 of the same chapter) *serving of tables,* is a service done to the Church or congregation: so that neither any one man, nor the whole church, could ever of their pastor say, he was their minister: but of a deacon, whether the charge he undertook were to serve tables, or distribute maintenance to the Christians, when they lived in each city on a common stock or upon collections, as in the first times, or to take a care of the house of prayer, or of the revenue, or other worldly business of the Church, the whole congregation might properly call him their minister.

For their employment, as deacons, was to serve the congregation; though upon occasion they omitted not to preach the gospel, and maintain the doctrine of Christ, every one according to his gifts, as St. Stephen did; and both to preach and baptize, as Philip did. For that Philip, which (*Acts* viii. 5) preached the gospel at Samaria, and (verse 38) baptized the Eunuch, was Philip the deacon, not Philip the apostle. For it is manifest (verse 1) that when Philip preached in Samaria, the apostles were at Jerusalem, and (verse 14) *when they heard that Samaria had received the word of God, sent Peter and John to them;* by imposition of whose hands, they that were baptized (verse 15), received, which before by the baptism of Philip they had not received, the Holy Ghost. For it was necessary for the conferring of the Holy Ghost, that their baptism should be administered or confirmed by a minister of the Church. And therefore to confirm the baptism of those that Philip the deacon had baptized, the apostles sent out of their own number from Jerusalem to Samaria, Peter and John; who conferred on them that before were but baptized, those graces that were signs of the Holy Spirit, which at that time did accompany all true believers; which what they were may be understood by that which St. Mark saith (chap. xvi. 17), *these signs follow them that believe in my name; they shall cast out devils; they shall speak with new tongue; they shall take up serpents; and if they drink any deadly thing, it shall not hurt them; they shall lay hands on the sick, and they shall recover.* This to do, was it that Philip could not give; but the apostles could, and, as appears by this place, effectually did to every man that truly believed and was by a minister of Christ himself baptized: which power either Christ's ministers in this age cannot confer, or else there are very few true believers, or Christ hath very few ministers.

*And how chosen.* That the first deacons were chosen, not by the apostles, but by a congregation of the disciples, that is, of Christian men of all sorts, is manifest out of *Acts* vi, where we read that the *Twelve*, after the number of disciples was multiplied, called them together, and having told them, that it was not fit that the apostles should leave the word of God and serve tables, said unto them, (verse 3) *Brethren, look you out among you seven men of honest report, full of the Holy Ghost and of wisdom, whom we may appoint over this business.* Here it is manifest, that though the apostles declared them elected; yet the congregation chose them; which also (verse 5) is more expressly said, where it is written, that *the saying pleased the whole multitude, and they chose seven, &c.*

*Of ecclesiastical revenue, under the law of Moses.* Under the Old Testament, the tribe of Levi were only capable of the priesthood, and other inferior offices of the Church. The land was divided amongst the other tribes, Levi excepted, which, by the subdivision of the tribe of Joseph into Ephraim and Manasseh, were still twelve. To the tribe of Levi were assigned certain cities for their habitation, with the suburbs for their cattle: but for their portion, they were to have the tenth of the fruits of the land of their brethren. Again, the priests for their maintenance had the tenth of that tenth, together with part of the oblations and sacrifices. For God had said to Aaron (*Numb.* xviii. 20) *Thou shalt have no inheritance in their land; neither shalt thou have any part amongst them; I am thy part and thine inheritance amongst the children of Israel.* For God being then king, and having constituted the tribe of Levi to be his public ministers, he allowed them for their maintenance the public revenue, that is to say, the part that God had reserved to himself; which were tithes and offerings: and that is it which is meant, where God saith, *I am thine inheritance.* And therefore to the Levites might not unfitly be attributed the name of *clergy*, from κλῆρος, which signifieth lot or inheritance; not that they were heirs of the kingdom of God, more than other; but that God's inheritance was their maintenance. Now, seeing in this time God himself was their king, and Moses, Aaron, and the succeeding high-priests, were his lieutenants; it is manifest, that the right of tithes and offerings was constituted by the civil power.

After their rejection of God in the demanding of a king, they enjoyed still the same revenue; but the right thereof was derived from that, that the kings did never take it from them: for the public revenue was at the disposing of him that was the public person; and that, till the Captivity, was the king. And again, after the return from the Captivity, they paid their tithes as before to the priest. Hitherto therefore Church livings were determined by the civil sovereign.

*In our Saviour's time, and after.* Of the maintenance of our Saviour and his apostles, we read only they had a purse, which was carried by Judas Iscariot; and that of the apostles, such as were fishermen did sometimes use their trade; and that when our Saviour sent the twelve apostles to preach, he forbad them (*Matt.* x. 9, 10): *to carry gold, and silver, and brass in their purses, for that the workman is worthy of his hire.* By which it is probable, their ordinary maintenance was not unsuitable to their employment; for their employment was (verse 8) *freely to give, because they had freely received;* and their maintenance was the *free gift* of those that believed the good tiding they carried about of the coming of the Messiah their Saviour. To which we may add, that which was contributed out of gratitude by such as our Saviour had healed of diseases; of which are mentioned (*Luke* viii. 2, 3) *Certain women which had been healed of evil spirits and infirmities; Mary Magdalen, out of whom went seven devils; and Joanna the wife of Chuza, Herod's steward, and Susanna, and many others, which ministered unto him of their substance.*

After our Saviour's ascension, the Christians of every city lived in common (*Acts* iv. 34, 35) upon the money which was made of the sale of their lands and possessions, and laid down at the feet of the apostles, of good will, not of duty; for, *whilst the land remained,* saith St. Peter to Ananias (*Acts* v. 4), *was it not thine? and after it was sold, was it not in thy power?* which sheweth he needed not have saved his land nor his money by lying, as not being bound to contribute any thing at all, unless he had pleased. And as in the time of the apostles, so also all the time downward, till after Constantine the Great, we shall find that the maintenance of the bishops and pastors of the Christian Church was nothing but the voluntary contribution of them that had embraced their doctrine. There was yet no mention of tithes: but such was in the time of Constantine and his sons the affection of Christians to their pastors, as Ammianus Marcellinus saith, describing the sedition of Damascus and Ursicinus about the bishopric, that it was worth their contention, in that the bishops of those times, by the liberality of their flock, and especially of matrons, lived splendidly, were carried in coaches, and were sumptuous in their fare and apparel.

*The ministers of the Gospel lived on the benevolence of their flocks.* But here may some ask, whether the pastors were then bound to live upon voluntary contribution, as upon alms; *For who,* saith St. Paul (1 *Cor.* ix. 7) *goeth to war at his own charges? or who feedeth a flock, and eateth not of the milk of the flock?* And again, (verse 13) *Do ye not know that they which minister about holy things, live of the things of the temple; and they which wait at the altar, partake with the altar;* that is to say, have part of that which is offered at the altar for their maintenance? And then he concludeth, (verse 14) *Even so hath the Lord appointed, that they which preach the gospel should live of the gospel.* From which place may be inferred indeed, that the pastors of the Church ought to be maintained by their flocks; but not that the pastors were to determine, either the quantity, or the kind of their own allowance, and be, as it were, their own carvers. Their allowance must needs therefore be determined, either by the gratitude and liberality of every particular man of their flock, or by the whole congregation. By the whole congregation it could not be, because their acts were then no laws; therefore the maintenance of pastors before emperors and civil sovereigns had made laws to settle it, was nothing but benevolence. They that served at the altar lived on what was offered. So may the pastors also take what is offered them by their flock; but not exact what is not offered. In what court should they sue for it, who had no tribunals? Or, if they had arbitrators amongst themselves, who should execute their judgments, when they had no power to arm their officers? It remaineth, therefore, that there could be no certain maintenance assigned to any pastors of the Church, but by the whole congregation; and then only, when their decrees should have the force, not only of *canons*, but also of *laws;* which laws could not be made, but by emperors, kings, or other civil sovereigns. The right of tithes in Moses' law, could not be applied to the then ministers of the gospel; because Moses and the high-priests were the civil sovereigns of the people under God, whose kingdom amongst the Jews was present; whereas the kingdom of God by Christ is yet to come.

Hitherto hath been shewn what the pastors of the Church are; what are the points of their commission, as that they were to preach, to teach, to baptize, to be presidents in their several congregations; what is ecclesiastical censure, viz. excommunication, that is to say, in those places where Christianity was forbidden by the civil laws, a putting of themselves out of the company of the excommunicate, and where Christianity was by the civil law commanded, a putting the excommunicate out of the congregations of Christians; who elected the pastors and ministers of the Church, that it was the congregation; who consecrated and blessed them, that it was the pastor; what was their due revenue, that it was none but their own possessions, and their own labour, and the voluntary contributions of devout and grateful Christians. We are to consider now, what office in the Church those persons have, who being civil sovereigns, have embraced also the Christian faith.

*That the civil sovereign, being a Christian, hath the right of appointing pastors.* And first, we are to remember, that the right of judging what doctrines are fit for peace, and to be taught the subjects, is in all commonwealths inseparably annexed, as hath been already proved (chapter 13), to the sovereign power civil, whether it be in one man, or in one assembly of men. For it is evident to the meanest capacity, that men's actions are derived from the opinions they have of the good or evil, which from those actions redound unto themselves; and consequently, men that are once possessed of an opinion, that their obedience to the sovereign power will be more hurtful to them than their disobedience, will disobey the laws, and thereby overthrow the commonwealth, and introduce confusion and civil war; for the avoiding whereof, all civil government was ordained. And therefore in all commonwealths of the heathen, the sovereigns have had the name of pastors of the people, because there was no subject that could lawfully teach the people, but by their permission and authority.

This right of the heathen kings cannot be thought taken from them by their conversion to the faith of Christ; who never ordained that kings, for believing in him, should be deposed, that is, subjected to any but himself, or, which is all one, be deprived of the power necessary for the conservation of peace amongst their subjects, and for their defence against foreign enemies. And therefore Christian kings are still the supreme pastors of their people, and have power to ordain what pastors they please, to teach the Church, that is, to teach the people committed to their charge.

Again, let the right of choosing them be, as before the conversion of kings, in the Church; for so it was in the time of the apostles themselves, as hath been shown already in this chapter; even so also the right will be in the civil sovereign, Christian. For in that he is a Christian, he allows the teaching; and in that he is the sovereign, which is as much as to say, the Church by representation, the teachers he elects are elected by the Church. And when an assembly of Christians choose their pastor in a Christian commonwealth, it is the sovereign that electeth him, because it is done by his authority; in the same manner, as when a town choose their mayor, it is the act of him that hath the sovereign power: for every act done, is the act of him, without whose consent it is invalid. And therefore whatsoever examples may be drawn out of history, concerning the election of pastors by the people, or by the clergy, they are no arguments against the right of any civil sovereign, because they that elected them did it by his authority.

Seeing then in every Christian commonwealth, the civil sovereign is the supreme pastor, to whose charge the whole flock of his subjects is committed, and consequently that it is by his authority that all other pastors are made, and have power to teach, and perform all other pastoral offices; it followeth also, that it is from the civil sovereign that all other pastors derive their right of teaching, preaching, and other functions pertaining to that office, and that they are but his ministers; in the same manner as the magistrates of towns, judges in courts of justice, and commanders of armies, are all but ministers of him that is the magistrate of the whole commonwealth, judge of all causes, and commander of the whole militia, which is always the civil sovereign. And the reason hereof, is not because they that teach, but because they that are to learn, are his subjects. For let it be supposed, that a Christian king commit the authority of ordaining pastors in his dominions to another king, as divers Christian kings allow that power to the Pope; he doth not thereby constitute a pastor over himself, nor a sovereign pastor over his people; for that were to deprive himself of the civil power; which, depending on the opinion men have of their duty to him and the fear they have of punishment in another world, would depend also on the skill and loyalty of doctors, who are no less subject, not only to ambition, but also to ignorance, than any other sort of men. So that where a stranger hath authority to appoint teachers, it is given him by the sovereign in whose dominions he teacheth. Christian doctors are our schoolmasters to Christianity; but kings are fathers of families, and may receive schoolmasters for their subjects from the recommendation of a stranger, but not from the command; especially when the ill teaching them shall redound to the great and manifest profit of him that recommends them: nor can they be obliged to retain them, longer than it is for the public good; the care of which they stand so long charged withal, as they retain any other essential right of the sovereignty.

*The pastoral authority of sovereigns only is* jure divino; *that of other pastors is* jure civili. If a man therefore should ask a pastor, in the execution of his office, as the chief-priests and elders of the people (*Matt.* xxi. 23) asked our Saviour, *By what authority doest thou these things, and who gave thee this authority?* he can make no other just answer, but that he doth it by the authority of the commonwealth, given him by the king, or assembly that representeth it. All pastors, except the supreme, execute their charges in the right, that is by the authority of the civil sovereign, that is, *jure civili.* But the king, and every other sovereign, executeth his office of supreme pastor by immediate authority from God, that is to say, in *God's right* or *jure divino.* And therefore none but kings can put into their titles a mark of their submission to God only, *Dei gratiâ rex,* &c. Bishops ought to say in the beginning of their mandates, *By the favour of the King's Majesty, bishop of such a diocese;* or as civil minsters, *in His Majesty's name.* For in saying, *Divinâ providentiâ,* which is the same with *Dei gratiâ,* though disguised, they deny to have received their authority from the civil state; and slyly slip off the collar of their civil subjection, contrary to the unity and defence of the commonwealth.

*Christian kings have power to execute all manner of pastoral function.* But if every Christian sovereign be the supreme pastor of his own subjects, it seemeth that he hath also the authority, not only to preach, which perhaps no man will deny, but also to baptize and to administer the sacrament of the Lord's Supper: and to consecrate both temples and pastors to God's service; which most men deny; partly because they use not to do it, and partly because the administration of sacraments, and consecration of persons and places to holy uses, requireth the imposition of such men's hands, as by the like imposition successively from the time of the apostles have been ordained to the like ministry. For proof therefore that Christian kings have power to baptize, and to consecrate, I am to render a reason, both why they use not to do it, and how, without the ordinary ceremony of imposition of hands, they are made capable of doing it when they will.

There is no doubt but any king, in case he were skilful in the sciences, might by the same right of his office read lectures of them himself, by which he authorizeth others to read them in the universities. Nevertheless, because the care of the sum of the business of the commonwealth taketh up his whole time, it were not convenient for him to apply himself in person to that particular. A king may also, if he please, sit in judgment to hear and determine all manner of causes, as well as give others authority to do it in his name; but that the charge, that lieth upon him of command and government, constrain him to be continually at the helm, and to commit the ministerial offices to others under him. In the like manner our Saviour, who surely had power to baptize, baptized none (*John* iv. 2) himself, but sent his apostles and disciples to baptize. So also St. Paul, by the necessity of preaching in divers and far distant places, baptized few: amongst all the Corinthians he baptized only (1 *Cor.* i. 14, 16) Crispus, Gaius, and Stephanas; and the reason was, (1 *Cor.* i. 17) because his principal charge was to preach. Whereby it is manifest, that the greater charge, such as is the government of the Church, is a dispensation for the less. The reason therefore why Christian kings use not to baptize, is evident, and the same for which at this day there are few baptized by bishops, and by the Pope fewer.

And as concerning imposition of hands, whether it be needful for the authorizing of a king to baptize and consecrate, we may consider thus:

Imposition of hands, was a most ancient public ceremony amongst the Jews, by which was designed, and made certain, the person, or other thing intended in a man's prayer, blessing, sacrifice, consecration, condemnation, or other speech. So Jacob, in blessing the children of Joseph (*Gen.* xlviii. 14), *Laid his right hand on Ephraim the younger, and his left hand on Manasseh the first born;* and this he did *wittingly* (though they were so presented to him by Joseph, as he was forced in doing it to stretch out his arms across) to design to whom he intended the greater blessing. So also in the sacrificing of the burnt offering, Aaron is commanded (*Exod.* xxix. 10) *to lay his hands on the head of the bullock:* and (verse 15) *to lay his hand on the head of the ram.* The same is also said again *Levit.* i. 4, and viii. 14. Likewise Moses, when he ordained Joshua to be captain of the Israelites, that is, consecrated him to God's service, (*Numb.* xxvii. 23) *Laid his hands upon him, and gave him his charge,* designing and rendering certain, who it was they were to obey in war. And in the consecration of the Levites (*Numb.* viii. 10), God commanded that *the children of Israel should put their hands upon the Levites.* And in the condemnation of him that had blasphemed the Lord (*Levit.* xxiv. 14), God commanded that *all that heard him should lay their hands on his head, and that all the congregation should stone him.* And why should they only that heard him, lay their hands upon him, and not rather a priest, Levite, or other minister of justice, but that none else were able to design and to demonstrate to the eyes of the congregation, who it was that had blasphemed and ought to die? And to design a man or any other thing, by the hand to the eye, is less subject to mistake, than when it is done to the ear by a name.

And so much was this ceremony observed, that in blessing the whole congregation at once, which cannot be done by laying on of hands, yet Aaron (*Levit.* ix. 22) *did lift up his hand toward the people when he blessed them.* And we read also of the like ceremony of consecration of temples amongst the heathen, as that the priest laid his hands on some post of the temple, all the while he was uttering the words of consecration. So natural it is to design any individual thing, rather by the hand, to assure the eyes, than by words to inform the ear, in matters of God's public service.

This ceremony was not therefore new in our Saviour's time. For Jairus (*Mark* v. 23), whose daughter was sick, besought our Saviour, not to heal her, but *to lay his hands upon her that she might be healed.* And (*Matt.* xix. 13) *they brought unto him little children, that he should put his hands on them, and pray.*

According to this ancient rite, the apostles, and presbyters, and the presbytery itself, laid hands on them whom they ordained pastors, and withal prayed for them that they might receive the Holy Ghost; and that not only once, but sometimes oftener, when a new occasion was presented: but the end was still the same, namely a punctual and religious designation of the person, ordained either to the pastoral charge in general, or to a particular mission. So (*Acts* vi. 6) *The apostles prayed, and laid their hands* on the seven deacons; which was done, not to give them the Holy Ghost (for they were full of the Holy Ghost before they were chosen, as appeareth immediately before, verse 3) but to design them to that office. And after Philip the deacon had converted certain persons in Samaria, Peter and John went down (*Acts* viii. 17), *and laid their hands on them, and they received the Holy Ghost.* And not only an apostle, but a presbyter had this power: for St. Paul adviseth Timothy (1 *Tim.* v. 22) *Lay hands suddenly on no man;* that is, design no man rashly to the office of a pastor. The whole presbytery laid their hands on Timothy, as we read 1 *Tim.* iv. 14: but this is to be understood, as that some did it by the appointment of the presbytery, and most likely their προεστώς, or prolocutor, which it may be was St. Paul himself. For in his second Epistle to *Timothy*, (chap. i. 6) he saith to him, *Stir up the gift of God, which is in thee by the laying on of my hands:* where note by the way, that by the Holy Ghost, is not meant the third person in the Trinity, but the gifts necessary to the pastoral office. We read also, that St. Paul had imposition of hands twice; once from Ananias at Damascus, (*Acts* ix. 17, 18) at the time of his baptism; and again (*Acts* xiii. 3) at Antioch, when he was first sent out to preach. The use then of this ceremony, considered in the ordination of pastors, was to design the person to whom they gave such power. But if there had been then any Christian, that had had the power of teaching before; the baptizing of him, that is, the making him a Christian, had given him no new power, but had only caused him to preach true doctrine, that is, to use his power aright; and therefore the imposition of hands had been un-necessary; baptism itself had been sufficient. But every sov-ereign, before Christianity, had the power of teaching, and ordaining teachers; and therefore Christianity gave them no new right, but only directed them in the way of teaching truth; and consequently they needed no imposition of hands, besides that which is done in baptism, to authorize them to exercise any part of the pastoral function, as namely, to bap-tize and consecrate. And in the Old Testament, though the priest only had right to consecrate, during the time that the sovereignty was in the high-priest; yet is was not so when the sovereignty was in the king. For we read (1 *Kings* viii) that Solomon blessed the people, consecrated the Temple, and pronounced that public prayer which is the pattern now for consecration of all Christian churches and chapels: whereby it appears, he had not only the right of ecclesiastical government, but also of exercising ecclesiastical functions.

*The civil sovereign, if a Christian, is head of the Church in his own dominions.* From this consolidation of the right politic and ecclesiastic in Christian sovereigns, it is evident, they have all manner of power over their subjects, that can be given to man, for the government of men's external ac-tions, both in policy and religion; and may make such laws as themselves shall judge fittest, for the government of their own subjects, both as they are the commonmealth, and as they are the Church; for both State and Church are the same men.

If they please, therefore, they may, as many Christian kings now do, commit the government of their subjects in matters of religion to the Pope; but then the Pope is in that point subordinate to them, and exerciseth that charge in another's dominion *jure civili,* in the right of the civil sovereign; not *jure divino,* in God's right; and may therefore be discharged of that office, when the sovereign, for the good of his subjects, shall think it necessary. They may also, if they please, commit the care of religion to one supreme pastor, or to an assembly of pastors; and give them what power over the Church, or one over another, they think most convenient; and what titles of honour, as of archbishops, bishops, priests, or presbyters, they will; and make such laws for their maintenance, either by tithes or otherwise, as they please, so they do it out of a sincere conscience, of which God only is the judge. It is the civil sovereign that is to appoint judges and interpreters of the canonical Scriptures; for it is he that maketh them laws. It is he also that giveth strength to excommunications; which but for such laws and punishments, as may humble obstinate libertines, and reduce them to union with the rest of the Church, would be contemned. In sum, he hath the supreme power in all causes, as well ecclesiastical as civil, as far as concerneth actions and words, for those only are known and may be accused; and of that which cannot be accused, there is no judge at all but God, that knoweth the heart. And these rights are incident to all sovereigns, whether monarchs or assemblies: for they that are the representants of a Christian people, are representants of the Church: for a Church, and a commonwealth of Christian people, are the same thing.

*Cardinal Bellarmine's books,* De Summo Pontifice *considered.* Though this that I have here said, and in other places of this book, seem clear enough for the asserting of the supreme ecclesiastical power to Christian sovereigns; yet because the Pope of Rome's challenge to that power universally, hath been maintained chiefly, and I think, as strongly as is possible, by Cardinal Bellarmine, in his controversy *De Summo Pontifice;* I have thought it necessary, as briefly as I can, to examine the grounds and strength of his discourse.

*The first book.* Of five books he hath written of this subject, the first containeth three questions: one, which is simply the best government, *Monarchy, Aristocracy,* or *Democracy;* and concludeth for neither, but for a government mixed of all three: another, which of these is the best government of the Church; and concludeth for the mixed, but which should most participate of monarchy: the third, whether in this mixed monarchy, St. Peter had the place of monarch. Concerning his first conclusion, I have already sufficiently proved (chapter 18) that all governments which men are bound to obey, are simple and absolute. In monarchy there is but one man supreme; and all other men that have any kind of power in the state, have it by his commission, during his pleasure, and execute it in his name: and in aristocracy and democracy, but one supreme assembly, with the same power that in monarchy belongeth to the monarch, which is not a mixed, but an absolute sovereignty. And of the three sorts, which is the best, is not to be disputed, where any one of them is already established; but the present ought always to be preferred, maintained, and accounted best; because it is against both the law of nature, and the divine positive law, to do any thing tending to the subversion thereof. Besides, it maketh nothing to the power of any pastor, unless he have the civil sovereignty, what kind of government is the best; because their calling is not to govern men by commandment, but to teach them, and persuade them by arguments, and leave it to them to consider whether they shall embrace, or reject the doctrine taught. For monarchy, aristocracy, and democracy, do mark out unto us three sorts of sovereigns, not of pastors, or, as we may say, three sorts of masters of families, not three sorts of schoolmasters for their children.

And therefore the second conclusion, concerning the best form of government of the Church, is nothing to the question of the Pope's power without his own dominions. For in all other commonwealths his power, if he have any at all, is that of the schoolmaster only, and not of the master of the family.

For the third conclusion, which is, that St. Peter was monarch of the Church, he bringeth for his chief argument the place of St. Matthew (chap. xvi. 18, 19) *Thou art Peter, and upon this rock I will build my Church, &c. And I will give thee the keys of heaven; whatsoever thou shalt bind on earth, shall be bound in heaven, and whatsoever thou shalt loose on earth, shall be loosed in heaven.* Which place, well considered, proveth no more, but that the Church of Christ hath for foundation one only article; namely, that which Peter in the name of all the apostles professing, gave occasion to our Saviour to speak the words here cited. Which that we may clearly understand, we are to consider, that our Saviour preached by himself, by John the Baptist, and by his apostles, nothing but this article of faith, *that he was the*

*Christ;* all other articles requiring faith no otherwise, than as founded on that. John began first, *(Matt.* iii. 2) preaching only this, *the kingdom of God is at hand.* Then our Saviour himself *(Matt.* iv. 17) preached the same: and to his twelve apostles, when he gave them their commission, *(Matt.* x. 7), there is no mention of preaching any other article but that. This was the fundamental article, that is the foundation of the Church's faith. Afterwards the apostles being returned to him, he *(Matt.* xvi. 13) asketh them all, not Peter only, *who men said he was;* and they answered, that *some said he was John the Baptist, some Elias, and others Jeremiah, or one of the Prophets.* Then (verse 15) he asked them all again, not Peter only, *whom say ye that I am?* Therefore St. Peter answered for them all, *Thou art Christ, the Son of the living God;* which I said is the foundation of the faith of the whole Church; from which our Saviour takes the occasion of saying, *upon this stone I will build my Church:* by which it is manifest, that by the foundation-stone of the Church, was meant the fundamental article of the Church's faith. But why then, will some object, doth our Saviour interpose these words, *thou art Peter?* If the original of this text had been rigidly translated, the reason would easily have appeared. We are therefore to consider, that the apostle Simon was surnamed *Stone,* which is the signification of the Syriac word *Cephas,* and of the Greek word Πετρος. Our Saviour therefore, after the confession of that fundamental article, alluding to his name, said (as if it were in English) thus, Thou art *Stone,* and upon this Stone I will build my Church: which is as much as to say, this article, that *I am the Christ,* is the foundation of all the faith I require in those that are to be members of my Church. Neither is this allusion to a name, an unusual thing in common speech. But it had been a strange and obscure speech, if our Saviour, intending to build his Church on the person of St. Peter, had said, *thou art a stone, and upon this stone I will build my Church;* when it was so obvious, without ambiguity, to have said, *I will build my Church on thee;* and yet there had been still the same allusion to his name.

And for the following words, *I will give thee the keys of heaven, &c.* it is no more than what our Saviour gave also to all the rest of his disciples, *(Matt.* xviii. 18), *Whatsoever ye shall bind on earth, shall be bound in heaven: and whatsoever ye shall loose on earth, shall be loosed in heaven.* But howsoever this be interpreted, there is no doubt but the power here granted belongs to all supreme pastors; such as are all Christian civil sovereigns in their own dominions. In so much, as if St. Peter, or our Saviour himself, had converted any of them to believe him, and to acknowledge his kingdom; yet, because his kingdom is not of this world, he had left the supreme care of converting his subjects to none but him; or else he must have deprived him of the sovereignty, to which the right of teaching is inseparably annexed. And thus much in refutation of his first book, wherein he would prove St. Peter to have been the monarch universal of the Church, that is to say, of all the Christians in the world.

*The second book.* The second book hath two conclusions: one, that St. Peter was Bishop of Rome, and there died: the other, that the Popes of Rome are his successors. Both which have been disputed by others. But supposing them true; yet if by Bishop of Rome, be understood either the monarch of the Church, or the supreme pastor of it; not Silvester, but Constantine, who was the first Christian emperor, was that bishop; and as Constantine, so all other Christian emperors, were of right supreme bishops of the Roman empire: I say, of the Roman empire, not of all Christendom; for other Christian sovereigns had the same right in their several territories, as to an office essentially adherent to their sovereignty. Which shall serve for answer to his second book.

*The third book.* In the third book he handleth the question, whether the Pope be Antichrist? For my part, I see no argument that proves he is so, in that sense the Scripture useth the name: nor will I take any argument from the quality of Antichrist, to contradict the authority he exerciseth, or hath heretofore exercised, in the dominions of any other prince or state.

It is evident that the prophets of the Old Testament foretold, and the Jews expected a Messiah, that is, a Christ, that should re-establish amongst them the kingdom of God, which had been rejected by them in the time of Samuel, when they required a king after the manner of other nations. This expectation of theirs made them obnoxious to the imposture of all such, as had both the ambition to attempt the attaining of the kingdom, and the art to deceive the people by counterfeit miracles, by hypocritical life, or by orations and doctrine plausible. Our Saviour therefore, and his apostles, forewarned men of false prophets and of false Christs. False Christs are such as pretend to be the *Christ,* but are not, and are called properly *Antichrist;* in such sense, as when there happeneth a schism in the Church, by the election of two Popes, the one calleth the other *Antipapa,* or the false Pope. And therefore Antichrist in the proper signification hath two essential marks; one, that he denieth Jesus to be Christ; and another that he professeth himself to be Christ. The first mark is set down by St. John in his first Epistle, iv. 3, *Every Spirit that confesseth not that Jesus Christ is come in the flesh, is not of God; and this is the spirit of Antichrist.* The other mark is expressed in the words of our Saviour, (*Matt.* xxiv. 5) *many shall come in my name, saying, I am Christ;* and again, (verse 23) *If any man shall say unto you, lo! here is Christ, there is Christ, believe it not.* And therefore Antichrist must be a false Christ; that is, some of them that shall pretend themselves to be Christ. And out of these two marks, *to deny Jesus to be the Christ,* and *to affirm himself to be the Christ,* it followeth, that he must also be an *adversary of Jesus the true Christ,* which is another usual signification of the word Antichrist. But of these many Antichrists, there is one special one, ὁ Ἀντίχριστος, *the Antichrist,* or *Antichrist* definitely, as one certain person; not indefinitely *an Antichrist.* Now, seeing the Pope of Rome neither pretendeth himself, nor denieth Jesus to be the Christ, I perceive not how he can be called Antichrist; by which word is not meant, one that falsely pretendeth to be *his lieutenant* or *vicar-general,* but to be *He.* There is also some mark of the time of this special Antichrist, as (*Matt.* xxiv. 15), when that abominable destroyer, spoken of by Daniel (*Dan.* ix. 27) shall stand in the Holy place, and such tribulation as was not since the beginning of the world, nor ever shall be again, insomuch as if it were to last long, (*Matt.* xxiv. 22) *no flesh could be saved; but for the elect's sake those days shall be shortened,* made fewer. But that tribulation is not yet come; for it is to be followed immediately (verse 29) by a darkening of the sun and moon, a falling of the stars, a concussion of the heavens, and the glorious coming again of our Saviour in the clouds. And therefore *the Antichrist* is not yet come; whereas, many Popes are both come and gone. It is true, the Pope, in taking upon him to give laws to all Christian kings and nations, usurpeth a kingdom in this world, which Christ took not on him: but he doth it not *as Christ,* but as *for Christ,* wherein there is nothing of *the Antichrist.*

*Fourth book.* In the fourth book, to prove the Pope to be the supreme judge in all questions of faith and manners, *which is as much as to be the absolute monarch of all Christians in the world,* he bringeth three propositions: the first, that his judgments are infallible: the second, that he can make very laws, and punish those that observe them not: the third, that our Saviour conferred all jurisdiction ecclesiastical on the Pope of Rome.

*Texts for the infallibility of the Pope's judgment in points of faith.* For the infallibility of his judgments, he allegeth the Scriptures: and first, that of Luke xxii. 31, 32: *Simon, Simon, Satan hath desired you, that he may sift you as wheat; but I have prayed for thee, that thy faith fail not; and when thou are converted, strengthen thy brethren.* This, according to Bellarmine's exposition, is, that Christ gave here to Simon Peter two privileges: one, that neither his faith should fail, nor the faith of any of his successors: the other, that neither he, nor any of his successors, should ever define any point concerning faith or manners erroneously, or contrary to the definition of a former Pope: which is a strange, and very much strained interpretation. But he that with attention readeth that chapter, shall find there is no place in the whole Scripture that maketh more against the Pope's authority, than this very place. The Priests and Scribes seeking to kill our Saviour at the Passover, and Judas possessed with a resolution to betray him, and the day of killing the Passover being come, our Saviour celebrated the same with his apostles, which he said, till the kingdom of God was come he would do no more; and withal told them, that one of them was to betray him. Hereupon they questioned which of them it should be; and withal, seeing the next Passover their master would celebrate should be when he was king, entered into a contention, who should then be the greatest man. Our Saviour therefore told them, that the kings of the nations had dominion over their subjects, and are called by a name in Hebrew, that signifies bountiful; but I cannot be so to you, you must endeavour to serve one another; I ordain you a kingdom, but it is such as my Father had ordained me; a kingdom that I am now to purchase with my blood, and not to possess till my second coming; then ye shall eat and drink at my table, and sit on thrones judging the twelve tribes of Israel. And then addressing himself to St. Peter, he saith; Simon, Simon, Satan seeks, by suggesting a present domination, to weaken your faith of the future; but I have prayed for thee, that thy faith shall not fail; thou therefore note this, being converted, and understanding my kingdom as of an-

other world, confirm the same faith in thy brethren. To which
St. Peter answered, as one that no more expected any authority in this world, *Lord, I am ready to go with thee, not only
to prison, but to death*. Whereby it is manifest, St. Peter had
not only no jurisdiction given him in this world, but a charge
to teach all the other apostles, that they also should have
none. And for the infallibility of St. Peter's sentence definitive
in matter of faith, there is no more to be attributed to it out
of this text, than that Peter should continue in the belief of
this point, namely, that Christ should come again and possess
the kingdom at the day of judgment; which was not given by
this text to all his successors; for we see they claim it in the
world that now is.

The second place is that of Matt. xvi. 18, *Thou art Peter,
and upon this rock I will build my Church, and the gates of
hell shall not prevail against it*. By which, as I have already
shown in this chapter, is proved no more, than that the gates
of hell shall not prevail against the confession of Peter, which
gave occasion to that speech; namely this, that *Jesus is Christ
the Son of God*.

The third text is John xxi. 16, 17: *Feed my sheep;* which
contains no more but a commission of teaching. And if we
grant the rest of the apostles to be contained in that name of
*sheep;* then it is the supreme power of teaching; but it was
only for the time that there were no Christian sovereigns already possessed of that supremacy. But I have already proved
that Christian sovereigns are in their own dominions the
supreme pastors, and instituted thereto, by virtue of their
being baptized, though without other imposition of hands.
For such imposition, being a ceremony of designing the person, is needless, when he is already designed to the power of
teaching what doctrine he will, by his institution to an absolute power over his subjects. For as I have proved before,
sovereigns are supreme teachers, in general, by their office;
and therefore oblige themselves, by their baptism, to teach
the doctrine of Christ: and when they suffer others to teach
their people they do it at the peril of their own souls; for it
is at the hands of the heads of families that God will require
the account of the instruction of his children and servants.
It is of Abraham himself, not of a hireling, that God saith
(*Gen*. xviii. 19) *I know him that he will command his children, and his household after him, that they keep the way of
the Lord, and do justice and judgment*.

The fourth place is that of *Exod*. xxviii. 30: *Thou shalt put in the breast-plate of judgment, the Urim and the Thummim:* which he saith is interpreted by the Septuagint δήλωσιν καὶ ἀλήθειαν; that is, *evidence* and *truth:* and thence concludeth, God hath given evidence and truth, which is almost infallibility, to the high-priest. But be it evidence and truth itself that was given; or be it but admonition to the priest to endeavour to inform himself clearly, and give judgment uprightly; yet in that it was given to the high-priest, it was given to the civil sovereign; (for such next under God was the high-priest in the commonwealth of Israel); and is an argument for evidence and truth, that is, for the ecclesiastical supremacy of civil sovereigns over their own subjects, against the pretended power of the Pope. These are all the texts he bringeth for the infallibility of the judgment of the Pope in point of faith.

*Texts for the same, in point of manners.* For the infallibility of his judgment concerning manners, he bringeth one text, which is that of John xvi. 13: *When the Spirit of truth is come, he will lead you into all truth:* where, saith he, by *all truth,* is meant, at least *all truth necessary to salvation.* But with this mitigation, he attributeth no more infallibility to the Pope, than to any man that professeth Christianity and is not to be damned. For if any man err in any point, wherein not to err is necessary to salvation, it is impossible he should be saved; for that only is necessary to salvation, without which to be saved is impossible. What points these are, I shall declare out of the Scripture in the chapter following. In this place I say no more, but that though it were granted, the Pope could not possibly teach any error at all, yet doth not this entitle him to any jurisdiction in the dominions of another prince; unless we shall also say, a man is obliged in conscience to set on work upon all occasions the best workman, even then also when he hath formerly promised his work to another.

Besides the text, he argueth from reason, thus. If the Pope could err in necessaries, then Christ hath not sufficiently provided for the Church's salvation; because he hath commanded her to follow the Pope's directions. But this reason is invalid, unless he shew when and where Christ commanded that, or took at all any notice of a Pope. Nay, granting whatsoever was given to St. Peter, was given to the Pope; yet seeing there is in the Scripture no command to any man to obey St. Peter, no man can be just, that obeyeth him, when his commands are contrary to those of his lawful sovereign.

Lastly, it hath not been declared by the Church, nor by

the Pope. himself, that he is the civil sovereign of all the Christians in the world; and therefore all Christians are not bound to acknowledge his jurisdiction in point of manners. For the civil sovereignty, and supreme judicature in controversies of manners, are the same thing: and the makers of civil laws, are not only declarers, but also makers of the justice and injustice of actions; there being nothing in men's manners that make them righteous or unrighteous, but their conformity with the law of the sovereign. And therefore, when the Pope challengeth supremacy in controversies of manners, he teacheth men to disobey the civil sovereign; which is an erroneous doctrine, contrary to the many precepts of our Saviour and his apostles, delivered to us in the Scripture.

To prove the Pope has power to make laws, he allegeth many places; as first, (*Deut.* xvii. 12), *The man that will do presumptuously, and will not hearken unto the priest, that standeth to minister there before the Lord thy God, or unto the judge, even that man shall die; and thou shalt put away the evil from Israel.* For answer whereunto, we are to remember that the high-priest, next and immediately under God, was the civil sovereign; and all judges were to be constituted by him. The words alleged sound therefore thus: *The man that will presume to disobey the civil sovereign for the time being, or any of his officers in the execution of their places, that man shall die, &c.;* which is clearly for the civil sovereignty, against the universal power of the Pope.

Secondly, he allegeth that of *Matt.* xvi. 19, *Whatsoever ye shall bind, &c.* and interpreteth it for such *binding* as is attributed (*Matt.* xxiii. 4) to the Scribes and Pharisees. *They bind heavy burthens, and grievous to be borne, and lay them on men's shoulders;* by which is meant, he says, making of laws; and concludes thence, that the Pope can make laws. But this also maketh only for the legislative power of civil sovereigns. For the Scribes and Pharisees sat in Moses' chair; but Moses next under God was sovereign of the people of Israel: and therefore our Saviour commanded them to do all that they should say, but not all that they should do: that is, to obey their laws, but not follow their example.

The third place is *John* xxi. 16, *Feed my sheep;* which is not a power to make laws, but a command to teach. Making laws belongs to the lord of the family; who by his own discretion chooseth his chaplain, as also a schoolmaster to teach his children.

The fourth place (*John* xx. 21) is against him. The words

are, *As my father sent me, so send I you.* But our Saviour
was sent to redeem by his death such as should believe, and
by his own and his apostles' preaching to prepare them for
their entrance into his kingdom; which he himself saith, is
not of this world, and hath taught us to pray for the coming
of it hereafter, though he refused (*Acts* i. 6, 7) to tell his
apostles when it should come; and in which, when it comes,
the twelve apostles shall sit on twelve thrones, every one perhaps as high as that of St. Peter, to judge the twelve tribes of
Israel. Seeing then God the Father sent not our Saviour to
make laws in this present world, we may conclude from the
text, that neither did our Saviour send St. Peter to make
laws here, but to persuade men to expect his second coming
with a steadfast faith; and in the meantime, if subjects, to
obey their princes; and if princes, both to believe it themselves, and to do their best to make their subjects do the
same; which is the office of a bishop. Therefore this place
maketh most strongly for the joining of the ecclesiastical
supremacy to the civil sovereignty, contrary to that which
Cardinal Bellarmine allegeth it for.

The fifth place is *Acts* xv. 28, 29, *It hath seemed good to
the Holy Spirit and to us, to lay upon you no greater burthen,
than these necessary things, that ye abstain from meats
offered to idols, and from blood, and from things strangled,
and from fornication.* Here he notes the word *laying of
burthens* for the legislative power. But who is there, that
reading this text, can say, this style of the apostles may not
as properly be used in giving counsel, as in making laws?
The style of a law is, *we command:* but, *we think good,* is
the ordinary style of them, that but give advice; and they
lay a burthen that give advice, though it be conditional, that
is, if they to whom they give it, will attain their ends: and
such is the burthen of abstaining from things strangled, and
from blood; not absolute, but in case they will not err. I have
shown before, (chapter 25) that law is distinguished from
counsel in this, that the reason of a law is taken from the
design and benefit of him that prescribeth it; but the reason
of a counsel, from the design and benefit of him to whom
the counsel is given. But here, the apostles aim only at the
benefit of the converted Gentiles, namely their salvation; not
at their own benefit; for having done their endeavour, they
shall have their reward, whether they be obeyed or not. And
therefore the acts of this council, were not laws, but counsels.

The sixth place is that of *Rom.* xiii, *Let every soul be sub-*

ject to the higher powers, for there is no power but of God; which is meant, he saith, not only of secular, but also of ecclesiastical princes. To which I answer, first, that there are no ecclesiastical princes but those that are also civil sovereigns; and their principalities exceed not the compass of their civil sovereignty; without those bounds, though they may be received for doctors, they cannot be acknowledged for princes. For if the apostle had meant, we should be subject both to our own princes, and also to the Pope, he had taught us a doctrine, which Christ himself hath told us is impossible, namely, *to serve two masters*. And though the apostle say in another place, (2 *Cor.* xiii. 10) *I write these things being absent, lest being present I should use sharpness, according to the power which the Lord hath given me;* it is not, that he challenged a power either to put to death, imprison, banish, whip, or fine any of them, which are punishments; but only to excommunicate, which, without the civil power, is no more but a leaving of their company, and having no more to do with them than with a heathen man or a publican; which in many occasions might be a greater pain to the excommunicant, than to the excommunicate.

The seventh place is 1 *Cor.* iv. 21, *Shall I come unto you with a rod, or in love, and the spirit of lenity?* But here again, it is not the power of a magistrate to punish offenders, that is meant by a rod; but only the power of excommunication, which is not in its own nature a punishment, but only a denouncing of punishment, that Christ shall inflict when he shall be in possession of his kingdom, at the day of judgment. Nor then also shall it be properly a punishment, as upon a subject that hath broken the law; but a revenge, as upon an enemy or revolter, that denieth the right of our Saviour to the kingdom. And therefore this proveth not the legislative power of any bishop, that has not also the civil power.

The eighth place is 1 *Timothy* iii. 2; *A bishop must be the husband of but one wife, vigilant, sober, &c.:* which he saith was a law. I thought that none could make a law in the Church, but the monarch of the Church, St. Peter. But suppose this precept made by the authority of St. Peter; yet I see no reason why to call it a law, rather than an advice, seeing Timothy was not a subject, but a disciple of St. Paul; nor the flock under the charge of Timothy, his subjects in the kingdom, but his scholars in the school of Christ. If all the precepts he giveth Timothy be laws, why is not this also a law, (1 *Tim.* v. 23) *Drink no longer water, but use a little wine for thy health's sake.* And why are not also the precepts of good physicians so many laws, but that it is not the imperative manner of speaking, but an absolute subjection to a person, that maketh his precepts laws?

In like manner, the ninth place, 1 *Tim.* v. 19, *Against an elder receive not an accusation, but before two or three witnesses,* is a wise precept, but not a law.

The tenth place is *Luke* x. 16, *He that heareth you, heareth me; and he that despiseth you, despiseth me.* And there is no doubt, but he that despiseth the counsel of those that are sent by Christ, despiseth the counsel of Christ himself. But who are those now that are sent by Christ, but such as are ordained pastors by lawful authority? And who are lawfully ordained, that are not ordained by the sovereign pastor? And who is ordained by the sovereign pastor in a Christian commonwealth, that is not ordained by the authority of the sovereign thereof? Out of this place therefore it followeth, that he which heareth his sovereign, being a Christian, heareth Christ; and he that despiseth the doctrine which his king, being a Christian, authorizeth, despiseth the doctrine of Christ: which is not that which Bellarmine intendeth here to prove, but the contrary. But all this is nothing to a law. Nay more, a Christian king, as a pastor and teacher of his subjects, makes not thereby his doctrines laws. He cannot oblige men to believe; though as a civil sovereign he may make laws suitable to his doctrine, which may oblige men to certain actions, and sometimes to such as they would not otherwise do, and which he ought not to command; and yet when they are commanded, they are laws; and the external actions done in obedience to them, without the inward approbation, are the actions of the sovereign, and not of the subject, which is in that case but as an instrument, without any motion of his own at all; because God hath commanded to obey them.

The eleventh is every place where the people for counsel putteth some word, by which men use to signify command; or calleth the following of his counsel by the name of obedience. And therefore they are alleged out of 1 *Cor.* xi. 2, *I commend you for keeping my precepts as I delivered them to you.* The Greek is, *I commend you for keeping those things I delivered to you, as I delivered them.* Which is far from signifying that they were laws, or any thing else, but good counsel. And that of 1 *Thess.* iv. 2, *You know what commandments we gave you:* where the Greek word is παραγγελίας ἐδώκαμεν, equivalent to παρεδώκαμεν, *what we delivered to you*, as in the place next before alleged, which does not prove the traditions of the apostles to be any more than counsels; though as is said in the 8th verse, *he that despiseth them, despiseth not man, but God*. For our Saviour himself came not to judge, that is, to be king in the world; but to sacrifice himself for sinners, and leave doctors in his Church to lead, not to drive men to Christ, who never accepteth forced actions, (which is all the law produceth,) but the inward conversion of the heart; which is not the work of laws, but of counsel and doctrine.

And that of 2 *Thess.* iii. 14, *If any man obey not our word by this Epistle, note that man, and have no company with him, that he may be ashamed:* where from the word *obey*, he would infer, that this epistle was a law to the Thessalonians. The epistles of the emperors were indeed laws. If therefore the epistle of St. Paul were also a law, they were to obey two masters. But the word *obey*, as it is in the Greek ὑπακούει, signifieth *hearkening to* or *putting in practice*, not only that which is commanded by him that has right to punish, but also that which is delivered in a way of counsel for our good; and therefore St. Paul does not bid kill him that disobeys; nor beat, nor imprison, nor amerce him, which legislators may all do; but avoid his company, that he may be ashamed: whereby it is evident, it was not the empire of an apostle, but his reputation amongst the faithful, which the Christians stood in awe of.

The last place is that of *Heb.* xiii. 17, *Obey your leaders, and submit yourselves to them; for they watch for your souls, as they that must give account:* and here also is intended by obedience, a following of their counsel. For the reason of our obedience is not drawn from the will and command of our pastors, but from our own benefit, as being the salvation of our souls, they watch for, and not for the exaltation of their own power and authority. If it were meant here, that all they teach were laws, then not only the Pope, but every pastor in his parish should have legislative power. Again, they that are bound to obey their pastors, have no power to examine their commands. What then shall we say to St. John, who bids us (1 *John* iv. 1) *Not to believe every spirit, but to try the spirits whether they are of God; because many false prophets are gone out into the world?* It is therefore manifest, that we may dispute the doctrine of our pastors; but no man can dispute a law. The commands of civil sovereigns are on all sides granted to be laws: if any else can make a law besides himself, all commonwealth, and consequently all peace and justice must cease; which is contrary to all laws both divine and human. Nothing therefore can be drawn from these, or any other places of Scripture, to prove the decrees of the Pope, where he has not also the civil sovereignty, to be laws.

*The question of superiority between the Pope and other bishops.* The last point he would prove, is this, *That our Saviour Christ has committed ecclesiastical jurisdiction immediately to none but the Pope.* Wherein he handleth not the question of supremacy between the Pope and Christian kings, but between the Pope and other bishops. And first, he says, it is agreed that the jurisdiction of bishops is at least in the general *de jure divino,* that is, in the right of God; for which he alleges St. Paul, *Eph.* iv. 11, where he says, that Christ after his ascension into heaven, *gave gifts to men, some apostles, some prophets, and some evangelists, and some pastors, and some teachers;* and thence infers, they have indeed their juridsiction in God's right; but will not grant they have it immediately from God, but derived through the Pope. But if a man may be said to have his jurisdiction *de jure divino,* and yet not immediately; what lawful jurisdiction, though but civil, is there in a Christian commonwealth, that is not also *de juro divino?* For Christian kings have their civil power from God immediately; and the magistrates under him exercise their several charges in virtue of his commission; wherein that which they do, is no less *de jure divino mediato,* than that which the bishops do in virtue of the Pope's ordination. All lawful power is of God, immediately in the Supreme Governor, and mediately in those that have authority under him: so that either he must grant every constable in the state, to hold his office in the right of God; or he must not hold that any bishop holds his so, besides the Pope himself.

But this whole dispute, whether Christ left the jurisdiction to the Pope only, or to other bishops also, if considered out of those places where the Pope has the civil sovereignty, is a contention *de lana caprina:* for none of them, where they are not sovereigns, has any jurisdiction at all. For jurisdiction is the power of hearing and determining causes between man and man; and can belong to none but him that hath the power to prescribe the rules of right and wrong; that is, to make laws; and with the sword of justice to compel men to obey his decisions, pronounced either by himself, or by the judges he ordaineth thereunto; which none can lawfully do but the civil sovereign.

Therefore when he allegeth out of chapter vi of *Luke*, that our Saviour called his disciples together, and chose twelve of them, which he named apostles, he proveth that he elected them (all, except Matthias, Paul and Barnabas,) and gave them power and command to preach, but not to judge of causes between man and man: for that is a power which he refused to take upon himself, saying, *Who made me a judge, or a divider, amongst you?* and in another place, *My kingdom is not of this world.* But he that hath not the power to hear and determine causes between man and man, cannot be said to have any jurisdiction at all. And yet this hinders not, but that our Saviour gave them power to preach and baptize in all parts of the world, supposing they were not by their own lawful sovereign forbidden: for to our own sovereigns Christ himself, and his apostles, have in sundry places expressly commanded us in all things to be obedient.

The arguments by which he would prove, that bishops receive their jurisdiction from the Pope (seeing the Pope in the dominions of other princes hath no jurisdiction himself,) are all in vain. Yet because they prove, on the contrary, that all bishops receive jurisdiction, when they have it, from their civil sovereigns, I will not omit the recital of them.

The first is from chapter xi of *Numbers*, where Moses not being able alone to undergo the whole burthen of administering the affairs of the people of Israel, God commanded him to choose seventy elders, and took part of the spirit of Moses, to put it upon those seventy elders: by which is understood, not that God weakened the spirit of Moses; for that had not eased him at all; but that they had all of them their authority from him; wherein he doth truly and ingenuously interpret that place. But seeing Moses had the entire sovereignty in the commonwealth of the Jews, it is manifest, that it is thereby signified, that they had their authority from the civil sovereign: and therefore that place proveth that bishops in every Christian commonwealth have their authority from the civil sovereign; and from the Pope in his own territories only, and not in the territories of any other state.

The second argument, is from the nature of monarchy; wherein all authority is in one man, and in others by derivation from him. But the government of the Church, he says, is monarchical. This also makes for Christian monarchs. For they are really monarchs of their own people; that is, of their own Church; for the Church is the same thing with a Christian people; whereas the power of the Pope, though he were St. Peter, is neither monarchy, nor hath any thing of *archical*, nor *cratical*, but only of *didactical;* for God accepteth not a forced, but a willing obedience.

The third, is from that the *see* of St. Peter is called by St. Cyprian, the *head*, the *source*, the *root*, the *sun*, from whence the authority of bishops is derived. But by the law of nature, which is a better principle of right and wrong than the word of any doctor that is but a man, the civil sovereign in every commonwealth, is the *head*, the *source*, the *root*, and the *sun*, from which all jurisdiction is derived. And therefore the jurisdiction of bishops, is derived from the civil sovereign.

The fourth, is taken from the inequality of their jurisdictions. For if God, saith he, had given it them immediately, he had given as well equality of jurisdiction, as of order: but we see, some are bishops but of one town, some of a hundred towns, and some of many whole provinces; which differences were not determined by the command of God; their jurisdiction therefore is not of God, but of man; and one has a greater, another a less, as it pleaseth the Prince of the Church. Which argument, if he had proved before, that the Pope had an universal jurisdiction over all Christians, had been for his purpose. But seeing that hath not been proved, and that it is notoriously known, the large jurisdiction of the Pope was given him by those that had it, that is, by the Emperors of Rome, (for the Patriarchs of Constantinople, upon the same title, namely of being bishop of the capital city of the empire, and seat of the emperor, claimed to be equal to him), it followeth, that all other bishops have their jurisdiction from the sovereigns of the place wherein they exercise the same. And as for that cause they have not their authority *de jure divino;* so neither hath the Pope his *de jure divino*, except only where he is also the civil sovereign.

His fifth argument is this: *If bishops have their jurisdiction immediately from God, the Pope could not take it from them, for he can do nothing contrary to God's ordination;* and this consequence is good, and well proved. *But,* saith he, *the Pope can do this, and has done it.* This also is granted, so he do it in his own dominions, or in the dominions of any other prince that hath given him that power; but not universally, in right of the Popedom: for that power belongeth to every Christian sovereign, with the bounds of his own empire, and is inseparable from the sovereignty. Before the people of

Israel had, by the commandment of God to Samuel, set over themselves a king, after the manner of other nations, the high-priest had the civil government; and none but he could make or depose an inferior priest. But that power was afterwards in the king, as may be proved by this same argument of Bellarmine; for if the priest, be he the high-priest or any other, had his jurisdiction immediately from God, then the king could not take it from him; *for he could do nothing contrary to God's ordinance*. But it is certain that king Solomon (1 *Kings* ii. 26, 27) deprived Abiathar the high-priest of his office, and placed Zadok (verse 35) in his room. Kings therefore may in like manner ordain and deprive bishops, as they shall think fit for the well-governing of their subjects.

His sixth argument is this, if bishops have their jurisdiction *de jure divino*, that is, *immediately from God*, they that maintain it, should bring some word of God to prove it: but they can bring none. The argument is good; I have therefore nothing to say against it. But it is an argument no less good, to prove the Pope himself to have no jurisdiction in the dominion of any other prince.

Lastly, he bringeth for argument the testimony of two popes, Innocent and Leo; and I doubt not he might have alleged, with as good reason, the testimonies of all the popes almost since St. Peter. For considering the love of power naturally implanted in mankind, whosoever were made Pope, he would be tempted to uphold the same opinion. Nevertheless, they should therein but do, as Innocent and Leo did, bear witness of themselves, and therefore their witness should not be good.

*Of the Pope's temporal power*. In the fifth book he hath four conclusions. The first is, *that the Pope is not lord of all the world*: the second, *that the Pope is not the lord of all the Christian world*: the third, *that the Pope, without his own territory, has not any temporal jurisdiction* DIRECTLY. These three conclusions are easily granted. The fourth is, *that the Pope has, in the dominions of other princes, the supreme temporal power* INDIRECTLY: which is denied; unless he mean by *indirectly*, that he has gotten it by indirect means, then is that also granted. But I understand, that when he saith he hath it *indirectly*, he means, that such temporal jurisdiction belongeth to him of right, but that this right is but a consequence of this pastoral authority, the which he could not exercise unless he have the other with it: and therefore to the pastoral power, which he calls spiritual, the supreme power civil is necessarily annexed; and that thereby he hath a right to change kingdoms, giving them to one and taking them from another, when he shall think it conduces to the salvation of souls.

Before I come to consider the arguments by which he would prove this doctrine, it will not be amiss to lay open the consequences of it; that princes and states, that have the civil sovereignty in their several commonwealths, may bethink themselves, whether it be convenient for them, and conducing to the good of their subjects, of whom they are to give an account at the day of judgment, to admit the same.

When it is said, the Pope hath not, in the territories of other states, the supreme civil power *directly;* we are to understand, he doth not challenge it, as other civil sovereigns do, from the original submission thereto of those that are to be governed. For it is evident, and has already been sufficiently in this treatise demonstrated, that the right of all sovereigns is derived originally from the consent of every one of those that are to be governed; whether they that choose him, do it for their common defence against an enemy, as when they agree amongst themselves to appoint a man or an assembly of men to protect them; or whether they do it, to save their lives, by submission to a conquering enemy. The Pope therefore, when he disclaimeth the supreme civil power over other states *directly,* denieth no more, but that his right cometh to him by that way; he ceaseth not for all that, to claim it another way; and that is, without the consent of them that are to be governed, by a right given him by God, which he calleth *indirectly,* in his assumption to the papacy. But by what way soever he pretend, the power is the same; and he may, if it be granted to be his right, depose princes and states, as often as it is for the salvation of souls, that is, as often as he will; for he claimeth also the sole power to judge whether it be to the salvation of men's souls or not. And this is the doctrine, not only that Bellarmine here, and many other doctors, teach in their sermons and books, but also that some councils have decreed, and the Popes have accordingly, when the occasion hath served them, put in practice. For the fourth council of Lateran, held under Pope Innocent the Third, in the third chapter *De Hæreticis,* hath this canon: *If a king, at the Pope's admonition, do not purge his kingdom of heretics, and being excommunicate for the same, make not satisfaction within a year, his subjects are absolved of their obedience.* And the practice hereof hath been seen on divers occasions; as in the deposing of Childeric, king of France; in the translation of the Roman empire to Charlemagne; in the oppression of John, king of England; in transferring the kingdom of Navarre; and of late years, in the League against Henry the Third of France, and in many more occurrences. I think there be few princes that consider not this as unjust, and inconvenient; but I wish they would all resolve to be kings or subjects. Men cannot serve two masters. They ought therefore to ease them, either by holding the reins of government wholly in their own hands; or by wholly delivering them into the hands of the Pope; that such men as are willing to be obedient, may be protected in their obedience. For this distinction of temporal and spiritual power is but words. Power is as really divided, and as dangerously to all purposes, by sharing with another *indirect* power, as with a *direct* one. But to come now to his arguments.

The first is this, *The civil power is subject to the spiritual: therefore he that hath the supreme power spiritual, hath right to command temporal princes, and dispose of their temporals in order to the spiritual.* As for the distinction of temporal and spiritual, let us consider in what sense it may be said intelligibly, that the temporal or civil power is subject to the spiritual. There be but two ways that those words can be made sense. For when we say, one power is subject to another power, the meaning either is, that he which hath the one, is subject to him that hath the other; or that one power is to the other, as the means to the end. For we cannot understand, that one power hath power over another power; or that one power can have right or command over another. For subjection, command, right, and power, are accidents, not of powers, but of persons. One power may be subordinate to another, as the art of a saddler to the art of a rider. If then it be granted, that the civil government be ordained as a means to bring us to a spiritual felicity; yet it does not follow, that if a king have the civil power, and the Pope the spiritual, that therefore the king is bound to obey the Pope, more than every saddler is bound to obey every rider. Therefore as from subordination of an art, cannot be inferred the subjection of the professor; so from the subordination of a government, cannot be inferred the subjection of the governor. When therefore he saith, the civil power is subject to the spiritual, his meaning is, that the civil sovereign is subject to the spiritual sovereign. And the argument stands thus, *The civil sovereign is subject to the spiritual; therefore the spiritual prince may command temporal princes.* Where the conclusion is the same with the antecedent he should have proved. But to prove it, he allegeth first, this reason: *Kings and popes, clergy and laity, make but one commonwealth; that is to say, but one Church: and in all bodies the members depend one upon another: but things spiritual depend not of things temporal: therefore temporal depend on spiritual, and therefore are subject to them.* In which argumentation there be two gross errors: one is, that all Christian kings, popes, clergy, and all other Christian men, make but one commonwealth. For it is evident that France is one commonwealth, Spain another, and Venice a third, &c. And these consist of Christians; and therefore also are several bodies of Christians; that is to say, several Churches: and their several sovereigns represent them, whereby they are capable of commanding and obeying, of doing and suffering, as a natural man; which no general or universal Church is, till it have a representant; which it hath not on earth: for if it had, there is no doubt but that all Christendom were one commonwealth, whose sovereign were that representant, both in things spiritual and temporal. And the Pope, to make himself this representant, wanteth three things that our Saviour hath not given him, to *command,* and to *judge,* and to *punish,* otherwise than, by excommunication, to run from those that will not learn of him. For though the Pope were Christ's only vicar, yet he cannot exercise his government, till our Saviour's second coming: and then also it is not the Pope, but St. Peter himself with the other apostles, that are to be judges of the world.

The other error in this his first argument is, that he says, the members of every commonwealth, as of a natural body, depend one of another. It is true, they cohere together; but they depend only on the sovereign, which is the soul of the commonwealth; which failing, the commonwealth is dissolved into a civil war, no one man so much as cohering to another, for want of a common dependence on a known sovereign; just as the members of the natural body dissolve into earth, for want of a soul to hold them together. Therefore there is nothing in this similitude, from whence to infer a dependence of the laity on the clergy, or of the temporal officers on the spiritual; but of both on the civil sovereign; which ought indeed to direct his civil commands to the salvation of souls; but is not therefore subject to any but God himself. And thus you see the laboured fallacy of the first argument, to deceive such men as distinguished not between the subordination of actions in the way to the end; and the subjection of persons one to another in the administration of the means. For to every end, the means are determined by nature, or by God himself supernaturally: but the power to make men use the means, is in every nation resigned, by the law of nature, which forbiddeth men to violate their faith given, to the civil sovereign.

His second argument is this; *Every commonwealth, because it is supposed to be perfect and sufficient in itself, may command any other commonwealth not subject to it, and force it to change the administration of the government; nay, depose the prince, and set another in his room, if it cannot otherwise defend itself against the injuries he goes about to do them: much more may a spiritual commonwealth command a temporal one to change the administration of their government, and may depose princes, and institute others, when they cannot otherwise defend the spiritual good.*

That a commonwealth, to defend itself against injuries, may lawfully do all that he hath here said, is very true; and hath already in that which hath gone before been sufficiently demonstrated. And if it were also true, that there is now in this world a spiritual commonwealth, distinct from a civil commonwealth, then might the prince thereof, upon injury done him, or upon want of caution that injury be not done him in time to come, repair and secure himself by war; which is, in sum, deposing, killing, or subduing, or doing any act of hostility. But by the same reason, it would be no less lawful for a civil sovereign, upon the like injuries done, or feared, to make war upon the spiritual sovereign; which I believe is more than Cardinal Bellarmine would have inferred from his own proposition.

But spiritual commonwealth there is none in this world: for it is the same thing with the kingdom of Christ, which he himself saith, is not of this world; but shall be in the next world at the resurrection, when they that have lived justly, and believed that he was the Christ, shall, though they died *natural* bodies, rise *spiritual* bodies; and then it is, that our Saviour shall judge the world, and conquer his adversaries, and make a spiritual commonwealth. In the meantime, seeing there are no men on earth whose bodies are spiritual, there can be no spiritual commonwealth amongst men that are yet in the flesh; unless we call preachers, that have commission to teach, and prepare men for their reception into the kingdom of Christ at the resurrection, a commonwealth; which I have proved already to be none.

The third argument is this; *It is not lawful for Christians to tolerate an infidel, or heretical king, in case he endeavour to draw them to his heresy or infidelity. But to judge whether a king draw his subjects to heresy or not, belongeth to the Pope. Therefore hath the Pope right to determine whether the prince be to be deposed, or not deposed.*

To this I answer, that both these assertions are false. For Christians, or men of what religion soever, if they tolerate not their king, whatsoever law he maketh, though it be concerning religion, do violate their faith, contrary to the divine law, both *natural* and *positive:* nor is there any judge of heresy amongst subjects, but their own civil sovereign. For *heresy is nothing else but a private opinion obstinately maintained, contrary to the opinion which the public person, that is to say, the representant of the commonwealth, hath commanded to be taught.* By which it is manifest, that an opinion publicly appointed to be taught, cannot be heresy; nor the sovereign princes that authorize them, heretics. For heretics are none but private men, that stubbornly defend some doctrine, prohibited by their lawful sovereigns.

But to prove that Christians are not to tolerate infidel or heretical kings, he allegeth a place in *Deut.* xvii. 15, where God forbiddeth the Jews, when they shall set a king over themselves, to choose a stranger: and from thence inferreth, that it is unlawful for a Christian to choose a king that is not a Christian. And it is true, that he that is a Christian, that is, he that hath already obliged himself to receive our Saviour, when he shall come, for his king, shall tempt God too much in choosing for king in this world, one that he knoweth will endeavour, both by terror and persuasion, to make him violate his faith. But it is, saith he, the same danger, to choose one that is not a Christian, for king, and not to depose him when he is chosen. To this I say, the question is not of the danger of not deposing; but of the justice of deposing him. To choose him, may in some cases be unjust; but to depose him when he is chosen, is in no case just. For it is always violation of faith, and consequently against the law of nature, which is the eternal law of God. Nor do we read that any such doctrine was accounted Christian in the time of the apostles; nor in the time of the Roman emperors, till the Popes had the civil sovereignty of Rome. But to this he hath replied, that the Christians of old deposed not Nero, nor

Diocletian, nor Julian, nor Valens an Arian, for this cause only, that they wanted temporal forces. Perhaps so. But did our Saviour, who for calling for, might have had twelve legions of immortal, invulnerable angels to assist him, want forces to depose Cæsar, or at least Pilate, that unjustly, without finding fault in him, delivered him to the Jews to be crucified? Or if the apostles wanted temporal forces to depose Nero, was it therefore necessary for them, in their epistles to the new made Christians, to teach them, as they did, to obey the powers constituted over them, whereof Nero in that time was one, and that they ought to obey them, not for fear of their wrath, but for conscience sake? Shall we say they did not only obey, but also teach what they meant not, for want of strength? It is not therefore for want of strength, but for conscience sake, that Christians are to tolerate their heathen princes, or princes (for I cannot call any one whose doctrine is the public doctrine, an heretic) that authorize the teaching of an error. And whereas for the temporal power of the Pope, he allegeth further, that St. Paul (1 *Cor.* vi) appointed judges under the heathen princes of those times, such as were not ordained by those princes; it is not true. For St. Paul does but advise them, to take some of their brethren to compound their differences as arbitrators, rather than to go to law one with another before the heathen judges; which is a wholesome precept, and full of charity, fit to be practised also in the best Christian commonwealths. And for the danger that may arise to religion, by the subjects tolerating of a heathen, or an erring prince, it is a point of which a subject is no competent judge; or if he be, the Pope's temporal subjects may judge also of the Pope's doctrine. For every Christian prince, as I have formerly proved, is no less supreme pastor of his own subjects, than the Pope of his.

The fourth argument, is taken from the baptism of kings; wherein, that they may be made Christians, they submit their sceptres to Christ; and promise to keep and defend the Christian faith. This is true; for Christian kings are no more but Christ's subjects: but they may, for all that, be the Pope's fellows; for they are supreme pastors of their own subjects; and the Pope is no more but king and pastor, even in Rome itself.

The fifth argument, is drawn from the words spoken by our Saviour, *Feed my sheep;* by which was given all power necessary for a pastor; as the power to chase away wolves, such as are heretics; the power to shut up rams, if they be

mad, or push at the other sheep with their horns, such as are
evil, though Christian, kings; and power to give the flock
convenient food. From whence he inferreth, that St. Peter
had these three powers given him by Christ. To which I
answer, that the last of these powers is no more than the
power, or rather command, to teach. For the first, which is to
chase away wolves, that is, heretics, the place he quoteth is
(*Matt.* vii. 15) *Beware of false prophets, which come to you
in sheep's clothing, but inwardly are ravening wolves.* But
neither are heretics false prophets, or at all prophets: nor,
admitting heretics for the wolves there meant, were the
apostles commanded to kill them, or if they were kings, to
depose them; but to beware of, fly, and avoid them: nor was
it to St. Peter, nor to any of the apostles, but to the multitude
of the Jews that followed him into the mountain, men for the
most part not yet converted, that he gave this counsel, to
beware of false prophets: which therefore, if it confer a
power of chasing away kings, was given, not only to private
men, but to men that were not at all Christians. And as to
the power of separating, and shutting up of furious rams, by
which he meaneth Christian kings that refuse to submit themselves to the Roman pastor, our Saviour refused to take upon
him that power in this world himself, but advised to let the
corn and tares grow up together till the day of judgment:
much less did he give it to St. Peter, or can St. Peter give it
to the Popes. St. Peter, and all other pastors, are bidden to
esteem those Christians that disobey the Church, that is, that
disobey the Christian sovereign, as heathen men, and as publicans. Seeing then, men challenge to the Pope no authority
over heathen princes, they ought to challenge none over those
that are to be esteemed as heathen.

But from the power to teach only, he inferreth also a
coercive power in the Pope over kings. The pastor, saith he,
must give his flock convenient food: therefore the Pope may,
and ought to compel kings to do their duty. Out of which it
followeth, that the Pope, as pastor of Christian men, is king
of kings: which all Christian kings ought indeed either to
confess, or else they ought to take upon themselves the
supreme pastoral charge, every one in his own dominion.

His sixth and last argument, is from examples. To which
I answer, first, that examples prove nothing: secondly, that
the examples he allegeth make not so much as a probability
of right. The fact of Jehoiada, in killing Athaliah, (2 *Kings*
xi) was either by the authority of king Joash, or it was a

horrible crime in the high-priest, which ever after the election of king Saul was a mere subject. The fact of St. Ambrose, in excommunicating Theodosius the emperor, if it were true he did so, was a capital crime. And for the Popes, Gregory I, Gregory II, Zachary, and Leo III, their judgments are void, as given in their own cause; and the acts done by them conformably to this doctrine, are the greatest crimes, especially that of Zachary, that are incident to human nature. And thus much of Power Ecclesiastical; wherein I had been more brief, forbearing to examine these arguments of Bellarmine, if they had been his as a private man, and not as the champion of the Papacy against all other Christian Princes and States.

# Chapter 43

## Of what is Necessary for a Man's Reception into the Kingdom of Heaven

*The difficulty of obeying God and man both at once.* The most frequent pretext of sedition, and civil war, in Christian commonwealths, hath a long time proceeded from a difficulty, not yet sufficiently resolved, of obeying at once both God and man, then when their commandments are one contrary to the other. It is manifest enough, that when a man receiveth two contrary commands, and knows that one of them is God's, he ought to obey that, and not the other, though it be the command even of his lawful sovereign (whether a monarch, or a sovereign assembly), or the command of his father. The difficulty therefore consisteth in this, that men, when they are commanded in the name of God, know not in divers cases, whether the command be from God, or whether he that commandeth do but abuse God's name for some private ends of his own. For as there were in the Church of the Jews, many false prophets, that sought reputation with the people, by feigned dreams and visions; so there have been in all times in the Church of Christ, false teachers, that seek reputation with the people, by fantastical and false doctrines; and by such reputation, (as is the nature of ambition), to govern them for their private benefit.

*Is none to them that distinguish between what is, and what is not necessary to salvation.* But this difficulty of obeying both God and the civil sovereign on earth, to those that can distinguish between what is *necessary*, and what is not *necessary for their reception into the kingdom of God*, is of no moment. For if the command of the civil sovereign be such, as that it may be obeyed without the forfeiture of life eternal; not to obey it is unjust; and the precept of the apostle takes place: *Servants obey your masters in all things;* and *Children obey your parents in all things;* and the precept of our Saviour, *The Scribes and Pharisees sit in Moses' chair; all therefore they shall say, that observe and do.* But if the command be such as cannot be obeyed, without being damned to eternal death; then it were madness to obey it, and the council of our Saviour takes place, (*Matt.* x. 28), *Fear not those that kill the body, but cannot kill the soul.* All men therefore that would avoid, both the punishments that are to be in this world inflicted, for disobedience to their earthly sovereign, and those that shall be inflicted in the world to come, for disobedience to God, have need be taught to distinguish well between what is, and what is not necessary to eternal salvation.

*All that is necessary to salvation is contained in faith and obedience.* All that is NECESSARY *to salvation,* is contained in two virtues, *faith in Christ,* and *obedience to laws.* The latter of these, if it were perfect, were enough to us. But because we are all guilty of disobedience to God's law, not only originally in Adam, but also actually by our own transgressions, there is required at our hands now, not only *obedience* for the rest of our time, but also a *remission of sins* for the time past; which remission is the reward of our faith in Christ. That nothing else is necessarily required to salvation, is manifest from this, that the kingdom of heaven is shut to none but to sinners; that is to say, to the disobedient, or transgressors of the law; nor to them, in case they repent, and believe all the articles of Christian faith necessary to salvation.

*What obedience is necessary.* The obedience required at our hands by God, that accepteth in all our actions the will for the deed, is a serious endeavour to obey him; and is called also by all such names as signify that endeavour. And therefore obedience is sometimes called by the names of *charity* and *love,* because they imply a will to obey; and our Saviour himself maketh our love to God, and to one another, a fulfilling of the whole law: and sometimes by the name of *righteousness;* for righteousness is but the will to give to every one his own; that is to say, the will to obey the laws: and sometimes by the name of *repentance;* because to repent, implieth a turning away from sin, which is the same with the return of the will to obedience. Whosoever therefore unfeignedly desireth to fulfil the commandments of God, or repenteth him truly of his transgressions, or that loveth God with all his heart, and his neighbour as himself, hath all the obedience necessary to his reception into the kingdom of God. For if God should require perfect innocence, there could no flesh be saved.

*And to what laws.* But what commandments are those that God hath given us? Are all those laws which were given to the Jews by the hand of Moses, the commandments of God? If they be, why are not Christians taught to obey them? If they be not, what others are so, besides the law of nature? For our Saviour Christ hath not given us new laws, but counsel to observe those we are subject to; that is to say, the laws of nature, and the laws of our several sovereigns: nor did he make any new law to the Jews in his sermon on the Mount, but only expounded the law of Moses, to which they were subject before. The laws of God therefore are none but the laws of nature, whereof the principal is, that we should not violate our faith, that is, a commandment to obey our civil sovereigns, which we constituted over us by mutual pact one with another. And this law of God, that commandeth obedience to the law civil, commandeth by consequence obedience to all the precepts of the Bible; which, as I have proved in the precedent chapter, is there only law, where the civil sovereign hath made it so; and in other places, but counsel; which a man at his own peril may without injustice refuse to obey.

*In the faith of a Christian, who is the person believed.* Knowing now what is the obedience necessary to salvation, and to whom it is due; we are to consider next concerning faith, whom, and why we believe; and what are the articles, or points necessary to be believed by them that shall be saved. And first, for the person whom we believe, because it is impossible to believe any person, before we know what he saith, it is necessary he be one that we have heard speak. The person, therefore, whom Abraham, Isaac, Jacob, Moses, and the prophets, believed, was God himself, that spake unto them supernaturally: and the person, whom the apostles and disciples that conversed with Christ believed, was our Saviour himself. But of them, to whom neither God the Father, nor our Saviour, ever spake, it cannot be said that the person whom they believed, was God. They believed the apostles, and after them the pastors and doctors of the Church, that recommended to their faith the history of the Old and New Testament: so that the faith of Christians ever since our Saviour's time, hath had for foundation, first, the reputation of their pastors, and afterward, the authority of those that made the Old and New Testament to be received for the rule of faith; which none could do but Christian sovereigns; who are therefore the supreme pastors, and the only persons whom Christians now hear speak from God; except such as God speaketh to in these days supernaturally. But because there be many false prophets *gone out into the world*, other men are to examine such spirits, as St. John adviseth us, (1 *John*

iv. 1) *whether they be of God, or not.* And therefore, seeing the examination of doctrines belongeth to the supreme pastor, the person, which all they that have no special revelation are to believe, is, in every commonwealth, the supreme pastor, that is to say, the civil sovereign.

*The causes of Christian faith.* The causes why men believe any Christian doctrine, are various. For faith is the gift of God; and he worketh it in each several man, by such ways as it seemeth good unto himself. The most ordinary immediate cause of our belief, concerning any point of Christian faith, is, that we believe the Bible to be the word of God. But why we believe the Bible to be the word of God, is much disputed, as all questions must needs be, that are not well stated. For they make not the question to be, *why we believe it,* but, *how we know it;* as if *believing* and *knowing* were all one. And thence while one side ground their knowledge upon the infallibility of the Church, and the other side, on the testimony of the private spirit, neither side concludeth what it pretends. For how shall a man know the infallibility of the Church, but by knowing first the infallibility of the Scripture? Or how shall a man know his own private spirit to be other than a belief, grounded upon the authority and arguments of his teachers, or upon a presumption of his own gifts? Besides, there is nothing in the Scripture, from which can be inferred the infallibility of the Church; much less, of any particular Church; and least of all, the infallibility of any particular man.

*Faith comes by hearing.* It is manifest therefore, that Christian men do not know, but only believe the Scripture to be the word of God; and that the means of making them believe, which God is pleased to afford men ordinarily, is according to the way of nature, that is to say, from their teachers. It is the doctrine of St. Paul concerning Christian faith in general (*Rom.* x. 17), *Faith cometh by hearing,* that is, by hearing our lawful pastors. He saith also, (verses 14, 15, of the same chapter), *How shall they believe in him of whom they have not heard? and how shall they hear without a preacher? and how shall they preach, except they be sent?* Whereby it is evident, that the ordinary cause of believing that the Scriptures are the word of God, is the same with the cause of the believing of all other articles of our faith, namely, the hearing of those that are by the law allowed and appointed to teach us, as our parents in their houses, and our pastors in the churches. Which also is made more manifest by experience.

For what other cause can there be assigned, why in Christian commonwealths all men either believe, or at least profess the Scripture to be the word of God, and in other commonwealths scarce any; but that in Christian commonwealths they are taught it from their infancy; and in other places they are taught otherwise?

But if teaching be the cause of faith, why do not all believe? It is certain therefore that faith is the gift of God, and he giveth it to whom he will. Nevertheless, because to them to whom he giveth it, he giveth it by the means of teachers, the immediate cause of faith is hearing. In a school, where many are taught, and some profit, others profit not, the cause of learning in them that profit, is the master; yet it cannot be thence inferred, that learning is not the gift of God. All good things proceed from God; yet cannot all that have them, say they are inspired; for that implies a gift supernatural, and the immediate hand of God; which he that pretends to, pretends to be a prophet, and is subject to the examination of the Church.

But whether men *know*, or *believe*, or *grant* the Scriptures to be the word of God; if out of such places of them, as are without obscurity, I shall show what articles of faith are necessary, and only necessary for salvation, those men must needs *know*, *believe*, or *grant* the same.

*The only necessary article of Christian faith.* The, *unum necessarium*, only article of faith, which the Scripture maketh simply necessary to salvation, is this, that JESUS IS THE CHRIST. By the name of *Christ* is understood the king, which God had before promised by the prophets of the Old Testament, to send into the world, to reign (over the Jews, and over such of other nations as should believe in him), under himself eternally; and to give them that eternal life, which was lost by the sin of Adam. Which when I have proved out of Scripture, I will further show when, and in what sense, some other articles may be also called *necessary*.

*Proved from the scope of the Evangelists.* For proof that the belief of this article, *Jesus is the Christ*, is all the faith required to salvation, my first argument shall be from the scope of the Evangelists; which was by the description of the life of our Saviour, to establish that one article, *Jesus is the Christ*. The sum of St. Matthew's Gospel is this, that Jesus was of the stock of David, born of a Virgin; which are the marks of the true Christ: that the Magi came to worship him as King of the Jews: that Herod for the same cause

sought to kill him: that John the Baptist proclaimed him:
that he preached by himself and his apostles that he was that
king: that he taught the law, not as a scribe, but as a man
of authority: that he cured diseases by his word only, and
did many other miracles, which were foretold the Christ
should do: that he was saluted king when he entered into
Jerusalem: that he forewarned them to beware of all others
that should pretend to be Christ: that he was taken, accused,
and put to death, for saying he was king: that the cause of
his condemnation written on the cross was, JESUS OF
NAZARETH, THE KING OF THE JEWS. All which tend
to no other end than this, that men should believe that *Jesus
is the Christ*. Such therefore was the scope of St. Matthew's
Gospel. But the scope of all the evangelists, as may appear
by reading them, was the same. Therefore the scope of the
whole Gospel was the establishing of that only article. And
St. John expressly makes it his conclusion, (*John* xx. 31),
*These things are written, that you may know that Jesus is
the Christ, the Son of the living God.*

*From the sermons of the apostles.* My second argument is
taken from the subjects of the sermons of the apostles, both
whilst our Saviour lived on earth, and after his ascension.
The apostles, in our Saviour's time, were sent, (*Luke* ix. 2)
*to preach the kingdom of God.* For neither there, nor, *Matt.*
x. 7, giveth he any commission to them other than this, *As
ye go, preach, saying, the kingdom of heaven is at hand;* that
is, that Jesus is the *Messiah*, the *Christ*, the *King* which was
to come. That their preaching also after his ascension was
the same, is manifest out of *Acts* xvii. 6, 7, *They drew*, saith
St. Luke, *Jason and certain brethren unto the rulers of the
city, crying, these that have turned the world upside down
are come hither also, whom Jason hath received: and these
all do contrary to the decrees of Cæsar, saying, that there is
another king, one Jesus.* And out of the 2nd and 3rd verses
of the same chapter, where it is said, that St. Paul, *as his
manner was, went in unto them; and three sabbath days
reasoned with them out of the Scriptures; opening and alleging, that Christ must needs have suffered, and risen again
from the dead, and that this Jesus, whom he preached, is
Christ.*

*From the easiness of the doctrine.* The third argument is
from those places of Scripture, by which all the faith required
to salvation is declared to be easy. For if an inward assent
of the mind to all the doctrines concerning Christian faith

now taught, whereof the greatest part are disputed, were necessary to salvation, there would be nothing in the world so hard as to be a Christian. The thief upon the cross, though repenting, could not have been saved for saying, *Lord remember me when thou comest into thy kingdom;* by which he testified no belief of any other article, but this, that *Jesus was the king.* Nor could it be said (as it is, *Matt.* xi. 30), that *Christ's yoke is easy, and his burthen light:* nor that *little children believe in him,* as it is *Matt.* xviii. 6. Nor could St. Paul have said, (1 *Cor.* i. 21), *It pleased God by the foolishness of preaching, to save them that believe.* Nor could St. Paul himself have been saved, much less have been so great a doctor of the Church so suddenly, that never perhaps thought of transubstantiation nor purgatory, nor many other articles now obtruded.

*From formal and clear texts.* The fourth argument is taken from places express, and such as receive no controversy of interpretation; as first, *John* v. 39; *Search the Scriptures; for in them ye think ye have eternal life; and they are they that testify of me.* Our Saviour here speaketh of the Scriptures only of the Old Testament; for the Jews at that time could not search the Scriptures of the New Testament, which were not written. But the Old Testament hath nothing of Christ, but the marks by which men might know him when he came; as that he should descend from David; be born at Bethlehem, and of a Virgin; do great miracles, and the like. Therefore to believe that this Jesus was He, was sufficient to eternal life: but more than sufficient is not necessary; and consequently no other article is required. Again, (*John* xi. 26) *Whosoever liveth and believeth in me, shall not die eternally.* Therefore, to believe in Christ, is faith sufficient to eternal life; and consequently no more faith than that is necessary. But to believe in Jesus, and to believe that Jesus is the Christ, is all one, as appeareth in the verses immediately following. For when our Saviour (verse 26) had said to Martha, *Believest thou this?* she answereth (verse 27), *Yea, Lord, I believe that thou art the Christ, the Son of God, which should come into the world.* Therefore this article alone is faith sufficient to life eternal; and more than sufficient is not necessary. Thirdly, *John* xx. 31: *These things are written that ye might believe, that Jesus is the Christ, the Son of God, and that believing ye might have life through his name.* There, to believe that *Jesus is the Christ,* is faith sufficient to the obtaining of life; and therefore no other article is necessary. Fourthly, 1 *John* iv.

2: *Every spirit that confesseth that Jesus Christ is come in
the flesh, is of God.* And 1 John v. 1: *Whosoever believeth
that Jesus is the Christ, is born of God.* And verse 5, *Who
is he that overcometh the world, but he that believeth that
Jesus is the Son of God?* Fifthly, *Acts* viii. 36, 37: *see*, saith
the Eunuch, *here is water, what doth hinder me to be baptized? And Philip said, if thou believest with all thy heart,
thou mayst. And he answered and said, I believe that Jesus
is the Son of God.* Therefore this article believed, *Jesus is tde
Christ*, is sufficient to baptism, that is to say, to our reception
into the kingdom of God, and by consequence, only necessary. And generally in all places where our Saviour saith to
any man, *Thy faith hath saved thee*, the cause he saith it, is
some confession, which directly, or by consequence, implieth
a belief, that *Jesus is the Christ*.

*From that it is the foundation of all other articles.* The last
argument is from the places, where this article is made the
foundation of faith: for he that holdeth the foundation, shall
be saved. Which places are first, *Matt.* xxiv. 23, 24: *If any
man shall say unto you, Lo here is Christ, or there, believe it
not; for there shall arise false Christs, and false prophets, and
shall shew great signs and wonders, &c.* Here we see this
article, *Jesus is the Christ*, must be held, though he that shall
teach the contrary should do great miracles. The second
place is, *Gal.* i. 8: *Though we, or an angel from heaven,
preach any other gospel unto you, than that we have preached
unto you, let him be accursed.* But the gospel which Paul,
and the other apostles, preached, was only this article, that
*Jesus is the Christ:* therefore for the belief of this article, we
are to reject the authority of an angel from heaven; much
more of any motal man, if he teach the contrary. This is
therefore the fundamental article of Christian faith. A third
place is, 1 *John* iv. 1, 2: *Beloved, believe not every spirit:
hereby ye shall know the Spirit of God; every spirit that confesseth that Jesus Christ is come in the flesh, is of God.* By
which it is evident, that this article, is the measure and rule,
by which to estimate and examine all other articles; and is
therefore only fundamental. A fourth is *Matt.* xvi. 16, 18,
where after St. Peter had professed this article, saying to our
Saviour, *Thou art Christ the son of the living God*, our
Saviour answered, *Thou art Peter, and upon this rock I will
build my Church;* from whence I infer, that this article is
that, on which all other doctrines of the Church are built,
as on their foundation. A fifth is 1 *Cor.* iii. 11, 12, &c. *Other*

*foundation can no man lay, than that which is laid, Jesus is the Christ. Now if any man build upon this foundation, gold, silver, precious stones, wood, hay, stubble; every man's work shall be made manifest; for the day shall declare it, because it shall be revealed by fire, and the fire shall try every man's work of what sort it is. If any man's work abide, which he hath built thereupon, he shall receive a reward. If any man's work shall be burnt, he shall suffer his loss; but he himself shall be saved, yet so as by fire.* Which words, being partly plain and easy to understand, and partly allegorical and difficult; out of that which is plain, may be inferred, that pastors that teach this foundation, that *Jesus is the Christ,* though they draw from it false consequences, which all men are sometimes subject to, they may nevertheless be saved; much more that they may be saved, who being no pastors, but hearers, believe that which is by their lawful pastors taught them. Therefore the belief of this article is sufficient; and by consequence, there is no other article of faith necessarily required to salvation.

Now for the part which is allegorical, as *that the fire shall try every man's work,* and that *they shall be saved, but so as by fire,* or *through fire,* (for the original is διὰ πυρὸς,) it maketh nothing against this conclusion which I have drawn from the other words, that are plain. Nevertheless, because upon this place there hath been an argument taken, to prove the fire of purgatory, I will also here offer you my conjecture concerning the meaning of this trial of doctrines, and saving of men as by fire. The apostle here seemeth to allude to the words of the prophet *Zechariah,* (xiii. 8, 9), who speaking of the restoration of the kingdom of God, saith thus; *Two parts therein shall be cut off, and die, but the third shall be left therein; and I will bring the third part through the fire, and will refine them as silver is refined, and will try them as gold is tried; they shall call on the name of the Lord, and I will hear them.* The day of judgment is the day of the restoration of the kingdom of God; and at that day it is, that St. Peter tells us (2 *Pet.* iii. 7, 10, 12) shall be the conflagration of the world, wherein the wicked shall perish; but the remnant which God will save, shall pass through that fire unhurt, and be therein, (as silver and gold are refined by the fire from their dross,) tried, and refined from their idolatry, and be made to call upon the name of the true God. Alluding whereto, St. Paul here saith, that *the day,* that is, the day of judgment, the great day of our Saviour's coming to restore the kingdom of God in Israel, shall try every man's doctrine, by judging which are gold, silver, precious stones, wood, hay, stubble; and then they that have built false consequences on the true foundation, shall see their doctrines condemned; nevertheless they themselves shall be saved, and pass unhurt through this universal fire, and live eternally, to call upon the name of the true and only God. In which sense there is nothing that accordeth not with the rest of Holy Scripture, or any glimpse of the fire of purgatory.

*In what sense other articles may be called necessary.* But a man may here ask, whether it be not as necessary to salvation, to believe, that God is omnipotent; Creator of the world; that Jesus Christ is risen; and that all men else shall rise again from the dead at the last day; as to believe that *Jesus is the Christ.* To which I answer, they are; and so are many more articles: but they are such, as are contained in this one, and may be deduced from it, with more or less difficulty. For who is there that does not see, that they who believe Jesus to be the Son of the God of Israel, and that the Israelites had for God the Omnipotent Creator of all things, do therein also believe, that God is the Omnipotent Creator of all things? Or how can a man believe, that Jesus is the king that shall reign eternally, unless he believe him also risen again from the dead? For a dead man cannot exercise the office of a king. In sum, he that holdeth this foundation, *Jesus is the Christ,* holdeth expressly all that he seeth rightly deduced from it, and implicitly all that is consequent thereunto, though he have not skill enough to discern the consequence. And therefore it holdeth still good, that the belief of this one article is sufficient faith to obtain remission of sins to the *penitent,* and consequently to bring them into the kingdom of heaven.

*That faith and obedience are both of them necessary to salvation.* Now that I have shown, that all the obedience required to salvation, consisteth in the will to obey the law of God, that is to say, in repentance; and all the faith required to the same, is comprehended in the belief of this article, *Jesus is the Christ;* I will further allege those places of the Gospel, that prove, that all that is necessary to salvation is contained in both these joined together. The men to whom St. Peter preached on the day of Pentecost, next after the ascension of our Saviour, asked him, and the rest of the apostles, saying, (*Acts* ii. 37), *Men and brethren, what shall we do?* To whom St. Peter answered (in the next verse) *Repent, and be bap-*

*tized every one of you, for the remission of sins, and ye shall
receive the gift of the Holy Ghost.* Therefore repentance, and
baptism, that is, believing that *Jesus is the Christ,* is all that
is necessary to salvation. Again, our Saviour being asked by
a certain ruler (*Luke* xviii. 18), *What shall I do to inherit
eternal life?* answered, (verse 20) *Thou knowest the commandments, do not commit adultery, do not kill, do not steal,
do not bear false witness, honour thy father and thy mother.*
Which when he said he had observed, our Saviour added,
(verse 22) *Sell all thou hast, give it to the poor, and come
and follow me:* which was as much to say, rely on me that
am the king. Therefore to fulfil the law, and to believe that
Jesus is the king, is all that is required to bring a man to
eternal life. Thirdly, St. Paul saith (*Rom.* i. 17), *The just
shall live by faith;* not every one, but the *just;* therefore *faith*
and *justice* (that is, the *will to be just,* or *repentance*) are all
that is necessary to life eternal. And (*Mark* i. 15) our
Saviour preached, saying, *The time is fulfilled, and the kingdom of God is at hand, repent and believe the evangel,* that
is, the good news that the Christ was come. Therefore, to
repent, and to believe that Jesus is the Christ, is all that is
required to salvation.

*What each of them contributes thereunto.* Seeing then it
is necessary that faith and obedience, implied in the word repentance, do both concur to our salvation; the question by
which of the two we are justified, is impertinently disputed.
Nevertheless, it will not be impertinent, to make manifest in
what manner each of them contributes thereunto; and in
what sense it is said, that we are to be justified by the one,
and by the other. And first, if by righteousness be understood the justice of the works themselves, there is no man
that can be saved; for there is none that hath not transgressed
the law of God. And therefore when we are said to be justified by works, it is to be understood of the will, which God
doth always accept for the work itself, as well in good, as in
evil men. And in this sense only it is, that a man is called
*just,* or *unjust;* and that his justice justifies him, that is, gives
him the title, in God's acceptation, of *just;* and renders him
capable of *living by his faith,* which before he was not. So
that justice justifies in that sense, in which to *justify,* is the
same as that to *denominate a man just;* and not in the signification of discharging the law; whereby the punishment of
his sins should be unjust.

But a man is then also said to be justified, when his plea,

though in itself insufficient, is accepted; as when we plead our will, our endeavour to fulfil the law, and repent us of our failings, and God accepteth it for the performance itself. And because God accepteth not the will for the deed, but only in the faithful; it is therefore faith that makes good our plea; and in this sense it is, that faith only justifies. So that *faith* and *obedience* are both necessary to salvation; yet in several senses each of them is said to justify.

*Obedience to God and to the civil sovereign not inconsistent, whether Christian, or infidel.* Having thus shown what is necessary to salvation; it is not hard to reconcile our obedience to God, with our obedience to the civil sovereign; who is either Christian, or infidel. If he be a Christian, he alloweth the belief of this article, that *Jesus is the Christ;* and of all the articles that are contained in, or are by evident consequence deduced from it: which is all the faith necessary to salvation. And because he is a sovereign, he requireth obedience to all his own, that is, to all the civil laws; in which also are contained all the laws of nature, that is all the laws of God: for besides the laws of nature, and the laws of the Church, which are part of the civil law, (for the Church that can make laws is the commonwealth), there be no other laws divine. Whosoever therefore obeyeth his Christian sovereign, is not thereby hindered, neither from believing, nor from obeying God.

*Obedience to God and to the civil sovereign not inconsistent, whether Christian.* But suppose that a Christian king should from this foundation *Jesus is the Christ,* draw some false consequences, that is to say, make some superstructions of hay or stubble, and command the teaching of the same; yet seeing St. Paul says he shall be saved; much more shall he be saved, that teacheth them by his command; and much more yet, he that teaches not, but only believes his lawful teacher. And in case a subject be forbidden by the civil sovereign to profess some of those his opinions, upon what just ground can he disobey? Christian kings may err in deducing a consequence, but who shall judge? Shall a private man judge, when the question is of his own obedience? Or shall any man judge but he that is appointed thereto by the Church, that is, by the civil sovereign that representeth it? Or if the Pope, or an apostle judge, may he not err in deducing of a consequence? Did not one of the two, St. Peter or St. Paul, err in a superstructure, when St. Paul withstood St. Peter to his face? There can therefore be no contradiction between the laws of God, and the laws of a Christian commonwealth.

*Or infidel.* And when the civil sovereign is an infidel, every one of his own subjects that resisteth him, sinneth against the laws of God (for such are the laws of nature), and rejecteth the counsel of the apostles, that admonisheth all Christians to obey their princes, and all children and servants to obey their parents and masters in all things. And for their *faith,* it is internal, and invisible; they have the licence that Naaman had, and need not put themselves into danger for it. But if they do, they ought to expect their reward in heaven, and not complain of their lawful sovereign; much less make war upon him. For he that is not glad of any just occasion of martyrdom, has not the faith he professeth, but pretends it only, to set some colour upon his own contumacy. But what infidel king is so unreasonable, as knowing he has a subject, that waiteth for the second coming of Christ, after the present world shall be burnt, and intendeth then to obey him, (which is the intent of believing that Jesus is the Christ,) and in the meantime thinketh himself bound to obey the laws of that infidel king, (which all Christians are obliged in conscience to do), to put to death or to persecute such a subject?

*Conclusion.* And thus much shall suffice, concerning the kingdom of God, and policy ecclesiastical. Wherein I pretend not to advance any position of my own, but also to show what are the consequences that seem to me deducible from the principles of Christian politics, (which are the holy Scriptures,) in confirmation of the power of civil sovereigns, and the duty of their subjects. And in the allegation of Scripture, I have endeavoured to avoid such texts as are of obscure or controverted interpretation; and to allege none, but in such sense as is most plain, and agreeable to the harmony and scope of the whole Bible; which was written for the reestablishment of the kingdom of God in Christ. For it is not the bare words, but the scope of the writer, that giveth the true light, by which any writing is to be interpreted; and they that insist upon single texts, without considering the main design, can derive nothing from them clearly; but rather by casting atoms of Scripture, as dust before men's eyes, make everything more obscure than it is; an ordinary artifice of those that seek not the truth, but their own advantage.

# THE FOURTH PART
# OF THE KINGDOM OF DARKNESS

## Chapter 44

### Of Spiritual Darkness, from Misinterpretation of Scripture

*The kingdom of Darkness, what.* Besides these sovereign powers, *divine*, and *human*, of which I have hitherto discoursed, there is mention in Scripture of another power, namely, (*Eph.* vi. 12) that of *the rules of the darkness of this world;* (*Matt.* xii. 26) *the kingdom of Satan;* and (*Matt.* ix. 34) *the principality of Beelzebub over demons,* that is to say, over phantasms that appear in the air: for which cause Satan is also called, (*Eph.* ii. 2) *the prince of the power of the air;* and, because he ruleth in the darkness of this world, (*John* xvi. 11) *the prince of this world:* and in consequence hereunto, they who are under his dominion, in opposition to the faithful, (who are the *children of the light,*) are called the *children of darkness.* For seeing Beelzebub is prince of phantasms, inhabitants of his dominion of air and darkness, the children of darkness, and these demons, phantasms, or spirits of illusion, signify allegorically the same thing. This considered, the kingdom of darkness, as it is set forth in these and other places of the Scripture, is nothing else but a *confederacy of deceivers, that to obtain dominion over men in this present world, endeavour by dark and erroneous doctrines, to extinguish in them the light, both of nature, and of the gospel; and so to disprepare them for the kingdom of God to come.*

*The Church not yet fully freed of darkness.* As men that are utterly deprived from their nativity, of the light of the bodily eye, have no idea at all of any such light; and no man conceives in his imagination any greater light, than he hath at some time or other perceived by his outward senses: so also is it of the light of the gospel, and of the light of the understanding, that no man can conceive there is any greater degree of it, than that which he hath already attained unto.

And from hence it comes to pass, that men have no other means to acknowledge their own darkness, but only by reasoning from the unforeseen mischances, that befall them in their ways. The darkest part of the kingdom of Satan, is that which is without the Church of God; that is to say, amongst them that believe not in Jesus Christ. But we cannot say, that therefore the Church enjoyeth, as the land of Goshen, all the light, which to the performance of the work enjoined us by God, is necessary. Whence comes it, that in Christendom there has been, almost from the time of the Apostles, such jostling of one another out of their places, both by foreign and civil war; such stumbling at every little asperity of their own fortune, and every little eminence of that of other men; and such diversity of ways in running to the same mark, *felicity,* if it be not night amongst us, or at least a mist? We are therefore yet in the dark.

*Four causes of spiritual darkness.* The enemy has been here in the night of our natural ignorance, and sown the tares of spiritual errors; and that, first, by abusing, and putting out the light of the Scriptures: for we err, not knowing the Scriptures. Secondly, by introducing the demonology of the heathen poets, that is to say, their fabulous doctrine concerning demons, which are but idols, or phantasms of the brain, without any real nature of their own, distinct from human fancy; such as are dead men's ghosts, and fairies, and other matter of old wives' tales. Thirdly, by mixing with the Scripture divers relics of the religion, and much of the vain and erroneous philosophy, of the Greeks, especially of Aristotle. Fourthly, by mingling with both these, false, or uncertain traditions, and feigned, or uncertain history. And so we come to err, *by giving heed to seducing spirits,* and the demonology of such *as speak lies in hypocrisy;* or as it is in the original, (1 *Tim.* iv. 1, 2) *of those that play the part of liars, with a seared conscience,* that is, contrary to their own knowledge. Concerning the first of these, which is the seducing of men by abuse of Scripture, I intend to speak briefly in this chapter.

*Errors from misinterpreting the Scriptures, concerning the kingdom of God.* The greatest and main abuse of Scripture, and to which almost all the rest are either consequent or subservient, is the wresting of it, to prove that the kingdom of God, mentioned so often in the Scripture, is the present Church, or multitude of Christian men now living, or that being dead, are to rise again at the last day: whereas the kingdom of God was first instituted by the ministry of Moses, over the Jews only; who were therefore called his peculiar people; and ceased afterward, in the election of Saul, when they refused to be governed by God any more, and demanded a king after the manner of the nations; which God himself consented unto, as I have more at large proved before in chapter 35. After that time, there was no other kingdom of God in the world, by any pact, or otherwise, than he ever was, is, and shall be king of all men, and of all creatures, as governing according to his will, by his infinite power. Nevertheless, he promised by his prophets to restore this his government to them again, when the time he hath in his secret counsel appointed for it shall be fully come, and when they shall turn unto him by repentance and amendment of life. And not only so, but he invited the Gentiles to come in, and enjoy the happiness of his reign, on the same conditions of conversion and repentance; and he promised also to send his Son into the world, to expiate the sins of them all by his death, and to prepare them by his doctrine, to receive him at his second coming. Which second coming not yet being, the kingdom of God is not yet come, and we are not now under any other kings by pact, but our civil sovereigns; saving only, that Christian men are already in the kingdom of grace, in as much as they have already the promise of being received at his coming again.

*As that the kingdom of God is the present Church.* Consequent to this error, that the present Church is Christ's kingdom, there ought to be some one man, or assembly, by whose mouth our Saviour, now in heaven, speaketh, giveth law, and which representeth his person to all Christians; or divers men, or divers assemblies that do the same to divers parts of Christendom. This power regal under Christ, being challenged, universally by the Pope, and in particular commonwealths by assemblies of the pastors of the place, (when the Scripture gives it to none but to civil sovereigns) comes to be so passionately disputed, that it putteth out the light of nature, and causeth so great a darkness in men's understanding, that they see not who it is to whom they have engaged their obedience.

*And that the Pope is his vicar general:* Consequent to this claim of the Pope to be vicar-general of Christ in the present Church, (supposed to be that kingdom of his to which we are addressed in the gospel) is the doctrine, that it is necessary for a Christian king to receive his crown by a bishop; as if it were from that ceremony, that he derives the clause of

*Dei gratiâ* in his title; and that then only he is made king by the favour of God, when he is crowned by the authority of God's universal vicegerent on earth; and that every bishop, whosoever be his sovereign, taketh at his consecration an oath of absolute obedience to the Pope. Consequent to the same, is the doctrine of the fourth Council of Lateran, held under Pope Innocent the Third, (chap. III. *De Hereticis*), *that if a king at the Pope's admonition, do not purge his kingdom of heresies, and being excommunicate for the same, do not give satisfaction within a year, his subjects are absolved of the bond of their obedience.* Where, by heresies are understood all opinions which the Church of Rome hath forbidden to be maintained. And by this means, as often as there is any repugnancy between the political designs of the Pope, and other Christian princes, as there is very often, there ariseth such a mist amongst their subjects, that they know not a stranger that thrusteth himself into the throne of their lawful prince, from him whom they had themselves placed there; and in this darkness of mind, are made to fight one against another, without discerning their enemies from their friends, under the conduct of another man's ambition.

*And that the pastors are the clergy.* From the same opinion, that the present Church is the kingdom of God, it proceeds that pastors, deacons, and all other ministers of the Church, take the name to themselves of the *clergy;* giving to other Christians the name of *laity,* that is, simply *people.* For clergy signifies those, whose maintenance is that revenue, which God having reserved to himself during his reign over the Israelites, assigned to the tribe of Levi, (who were to be his public ministers, and had no portion of land set them out to live on, as their brethren,) to be their inheritance. The Pope therefore, pretending the present Church to be, as the realm of Israel, the kingdom of God, challenging to himself and his subordinate ministers, the like revenue, as the inheritance of God, the name of clergy was suitable to that claim. And thence it is, that tithes, and other tributes paid to the Levites, as God's right, amongst the Israelites, have a long time been demanded, and taken of Christians, by ecclesiastics, *jure divino,* that is, in God's right. By which means, the people everywhere were obliged to a double tribute; one to the state, another to the clergy; whereof, that to the clergy, being the tenth of their revenue, is double to that which a king of Athens, and esteemed a tyrant, exacted of his subjects for the defraying of all public charges: for he demanded no more but the twentieth part, and yet abundantly maintained therewith the commonwealth. And in the kingdom of the Jews, during the sacerdotal reign of God, the tithes and offerings were the whole public revenue.

From the same mistaking of the present Church for the kingdom of God, came in the distinction between the *civil* and the *canon* laws: the civil law being the acts of *sovereigns* in their own dominions, and the canon law being the acts of the *Pope* in the same dominion. Which canons, though they were but canons, that is, *rules propounded,* and but voluntarily received by Christian princes, till the translation of the empire to Charlemagne; yet afterwards, as the power of the Pope increased, became *rules commanded,* and the emperors themselves, to avoid greater mischiefs, which the people blinded might be led into, were forced to let them pass for laws.

From hence it is, that in all dominions where the Pope's ecclesiastical power is entirely received, Jews, Turks, and Gentiles, are in the Roman Church tolerated in their religion, as far forth, as in the exercise and profession thereof they offend not against the civil power: whereas in a Christian, though a stranger, not to be of the Roman religion, is capital; because the Pope pretendeth, that all Christians, are his subjects. For otherwise it were as much against the law of nations, to persecute a Christian stranger, for professing the religion of his own country, as an infidel; or rather more, in as much as they that are not against Christ, are with him.

From the same it is, that in every Christian state there are certain men, that are exempt, by ecclesiastical liberty, from the tributes, and from the tribunals of the civil state; for so are the secular clergy, besides monks and friars, which in many places bear so great a proportion to the common people, as if need were, there might be raised out of them alone, an army, sufficient for any war the Church militant should employ them in, against their own, or other princes.

*Error from mistaking consecration for conjuration.* A second general abuse of Scripture, is the turning of consecration into conjuration, or enchantment. To *consecrate,* is, in Scripture, to offer, give, or dedicate, in pious and decent language and gesture, a man, or any other thing to God, by separating of it from common use; that is to say, to sanctify, or make it God's, and to be used only by those, whom God hath appointed to be his public ministers, (as I have already proved at large in the 35th chapter), and thereby to change, not the thing consecrated, but only the use of it, from being profane and common, to be holy, and peculiar to God's service. But when by such words, the nature or quality of the thing itself, is pretended to be changed, it is not consecration, but either an extraordinary work of God, or a vain and impious conjuration. But seeing, for the frequency of pretending the change of nature in their consecrations, it cannot be esteemed a work extraordinary, it is no other than a *conjuration* or *incantation*, whereby they would have men to believe an alteration of nature that is not, contrary to the testimony of man's sight, and of all the rest of his senses. As for example, when the priest, instead of consecrating bread and wine to God's peculiar service in the sacrament of the Lord's Supper, (which is but a separation of it from the common use, to signify, that is, to put men in mind of their redemption, by the passion of Christ, whose body was broken, and blood shed upon the cross for our transgressions,) pretends, that by saying of the words of our Saviour, *This is my body,* and *this is my blood,* the nature of bread is no more there, but his very body; notwithstanding there appeareth not to the sight, or other sense of the receiver, any thing that appeared not before the consecration. The Egyptian conjurers, that are said to have turned their rods to serpents, and the water into blood, are thought but to have deluded the senses of the spectators, by a false show of things, yet are esteemed enchanters. But what should we have thought of them, if there had appeared in their rods nothing like a serpent, and in the water enchanted, nothing like blood, nor like any thing else but water, but that they had faced down the king, that they were serpents that looked like rods, and that it was blood that seemed water? That had been both enchantment, and lying. And yet in this daily act of the priest, they do the very same, by turning the holy words into the manner of a charm, which produceth nothing new to the sense; but they face us down, that it hath turned the bread into a man; nay more, into a God; and require men to worship it, as if it were our Saviour himself present God and man, and thereby to commit most gross idolatry. For if it be enough to excuse it of idolatry, to say it is no more bread, but God; why should not the same excuse serve the Egyptians, in case they had the faces to say, the leeks and onions they worshipped, were not very leeks and onions, but a divinity under their *species,* or likeness. The words, *This is my body,* are equivalent to these, *this signifies,* or *represents my body;* and it is an ordinary figure of speech: but to take it literally, is an abuse; nor though so taken, can it extend any further, than to the bread which Christ himself with his own hands consecrated. For he never said, that of what bread soever, any priest whatsoever, should say, *This is my body,* or, *this is Christ's body,* the same should presently be transubstantiated. Nor did the Church of Rome ever establish this transubstantiation, till the time of Innocent the Third; which was not above 500 years ago, when the power of popes was at the highest, and the darkness of the time grown so great, as men discerned not the bread that was given them to eat, especially when it was stamped with the figure of Christ upon the cross, as if they would have men believe it were transubstantiated, not only into the body of Christ, but also into the wood of his cross, and that they did eat both together in the sacrament.

*Incantation in the ceremonies of baptism:* The like incantation, instead of consecration, is used also in the sacrament of baptism: where the abuse of God's name in each several person, and in the whole Trinity, with the sign of the cross at each name, maketh up the charm. As first, when they make the holy water, the priest saith, *I conjure thee, thou creature of water, in the name of God the Father Almighty, and in the name of Jesus Christ his only Son our Lord, and in virtue of the Holy Ghost, that thou become conjured water, to drive away all the powers of the enemy, and to eradicate, and supplant the enemy, &c.* And the same in the benediction of the salt to be mingled with it: *That thou become conjured salt, that all phantasms, and knavery of the devil's fraud may fly and depart from the place wherein thou are sprinkled; and every unclean spirit be conjured by Him that shall come to judge the quick and the dead.* The same in the benediction of the oil; *That all the power of the enemy, all the host of the devil, all assaults and phantasms of Satan, may be driven away by this creature of oil.* And for the infant that is to be baptized, he is subject to many charms: first, at the church door the priest blows thrice in the child's face, and says: *Go out of him unclean spirit, and give place to the Holy Ghost the comforter.* As if all children, till blown on by the priest, were demoniacs. Again, before his entrance into the church, he saith as before, *I conjure thee, &c. to go out, and depart from this servant of God.* And again the same exorcism is repeated once more before he be baptized. These, and some other incantations, are those that are used instead of benedictions, and consecrations, in administration of the sacraments of baptism, and the Lord's supper; wherein every thing that serveth to those holy uses, except the unhallowed spittle of the priest, hath some set form of exorcism.

*And in marriage, in visitation of the sick, and in consecration of places.* Nor are the other rites, as of marriage, of extreme unction, of visitation of the sick, of consecrating churches and churchyards, and the like, exempt from charms; inasmuch as there is in them the use of enchanted oil and water, with the abuse of the cross, and of the holy word of David, *asperges me Domine hyssopo*, as things of efficacy to drive away phantasms, and imaginary spirits.

*Errors from mistaking eternal life, and everlasting death:* Another general error, is from the misinterpretation of the words *eternal life, everlasting death,* and the *second death.* For though we read plainly in Holy Scripture, that God created Adam in an estate of living for ever, which was conditional, that is to say, if he disobeyed not his commandment; which was not essential to human nature, but consequent to the virtue of the tree of life; whereof he had liberty to eat, as long as he had not sinned; and that he was thrust out of Paradise after he had sinned, lest he should eat thereof, and live for ever; and that Christ's Passion is a discharge of sin to all that believe on him; and by consequence, a restitution of eternal life to all the faithful, and to them only: yet the doctrine is now, and hath been a long time far otherwise; namely, that every man hath eternity of life by nature, inasmuch as his soul is immortal. So that the flaming sword at the entrance of Paradise, though it hinder a man from coming to the tree of life, hinders him not from the immortality which God took from him for his sin; nor makes him to need the sacrificing of Christ, for the recovering of the same; and consequently, not only the faithful and righteous, but also the wicked and the heathen, shall enjoy eternal life, without any death at all; much less a second, and everlasting death. To salve this, it is said, that by second, and everlasting death, is meant a second, and everlasting life, but in torments; a figure never used but in this very case.

All which doctrine is founded only on some of the obscurer places of the New Testament; which nevertheless, the whole scope of the Scripture considered, are clear enough in a different sense, and unnecessary to the Christian faith. For supposing that when a man dies, there remaineth nothing of him but his carcass; cannot God, that raised inanimated dust and clay into a living creature by his word, as easily raise a dead carcass to life again, and continue him alive for ever, or make him die again, by another word? The *soul* in Scripture, signifieth always, either the life, or the living creature; and the body and soul jointly, the *body alive*. In the fifth day of creation, God said: Let the waters produce *reptile animæ viventis*, the creeping thing that hath in it a living soul; the English translate it, *that hath life*. And again, God created whales, *et omnem animam viventem;* in which in the English is, *every living creature*. And likewise of man, God made him of the dust of the earth, and breathed in his face the breath of life, *et factus est homo in animam viventem*, that is, *and man was made a living creature*. And after Noah came out of the ark, God saith, he will no more smite *omnem animam viventem*, that is, *every living creature*. And (*Deut.* xii. 23), *Eat not the blood, for the blood is the soul;* that is, *the life*. From which places, if by *soul* were meant a *substance incorporeal*, with an existence separated from the body, it might as well be inferred of any other living creature as of man. But that the souls of the faithful, are not of their own nature, but by God's special grace, to remain in their bodies, from the resurrection to all eternity, I have already, I think, sufficiently proved out of the Scriptures, in chapter 38. And for the places of the New Testament, where it is said that any man shall be cast body and soul into hell fire, it is no more than body and life; that is to say, they shall be cast alive into the perpetual fire of Gehenna.

*As the doctrine of purgatory, and exorcisms, and invocation of saints.* This window it is, that gives entrance to the dark doctrine, first, of eternal torments; and afterwards of purgatory, and consequently of the walking abroad, especially in places consecrated, solitary, or dark, of the ghosts of men deceased; and thereby to the pretences of exorcism and conjuration of phantasms; as also of invocation of men dead; and to the doctrine of indulgences, that is to say, of exemption for a time, or for ever, from the fire of purgatory, wherein these incorporeal substances are pretended by burning to be cleansed, and made fit for heaven. For men being generally possessed before the time of our Saviour, by contagion of the demonology of the Greeks, of an opinion, that the souls of men were substances distinct from their bodies, and therefore that when the body was dead, the soul of every man, whether godly or wicked, must subsist somewhere by virtue of its own nature, without acknowledging therein any supernatural gift of God; the doctors of the Church doubted a long time, what was the place, which they were to abide in, till they should be reunited to their bodies in the resurrection; supposing for a while, they lay under the altars; but afterward the Church of Rome found it more profitable to build for them this place of purgatory; which by some other Churches in this latter age has been demolished.

*The texts alleged for the doctrines aforementioned have been answered before.* Let us now consider what texts of Scripture seem most to confirm these three general errors, I have here touched. As for those which Cardinal Bellarmine hath alleged, for the present kingdom of God administered by the Pope, than which there are none that make a better show of proof; I have already answered them; and made it evident, that the kingdom of God, instituted by Moses, ended in the election of Saul; after which time the priest of his own authority never deposed any king. That which the high-priest did to Athaliah, was not done in his own right, but in the right of the young king Joash her son: but Solomon in his own right deposed the high-priest Abiathar, and set up another in his place. The most difficult place to answer, of all those that can be brought to prove the kingdom of God by Christ is already in this world, is alleged, not by Bellarmine, nor any other of the Church of Rome; but by Beza, that will have it to begin from the resurrection of Christ. But whether he intend thereby, to entitle the Presbytery to the supreme power ecclesiastical in the commonwealth of Geneva, and consequently to every presbytery in every other commonwealth, or to princes, and other civil sovereigns, I do not know. For the presbytery hath challenged the power to excommunicate their own kings, and to be the supreme moderators in religion, in the places where they have that form of Church-government, no less than the Pope challengeth it universally.

*Answer to the text on which Beza infereth that the kingdom of Christ began at the resurrection.* The words are (*Mark* ix. 1), *Verily I say unto you, that there be some of them that stand here, which shall not taste of death, till they have seen the kingdom of God come with power.* Which words if taken grammatically, make it certain, that either some of those men that stood by Christ at that time, are yet alive; or else, that the kingdom of God must be now in this present world. And then there is another place more difficult. For when the apostles, after our Saviour's resurrection, and immediately before his ascension, asked our Saviour, saying, (*Acts* i. 6), *Wilt thou at this time restore again the kingdom to Israel?* he answered them, *It is not for you to know the times and the seasons, which the Father hath put in his own power; but ye shall receive power by the coming of the Holy Ghost upon you, and ye shall be my (martyrs) witnesses both in Jerusalem, and in all Judea, and in Samaria, and unto the uttermost part of the earth.* Which is as much as to say, My kingdom is not yet come, nor shall you fore-know when it shall come; for it shall come as a thief in the night; but I will send you the Holy Ghost, and by him you shall have power to bear witness to all the world, by your preaching, of my resurrection, and the works I have done, and the doctrine I have taught, that they may believe in me, and expect eternal life, at my coming again. How does this agree with the coming of Christ's kingdom at the resurrection? And that which St. Paul says (1 *Thess.* i. 9, 10), *That they turned from idols, to serve the living and true God, and to wait for his Son from heaven;* where to wait for his Son from heaven, is to wait for his coming to be king in power; which were not necessary, if his kingdom had been then present. Again, if the kingdom of God began, as Beza on that place (*Mark* ix. 1) would have it, at the resurrection; what reason is there for Christians ever since the resurrection to say in their prayers, *Let thy kingdom come?* It is therefore manifest, that the words of St. Mark are not so to be inter-preted. There be some of them that stand here, saith our Saviour, that shall not taste of death till they have seen the kingdom of God come in power. If then this kingdom were to come at the resurrection of Christ, why is it said, *some of them*, rather than *all?* For they all lived till after Christ was risen.

*Explication of the place in Mark ix.* 1. But they that re-quire interpretation of this text, let them interpret first the like words of our Saviour to St. Peter, concerning St. John, (chap. xxi. 22), *If I will that he tarry till I come, what is that to thee?* upon which was grounded a report that he should not die. Nevertheless the truth of that report was neither con-firmed, as well grounded; nor refuted, as ill grounded on those words; but left as a saying not understood. The same difficulty is also in the place of *St. Mark.* And if it be lawful to conjecture at their meaning, by that which immediately follows, both here, and in *St. Luke,* where the same is again repeated, it is not improbable, to say they have relation to the Transfiguration, which is described in the verses immediately following: where it is said, that *after six days Jesus taketh with him Peter, and James, and John* (not all, but some of his disciples), *and leadeth them up into a high mountain apart by themselves, and was transfigured before them: and his raiment became shining, exceeding white as snow; so as no fuller on earth can white them: and there appeareth unto them, Elias with Moses, and they were talking with Jesus, &c.* So that they saw Christ in glory and majesty, as he is to come; insomuch as *they were sore afraid.* And thus the promise of our Saviour was accomplished by way of *vision.* For it was a vision, as may probably be inferred out of *St. Luke,* that reciteth the same story (chap. ix. 28, &c.), and saith, that Peter and they that were with him, were heavy with sleep: but most certainly out of *Matt.* xvii. 9, where the same is again related; for our Saviour charged them, saying, *Tell no man the vision until the Son of Man be risen from the dead.* Howsoever it be, yet there can from thence be taken no argument, to prove that the kingdom of God taketh beginning till the day of judgment.

*Abuse of some other texts in defence of the power of the Pope.* As for some other texts, to prove the Pope's power over civil sovereigns, (besides those of Bellarmine), as that the two swords that Christ and his apostles had amongst them, were the spiritual and the temporal sword, which they say St. Peter had given him by Christ: and, that of the two luminaries, the greater signifies the Pope, and the lesser the King; one might as well infer out of the first verse of the Bible, that by heaven is meant the Pope, and by earth the King. Which is not arguing from Scripture, but a wanton insulting over princes, that came in fashion after the time the Popes were grown so secure of their greatness, as to contemn all Christian kings; and treading on the necks of emperors, to mock both them and the Scripture, in the words of Psalm xci. 13, *Thou shalt tread upon the lion and the adder; the young lion and the dragon thou shalt trample under thy feet.*

*The manner of consecrations in the Scripture, was without exorcisms.* As for the rites of consecration, though they depend for the most part upon the discretion and judgment of the governors of the Church, and not upon the Scriptures; yet those governors are obliged to such direction, as the nature of the action itself requireth; as that the ceremonies, words, and gestures, be both decent and significant, or at least comformable to the action. When Moses consecrated the tabernacle, the altar, and the vessels belonging to them, (*Exod*. xl. 9), he anointed them with the oil which God had commanded to be made for that purpose: and they were holy: there was nothing exorcised, to drive away phantasms. The same Moses, the civil sovereign of Israel, when he consecrated Aaron, the high-priest, and his sons, did wash them with water, not exorcised water, put their garments upon them, and anointed them with oil; and they were sanctified, to minister unto the Lord in the priest's office; which was a simple and decent cleansing, and adorning them, before he presented them to God, to be his servants. When King Solomon, the civil sovereign of Israel, consecrated the temple he had built, (1 *Kings* viii), he stood before all the congregation of Israel; and having blessed them, he gaves thanks to God, for putting into the heart of his father to build it; and for giving to himself the grace to accomplish the same; and then prayed unto him, first, to accept that house, though it were not suitable to his infinite greatness; and to hear the prayers of his servants that should pray therein, or, if they were absent, towards it; and lastly, he offered a sacrifice of peace-offering, and the house was dedicated. Here was no procession; the king stood still in his first place; no exorcised water; no *Asperges me*, nor other impertinent application of words spoken upon another occasion; but a decent and rational speech, and such as in making to God a present of his new-built house, was most conformable to the occasion.

We read not that St. John did exorcise the water of Jordan; nor Philip the water of the river wherein he baptized the Eunuch; nor that any pastor in the time of the apostles, did take his spittle, and put it to the nose of the person to be baptized, and say, in *odorem suavitatis*, that is, *for a sweet savour unto the Lord;* wherein neither the ceremony of spittle, for the uncleanness; nor the application of that Scripture for the levity, can by any authority of man be justified.

*The immortality of man's soul, not proved by Scripture to be of nature, but of grace.* To prove that the soul separated from the body, liveth eternally, not only the souls of the elect, by especial grace, and restoration of the eternal life which Adam lost by sin, and our Saviour restored by the sacrifice of himself, to the faithful; but also the souls of reprobates, as a property naturally consequent to the essence of mankind, without other grace of God, but that which is universally given to all mankind; there are divers places, which at the first sight seem sufficiently to serve the turn: but such, as when I compare them with that which I have before (chapter 38) alleged out of the fourteenth of *Job*, seem to me much more subject to a diverse interpretation, than the words of Job.

And first there are the words of Solomon (*Eccles.* xii. 7), *Then shall the dust return to dust, as it was, and the spirit shal return to God that gave it.* Which may bear well enough, if there be no other text directly against it, this interpretation, that God only knows, but man not, what becomes of a man's spirit, when he expireth; and the same Solomon, in the same book, (chapter iii. 20, 21) delivereth the same sentence in the same sense I have given it. His words are: *All go,* (man and beast), *to the same place; all are of the dust, and all turn to dust again; who knoweth that the spirit of man goeth upward, and that the spirit of the beast goeth downward to the earth?* That is, none knows but God; nor is it an unusual phrase to say of things we understand not, *God knows what,* and, *God knows where.* That of (*Gen.* v. 24) *Enoch walked with God, and he was not; for God took him;* which is expounded, (*Heb.* xi. 5), *He was translated, that he should not die; and was not found, because God had translated him.* For before his translation, he had this testimony, that he pleased God; making as much for the immortality of the body, as of the soul, proveth, that this his translation was peculiar to them that please God; not common to them with the wicked, and depending on grace, not on nature. But on the contrary, what interpretation shall we give besides the literal sense, of the words of Solomon (*Eccles.* iii. 19), *That which befalleth the sons of men, befalleth beasts; even one thing befalleth them; as the one dieth, so doth the other; yea, they have all one breath,* (one spirit); *so that a man hath no preeminence above a beast, for all is vanity.* By the literal sense, here is no natural immortality of the soul; nor yet any repugnancy with the life eternal, which the elect shall enjoy by grace. And (*Eccles.* chap. iv. 3) *Better is he that hath not yet been, than both they;* that is, than they that live, or have lived; which, if the soul of all them that have lived, were immortal, were a hard saying; for then to have an immortal soul, were worse than to have no soul at all. And again, (chapter ix. 5), *The living know they shall die, but the dead know not anything;* that is, naturally, and before the resurrection of the body.

Another place which seems to make for a natural immortality of the soul, is that, where our Saviour saith, that Abraham, Isaac, and Jacob, are living: but this is spoken of the

promise of God, and of their certitude to rise again, not of a
life then actual; and in the same sense that God said to
Adam, that on the day he should eat of the forbidden fruit,
he should certainly die; from that time forward he was a
dead man by sentence; but not by execution, till almost a
thousand years after. So Abraham, Isaac, and Jacob were
alive by promise, then, when Christ spake; but are not actually till the resurrection. And the history of Dives and
Lazarus, makes nothing against this, if we take it, as it is, for
a parable.

But there be other places of the New Testament, where an
immortality seemeth to be directly attributed to the wicked.
For it is evident that they shall all rise to judgment. And it is
said besides in many places, that they shall go into *everlasting
fire, everlasting torments, everlasting punishments; and that
the worm of conscience never dieth;* and all this is comprehended in the word *everlasting death,* which is ordinarily interpreted *everlasting life in torments.* And yet I can find no
where that any man shall live in torments everlastingly. Also,
it seemeth hard, to say, that God who is the father of mercies;
that doth in heaven and earth all that he will; that hath the
hearts of all men in his disposing; that worketh in men both
to do, and to will; and without whose free gift a man hath
neither inclination to good, nor repentance of evil, should
punish men's transgressions without any end of time, and
with all the extremity of torture, that men can imagine, and
more. We are therefore to consider, what the meaning is, of
*everlasting fire,* and other the like phrases of Scripture.

I have showed already, that the kingdom of God by Christ
beginneth at the day of judgment: that in that day the faithful shall rise again, with glorious and spiritual bodies, and
be his subjects in that his kingdom, which shall be eternal:
that they shall neither marry nor be given in marriage, nor
eat and drink, as they did in their natural bodies; but live
for ever in their individual persons, without the specifical
eternity of generation: and that the reprobates also shall rise
again, to receive punishments for their sins: as also, that
those of the elect, which shall be alive in their earthly bodies
at that day, shall have their bodies suddenly changed, and
made spiritual and immortal. But that the bodies of the reprobate, who make the kingdom of Satan, shall also be
glorious, or spiritual bodies, or that they shall be as the angels
of God, neither eating, nor drinking, nor engendering; or
that their life shall be eternal in their individual persons, as

the life of every faithful man, or as the life of Adam had been if he had not sinned, there is no place of Scripture to prove it; save only these places concerning eternal torments; which may otherwise be interpreted.

From whence may be inferred, that as the elect after the resurrection shall be restored to the estate, wherein Adam was before he had sinned; so the reprobate shall be in the estate, that Adam and his posterity were in after the sin committed; saving that God promised a Redeemer to Adam, and such of his seed as should trust in him, and repent; but not to them that should die in their sins, as do the reprobate.

*Eternal torments, what.* These things considered, the texts that mention *eternal fire, eternal torments, or the worm that never dieth,* contradict not the doctrine of a second, and everlasting death, in the proper and natural sense of the word *death.* The fire, or torments prepared for the wicked in Gehenna, Tophet, or in what place soever, may continue for ever; and there may never want wicked men to be tormented in them; though not every, nor any one eternally. For the wicked being left in the estate they were in after Adam's sin, may at the resurrection live as they did, marry, and give in marriage, and have gross and corruptible bodies, as all mankind now have; and consequently may engender perpetually, after the resurrection, as they did before: for there is no place in Scripture to the contrary. For St. Paul, speaking of the resurrection (1 *Cor.* xv) understandeth it only of the resurrection to life eternal; and not the resurrection to punishment. And of the first, he saith, that the body is *sown in corruption, raised in incorruption; sown in dishonour, raised in honour; sown in weakness, raised in power; sown a natural body, raised a spiritual body.* There is no such thing can be said of the bodies of them that rise to punishment. So also our Saviour, when he speaketh of the nature of man after the resurrection, meaneth the resurrection to life eternal, not to punishment. The text is, *Luke* xx, verses 34, 35, 36, a fertile text: *The children of this world marry, and are given in marriage; but they that shall be counted worthy to obtain that world, and the resurrection from the dead, neither marry, nor are given in marriage: neither can they die any more; for they are equal to the angels, and are the children of God, being the children of the resurrection.* The children of this world, that are in the estate which Adam left them in, shall marry, and be given in marriage; that is, corrupt, and generate successively; which is an immortality of the kind, but not of the persons of men: they are not worthy to be counted amongst them that shall obtain the next world, and an absolute resurrection from the dead; but only a short time, as inmates of that world; and to the end only to receive condign punishment for their contumacy. The elect are the only children of the resurrection; that is to say, the sole heirs of eternal life: they only can die no more, it is they that are equal to the angels, and that are the children of God; and not the reprobate. To the reprobate there remaineth after the resurrection, a *second* and *eternal* death: between which resurrection, and their second and eternal death, but a time of punishment and torment; and to last by succession of sinners thereunto, as long as the kind of man by propagation shall endure; which is eternally.

*Answer of the texts alleged for purgatory.* Upon this doctrine of the natural eternity of separated souls, is founded, as I said, the doctrine of purgatory. For supposing eternal life by grace only, there is no life but the life of the body; and no immortality till the resurrection. The texts for purgatory alleged by Bellarmine out of the canonical Scripture of the Old Testament, are, first, the fasting of David for Saul and Jonathan, mentioned 2 *Sam*. i. 12, and again, 2 *Sam*. iii. 35, for the death of Abner. This fasting of David, he saith, was for the obtaining of something for them at God's hands, after their death: because after he had fasted to procure the recovery of his own child, as soon as he knew it was dead, he called for meat. Seeing then the soul hath an existence separate from the body, and nothing can be obtained by men's fasting for the souls that are already either in heaven or hell, it followeth that there be some souls of dead men, that are neither in heaven, nor in hell; and therefore they must be in some third place, which must be purgatory. And thus with hard straining, he has wrested those places to the proof of a purgatory: whereas it is manifest, that the ceremonies of mourning, and fasting, when they are used for the death of men, whose life was not profitable to the mourners, they are used for honour's sake to their persons; and when it is done for the death of them by whose life the mourners had benefit, it proceeds from their particular damage. And so David honoured Saul and Abner, with his fasting; and in the death of his own child, recomforted himself, by receiving his ordinary food.

In other places, which he allegeth out of the Old Testament, there is not so much as any show, or colour of proof.

He brings in every text wherein there is the word *anger,* or *fire,* or *burning,* or *purging,* or *cleansing,* in case any of the fathers have but in a sermon rhetorically applied it to the doctrine of purgatory, already believed. The first verse of *Psalm* xxxvii; *O Lord, rebuke me not in thy wrath, nor chasten me in thy hot displeasure:* what were this to purgatory, if Augustine had not applied the *wrath* to the fire of hell, and the *displeasure* to that of purgatory? And what is it to purgatory, that of *Psalm* lxvi. 12, *We went through fire and water, and thou broughtest us to a moist place;* and other the like texts, with which the doctors of those times intended to adorn, or extend their sermons, or commentaries, haled to their purposes by force of wit?

*Places of the New Testament for purgatory answered.* But he allegeth other places of the New Testament, that are not so easy to be answered. And first that of *Matt.* xii. 32: *Whosoever speaketh a word against the Son of Man, it shall be forgiven him; but whosoever speaketh against the Holy Ghost, it shall not be forgiven him neither in this world, nor in the world to come:* where he will have purgatory to be the world to come, wherein some sins may be forgiven, which in this world were not forgiven: notwithstanding that it is manifest, there are but three worlds; one from the creation to the flood, which was destroyed by water, and is called in Scripture *the old world;* another from the flood, to the day of judgment, which is *the present world,* and shall be destroyed by fire; and the third, which shall be from the day of judgment forward, everlasting, which is called *the world to come;* and in which it is agreed by all, there shall be no purgatory: and therefore the world to come, and purgatory, are inconsistent. But what then can be the meaning of those our Saviour's words? I confess they are very hardly to be reconciled with all the doctrines now unanimously received: nor is it any shame, to confess the profoundness of the Scripture to be too great to be sounded by the shortness of human understanding. Nevertheless, I may propound such things to the consideration of more learned divines, as the text itself suggesteth. And first, seeing to speak against the Holy Ghost, as being the third person of the Trinity, is to speak against the Church, in which the Holy Ghost resideth; it seemeth the comparison is made, between the easiness of our Saviour, in bearing with offences done to him while he himself taught the world, that is, when he was on earth, and the severity of the pastors after him, against those which should deny their au-

thority, which was from the Holy Ghost. As if he should say,
you that deny my power; nay you that shall crucify me, shall
be pardoned by me, as often as you turn unto me by repentance: but if you deny the power of them that teach you hereafter, by virtue of the Holy Ghost, they shall be inexorable,
and shall not forgive you, but persecute you in this world,
and leave you without absolution, (though you turn to me,
unless you turn also to them), to the punishments, as much
as lies in them, of the world to come. And so the words may
be taken as a prophecy, or prediction concerning the times,
as they have along been in the Christian Church. Or if this
be not the meaning, (for I am not peremptory in such difficult places), perhaps there may be places left after the resurrection, for the repentance of some sinners. And there is also
another place, that seemeth to agree therewith. For considering the words of St. Paul (1 *Cor.* xv. 29), *What shall they do
which are baptized for the dead, if the dead rise not at all?
why also are they baptized for the dead?* a man may probably
infer, as some have done, that in St. Paul's time, there was a
custom, by receiving baptism for the dead man, (as men that
now believe, are sureties and undertakers for the faith of in-
fants, that are not capable of believing), to undertake for the
persons of their deceased friends, that they should be ready
to obey, and receive our Saviour for their king, at his coming
again; and then the forgiveness of sins in the world to come,
has no need of a purgatory. But in both these interpretations,
there is so much of paradox, that I trust not to them; but
propound them to those that are thoroughly versed in the
Scripture, to inquire if there be no clearer place that contra-
dicts them. Only of thus much, I see evident Scripture, to
persuade me, that there is neither the word, nor the thing of
purgatory, neither in this, nor any other text; nor anything
that can prove a necessity of a place for the soul without the
body; neither for the soul of Lazarus during the four days
he was dead; nor for the souls of them which the Roman
Church pretend to be tormented now in purgatory. For God,
that could give a life to a piece of clay, hath the same power
to give life again to a dead man, and renew his inanimate,
and rotten carcass, into a glorious, spiritual, and immortal
body.

Another place is that of 1 *Cor.* iii, where it is said, that
they which build stubble, hay, &c. on the true foundation,
their work shall perish; but *they themselves shall be saved,
but as through fire:* this fire, he will have to be the fire of

purgatory. The words, as I have said before, are an allusion to those of *Zech.* xiii. 9, where he saith, *I will bring the third part through the fire, and refine them as silver is refined, and will try them as gold is tried:* which is spoken of the coming of the Messiah in power and glory; that is, at the day of judgment, and conflagration of the present world; wherein the elect shall not be consumed, but be refined; that is, depose their erroneous doctrines and traditions, and have them as it were singed off; and shall afterwards call upon the name of the true God. In like manner, the apostle saith of them, that holding this foundation, *Jesus is the Christ,* shall build thereon some other doctrines that be erroneous, that they shall not be consumed in that fire which reneweth the world, but shall pass through it to salvation; but so as to see, and relinquish their former errors. The builders, are the *pastors;* the foundation, that *Jesus is the Christ;* the stubble and hay, *false consequences drawn from it through ignorance, or frailty;* the gold, silver, and precious stones, are their *true doctrines;* and their refining or purging, the *relinquishing of their errors.* In all which there is no colour at all for the burning of incorporeal, that is to say, impatible souls.

*Baptism for the dead, how understood.* A third place is that of 1 *Cor.* xv. 29, before mentioned, concerning baptism for the dead: out of which he concludeth, first, that prayers for the dead are not unprofitable; and out of that, that there is a fire of purgatory: but neither of them rightly. For of many interpretations of the word baptism, he approveth this in the first place, that by baptism is meant, metaphorically, a baptism of penance; and that men are in this sense baptized, when they fast, and pray, and give alms: and so, baptism for the dead, and prayer for the dead, is the same thing. But this is a metaphor, of which there is no example, neither in the Scripture, nor in any other use of language; and which is also discordant to the harmony, and scope of the Scripture. The word baptism is used (*Mark* x. 38, and *Luke* xii. 50), for being dipped in one's own blood, as Christ was upon the cross, and as most of the apostles were, for giving testimony of him. But it is hard to say, that prayer, fasting, and alms, have any similitude with dipping. The same is used also *Matt.* iii. 11 (which seemeth to make somewhat for purgatory) for a purging with fire. But it is evident the fire and purging here mentioned, is the same whereof the prophet Zechariah speaketh (chapter xiii. 9) *I will bring the third part through the fire, and will refine them,* &c. And St. Peter after him (1

Epistle i. 7), *That the trial of your faith, which is much more precious than of gold that perisheth, though it be tried with fire, might be found unto praise, and honour, and glory at the appearing of Jesus Christ;* and St. Paul (1 *Cor.* iii. 13), *The fire shall try every man's work of what sort it is.* But St. Peter and St. Paul speak of the fire that shall be at the second appearing of Christ; and the prophet Zechariah of the day of judgment. And therefore this place of St. Matthew may be interpreted of the same; and then there will be no necessity of the fire of purgatory.

Another interpretation of baptism for the dead, is that which I have before mentioned, which he preferreth to the second place of probability: and thence also he inferreth the utility of prayer for the dead. For if after the resurrection, such as have not heard of Christ, or not believed in him, may be received into Christ's kingdom; it is not in vain, after their death, that their friends should pray for them, till they should be risen. But granting that God, at the prayers of the faithful, may convert unto him some of those that have not heard Christ preached, and consequently cannot have rejected Christ, and that the charity of men in that point cannot be blamed; yet this concludeth nothing for purgatory; because to rise from death to life, is one thing; to rise from purgatory to life is another; as being a rising from life to life, from a life in torments to a life in joy.

A fourth place is that of *Matt.* v. 25, 26: *Agree with thine adversary quickly, whilst thou art in the way with him, lest at any time the adversary deliver thee to the judge, and the judge deliver thee to the officer, and thou be cast into prison: verily I say unto thee, thou shalt by no means come out thence, till thou hast paid the uttermost farthing.* In which allegory, the offender is the *sinner;* both the adversary and the judge is *God;* the way is this *life;* the prison is the *grave;* the officer, *death;* from which, the sinner shall not rise again to life eternal, but to a second death, till he have paid the utmost farthing, or Christ pay it for him by his passion, which is a full ransom for all manner of sins, as well lesser sins, as greater crimes; both being made by the passion of Christ equally venial.

The fifth place, is that of *Matt.* v. 22: *Whosoever is angry with his brother without a cause, shall be guilty in judgment: and whosoever shall say to his brother, Raca, shall be guilty in the council; but whosoever shall say, thou fool, shall be guilty to hell fire.* From which words he inferreth three sorts of sins, and three sorts of punishments; and that none of those sins, but the last, shall be punished with hell fire; and consequently, that after this life, there is punishment of lesser sins in purgatory. Of which inference, there is no colour in any interpretation that hath yet been given of them. Shall there be a distinction after this life of courts of justice, as there was amongst the Jews in our Saviour's time, to hear, and determine divers sorts of crimes, as the judges, and the council? Shall not all judicature appertain to Christ and his apostles? To understand therefore this text, we are not to consider it solitarily, but jointly with the words precedent, and subsequent. Our Saviour in this chapter interpreteth the law of Moses; which the Jews thought was then fulfilled, when they had not transgressed the grammatical sense thereof, howsoever they had transgressed against the sentence, or meaning of the legislator. Therefore whereas they thought the sixth commandment was not broken, but by killing a man: nor the seventh, but when a man lay with a woman, not his wife, our Saviour tells them the inward anger of a man against his brother, if it be without just cause, is homicide. You have heard, saith he, the Law of Moses, *Thou shalt not kill*, and that *Whosoever shall kill, shall be condemned before the judges*, or before the session of the Seventy: but I say unto you, to be angry with one's brother without cause, or to say unto him *Raca*, or *Fool*, is homicide, and shall be punished at the day of judgment, and session of Christ, and his apostles, with hell fire. So that those words were not used to distinguish between divers crimes, and divers courts of justice, and divers punishments; but to tax the distinction between sin and sin, which the Jews drew not from the difference of the will in obeying God, but from the difference of their temporal courts of justice; and to show them that he that had the will to hurt his brother, though the effect appear but in reviling, or not at all, shall be cast into hell fire, by the judges, and by the session, which shall be the same, not different, courts at the day of judgment. This considered, what can be drawn from this text, to maintain purgatory, I cannot imagine.

The sixth place is *Luke* xvi. 9: *Make ye friends of the unrighteous Mammon; that when ye fail, they may receive you into everlasting tabernacles.* This he alleges to prove invocation of saints departed. But the sense is plain, that we should make friends with our riches, of the poor; and thereby obtain their prayers whilst they live. *He that giveth to the poor, lendeth to the Lord.*

The seventh is *Luke* xxiii. 42: *Lord, remember me, when thou comest into thy kingdom.* Therefore, saith he, there is remission of sins after this life. But the consequence is not good. Our Saviour then forgave him; and at his coming again in glory, will remember to raise him again to life eternal.

The eighth is *Acts* ii. 24, where St. Peter saith of Christ, *that God had raised him up, and loosed the pains of death, because it was not possible he should be holden of it:* which he interprets to be a descent of Christ into purgatory, to loose some souls there from their torments: whereas it is manifest, that it was Christ that was loosed; it was he that could not be holden of death, or the grave; and not the souls in purgatory. But if that which Beza says, in his notes on this place, be well observed, there is none that will not see, that instead of *pains*, it should be *bands;* and then there is no further cause to seek for purgatory in this text.

# Chapter 45

## Of Demonology, and other Relics of the Religion of the Gentiles

*The original of demonology*. The impression made on the organs of sight by lucid bodies, either in one direct line, or in many lines, reflected from opaque, or refracted in the passage through diaphanous bodies produceth in living creatures, in whom God hath placed such organs, an imagination of the object, from whence the impression proceedeth; which imagination is called *sight;* and seemeth not to be a mere imagination, but the body itself without us; in the same manner, as when a man violently presseth his eye, there appears to him a light without, and before him, which no man perceiveth but himself; because there is indeed no such thing without him, but only a motion in the interior organs, pressing by resistance outward, that makes him think so. And the motion made by this pressure, continuing after the object which caused it is removed, is that we call *imagination* and *memory;* and, in sleep, and sometimes in great distemper of the organs by sickness or violence, a *dream;* of which things I have already spoken briefly, in the second and third chapters.

This nature of sight having never been discovered by the ancient pretenders to natural knowledge; much less by those that consider not things so remote, as that knowledge is, from their present use; it was hard for men to conceive of those images in the fancy and in the sense, otherwise, than of things really without us: which some, because they vanish away, they know not whither nor how, will have to be absolutely incorporeal, that is to say immaterial, or forms without matter; colour and figure, without any coloured or figured body; and that they can put on airy bodies, as a garment, to make them visible when they will to our bodily eyes; and others say, are bodies and living creatures, but made of air, or other more subtle and ethereal matter, which is, then, when they will be seen, condensed. But both of them agree on one general appellation of them, DEMONS. As if the dead of whom they dreamed, were not inhabitants of their own brain, but of the air, or of heaven, or hell; not phantasms, but ghosts; with just as much reason as if one should say, he saw his own ghost in a looking-glass, or the ghosts of the stars in a river; or call the ordinary apparition of the sun, of the quantity of about a foot, the *demon*, or ghost of that great sun that enlighteneth the whole visible world: and by that means have feared them, as things of an unknown, that is, of an unlimited power to do them good or harm; and consequently, given occasion to the governors of the heathen commonwealths to regulate this their fear, by establishing that DEMONOLOGY, (in which the poets, as principal priests of the heathen religion, were specially employed or reverenced,) to the public peace, and to the obedience of subjects necessary thereunto; and to make some of them good *demons*, and others evil; the one as a spur to the observance, the other as reins to withhold them from violation of the laws.

*What were the demons of the ancients*. What kind of things they were, to whom they attributed the name of *demons*, appeareth partly in the genealogy of their gods, written by Hesiod, one of the most ancient poets of the Grecians; and partly in other histories; of which I have observed some few before, in the twelfth chapter of this discourse.

*How that doctrine was spread. How far received by the Jews*. The Grecians, by their colonies and conquests, communicated their language and writings into Asia, Egypt, and Italy; and therein, by necessary consequence their *demonology*, or, as St. Paul calls it, (1 *Tim.* iv. 1) *their doctrines of devils*. And by that means the contagion was derived also to the Jews, both of Judea and Alexandria, and other parts, whereinto they were dispersed. But the name of *demon* they did not, as the Grecians, attribute to spirits both good and evil; but to the evil only: and to the good *demons* they gave the name of the spirit of God; and esteemed those into whose bodies they entered to be prophets. In sum, all singularity, if good, they attributed to the spirit of God; and if evil, to some *demon*, but a κακοδαίμων, an evil *demon*, that is a *devil*. And therefore, they called *demoniacs*, that is *possessed by the devil*, such as we call madmen or lunatics; or such as had the falling sickness, or that spoke anything which they, for want of understanding, thought absurd. As also of an unclean person in a notorious degree, they used to say he had an unclean spirit; of a dumb man, that he had a dumb devil; and of John the Baptist (*Matt.* xi. 18), for the singularity of his fasting, that he had a devil; and of our Saviour, because he said, he that keepeth his sayings should not see death in *æternum*, (*John* viii. 52), *Now we know thou hast a devil*;

*Abraham is dead, and the prophets are dead:* and again, because he said (*John* vii. 20), *They went about to kill him,* the people answered, *Thou hast a devil; who goeth about to kill thee?* Whereby it is manifest, that the Jews had the same opinions concerning phantasms, namely, that they were not phantasms, that is, idols of the brain, but things real, and independent on the fancy.

*Why our Saviour controlled it not.* Which doctrine, if it be not true, why, may some say, did not our Saviour contradict it, and teach the contrary? Nay, why does he use on divers occasions such forms of speech as seem to confirm it? To this I answer, that first, where Christ saith, (*Luke* xxiv. 39) *A spirit hath not flesh and bone,* though he show that there be spirits, yet he denies not that they are bodies. And where St. Paul says, (1 *Cor.* xv. 44) *we shall rise spiritual bodies,* he acknowledgeth the nature of spirits, but that they are bodily spirits; which is not difficult to understand. For air and many other things are bodies, though not flesh and bone, or any other gross body to be discerned by the eye. But when our Saviour speaketh to the devil, and commandeth him to go out of a man, if by the devil, he meant a disease, as frenzy, or lunacy, or a corporeal spirit, is not the speech improper? Can diseases hear? Or can there be a corporeal spirit in a body of flesh and bone, full already of vital and animal spirits? Are there not, therefore spirits, that neither have bodies, nor are mere imaginations? To the first I answer, that the addressing of our Saviour's command to the madness, or lunacy he cureth, is no more improper than was his rebuking of the fever, or of the wind and sea; for neither do these hear; or than was the command of God, to the light, to the firmament, to the sun, and stars, when he commanded them to be; for they could not hear before they had a being. But those speeches are not improper, because they signify the power of God's word; no more therefore is it improper, to command madness, or lunacy, under the appellation of devils by which they were then commonly understood, to depart out of a man's body. To the second, concerning their being incorporeal, I have not yet observed any place of Scripture, from whence it can be gathered, that any man was ever possessed with any other corporeal spirit, but that of his own, by which his body is naturally moved.

*The Scriptures do not teach that spirits are incorporeal.* Our Saviour, immediately after the Holy Ghost descended upon him in the form of a dove, is said by St. Matthew (chapter iv. 1), to have been *led up by the Spirit into the wilderness;* and the same is recited (*Luke* iv. 1) in these words, *Jesus being full of the Holy Ghost, was led in the Spirit into the wilderness;* whereby it is evident that by *spirit* there, is meant the Holy Ghost. This cannot be interpreted for a possession; for Christ, and the Holy Ghost, are but one and the same substance; which is no possession of one substance, or body, by another. And whereas in the verses following he is said to *have been taken up by the devil into the holy city, and set upon a pinnacle of the temple,* shall we conclude thence that he was possessed of the devil, or carried thither by violence? And again, *carried thence by the devil into an exceeding high mountain, who showed him thence all the kingdoms of the world:* wherein we are not to believe he was either possessed, or forced by the devil; nor that any mountain is high enough, according to the literal sense, to show him one whole hemisphere. What then can be the meaning of this place, other than that he went of himself into the wilderness; and that this carrying of him up and down from the wilderness to the city, and from thence into a mountain, was a vision? Comformable whereunto, is also the phrase of St. Luke, that he was led into the wilderness, not *by,* but *in,* the Spirit; whereas, concerning his being taken up into the mountain, and unto the pinnacle of the temple, he speaketh as St. Matthew doth: which suiteth with the nature of a vision.

Again, where St. Luke (chap. xxii. 3, 4) says of Judas Iscariot, that *Satan entered into him, and thereupon that he went and communed with the chief priests, and captains, how he might betray Christ unto them;* it may be answered, that by the entering of Satan, that is the *enemy,* into him, is meant, the hostile and traitorous intention of selling his Lord and Master. For as by the Holy Ghost, is frequently in Scripture understood, the graces and good inclinations given by the Holy Ghost; so by the entering of Satan may be understood the wicked cogitations, and designs of the adversaries of Christ, and his disciples. For as it is hard to say, that the devil was entered into Judas, before he had any such hostile design; so it is impertinent to say, he was first Christ's enemy in his heart, and that the devil entered into him afterwards. Therefore the entering of Satan, and his wicked purpose, was one of the same thing.

But if there be no immaterial spirit, or any possession of men's bodies by any spirit corporeal, it may again be asked, why our Saviour and his apostles did not teach the people so; and in such clear words, as they might no more doubt thereof. But such questions as these, are more curious, than necessary for a Christian man's salvation. Men may as well ask why Christ, that could have given to all men faith, piety, and all manner of moral virtues, gave it to some only, and not to all: and why he left the search of natural causes, and sciences, to the natural reason and industry of men, and did not reveal it to all, or any man supernaturally; and many other such questions. Of which nevertheless there may be alleged probable and pious reasons. For as God, when he brought the Israelites into the land of Promise, did not secure them therein, by subduing all the nations round about them; but left many of them, as thorns in their sides, to awaken from time to time their piety and industry: so our Saviour, in conducting us toward his heavenly kingdom, did not destroy all the difficulties of natural questions; but left them to exercise our industry, and reason; the scope of his preaching, being only to show us this plain and direct way to salvation, namely, the belief of this article, *that he was the Christ, the Son of the living God, sent into the world to sacrifice himself for our sins, and at his coming again, gloriously to reign over his elect, and to save them from their enemies eternally.* To which, the opinion of possession by spirits, or phantasms, is no impediment in the way; though it be to some an occasion of going out of the way, and to follow their own inventions. If we require of the Scripture an account of all questions, which may be raised to trouble us in the performance of God's commands, we may as well complain of Moses for not having set down the time of the creation of such spirits, as well as of the creation of the earth and sea, and of men and and beasts. To conclude; I find in Scripture that there be angels, and spirits, good and evil; but not that they are incorporeal, as are the apparitions men see in the dark, or in a dream, or vision; which the Latins call *spectra,* and took for *demons.* And I find that there are spirits corporeal, though subtle and invisible; but not that any man's body was possessed or inhabited by them; and that the bodies of the saints shall be such, namely, spiritual bodies, as St. Paul calls them.

*The power of casting out devils, not the same it was in the primitive church.* Nevertheless, the contrary doctrine, namely, that there be incorporeal spirits, hath hitherto so prevailed in the Church, that the use of exorcism, that is to say, of ejection of devils by conjuration, is thereupon built; and, though rarely and faintly practised, is not yet totally given over. That there were many demoniacs in the primitive Church, and few madmen, and other such singular diseases; whereas in these times we hear of, and see many madmen, and few demoniacs, proceeds not from the change of nature, but of names. But how it comes to pass that whereas heretofore the apostles, and after them for a time, the pastors of the Church, did cure those singular diseases, which now they are not seen to do; as likewise, why it is not in the power of every true believer now, to do all that the faithful did then, that is to say, as we read (*Mark* xvi. 17, 18), *in Christ's name to cast out devils, to speak with new tongues, to take up serpents, to drink deadly poison without harm-taking, and to cure the sick by the laying on of their hands,* and all this without other words, but *in the name of Jesus,* is another question. And it is probable that those extraordinary gifts were given to the Church, for no longer a time, than men trusted wholly to Christ, and looked for their felicity only in his kingdom to come; and consequently, that when they sought authority, and riches, and trusted to their own subtlety for a kingdom of this world, these supernatural gifts of God were again taken from them.

*Another relic of Gentilism, worshipping of images, left in the Church, not brought into it.* Another relic of Gentilism is, the *worship of images,* neither instituted by Moses in the Old, nor by Christ in the New Testament; nor yet brought in from the Gentiles; but left amongst them after they had given their names to Christ. Before our Saviour preached, it was the general religion of the Gentiles to worship for gods those appearances that remain in the brain from the impression of external bodies upon the organs of their senses, which are commonly called *ideas, idols, phantasms, conceits,* as being representations of those external bodies which cause them, and have nothing in them of reality, no more than there is in the things that seem to stand before us in a dream. And this is the reason why St. Paul says, (1 *Cor.* viii. 4) *we know that an idol is nothing;* not that he thought that an image of metal, stone, or wood, was nothing; but that the thing which they honoured, or feared in the image, and held for a god, was a mere figment, without place, habitation, motion, or existence, but in the motions of the brain. And the worship of these with divine honour, is that which is in the Scripture called idolatry, and rebellion against God. For God being King of the Jews, and his lieutenant being first Moses, and afterwards the high-priest; if the people had been permitted to worship, and pray to images, which are representations of their own fancies, they had had no further dependence on the true God, of whom there can be no similitude; nor on his prime-ministers, Moses and the high-priests; but every man had governed himself according to his own appetite, to the utter eversion of the commonwealth, and their own destruction for want of union. And therefore the first law of God was, *they should not take for gods,* ALIENOS DEOS, *that is, the gods of other nations, but that only true God, who vouchsafed to commune with Moses, and by him to give them laws and directions, for their peace, and for their salvation from their enemies.* And the second was, that *they should not make to themselves any image to worship, of their own invention.* For it is the same deposing of a king, to submit to another king, whether he be set up by a neighbour nation, or by ourselves.

*Answer to certain seeming texts for images.* The places of Scripture pretended to countenance the setting up of images, to worship them; or to set them up at all in the places where God is worshipped, are first, two examples; one of the cherubims over the ark of God; the other of the brazen serpent. Secondly, some texts whereby we are commanded to worship certain creatures for their relation to God; as to worship his footstool. And lastly, some other texts, by which is authorized a religious honouring of holy things. But before I examine the force of those places, to prove that which is pretended, I must first explain what is to be understood by *worshipping,* and what by *images* and *idols.*

*What is worship.* I have already shown in chapter twenty of this discourse, that to honour, is to value highly the power of any person: and that such value is measured, by our comparing him with others. But because there is nothing to be compared with God in power; we honour him not, but dishonour him by any value less than infinite. And thus honour is properly of its own nature, secret, and internal in the heart. But the inward thoughts of men, which appear outwardly in their words and actions, are the signs of our honouring, and these go by the name of *worship;* in Latin, *cultus.* Therefore, to pray to, to swear by, to obey, to be diligent and officious in serving: in sum, all words and actions that betoken fear to offend, or desire to please, is *worship,* whether those words and actions be sincere, or feigned: and because they appear as signs of honouring, are ordinarily also called *honour*.

*Distinction between divine and civil worship.* The worship we exhibit to those we esteem to be but men, as to kings, and men in authority, is *civil worship;* but the worship we exhibit to that which we think to be God, whatsoever the words, ceremonies, gestures or other actions be, is *divine worship*. To fall prostrate before a king, in him that thinks him but a man, is but civil worship: and he that putteth off his hat in the church, for this cause, that he thinketh it the house of God, worshippeth with divine worship. They that seek the distinction of divine and civil worship, not in the intention of the worshipper, but in the words δουλεία and λατρεία, deceive themselves. For whereas there be two sorts of servants: that sort, which is of those that are absolutely in the power of their masters, as slaves taken in war, and their issue, whose bodies are not in their own power, (their lives depending on the will of their masters, in such manner as to forfeit them upon the least disobedience), and that are bought and sold as beasts, were called δοῦλοι, that is, properly slaves, and their service δουλεία: the other, which is of those that serve (for hire, or in hope of benefit from their masters) voluntarily, are called θῆτες; that is, domestic servants, to whose service the masters have no further right, than is contained in the covenants made betwixt them. These two kinds of servants have thus much common to them both, that their labour is appointed them by another: and the word λάτρις, is the general name of both, signifying him that worketh for another, whether as a slave, or a voluntary servant. So that λατρεία signifieth generally all service: but δουλεία the service of bond-men only, and the condition of slavery: and both are used in Scripture, (to signify our service of God) promiscuously; δουλεία, because we are God's slaves; λατρεία, because we serve him. And in all kinds of service is contained, not only obedience, but also worship; that is, such actions, gestures, and words, as signify *honour*.

*An image, what. Phantasms.* An *image*, in the most strict signification of the word, is the resemblance of something visible: in which sense the phantastical forms, apparitions, or seemings of visible bodies to the sight, are only *images;* such as are the show of a man, or other thing in the water, by reflection, or refraction; or of the sun, or stars by direct vision in the air; which are nothing real in the things seen, nor in the place where they seem to be; nor are their magnitudes and figures the same with that of the object; but changeable, by the variation of the organs of sight, or by glasses, and are present oftentimes in our imagination, and in our dreams, when the object is absent; or changed into other colours and shapes, as things that depend only upon the fancy. And these are the *images,* which are originally and most properly called *ideas,* and *idols,* and derived from the language of the Grecians, with whom the word εἴδω signifieth *to see.* They are also called *phantasms,* which is in the same language, *apparitions.* And from these images it is, that one of the faculties of man's nature, is called the *imagination.* And from hence it is manifest, that there neither is, nor can be, any image made of a thing invisible.

It is also evident, that there can be, no image of a thing infinite: for all the images, and phantasms that are made by the impression of things visible, are figured; but figure is a quantity every way determined. And therefore there can be no image of God; nor of the soul of man; nor of spirits; but only of bodies visible; that is, bodies that have light in themselves, or are by such enlightened.

*Fictions. Material images.* And whereas a man can fancy shapes he never saw; making up a figure out of the parts of divers creatures; as the poets make their centaurs, chimeras, and other monsters never seen: so can he also give matter to those shapes, and make them in wood, clay, or metal. And these are also called images, not for the resemblance of any corporeal thing, but for the resemblance of some phantastical inhabitants of the brain of the maker. But in these idols, as they are originally in the brain, and as they are painted, carved, moulded, or moulten in matter, there is a similitude of the one to the other, for which the material body made by art, may be said to be the image of the fantastical idol made by nature.

But in a large use of the word image, is contained also, any representation of one thing by another. So an earthly sovereign may be called the image of God: and an inferior magistrate, the image of an earthly sovereign. And many times in the idolatry of the Gentiles there was little regard to the similitude of their material idol to the idol in their fancy, and yet it was called the image of it. For a stone unhewn has been set up for Neptune, and divers other shapes far different from the shapes they conceived of their gods. And at this day we see many images of the Virgin Mary, and other saints, unlike one another, and without correspondence to any one man's fancy; and yet serve well enough for the purpose they were erected for; which was no more but by the names only, to represent the persons mentioned in the history; to which every man applieth a mental image of his own making, or none at all. And thus an image in the largest sense, is either the resemblance, or the representation of some thing visible; or both together, as it happeneth for the most part.

But the name of idol is extended yet further in Scripture, to signify also the sun, or a star, or any other creature, visible or invisible, when they are worshipped for gods.

*Idolatry, what.* Having shown what is *worship,* and what an *image;* I will now put them together, and examine what that IDOLATRY is, which is forbidden in the second commandment, and other places of the Scripture.

To worship an image, is voluntarily to do those external acts, which are signs of honouring either the matter of the image, which is wood, stone, metal, or some other visible creature; or the phantasm of the brain, for the resemblance, or representation whereof, the matter was formed or figured; or both together, as one animate body, composed of the matter and the phantasm, as of a body and soul.

To be uncovered, before a man of power and authority, or before the throne of a prince, or in such other places as he ordaineth to that purpose in his absence, is to worship that man, or prince with civil worship; as being a sign, not of honouring the stool or place, but the person; and is not idolatry. But if he that doth it, should suppose the soul of the prince to be in the stool, or should present a petition to the stool, it were divine worship, and idolatry.

To pray to a king for such things, as he is able to do for us, though we prostrate ourselves before him, is but civil worship; because we acknowledge no other power in him, but human: but voluntarily to pray unto him for fair weather, or for any thing which God only can do for us, is divine worship, and idolatry. On the other side, if a king compel a man to it by the terror of death, or other great corporal punishment, it is not idolatry: for the worship which the sovereign commandeth to be done unto himself by the terror of his laws, is not a sign that he that obeyeth him, does inwardly honour him as a God, but that he is desirous to save himself from death, or from a miserable life; and that which is not a sign of internal honour, is no worship, and therefore no idolatry. Neither can it be said, that he that does it, scandalizeth, or layeth any stumbling block before his brother; because how wise, or learned soever he be that worshippeth in that manner, another man cannot from thence argue, that he approveth it; but that he doth it for fear; and that it is not his act, but the act of his sovereign.

To worship God, in some peculiar place, or turning a man's face towards an image, or determinate place, is not to worship, or honour the place, or image; but to acknowledge it holy, that is to say, to acknowledge the image, or the place to be set apart from common use. For that is the meaning of the word *holy;* which implies no new quality in the place or image, but only a new relation by appropriation to God; and therefore is not idolatry; no more than it was idolatry to worship God before the brazen serpent; or for the Jews, when they were out of their own country, to turn their faces, when they prayed, towards the temple of Jerusalem; or for Moses to put off his shoes when he was before the flaming bush, the ground appertaining to Mount Sinai, which place God had chosen to appear in, and to give his laws to the people of Israel, and was therefore holy ground, not by inherent sanctity, but by separation to God's use; or for Christians to worship in the churches, which are once solemnly dedicated to God for that purpose, by the authority of the king, or other true representant of the Church. But to worship God, as inanimating, or inhabiting such image, or place; that is to say, in infinite substance in a finite place, is idolatry: for such finite gods, are but idols of the brain, nothing real; and are commonly called in the Scripture by the names of *vanity,* and *lies,* and *nothing.* Also to worship God, not as inanimating, or present in the place, or image; but to the end to be put in mind of him, or of some works of his, in case the place, or image be dedicated, or set up by private authority, and not by the authority of them that are our sovereign pastors, is idolatry. For the commandment is, *thou shalt not make to thyself any graven image.* God commanded Moses to set up the brazen serpent; he did not make it to himself; it was not therefore against the commandment. But the making of the golden calf by Aaron, and the people, as being done without authority from God, was idolatry; not only because they held it for God, but also because they made it for a religious use, without warrant either from God their sovereign, or from Moses, that was his lieutenant.

The Gentiles worshipped for gods, Jupiter and others; that

living, were men perhaps that had done great and glorious acts: and for the children of God, divers men and women, supposing them gotten between an immortal deity, and a mortal man. This was idolatry, because they made them so to themselves, having no authority from God, neither in his eternal law of reason, nor in his positive and revealed will. But though our Saviour was a man, whom we also believe to be God immortal, and the Son of God, yet this is no idolatry; because we build not that belief upon our own fancy, or judgment, but upon the Word of God revealed in the Scriptures. And for the adoration of the Eucharist, if the words of Christ, *this is my body,* signify, *that he himself, and the seeming bread in his hand, and not only so, but that all the seeming morsels of bread that have ever since been, and any time hereafter shall be consecrated by priests, be so many Christ's bodies, and yet all of them but one body;* then is that no idolatry, because it is authorized by our Saviour: but if that text do not signify that, (for there is no other that can be alleged for it) then, because it is a worship of human institution, it is idolatry. For it is not enough to say, God can transubstantiate the bread into Christ's body: for the Gentiles also held God to be omnipotent, and might upon that ground no less excuse their idolatry, by pretending, as well as others, a transubstantiation of their wood, and stone into God Almighty.

Whereas there be, that pretend divine inspiration to be the supernatural entering of the Holy Ghost into a man, and not an acquisition of God's graces, by doctrine, and study; I think they are in a very dangerous dilemma. For if they worship not the man whom they believe to be so inspired, they fall into impiety; as not adoring God's supernatural presence. And again, if they worship them, they commit idolatry; for the apostles would never permit themselves to be so worshipped. Therefore the safest way is to believe, that by the descending of the dove upon the apostles; and by Christ's breathing on them, when he gave them the Holy Ghost; and by the giving of it by imposition of hands, are understood the signs which God has been pleased to use, or ordain to be used, of his promise to assist those persons in their study to preach his kingdom, and in their conversation, that it might not be scandalous, but edifying to others.

*Scandalous worship of images.* Besides the idolatrous worship of images, there is also a scandalous worship of them; which is also a sin, but not idolatry. For *idolatry* is to worship by signs of an internal, and real honour: but *scandalous worship*, is but seeming worship, and may sometimes be joined with an inward, and hearty detestation, both of the image, and of the phantastical *demon*, or idol, to which it is dedicated; and proceed only from the fear of death, or other grievous punishment; and is nevertheless a sin in them that so worship, in case they be men whose actions are looked at by others, as lights to guide them by; because following their ways, they cannot but stumble, and fall in the way of religion: whereas the example of those we regard not, works not on us at all, but leaves us to our own diligence and caution; and consequently are no causes of our falling.

If therefore a pastor lawfully called to teach and direct others, or any other, of whose knowledge there is a great opinion, do external honour to an idol for fear; unless he make his fear and unwillingness to it, as evident as the worship; he scandalizeth his brother, by seeming to approve idolatry. For his brother arguing from the action of his teacher, or of him whose knowledge he esteemeth great, concludes it to be lawful in itself. And this scandal is sin, and a *scandal given*. But if one being no pastor, nor of eminent reputation for knowledge in Christian doctrine, do the same, and another follow him; this is no scandal given; for he had no cause to follow such example: but is a pretence of scandal, which he taketh of himself for an excuse before men. For an unlearned man, that is in the power of an idolatrous king, or state, if commanded on pain of death to worship before an idol, he detesteth the idol in his heart, he doth well; though if he had the fortitude to suffer death, rather than worship it, he should do better. But if a pastor, who as Christ's messenger, has undertaken to teach Christ's doctrine to all nations, should do the same, it were not only a sinful scandal, in respect of other Christian men's consciences, but a perfidious forsaking of his charge.

The sum of that which I have saith hitherto, concerning the worship of images, is this, that he that worshippeth in an image, or any creature, either the matter thereof, or any fancy of his own, which he thinketh to dwell in it; or both together; or believeth that such things hear his prayers, or see his devotions, without ears or eyes, committeth idolatry: and he that counterfeiteth such worship for fear of punishment, if he be a man whose example hath power amongst his brethren, committeth a sin. But he that worshippeth the Creator of the world before such an image, or in such a place as he hath not made, or chosen of himself, but taken from the commandment of God's word, as the Jews did in worshipping God before the cherubims, and before the brazen serpent for a time, and in, or towards the Temple of Jerusalem, which was also but for a time, committeth no idolatry.

Now for the worship of saints, and images, and relics, and other things at this day practised in the Church of Rome, I say they are not allowed by the Word of God, nor brought into the Church of Rome, from the doctrine there taught; but partly left in it at the first conversion of the Gentiles; and afterwards countenanced, and confirmed, and augmented by the bishops of Rome.

*Answer to the argument from the cherubims, and brazen serpent.* As for the proofs alleged out of Scripture, namely, those examples of images appointed by God to be set up; they were not set up for the people, or any man to worship, but that they should worship God himself before them; as before the cherubims over the ark, and the brazen serpent. For we read not, that the priest, or any other did worship the cherubims; but contrarily we read (2 *Kings* xviii. 4) that Hezekiah brake in pieces the brazen serpent which Moses had set up, because the people burnt incense to it. Besides, those examples are not put for our imitation, that we also should set up images, under pretence of worshipping God before them; because the words of the second commandment, *thou shalt not make to thyself any graven image, &c.* distinguish between the images that God commanded to be set up, and those which we set up to ourselves. And therefore from the cherubims or brazen serpent, to the images of man's devising; and from the worship commanded by God, to the will-worship of men, the argument is not good. This also is to be considered, that as Hezekiah brake in pieces the brazen serpent, because the Jews did worship it, to the end they should do so no more; so also Christian sovereigns ought to brake down the images which their subjects have been accustomed to worship, that there be no more occasion of such idolatry. For at this day, the ignorant people, where images are worshipped, do really believe there is a divine power in the images; and are told by their pastors, that some of them have spoken; and have bled; and that miracles have been done by them; which they apprehend as done by the saint, which they think either is the image itself, or in it. The Israelites, when they worshipped the calf, did think they worshipped the God that brought them out of Egypt; and yet it was idolatry, because they thought the calf either was that God, or had him in his belly. And though some man may think it impossible for people to be so stupid, as to think the image to be God, or a saint; or to worship it in that notion; yet it is manifest in Scripture to the contrary; where when the golden calf was made, the people said, (*Exod.* xxxii. 4) *These are thy gods, O Israel;* and where the images of Laban (*Gen.* xxxi. 30) are called his gods. And we see daily by experience in all sorts of people, that such men as study nothing but their food and ease, are content to believe any absurdity, rather than to trouble themselves to examine it; holding their faith as it were by entail unalienable, except by an express and new law.

*Painting of fancies no idolatry; but abusing them to religious worship is.* But they infer from some other places, that it is lawful to paint angels, and also God himself: as from God's walking in the garden; from Jacob's seeing God at the top of the ladder; and from other visions, and dreams. But visions, and dreams, whether natural, or supernatural, are but phantasms: and he that painteth an image of any of them, maketh not an image of God, but of his own phantasm, which is making of an idol. I say not, that to draw a picture after a fancy, is a sin; but when it is drawn, to hold it for a representation of God, is against the second commandment; and can be of no use, but to worship. And the same may be said of the images of angels, and of men dead; unless as monuments of friends, or of men worthy remembrance. For such use of an image, is not worship of the image; but a civil honouring of the person, not that is, but that was. But when it is done to the image which we make of a saint, for no other reason, but that we think he heareth our prayers, and is pleased with the honour we do him, when dead, and without sense, we attribute to him more than human power; and therefore it is idolatry.

Seeing therefore there is no authority, neither in the law of Moses, nor in the Gospel, for the religious worship of images, or other representations of God, which men set up to themselves; or for the worship of the image of any creature in heaven or earth, or under the earth: and whereas Christian kings, who are living representants of God, are not to be worshipped by their subjects, by any act that signifieth a greater esteem of his power, than the nature of mortal man is capable of; it cannot be imagined, that the religious worship now in use, was brought into the Church by misunderstanding of the Scripture. It resteth therefore, that it was left in it, by not destroying the images themselves, in the conversion of the Gentiles that worshipped them.

*How idolatry was left in the Church.* The cause whereof, was the immoderate esteem, and prices set upon the workmanship of them, which made the owners, though converted from worshipping them as they had done religiously for demons, to retain them still in their houses, upon pretence of doing it in the honour of Christ, of the Virgin Mary, and of the Apostles, and other the pastors of the primitive Church; as being easy, by giving them new names, to make that an image of the Virgin Mary, and of her son our Saviour, which before perhaps was called the image of Venus, and Cupid; and so of a Jupiter to make a Barnabas, and of Mercury a Paul, and the like. And as worldly ambition creeping by degrees into the pastors, drew them to an endeavour of pleasing the new-made Christians; and also to a liking of this kind of honour, which they also might hope for after their decease, as well as those that had already gained it: so the worshipping of the images of Christ and his apostles, grew more and more idolatrous; save that somewhat after the time of Constantine, divers emperors, and bishops, and general councils, observed and opposed the unlawfulness thereof; but too late, or too weakly.

*Canonizing of saints.* The canonizing of saints, is another relic of Gentilism: it is neither a misunderstanding of Scripture, nor a new invention of the Roman Church, but a custom as ancient as the commonwealth of Rome itself. The first that ever was canonized at Rome, was Romulus, and that upon the narration of Julius Proculus, that swore before the senate, he spake with him after his death, and was assured by him, he dwelt in heaven, and was there called *Quirinus,* and would be propitious to the state of their new city: and thereupon the senate gave *public testimony* of his sanctity. Julius Cæsar, and other emperors after him, had the like *testimony;* that is, were canonized for saints; for by such testimony is CANONIZATION now defined; and is the same with the ἀποθέωσις of the heathen.

*The name of Pontifex.* It is also from the Roman Heathen, that the Popes have received the name, and power of PONTIFEX MAXIMUS. This was the name of him that in the ancient commonwealth of Rome, had the supreme authority under the senate and people, of regulating all ceremonies and doctrines concerning their religion: and when Augustus Cæsar changed the state into a monarchy, he took to himself no more but this office, and that of tribune of the people, that is to say, the supreme power both in state, and religion; and the succeeding emperors enjoyed the same. But when the emperor Constantine lived, who was the first that professed and authorized Christian religion, it was consonant to his profession, to cause religion to be regulated, under his authority, by the Bishop of Rome: though it do not appear they had so soon the name of Pontifex; but rather, that the succeeding bishops took it of themselves, to countenance the power they exercised over the bishops of the Roman provinces. For it is not any privilege of St. Peter, but the privilege of the city of Rome, which the emperors were always willing to uphold, that gave them such authority over other bishops; as may be evidently seen by that, that the bishop of Constantinople, when the emperor made that city the seat of the empire, pretended to be equal to the bishop of Rome; though at last, not without contention, the Pope carried it, and became the *Pontifex Maximus;* but in right only of the emperor; and not without the bounds of the empire; nor any where, after the emperor had lost his power in Rome; though it were the Pope himself that took his power from him. From whence we may by the way observe, that there is no place for the superiority of the Pope over other bishops, except in the territories whereof he is himself the civil sovereign, and where the emperor having sovereign power civil, hath expressly chosen the Pope for the chief pastor under himself, of his Christian subjects.

*Procession of images.* The carrying about of images in *procession,* is another relic of the religion of the Greeks, and Romans. For they also carried their idols from place to place, in a kind of chariot, which was peculiarly dedicated to that use, which the Latins called *thensa,* and *vehiculum Deorum;* and the image was placed in a frame, or shrine, which they called *ferculum:* and that which they called *pompa,* is the same that now is named *procession.* According whereunto, amongst the divine honours which were given to Julius Cæsar by the senate, this was one, that in the pomp, or procession, at the Circæan games, he should have *thensam et ferculum,* a sacred chariot and a shrine; which was as much, as to be carried up and down as a god: just as at this day the Popes are carried by Switzers under a canopy.

*Wax candles, and torches lighted.* To these processions also belonged the bearing of burning torches, and candles, before the images of the gods, both amongst the Greeks and

Romans. For afterwards the emperors of Rome received the same honour; as we read of Caligula, that at his reception to the empire, he was carried from Misenum to Rome, in the midst of a throng of people, the ways beset with altars, and beasts for sacrifice, and burning *torches:* and of Caracalla, that was received into Alexandria with incense, and with casting of flowers, and δαδουχίαις, that is, with torches; for δαδοῦχοι were they that amongst the Greeks carried torches lighted in the processions of their gods. And in process of time, the devout, but ignorant people, did many times honour their bishops with the like pomp of wax candles, and the images of our Saviour, and the saints, constantly, in the church itself. And thus came in the use of wax candles; and was also established by some of the ancient Councils.

The heathens had also their *aqua lustralis,* that is to say, *holy water.* The Church of Rome imitates them also in their *holy days.* They had their *bacchanalia;* and we have our *wakes,* answering to them: they their *saturnalia,* and we our *carnivals,* and Shrove-Tuesday's liberty of servants: they their procession of *Priapus;* we our fetching in, erection, and dancing about *May-poles;* and dancing is one kind of worship: they had their procession called *Ambarvalia;* and we our procession about the fields in the *Rogation-week.* Nor do I think that these are all the ceremonies that have been left in the Church, from the first conversion of the Gentiles; but they are all that I can for the present call to mind; and if a man would well observe that which is delivered in the histories, concerning the religious rites of the Greeks and Romans, I doubt not but he might find many more of these old empty bottles of Gentilism, which the doctors of the Roman Church, either by negligence or ambition, have filled up again with the new wine of Christianity, that will not fail in time to break them.

## Chapter 46

## Of Darkness from Vain Philosophy, and Fabulous Traditions

*What philosophy is.* By PHILOSOPHY is understood *the knowledge acquired by reasoning, from the manner of the generation of any thing, to the properties; or from the properties, to some possible way of generation of the same; to the end to be able to produce, as far as matter, and human force permit, such effects, as human life requireth.* So the geometrician, from the construction of figures, findeth out many properties thereof; and from the properties, new ways of their construction, by reasoning; to the end to be able to measure land, and water; and for infinite other uses. So the astronomer, from the rising, setting, and moving of the sun, and stars, in divers parts of the heavens, findeth out the causes of day, and night, and of the different seasons of the year; whereby he keepeth an account of time; and the like of other sciences.

*Prudence no part of philosophy.* By which definition it is evident, that we are not to account as any part thereof, that original knowledge called experience, in which consisteth prudence: because it is not attained by reasoning, but found as well in brute beasts, as in man; and is but a memory of successions of events in times past, wherein the omission of every little circumstance altering the effect, frustrateth the expectation of the most prudent: whereas nothing is produced by reasoning aright, but general, eternal, and immutable truth.

*No false doctrine is part of philosophy.* Nor are we therefore to give that name to any false conclusions: for he that reasoneth aright in words he understandeth, can never conclude an error.

*No more is revelation supernatural.* Nor to that which any man knows by supernatural revelation; because it is not acquired by reasoning.

*Nor learning taken upon credit of authors.* Nor that which is gotten by reasoning from the authority of books; because it is not by reasoning from the cause to the effect, nor from the effect to the cause; and is not knowledge but faith.

*Of the beginnings and progress of philosophy.* The faculty of reasoning being consequent to the use of speech, it was not possible, but that there should have been some general truths found out by reasoning, as ancient almost as language itself. The savages of America, are not without some good moral sentences; also they have a little arithmetic, to add, and divide in numbers not too great: but they are not, therefore, philosophers. For as there were plants of corn and wine in small quantity dispersed in the fields and woods, before men knew their virtue, or made use of them for their nourishment, or planted them apart in fields and vineyards; in which time they fed on acorns, and drank water: so also there have been divers true, general, and profitable speculations from the beginning; as being the natural plants of human reason. But they were at first but few in number; men lived upon gross experience; there was no method; that is to say, no sowing, nor planting of knowledge by itself, apart from the weeds, and common plants of error and conjecture. And the cause of it being the want of leisure from procuring the necessities of life, and defending themselves against their neighbours, it was impossible, till the erecting of great commonwealths, it should be otherwise. *Leisure* is the mother of *philosophy;* and *Commonwealth*, the mother of *peace* and *leisure.* Where first were great and flourishing *cities*, there was first the study of *philosophy*. The *Gymnosophists* of India, the *Magi* of Persia, and the *Priests* of Chaldea and Egypt, are counted the most ancient philosophers; and those countries were the most ancient of kingdoms. *Philosophy* was not risen to the Grecians, and other people of the west, whose *commonwealths*, no greater perhaps than Lucca or Geneva, had never *peace,* but when their fears of one another were equal; nor the *leisure* to observe anything but one another. At length, when war had united many of these Grecian lesser cities, into fewer, and greater; then began *seven men*, of several parts of Greece, to get the reputation of being *wise;* some of them for *moral* and *politic* sentences; and others for the learning of the Chaldeans and Egyptians, which was *astronomy*, and *geometry*. But we hear not yet of any *schools of philosophy*.

*Of the schools of philosophy amongst the Athenians.* After the Athenians, by the overthrow of the Persian armies, had gotten the dominion of the sea; and thereby, of all the islands, and maritime cities of the Archipelago, as well of Asia as Europe; and were grown wealthy; they that had no employment, neither at home nor abroad, had little else to employ themselves in, but either (as St. Luke says, *Acts* xvii. 21), *in telling and hearing news*, or in discoursing of *philosophy* publicly to the youth of the city. Every master took some place for that purpose. Plato, in certain public walks called *Academia,* from one *Academus:* Aristotle in the walk of the temple of Pan, called *Lyceum:* others in the *Stoa,* or covered walk, wherein the merchants' goods were brought to land: others in other places; where they spent the time of their leisure, in teaching or in disputing of their opinions: and some in any place, where they could get the youth of the city together to hear them talk. And this was it which Carneades also did at Rome, when he was ambassador: which caused Cato to advise the senate to dispatch him quickly, for fear of corrupting the manners of the young men, that delighted to hear him speak, as they thought, fine things.

From this it was, that the place where any of them taught, and disputed, was called *schola,* which in their tongue signifieth *leisure;* and their disputations, *diatribæ,* that is to say, *passing of the time.* Also the philosophers themselves had the name of their sects, some of them from these their Schools: for they that followed Plato's doctrine, were called *Academics;* the followers of Aristotle *Peripatetics,* from the walk he taught in; and those that Zeno taught *Stoics,* from the *Stoa;* as if we should denominate men from *Moor-fields,* from *Paul's Church,* and from the *Exchange,* because they meet there often, to prate and loiter.

Nevertheless, men were so much taken with this custom, that in time it spread itself over all Europe, and the best part of Africa; so as there were schools publicly erected and maintained, for lectures and disputations, almost in every commonwealth.

*Of the schools of the Jews.* There were also schools, anciently, both before and after the time of our Saviour, amongst the Jews; but they were schools of their law. For though they were called *synagogues,* that is to say, congregations of the people; yet, inasmuch as the law was every sabbath-day read, expounded, and disputed in them, they differed not in nature, but in name only, from public schools; and were not only in Jerusalem, but in every city of the Gentiles, where the Jews inhabited. There was such a school at Damascus, whereinto Paul entered, to persecute. There were others at Antioch, Iconium, and Thessalonica, whereinto he entered to dispute: and such was the synagogue of the *Libertines, Cyrenians, Alexandrians, Cilicians,* and those of Asia; that is to say, the school of *Libertines,* and of Jews that were strangers in Jerusalem; and of this school they were that disputed (*Acts* vi. 9) with St. Stephen.

*The schools of the Grecians unprofitable.* But what has been the utility of those schools? What science is there at this day acquired by their readings and disputings? That we have of geometry, which is the mother of all natural science, we are not indebted for it to the schools. Plato, that was the best philosopher of the Greeks, forbad entrance into his school to all that were not already in some measure geometricians. There were many that studied that science to the great advantage of mankind: but there is no mention of their schools; nor was there any sect of geometricians; nor did they then pass under the name of philosophers. The natural philosophy of those schools was rather a dream than science, and set forth in senseless and insignificant language; which cannot be avoided by those that will teach philosophy, without having first attained great knowledge in geometry. For nature worketh by motion; the ways and degrees whereof cannot be known, without the knowledge of the proportions and properties of lines and figures. Their moral philosophy is but a description of their own passions. For the rule of manners, without civil government, is the law of nature; and in it, the law civil, that determineth what is *honest* and *dishonest,* what is *just* and *unjust,* and generally what is *good* and *evil.* Whereas they make the rules of *good* and *bad,* by their own *liking* and *disliking:* by which means, in so great diversity of taste, there is nothing generally agreed on; but every one doth, as far as he dares, whatsoever seemeth good in his own eyes, to the subversion of commonwealth. Their *logic,* which should be the method of reasoning, is nothing else but captions of words, and inventions how to puzzle such as should go about to pose them. To conclude, there is nothing so absurd, that the old philosophers, as Cicero saith (who was one of them,) have not some of them maintained. And I believe that scarce anything can be more absurdly said in natural philosophy, than that which now is called *Aristotle's Metaphysics;* nor more repugnant to government, that much of that he hath said in his *Politics;* nor more ignorantly, than a great part of his *Ethics.*

*The schools of the Jews unprofitable.* The school of the Jews was originally a school of the law of Moses; who commanded (*Deut.* xxxi. 10) that at the end of every seventh year, at the Feast of the Tabernacles, it should be read to all the people, that they might hear and learn it. Therefore the reading of the law, which was in use after the Captivity, every Sabbath day, ought to have had no other end, but the acquainting of the people with the Commandments which they were to obey, and to expound unto them the writings of the prophets. But it is manifest, by the many reprehensions of them by our Saviour, that they corrupted the text of the law with their false commentaries, and vain traditions; and so little understood the prophets, that they did neither acknowledge Christ, nor the works he did, of which the prophets prophesied. So that by their lectures and disputations in their synagogues, they turned the doctrine of their law into a fantastical kind of philosophy, concerning the incomprehensible nature of God, and of spirits; which they compounded of the vain philosophy and theology of the Grecians, mingled with their own fancies, drawn from the obscurer places of the Scripture, and which might most easily be wrested to their purpose; and from the fabulous traditions of their ancestors.

*University, what it is.* That which is now called an *University*, is a joining together, and an incorporation under one government, of many public schools, in one and the same town or city. In which, the principal schools were ordained for the three professions, that is to say, of the Roman religion, of the Roman law, and of the art of medicine. And for the study of philosophy, it hath no otherwise place, than as a handmaid to the Roman religion: and since the authority of Aristotle is only current there, that study is not properly philosophy, (the nature whereof dependeth not on authors,) but *Aristotelity*. And for geometry, till of very late times it had no place at all; as being subservient to nothing but rigid truth. And if any man by the ingenuity of his own nature, had attained to any degree of perfection therein, he was commonly thought a magician, and his art diabolical.

*Errors brought into religion from Aristotle's metaphysics.* Now to descend to the particular tenets of vain philosophy, derived to the Universities, and thence into the Church, partly from Aristotle, partly from blindness of understanding; I shall first consider their principles. There is a certain *philosophia prima*, on which all other philosophy ought to depend; and consisteth principally, in right limiting of the significations of such appellations, or names, as are of all others the most universal; which limitations serve to avoid ambiguity and equivocation in reasoning; and are commonly called definitions: such as are the definitions of body, time, place, matter, form, essence, subject, substance, accident, power, act, finite, infinite, quantity, quality, motion, action, passion, and divers others, necessary to the explaining of a man's conceptions concerning the nature and generation of bodies. The explication, that is, the settling of the meaning, of which, and the like terms, is commonly in the Schools called *metaphysics:* as being a part of the philosophy of Aristotle, which hath that for title. But it is in another sense; for there it signifieth as much as *books written or placed after his natural philosophy:* but the Schools take them for *books of supernatural philosophy:* for the word *metaphysics* will bear both these senses. And indeed that which is there written, is for the most part so far from the possibility of being understood, and so repugnant to natural reason, that whosoever thinketh there is anything to be understood by it, must needs think it supernatural.

*Errors concerning abstract essences.* From these metaphysics, which are mingled with the Scripture to make School divinity, we are told, there be in the world certain essences separated from bodies, which they call *abstract essences, and substantial forms.* For the interpreting of which jargon, there is need of somewhat more than ordinary attention in this place. Also I ask pardon of those that are not used to this kind of discourse, for applying myself to those that are. The world, (I mean not the earth only, that denominates the lovers of it *worldly men,* but the *universe,* that is, the whole mass of all things that are), is corporeal, that is to say, body; and hath the dimensions of magnitude, namely, length, breadth, and depth: also every part of body, is likewise body, and hath the like dimensions; and consequently every part of the universe, is body, and that which is not body, is no part of the universe: and because the universe is all, that which is no part of it, is *nothing;* and consequently *nowhere.* Nor does it follow from hence, that spirits are *nothing:* for they have dimensions, and are therefore really *bodies;* though that name in common speech be given to such bodies only, as are visible, or palpable; that is, that have some degree of opacity. But for spirits, they call them incorporeal; which is a name of more honour, and may therefore with more piety be attributed to God himself; in whom we consider not what attribute expresseth best his nature, which is incomprehensible; but what best expresseth our desire to honour Him.

To know now upon what grounds they say there be *essence abstract,* or *substantial forms,* we are to consider what those words do properly signify. The use of words, is to register to ourselves, and make manifest to others the thoughts and conceptions of our minds. Of which words, some are the names of the things conceived; as the names of all sorts of bodies, that work upon the senses, and leave an impression in the imagination. Others are the names of the imaginations themselves; that is to say, of those ideas, or mental images we have of all things we see, or remember. And others again are names of names; or of different sorts of speech: as *universal, plural, singular,* are the names of names; and *definition, affirmation, negation, true, false, syllogism, interrogation, promise, covenant,* are the names of certain forms of speech. Others serve to show the consequence or repugnance of one name to another; as when one saith, *a man is a body,* he intendeth that the name of *body* is necessarily consequent to the name of *man;* as being but several names of the same thing, *man;* which consequence is signified by coupling them together with the word *is.* And as we use the verb *is,* so the Latins use their verb *est,* and the Greeks their Ἔστι through all its declinations. Whether all other nations of the world have in their several languages a word that answereth to it, or not, I cannot tell; but I am sure they have not need for it. For the placing of two names in order may serve to signify their consequence, if it were the custom, (for custom is it, that gives words their force,) as well as the words *is,* or *be,* or *are,* and the like.

And if it were so, that there were a language without any verb answerable to *est,* or *is,* or *be;* yet the men that used it would be not a jot the less capable of inferring, concluding, and of all kind of reasoning, than were the Greeks, and Latins. But what then would become of these terms, of *entity, essence, essential, essentiality,* that are derived from it, and of many more than depend on these, applied as most commonly they are? They are therefore no names of things; but signs, by which we make known, that we conceive the consequence of one name or attribute to another: as when we say, *a man is a living body,* we mean not that the *man* is one thing, the *living body* another, and the *is,* or *being* a third; but that the *man,* and the *living body,* is the same thing; because the consequence, *if he be a man, he is a living body,* is a true consequence, signified by that word *is.* Therefore, *to be a body, to walk, to be speaking, to live, to see,* and the like infinitives; also *corporeity, walking, speaking, life, sight,* and the like, that signify just the same, are the names of *nothing;* as I have elsewhere more amply expressed.

But to what purpose, may some man say, is such subtlety in a work of this nature, where I pretend to nothing but what is necessary to the doctrine of government and obedience? It is to this purpose, that men may no longer suffer themselves to be abused, by them, that by this doctrine of *separated essences,* built on the vain philosophy of Aristotle, would fright them from obeying the laws of their country, with empty names; as men fright birds from the corn with an empty doublet, a hat, and a crooked stick. For it is upon this ground, that when a man is dead and buried, they say his soul, that is his life, can walk separated from his body, and is seen by night amongst the graves. Upon the same ground they say, that the figure, and colour, and taste of a piece of bread, has a being, there, where they say there is no bread. And upon the same ground they say, that faith, and wisdom, and other virtues, are sometimes *poured* into a man, sometimes *blown* into him from Heaven, as if the virtuous and their virtues could be asunder; and a great many other things that serve to lessen the dependence of subjects on the sovereign power of their country. For who will endeavour to obey the laws, if he expect obedience to be poured or blown into him? Or who will not obey a priest, that can make God, rather than his sovereign, nay than God himself? Or who, that is in fear of ghosts, will not bear great respect to those that can make the holy water, that drives them from him? And this shall suffice for an example of the errors, which are brought into the Church, from the *entities* and *essences* of Aristotle: which it may be he knew to be false philosophy; but writ it as a thing consonant to, and corroborative of their religion; and fearing the fate of Socrates.

Being once fallen into this error of *separated essences,* they are thereby necessarily involved in many other absurdities that follow it. For seeing they will have these forms to be real, they are obliged to assign them *some place.* But because they hold them incorporeal, without all dimension of quantity, and all men know that place is dimension, and not to be filled, but by that which is corporeal; they are driven to uphold their credit with a distinction, that they are not indeed anywhere *circumscriptive,* but *definitive;* which terms being mere words, and in this occasion insignificant, pass only in Latin, that the vanity of them may be concealed. For the circumscription of a thing, is nothing else but the determination, or defining of its place; and so both the terms of the distinction are the same. And in particular, of the essence of a man, which, they say, is his soul, they affirm it, to be all of it in his little finger, and all of it in every other part, how small soever, of his body; and yet no more soul in the whole body, than in any one of those parts. Can any man think that God is served with such absurdities? And yet all this is necessary to believe, to those that will believe the existence of an incorporeal soul, separated from the body.

And when they come to give account how an incorporeal substance can be capable of pain, and be tormented in the fire of hell or purgatory, they have nothing at all to answer, but that it cannot be known how fire can burn souls.

Again, whereas motion is change of place, and incorporeal substances are not capable of place, they are troubled to make it seem possible, how a soul can go hence, without the body, to heaven, hell, or purgatory; and how the ghosts of men, and I may add of their clothes which they appear in, can walk by night in churches, churchyards, and other places of sepulture. To which I know not what they can answer, unless they will say, they walk *definitivè*, not *circumscriptivè*, or *spiritually*, not *temporally:* for such egregious distinctions are equally applicable to any difficulty whatsoever.

*Nunc-stans.* For the meaning of *eternity*, they will not have it to be an endless succession of time; for then they should not be able to render a reason how God's will, and preordaining of things to come, should not be before his prescience of the same, as the efficient cause before the effect, or agent before the action; nor of many other their bold opinions concerning the incomprehensible nature of God. But they will teach us, that eternity is the standing still of the present time, a *nunc-stans*, as the Schools call it; which neither they, nor any else understand, no more than they would a *hic-stans* for an infinite greatness of place.

*One body in many places, and many bodies in one place at once*. And whereas men divide a body in their thought, by numbering parts of it, and, in numbering those parts, number also the parts of the place it filled; it cannot be, but in making many parts, we make also many places of those parts; whereby there cannot be conceived in the mind of any man, more, or fewer parts, than there are places for: yet they will have us believe, that by the Almighty power of God, one body may be at one and the same time in many places; and many bodies at one and the same time in one place: as if it were an acknowledgment of the Divine Power to say, that which is, is not; or that which has been, has not been. And these are but a small part of the incongruities they are forced to, from their disputing philosophically, instead of admiring, and adoring of the divine and incomprehensible nature; whose attributes cannot signify what he is, but ought to signify our desire to honour him, with the best appellations we can think on. But they that venture to reason of his nature, from these attributes of honour, losing their understanding in the very first attempt, fall from one inconvenience into another, without end, and without number; in the same manner, as when a man ignorant of the ceremonies of court, coming into the presence of a greater person that he is used to speak to, and stumbling at his entrance, to save himself from falling, lets slip his cloak; to recover his cloak, lets fall his hat; and with one disorder after another, discovers his astonishment and rusticity.

*Absurdities in natural philosophy, as gravity the cause of heaviness.* Then for *physics*, that is, the knowledge of the subordinate and secondary causes of natural events; they render none at all, but empty words. If you desire to know why some kind of bodies sink naturally downwards toward the earth, and others go naturally from it; the Schools will tell you out of Aristotle, that the bodies that sink downwards, are *heavy;* and that this heaviness is it that causes them to descend. But if you ask what they mean by *heaviness,* they will define it to be an endeavour to go to the centre of the earth. So that the cause why things sink downward, is an endeavour to be below: which is as much as to say, that bodies descend, or ascend, because they do. Or they will tell you the centre of the earth is the place of rest, and conservation for heavy things; and therefore they endeavour to be there: as if stones and metals had a desire, or could discern the place they would be at, as man does; or loved rest, as man does not; or that a piece of glass were less safe in the window, than falling into the street.

*Quantity put into body already made.* If we would know why the same body seems greater, without adding to it, one time, than another; they say, when it seems less, it is *condensed;* when greater, *rarefied.* What is that *condensed,* and *rarefied?* Condensed, is when there is in the very same matter, less quantity than before; and rarefied, when more. As if there could be matter, that had not some determined quantity; when quantity is nothing else but the determination of matter; that is to say, of body, by which we say, one body is greater or lesser than another, by thus, or thus much. Or as if a body were made without any quantity at all, and that afterwards more or less were put into it, according as it is intended the body should be more or less dense.

*Pouring in of souls.* For the cause of the soul of man, they say, *creatur infundendo,* and *creando infunditur:* that is, *it is created by pouring it in, and poured in by creation.*

*Ubiquity of apparition.* For the cause of sense, an ubiquity of *species;* that is, of the *shows* or *apparitions* of objects; which when they be apparitions to the eye, is *sight;* when to the ear, *hearing;* to the palate, *taste;* to the nostril, *smelling;* and to the rest of the body, *feeling.*

*Will, the cause of willing.* For cause of the will to do any particular action, which is called *volitio,* they assign the faculty, that is to say, the capacity in general, that men have, to will sometimes one thing, sometimes another, which is called *voluntas;* making the *power* the cause of the *act.* As if one should assign for cause of the good or evil acts of men, their ability to do them.

*Ignorance an occult cause.* And in many occasions they put for cause of natural events, their own ignorance; but disguised in other words: as when they say, fortune is the cause of things contingent; that is, of things whereof they know no cause: and as when they attribute many effects to *occult qualities;* that is, qualities not known to them; and therefore also, as they think, to no man else. And to *sympathy, antipathy, antiperistasis, specifical qualities,* and other like terms, which signify neither the agent that produceth them, nor the operation by which they are produced.

*One makes the things incongruent, another the incongruity.* And for their moral, and civil philosophy, it hath the same, or greater absurdities. If a man do an action of injustice, that is to say, an action contrary to the law, God they say is the prime cause of the law, and also the prime cause of that, and all other actions; but no cause at all of the injustice; which is the inconformity of the action to the law. This is vain philosophy. A man might as well say, that one man maketh both a straight line, and a crooked, and another maketh their incongruity. And such is the philosophy of all men that resolve of their conclusions, before they know their premises; pretending to comprehend, that which is incomprehensible; and of attributes of honour to make attributes of nature; as this distinction was made to maintain the doctrine of free-will, that is, of a will of man, not subject to the will of God.

*Private appetite the rule of public good.* Aristotle, and other heathen philosophers, define good and evil, by the appetite of men; and well enough, as long as we consider them governed every one by his own law; for in the condition of men that have no other law but their own appetites, there can be no general rule of good, and evil actions. But in a commonwealth this measure is false: not the appetite of private men, but the law, which is the will and appetite of the state, is the measure. And yet is this doctrine still practised; and men judge the goodness or wickedness of their own, and of other men's actions, and of the actions of the commonwealth itself, by their own passions; and no man calleth good or evil, but that which is so in his own eyes, without any regard at all to the public laws; except only monks, and friars, that are bound by vow to that simple obedience to their superior, to which every subject ought to think himself bound by the law of nature to the civil sovereign. And this private measure of good, is a doctrine, not only vain, but also pernicious to the public state.

*And that lawful marriage is unchastity.* It is also vain and false philosophy, to say the work of marriage is repugnant to chastity, or continence, and by consequence to make them moral vices; as they do, that pretend chastity, and continence, for the ground of denying marriage to the clergy. For they confess it is no more, but a constitution of the Church, that requireth in those holy orders that continually attend the altar and administration of the eucharist, a continual abstinence from women, under the name of continual chastity, continence, and purity. Therefore they call the lawful use of wives, want of chastity and continence; and so make marriage a sin, or at least a thing so impure, and unclean, as to render a man unfit for the altar. If the law were made because the use of wives is incontinence, and contrary to chastity, then all marriage is vice: if because it is a thing too impure, and unclean, for a man consecrated to God; much more should other natural, necessary, and daily works which all men do, render men unworthy to be priests, because they are more unclean.

But the secret foundation of this prohibition of marriage of priests, is not likely to have been laid so slightly, as upon such errors in moral philosophy; nor yet upon the preference of single life, to the estate of matrimony; which proceeded from the wisdom of St. Paul, who perceived how inconvenient a thing it was, for those that in those times of persecution were preachers of the gospel, and forced to fly from one country to another, to be clogged with the care of wife and children; but upon the design of the Popes, and priests of after times, to make themselves the clergy, that is to say, sole heirs of the kingdom of God in this world; to which it was necessary to take from them the use of marriage; because our Saviour saith, that at the coming of his kingdom the children of God *shall neither marry, nor be given in marriage, but shall be as the angels in heaven;* that is to say, spiritual. Seeing then they had taken on them the name of spiritual, to have allowed themselves, when there was no need, the propriety of wives, had been an incongruity.

*And that all government but popular is tyranny.* From Aristotle's civil philosophy, they have learned, to call all manner of commonwealths but the popular, (such as was at that time the state of Athens), *tyranny.* All kings they called tyrants; and the aristocracy of the thirty governors set up there by the Lacedemonians that subdued them, the thirty tyrants. As also to call the condition of the people under the democracy, *liberty.* A *tyrant* originally signified no more simply, but a *monarch.* But when afterwards in most parts of Greece that kind of government was abolished, the name began to signify, not only the thing it did before, but with it, the hatred which the popular states bare towards it. As also the name of king became odious after the deposing of the kings in Rome, as being a thing natural to all men, to conceive some great fault to be signified in any attribute, that is given in despite, and to a great enemy. And when the same men shall be displeased with those that have the administration of the democracy, or aristocracy, they are not to seek for disgraceful names to express their anger in; but call readily the one *anarchy,* and the other *oligarchy,* or the *tyranny of a few.* And that which offendeth the people, is no other thing, but that they are governed, not as every one of them would himself, but as the public represantant, be it one man, or an assembly of men, thinks fit; that is, by an arbitrary government: for which they give evil names to their superiors; never knowing, till perhaps a little after a civil war, that without such arbitrary government, such war must be perpetual; and that it is men, and arms, not words and promises, that make the force and power of the laws.

*That not men, but law governs.* And therefore this is another error of Aristotle's politics, that in a well-ordered commonwealth, not men should govern, but the laws. What man, that has his natural senses, though he can neither write nor read, does not find himself governed by them he fears, and believes can kill or hurt him when he obeyeth not? Or that believes the law can hurt him; that is, words and paper, without the hands and swords of men? And this is of the number of pernicious errors: for they induce men, as oft as they like not their governors, to adhere to those that call them tyrants, and to think it lawful to raise war against them: and yet they are many times cherished from the pulpit, by the clergy.

*Laws over the conscience.* There is another error in their civil philosophy, which they never learned of Aristotle, nor Cicero, nor any other of the heathen, to extend the power of the law, which is the rule of actions only, to the very thoughts and consciences of men, by examination, and *inquisition* of what they hold, notwithstanding the conformity of their speech and actions. By which, men are either punished for answering the truth of their thoughts, or constrained to answer an untruth for fear of punishment. It is true, that the civil magistrate, intending to employ a minister in the charge of teaching, may enquire of him, if he be content to preach such and such doctrines; and in case of refusal, may deny him the employment. But to force him to accuse himself of opinions, when his actions are not by law forbidden, is against the law of nature; and especially in them, who teach, that a man shall be damned to eternal and extreme torments, if he die in a false opinion concerning an article of the Christian faith. For who is there, that knowing there is so great danger in an error, whom the natural care of himself, compelleth not to hazard his soul upon his own judgment, rather than that of any other man that is unconcerned in his damnation?

*Private interpretation of law.* For a private man, without the authority of the commonwealth, that is to say, without permission from the representant thereof, to interpret the law by his own spirit, is another error in the politics: but not drawn from Aristotle, nor from any other of the heathen philosophers. For none of them deny, but that in the power of making laws, is comprehended also the power of explaining them when there is need. And are not the Scriptures, in all places where they are law, made law by the authority of the commonwealth, and consequently, a part of the civil law?

Of the same kind it is also, when any but the sovereign restraineth in any man that power which the commonwealth hath not restrained; as they do, that impropriate the preaching of the gospel to one certain order of men, where the laws have left it free. If the state give me leave to preach, or teach; that is, if it forbid me not, no man can forbid me. If I find myself amongst the idolaters of America, shall I that am a Christian, though not in orders, think it a sin to preach Jesus Christ, till I have received orders from Rome? Or when I have preached, shall not I answer their doubts, and expound the Scriptures to them; that is, shall I not teach? But for this may some say, as also for administering to them the sacraments, the necessity shall be esteemed for a sufficient mission; which is true: but this is true also, that for whatsoever, a dispensation is due for the necessity, for the same there needs no dispensation, where there is no law that forbids it. Therefore to deny these functions to those, to whom the civil sovereign hath not denied them, is a taking away of a lawful liberty, which is contrary to the doctrine of civil government.

*Language of School divines.* More examples of vain philosophy, brought into religion by the doctors of School divinity, might be produced; but other men may if they please observe them of themselves. I shall only add this, that the writings of School divines, are nothing else for the most part, but insignificant trains of strange and barbarous words, or words otherwise used, than in the common use of the Latin tongue; such as would pose Cicero, and Varro, and all the grammarians of ancient Rome. Which if any man would see proved, let him, as I have said once before, see whether he can translate any School divine into any of the modern tongues, as French, English, or any other copious language: for that which cannot in most of these be made intelligible, is not intelligible in the Latin. Which insignificancy of language, though I cannot note it for false philosophy; yet it hath a quality, not only to hide the truth, but also to make men think they have it, and desist from further search.

*Errors from tradition.* Lastly, for the errors brought in from false, or uncertain history, what is all the legend of fictitious miracles, in the lives of the saints; and all the histories of apparitions, and ghosts, alleged by the doctors of the Roman Church, to make good their doctrines of hell, and purgatory, the power of exorcism, and other doctrines which have no warrant, neither in reason, nor Scripture; as also all those traditions which they call the unwritten word of God: but old wives' fables? Whereof, though they find dispersed somewhat in the writings of the ancient fathers; yet those fathers were men, that might too easily believe false reports; and the producing of their opinions for testimony of the truth of what they believed, hath no other force with them that, according to the counsel of St. John (1 *John* iv. 1), examine spirits, than in all things that concern the power of the Roman Church, (the abuse whereof either they suspected not, or had benefit by it), to discredit their testimony, in respect of too rash belief of reports; which the most sincere men, without great knowledge of natural causes, such as the fathers were, are commonly the most subject to. For naturally, the best men are the least suspicious of fraudulent purposes. Gregory the Pope, and St. Bernard have somewhat of apparitions of ghosts, that said they were in purgatory; and so has our Bede: but nowhere, I believe, but by report from others. But if they, or any other, relate any such stories of their own knowledge, they shall not thereby confirm the more such vain reports; but discover their own infirmity, or fraud.

*Suppression of reason.* With the introduction of false, we may join also the suppression of true philosophy, by such men, as neither by lawful authority, nor sufficient study, are competent judges of the truth. Our own navigations make manifest, and all men learned in human sciences, now acknowledge there are antipodes: and every day it appeareth more and more, that years and days are determined by motions of the earth. Nevertheless, men that have in their writings but supposed such doctrine, as an occasion to lay open the reasons for, and against it, have been punished for it by authority ecclesiastical. But what reason is there for it? Is it because such opinions are contrary to true religion? That cannot be, if they be true. Let therefore the truth be first examined by competent judges, or confuted by them that pretend to know the contrary. Is it because they be contrary to the religion established? Let them be silenced by the laws of those, to whom the teachers of them are subject; that is, by the laws civil. For disobedience may lawfully be punished in them, that against the laws teach even true philosophy. Is it because they tend to disorder in government, as countenancing rebellion, or sedition? Then let them be silenced, and the teachers punished by virtue of his power to whom the care of the public quiet is committed; which is the authority civil. For whatsoever power ecclesiastics take upon themselves, (in any place where they are subject to the state), in their own right, though they call it God's right, is but usurpation.

## Chapter 47

### Of the Benefit that proceedeth from such Darkness; and to whom it accrueth

*He that receiveth benefit by a fact, is presumed to be the author.* CICERO maketh honourable mention of one of the Cassii, a severe judge amongst the Romans, for a custom he had, in criminal causes, when the testimony of the witnesses was not sufficient, to ask the accusers, *cui bono;* that is to say, what profit, honour, or other contentment, the accused obtained, or expected by the fact. For amongst presumptions, there is none that so evidently declareth the author, as doth the benefit of the action. By the same rule I intend in this place to examine, who they may be that have possessed the people so long in this part of Christendom, with these doctrines, contrary to the peaceable societies of mankind.

*That the Church militant is the kingdom of God, was first taught by the Church of Rome.* And first, to this error, *that the present Church now militant on earth, is the kingdom of God,* (that is, the kingdom of glory, or the land of promise; not the kingdom of grace, which is but a promise of the land), are annexed these worldly benefits; first, that the pastors and teachers of the Church, are entitled thereby, as God's public ministers, to a right of governing the Church; and consequently, because the Church and commonwealth are the same persons, to be rectors, and governors of the commonwealth. By this title it is, that the Pope prevailed with the subjects of all Christian princes, to believe, that to disobey him, was to disobey Christ himself; and in all differences between him and other princes, (charmed with the word *power spiritual*), to abandon their lawful sovereigns; which is in effect an universal monarchy over all Christendom. For though they were first invested in the right of being supreme teachers of Christian doctrine, by and under Christian emperors, within the limits of the Roman empire, as is acknowledged by themselves, by the title of *Pontifex Maximus,* who was an officer subject to the civil state; yet after the empire was divided, and dissolved, it was not hard to obtrude upon the people already subjected to them, another title, namely, the right of St. Peter, not only to save entire their pretended power; but also to extend the same over the same Christian provinces, though no more united in the empire of Rome. This benefit of an universal monarchy, (considering the desire of men to bear rule), is a sufficient presumption, that the Popes that pretended to it, and for a long time enjoyed it, were the authors of the doctrine, by which it was obtained; namely, that the Church now on earth, is the kingdom of Christ. For that granted, it must be understood, that Christ hath some lieutenant amongst us, by whom we are to be told what are his commandments.

After that certain Churches had renounced this universal power of the Pope, one would expect in reason, that the civil sovereigns in all those Churches, should have recovered so much of it, as before they had unadvisedly let it go, was their own right, and in their own hands. And in England it was so in effect; saving that they, by whom the kings administered the government of religion, by maintaining their employment to be in God's right, seemed to usurp, if not a supremacy, yet an independency on the civil power: and they but seemed to usurp it, inasmuch as they acknowledged a right in the king, to deprive them of the exercise of their function at his pleasure.

*And maintained also by the Presbytery*. But in those places where the presbytery took that office, though many other doctrines of the Church of Rome were forbidden to be taught; yet this doctrine, that the kingdom of Christ is already come, and that it began at the resurrection of our Saviour, was still retained. But *cui bono?* What profit did they expect from it? The same which the Popes expected: to have a sovereign power over the people. For what is it for men to excommunicate their lawful king, but to keep him from all places of God's public service in his own kingdom; and with force to resist him, when he with force endeavoureth to correct them? Or what is it, without authority from the civil sovereign, to excommunicate any person, but to take from him his lawful liberty, that is, to usurp an unlawful power over their brethren? The authors therefore of this darkness in religion, are the Roman, and the presbyterian clergy.

*Infallibility*. To this head, I refer also all those doctrines, that serve them to keep the possession of this spiritual sovereignty after it is gotten. As first, that the *Pope in his public capacity cannot err*. For who is there, that believing this to be true, will not readily obey him in whatsoever he commands?

*Subjection of bishops.* Secondly, that all other bishops, in what commonwealth soever, have not their right, neither immediately from God, nor mediately from their civil sovereigns, but from the Pope, is a doctrine, by which there comes to be in every Christian commonwealth many potent men, (for so are bishops), that have their dependence on the Pope, and owe obedience to him, though he be a foreign prince; by which means he is able, as he hath done many times, to raise a civil war against the state that submits not itself to be governed according to his pleasure and interest.

*Exemptions of the clergy.* Thirdly, the exemption of these, and of all other priests, and of all monks, and friars, from the power of the civil laws. For by this means, there is a great part of every commonwealth, that enjoy the benefit of the laws, and are protected by the power of the civil state, which nevertheless pay no part of the public expense; nor are liable to the penalties, as other subjects, due to their crimes; and consequently, stand not in fear of any man, but the Pope; and adhere to him only, to uphold his universal monarchy.

*The names of* sacerdotes, *and sacrificers.* Fourthly, the giving to their priests, which is no more in the New Testament but presbyters, that is, elders, the name of *sacerdotes*, that is, sacrificers, which was the title of the civil sovereign, and his public ministers, amongst the Jews, whilst God was their king. Also, the making the Lord's Supper a sacrifice, serveth to make the people believe the Pope hath the same power over all Christians, that Moses and Aaron had over the Jews; that is to say, all power, both civil and ecclesiastical, as the high-priest then had.

*The sacramentation of marriage.* Fifthly, the teaching that matrimony is a sacrament, giveth to the clergy the judging of the lawfulness of marriages; and thereby, of what children are legitimate; and consequently, of the right of succession to hereditary kingdoms.

*The single life of priests.* Sixthly, the denial of marriage to priests, serveth to assure this power of the Pope over kings. For if a king be a priest, he cannot marry, and transmit his kingdom to his posterity; if he be not a priest, then the Pope pretendeth this authority ecclesiastical over him, and over his people.

*Auricular confession.* Seventhly, from auricular confession, they obtain, for the assurance of their power, better intelligence of the designs of princes, and great persons in the civil state, than these can have of the designs of the state ecclesiastical.

*Canonization of saints, and declaring of martyrs.* Eighthly, by the canonization of saints, and declaring who are martyrs, they assure their power, in that they induce simple men into an obstinacy against the laws and commands of their civil sovereigns even to death, if by the Pope's excommunication, they be declared heretics or enemies to the Church; that is, as they interpret it, to the Pope.

*Transubstantiation, penance, absolution.* Ninthly, they assure the same, by the power they ascribe to every priest, of making Christ; and by the power of ordaining penance; and of remitting, and retaining of sins.

*Purgatory, indulgences, external works.* Tenthly, by the doctrine of purgatory, of justification by external works, and of indulgences, the clergy is enriched.

*Demonology and exorcism.* Eleventhly, by their demonology, and the use of exorcism, and other things appertaining thereto, they keep, or think they keep, the people more in awe of their power.

*School divinity.* Lastly, the metaphysics, ethics, and politics of Aristotle, the frivolous distinctions, barbarous terms, and obscure language of the Schoolmen, taught in the universities, which have been all erected and regulated by the Pope's authority, serve them to keep these errors from being detected, and to make men mistake the *ignis fatuus* of vain philosophy, for the light of the Gospel.

*The authors of spiritual darkness, who they be.* To these, if they sufficed not, might be added other of their dark doctrines, the profit whereof redoundeth manifestly, to the setting up of an unlawful power over the lawful sovereigns of Christian people; or for the sustaining of the same, when it is set up; or to the worldly riches, honour, and authority of those that sustain it. And therefore by the aforesaid rule, of *cui bono*, we may justly pronounce for the authors of all this spiritual darkness, the Pope, and Roman clergy, and all those besides that endeavour to settle in the minds of men this erroneous doctrine, that the Church now on earth, is that kingdom of God mentioned in the Old and New Testament.

But the emperors, and other Christian sovereigns, under whose government these errors, and the like encroachments of ecclesiastics upon their office, at first crept in, to the disturbance of their possessions, and of the tranquillity of their subjects, though they suffered the same for want of foresight of the sequel, and of insight into the designs of their teachers, may nevertheless be esteemed accessories to their own, and the public damage. For without their authority there could at first no seditious doctrine have been publicly preached. I say they might have hindered the same in the beginning: but when the people were once possessed by those spiritual men, there was no human remedy to be applied, that any man could invent. And for the remedies that God should provide, who never faileth in his good time to destroy all the machinations of men against the truth, we are to attend his good pleasure, that suffereth many times the prosperity of his enemies, together with their ambition, to grow to such a height, as the violence thereof openeth the eyes, which the wariness of their predecessors had before sealed up, and makes men by too much grasping let go all, as Peter's net was broken, by the struggling of too great a multitude of fishes; whereas the impatience of those, that strive to resist such encroachment, before their subjects' eyes were opened, did but increase the power they resisted. I do not therefore blame the emperor Frederic for holding the stirrup to our country-man Pope Adrian; for such was the disposition of his subjects then, as if he had not done it, he was not likely to have succeeded in the empire. But I blame those, that in the beginning, when their power was entire, by suffering such doctrines to be forged in the universities of their own dominions, have holden the stirrup to all the succeeding Popes, whilst they mounted into the thrones of all Christian sovereigns, to ride, and tire, both them, and their people at their pleasure.

But as the inventions of men are woven, so also are they ravelled out; the way is the same, but the order is inverted. The web begins at the first elements of power, which are wisdom, humility, sincerity, and other virtues of the Apostles, whom the people, converted, obeyed out of reverence, not by obligation. Their consciences were free, and their words and actions subject to none but the civil power. Afterwards the presbyters, as the flocks of Christ increased, assembling to consider what they should teach, and thereby obliging themselves to teach nothing against the decrees of their assemblies, made it to be thought the people were thereby obliged to follow their doctrine, and when they refused, refused to keep them company, (that was then called excommunication), not as being infidels, but as being disobedient: and this was the first knot upon their liberty. And the number of presbyters increasing, the presbyters of the chief city or province, got themselves an authority over the parochial presbyters, and appropriated to themselves the names of bishops: and this was a second knot on Christian liberty. Lastly, the bishop of Rome, in regard of the imperial city, took upon him an authority, (partly by the wills of the emperors themselves, and by the title of *Pontifex Maximus*, and at last when the emperors were grown weak, by the privileges of St. Peter), over all other bishops of the empire: which was the third and last knot, and the whole *synthesis* and *construction*, of the pontifical power.

And therefore the *analysis*, or *resolution*, is by the same way; but beginneth with the knot that was last tied; as we may see in the dissolution of the preterpolitical Church in England. First, the power of the Popes was dissolved totally by Queen Elizabeth; and the bishops, who before exercised their functions in right of the Pope, did afterwards exercise the same in right of the Queen and her successors; though by retaining the phrase of *jure divino*, they were thought to demand it by immediate right from God: and so was untied the third knot. After this, the presbyterians lately in England obtained the putting down of episcopacy: and so was the second knot dissolved. And almost at the same time, the power was taken also from the presbyterians: and so we are reduced to the independency of the primitive Christians, to follow Paul, or Cephas, or Apollos, every man as he liketh best: which, if it be without contention, and without measuring the doctrine of Christ, by our affection to the person of his minister, (the fault the apostle reprehended in the Corinthians), is perhaps the best. First, because there ought to be no power over the consciences of men, but of the Word itself, working faith in every one, not always according to the purpose of them that plant and water, but of God himself, that giveth the increase. And secondly, because it is unreasonable in them, who teach there is such danger in every little error, to require of a man endued with reason of his own, to follow the reason of any other man, or of the most voices of any other men, which is little better than to venture his salvation at cross and pile. Nor ought those teachers to be displeased with this loss of their ancient authority. For there is none should know better than they, that power is preserved by the same virtues by which it is acquired; that is to say, by wisdom, humility, clearness of doctrine, and sincerity of conversation; and not by suppression of the natural sciences, and of the morality of natural reason; nor by obscure language; nor by arrogating to themselves more knowledge than they make appear; nor by pious frauds; nor by such other faults, as in the pastors of God's Church are not only faults, but also scandals, apt to make men stumble one time or other upon the suppression of their authority.

*Comparison of the papacy with the kingdom of fairies.* But after this doctrine, *that the Church now militant, is the kingdom of God spoken of in the Old and New Testament,* was received in the world; the ambition, and canvassing for the offices that belong thereunto, and especially for that great office of being Christ's lieutenant, and the pomp of them that obtained therein the principal public charges, became by degrees so evident, that they lost the inward reverence due to the pastoral function: insomuch as the wisest men, of them that had any power in the civil state, needed nothing but the authority of their princes, to deny them any further obedience. For, from the time that the Bishop of Rome had gotten to be acknowledged for bishop universal, by pretence of succession to St. Peter, their whole hierarchy, or kingdom of darkness, may be compared not unfitly to the *kingdom of fairies;* that is, to the old wives' *fables* in England, concerning *ghosts* and *spirits,* and the feats they play in the night. And if a man consider the original of this great ecclesiastical dominion, he will easily perceive that the Papacy is no other than the *ghost* of the deceased *Roman empire,* sitting crowned upon the grave thereof. For so did the Papacy start up on a sudden out of the ruins of that heathen power.

The *language* also, which they use, both in the churches, and in their public acts, being *Latin,* which is not commonly used by any nation now in the world, what is it but the *ghost* of the old *Roman* language?

The *fairies* in what nation soever they converse, have but one universal king, which some poets of ours call King Oberon; but the Scripture calls Beelzebub, prince of *demons.* The *ecclesiastic* likewise, in whose dominions soever they be found, acknowledge but one universal king, the *Pope.*

The *ecclesiastics* are *spiritual* men, and *ghostly* fathers. The fairies are *spirits,* and *ghosts. Fairies* and *ghosts* inhabit darkness, solitudes and graves. The *ecclesiastics* walk in obscurity of doctrine, in monasteries, churches, and churchyards .

The *ecclesiastics* have their cathedral churches, which, in what town soever they be erected, by virture of holy water, and certain charms called exorcisms, have the power to make those towns, cities, that is to say, seats of empire. The *fairies* also have their enchanted castles, and certain gigantic ghosts, that domineer over the regions round about them.

The *fairies* are not to be seized on; and brought to answer for the hurt they do. So also the *ecclesiastics* vanish away from the tribunals of civil justice.

The *ecclesiastics* take from young men the use of reason, by certain charms compounded of metaphysics, and miracles, and traditions, and abused Scripture, whereby they are good for nothing else, but to execute what they command them. The *fairies* likewise are said to take young children out of their cradles, and to change them into natural fools, which common people do therefore call *elves,* and are apt to mischief.

In what shop, or operatory the fairies make their enchantment, the old wives have not determined. But the operatories of the *clergy* are well enough known to be the universities, that received their discipline from authority pontifical.

When the *fairies* are displeased with anybody, they are said to send their elves, to pinch them. The *ecclesiastics,* when they are displeased with any civil state, make also their elves, that is, superstitious, enchanted subjects, to pinch their princes, by teaching sedition; or one prince enchanted with promises, to pinch another.

The *fairies* marry not; but there be amongst them *incubi,* that have copulation with flesh and blood. The *priests* also marry not.

The *ecclesiastics* take the cream of the land, by donations of ignorant men, that stand in awe of them, and by tithes. So also it is in the fable of *fairies,* that they enter into the dairies, and feast upon the cream, which they skim from the milk.

What kind of money is current in the kingdom of *fairies,* is not recorded in the story. But the *ecclesiastics* in their receipts accept of the same money that we do; though when they are to make any payment, it is in canonizations, indulgences, and masses.

To this, and such like resemblances between the *papacy,* and the kingdom of *fairies,* may be added this, that as the *fairies* have no existence, but in the fancies of ignorant people, rising from the traditions of old wives, or old poets: so the spiritual power of the *Pope,* without the bounds of his own civil dominion, consisteth only in the fear that seduced people stand in, of their excommunications; upon hearing of false miracles, false traditions, and false interpretations of the Scripture.

It was not therefore a very difficult matter, for Henry VIII by his exorcism; nor for Queen Elizabeth by hers, to cast them out. But who knows that this spirit of Rome, now gone out, and walking by missions through the dry places of China, Japan, and the Indies, that yield him little fruit, may not return, or rather an assembly of spirits worse than he, enter, and inhabit this clean swept house, and make the end thereof worse than the beginning? For it is not the Roman clergy only, that pretends the kingdom of God to be of this world, and thereby to have a power therein, distinct from that of the civil state. And this is all I had a design to say, concerning the doctrine of the POLITICS. Which when I have reviewed, I shall willingly expose it to the censure of my country.

# A Review, and Conclusion

FROM THE CONTRARIETY of some of the natural faculties of the mind, one to another, as also of one passion to another, and from their reference to conversation, there has been an argument taken, to infer an impossibility that any one man should be sufficiently disposed to all sorts of civil duty. The severity of judgment, they say, makes men censorious, and unapt to pardon the errors and infirmities of other men: and on the other side, celerity of fancy, makes the thoughts less steady than is necessary, to discern exactly between right and wrong. Again, in all deliberations, and in all pleadings, the faculty of solid reasoning is necessary: for without it, the resolutions of men are rash, and their sentences unjust: and yet if there be not powerful eloquence, which procureth attention and consent, the effect of reason will be little. But these are contrary faculties; the former being grounded upon principles of truth; the other upon opinions already received, true or false; and upon the passions and interests of men, which are different and mutable.

And amongst the passions, *courage*, (by which I mean the contempt of wounds, and violent death) inclineth men to private revenges, and sometimes to endeavour the unsettling of the public peace: and *timorousness*, many times disposeth to the desertion of the public defence. Both these, they say, cannot stand together in the same person.

And to consider the contrariety of men's opinions, and manners, in general, it is, they say, impossible to entertain a constant civil amity with all those, with whom the business of the world constrains us to converse: which business consisteth almost in nothing else but a perpetual contention for honour, riches, and authority.

To which I answer, that these are indeed great difficulties, but not impossibilities: for by education, and discipline, they may be, and are sometimes reconciled. Judgment and fancy may have place in the same man; but by turns; as the end which he aimeth at requireth. As the Israelites in Egypt, were sometimes fastened to their labour of making bricks, and other times were ranging abroad to gather straw: so also may the judgment sometimes be fixed upon one certain consideration, and the fancy at another time wandering about the

503

world. So also reason, and eloquence, though not perhaps in the natural sciences, yet, in the moral, may stand very well together. For wheresoever there is place for adorning and preferring of error, there is much more place for adorning and preferring of truth, if they have it to adorn. Nor is there any repugnancy between fearing the laws, and not fearing a public enemy; nor between abstaining from injury, and pardoning it in others. There is therefore no such inconsistence of human nature, with civil duties, as some think. I have known clearness of judgment, and largeness of fancy; strength of reason, and graceful elocution; a courage for the war, and a fear for the laws, and all eminently in one man; and that was my most noble and honoured friend, Mr. Sidney Godolphin; who hating no man, nor hated of any, was unfortunately slain in the beginning of the late civil war, in the public quarrel, by an undiscerned and an undiscerning hand.

To the Laws of Nature, declared in Chapter 15, I would have this added, *that every man is bound by nature, as much as in him lieth, to protect in war the authority, by which he is himself protected in time of peace.* For he that pretendeth a right of nature to preserve his own body, cannot pretend a right of nature to destroy him, by whose strength he is preserved: it is a manifest contradiction of himself. And though this law may be drawn by consequence, from some of those that are there already mentioned; yet the times require to have it inculcated, and remembered.

And because I find by divers English books lately printed, that the civil wars have not yet sufficiently taught men in what point of time it is, that a subject becomes obliged to the conqueror; nor what is conquest; nor how it comes about, that it obliges men to obey his laws: therefore for further satisfaction of men therein, I say, the point of time, wherein a man becomes subject to a conqueror, is that point, wherein having liberty to submit to him, he consenteth, either by express words, or by other sufficient sign, to be his subject. When it is that a man hath the liberty to submit, I have showed before in the end of Chapter 21; namely, that for him that hath no obligation to his former sovereign but that of an ordinary subject, it is then, when the means of his life are within the guards and garrisons of the enemy; for it is then, that he hath no longer protection from him, but is protected by the adverse party for his contribution. Seeing therefore such contribution is everywhere, as a thing inevitable, notwithstanding it be an assistance to the enemy, esteemed lawful; a total submission, which is but an assistance to the enemy, cannot be esteemed unlawful. Besides, if a man consider that they who submit, assist the enemy but with part of their estates, whereas they that refuse, assist him with the whole, there is no reason to call their submission, or composition, an assistance; but rather a detriment to the enemy. But if a man, besides the obligation of a subject, hath taken upon him a new obligation of a soldier, then he hath not the liberty to submit to a new power, as long as the old one keeps the field, and giveth him means of subsistence, either in his armies, or garrisons: for in this case, he cannot complain of want of protection, and means to live as a soldier. But when that also fails, a soldier also may seek his protection wheresoever he has most hope to have it; and may lawfully submit himself to his new master. And so much for the time when he may do it lawfully, if he will. If therefore he do it, he is undoubtedly bound to be a true subject: for a contract lawfully made, cannot lawfully be broken.

By this also a man may understand, when it is, that men may be said to be conquered; and in what the nature of conquest, and the right of a conqueror consisteth: for this submission in itself implieth them all. Conquest, is not the victory itself; but the acquisition, by victory, of a right over the persons of men. He therefore that is slain, is overcome, but not conquered: he that is taken, and put into prison, or chains, is not conquered, though overcome; for he is still an enemy, and may save himself if he can: but he that upon promise of obedience, hath his life and liberty allowed him, is then conquered, and a subject; and not before. The Romans used to say, that their general had *pacified* such a *province*, that is to say, in English, *conquered* it; and that the country was *pacified* by victory, when the people of it had promised *imperata facere*, that is, *to do what the Roman people commanded them:* this was to be conquered. But this promise may be either express, or tacit: express, by promise: tacit, by other signs. As for example, a man that hath not been called to make such an express promise, because he is one whose power perhaps is not considerable; yet if he live under their protection openly, he is understood to submit himself to the government: but if he live there secretly, he is liable to anything that may be done to a spy, and enemy of the state. I say not, he does any injustice; for acts of open hostility bear not that name; but that he may be justly put to death. Likewise, if a man, when his country is conquered, be out of it, he is not conquered, nor subject: but if at his return, he submit to the government, he is bound to obey it. So that *conquest*, to define it, is the acquiring of the right of sovereignty by victory. Which right, is acquired in the people's submission, by which they contract with the victor, promising obedience, for life and liberty.

In Chapter 29, I have set down for one of the causes of the dissolutions of commonwealths, their imperfect generation, consisting in the want of an absolute and arbitrary legislative power; for want whereof, the civil sovereign is fain to handle the sword of justice unconstantly, and as if it were too hot for him to hold. One reason whereof, which I have not there mentioned, is this, that they will all of them justify the war, by which their power was at first gotten, and whereon, as they think, their right dependeth, and not on the possession. As if, for example, the right of the kings of England did depend on the goodness of the cause of William the Conqueror, and upon their lineal, and directest descent from him; by which means, there would perhaps be no tie of the subjects' obedience to their sovereign at this day in all the world: wherein whilst they needlessly think to justify themselves, they justify all the successful rebellions that ambition shall at any time raise against them, and their successors. Therefore I put down for one of the most effectual seeds of the death of any state, that the conquerors require not only a submission of men's actions to them for the future, but also an approbation of all their actions past; when there is scarce a commonwealth in the world, whose beginnings can in conscience be justified.

And because the name of tyranny, signifieth nothing more, nor less, than the name of sovereignty, be it in one, or many men, saving that they that use the former word, are understood to be angry with them they call tyrants; I think the toleration of a professed hatred of tyranny, is a toleration of hatred to commonwealth in general, and another evil seed, not differing much from the former. For to the justification of the cause of a conqueror, the reproach of the cause of the conquered, is for the most part necessary: but neither of them necessary for the obligation of the conquered. And thus much I have thought fit to say upon the review of the first and second part of this discourse.

In Chapter 35, I have sufficiently declared out of the Scripture, that in the commonwealth of the Jews, God himself was made the sovereign, by pact with the people; who were therefore called his *peculiar people*, to distinguish them from the rest of the world, over whom God reigned not by their consent, but by his own power: and that in this kingdom Moses was God's lieutenant on earth; and that it was he that told them what laws God appointed them to be ruled by. But I have omitted to set down who were the officers appointed to do execution; especially in capital punishments; not then thinking it a matter of so necessary consideration, as I find it since. We know that generally in all commonwealths, the execution of corporal punishments, was either put upon the guards, or other soldiers of the sovereign power; or given to those, in whom want of means, contempt of honour, and hardness of heart, concurred, to make them sue for such an office. But amongst the Israelites it was a positive law of God their sovereign, that he that was convicted of a capital crime, should be stoned to death by the people; and that the witnesses should cast the first stone, and after the witnesses, then the rest of the people. This was a law that designed who were to be the executioners; but not that any one should throw a stone at him before conviction and sentence, where the congregation was judge. The witnesses were nevertheless to be heard before they proceeded to execution, unless the fact were committed in the presence of the congregation itself, or in sight of the lawful judges; for then there needed no other witnesses but the judges themselves. Nevertheless, this manner of proceeding being not thoroughly understood, hath given occasion to a dangerous opinion, that any man may kill another, in some cases, by a right of zeal; as if the executions done upon offenders in the kingdom of God in old time, proceeded not from the sovereign command, but from the authority of private zeal: which, if we consider the texts that seem to favour it, is quite contrary.

First, where the Levites fell upon the people, that had made and worshipped the Golden Calf, and slew three thousand of them; it was by the commandment of Moses, from the mouth of God; as is manifest, *Exod.* xxxii. 27. And when the son of a woman of Israel had blasphemed God, they that heard it, did not kill him, but brought him before Moses, who put him under custody, till God should give sentence against him; as appears, *Levit.* xxiv. 11, 12. Again, (*Numb.* xxv. 6, 7), when Phinehas killed Zimri and Cozbi, it was not by right of private zeal: their crime was committed in the sight of the assembly; there needed no witness; the law was known, and he the heir-apparent to the sovereignty; and, which is the principal point, the lawfulness of his act depended wholly upon a subsequent ratification by Moses, whereof he had no cause to doubt. And this presumption of a future ratification, is sometimes necessary to the safety of a commonwealth; as in a sudden rebellion, any man that can suppress it by his own power in the country where it begins, without express law or commission, may lawfully do it, and provide to have it ratified, or pardoned whilst it is in doing, or after it is done. Also *Numb.* xxxv. 30, it is expressly said, *Whosoever shall kill the murderer, shall kill him upon the word of witnesses:* but witnesses suppose a formal judicature, and consequently condemn that pretence of *jus zelotarum*. The law of Moses concerning him that enticeth to idolatry, that is to say, in the kingdom of God to a renouncing of his allegiance, (*Deut.* xiii. 8, 9), forbids to conceal him, and commands the accuser to cause him to be put to death, and to cast the first stone at him; but not to kill him before he be condemned. And (*Deut.* xvii. 4, 5, 6, 7), the process against idolatry is exactly set down: for God there speaketh to the people, as judge, and commandeth them, when a man is accused of idolatry, to enquire diligently of the fact, and finding it true, then to stone him; but still the hand of the witness throweth the first stone. This is not private zeal, but public condemnation. In like manner when a father hath a rebellious son, the law is, (*Deut.* xxi. 18-21), that he shall bring him before the judges of the town, and all the people of the town shall stone him. Lastly, by pretence of these laws it was, that St. Stephen was stoned, and not by pretence of private zeal: for before he was carried away to execution, he had pleaded his cause before the high-priest. There is nothing in all this, nor in any other part of the Bible, to countenance executions by private zeal; which being oftentimes but a conjunction of ignorance and passion, is against both the justice and peace of a commonwealth.

In Chapter 36, I have said, that it is not declared in what manner God spake supernaturally to Moses: nor that he spake not to him sometimes by dreams and visions, and by a supernatural voice, as to other prophets: for the manner how he spake unto him from the mercy-seat, is expressly set down, *Numb.* vii. 89, in these words, *From that time forward, when Moses entered into the Tabernacle of the congregation to speak with God, he heard a voice which spake unto him from over the mercy-seat, which is over the Ark of the testimony; from between the cherubims he spake unto him.* But it is not declared in what consisteth the preeminence of the manner of God's speaking to Moses, above that of his speaking to other prophets, as to Samuel, and to Abraham, to whom he also spake by a voice, (that is, by vision), unless the difference consist in the clearness of the vision. For *face to face,* and *mouth to mouth,* cannot be literally understood of the infiniteness, and incomprehensibility of the Divine nature.

And as to the whole doctrine, I see not yet, but the principles of it are true and proper; and the ratiocination solid. For I ground the civil right of sovereigns, and both the duty and liberty of subjects, upon the known natural inclinations of mankind, and upon the articles of the law of nature; of which no man, that pretends but reason enough to govern his private family, ought to be ignorant. And for the power ecclesiastical of the same sovereigns, I ground it on such texts, as are both evident in themselves, and consonant to the scope of the whole Scripture. And therefore am persuaded, that he that shall read it with a purpose only to be informed, shall be informed by it. But for those that by writing, or public discourse, or by their eminent actions, have already engaged themselves to the maintaining of contrary opinions, they will not be so easily satisfied. For in such cases, it is natural for men, at one and the same time, both to proceed in reading, and to lose their attention, in the search of objections to that they had read before. Of which in a time wherein the interests of men are changed, (seeing much of that doctrine, which serveth to the establishing of a new government, must needs be contrary to that which conduced to the dissolution of the old), there cannot choose but be very many.

In that part which treateth of a Christian commonwealth, there are some new doctrines, which, it may be, in a state where the contrary were already fully determined, were a fault for a subject without leave to divulge, as being an usurpation of the place of a teacher. But in this time, that men call not only for peace, but also for truth, to offer such doctrines as I think true, and that manifestly tend to peace and loyalty, to the consideration of those that are yet in deliberation, is no more, but to offer new wine, to put into new casks, that both may be preserved together. And I suppose, that then, when novelty can breed no trouble nor disorder in a state, men are not generally so much inclined to the reverence of antiquity, as to prefer ancient errors, before new and well-proved truth.

There is nothing I distrust more than my elocution, which nevertheless I am confident, excepting the mischances of the press, is not obscure. That I have neglected the ornament of quoting ancient poets, orators, and philosophers, contrary to the custom of late time, whether I have done well or ill in it, proceedeth from my judgment, grounded on many reasons. For first, all truth of doctrine dependeth either upon *reason*, or upon *Scripture;* both which give credit to many, but never receive it from any writer. Secondly, the matters in question are not of *fact*, but of *right*, wherein there is no place for *witnesses*. There is scarce any of those old writers, that contradicteth not sometimes both himself and others; which makes their testimonies insufficient. Fourthly, such opinions as are taken only upon credit of antiquity, are not intrinsically the judgment of those that cite them, but words that pass, like gaping, from mouth to mouth. Fifthly, it is many times with a fraudulent design that men stick their corrupt doctrine with the cloves of other men's wit. Sixthly, I find not that the ancients they cite, took it for an ornament, to do the like with those that wrote before them. Seventhly, it is an argument of indigestion, when Greek and Latin sentences unchewed come up again, as they used to do, unchanged. Lastly, though I reverence those men of ancient time, that either have written truth perspicuously, or set us in a better way to find it out ourselves; yet to the antiquity itself I think nothing due. For if we will reverence the age, the present is the oldest. If the antiquity of the writer, I am not sure, that generally they to whom such honour is given, were more ancient when they wrote, than I am that am writing. But if it be well considered, the praise of ancient authors, proceeds not from the reverence of the dead, but from the competition, and mutual envy of the living.

To conclude, there is nothing in this whole discourse, nor in that I writ before of the same subject in Latin, as far as I can perceive, contrary either to the Word of God, or to good manners; or to the disturbance of the public tranquillity. Therefore I think it may be profitably printed, and more profitably taught in the Universities, in case they also think so, to whom the judgment of the same belongeth. For seeing the Universities are the fountains of civil and moral doctrine, from whence the preachers, and the gentry, drawing such water as they find, use to sprinkle the same (both from the pulpit and in their conversation), upon the people, there ought certainly to be great care taken, to have it pure, both from the venom of heathen politicians, and from the incantation of deceiving spirits. And by that means the most men, knowing their duties, will be the less subject to serve the ambition of a few discontented persons, in their purposes against the state; and be the less grieved with the contributions necessary for their peace, and defence; and the governors themselves have the less cause, to maintain at the common charge any greater army, than is necessary to make good the public liberty, against the invasions and encroachments of foreign enemies.

And thus I have brought to an end my Discourse of Civil and Ecclesiastical Government, occasioned by the disorders of the present time, without partiality, without application, and without other design than to set before men's eyes the mutual relation between protection and obedience; of which the condition of human nature, and the laws divine, both natural and positive, require an inviolable observation. And though in the revolution of states, there can be no very good constellation for truths of this nature to be born under, (as having an angry aspect from the dissolvers of an old government, and seeing but the backs of them that erect a new), yet I cannot think it will be condemned at this time, either by the public judge of doctrine, or by any that desires the continuance of public peace. And in this hope I return to my interrupted speculation of bodies natural; wherein, if God give me health to finish it, I hope the novelty will as much please, as in the doctrine of this artificial body it useth to offend. For such truth, as opposeth no man's profit, nor pleasure, is to all men welcome.